A History of the English Language

The history and development of English, from the earliest known writings to its status today as a dominant world language, is a subject of major importance to linguists and historians. In this authoritative volume, a team of international experts cover the entire recorded history of the English language, outlining its development over fifteen centuries. With an emphasis on more recent periods, every key stage in the history of the language is discussed, with full accounts of standardisation, names, the distribution of English in Britain and North America, and its global spread. New historical surveys of the crucial aspects of the language (sounds, word structure, grammar and vocabulary) are presented, and historical changes that have affected English are treated as a continuing process, helping to explain the shape of the language today. Comprehensive and fully up-to-date, the volume will be indispensable to all advanced students, scholars and teachers in this prominent field.

RICHARD HOGG is Smith Professor of Language and Medieval English at the University of Manchester. He is editor of volume 1 of *The Cambridge History of the English Language* (six volumes, 1992–2001) and one of the founding editors of the journal *English Language and Linguistics* (also published by Cambridge University Press). He is author of *Metrical Phonology* with Christopher McCully (Cambridge University Press, 1986), *A Grammar of Old English* (1992) and *An Introduction to Old English* (2002). He is Fellow of the British Academy (1994), and Fellow of the Royal Society of Edinburgh (2004).

DAVID DENISON is Professor of English Linguistics at the University of Manchester, and has held visiting appointments at the universities of Amsterdam, British Columbia, Santiago de Compostela and Paris 3. He is one of the founding editors of the journal *English Language and Linguistics* (published by Cambridge University Press), and author of *English Historical Syntax* (1993/2004) and of the 'Syntax' chapter in volume 4 of *The Cambridge History of the English Language* (1998). He is also co-editor of *Fuzzy Grammar* (2004).

Frontispiece: *Map of England*

A History of the English Language

Edited by

RICHARD HOGG AND DAVID DENISON

CAMBRIDGE
UNIVERSITY PRESS

CAMBRIDGE UNIVERSITY PRESS
Cambridge, New York, Melbourne, Madrid, Cape Town, Singapore, São Paulo, Delhi

Cambridge University Press
The Edinburgh Building, Cambridge CB2 8RU, UK

Published in the United States of America by Cambridge University Press, New York

www.cambridge.org
Information on this title: www.cambridge.org/9780521717991

First published 2006
First paperback edition 2008

Printed in the United Kingdom at the University Press, Cambridge

A catalogue record for this publication is available from the British Library

Library of Congress Cataloguing in Publication data
A history of the English language / edited by Richard Hogg and David Denison.
  p.   cm.
Includes bibliographical references and index.
ISBN 0-521-66227-3
1. English language – History.   I. Hogg, Richard M.   II. Denison, David, 1950–   III. Title.
PE1075.H57   2006
420.9 – dc22   2005032565

ISBN 978-0-521-66227-7 hardback
ISBN 978-0-521-71799-1 paperback

Contents

List of figures   *page* vi
List of tables   viii
List of contributors   ix
Preface   xi
Acknowledgements   xiii

1 Overview   1
David Denison and Richard Hogg

2 Phonology and morphology   43
Roger Lass

3 Syntax   109
Olga Fischer and Wim van der Wurff

4 Vocabulary   199
Dieter Kastovsky

5 Standardisation   271
Terttu Nevalainen and Ingrid Tieken-Boon van Ostade

6 Names   312
Richard Coates

7 English in Britain   352
Richard Hogg

8 English in North America   384
Edward Finegan

9 English worldwide   420
David Crystal

Further reading   440
References   445
Index   479

Figures

Frontispiece: Map of England

1.1   Anglo-Saxon England (from Hill, 1981)   *page* 4
1.2   The Indo-European languages   5
1.3   The Germanic languages   5
1.4   Wave representation of Germanic (after Trask, 1996)   6
1.5   The homeland of the Angles   9
1.6   Scandinavian place-names (from Hill, 1981)   13
1.7   Domesday population (from Hill, 1981)   19
1.8   The Caistor runes (from Page, 1973)   30
1.9   Prefaces to the *Cura Pastoralis* (from Brook, 1955)   31
1.10   S-curve   37
7.1   Anglo-Saxon England (from Hogg, 1992a: 419)   354
7.2   Survey points used for the *Linguistic Atlas of Late Mediaeval English*   363
7.3   Traditional dialect areas (from Trudgill, 1999b)   372
7.4   Modern dialect areas (from Trudgill, 1999b)   373
7.5   Limits of postvocalic /r/ in present-day dialects (from Trudgill, 1999b)   377
8.1   *DARE* map and conventional map, with state names (from *Dictionary of American Regional English*, I, 1985)   400
8.2   Distribution of HERO on a *DARE* map (from *Dictionary of American Regional English*, II, 1991)   401
8.3   Distribution of HOAGIE on a *DARE* map (from *Dictionary of American Regional English*, II, 1991)   401
8.4   Distribution of POORBOY on a *DARE* map (from *Dictionary of American Regional English*, II, 1991)   402
8.5   Distribution of SUBMARINE SANDWICH on a *DARE* map (from *Dictionary of American Regional English*, IV, 2002)   402
8.6   Kurath's dialect regions of the eastern states, based on vocabulary (from Kurath, 1949)   403
8.7   Carver's dialect regions of the USA, based on vocabulary (from Carver, 1987)   404

8.8   Northern Cities Shift (adapted from Labov, forthcoming)   405
8.9   Southern Shift (adapted from Labov, forthcoming)   406
8.10 Dialect areas of North America, based on vowel
      pronunciation (adapted from Labov, forthcoming)   407
8.11 Pronunciation of *-ing* as /IN/ by four SES groups in three
      situations in New York City (from Labor, 1996)   409

Tables

1.1   Some sources of English words (*OED*^{2})   *page* 2
1.2   An example of comparative reconstruction   7
1.3   National GDP in 1890   21
1.4   National GDP and population in 2003   27
1.5   Two quantifiers   38
3.1   The main syntactic changes   111
3.2   Element order within the NP in PDE   114
3.3   Combinations of auxiliaries in the verbal group (adapted
      from Denison, 2000a: 139)   159
5.1   Concord patterns in conversation (from Biber et al.,
      1999: 191)   298
7.1   Some Middle English texts   365
9.1   Some recent estimates of world English speakers as a
      first, second and foreign language (in millions)   424
9.2   Annual growth rate in population, 1998–2003: selected
      countries. Data from Encyclopaedia Britannica (2004)   426

Contributors

Richard Coates, Professor of Linguistics, University of Sussex.

David Crystal, Honorary Professor of Linguistics, University of Wales, Bangor.

David Denison, Professor of English Linguistics, University of Manchester.

Edward Finegan, Professor of Linguistics and Law, University of Southern California.

Olga Fischer, Professor of Germanic Linguistics, University of Amsterdam.

Richard Hogg, Smith Professor of English Language and Medieval English Literature, University of Manchester.

Dieter Kastovsky, Professor of English Linguistics, University of Vienna.

Roger Lass, Professor Emeritus of Linguistics, Senior Professorial Fellow and Honorary Research Associate in English, University of Cape Town.

Terttu Nevalainen, Professor of English Philology, University of Helsinki.

Ingrid Tieken-Boon van Ostade, Senior Lecturer in Historical Linguistics, University of Leiden.

Wim van der Wurff, Senior Lecturer in English Language and Linguistics, University of Newcastle upon Tyne.

Preface

Who is this book written for? There are already so many books on the history of English, both large and small, that another one might at first sight seem otiose, redundant and unnecessary. But one of the beauties of the language is its ability to show continuous change and flexibility while in some sense remaining the same. And if that is true of the language, it is also true of the study of the language, whether undertaken for strictly academic purposes or not. This book is pitched at senior undergraduates in the main, though we trust that the general reader will also find in it much that is enlightening and enjoyable. Our justification for this work, then, is that knowledge of the history of English is a part of our common culture which needs – and repays – constant renewal.

But there is more to it than that. There are indeed many good existing accounts, including, in particular, Barbara Strang's first-class *A History of English* (1970). In the thirty-five years since its publication, the language has continued to change, and scholarship has advanced along several different paths. Most obviously, the advent of computerised material has enabled us to analyse and hence understand much material which was previously impractical for the individual scholar to assimilate. Secondly, the (very different) Chomskyan and Labovian revolutions in linguistics, both in their infancy in 1970, have had repercussions in many domains relevant to this book. While the essence of the subject remains the same, the focus of attention may have shifted.

How does the current work relate to *The Cambridge History of the English Language* (*CHEL*; six volumes, 1992–2001)? A mixture of old and new contributors will be apparent, albeit with some of the 'old' contributors working on 'new' areas (and the whole book in any case written afresh). More important is the fact that the orientation of this work is rather different from that of *CHEL*. The most obvious difference is in emphasis, now tilted (within a full account of the history of the language) slightly more towards the later than the earlier periods. A further shift is the emphasis on variation, both in terms of standard and non-standard varieties and of different Englishes – in Britain, North America and worldwide.

On the other hand, we do attempt to cover, if more concisely than was possible in *CHEL*, the 'core' structural elements of the language. To make a slightly artificial division, Chapters 2 to 4 deal with major domains of the internal, structural history of English, while Chapters 5 to 9 tackle aspects of its use, distribution and variation. All eight are individual, coherent and linguistically informed accounts, taking their subject-matter through the whole sweep of the recorded history of

English. In the opening chapter, and continuing throughout the book, we attempt to situate these linguistic developments in their historical and social context. From the continual, dynamic interaction of internal and external factors comes what is by any standards a richly varied language.

Richard Hogg and David Denison, Manchester, May 2005

Acknowledgements

Richard Hogg and David Denison wish to thank Sylvia Adamson, Jeff Denton, Robert Fulk, Willem Hollmann, Jussi Klemola, Meg Laing, Steve Rigby and Mary Syner for help with or comments on Chapter 1. Olga Fischer and Wim van der Wurff particularly wish to thank Willem Koopman for reading Chapter 3 with great care and meticulousness; their chapter was also improved by comments from students on van der Wurff's course 'English Historical Syntax' at the University of Leiden in 2003. Ed Finegan is grateful to Richard W. Bailey and Michael B. Montgomery for comments and suggestions on a draft of Chapter 8.

1   Overview

David Denison and Richard Hogg

1.1   Introduction

David Crystal estimates that about 400 million people have English as their first language, and that in total as many as 1500 million may be to a greater or lesser extent fluent speakers of English (see Chapter 9, Table 9.1). The two largest countries (in terms of population) where English is the inherited national language are Britain and the USA. But it is also the majority language of Australia and New Zealand, and a national language in both Canada and South Africa. Furthermore, in other countries it is a second language, in others an official language or the language of business.

If, more parochially, we restrict ourselves to Britain and the USA, the fact that it is the inherited national language of both does not allow us to conclude that English shows a straightforward evolution from its ultimate origins. Yet originally English was imported into Britain, as also happened later in North America. And in both cases the existing languages, whether Celtic, as in Britain, or Amerindian languages, as in North America, were quickly swamped by English. But in both Britain and the USA, English was much altered by waves of immigration. Chapter 8 will demonstrate how that occurred in the USA.

In Britain, of course, the Germanic-speaking Anglo-Saxons brought their language with them as immigrants. The eighth and ninth centuries saw Scandinavian settlements and then the Norman Conquest saw significant numbers of French-speaking settlers. Both these invasions had a major impact on the language, which we shall discuss later in this chapter. However, they should not obscure the constant influence of other languages on English, whether through colonisation or through later immigration. Some idea of the polyglot nature of the language (as opposed to its speakers) can be gleaned from the figures presented in Table 1.1, based upon etymologies in the *Oxford English Dictionary*. (Note that the already-existing language English did not get its basic vocabulary and structure from any of the languages in Table 1.1; the origins of English will be introduced shortly.)

The *OED* is probably the most complete historical dictionary of any language. The languages in Table 1.1 have been chosen (from over 350 in *OED*!) only in order to demonstrate the variety of linguistic sources for English. The figures in Table 1.1 remain imprecise, despite elaborate electronic searches of the entire *OED* (with its 20+ ways of marking a French loan and 50+ for Scandinavian): exact figures are beside the point and in fact unattainable.

Table 1.1 *Some sources of English words (OED[2])*

Latin	24,940
French	9,470
Scandinavian	1,530
Spanish	1,280
Dutch, including Afrikaans	860
Arabic	615
Turkish	125
Hindi	120
Hungarian	26
Cherokee	1–3

Even when we are dealing with only one country, say Britain or the USA, there are a wide range of varieties of English available. These varieties are dependent on various factors. Each speaker is different from every other speaker, and often in non-trivial ways. Thus speaker A may vary from speaker B in geographical dialect. And the context of speech varies according to register, or the social context in which the speaker is operating at the time. Register includes, for example, occupational varieties, and it interacts with such features as the contrast between written and spoken language (medium) or that between formal and colloquial language.

It will be clear that the above points raise the question of what this volume purports to be a history *of*. There are, we can now see, many different Englishes. And these Englishes can interact in an intricate fashion. To take a single example, how might we order the relationships between written colloquial English and spoken formal English? Not, surely, on a single scale. And as English becomes more and more of a global language, the concept of dialect becomes more and more opaque. In writing this volume, therefore, we have had to make some fundamental decisions about what English is, and what history we might be attempting to construct.

In making these decisions we have had to bear two different aims in mind. One is to be able to give some plausible account of where English is situated today. Therefore many of the chapters pay particular attention to the present-day language, the chapter on English worldwide almost exclusively so. But this is a history, and therefore our other aim is to demonstrate how English has developed over the centuries. And not merely for its own sake, but because of our joint belief that it is only through understanding its history that we can hope adequately to understand the present.

At this point we first introduce some conventional labels for periods in the recorded history of English. From its introduction on the island of Britain to the end of the eleventh century, the language is nowadays known as Old English (OE). From c.1100 to around the end of the fifteenth century is called the Middle English

(ME) period, and from c.1500 to the present day is called Modern English (ModE). ModE is distinct therefore from present-day English (PDE), which, if a period at all, extends at most to the childhoods of people now living, say from the early twentieth century to the present. Division into periods is to a large extent arbitrary, if convenient for reference and sanctioned by scholarly tradition. There is both linguistic and non-linguistic justification for identifying (roughly) those periods, though sometimes with slightly differing transition dates, and sometimes with the main periods of OE, ME and ModE divided into early and late sub-periods. Other periodisations have been proposed, however, and in any case the transition dates suggested above should not be taken too seriously. There is no point in further discussion until more evidence of the detailed history has been presented.

1.2   The roots of English

What is English? Who are the people who have spoken it? Before we begin our exploration of the internal history of English, it is questions such as these which must be answered. If we trace history back, then, wherever English is spoken today, whether it be in Bluff, New Zealand, or Nome, Alaska, in every case its ultimate origins lie in Anglo-Saxon England. If we consider the map of Anglo-Saxon England (Figure 1.1), based on the place-names in Bede's *Historia Ecclesiastica* of the early eighth century, we get some impression of what the Anglo-Saxons might have thought of as their heartland. This map is, of course, incomplete in that it relies on only a single, albeit contemporary, source. Further-more, Bede lived his whole life at Jarrow in County Durham, and his material is necessarily centred on Northumbria and ecclesiastical life. Nevertheless, it is a useful reminder that the original English settlements of Britain concentrated on the east and south coasts of the country.

Of course, this is not unexpected. The Anglo-Saxon speakers of English had started to come to Britain early in the fifth century from the lands across the North Sea – roughly speaking, the largely coastal areas between present-day Denmark and the Netherlands and the immediate hinterland. Bede himself states that the Anglo-Saxon invaders came from three tribes, the Angles, the Saxons and the Jutes. He equates the Angles with Anglian, the Saxons with Saxon, and the Jutes with Kentish. Certainly, it is safe to conclude that the earliest settlements were in East Anglia and the southeast, with a steady spread along the Thames valley, into the midlands, and northwards through Yorkshire and into southern Scotland.

Looking further afield, both in geography and time, English was a dialect of the Germanic branch of Indo-European. What does this mean? Indo-European refers to a group of languages, some with present-day forms, such as English, Welsh, French, Russian, Greek and Hindi, others now 'dead', such as Latin, Cornish (though revived by enthusiasts), Tocharian and Sanskrit, which are all believed to have a common single source. We do not have texts of Germanic, which is usually held to have existed in a generally common core between about 500 BC and about

Figure 1.1   *Anglo-Saxon England (from Hill, 1981)*

Figure 1.2   *The Indo-European languages*

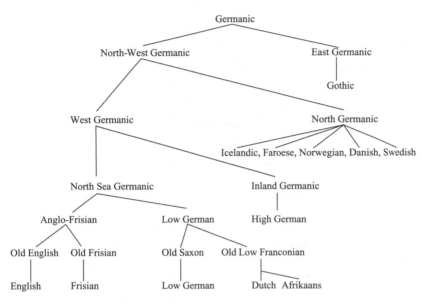

Figure 1.3   *The Germanic languages*

AD 200. Still less is there any textual evidence for the language we call Indo-European. The most usual view is that Indo-European originated in the southern steppes of Russia, although an alternative view holds that it spread from Anatolia in modern-day Turkey. The variety of opinions can be found in works such as Lehmann (1993), Gimbutas (1982), Renfrew (1987), and the excellent discussion in Mallory (1989). Many older works are equally important, and Meillet (1937) remains indispensable.

Whatever the actual shape of Indo-European (much work has been done to define this over the last two centuries), and wherever and whenever it may have been spoken, it will be obvious that any language which is the source of present-day languages as diverse as Hindi, Russian, Latin and English has everywhere undergone substantial change. The normal method of displaying the later developments of Indo-European is by a family tree such as that shown in Figure 1.2. Although family trees such as this are the staple diet of most books on historical linguistics, they should always be treated with caution. Indo-European is necessarily a vague, or at least fuzzy, entity, and the same is true of its branches.

In order to see that, consider a fairly standard family tree of Germanic, of which English is one part, such as that shown in Figure 1.3. Such a tree obscures a variety of problems, and one reason for this is that it forces a strict separation

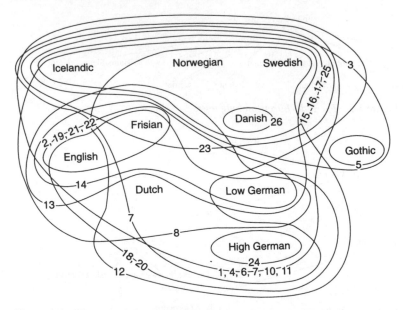

Figure 1.4   *Wave representation of Germanic (after Trask, 1996)*

between languages which certainly could only have emerged over a period of time and where various features may be shared by apparently discrete languages.

It is, therefore, worth comparing the family tree in Figure 1.3 with an alternative arrangement derived from the wave theory of language relationship, where languages are placed on an abstract map according to their degree of similarity. Figure 1.4 is one such diagram, based on significant shared linguistic features – the lines marking off the spread of features are called isoglosses. What both this wave diagram and the family tree demonstrate in their different ways is that the closest language to English in purely linguistic terms is Frisian, still spoken by about 400,000 Frisian–Dutch bilinguals in the Dutch province of Friesland and a few thousand speakers in Germany, most of them in Schleswig-Holstein.

How can we tell that the origins of English are as we have described? After all, the oldest English texts, apart from tiny fragments, date from about AD 700, and the only older Germanic texts are from Gothic, about 200–300 years earlier. And perhaps the earliest other Indo-European texts – the Anatolian languages, principally Hittite and Luwian – are from about 1400 BC. The method by which we attempt to deduce prehistoric stages of a language is called comparative reconstruction, and it is useful to consider one simple, but nevertheless important, example of this as shown in Table 1.2.

If you compare the forms language by language, then a number of features should become clear:

- where Sanskrit, Greek and Latin have /p/, English has /f/
- where Sanskrit, Greek and Latin have /t/, English has /θ/ (= OE þ)
- where Greek and Latin have /k/, and Sanskrit has /ś/, English has /h/

Table 1.2 *An example of comparative reconstruction*

Sanskrit	Greek	Latin	Old English	PD English
pitā	patêr	pater	fæder	father
tráyas	treîs	trēs	þrēo	three
śatám	he-katón	centum	hund	hundred
kás	tís	quis	hwā	who

and furthermore the similarity of all the forms is so great that this cannot be the result of accident.

If we assume that English /h/ was originally the voiceless fricative /x/, for which there is early spelling evidence, then we can note that, with one exception to the above, wherever Sanskrit, Greek and Latin have a voiceless stop, English has a voiceless fricative. The principles of comparative reconstruction then say that, all other things being equal, the earliest texts show the older state of affairs. Therefore, the four languages concerned must have shared a common origin in which the initial consonants were */p, t, k/, where * indicates a reconstructed form. In order to explain the apparently aberrant Sanskrit form *śatám* we have to claim that the original form was **katam* and that /k/ later became /ś/. We have so far ignored the forms of *who* in the fourth row. Rather than explaining these here, it might be instructive to see if you can work out why the Indo-European form might have been **/kwis/*. The example which we have just worked through, and which is called Grimm's Law after its discoverer, the nineteenth-century linguist and folklorist Jacob Grimm, is much more complex than we have suggested. Nevertheless it may give some indication of the methods of comparative reconstruction.

Exercises like the one just sketched form part of an edifice of scholarly knowledge built up over many years. Their success gives plausibility to hypotheses about the historical relationships between attested languages. Comparative reconstruction also allows one to fill in stages of language history for which there is no surviving historical evidence. It works most obviously in the areas of phonology, morphology and lexis, but even the syntax of Germanic and of Indo-European have been reconstructed in some detail. There is a danger that by *assuming* a single common ancestor one inevitably *produces* a single reconstructed proto-language. Potential circularity of this kind can be mitigated in ways to be discussed in a moment. In fact, much of what we think we know about the history of English is so tightly held in place in the accumulated mesh of interlocking hypotheses that its correctness is virtually certain. What appeals to the writers of this book is that there is so much still to discover.

In this process of intellectual discovery, the linguistic data are primary, but we can anchor our mesh of assumptions by means of certain 'reality checks' external to the language. Some are methodological. The greater the explanatory power of a hypothesis and the fewer special cases which have to be pleaded, the more likely it is to be correct. Second, hypothesised states of the language and the necessary changes between such states are only acceptable if they can be paralleled by states and changes which have actually been attested elsewhere (the Uniformitarian Hypothesis, that the types of possible language and language change have not changed over time). Some are non-linguistic: we require our internal history of the language to fit in with what can be discovered of its external history, which in turn is enmeshed with the cultural, political, economic and archaeological histories of its speakers. (Much of this chapter is concerned with those particular kinds of relation.) And some anchors involve the histories of other languages, which have their own complex mesh of assumptions and reconstructions: when a good sideways link is found between two such language histories, each may be strengthened. Relevant examples include the values of the letters used in the Latin alphabet when it was applied to the spelling of English, and the borrowing of words at various times from other languages into English and from English into other languages. Notice that these constraints on the construction of linguistic history are as necessary for historical periods as for prehistory. Even when we have actual texts to work on, all but the most basic description is still no more than inference or hypothesis. Like all scientific endeavour, the findings of historical linguistics are provisional.

1.3   Early history: immigration and invasion

We have already noted that English is a member of the Germanic branch of Indo-European. As such it was brought to Britain by Germanic speakers. (This section has for convenience been given a rather anglocentric subtitle; after all, the Anglo-Saxon and indeed Viking invasions are *emigrations* from the point of view of the people(s) left behind.) Of course, when these speakers came to Britain, the island was already occupied, and by two groups. Firstly, by speakers of a number of languages belonging to the Celtic branch of Indo-European: Welsh, Scots Gaelic, Cumbric, Cornish and Manx. At the beginning of the fifth century Celtic speakers occupied all parts of Britain. Secondly, and at least until 410, there were Latin speakers, since Britain as far north as southern Scotland was a part of the Roman Empire. The withdrawal of Rome from Britain in 410 may well have been the catalyst for the Germanic settlement. In linguistic terms, obvious Celtic influence on English was minimal, except for place- and river-names (see Section 6.5.2), *pace* the important series of articles incorporated in Preusler (1956). Latin influence was much more important, particularly for vocabulary (see Section 4.2.3). However, recent work has revived the suggestion that Celtic may have had considerable effect on low-status, spoken varieties of Old English, effects which only became evident in the morphology and syntax of written English after the Old English period; see particularly Poussa (1990), Vennemann (2001) and the collections edited by Tristram (1997, 2000, 2003). Advocates of this still controversial approach variously provide some striking evidence of coincidence of

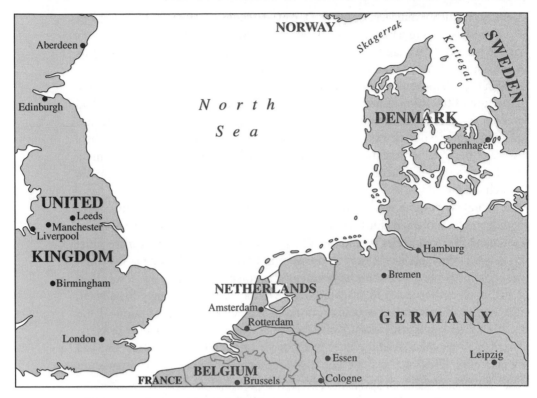

Figure 1.5   *The homeland of the Angles*

forms between Celtic languages and English, a historical framework for contact, parallels from modern creole studies, and – sometimes – the suggestion that Celtic influence has been systematically downplayed because of a lingering Victorian concept of condescending English nationalism.

As we have already mentioned, the Anglo-Saxon settlement of Britain began along the east and south coasts. The first settlements appear to have been in East Anglia. Exactly who these settlers were is hard to tell. Even the name 'Anglo-Saxon' is not of great help. The terms are not strictly comparable. The Angles probably formed a group of coastal dwellers in the area between, approximately, modern Amsterdam and southern Denmark (see Figure 1.5).

The Saxons, on the other hand, were a group of confederate tribes which may have included the Angles. Bede also tells us of the Jutes, about whom we know little more than that. But it seems significant that Kent and the Isle of Wight, where the Jutes seem to have been based, had distinctive features of their own, both linguistic and non-linguistic, throughout the Anglo-Saxon period. Deira, in Yorkshire, and Bernicia, in Northumberland, show linguistic and other signs of having been settled by somewhat different, more northerly, groups than elsewhere.

During the fifth century it is likely that the settlements were on the coast and along valleys, but within about a century settlement was extensive throughout the country, from Northumbria down to Dorset, excluding only the hilliest areas of the Pennines. It is remarkable how quickly the settlement of much of the country was achieved. If we are to believe Bede's account of Hengest and Horsa, this would suggest that the first Germanic invaders came as warriors to help local British (i.e. Celtic) rulers as they fought amongst themselves. In other words, the departure of the Romans meant that the organisational structures which they had erected for the governance of the country had begun to decay. Thus a vacuum of authority and power was created by their departure, and the Germanic tribes, aware of the attractions of the country, perhaps because their fathers or forefathers had been mercenaries in the Roman army, were eager and willing to step into the breach.

But that is not quite enough to explain the rapidity of the Germanic settlement, which was far more a conquest of Britain, linguistically speaking, than the Norman Conquest 500 years later would be. What its speed suggests is that there must have been considerable population pressure in northwestern Europe at the time, perhaps partly because in the fifth century the average temperature was lower than it had been earlier and would again be later. Whatever the case may have been, this conquest saw an overwhelmingly rapid replacement or absorption of the existing Celtic linguistic community by the newly arrived Germanic speakers. There is now some genetic evidence for mass immigration to central England (Weale et al., 2002), consistent with displacement of the *male* Celtic population by Anglo-Saxons but saying nothing about females. Before long Celtic speakers had been confined to the lands west of Offa's Dyke, to Cornwall, the northwest, and north of the Borders of Scotland. The gradual elimination of Celtic has continued remorselessly, albeit slowly, ever since. It may only have been with the coming of Christianity and the establishment of churches and abbeys that Anglo-Saxon England started to achieve the beginning of the types of political and social structure which we associate with later centuries.

After this first phase we witness the consolidation of Anglo-Saxon authority over their newly won territory in the seventh century with the emergence of what we now call the Heptarchy, or the rule of the seven kingdoms. These were the kingdoms of Wessex, Essex, Sussex, Kent, East Anglia, Mercia and Northumbria. It would be misleading, however, to think of these 'kingdoms' in modern terms: they were more like tribal groups, their boundaries vague and subject to change, not susceptible to the precise delineation of the kind that we are accustomed to today. Even their number, although hallowed by antiquity, may be due as much to numerology as to historical fact.

We shall return to the issues surrounding the Heptarchy, but not the Heptarchy itself, when considering political and cultural history. At the moment we need only observe that by the later seventh century the major centres of power appear to have been amongst the northern kingdoms, and especially Northumbria. In the following century Mercia gradually became the key centre of power. But this was to change. For at the very end of the eighth century, in 793, as the *Anglo-Saxon Chronicle reports*, 'the harrying of the heathen miserably destroyed God's church in Lindisfarne by rapine and slaughter' (Garmonsway, 1954: 56). For now Britain was to be invaded once more. This time, however, the invasions were to come from fellow-speakers of Germanic, namely Scandinavian Vikings from Denmark and Norway.

For the next half-century or more, these invasions constituted no more than sporadic raids, particularly along the whole of the eastern and southern coasts. But from 835 onwards, when the Vikings attacked Sheppey on the Thames estuary, raids became more frequent until, in 865, a Viking army over-wintered in East Anglia. By 870 these Danes had overrun all the eastern parts of Mercia and Northumbria as well as East Anglia, whilst Norwegians had occupied northwestern parts as well as the Isle of Man, having first established a base in Dublin. The languages spoken by these invaders could not have been grossly different from the language of the Anglo-Saxons: at most they would have differed to much the same degree as spoken Glaswegian and Bronx English differ from each other today. Nevertheless, we can be certain that if it had not been for the resistance of Wessex, led by Alfred, the English spoken today would be much more like a language such as Danish.

Alfred came to the throne of Wessex in 871, at the height of the Danish invasions. Through his strategy and tactics in both war and diplomacy he was able, first, to regroup the Wessex forces and, then, to establish a truce with the Danes by the Treaty of Wedmore in 878. From our point of view, the most important feature of that treaty was that it recognised Danish settlement roughly speaking northeast of a line from London to Chester. This area was known as the Danelaw. In the Danelaw there must have been many Danish speakers living alongside English speakers, apparently with relatively little mutual hostility and their languages to some degree mutually intelligible.

As we shall see later, the success of Wessex in resisting the Danes had important repercussions for the political structure of the country, but the point to note at present is that this ensured the long-term dominance of English as the language of a more obviously national kingdom than had previously existed. Over time, the Viking invaders were assimilated into the native population. It is not surprising that, as this assimilation took place, Scandinavian linguistic features entered English quite extensively. Remarkably, however, there is little evidence for such features before the eleventh century. Indeed, of the most obvious Scandinavian features in the present-day language, namely the third-person pronoun *they*, which replaced Old English *hi*, and *are*, which replaced Old English *synt*, the latter is first found in northern dialects towards the very end of the tenth century and the former is a twelfth-century phenomenon. The earliest Scandinavian words are those such as *lagu* 'law' and *wicing* 'Viking, pirate', which have clear relations with the time of the Viking settlements. Other, everyday words which entered English from the settlements, such as *egg*, *guess*, *leg*, *sky*, *window*, only became apparent in later centuries.

And because English, Danish and Norse were so similar at the time of the settlements, there are quite a number of pairs of words, historically identical in origin, which were typical of different areas. One such pair is *church* ~ *kirk*, where the former is English, the latter Scandinavian, for Scandinavian retains a velar stop where English shows palatalisation. One particularly interesting example of this is the place-element *-chester* (originally from Lat. *caster* or *castra*), for the variation between that form and *-caster* (phonologically modified by Scandinavian settlers), as in *Manchester* ~ *Lancaster*, helps us to assess the degree of Scandinavianisation in different parts of the country. We will return to this question below. An even more accurate picture of Scandinavian influence in Britain can be obtained by inspecting the distribution of Scandinavian place-names in Britain, as shown on the map, Figure 1.6.

A noteworthy feature of the eleventh century is that the beginning of the century saw an Anglo-Saxon king, Ethelred, on the throne, but by 1016 the Dane Cnut (Canute) was king; twenty-five years or so later, there was once more an Anglo-Saxon king, but from 1066 the king of England was a Norman. The first point to make here is that when Cnut came to the throne it was after prolonged warfare between the Anglo-Saxon king and the Danes, but during that period there were important English leaders on both sides (and neither), and that Cnut's accession to the throne after the death of Ethelred was not particularly hostile by the temper of the times (indeed, Cnut married Ethelred's widow, Emma, even if it was primarily a marriage of convenience and even if the fact that Cnut was not monogamous seems, not unnaturally, to have been a source of tension between them). But the linguistic distinctions between English and Danes seem not to have been the cause of serious hostility. On the Scandinavian presence in England, see further Chapter 6, especially Section 6.5.6.

When Edward the Confessor came to the throne in 1042, he was more a harbinger of Norman French influence than a restorer of the English tongue. He had spent a long time in exile, during which he cultivated close relations with the dukes of Normandy. He even appointed a Frenchman as bishop of London in 1050; furthermore, when he died in January 1066 he had managed to muddy the succession sufficiently to ensure that Harold and William of Normandy could both reasonably claim the throne, and neither was reluctant to do so. Famously it was William who triumphed.

The most important immediate effects of the Norman Conquest were political, for example in the appointment of Norman bishops and the redistribution of land to the Normans, as witnessed in the *Domesday Book*. Cultural, including linguistic, effects were much more long-term. That is to say, the eventual influence of French on English can be ascribed to the cultural patterns imposed on England as a consequence of the Conquest. (The situation was more complex in Scotland, still predominantly Gaelic-speaking, where some Normans and Saxons settled.) We noted earlier that Scandinavian structures took a long time to be embedded into the structure of English; the same is certainly true of French. One reason for this was undoubtedly the fact that French, belonging to an entirely different form of Indo-European, had developed independently from Germanic for a period stretching over many centuries. Consequently the structures of French were, and

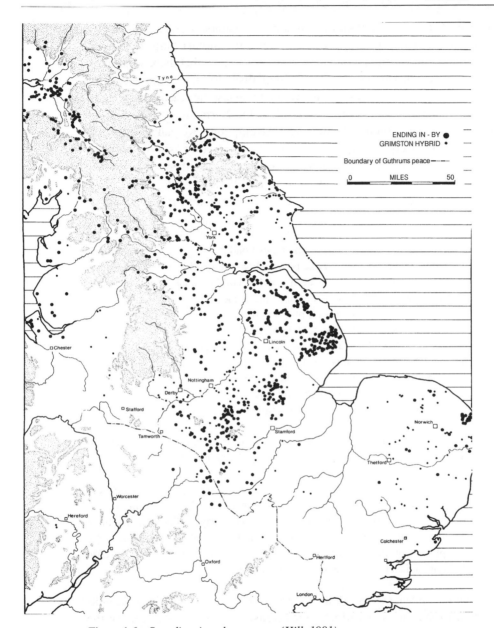

Figure 1.6   *Scandinavian place-names (Hill, 1981)*

remain, quite different from those of English. Thus there was no possibility of simple admixture, as there had been with Scandinavian. This, of course, meant that bilingualism, as the consequence of linguistic similarity, was far less likely.

To add to this, the pattern of social structures was very different from that obtaining in the Danelaw and eventually still larger parts of the country. Unlike the Scandinavians, the Norman French came as a superordinate power. It is true that the Normans, themselves in origin Franco-Viking, did not bring with them some superordinate culture, but they brought power, authority and an aristocratic élite. We know that the new rulers had French as their mother tongue for many generations, but amongst the landowning classes we know that there were inter-marriages and that to that extent there was bilingualism. But it is far more difficult to assess the degree of that bilingualism. We can make some reasonable sugges-tions based on social class and on the basis that the Normans were very much a minority group in the country. Under these assumptions, we can surmise that the Normans were likely to acquire a degree of bilingualism simply in order to communicate with the far from silent majority. On the other hand, English speakers had to acquire French if they wished to prosper in aristocratic circles. The point is made more eloquently in the *Chronicle of Robert of Gloucester* in about 1325:

> Þus com, lo, Englelond in-to Normandies hond:
> And þe Normans ne couþe speke þo bote hor owe speche,
> And speke French as hii dude atom, and hor children dude also teche,
> So þat heiemen of þis lond, þat of hor blod come,
> Holdeþ alle þulke speche þat hii of hom nome;
> Vor bote a man conne Frenss me telþ of him lute.
> Ac lowe men holdeþ to Engliss, and to hor owe speche ȝute.
> Ich wene þer ne beþ in al þe world contreys none
> Þat ne holdeþ to hor owe speche, bote Englelond one.
> Ac wel me wot uor to conne boþe wel it is,
> Vor þe more þat a mon can, þe more wurþe he is.

> Lo, in this way England came into the hands of Normandy: and the Normans could only speak their own language and spoke French, as they did at home, and also had their children taught it, so that the noblemen of this land, that came from their blood, all keep to the same language as they received from them; for unless a man knows French he is held in little regard. But men of low estate keep with English, and to their own language still. I think that there are no countries in the world where they do not keep with their own language, except England alone. But people know that it is good to know both, because the more a man knows, the more he is honoured.

There are a significant number of differences in the ways in which the Scandi-navian and the French invasions affected the English language. Firstly, there is the matter of date. We have already noticed that Scandinavian influences only become apparent in the eleventh century. French influence too takes some time to perco-late through the system. The time-lag is about one or two centuries. If we look at the *Peterborough Chronicle*, the last part of which (and equally the last rem-nant of the *Anglo-Saxon Chronicle*) was written in 1155, a few French loanwords appear, for example *iustise* replaces the Old English *rihtwisnesse*; a particularly interesting example is the replacement of *gersume* by *tresor* 'treasure', since the former is itself a loanword from Norse. Generally the number of French loans only becomes great in the following century. Furthermore, there is a dialectal problem with French influence. The Normans who invaded spoke their regional dialect, which itself had been altered by Viking invasions. This dialect, therefore, was very different from the central French dialect of the areas around Paris and Orleans. Until the end of the twelfth century and the reign of Henry II, the French of the court was Anglo-Norman, but from then on the court became associated with Paris and Orleans, and the language changed accordingly. Chaucer makes the distinction clear in his description of the Prioress in his *General Prologue*:

> And Frenssh she spak ful faire and fetisly,
> After the scole of Stratford atte Bow,
> For Frenssh of Parys was to hire unknowe.

One example of the differences between Norman French and Central French is the word *chancellor*. When it first came into English it had the Norman form *canceller*, with an initial velar stop. The Central French form, which had palatal /ʃ/ (cf. *kirk* vs *church* discussed earlier, also the result of Scandinavian influence), first appears only at the end of the thirteenth century.

A second feature which contrasts Scandinavian and French influence is linguistic variation in Britain. This shows itself in two different ways. We have already noted that Scandinavian influence was originally predominant in the Danelaw. In a moment or two we shall see that eventually many Scandinavian elements entered southern dialects as well, but this is a two-stage process. There is the original contact between the two languages which brought Scandinavian features into the English of the Danelaw. Then, later, there is spread within English by means of interdialectal contact. Contact between French and English, on the other hand, shows a much lesser geographical variation. The key here is register. That is to say, the variables which affect English in respect of French are far more to do with a contrast between types of social language than geography. Thus, if a text is concerned with, say, religion or science, or it is a formal piece, then it is probable that it will contain a higher proportion of French loanwords than a text which is purely secular or colloquial, whichever part of the country the text comes from. In this respect we should also note that Scandinavian loans are more likely to be colloquial (or everyday).

This feature is one which persists even in the present-day language, where, as in Middle English, we often find pairs of words with related meanings, one of which is English in origin, the other French. A typical example of such a doublet is *house* ~ *mansion* (cf. present-day French *maison*). The difference between the two words is essentially one of social prestige. This discussion naturally leads into a discussion of another language which influences English and has done so since the sixth century, namely Latin. In the Old English period Latin had contributed significantly to the lexical stock of English, but the Middle English period saw an even greater influx of Latin words. In part this was due to the fact that French, a Romance language, derived most of its structure and vocabulary from Latin. Consequently, it is often quite difficult, indeed sometimes impossible, to determine whether a word has been taken from French or from its antecedent language. Sometimes it is possible to find triplets, that is to say, three words, one each from Latin, French and (home-grown) English, all with the same basic meaning. So we find *regal, royal* and *kingly* and, as with doublets, the social prestige typically varies between high-prestige Latin and low-prestige English.

None of the above is intended to deny the growing presence of French loanwords in everyday language. However, we have to be careful about some aspects of that vocabulary. For example, the introduction of French loans for food, such as *beef, pork* and *mutton*, is sometimes held to demonstrate a considerable degree of bilingualism. This view owes a great deal to Scott's *Ivanhoe*, which claims that animals on the hoof were called by their English names, but by French names when cooked. The initial reaction is to believe that; it is only when we recall terms such as English *lamb* (alongside *mutton*) or Anglo-Norman *cattle* alongside English *cow* that its plausibility diminishes. It is more likely, although less romantically appealing, to suggest that French loans were most probable in administration and learning, and that by and large 'ordinary' words were only borrowed in the few areas where there was constant interaction between English and French speakers. This neither demonstrates extensive bilingualism nor even that there was extensive borrowing beyond a few specific areas.

It is too easy to slip into the view that either the Danish Conquest or the Norman Conquest was the more important linguistically. The more likely position is that, throughout, the language remained fundamentally *English*. What we find is that the Danish Conquest had important consequences in some areas of the language. In particular, and as we have mentioned briefly already, some key elements in the present-day language come from Danish, above all many parts of the third-person pronoun system and part of the present tense of the verb *be*. The verbal inflexion *-s* is also probably due to Scandinavian influence. It has been argued that the simplification and loss of other inflections, particularly nominal and adjectival ones, might have been hastened by the intermingling of languages with similar vocabulary but noticeably different endings – even that there was extensive pidginisation in the Danelaw. It is in the core inflectional morphology of the language, plus such function words as *till* and *though*, that the most striking influences are seen.

What exactly was the linguistic contact situation in the Danelaw? Poussa (1982) argues that the language which developed there – and which was later to form the basis of standard English – was actually an Anglo-Scandinavian creole, though most others are sceptical of such a radical degree of intermixing. There is now an extensive literature on the question, with useful summaries by Danchev (1997), Görlach (1986), Hansen (1984), McWhorter (2002), Thomason & Kaufman (1988: 263–342) and Wallmannsberger (1988). Syntactic work by Kroch & Taylor (1997, and with Ringe, 2000) exploits the related idea that a Scandinavianised dialect of Middle English could have developed different rules of cliticisation and word order from dialects in the south, and that contact between such a northern dialect and more southerly dialects might have triggered the changes which led to modern English word order; see Sections 3.5.2, 3.5.3.

If an early Anglo-Celtic creole is at least a tenable hypothesis, and an Anglo-Danish creole even a plausible one, the case for an Anglo-French creole is much less so, though it too has been advocated; for details see the surveys just mentioned. Although we shall not examine the possibility any further, we should still look at French influence outside the borrowing of vocabulary. It is best to start by saying that French influence is largely absent from inflectional morphology. The only possibilities concern the eventual domination of the plural inflection -s at the expense of -en (hence *shoes* rather than *shoon*) and the rise of the personal pronoun *one*. Although there are parallels in French, it is virtually certain that the English developments are entirely independent.

The strongest influence of French can be best seen in two other areas, apparently unrelated but in fact closely connected to each other. These are: (i) derivational morphology; (ii) stress. Like all the other Germanic languages, Old English had a rich range of derivational prefixes and suffixes, and new words were routinely created by affixation and by compounding. When a gap in vocabulary was felt, native word formation was the default and foreign borrowing relatively the exception. One effect of the influx of French words into Middle English was that subsequently a recourse to foreign sources became quite normal – not that native word formation died out. (There is an obvious contrast with German, where until recently the use of native processes was overwhelmingly dominant.) Over time the inventory of affixes underwent a big change, with the loss of some items productive in OE and the adoption of many affixes, for example -*ment* for abstract nouns and -*able* for adjectives, deduced from their presence in loanwords. Furthermore the stress pattern of English words lost its simple, fixed pattern – primary stress carried by the first syllable apart from specific kinds of prefix – with the adoption of many words with the level stress of French. There was a period of uncertainty in the stressing of many borrowed words, in some cases lasting to the present day (*adult*, *controversy*), before most settled either into the traditional, Germanic pattern or the novel, Romance distribution. (A detailed discussion in terms of stress rules will be found in Section 2.6.2.4.) And these two areas of influence are linked by the fact that modern English derivational morphology seems to operate in two strata, roughly Germanic and Romance, which have separate distributions, different effects on the stressing of the resultant word, and which, when combined, typically put the Germanic affix closer to the stem.

1.4   Later history: internal migration, emigration, immigration again

The previous section dealt with three major invasions of the British Isles. For nearly a millennium now, England has had no hostile foreign armies marching over it, a remarkable record by European standards (even Switzerland's is shorter). The potential importance of this fact can be seen in a thought-experiment. Imagine a country of utter stability, where every local speech community develops undisturbed through the generations from the late eleventh century to the present. If the homeland of English had really been such a country, the history of the language would have been a lot simpler, if duller. Admittedly, some English rural dialects do reflect long periods of continuity (see Section 7.6). But 'English-land' has not generally resembled our imaginary country, and indeed English is not confined to England, nor even for centuries now to the British Isles. This guides us in our necessarily selective sketch of the external history of the language. What are the events that have particularly tended to disrupt or deflect the smooth, geographically stable development of English? Major population movements will certainly figure largely in such a story. However, even where populations remain *in situ*, linguistic influence takes place by other means, so that we must look too at certain developments in cultural history and in the history of transportation and communication.

By the twelfth century Westminster had supplanted Winchester as the seat of national government. Westminster was still geographically (albeit only by a couple of miles) and linguistically separate from London in the ME period. London was the largest town in northern Europe (10,000–15,000 people in 1085) and commercially the most important in England, though Norwich, York, Lincoln and Exeter were major centres too. An indication of population distribution in late-eleventh-century England can be gleaned from the map, Figure 1.7.

Immigration to London from particular parts of the country is of great significance to the future development of London English – and, given the then importance of London, to English in general. The newcomers brought new dialect forms into London speech, which changed not just what was said but also social judgements as to what was acceptable and, sometimes, what forms could serve as practical compromises among such a mixed population. Historians have made ingenious use of taxation records and other documents to count and often to identify by name and locality the individuals who moved to London (Keene, 2000: 104–11 is an important recent survey). In the early fourteenth century, Norfolk, in East Anglia, and Essex and Hertfordshire, in the east midlands, were the major source areas. Later in the century the central midlands (Leicestershire, Northamptonshire, Bedfordshire) preponderated.

The disproportionate growth of London in the late Middle Ages and beyond, and the convergence of commercial and political power in what was increasingly a single location, had many important consequences for the history of English, including the dialect mixture and incipient standardisation which will be examined in detail in Section 5.2.1. In 1550 the population of London was already about 120,000, well above that of Florence, Rome, Madrid or Amsterdam and a little below Venice's, while Naples and Paris were nearly twice as big, and Constantinople about three times (Beier & Finlay, 1986: 3). By 1750 London had overtaken all of them.

Indeed the growth and dispersal of the overall English-speaking population is an important factor in itself. Up to the seventeenth century it was almost entirely confined to mainland Britain and amounted to only some two million speakers in

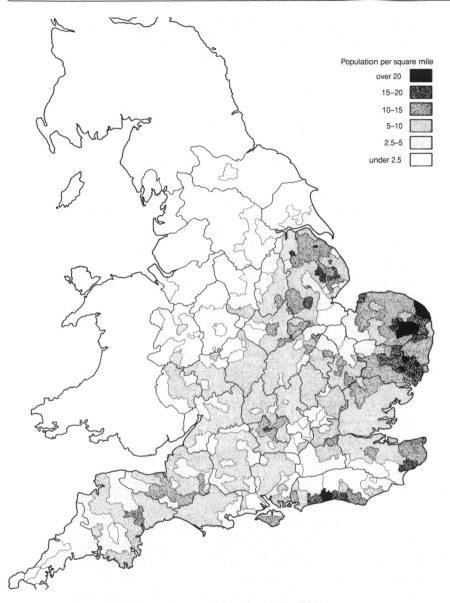

Population per square mile

over 20

15–20

10–15

5–10

2.5–5

under 2.5

Figure 1.7   *Domesday population (from Hill, 1981)*

1500 and 5–8½ million in 1700: compare that with the present-day figures quoted at the start of this chapter. (Incidentally, growth was not unidirectional: plague in particular – 'the Black Death', as it was rather later called – could reduce a population by a half or two-thirds in a matter of months; in England there were substantial outbreaks at various times between 1348 and 1666.) With the spread of the British Empire and the appearance of increasingly important populations of English speakers in other continents, the geographical and social shape of English became rather different, reinforcing the need to speak of plural *Englishes*.

The two medieval English universities were founded in small midlands towns within 60 miles of London, at Oxford in the late twelfth century and Cambridge in 1209. Many young men attended for anything from a short period to five years; a third or so did not achieve a degree. There was frequent interchange of scholars between the two. The number of Englishmen in residence at any one time is estimated at 1,900–2,600 in the 1370s, rising to 3,000 by 1450, a probable participation rate of somewhere between 1.8 per cent and 3.2 per cent of the relevant male age group. Later, in the 1630s, it is conservatively estimated to have been 2½ per cent. These were the only universities in England right up to the nineteenth century. (Now there are over seventy, and no longer men-only.) Even though university populations cannot match the early urban growth of London, attendance at university is nevertheless thought to have played some significant part in dialect mixing and national standardisation towards the end of the ME period and beyond. From the fourteenth century or so another venue for higher education was the four Inns of Court in London. In Scotland the earliest university foundations were St Andrews (1411–13), Glasgow (1451), Aberdeen (one constituent college c.1495) and Edinburgh (1583).

Outside England there were significant English-speaking populations in Edinburgh and (from 1170) Dublin, which became the centre of a small area of Anglo-Norman settlement in Ireland, the Pale – a word whose meanings have moved from 'fence-post' to 'fence' to 'boundary' to 'area under (English) jurisdiction'; hence the much later and typically English usage *beyond the Pale* 'unacceptable'. From the fourteenth to the seventeenth centuries, the forms of English used in Scotland began to diverge from those used in England. The impetus for this divergence was political and the result of the Three Hundred Years' War between Scotland and England, in which, for a long time, the Scots were able to assert their independence. Paradoxically, the success of a distinct Scottish form of the language came at the expense of Scots Gaelic, as the lowland English-speaking leaders ousted Gaelic leaders, symbolised by the transferral of the capital from Perth to Edinburgh. It is to this period that we owe most of, for example, the distinctive Scots legal terminology, such as *feu* 'land duty'. That word also highlights another feature of the Scots of the time, namely the considerable number of French loanwords found exclusively in Scots, such as *tassie* 'cup'. These loans are often connected to the Franco-Scottish alliance of the period, as they fought together against the 'Auld Enemy', England.

The demise of Scots as a distinct, partly standardised, language came about not merely because of the Union of the Crowns in 1603, but for other, more pressing reasons. Two are of particular importance. Firstly, the Reformation brought with it the Bible in English, and an English, rather than Scots, form of the Bible at that (even before the Authorised Version). Secondly, Anglo-Scottish trade encouraged the use of English rather than Scots. As we enter the twenty-first century, it remains to be seen to what extent devolution will result in Scots once more having a distinctive form of the language. Once again, that is likely to be determined by political decisions.

Table 1.3 *National GDP in 1890. Figures from Maddison (1991: Tables A.2, B.7). GDPs are expressed in 1985 US dollars*

Country	GDP in 1890 US $billion	Ranking out of 16	Population million
United States	196.4	1	63.3
United Kingdom, including Ireland	118.4	2	35.0
France	77.9	3	40.1
Germany	50.5	4	30.0
Australia	12.2	8	3.1
Canada	9.1	11	4.9

Britain was (with Spain, Portugal, France and the Netherlands) one of the European colonial powers which between them came to dominate much of the rest of the world for hundreds of years. The British maritime expansion only became significant from the seventeenth century onwards, when colonies were established in India, Southeast Asia, North America, the West Indies, Central America and Africa. These were essentially commercial ventures at first, sometimes acquired from another colonial power (whether by direct assault or as the prize for some other victory). From 1651 to the early 1800s, colonial trade was firmly controlled by Navigation Acts enacted in Britain: what cargoes, whose ships and which destinations; mostly, of course, British shipping to, from or via British ports. In the mid-eighteenth century Britain became the dominant power in Canada and India, and later added (among others) Australia, New Zealand, Hong Kong, Burma, Malta, Cyprus, Pacific islands, and large swathes of east, west and southern Africa. After the Napoleonic Wars it had taken over economic leadership of the world from Holland (see Maddison, 1991: 30). By the end of the nineteenth century the British Empire, as it was by then known, accounted for nearly a quarter of the land and over a quarter of the population of the world. (Compare the estimates of English speakers now in Chapter 9, Table 9.1.) For one small country to project its power so widely was remarkable. Almost the only check to its expansion to date had been the loss of the important American colonies after 1776, and indeed by the second half of the nineteenth century, the US had overtaken Britain in absolute measures of wealth and economic performance, and Britain was already in slow decline. In 1890 the relative economic status of Britain, the United States and the rest of the industrialised world can be indicated by the estimates of Gross Domestic Product shown in Table 1.3.

One obvious linguistic effect on English of Britain's imperial expansion was the incorporation of lexical borrowings from a wide range of languages (see Section 4.4.2). The more important effect was to transplant the English language to lands in at least four continents beyond Europe, some of which would eventually come to rival and even overtake the homeland in importance – whatever measure of 'importance' is taken, including linguistic – and to sow the seeds of English as the principal language of international communication (see Section 9.3).

As mentioned above, the American colonists successfully fought their War of Independence in 1776–83. The new country was already substantial in population and in area, but still around a tenth of its later extension. The nineteenth century saw a remarkable westward movement of the frontier of the United States, the white European-American expansion rolling over and sometimes almost wiping out indigenous tribes ('[Red] Indians', as they were collectively known in English, later called Native Americans, or in Canada, First Peoples). There were modest lexical gains to American English, for example *canyon* from Spanish, *pemmican* from Cree. The economic centre of gravity moved westwards over time, with Texas and California gaining their current heavyweight status comparatively recently. Large numbers of settlers were drawn in from around the world, but especially Europe. Later many more nationalities came to the USA, from Europe, Asia and Latin America above all, as refugees or economic migrants. Interestingly, the largest ancestry groups self-reported in the 2000 US census (numbers scaled up from a sample, and not mutually exclusive) were: German 46.5 million, Irish 33.1 m, various Hispanic 34.3 m, Afro-American 31.6 m, English 28.3 m, American 19.6 m, Italian 15.9 m, Scotch-Irish/Scottish 10.6 m. The same census estimated that about 18 per cent of Americans aged five or over lived in households where a language other than English was spoken. We illustrate more recent trends from the University of California at Los Angeles, which encourages the 'heritage languages' of those of its US students with a non-English language spoken in the family home. In 1999 the languages Spanish, Chinese, Korean, Russian, Vietnamese, Tagalog [Philippines], Egyptian, Colloquial Arabic, Hindi, Persian, Hebrew, Japanese, Polish, Thai, Ukrainian and Indonesian were listed by UCLA, the first five involving over fifty 'heritage speakers' each. The many languages which flourish in the USA have enriched American English enormously. Note, however, that there is a strong emphasis on the learning of English as part of the acquisition of US citizenship. (Is it a coincidence that American road signs and clothes-care labels have more text and fewer symbols than British ones?)

Canada was the part of North America whose British colonists did not secede. They had already overcome their French rivals, who remained important minorities in Ontario and elsewhere, and a majority in Quebec. (The Cajun community had been expelled to Louisiana in 1755.) Anglo-French rivalry, in the beginning European-based, latterly home-grown, has dominated the entire history of Canada. Both English and French are national languages, and certain parts of the rapidly growing country are now, like the USA, something of an international melting-pot. The same can be said of twentieth-century Australia, although here the original settlers were overwhelmingly English and Irish. Indeed, the earliest ones were convicts and their gaolers: about 150,000 convicts had been transported to eastern Australia by the mid-nineteenth century – about one-third Irish, one in five female – and nearly 10,000 to Western Australia. Free settlers joined the population from early in the century. As in Canada, a huge country was only gradually explored and its wildernesses never populated, while native peoples fared badly at the hands of the colonists. Also as in Canada, a federal national government was belatedly formed: Canada's in 1867, Australia's in 1900–1. New Zealand was settled by traders, at first as an offshoot of Australia, and by the 1830s was being settled direct from Europe. It was annexed by Britain in the 1840s. The remainder of the century saw great growth in the economy, especially from farming, and the suppression of the native Maori peoples.

Britain's long and complex relationship with India began in a trading relationship with parts of the Mughal Empire around 1600, when the East India Company was founded. There was rivalry with other colonial powers, and the British gradually became the dominant foreign trading power over the next two centuries, many individuals making huge fortunes. Military involvement began at the end of the seventeenth century, but the size and development of the country meant that the British worked more by political alliances and trade than by conquest. From 1784 the administration of British India was divided between the East India Company and crown appointees, and during the first half of the nineteenth century the whole country fell under British rule, directly or through Indian potentates; the company lost its position in 1858. In many ways India was the most important part of the empire. Large numbers of Britons went out as administrators, developing a system which partially westernised the country in a combination of English and indigenous law and practice. Not until 1947 was Britain forced to give India up, partitioning the country into (mainly Hindu) India and (Muslim) Pakistan, the latter of which subsequently broke up into the already geographically split Pakistan and Bangladesh.

South Africa is different again. Its spoils were tussled over by the Dutch and the British from the time of the first small settlements on the Cape of Good Hope in the seventeenth century, and the history of South Africa – not a single country until 1910 – is a complex web involving also Xhosa, Zulu and many other tribal groups. An economy that had been largely agricultural took off in the late nineteenth century with the discovery of diamonds and gold. From 1899 to 1902 the brutal 'Boer War' or 'South African War' between the British and the Afrikaners (Dutch settlers) led in the end to a costly British victory. In the twentieth century the dominion enshrined both English and Dutch (later replaced by Afrikaans) as official languages. It was an increasingly racially segregated country, especially from the 1940s onwards, and a policy of separate development, latterly known as *apartheid*, remained in force until 1991. Black majority rule arrived in 1994.

The main ex-British colonies where the settler stock was in the majority had all gained full independence by the middle of the twentieth century – some long before, and some retaining the British monarch as head of state – and in the remainder of the century nearly all of the rest of the empire followed, notably India and Pakistan in 1947 and much of east and west Africa in the 1960s (long after the very different South Africa). Colonisation and decolonisation presents a varied picture as far as migration to and from Britain is concerned. There has been at times large-scale emigration from Britain and Ireland to North America and Australasia above all, and from Ireland to Britain. Significant twentieth-century immigration to Britain has come from the Caribbean, from various parts of Africa, including many east African Asians, and from the Indian subcontinent (including ex-settlers and administrators of British ancestry). These arrivals have altered the language mix in contemporary Britain by introducing new varieties of English, such as Jamaican patois, and also such languages as Urdu, Bengali, Gujarati, and (Cypriot) Turkish and Greek.

To return to intra-national matters, there has been a drift from rural to urban living throughout the world, but in England the pattern was different from the rest of Europe (Finlay & Shearer, 1986: 40). By 1600 about 7.9 per cent of the population of England lived in towns; in 1800 the figure was 27.5 per cent. It was in England that the industrial revolution started in the mid-eighteenth century, bringing the factory system, new machinery, the widespread use of iron and steel, new means of transport, new relationships between science and commerce. It accelerated the depopulation of the countryside and the growth of towns especially in the midlands and north of England – Manchester, for example, growing thirty-fold between 1717 and 1851. And it was a major factor in the world economic dominance successively of Britain and the USA.

Here we may note the large-scale building of canals (only significant from the late eighteenth century in Britain and the early nineteenth in the US) and, a few decades later, of railways. Dialect isoglosses tend to reflect political and ecclesiastical boundaries and natural barriers (rivers, mountains, and so on): limited communication inhibits linguistic contact. New methods of transport can link distant centres linguistically, so that changes no longer just spread smoothly across the country but may instead leapfrog the hinterland and jump from town to town. Canals were a very important accompaniment of the industrialisation of Britain, but unlike riverboats in parts of the USA were never a means of mass transportation of people. Railways certainly were (even if the very earliest British ones were for freight only). Railways were of particular importance in tying together far-separated parts of big countries like the USA, Canada, South Africa, Australia and India. By 1914 in Britain (Schwartz, 1999) and America, the rail networks had reached their peak in extent – subsequently they were cut back in Britain, Canada and the US – and road transport too was beginning to be responsible for the movement of large numbers of people, exposing travellers to forms of English which previously would have remained outside their experience. In the late twentieth century the growth of mass air travel for tourism was allowing a significant proportion of the British population to travel abroad for their holidays – 35 million holiday visits in 1999 by air, sea and tunnel – whether or not with significant exposure to the Spanish, French and other languages of the most popular destinations. In the USA there has been a proportionally much smaller take-up of foreign travel, but then again there is widespread exposure to other languages, particularly Spanish, within the country's own borders.

English-speaking Canadians have significant contact with Canadian French, officially at any rate, while the English of South Africa interacts with Afrikaans and with Bantu languages.

Recall now our earlier thought-experiment. The effect of war on the English language has not in fact been negligible at all, and we must note a number of conflicts which affect our story. There was terrible suffering during the civil war between Stephen and Matilda in the mid-twelfth century. During this anarchic time Winchester was burned down and power finally passed to Westminster. The Hundred Years' War between England and France lasted on and off from 1337 to 1453. Its effects were greater on France, where the fighting took place, but it cost England dear in lives, resources, and all but a fragment of its once large French territories, of relevance too in the growth of English nationalism and the decline of Anglo-French. Furthermore, it interacted with the Scottish Wars of Independence, which helped in the spread of a distinctively Scots form of the language (see above). The Wars of the Roses, a struggle for the English throne between the Houses of York and Lancaster, involved major battles in several parts of England. They lasted from 1455 to 1485, destroying in the process much of the old nobility. The English Civil Wars lasted from 1642 to 1649, with Puritan rule from then until the restoration of the Stuart monarchy in 1660. There were several brutal military campaigns which swept across large parts of the midlands – deaths have been estimated at 100,000 – and a large 'New Model Army' created in 1645 was national rather than local, yet cohesive, with consequences for the mixing of dialects (Morrill, 1991: 9, cited from Nevalainen & Raumolin-Brunberg, 2003: 31–2). Multiple reversals of fortune between Parliamentarians and Royalists ensured a period of rapid social change (see Nevalainen & Raumolin-Brunberg, 2003: 31–2). As far as major wars in 'English-land' are concerned, we must not forget the American Civil War of 1861–5, an enormous conflict which killed over 600,000 men. Its consequences for the future path of the USA, for black–white relations, for the slave and the cotton trades, were of course huge. Cassidy & Hall (2001: 201–5) assert its lexical importance in the history of American English, citing special senses like *doughboy* 'infantryman' (1865–) and new lexical items like *Ku-Klux-Klan* (1867–), while the increasing prestige of rhotic (*r*-pronouncing) dialects at the turn of the twentieth century may have been due in some part to the fact that the losers of the Civil War were non-rhotic (Fisher, 2001: 77). On the continued advance of rhotic accents, see further below.

After the seventeenth century it is doubtful that English/British military campaigns abroad had very much direct effect on the development of English, except insofar as territorial gains were concerned, until the twentieth century. The South African War drew the attention of the British to that part of the world, and some lexical innovations resulted from it, including that British invention, the *concentration camp*; the *Kop*, a raised stand at Liverpool's football ground (1926, from Spion Kop, scene of a battle in 1900, Afrikaans *kop* 'head, hill'); and the short-lived journalistic humorism *maffick* 'celebrate boisterously' (1900–10), back-formed from *mafficking* = Mafeking, scene of the lifting of a famous siege.

Further into the century the two world wars led to truly colossal upheaval. The First World (or 'Great') War is dated 1914–18 in Britain and its colonies, with the United States becoming decisively involved from 1917. About 8.9 million men were mobilised in the British Empire, of whom some 12 per cent were listed as dead or missing; the US figures are nearly 4.4 million and under 3 per cent. Overall some 65 million men were called up on all sides, 37½ million of whom became casualties, including 8½ million dead. Another 10 million civilians died as well. Usage of First World War origin includes *trench warfare* and *have (got) NP taped* 'be on top of a problem' (from having an enemy position in precise artillery range, as if measured by tape).

The Second World War, the deadliest so far waged, involved Britain and the Dominions from 1939, the USA from 1941, and lasted until 1945. Again a large proportion of men of military age were conscripted. Overall deaths, military and civilian, are estimated at 357,000 for the UK, 86,000 for the Dominions and colonies, 298,000 for the USA. The military losses, though terrible enough, are lower than for the Great War. (Losses by other nations, especially the USSR, Poland, Japan and Germany, were almost inconceivably higher. The Second World War is notorious for the Nazi slave labour and extermination programmes, and for the use of terror bombing by both sides, by which urban civilian populations became victim-combatants.) Civilian deaths were some 93,000 in the UK, including 61,000 from bombing. Three million people moved from target areas to the countryside at the height of the campaign, and maybe a third of the UK's housing stock was destroyed. Large American forces were stationed in Britain during the war ('overpaid, over-sexed and over here', as the well-worn contemporary *bon mot* had it); the effect on British civilian life was considerable, and there have been American military bases in Britain ever since. From this period date *blitz* 'heavy air-raid(s)', from German *Blitzkrieg* 'lightning war'; *block-buster* 'large bomb'; *kamikaze* 'suicide attack(er)', from a Japanese compound meaning 'divine wind'; *jeep* 'four-wheel-drive car', (mainly) from General Purpose vehicle – for the rise of acronyms see Sections 4.4.3 and 4.5.3.

The world wars have hastened the decline of Britain as a major world power (though still one of the largest foreign investors) and the long-established rise of the United States. An idea of relative economic power in the year 2003 can be seen in the Gross Domestic Products of some English-speaking (or partially so) countries; see Table 1.4 (figures taken from World Bank data-sheets).

Warfare since 1945 has certainly contributed to lexis at least: from America's wars in Korea, Vietnam and Iraq and Britain's in the Falklands we find such items as *brain-washing* (1950–), *frag* 'attack superior officer with a fragmentation grenade' (1971–), *yomp* 'march with heavy equipment over difficult terrain' (1982–), *Gulf War syndrome* (1992–), *weapons of mass destruction* (1980–) or *WMD* (2002–). Although such wars have been conducted well away from the

Table 1.4 *National GDP and population in 2003*

Country	GDP in 2003 US $billion	World Bank ranking by GDP	Population million
United States	10881.6	1	291.0
United Kingdom	1794.9	4	59.3
Canada	834.4	9	31.6
India	599.0	12	1064.4
Australia	518.4	13	19.9
Ireland	148.6	32	3.9
Malaysia	103.2	37	24.8
Singapore	91.3	38	4.3
New Zealand	76.3	45	4.0
OECD total	29664.8		

English-speaking countries, enlisted soldiers and airmen can get caught up in the campaigns for years at a time, while the populations back home have had access to increasing amounts of live or at least very recent reportage. All this must have had linguistic repercussions.

We turn now to more abstract events which do not involve large-scale movements of people or armies. A cultural movement of great linguistic (and other) importance is the Renaissance, a revival of learning in fifteenth-century Italy which spread across Europe, bringing new interest in the arts and sciences, in classical learning, and so on. One obvious effect on English was the adoption of much lexis from Latin, Greek, Italian and other languages. For example, of the 25,000-odd words in *OED* borrowed from Latin over the recorded history of English (see Table 1.1), over 40 per cent arrived between 1450 and 1650. A fashion for interlarding English with bookish words often borrowed from the classical languages (disparagingly called *Ynkehorne termes* in 1543, 'terms found in the inkhorn, or ink-well') had grown noticeable enough by the mid-sixteenth century to provoke a reaction, often expressed in satire or parody. See Section 4.4 for the effects of the Renaissance and the so-called Inkhorn Controversy on English lexis.

One aspect of the general Renaissance of learning, a growth of interest in science, has continued to have great influence on all aspects of society, especially from the nineteenth century onwards. New scientific and technical vocabulary is needed all the time, and characteristic sources include coining on a pseudo-classical basis using word fragments from Greek or Latin (the Neo-Latin/Greek internationalisms, or NGIs, discussed in Section 5.3.4), e.g. *photosynthesis* 1898 from Greek *phos/photo-* 'light' + Latin-from-Greek *synthesis* 'composition'; and *television*, first used anticipatively in 1907, from Greek *tele-* 'afar' + French-from-Latin *vision*. There are also adaptations of names of scientists and inventors

(*Parkinsonism* from James Parkinson, *volt* from Alessandro Volta); and borrowings and loan-translations from German (*quartz* 1756–, *leitmotiv* 1876–, *superman* calqued in 1903 on *Übermensch*). Many such coinages are effectively international rather than purely English.

The Renaissance also revived the study of Hebrew and Greek, languages of the Bible. Here it is convenient to consider how Christianity has played its part in shaping the English language, starting with the impetus to bring in a new writing system in early Anglo-Saxon times and, largely through translation from Latin in the reigns of Alfred and his successors, to develop an English prose. Much specialist vocabulary was adapted, coined or borrowed for religious purposes in Old and Middle English times, and education has often been wholly or in part the responsibility of the church. Although sermons were written and delivered in English at all periods, the Bible itself was generally kept in the Latin of the Vulgate translation. There were partial Old English translations from both Old and New Testaments, and in the late fourteenth century the Wycliffites sponsored two complete Middle English translations. It was not in conformity with Church of Rome practice to make the Bible available in the vernacular without a priest as intermediary, and both the Wycliffite translations and the important early-sixteenth-century English bibles of Tyndale and (to a lesser extent) Coverdale were potentially dangerous and subversive publications. Around this time the Church of England was made legally independent of Rome as a result of Henry VIII's dynastic needs. Despite temporary restorations of Catholicism as the official faith, once the English Reformation had taken permanent hold, two Protestant books made their way into the fabric of English culture: the Book of Common Prayer (first published in 1549 and amended at various times up to 1662) and the Authorised Version of the Bible (1611). They brought into the language all sorts of coinages, phraseology, rhythms and cadences which they made familiar (some of it taken via Tyndale almost direct from the Old Testament Hebrew), and they had a lasting influence on English prose style. One specific effect was to change the status of the pronoun *thou/thee/thy/thine*. For Tyndale, this had been the natural pronoun to use in address to God, as it was the second person singular. By the seventeenth century, *thou* had in most circumstances been supplanted by the pronoun *you* – originally plural, later also polite, later neutral (see Section 2.7.7.3) – but the committee which produced the Authorised Version retained Tyndale's choice of pronoun, thereby investing *thou* for later generations with an air of archaism and formality rather than intimacy.

The Reformation took schooling for the most part out of the control of Catholic religious institutions, and it encouraged the spread of lay literacy. As time has passed, school education has tended to be spread more widely through the population and to be continued to a greater age throughout the English-speaking world. Elementary education became legally required for all children in England and Wales from 1880, secondary education to age fourteen from 1918 (a public system of secondary schools was established in 1889 in Wales and 1902 in England).

Scotland had a stronger tradition of widespread education, and from an earlier date. The school-leaving age became fifteen in 1944 (Scotland 1947) and sixteen in 1972–3. In the United States, Canada and Australia, elementary education was becoming compulsory by the late nineteenth century. The first high school in the USA was founded in 1821. Schooling has obvious consequences for literacy, for knowledge of the English of other times and other places, for social contact, and – to varying degrees – for deliberate regulation of dialect and grammar and attempts at standardisation. Education changes language use.

The public schools (defined originally as 'founded or endowed for the use of the public', now 'independent, not funded by the state, i.e. private') grew up in all parts of England through the eighteenth and nineteenth centuries as the schools of the governing élite, preparing boys for positions in government at home and in the empire, and for the universities and the professions. Their linguistic importance is considerable, since there appeared a non-localised accent – later known as Received Pronunciation (RP) – which was particularly fostered by these schools, whose pupils mostly lived in as boarders during term-time. From the late nineteenth century there were girls' public schools too. In adulthood these people were disproportionately influential in British public life and later in broadcasting (which, arguably, *is* public life now). The importance of both RP and the public schools in England has waned since the mid-twentieth century, though it has by no means disappeared.

From the 1920s we can point to the cultural impact of America on the rest of the world, including the rest of the English-speaking world. The legacy of British influence and the continuing domination of America are mostly responsible for the phenomenon of English as a world language (see Section 9.3).

1.5   The form of historical evidence

Until the late nineteenth century, everything we have of older states of the language comes to us in written form. The relationship between writing and speech is not always a direct one. Here we look at the form in which texts were transmitted and the various media used.

A writing system used by Germanic tribes from maybe the second century AD was the runic futhork, a system, originally of twenty-four letters, derived from contact with Italic peoples using an Etruscan alphabet. (This, like almost all such Mediterranean writing systems, was ultimately derived from a Semitic alphabet. The derivational histories of writing systems can be considerably different from those of the languages they are used to represent, not least because they are shaped by conscious creativeness on the part of individuals.) Runes were straight-sided symbols suitable for carving on wood or stone. The later history of the runic alphabet involves changes to the form and value of individual runes as well as their overall inventory, and they play a bigger role in the history of Scandinavia

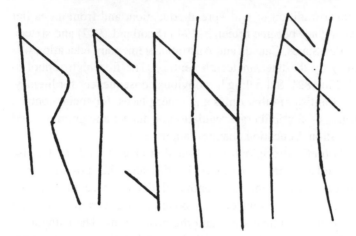

Figure 1.8   *The Caistor runes* (source: Page, 1973)

and its North Germanic languages than in England and English, where in fact
the three-dimensional remains are hardly more extensive than the manuscript
evidence of runes. The bone-carving shown in Figure 1.8 could be tentatively
regarded as the earliest surviving fragment of the English language.

According to Page (1973: 19–21) it is the earliest (at latest, fourth- or early
fifth-century) surviving runic text found in England, in a cremation-urn at Caistor-
by-Norwich, carved on a deer's ankle-joint. Its six runes read *ræȝæn*, possibly meaning 'roe-deer' – but the language (as well as the runes) may be North
Germanic rather than pre-English.

The absorption of Anglo-Saxon England into the Church of Rome was followed by the creation of a new writing system for Old English. The missionaries
who devised it naturally used the Latin alphabet. They augmented its nineteen
main symbols <a, b, c, d, e, f, g, h, i, l, m, n, o, p, r, s, t, u, y> to allow for OE
phonological distinctions which the Latin alphabet couldn't easily handle; the
letters <k, q, x, z, œ> were also used, if rarely, while <i, u> each served both as
vowel and semi-vowel/consonant, depending on the syllabic function of the sound
represented. The principal additions were <Ææ> 'ash', <Þþ> 'thorn', <Ðð>
'eth' and <Ᵽp> 'wynn', to give both upper- and lower-case versions of these
less familiar letters. Apart from eth or edh, a modern name (the contemporary
name was *ðæt* 'that'), the letter-names come from the runic alphabet, as did the
actual shapes of thorn and wynn. A combined <ae> letter was sporadically used
in Latin, and eth may have been of Irish origin. Just as in Modern English, combinations of letters – mainly digraphs – could become symbols in the orthographic
system. Texts were handwritten on parchment – treated animal skin – or vellum,
a higher-quality version made from the skins of kids, lambs or calves. Both were
expensive materials, but durable. Script had letter-shapes which in some cases
were surprisingly distant from those now used, for example <r> and <s>. The
opening of a preface by King Alfred is shown in Figure 1.9.

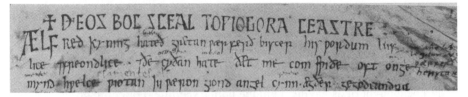

Figure 1.9   *Preface to* Cura Pastoralis *(source: Brook, 1955)*

†ÐEOS BOC SCEAL TOÞIOGORA CEASTRE
ÆLFRed kyning hateð gretan pærferð biscep his pordum luf
lice &freondlice

This book shall to Worcester
Alfred king commands [to] greet Wærferth bishop [by/with] his words lov-
ingly and friendlily

'This book is intended for Worcester. King Alfred sends loving and friendly
greetings to Bishop Wærferth . . .'

It has become the modern convention to print editions of OE texts with modern
word division and letter shapes, usually incorporating <æ, þ, ð > into the font but
replacing <p> by its later equivalent, <w>.

After the Norman Conquest there were significant changes in handwriting, in
the inventory of letters and in the phonological values some of them represented.
Here we note merely the principal changes in inventory. Wynn, eth and ash were
lost by the thirteenth century. The digraph <uu> crystallised into the single letter
<w>; <k, q, x, z> came into more general use; and scribes started distinguishing
systematically between two forms of <g>, an open shape based on the Insular
script, <ʒ>, and <g> from the rounded Carolingian handwriting introduced from
the continent in the eleventh century; the former is now called yogh, pronounced
[jɒg] or [jɒx], the second pronunciation handily encapsulating its two commonest
values. Yogh and thorn both died out around the fifteenth century, the latter
generally being replaced by <th> but surviving long enough to be represented in
early printing founts as <y>, especially in the common pairings *y^e* 'the' and *y^t*
'that', leading to the pseudo-archaism of *Ye Olde Worlde Shoppe* and the like: the
definite article was never genuinely pronounced with initial [j]. Yogh was usually
replaced by one of <y, g, gh>, depending on the sound it represented, but its latest
shape was indistinguishable from one form of <z>, leading to odd spellings for
the Scots names *Dalziel* [ˌdiːˈel] and *Menzies* [ˈmɪŋɪs] – now generally interpreted
outside Scotland, of course, as names whose historic *pronunciations* (if known)
are odd. The last changes in alphabetic inventory were the systematic separation of
<i, j> and of <u, v>, completed by the end of the eighteenth century. (Although
non-alphabetic, certain currency symbols and items like <@>, originally an
abbreviation, are arguably beginning to function in computer-mediated systems
on a par with letters and digits.)

The two premodern authors who are widely read, at least in schools, are Chaucer, who wrote in the late fourteenth century, and Shakespeare, around 1600. Chaucerian manuscripts predate the decisions made by early printers which helped to codify English spelling, while Shakespeare's plays were first published before the changes in linguistic sensibility and printing technology which made it normal for every word to be thought of as having a unique public spelling. For commercial and pedagogic reasons it is common to modernise Chaucer's scribes' use of <u, v, i, j, þ>, while Shakespeare is not often presented in the actual spelling of his printers. Original spelling is not the hardest of barriers to the understanding of older texts, but it is an obvious and, for many, an alarming one.

Most spellings are now fixed in the standard language, though different British publishing houses prefer one or other of <judgement ~ judgment>, <recognize ~ recognise>, and there are a few other permitted variants. More noticeable but still relatively superficial are the differences settled on by the United States and Britain: <color ~ colour>, <center ~ centre>, and so on. The other national standards mostly adhere to the British conventions, though Canada's position is complex. Specifically American spellings generally codify (a modest subset of) the recommendations of the lexicographer Noah Webster (1758–1843), who avowedly sought to demonstrate America's independence of Britain in this respect. Other spelling issues will be handled in Chapters 2 and 5.

Two technological developments are of great importance. From the end of the fifteenth century paper became available in England as a much cheaper substitute for parchment and vellum, whose cost had meant that unneeded manuscripts would be scraped clean for re-use in monastic scriptoria. Paper was not re-usable (Lyall, 1989), so the amount of surviving material goes up from then on. Around the same time printing with movable type began to offer an alternative to scribal copying and would lead eventually to much wider availability of books than had previously been possible. With wider readership goes wider literacy, and there are implications too for standardisation of practice which will be followed up in Chapter 5, especially Section 5.3.2.

London-based newspapers appeared from 1621, provincial from 1690. The Civil War in the middle of that century had greatly stimulated demand. By early in the next century daily papers were being produced and mailed nationally in Britain. The distribution of newspapers is bound up with the development of postal and transport systems, both briefly considered below. In the nineteenth century, high newspaper circulations were associated with printing on an industrial scale. By then journalism had become truly influential. As Carlyle wrote in 1841:

> Burke said there were three Estates in Parliament, but in the Reporters' Gallery . . . there sat a fourth Estate more important far than they all.

American papers sprang up soon after Independence and likewise went on to become a central part of American culture. However, geographical and political considerations meant that there has never been a *national* press in the USA to the extent found in Britain.

Not just printed material is affected by the introduction of paper: letters too become more common. Already from the fifteenth century we have the first significant numbers of surviving letters written by traders and merchant families rather than just by kings, noblemen, ecclesiastics and monks. Letters now were written in many cases by their authors rather than by professional scribes. Sending them was still a matter of finding a trusted courier. National delivery systems for letters were developed between 1635 and 1720 from what had been the king's postal service (hence 'Royal Mail'), though with charges paid for by the recipient. From the late seventeenth century pre-paid postal delivery services were set up within London (1680) and other towns, from 1784 a national mail coach service began, and by 1840 a cheap, uniform, national pre-paid service was introduced in Britain – nearly 170 million letters were posted in that year – followed soon by a cheaper book post. Mail trains in the US first ran in 1832 and by 1860 were very important. The first US postage stamp was issued in 1847. The cumulative effect of such developments on the volume of mail and on the numbers of letter-writers and readers can be imagined. Here for the first time was a significant means of two-way communication across large distances. By 1900 there were 2.3 billion letters posted annually in the UK; or, to take another figure, there were 88 postal items per capita in the UK in 1900, and 95 in the USA. By now maybe 20 billion items are posted annually in the UK.

In small parts of the academic community from the 1970s and in general use from the 1990s, electronic mail has again transformed the speed and cost of two-way written communication, with potentially wider effects on the style and vocabulary of English than that other technological development of the same period, the facsimile (fax) machine. Widespread electronic mail (e-mail) drove the early development of the internet, on which so much communication now depends, including instant messaging. It is too early to tell whether significant linguistic changes (at least outside their own particular technological medium or commercial niche) will be caused by, say, hypertext on the worldwide web and elsewhere, e-books rather than conventional print, or abbreviated text messaging between mobile (= cellular) phones, though the last-named is already infiltrating the language of e-mail at least. An increasing amount of writing since the 1970s, personal and public, has been done on word processors. Moreover, the effects of spell-checkers, grammar-checkers and predictive completion of part-typed text may turn out to have some influence on knowledge and usage of English, as too will the spread of technologies which allow people to speak to and listen to machines rather than type on to keyboards and read from screens.

Of course the linguistic effects of these writing technologies are dwarfed by developments in transmission of the spoken word. The telephone entered local use around the turn of the twentieth century, and by the turn of the twenty-first in the developed world was very widely available, offering direct dialling to individuals both within and between countries. Mobile or cell phones are the current big growth area. (In the developing world, telephones are typically available to a minority of the population, with ownership as low as a twentieth of the figure in the most developed countries, according to one 1998 estimate.) The telephone is relevant to the history of the language as an important form of linguistic contact, but it may be having other, less predictable effects, such as the widely remarked 'telephone voice' (the expression is known from at least 1920), almost a kind of code-switching. Much more recently, developments in business practice have placed up to 2 per cent of the British workforce in 'call centres', often in areas where employment costs are low (Scotland, the northeast of England, etc.). Indeed many call centres servicing the UK are now located even further from most of their customers, in Ireland or India for instance, though attempts may be made to conceal this. The language of call centre operatives is often subject to rigid scripting (see Cameron, 2000). This, then, is an increasingly frequent if rather strange kind of interdialectal contact.

The telephone is a two-way, one-to-one medium. Broadcast radio and television are one-way, one-to-many media, and their commercial development (radio from the 1920s, television essentially from the 1950s, though there were small-scale experiments before the Second World War) has transformed modern societies. Even in stable and isolated communities broadcast media have created widespread, if partial, familiarity with many varieties of spoken English, with a possible contribution to standardisation and to change.

All these sound media are essentially 'live'. Mechanical and electronic recording media have also been of immense importance. Early (cylindrical) phonograph and (flat) gramophone discs were used for speech as well as music from the late nineteenth century, and records give us our earliest direct non-written evidence for historical states of the language, developing towards our own day through the compact disc and other technologies to give increasingly faithful reproduction. From around 1930 optical recording of soundtracks in the 'talkies' gives us much more widespread evidence of speech sounds. Tape recording developed from the 1920s to the 1940s and by the 1950s was portable enough to allow easy recording outside the studio. Significant corpora of recorded speech date from the 1950s, with really big collections starting to be made from the 1990s. Large collections of written material have also been made in electronically readable form. There are, for instance, huge amounts of newspaper writing, and there are systematic, balanced collections of different genres, as in the British National Corpus. Semi-automatic methods of transcription of speech, together with techniques of tagging (labelling for word class) and/or parsing (assigning structural analyses), mean that the academic study of naturally produced language is increasingly the study of speech as well as of writing.

Like television, sound films constitute a major engine of cultural – including linguistic – influence, both within nation-states and across the international English-speaking world. As for traffic between English and other languages, there has apparently been relatively little linguistic influence *into* English as a result of mass media, at least as far as Britain and the USA are concerned, though of course a great deal *from*. A recent *Dictionary of European Anglicisms* (Görlach, 2001) surveys sixteen languages and, to take two examples, cites the English word *globe-trotter* as appearing in nine of them, e.g. Polish *globtroter*, pronounced [gloptroter], Dutch *globetrotter* [ɣloːbətrɔtər], and translated in two more, while the more recent *(blue) jeans* has been borrowed in thirteen of the sixteen. And that is just the European picture. The French department store chain Monoprix ran a clothing promotion in 2004 under the banner 'Urban tendance', explicitly intended to be an anglicisation of the French *tendance urbaine* 'urban trend'. English doesn't have to be fully understood to be influential.

1.6 The surviving historical texts

If the main evidence for English pre-1900, indeed pre-1950, is written, the nature of the texts becomes important: it is clear that language varies considerably according to genre and register.

Much OE writing was lost by scraping and re-use of the parchment or vellum, by destruction in Viking raids, in Henry VIII's much later dissolution of the monasteries, or by other accidents. The total surviving to the present is some 3½ million words, though multiple copies of some major texts would add to that figure. It includes a body of poetry largely confined to four manuscripts, syntactically archaic, preserving a number of synonyms (of nouns above all) on which its alliterative metre depended, and all in a mixed dialect with midlands and northern characteristics. There are Anglo-Latin glossaries, and Latin texts glossed word for word in OE between the lines. And there is prose, much of it religious, much of it translated more or less faithfully from Latin, nearly all in the West Saxon dialect. The most important wholly non-translated prose is the *Anglo-Saxon Chronicle*, started under King Alfred in the late ninth century, backdated to the earliest historical or legendary time known to its first compilers, and added to more or less continuously right up to the twelfth century. The beautifully written sermons and saints' lives of Ælfric, in parts freely translated from Latin, are often described as being in rhythmical prose; they date from around AD 1000. Virtually the whole surviving corpus of OE is available in electronic form from the compilers of the Toronto *Dictionary of Old English*, and parts of it are currently being tagged and parsed by syntacticians.

Early ME texts include a number of late copies of OE works. In addition to text types evidenced in the OE period, there is poetry based on French models and prose and verse texts translated from French. The dialectal variety is much greater than in the OE period, yet the prose of the period is not evenly spread around the country. Later ME remains dialectally diverse but with more of the country represented in prose. As of October 2000, the largest electronic archive of Middle English held 19 million words, by no means the complete corpus.

By the early ModE period the effects of standardisation are reducing the dialectal variety found. On the other hand, the quantity and variety as far as genre is concerned goes up remarkably, and from this point it becomes difficult to make useful generalisations about the texts available. Incidentally, by *available* we mean 'on paper'. It would not be prudent to list the electronic corpora of ModE here, as the information dates rather quickly. Nor do we wish to imply that computer-readable texts are the be-all and end-all of linguistic research – certainly not without checking the context of each example.

1.7   Indirect evidence

We have said something of the forms of English which provide the main evidence for a history of the language. Simple inspection can give us much information about the language of a particular time and place. A single text may sometimes provide subtle evidence of language *change*. When Jane Austen's Emma says 'Cannot you imagine, Mr Knightley, what a *sensation* his coming will produce?', the textual italics may prompt us to suspect that Emma's usage – the sense 'communal excitement' – was newfangled or 'trendy' in 1816 (and just the kind of thing to provoke Mr Knightley), a suspicion nicely confirmed in one of *OED*'s citations from 1818: 'His death produced what in the phraseology of the present day is called, a great sensation.' Thus a detail of typography bears here on individual lexical history. Then again, a so-called 'occasional spelling' can be instructive. A letter of 1461 contains <seschyons> for *sessions*, from which we can be sure that the sound change from [sesiənz] or [sesjənz] to [seʃənz] had at least begun in that dialect by then. Or to take a more complex pair of examples, *OED* records <wright> as separate, occasional, seventeenth-century spellings for both *right* and *write*. Since *right* has never had an initial [w] sound, we may assume that the initial cluster [wr] of words like *wren* and *write* had been simplified to [r] by then, otherwise we could not explain the 'mistake'; likewise, since *write* has never had a [x] sound before the [t], such a 'reverse spelling' implies that [x] had by then been lost from words like *light* and *right*, which, as their historic spellings attest, did once have the cluster [xt] (cf. German *Licht, recht*). So from these occasional spellings we deduce a *terminus ante quem*, or latest possible date, for important sound changes.

Another useful source for reconstructing phonological or phonetic history is rhymes and puns, always making due allowance for bad puns, poor rhymes, near-rhymes and eye-rhymes. When Falstaff asserts, 'If Reasons were as plentie as Blackberries, I would giue no man a Reason vpon compulsion', a likely pun between *reasons* and *raisins* corroborates our belief (on other grounds) that those words shared the same first vowel in Shakespeare's English. And if that is so, we must explain how they have come to differ in most non-Irish varieties of English since the eighteenth century (see Section 2.7.2 and Section 7.7).

Finally here we can mention metalinguistic discussions, when speakers and writers explicitly consider language. Again, these can be within the history of English, as with the 'orthoepists' who discussed English pronunciation and

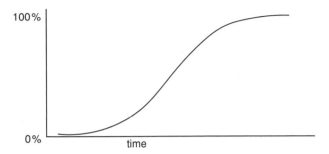

Figure 1.10   *S-curve*

spelling in the sixteenth and seventeenth centuries. They provide a wealth of information, albeit sometimes hard to interpret, about the sounds of English in their time (see Chapter 2). Or they can cross language boundaries, as when, say, a French writer provides a guidebook to England or a textbook on English for his fellow-countrymen, complete with a 'phonetic' spelling of English phrases in the contemporary conventions of French, or vice versa.

1.8   Why does language change?

All living languages are subject to change. How do they change? Many linguists distinguish between actuation or innovation on the one hand and propagation or diffusion on the other. Innovation is the introduction of a new variant, possibly initially characterisable as an error. Innovations may catch on or they may die off again. Diffusion is the spread of a variant from the point where it has become an option for a number of speakers. Diffusion is often observed to follow the pattern of an S-curve, presented in idealised form in Figure 1.10.

The diagram represents competition between two variants. The horizontal axis represents time, the vertical axis the proportion of available occasions on which an innovating variant is used rather than the older variant. At first the innovation is used sporadically, and for a long time its frequency increases slowly but remains low. Not till it is being used around 20 per cent of the time does the *rate* of increase start to grow noticeably. Now as the curve becomes steeper, the innovation becomes the dominant form within a relatively short period. By the time its relative frequency is running at some 80 per cent, the rate of increase is falling again, and the older form may survive at a low frequency – perhaps as a relic form in particular contexts – for a considerable time.

Diffusion of change requires the prior existence of variants – alternative ways of saying the same thing. Linguistic variation is familiar in our own speech communities. For example, many Englishes have the alternative pronunciations [iːðə] and [aɪðə] for *either*, with little apparent social marking attached to either variant. Other examples of variation in at least some current varieties of English are the

Table 1.5 *Two quantifiers*

	Older system		Newer system	
Mass noun	*less bread*	*more bread*	*less bread*	*more bread*
Count noun	**fewer loaves**	*more loaves*	*less loaves*	*more loaves*

negative interrogative patterns *Have you not seen X?* vs. *Haven't you seen X?*, and the lexical items *film* vs. *movie*. Some variation appears to be stable over long periods: variation is a necessary but not a sufficient condition for change to occur.

And why does language change? The answer to this question is dependent on the theoretical position of the analyst. If the most salient property of language is its grammar, an internalised set of rules unconsciously built up and used by an individual speaker–hearer, then language change may be seen as a consequence of new generations inducing a slightly different grammar from that internalised by their parents' generation, perhaps because of a slightly changed preponderance of some usage, the cause of which is not really grammatical in origin but some contingent 'performance' factor. The new grammar in turn leads to a further change in the output of its speakers, and so things move on. The process of language acquisition in childhood will be critical, and the favoured form of analysis will (usually) be formal and structural. Alternatively, if language is something which crucially belongs to and exists in a speech community, then speaker interaction and relative social status may be the fundamental engines of language change. Speakers may adjust their usage to (or against) community norms throughout adolescence and perhaps beyond, and change is not confined to the acquisition process. The requisite analysis will be sociolinguistic and statistical. Then again, if speakers and hearers are regarded as autonomous individuals, anxious above all to maximise their communicative efficiency, yet other considerations may be identified, typically involving speaker intentions.

This is not the place to decide between, or to reconcile, these and other theoretical positions. In the course of this book a number of explanatory models will be offered for particular changes in the history of English. All linguists can agree both that language does change and that certain factors seem to be widely relevant. We can group three main types of force for change under the headings *structural*, *social* and *functional*. Each has its own champions in the linguistic literature, though the dividing lines between them are not always clear-cut.

Structural pressure may develop in any part of the language system. A rather simple example would be the increasingly common use of the quantifier *less* with count nouns as well as mass nouns, whereas more conservative speakers prefer *fewer* with count nouns. The fact that *more* has co-occurred with both types of noun since the end of the sixteenth century must surely help to explain the replacement of *fewer* by *less*; see Table 1.5. The two systems have been in competition for over a century now, and the newer one appears to be on the verge of winning out.

For more complex phonological, morphological and syntactic examples see Chapters 2 and 3.

Social factors are relevant because one function of language, in addition to the apparently obvious one of communicating information, is to assert a speaker's identity, which is in large part to identify the speaker as part of one social grouping and not another. Transmission via social networks is an important mechanism of propagation of change; see Chambers (2002), Croft (2000), J. Milroy (1992, 1993), L. Milroy (1987), Nevalainen (2000b), Nevalainen & Raumolin-Brunberg (2003).

What we have called functional factors are relevant to innovation and perhaps also to propagation of change. Numerous types have been suggested. They include the avoidance of ambiguity, so that the obsolescence of the verb *let* 'hinder' (cf. the noun *let* in tennis) might be ascribed to an unfortunate clash with the more common verb *let* meaning 'allow', once phonetic change had made the two verbs (OE *lettan*, *lætan*, respectively) sound the same. A desire for expressiveness imposes pressure for change, which can be illustrated in the high turnover of intensifiers like *very, awfully, terribly, real, dead, way, well*, etc.: as one originally hyperbolic use becomes conventionalised, so the expressiveness of that choice begins to wane. Maintenance or development of iconicity, an explicit parallelism between linguistic form and meaning, is thought by some scholars (e.g. Haiman, 1983) to be an important motivating factor, as in a growing association by sound symbolism of initial /kr-/ with pejorative meaning – think of *Christ!* [as imprecation], *cramped, crabby, cracked, crafty, crank, crappy, crashing (bore), crass, crazy, creep, cretin, crime, cripple, crisis, crock, crooked, cross, crow, crude, cruel, crummy, crypto-*, etc. – and its possible role in the semantic change of *chronic* from 'long-lasting' to 'objectionable'. (This is as much structural as functional.) Economy of effort, too, may play a part – typically working in the opposite direction to iconicity – for example in phonological reduction, such as the loss of /t/ in *Christmas*.

Beyond these three broad categories there are extralinguistic factors to consider too. Changes in the world can play an obvious part, in that new concepts or inventions require new vocabulary. Cultural contact and population movement are further examples, as discussed above. (Note, however, that many historical linguists look first to internal factors in language change before having recourse to explanations from language contact.)

With all these pressures for change, you might expect language to be hopelessly unstable, and yet of course our parents can understand us – teenagers might disagree here – and even across gaps of centuries we can read Jane Austen, Shakespeare and even Chaucer without too much help. In other words, there is more inertia, more continuity, than change. The need to be understood, both by peers and by the older generation, applies a braking force on potential linguistic changes. The development of a written standard is another conservative influence, certainly on written English and plausibly also on some aspects of speech. (Spelling pronunciations like [ɒftən] instead of [ɒfən] for *often* are slightly different, as they may be reversals of a previous change.) And, more generally, most agents of change are *gentle* pressures which only gradually affect choices in a statistical way, rather as evolution alters species imperceptibly by selective reproductive success.

1.9   Recent and current change

The history of the English language is not merely a matter of the past, for PDE is not (except as a convenient idealisation) a fixed state of the language: change continues. Let us take a handful of examples from different linguistic domains.

New words and phrases enter the language in thousands every year. Recent examples include *sushi*, recorded from 1893 in *OED*[2] only as a specialist term in Japanese contexts but increasingly familiar in the English-speaking world; *docusoap* 'fly-on-the-wall TV documentary series' (1998–, from *documentary* + *soap opera*); *slaphead* 'bald person' (1990–); *twoc(k)* 'take without owner's consent, steal (a car)' (1990–, from British police usage); the *-gate* suffix for a political scandal (after the burgling of the Watergate building in 1972); *go postal* 'become (homicidally) enraged' (1994–, after workplace shootings associated with US postal workers). Some of these, of course, are restricted to certain varieties and may or may not generalise.

Existing words develop new meanings. For example, by an obvious extension of its spatial use and the phrase *ahead of (one's) time*, the preposition *ahead of* has started to mean 'before and in anticipation of (a specific event)' (1981–), especially in news bulletins. Ellipsis of the head noun from twentieth-century phrases like *security forces*, *security precautions*, as in 'There were renewed expressions of disquiet from scientists about the encroachment of security measures on personal freedom of speech and action' (1952, *OED*), has led to a new sense of *security* as an activity noun: 'On Oct. 30 delegations from Israel, Syria, Lebanon and Egypt and a joint Jordanian-Palestinian delegation finally took their seats, amid heavy security, at a negotiating table in Madrid' (1991, BNC). This new sense, attested probably since the 1970s and not yet in *OED*, has connotations not so much of safety but of (apprehension of) danger.

The verbs *substitute* and *replace* have long been used in similar contexts but with different complementation: 'An editor substituted a better expression for the phrase' = 'An editor replaced the phrase with/by a better expression.' Increasingly, *substitute* is used with the complementation of *replace*: 'An editor substituted the phrase with a better expression' ('incorrectly', according to *OED*, from 1974, although there is indirect evidence of occurrence from the 1920s). And the resulting confusion can lead to complete reversal of the original usage: 'Prizes are subject to availability. [The promoter] reserves the right to substitute any prize for one of an equal value' (2001 scratchcard, Thus plc). The outcome of these lexico-syntactic developments in *substitute* is not yet clear. Moving further into the area of grammar, we find that the long-term statistical decline of the modal verb *may/might* (mostly in favour of *can/could*) is being accompanied by numerous changes in what may be its death throes. The negative contraction *mayn't*, colloquial in the early twentieth century, is barely possible now. Fewer and fewer speakers treat *might* as the past tense of *may*, leading to past counterfactuals like 'If United had cracked down on Cantona, it may never have come to all this' (1998 *Daily Express*), where *might* would have been normal before the last decades of the twentieth century. And *may* is increasingly old-fashioned as a verb of permission ('May I have . . . ?' losing out to 'Can I have . . . ?').

In phonology, the Northern Cities Shift is a good example, with Chicago leading all the major cities in the Northern dialect area of the US in a cyclic pattern of change in vowels, including tensing and raising of /æ/, fronting of /o/, and lowering, centralisation and unrounding of long open /o/. First reports of the shift date from around 1968–9; Labov (1994: 177–201) recounts his bafflement when he first heard a Chicago teenager apparently saying *lacks* [læks] in a context which proved to require the word *locks*. For more detail see Section 8.3.4.

In plotting change, the obvious approach is to compare usage attested at two different times, whether close together – a corpus of 1991 material compared with one from 1961, say – or far apart. This is working with 'real time'. Sociolinguists have given us an alternative technique, that of 'apparent time'. Here all the data come from a single sampling, but differences in usage between generations can nevertheless indicate a change in progress. For example, a variable in some English speech communities is non-prevocalic /r/: that is, words such as *car* (except before a following vowel) or *hurt* are pronounced either with or without /r/ – rhotic vs. nonrhotic accents. This /r/ is generally absent in London English and RP, and absence was still the prestige variant in New York English of the 1930s. In Labov's classic studies of New York English in the 1960s, the younger the age-group of his upper-middle-class informants, the greater the use of non-prevocalic /r/. This indicated that the rhotic pronunciation was spreading. The apparent-time technique is most useful for present-day studies but can in principle be applied to older periods where there is sufficient data attributable to writers of varying ages, as in the Helsinki Corpus of Early English Correspondence.

We conclude this glance at the language of today with an intriguing and controversial development, the use of high rising tone – as if for an interrogative – at the end of a declarative sentence. The phenomenon has gone under various names in scholarly and journalistic treatments, among them uptalk, Australian Question Intonation or AQI, high rising terminal contour or HRT. It seems clear that the usage belongs essentially to the last thirty to forty years. It is widespread in Australia and New Zealand, is far more prevalent among the young (though may already be receding in California – Elizabeth Traugott, p.c., 2 May 2002) and is used more (though not exclusively) by females. It has reached Britain, where commentators have linked its spread to the popularity of the Australian soap opera *Neighbours*, perhaps strengthened by American imports like *Friends*. The researchers who used the term AQI had assumed that its origins lay in Sydney working-class speech in the 1960s. Yet American commentators have traced what seems to be the same linguistic phenomenon to 'ValSpeak' or 'Valley Speak', the speech of (San Fernando) 'Valley girls' in 1980s California, while earlier scholars described it as a Southern trait (noted as early as 1963), as also hinted at in this passage by a writer educated in Oklahoma City:

> Less than a minute later a tall brunette appeared and said, 'Mr Pope? Judge Whetstone will see you now?' She turned her statement into a question ... 'I'm Mary Sue Hethcox, Mr Pope, Judge Whetstone's secretary?' the brunette said over her shoulder. She made it yet another Southern question ... (1975 Ross Thomas, *The Money Harvest*)

The geographical provenance of this intonation pattern is, then, not yet clear. Sociolinguistically, it has been taken as a gender marker. And what is its discourse meaning? Suggestions include topicalisation, emphasis, deference, politeness, tentativeness, a desire for approval, 'to convey that the propositional content of the utterance should be added to speaker's and hearer's mutual belief space', verification that the hearer has understood (prompting speculation that it might have been fostered by major postwar immigration to Sydney of Italians, Greeks, Yugoslavs and others). How *non*-users interpret it is also an interesting question: in general, issues of interdialectal (mis)comprehension are being taken seriously both in their own right as facts of language and as a possible engine of change. In any event, to vary a point made early on in this chapter, a history of the language must concern not just *then* but *now*.

2 Phonology and morphology

Roger Lass

> The history of the Victorian Age will never be written: we know too much
> about it. For ignorance is the first requisite of the historian – ignorance, which
> simplifies and clarifies, which selects and omits, with a placid perfection
> unattainable by the highest art.
>
> Lytton Strachey, *Eminent Victorians* (1918)

2.1   History, change and variation

Any system *S* (a language, culture, art-style, organism . . .) can be
understood in a number of complementary ways. Two of the commonest are:

(a)   Structural: what is *S* made of? How is it put together, and what are the
        relations among the different components?
(b)   Functional: how do the components of *S* work to fulfil the overall
        function of the system, as well as their own special functions?

Such understanding often feels incomplete without a third dimension:

(c)   Historical: where did *S* and its parts come from? How much change
        has there been to produce what we see now, and what kind?

This can be split into some interesting subquestions, which define one way of
doing history:

(d)   How much of what we see at a given time is old, and how much is
        new?
(e)   Of the old: how much is doing what it used to? How much is doing new
        things? What is the new doing (e.g. has it taken over any old functions,
        or developed novel ones?); does anything appear to be 'junk', not
        doing anything at all?

The attempt to answer such questions can yield a rich and densely textured understanding. But there is a downside: the longer the history, the more data there
are, and the less clear the overall picture becomes. Historians have to steer a
difficult course between clarity and detail. Limitations of space encourage the
former – a clean narrative line – rather than the latter. So my picture will be 'true'

in the main, but also misleading and oversimplified. A better name for this chapter might be 'Great Moments in the history of English phonology and morphology'. I will restrict myself to a series of major events and transitions, each of which either contributes some crucial feature to the modern picture, or makes historical sense of what looks like enigmatic residue. But to keep myself honest and the reader sufficiently ill at ease, I will focus on the often remarkable complexity and disorder of real historical data whenever the story appears to be getting too clear.

A history should start at the beginning; but that is too far off to fit comfortably in this compass. The earliest attestations of English date from the seventh century; but since I have to end up in the twenty-first, I will gloss over much of the history of Old English itself, and begin with a quite late stage. What did the cluster of varieties we call 'English' look like in the late tenth or early eleventh century, and what does it look like now? What has happened during more than a millennium of continuous transmission, and when and how? The history of any aspect of an evolving system will show what biologists call 'punctuated equilibrium': long periods where little is happening, interspersed with sudden bursts of change. Our story is not only about change, but about the strikingly inhomogeneous language states that exist between the major episodes of change, and in fact enable them.

Around 1380, Geoffrey Chaucer remarks in *Troilus & Criseyde* (II, 22ff):

> Ye knowe ek that in forme of speche is chaunge
> Withinne a thousand yeer, and woordes tho
> That hadden pris, now wonder nyce and straunge
> Us thinketh hem, and yet thei spake hem so,
> And spedde as wel in love as men now do;
> Ek for to wynnen love in sondry ages,
> In sondry londes, sondry ben usages.

Compared to a sample of Modern English, this passage itself illustrates precisely what Chaucer is talking about. Here is a crude line-for-line prose translation:

> You know also that in (the) form of speech (there) is change
> Within a thousand years, and words then
> That had value, now wonderfully curious and strange
> (To) us they seem, and yet they spoke them so,
> And succeeded as well in love as men now do;
> Also to win love in sundry ages,
> In sundry lands, (there) are many usages.

Actually, if one *heard* this text it would be even harder to understand, even less like Modern English – the conservatism of our spelling hides some massive changes. For instance:

(1)   *Chaucer*   *ModE*
       knowe [knɔu(ə)]   know [nəʊ]
       speche [spɛːtʃ(ə)]   speech [spiːtʃ]
       thousand [θuːzənd]   thousand [θaʊzənd]

woordes [woːrdəs]	words [wɜː(r)dz]
wonder [wundər]	wonder [wʌndə(r)]
pris [priːs]	price [praɪs]
ages [aːdʒəs]	ages [ɛɪdʒəz]
do [doː]	do [duː]
that [θat]	that [ðæt]

Most stressed vowels have changed; initial /kn/ is disallowed; some dialects have lost postvocalic /r/; [ə] has dropped finally and in the plural ending except before certain consonants (*ag-es* vs *word-s*); the final consonant of the plural ending is now [z], not [s]; while initial voiceless [θ] remains in *thousand*, it has been voiced to [ð] in *that* and similar grammatical items. And we can no longer rhyme *usages* and *ages*; there has been an accent shift, as Chaucer must have *áges: uságes*.

Morphological changes are apparent on the surface, without the specialist knowledge required to determine Middle English pronunciation. The second-person pronoun no longer has the plural *ye*, but *you* for both numbers. Verbs had a suffix to mark agreement with plural subjects (*hadd-en*, *be-n*). The present third singular verb ending was *-th*, not *-s*. The infinitive was marked by a suffix *-en* (*to wynn-en*); the verb 'to be' used the *be-* stem for present plural (*be-n*) rather than modern *are* (though its ancestor existed in other dialects); the past of *speak* is now *spoke*, not *spake*; the third-person plural pronoun was *thei* in the nominative, but *hem* in the accusative. *Year* was a zero plural like *sheep*, whereas now it belongs to the 'regular' *s*-plural class.

There is also considerable grammatical variability. In modern standard Englishes it so happens that inflection is categorical (though in other dialects it is not): most verbs always take *-s* in present third-person singular, and a tiny subset never do (*he walk-s* vs *he can*). Chaucer's plural verbs sometimes have the *-en* ending (*woordes . . . hadd-en, sondry be-n*), sometimes not (*they spake . . . spedde*). Such variation is of great historical interest; it often indicates change in progress, and in fact is a necessary (but not sufficient) condition for there to be any change at all. That is: change is not simple 'transformation', in which X suddenly becomes Y. Historically, a language is best conceived, like a species or an art-style, as *a population of variants moving through time*, with differential selection pressures operating on different variants. A language is a heterogeneous system, where some categories exist in only one form, and others are sets of more and less common variants. And new variation is constantly being created. Sometimes the variation is unstable, and simply vanishes; sometimes it remains stable for centuries. But often − and this is what creates history − one variant is gradually selected at the expense of another. Because of the vicissitudes of survival we never have the entire population of variants at hand; and even if we did there would not be space in the compass of a short chapter like this to treat it in detail. But I assume it as background and illustrate it where useful.

The fact that all normal speech communities have some variable categories, and that change proceeds by gradual selection of variants, makes 'locating' particular changes in time nearly impossible. It forces historians to characterise complex changes with long temporal extensions as more or less punctual 'events'. All readers of all histories, whatever the subject, should take note of this piece of wisdom from Virginia Woolf's diaries (18 February 1921):

> But indeed nothing happens at one moment rather than another. The history books will make it much more definite than it is.

2.2   The extent of change: 'vertical' and 'horizontal' history

So in the five centuries or so since Chaucer change has continued, and English now looks very different. Yet his language and ours (or more accurately, the kind of language that this chapter is written in and the spoken varieties of its users) are still – if at times with some difficulty – recognisable as 'the same'. But consider this text from about a century less before Chaucer than we are after him:

(2)   Foxas habbað holu, and heofonan fuglas nest; soþlice mannes sunu næfð hwær he hys heafod ahylde.

The average modern reader would not recognise that this is even English, much less a familiar quotation from the New Testament. Even some of the letters are different, e.g. <þ, ð, æ>, and there are combinations we do not allow like <hw>. In fact this is the opening of Matthew 8:20, from an Old English translation of c. AD 1000. In the familiar Authorised Version ('King James Bible') of 1611 it reads:

(3)   The Foxes haue holes, and the birds of the ayre haue nests; but the sonne of man hath not where to lay his head.

Even this early Modern English (eModE) version, though more like our own English than Chaucer's, is still somewhat 'foreign': we now write *have*, *air*, *son*, not *haue*, *ayre*, *sonne*; we no longer say *hath* but *has*. But these differences are relatively superficial, not like the Old English ones; the relative 'modernness' is brought home by the fact that this text (here in its original form) is now usually printed with modernised spelling, but no changes in grammar. So we can take this, with a few minor reservations, as being as close to 'our English' as makes no real difference. Or so it seems from the written form. But even at this late date, there are still major phonological differences (using the modern spellings for convenience):

(4)

	1611	*ModE*
have	[hav]	[hæv]
holes	[hɔːlz]	[hǝʊlz]
birds	[birdz]	[bɜː(r)dz]
son	[sun]	[sʌn], Northern [sʊn]
lay	[lɛː]	[lɛɪ]

Some important historical points emerge from a more detailed consideration of the earliest version. Here is a literal translation of the Old English (with morpheme divisions marked, and rough glosses for grammatical endings):

(5)   *Fox-as   habb-að   hol-u   and heofon-an   fugl-as   nest*
        fox-nom.pl have-pres.pl hole-acc.pl and heaven-gen.sg bird-nom.pl nest

        soþ-lic-e   mann-es   sun-u   n-æf-ð
        true-ly-adv man-gen.sg son-nom.sg not-have-pres.3.sg

        hwær   he hys heafod ahyld-e
        where he his head   lay down-pres.subj.sg

Here is another translation of the same passage, in 'a different language' (the standard German Bible, based on Martin Luther's sixteenth-century translation):

(6)   *Füchs-e   hab-en Grub-e   und die   Vögel unter de-m*
        fox-nom.pl have-pl hole-acc.pl and the-nom.pl birds under the-dat.sg

        Himmel hab-en Nest-er   aber de-s   Mensch-en Sohn
        heaven have-pl nest-acc.pl but the-masc.gen.sg man-gen.sg son

        ha-t   nicht da   er sein Haupt hin-leg-e
        have-pres.3.sg not   there he his head down-lay-pres.subj.sg

The German does not look much (if at all) further from the later English than the Old English; it is an index of the extent of intervening change that we find our own distant ancestor more like German than like Modern English.

Further, both OE and German have a genitive in *-n* (*heofon-an*, *Mensch-en*), and Old and early Modern English (and ModE) and German a genitive in *-s* (*hy-s*, *hi-s*, *de-s*). And both Old English and German have a present subjunctive singular marker *-e* (*ahyld-e*, *hinleg-e*).

We are looking at a complex web of relationships: languages may be related 'vertically', as OE, ME and ModE are, by what Darwin famously called 'descent with modification'; or 'horizontally' in genetic networks, the way all stages of German and English are (i.e. there is a single common ancestor). Different languages may wander along divergent pathways from a common beginning; this is the source of both temporal and spatial linguistic 'biodiversity'.

2.3   Tale's end: a sketch of ModE phonology and morphology

2.3.1   Principles

On the face of it, histories should be narrated in 'proper order': start at the beginning . . . But this may not always be the best way. Any reader of this chapter will have some idea of 'what English is'; but how many, even native speakers, could produce a vowel or consonant inventory of any ModE dialect? Or have the details of ModE inflectional morphology (such as it is) at their fingertips? For this reason I am going to tell the story in two directions. I will start by characterising a kind of 'prototypical' ModE phonology and morphology, and then go back to OE and show (roughly) how we got where we are.

ModE dialects are more diverse phonologically than any other way, and more so in their vowels than their consonants. This leads to a major difficulty in defining 'English' – beyond the easy 'I know it when I see it.' But we have to make some choice; as the editors of this volume say in their 'Overview', it is not easy to answer the question of what this volume is 'a history *of*'. There are, as they note, 'many different Englishes'; but I need to target some specific variety to write any history at all. My choice – a 'prototypical' dialect of a broadly Southern English standard type – is the clearest endpoint for the story I have to tell, and the best basis for deducing the properties of others. Many readers will speak such dialects; all will be familiar with them. Those who speak quite different ones should not have much trouble mapping their own onto my exemplar. The purpose of this mini-phonology is essentially to name the characters in the story. Here, since the choice of symbols is skewed, for narrative reasons, to the southeast of England, the best way to interpret the keywords, even if the symbols look phonetically inappropriate, is as 'the vowel/consonant I have in word X'. For the most part this will make the history relatively transparent.

But there is still a profound equivocation: even with these stipulations I am taking one modern variety cluster as the target of a history which is not at all 'aimed' at it. There is, to start with, no Old English regional variety clearly ancestral to the language this chapter is written in. The same goes for the bulk of Middle English recorded before the fourteenth century. And yet historians appear to assume an unproblematic lineal connection. Conventionally we adopt the fiction of ancestry, and palliate the fiction by assuming that whatever is attested in early times can 'stand for' an ancestor. In a broad typological sense this is true enough to be relatively harmless – as long as we acknowledge it.

2.3.2   ModE vowel inventories

Defining the parameters for English vowel description is contentious; I choose a conservative model here, as close to the 'phonetic surface' as possible. I also generally avoid the term 'system' in favour of the more neutral 'inventory'. This is because I prefer not to ally myself with any theory that takes 'fixed' or 'exhaustive' systems of contrasting entities to be the basis for phonology. This preference is founded on a deeper principle: that the classical dichotomy between the 'synchronic' and the 'diachronic', between current states and their histories, is not a useful one (see Lass, 1997: ch. 1). I will often talk as if there were such things as 'vowel systems' in one or other classical 'structuralist' sense (as indeed on one level of exposition there perhaps ought to be: though see the arguments in Bybee, 2001). But my main interest is history, and therefore variation and variability, not hard-edged specification of categories and status. I will nonetheless use standard notations like // vs [ ] – with the *caveat* that they are not to be taken all that seriously.

I divide the vowels into three types – short, long and diphthongal; but the diphthongs group with the long vowels, both historically and synchronically. Structurally both are /VV/ clusters; across dialects (which means historically, since variation in space is a function of time) a 'long' category like *bone* can have either a long vowel like [oː] or one of a huge range of diphthongs, e.g. [əʊ, oʊ, œʊ . . .]; but whatever the phonetic quality of the *bed* vowel is, e.g. [ɛ] or [e], it is always a short monophthong.

(7)

	FRONT		CENTRAL		BACK	
	long	short	long	short	long	short
High	iː				uː	
High mid		ɪ		ə		ʊ
Low mid		ɛ	ɜː	ʌ	ɔː	
Low		æ			ɑː	ɒ

Diphthongs: FRONT-GLIDING: /ɛɪ/, /aɪ/, /ɒɪ/; BACK-GLIDING: /aʊ/, /əʊ/; CENTRING: /ɪə/, /ɛə/, /ʊə/; REDUCTION VOWEL 'schwa': /ə/ (only in some weak positions)

(8)   *Keywords* (multiple examples reflect multiple historical sources)
SHORT VOWELS: /ɪ/ *it, fill*; /ɛ/ *bed, head*; /æ/ *rat, cat*; /ʌ/ *son, blood*; /ʊ/ *full, good*; /ɒ/ *lot*; /ə/unstressed vowel in *Prussia*
LONG VOWELS: /iː/ *meet, be, read, week*; /ɜː/ *nurse, heard*; /uː/ *goose*; /ɔː/ *thought, all*; /ɑː/ *father, heart, arm*
DIPHTHONGS: /aɪ/ *bite*; /ɛɪ/ *name, mate*; /ɒɪ/ *joy*; /aʊ/ *house*; /əʊ/ *bone, coal*; /ɪə/ *near, theatre*; /ɛə/ *fair*; /ʊə/ *cure*

I characterise ModE as 'having contrastive vowel length'; most varieties do, though it has been lost in Scots and in many US dialects, at least away from the east coast. The choice of [uː] for *goose* is deliberately conservative: this ancient value persisted in most dialects of English until well into the twentieth century, but is now becoming increasingly rare. More modern dialects than not lack a high back vowel, and realise *goose* with central [ʉː] or front [yː].

The *bird* vowel (a collapse of older /ir, er, ur/) is distinctive only in dialects that have lost syllable-final /r/; its phonetic range covers almost the whole centre of the vowel-space. I use [ɜː] as a neutral and familiar placeholder. This collapse is absent or incomplete in Scots and Irish English. Contrastive /ʌ/ does not occur in Northern and North Midland dialects, nor in some forms of Irish English. These have the same vowel in *son* and *full*, so they are 'one contrast short' from a historical point of view – lack of this split is an archaism.

The *lot* vowel is often not rounded (West Country, Ireland, most of the US), and may be central or even front in areas of the US affected by the 'Northern Cities Shift', where *lot* has [æ] and *cat* [eə]. Many varieties have the same (normally short) vowel in *lot* and *bought*: Scots (Mainland and Ulster), Canadian English, and US dialects with a strong Scots input.

The centring diphthongs /ɛə/ and /ʊə/ result from changes before /r/, and occur only in words ending in orthographic <r>. This is not true of /ɪə/, which occurs without following <r>, if only in a few loans (*theatre, idea, -rrhoea*). More advanced varieties merge /ʊə/ with /ɔː/; many younger speakers (whether they have final /r/ or not) do not distinguish *poor* and *pour*; even those who keep these distinct do not generally distinguish *mourning* and *morning*, though if the development were fully regular they ought to. This highlights a crucial fact: *there is always a lexical element in phonological variation and change*. In a variable system not all words 'with the same phoneme' have the same variant sets, and changes frequently do not go to completion across the entire vocabulary.

2.3.3   ModE consonant inventories

The outline below holds for all dialects except in a few details. (In symbol pairs separated by a comma, the first is voiceless.)

(9)

	Labial	Dental	Alveolar	Palatal	Velar	Glottal
Stops	p, b		t, d	tʃ, dʒ	k, g	
Fricatives	f, v	θ, ð	s, z	ʃ, ʒ		h
Nasals	m		n		ŋ	
Liquids			r, l			
Semivowels	w		j			

For convenience I collapse palatals and palato-alveolars under 'palatal', and bilabials and labiodentals under 'labial', and take the 'affricates' as palatal stops; historically this conventional simplification loses no insights, and groups together categories that behave similarly.

Some dialects have a distinctive dorsal fricative we can call /x/. In Scots /x/ is a retained native segment of OE or Celtic origin (e.g. *nicht* 'night' /nɪxt/ < OE *niht*). 'Judaeo-English' varieties have it in nativised Yiddish loans (*Chanukah* /xanəkə/ 'Festival of Lights'). In South African English it occurs in loans from indigenous African languages (*quagga* /kwaxa/ from Khoe via Bantu); or from Afrikaans (e.g. *gemsbok* /xemsbok/). In some dialects (mainly Scots, Irish and eastern US), historical /xw-/, usually as a voiceless or partly voiced segment represented as [ʍ], still contrasts with /w-/ (*which* < OE *hwilc* vs *witch* < *wicca*). The velar nasal is normally contrastive (e.g. *sin* vs *sing*); but in northwest England final /g/ has been retained, so [ŋ] occurs only before velars (such dialects pronounce *sing, singer* as [sɪŋg], [sɪŋgə]).

(10)   *Keywords* (relevant segments in bold; as under vowels above, multiple examples represent multiple origins)
STOPS: /p/ *pit*; /b/ *bone*; /t/ *till*; /d/ *do*; /tʃ/ *chill, nature*; /dʒ/ *sedge, joy*; /k/ *cat*; /g/ *goose*
FRICATIVES: /f/ *few, rough*; /v/ *over, view*; /θ/ *thin*; /ð/ *this, other*; /s/ *sit*; /z/ *houses, zodiac*; /ʃ/ *ship, machine, ocean, nation*; /ʒ/ *vision, beige*; /h/ *hand*
NASALS: /m/ *meet*; /n/ *new*; /ŋ/ *sing*
LIQUIDS: /r/ *root, rough*; /l/ *lot, all*
SEMIVOWELS: /w/ *woe*; /j/ *you*

2.3.4   Stress

In languages with word accent or stress, some syllable in the word is particularly prominent – in loudness, length, pitch, pitch-movement, or any combination. In most English dialects stressed syllables are marked by relatively greater loudness and length, higher pitch or more pitch-movement than unstressed ones. In some languages stress always falls on the same syllable in the word (the first in Finnish, the penult in Polish, the final in Persian). Others, like English, are more complex; in this case due to partial morphological conditioning and the competition over centuries of native and foreign accentuation.

On the surface, ModE stress looks 'free': primary word accent can apparently fall on the first syllable (*kéttle, cháracter*), the second (*belíeve, divíde*), or the third (*violín, anthropólogy*). Morphology is involved as well: some suffixes do not affect word stress, while others attract it (*belíeve/belíev-er* vs *phótograph/ photógraph-y/photográph-ic*). Looking at stress patterns from the right word-edge rather than the left, we find stress final (*violín*), penultimate (*photográphic*) and antepenultimate (*photógraphy*). Here a regularity does surface: the main word accent normally cannot appear more than three syllables from the end. In a rather constricted nutshell, English stress starts out 'left-handed': the location of stress is computed from the beginning of the word. But through massive contact with a language of a very different type, English has also incorporated a 'right-handed' system, calculated from the word-end. The two types have been in competition since Middle English times; neither side has won or is likely to. Despite decades of attempts to define 'stress rules' for English, it is probably safe to say that it has none, but a set of competing (rather loose) patterns.

There are also patterns involving secondary stress (here marked by `): words of four syllables or more typically have two accented syllables (*ànthropólogy, ànthropológical, díctionàry*). Above the level of the single word, primary and secondary stress may be sensitive to grammatical structure: a compound word like *blackbird* is left-strong, but a phrase like *black bird* is right-strong.

2.3.5   Modern English morphology

In this chapter, morphology = inflection. That is, attachment to the edges of (or in some cases insertion into) lexical morphemes of markers that code categories or track grammatical relations. Very little of earlier English inflectional morphology remains; it now has a minimal relic system.

(a) *Case.* ModE nouns are invariant, except for an apparent genitive (*cat* vs *cat's, cats'*). If we define an inflectional affix as a marker attaching to a *word*, then this is not a case marker but a clitic which marks its host as a possessive modifier. The *s*-genitive can attach not only to words (as above), but to phrases and clauses: in [[*cat*]'*s*] it looks like an affix, but in [[*the king of England*]'*s nose*] -*s* attaches at phrase level, and in [[*the man who lives next door*]'*s brother*] at clause level.

True case marking remains only in the pronoun: aside from the modifying genitive (*my book, your dog*), there is only a two-way contrast, nominative vs objective or oblique: *I/me, he/him, she/her, they/them*. Even this vestige is lacking in the second person (invariant *you*), and the neuter third person (*it*: though this was unmarked even in Old English).

(b) *Number.* Number is coded on most nouns and all pronouns except *you*. (Though many dialects have reinvented a second-person plural, usually of the type /juːz/, i.e. *you* + plural *-s*.) Most plural marking on native nouns is regular: there is a 'sibilant suffix' (the same as in the genitive) appearing as /-s/ after voiceless non-sibilants, /-z/ after voiced non-sibilants, and /-Vz/ after sibilants (*cats* vs *dogs* vs *kisses*: /V-/ stands for whatever weak vowel occurs in a given lect). Of the older native plural types, only a few umlaut plurals (*mouse/mice, foot/feet*, etc.), and some zero plurals (*sheep*) remain. Most others have been replaced by the *s*-plural, which is now the only productive form: foreign plurals are generally restricted to the loanwords they came with (*stratum/strata, kibbutz/kibbutzim*). There is a fragmentary number (and person) concord between verb and subject: a suffix *-s* (with the same allomorphy as the plural) appears on non-modal present verbs with third-person subjects.

(c) *Gender.* There is no grammatical gender; pronouns agree with the 'natural' or semantic gender of their antecedents, except in the few cases where non-human or inanimate nouns can be referred to by pronouns other than *it* (ships as *she* and the like). These are metaphorical, not grammatical.

(d) *Tense and aspect.* The only morphological markings are for past tense, the past (perfective) participle, and the present participle. Most verbs in the past take a 'regular' *-ed* ending, whose allomorphy is in principle the same as that of the plural and third-person suffix: /-t/ after voiceless segments except /t/ (*kick-ed*), /-d/ after voiced (*lagg-ed*), and /-Vd/ after /t, d/ (*fitt-ed, hoard-ed*). There are however a good number of irregular past and participial formations, mostly relics of older, once regular alternations. Some reflect an ancient IE type that survived in a modified form into Old English (the 'strong' verbs, e.g. *ride/rode/ridden*); others have old length alternations which have become qualitative because of changes in long vowels that did not affect short ones (*keep/kept*: see Section 5.2.1). Still others are irregular in other ways, e.g. *buy/bought, seek/sought*.

2.4   Old English

2.4.1   Time, space and texts

The Old English record is fragmentary and discontinuous (see Chapter 1). The supposed 'language' Old English is actually a somewhat scrappy and often uncertainly provenanced collection of manuscript remains – much less unified than textbook introductions would suggest. A unitary Old English of course did not exist any more than a unitary Modern English; but since the remains are so scanty, what we really have is a collection of diverse scribal idiolects or 'text languages', and no very clear lines of descent. The apparently linear histories that the handbooks give us, and that I will be presenting here in modified form, are historians' constructs; but as long as the problems remain at least as background discomforts, this is relatively harmless.

2.4.2   The Old English vowels

Many details of the Old English dialect picture are unresolved. The exemplary inventories here are the most likely input to the Middle English varieties that grew into the most widely distributed forms of Modern English. The vowel system was highly symmetrical, with all monophthongs in qualitatively identical long/short pairs. There were at least two pairs of diphthongs, also contrasting in length; these appear not to have been of the modern /ai, au, iə/ types, but had two elements agreeing in height. There is no evidence for central vowels, but only front and back, and three contrasting heights, as opposed to the ModE and ME four.

(11)

	FRONT		BACK	
	long	short	long	short
High	iː, yː	i, y	uː	u
Mid	eː	e	oː	o
Low	æː	æ	ɑː	ɑ

Diphthongs: long: eːo, æːɑ; short: æɑ, eo

(12)   *Keywords*
SHORT VOWELS: /i/ *hit* 'it', *cild* 'child'; /y/ *fyllan* 'fill'; /e/ *bedd* 'bed', *mete* 'meat'; /æ/ *rætt* 'rat', *bæþ* 'bath'; /u/ *full* 'full', *lufu* 'love', *wund* 'wound'; /o/ *god* 'god', *nosu* 'nose'; /ɑ/ *catte* 'cat', *nama* 'name'
LONG VOWELS: /iː/ *bītan* 'bite'; /yː/ *hȳdan* 'hide'; /eː/ *mētan* 'meet'; /æː/ *lǣdan* 'lead'; /uː/ *hūs* 'house', *sūþerne* 'southern'; /oː/ *fōd* 'food', *gōd* 'good', *flōd* 'flood'; /ɑː/ *bān* 'bone'
SHORT DIPHTHONGS: /æɑ/ *earm* 'arm'; *eall* 'all'; /eo/ *heorte* 'heart', *heofon* 'heaven'
LONG DIPHTHONGS: /eːo/ *bēon* 'be'; *brēost* 'breast'; /æːɑ/ *lēaf* 'leaf'

The notation for the diphthongs is conventional but misleading: the 'short' diphthongs were non-steady-state short vowels, and the 'long' ones were the same length as long vowels. Some readers may note the absence here of the two diphthongs spelled <ie> in the standard grammars and dictionaries (e.g. *hīeran* 'to hear', *ieldra* 'older'). These were largely restricted to early West Saxon (tenth century), and play no independent part in the development of any later dialect; they had merged with /i(ː)/ or /y(ː)/ well before earliest Middle English.

Note that there is no /ʌ/. ModE words with this vowel descend either from /u/ (*full*), or shortening of /oː/ (*flood* < *flōd*). The diphthong in words like *joy, poison* appears later, in French and other loanwords. The standard view is that there was also a /ə/ in unstressed syllables, but I think it safer to assume that all vowels have their ordinary qualities in all positions until at least the transition to Middle English.

2.4.3   The Old English consonants

The consonant-quality system was smaller than that of ModE, but differently organised; there was contrastive length for most of its members, a parameter now completely lost:

(13)

	Labial	Dental	Alveolar	Palatal	Velar
Stops	p, pː, b, bː		t, tː, d, dː	tʃ, tʃː, dʒ dʒː	k, kː, g, gː
Fricatives	f, fː	θ, θː	s, sː	ʃ	x, xː
Nasals	m, mː	n, nː			
Liquids			l, lː r, rː		
Semivowels	w			j	

(14)   *Keywords* (relevant consonants in boldface)

STOPS: /p/ *pæþ* 'path'; /pː/ *æppel* 'apple'; /b/ *bæþ* 'bath'; /bː/ *cribb* 'crib'; /t/ *tellan* 'tell'; /tː/ *sette* 'set'; /tʃ/ *cinn* 'chin'; /tʃː/ *wrecca* 'exile, wretch'; /dʒ/ *sengean* 'singe'; /dʒː/ *ecg* 'edge'; /k/ *cynn* 'kin'; /kː/ *brocces* 'badger's' (gen. sg); /g/ *gold* 'gold'; /gː/ *hogg* 'hog'

FRICATIVES: /f/ *fæder* 'father'; /fː/ *pyffan* 'puff'; /θ/ *þēoh* 'thigh'; /θː/ *moþþe* 'moth'; /s/ *singan* 'sing'; /sː/ *cyssan* 'kiss'; /ʃ/ *scip* 'ship'; /x/ *hūs* 'house', *ni**h**t* 'night', *dwear**h*** 'dwarf'; /xː/ *hlæ**hh**an* 'laugh'

NASALS: /m/ *mann* 'man'; /mː/ *ramm* 'ram'; /n/ *nosu* 'nose'; /nː/ *cann* 'can'

LIQUIDS: /r/ *rætt* 'rat', *for* 'for'; /rː/ *feorr* 'far', *deorra* 'dearer'; /l/ *lufu* 'love', *hāl* 'whole'; /lː/ *eall* 'all', *feallan* 'fall'

SEMIVOWELS: /w/ *wæter* 'water'; /j/ *geoc* 'yoke'

There are no distinctive voiced fricatives: /f, θ, s/ are voiceless initially, finally and in clusters with other obstruents (including geminates or self-clusters, i.e. 'long consonants'), and voiced foot-medially (see Section 2.5.2.5); /ʃ/ is always voiceless. There is no distinctive /h/; this arises from the syllable-initial realisation of /x/ in the sixteenth to seventeenth centuries (Section 2.7.5.4). There is no phonemic velar nasal: [ŋ] occurs only before /k, g/.

The phonotactic restrictions were quite different from those of later periods. In particular there were a number of onset clusters that have subsequently been lost, including /kn, gn, wr, wl, xr, xl, xn, xw/. The first two remained as late as the eighteenth century in the southern standard. The /w-/ and /x-/ clusters were lost early in Middle English, except for /xw/, which persists in spelling as <wh> and may be distinct from /w/.

2.4.4   Stress

Old English stress was based on the Germanic Stress Rule (GSR), and a phrase-vs-compound rule more or less the same as the modern one. The general principles are: (a) primary stress is assigned to the first syllable of the lexical root (excluding prefixes), regardless of word length: *lágu* 'law', *lóppestre* 'lobster'; (b) most prefixes are unstressed: *ge-wríten* 'written', *wiþ-sácan* 'contend'; (c) certain prefixes, mainly on nouns, were stressable, and these received primary stress, with the root getting secondary stress: *wíðer-sàca* 'adversary'; (d) the pattern in (c) was that of compound nouns and adjectives: as in ModE, the left element was strong (primary stress) and the right weak (secondary): *mánn-hàta* 'man-hater'.

2.4.5   Old English morphology

2.4.5.1   The noun phrase: noun, pronoun and adjective

The ultimate ancestor of Old English, Proto-Indo-European (PIE), had eight noun cases: nominative, genitive, accusative, dative, ablative, locative, instrumental and vocative. In Germanic (by and large), nominative and accusative were already identical, the genitive remained distinct only in certain masculine and neuter declensions, and the dative, ablative, locative and instrumental had collapsed into a single case traditionally called 'dative' – though it often continues an old locative or instrumental. In some dialects fragments of an independent instrumental remain.

Old English also retains original grammatical gender (masculine vs feminine vs neuter), but with some irregularities. Gender is not 'sex': it is simply a classifying system, in which each noun has to belong to some category which predicts its agreement behaviour (forms of pronouns and adjectives). So *stān* 'stone' is masculine and takes *hē* as its agreeing pronoun, *cild* 'child' is neuter and takes *hit*, later *it*, *lufu* 'love' is feminine and takes *hēo*. Adjectives agree (roughly) in number, gender and case with the nouns they modify. PIE had three numbers (as still in Ancient Greek): singular, dual (two and two only) and plural. The dual remains only in the first and second personal pronouns.

There are many different noun paradigms; I illustrate with a few characteristic types, along with the so-called 'definite article' – really a determiner and pronoun that can also mark definiteness. Its plural is the same for all three genders, so I give it once only. (In general there are fewer distinctions in the OE plural than the singular: see pronouns and verbs below.)

(15)   *Some major OE noun-declension types*

	wulf 'wolf' a-stem (m)		*scip* 'ship' a-stem (n)		*lufu* 'love' ō-stem (f)	
	sg	pl	sg	pl	sg	pl
nom	se wulf	þā wulf-as	þæ-t scip	scip-u	luf-u	luf-a/-e
gen	þæ-s wulf-es	þā-r-a wulf-a	þæ-s scip-es	scip-a	þǣ-re luf-e	luf-a
dat	þā-m wulf-e	þā-m wulf-um	þā-m scip-e	scip-um	þǣ-re luf-e	luf-um
acc	þo-ne wulf	þā wulf-as	þæ-t scip	scip-u	þā luf-e	luf-a/-e

	sunu 'son' u-stem (m)		*nama* 'name' n-stem (m)		*fōt* 'foot' umlaut plural (m)	
	sg	pl	sg	pl	sg	pl
nom	sun-u	sun-a	nam-a	nam-an	fōt	fēt
gen	sun-a	sun-a	nam-an	nam-ena	fōt-es	fēt-a
dat	sun-a	sun-um	nam-an	nam-um	fēt	fōt-um
acc	sun-u	sun-a	nam-an	nam-an	fōt	fēt

(The declension names confusingly reflect the original Germanic stem-classes: *wulf* is called an '*a*-stem' because the endings were once connected to the root by an *-a*-: *wulf* < *wulβ-a-z*. These names are just mnemonics for future reference.)

There is less here than meets the eye; OE was not, as usually portrayed, a 'richly inflected' language. More often than not even the nominative and accusative (which should signal the prime grammatical relation – subject vs direct object) are identical in the singular, and always are in the plural. The real work in OE is done not by the forms of nouns but by adjectives, determiners and referring pronouns (and of course syntactic grouping and word order). I give the personal pronouns (the major reservoir for our current forms), and some examples of adjective inflection, to illustrate how information was apportioned among adjectives, determiners, pronouns and nouns. In the paradigms below, I omit a number of variants for reasons of space: they were not as neat as they look. Some of the OE variation will be recalled later. For convenience I give the modern reflexes where they survived.

(16)   *The OE personal pronouns*

1 PERSON

	sg	*dual*	*pl*		*sg*	*dual*	*pl*
nom	ic [*I*]	wit	wē [*we*]	þū [*thou*]	git	gē [*ye*]
gen	mīn [*my/mine*]	uncer	ūre [*our*]	þīn [*thy/thine*]	incer	ēower [*your*]
dat	mē [*me*]	unc	ūs [*us*]	þē [*thee*]	inc	ēow [*you*]
acc	mē	unc	ūs	þē	inc	ēow

2 PERSON (header appears above the second group)

3 PERSON

	masc sg	*neut sg*	*fem sg*	*pl all genders*
nom	hē [*he*]	hi-t [*it*]	hēo [?*she*]	hī(e)/hēo
gen	hi-s [*his*]	hi-s	hire/heora [*her*]	hira/heora
dat	hi-m [*him*]	hi-m	hire/heora	him/heom
acc	hi-ne	hi-t	hī(e)	hī(e)/ hēo

Note that there is no separate genitive for *it*, and no third-person plural *th*-forms (ancestors of *they*, etc.). These, along with *she*, are later developments. There is already considerable ambiguity: the feminine singular and all plurals show extensive overlap.

Our current determiner system comprises invariable *the* and two demonstratives (*this/these, that/those*); but in OE (see above) a great deal of syntactic information within the NP could be carried by determiners; the rest was handled by inflected adjectives. As to some extent in Modern German, the adjective acted as a kind of default: the less information carried by adjectives, the more by determiners, and vice versa. Thus the adjective had two paradigms: 'strong' (a mixture of old noun and pronoun endings), which marked a number of inflectional categories, and 'weak', rather like the paradigm of the *n*-stem noun, which marked very little. So even though the fully inflected masculine genitive singular of *gōd* 'good' would be *gōd-es*, the phrase 'of the good man' would normally be *þæ-s gōd-an mann-es*, where the *-an* says merely 'oblique case', but not genitive specifically. This system begins to fall apart in the transition to early Middle English, and the adjective becomes indeclinable by the fifteenth or sixteenth century.

2.4.5.2   The verb

The standard pedagogical Germanic verb paradigm is a complex historical accretion. It consists of the verb proper ('finite' = tensed and person/number marked forms), a deverbal noun in -n (the infinitive), and a deverbal adjective in -t/-d or -n (the past participle). The infinitive and past participle are traditionally 'part of' the verb; and indeed along with certain finite forms they constitute the 'principal parts', that set from which all other forms can be derived. This is clearest in the most archaic verb type, the so-called strong verb. These mark their major categories by root-internal vowel-alternations, and are generally divided into seven classes or 'ablaut series', as follows ('present' is represented by the infinitive; the hyphen before the past participle marks the attachment site for an optional prefix ge-):

(17)   *The OE strong verb classes*

	pres	*past sg*	*past pl*	*pp*
I 'bite'	bīt-an	bāt	bit-on	-bit-en
II 'creep'	crēop-an	crēap	crup-on	-crop-en
IIIa 'sing'	sing-an	sang	sung-on	-sung-en
IIIb 'help'	help-an	healp	hulp-on	-holpen
IV 'bear'	ber-an	bær	bǣr-on	-boren
V 'break'	brec-an	bræc	brǣc-on	-brecen
VI 'fare'	far-an	fōr	fōron	-faren
VII 'fall'	feall-an	fēoll	fēollon	-feallen

This system (which was not invariant even in OE) was quite irregularly restructured in Middle and early Modern English; the strong-verb vowel grades are still not fully reorganised or stable. Even within the same class, there are multiple types of histories: cf. *write/wrote/written* vs *bite/bit/bitten* vs *slide/slid/slid* vs *shit/shat/shat* or *shit/shit/shit*, all class I; and many verbs have appropriated bits of others (*break* has its past and past participle from the past participle of the *bear* type).

The weak verb, which forms its past and past participle by suffixation, is a Germanic innovation. There are a number of classes, but I will exemplify only by the two commonest. Here are the principal parts of three characteristic verbs of weak classes I and II:

(18)   *The main OE weak verb classes*

		pres	*past 3sg*	*past part*
Class I	'kiss'	cyss-an	cys-te	-cys-t
	'travel'	fēr-an	fēr-de	-fēr-ed
Class II	'love'	luf-i-an	luf-o-de	-luf-od

The person/number endings vary from class to class, but here is an outline that will guide us through the succeeding history. I take as my example the endings of a class I weak verb with a past in -d-:

(19)   *The OE verb endings (person/number/mood)*
                 pres ind   pres subj   past ind   past subj

	pres ind	pres subj	past ind	past subj
1sg	-e	-e	-de	-de
2sg	-(e)st	-e	-de	-de
3sg	-(e)þ	-e	-de	-de
pl	-aþ	-en	-on	-en

As in the noun, we see a much reduced system (virtually all these categories are distinct in Gothic, and the plural retains three persons in other early dialects, as it does today in Icelandic). The strong-verb conjugation differs in one important way from the weak: the past first and third singular are endingless, and the second-person singular has the vowel of the past plural with a suffix *-e*. So for *bītan* 'bite' the past singular would be *ic bāt, þū bit-e, hē bāt*. This difference explains one of the oddities of the modern modal auxiliaries, their lack of third-person singular *-s* (*he can*, **he can-s*). The ancestors of these verbs ('preterite-presents') have an old strong past form as present, and a new weak past. Some examples:

(20)   Preterite present verbs

	pres sg	pres pl	past sg
'can'	cann	cunn-on	cū-ðe
'shall'	sceal	scul-on	scol-de
'may'	mæg	mag-on	mih-te

There are many other irregular-verb subclasses, including the so-called 'anomalous verbs' like *go, will*. The details can be found in any OE grammar. But one exceedingly irregular verb deserves separate treatment, because of its text frequency, complexity and many functions: the verb (or rather the three verbs) 'to be'. This is made up of three paradigm fragments, a root in *s-*, one in *b-*, and one in *w-*.

(21)   The verb 'to be'

	PRESENT				PAST	
	indicative		*subjunctive*		*indicative*	*subjunctive*
	s-root	*b*-root	*s*-root	*b*-root	*w*-root only	
1sg	eom	bēo	sīe	bēo	wæs	wǣr-e
2sg	eart	bi-st	sīe	bēo	wǣr-e	wǣr-e
3sg	is	bi-þ	sīe	bēo	waes	wǣr-e
pl	sindon, sint, ear-on	bēo-þ	sīe-n	bēo-n	wǣr-on	wǣr-en

Non-finite forms: infinitive *bēon, wesan*; pres part *wesende*

Despite extensive reorganisation, the three roots remain; *are < earon* gradually took over the plural and second-person singular, and the *b*-root all non-finite forms. The *w*-root remains for the past. In late OE a new present participle *bēo-nd-e* (> *being*) appears, and in the eleventh century a past participle (*ge-*) *bēo-n* (> *been*).

2.4.6   Postlude as prelude

All this morphological detail is not given just for its own sake. These forms are the caterpillar innards that were remodelled by dissolution and reformation in the chrysalis of the next half-millennium. This larval material suggests some hypothetical but loaded questions, which touch on both phonology and morphology. For instance, recall the masculine and neuter dative pronoun *hi-m*, the dative determiner *þǣ-m*, the dative plural noun marker *-u-m*, and the accusative pronoun *hi-ne* and determiner *þo-ne*. Apparently *-m* marks dative and *-n* accusative. Now what would happen if syllable-final *-m* and *-n* tended to collapse in *-n*? For one thing, the dative/accusative third-person singular pronouns would merge. And if vowels in weak positions also tended to merge, the infinitive ending, the past indicative plural and present and past subjunctive plural of verbs and the oblique cases of weak nouns would become similar or identical. These processes were already beginning in OE. As early as the tenth century we find texts with the past plural, dative plural and infinitive marker (variably) collapsed in *-an*. But it was only about two centuries later that these changes went to completion.

2.5   The 'OE/ME transition' to c.1150

2.5.1   The Great Hiatus

Between the end of the eleventh century and the latter part of the twelfth, English textual attestation (apart from the continued copying of OE texts in some centres) appears to be sucked into a black hole. Oversimply, this is a historical contingency deriving from the change of administration after the Norman Conquest; this led to about a century of French-speaking hegemony and the dominance of French and Latin in the learned and public spheres. There is thus a period when very few texts composed in English come down to us; around the middle of the twelfth century English appears – falsely – to have been 'reborn' as something resembling OE in some ways but quite different in others. There was of course an unbroken transmission of the spoken language; but the habit of writing English was for a while largely superseded by different demands, which led to more writing in Latin and French than in English. Many of the major developments are therefore invisible – though we can tell pretty well what they must have been. Much of the surviving material, well into the thirteenth century, shows a mixture of Old English tradition and French and Latin devices, as well as considerable, often startlingly sophisticated, invention.

2.5.2   Phonology: major early changes

2.5.2.1   Early quantity adjustments

Many ModE words have the historically 'wrong' vowel: e.g. *child*, *field*, *bound* ought to have short vowels, and *southern*, *breast*, *kept* long ones. These oddities are especially salient in alternations: e.g. *south/southern*, *child/children*, *keep/kept*, where one member does not have the expected quantity. The source is a set of irregular shortenings and lengthenings that took place during the OE period, and were complete by the beginning of ME. The internal history and timing are generally unclear.

(i) *Homorganic lengthening*. Short (especially high) vowels tended to lengthen before clusters of nasal or liquid + homorganic voiced obstruent e.g. *cild* 'child' > *cīld, bŭnden* 'bound' > *būnden*. This failed if a third consonant followed: hence *cīld* vs pl *cildru*, giving modern *child/children*.

(ii) *Pre-cluster shortening*. Long vowels tended to shorten before clusters other than those in (i), including geminates. So *cēpan* 'keep', past *cēpte* > *cēpan/cĕpte, brēost* 'breast' > *brēost* > *brĕst*. This often failed before clusters of a kind that could serve as onsets as well as codas, especially /st/: hence short *breast* vs long *priest* < *prēost*.

(iii) *Trisyllabic shortening*. Long vowels shortened in the antepenults of trisyllabic words. There appear to have been two phases: first only if two consonants followed the vowel in question, and later also if one followed. Most of the clear examples are from the second phase (probably eleventh century). This can stand for the process as a whole, which has had important morphophonemic implications, and was late enough to affect French loanwords as well. Examples: OE *sūþ* 'south', *sūþerne* 'southern', later *sŭþerne*; French *divīn* 'divine', *divīniti*, later *diviniti*. (On these quantity adjustments in general see Ritt, 1994.)

2.5.2.2 The old diphthongs, low vowels and /y(ː)/

Beginning around the eleventh century the diphthong and low vowel systems were radically altered. First, /æ(ː)a/ monophthongised and merged with /æ(ː)/, and /e(ː)o/ > /ø(ː)/ (or so they say: but see below). At the same time short /æ/ merged with /a/, while long /æ(ː)/, itself now the product of a merger, remained unchanged, as did long /aː/.

According to the handbooks, the reflexes of /e(ː)o/ remained mid front rounded in the more westerly parts of the country, but elsewhere merged with /eː/. Similarly, /y(ː)/ remained unchanged in these areas, whereas elsewhere (N, EML) it either unrounded to /i(ː)/, or came down as /e(ː)/, reflecting a change that had already occurred in the southeast in OE times. Thus England is neatly divided into three areas by the reflexes of OE /y(ː)/. The texts chosen for most collections are usually short enough and 'typical' enough so that this appears really to be the case; but a close examination of the actual spellings in a large enough manuscript sample suggests something quite different. Here for instance are the accented vowel spellings for some OE /y(ː)/ words from Oxford, Bodleian Library, Digby 86 (Worcestershire, thirteenth century). This is an area in the SWML that according to the handbooks 'retained [y]', spelled <u>:

(22)   *dyde* 'did': <u> 6x, <e> 6x; *yfel* 'evil': <u> 1x, <e> 7x; *þyncan* 'seem':
             <u> 1x, <i> 7x, <e> 5x; *cyning* 'king' 13x; *hlystan* 'listen' <e> 4x

Curiously, no matter what the preponderant reflex of OE /y/ is in any area, the word 'king' always has <i>. The story of /y(:)/ has not yet been properly told, and that of /eo(:)/ looks to be even more complicated. I am sure the standard accounts are wrong. Rather, /y(:)/ simply merged with /u(:)/ in those areas where it is spelled <u>, and /e(:)o/ simply split and merged with either /e:/ or /o:/. There is no solid evidence that any front rounded vowels survived into ME (Lass & Laing, 2005.) Like much else dealing with early ME in this chapter, this is an interim report, which may (or may not) be corrected when the *Linguistic Atlas of Early Middle English* (*LAEME*), being prepared at Edinburgh, is completed.

It would be nice to be able to put all these changes in a chronological sequence; but they appear to overlap, as they do with a series of developments that produced a new set of diphthongs.

2.5.2.3   The new ME diphthongs

During this murky 'transitional' period, probably starting in the eleventh century, a new series of diphthongs were developing, from two sources:

(a)   'Middle English Breaking'. High vowel epenthesis between a non-high vowel and a velar or palatal continuant: /i/ after front vowels except new /a/, /u/ after back vowels and /a/. So *feohtan* 'fight' > *fehtan* [feçten] > [feiçten] *feiʒten, sōhte* 'sought' [so:xte] > [souxte] > [sɔuxte] *souʒte*.

(b)   Vocalisation. Syllable-final voiced continuants [j, w] became vowels, and [ɣ] (the intervocalic allophone of /g/) merged with /w/: so *dæg* 'day' [dæj] > [dæi] > [dai], *boga* 'bow' [bɔɣɑ] > [bowe] > [boue] > [bɔuc].

The eventual result was five diphthongs, all of the 'new' type with high second elements. With exemplary ModE forms and their OE sources:

(23)   /ai/ *day* <*dæg, way* < *weg*; /au/ *draw* < *dragan, saw* < *seah*; /ɛu/ *shrew* < *scrēawa*; /iu/ *rue* < *hrēowan, snow* < *snīwan*; /ɔu/ *own* < *āgan, know* < *cnāwan, dough* < *dāh, daughter* < *dohtor, grow* < *grōwan, sought* < *sōhte*

Some French diphthongs (and a triphthong) fell in with these: e.g. /au/ simply merged (*fault*), /ieu, yi/ (*rule, fruit*) > /iu/. French also contributed two diphthongs of its own, which occur only in foreign lexis: /oi/ (*joy*) and /ui/ (*poison*). These remained separate until the seventeenth century, though some words crossed from one category to the other (Section 2.7.4.7).

2.5.2.4   Weak vowel mergers

Vowel attrition in weak syllables had been occurring all through the history of Germanic; in OE historical /æ, e/ had already largely merged in /e/, long vowels were excluded from inflections, and only /i, e, u, o, a/ could occur in weak final syllables. Over the tenth to thirteenth centuries, these vowels merged, leading to a majority spelling <e> in most areas by 1400. The scholarly consensus suggests collapse in a 'neutral' /ə/; but neutralisation in /e/, without invocation of a special new vowel, is at least as likely for most regions except parts of the SWML, where there may have been some merger in /u/. (I will however represent this vowel as /e/ for convenience.) There is also evidence for a second, higher weak vowel throughout the rest of the history of English, especially before dentals; this is suggested by the frequent <-is/-ys>, <-id/-yd> plural and past spellings in the fourteenth to fifteenth centuries, and rhymes like Chaucer's *speres*: *here is* (*PF* 67ff).

2.5.2.5   The fricative voice contrast

In ModE, both voiced and voiceless fricatives can appear in any word position: *few/view, offer/over, staff/stave*. This is the contingent result of several unrelated changes converging over a considerable period. To arrive at the modern distribution, [v, ð, z] must be able to appear initially and finally, and [f, θ, s] medially. And this requires loss of consonantal length (in OE only long voiceless fricatives appeared between vowels).

French loans in *v-, z-* (*veal, virgin, zeal, zodiac*) began to appear after 1066: native/French pairs like *feel/veal, seal/zeal* became possible. Initial /v, z/ were established by about 1250. (The situation in parts of the south and SWML was rather different, since initial /f, s/ were voiced in late OE if not earlier: in these dialects what had to be established was initial /f, s/, which began to drift in from other areas during the ME period.) The initial /θ/: /ð/ contrast followed a different route: around the fourteenth century initial /θ/ started to voice in grammatical words (*this, though, thou*, etc.).

The word-final contrast develops mainly through loss of /-ə/; this began about 1100 and was completed during the fourteenth century. The original intervocalic environments were destroyed, exposing voiced fricatives in final position: OE *nosu* /nosu/[nozu] > [nɔːzə]> [nɔːz] 'nose', etc. Other instances are due to analogy: e.g. *drīfan* 'drive', past *drāf* should give ModE *drive/*drofe*; the /v/ has been extended from the present system.

The length contrast began to decay in the thirteenth century, and was lost by the fourteenth. Contrasts like [-fː-] vs [-v-] (*offrian* vs *ofer*) now became [-f-] vs [-v-], making voice distinctive between vowels. Like so many changes that can be described as if they were 'immediate', the restructuring has a long and irregular history.

2.6   Middle English, c.1150–1450

2.6.1   The problem of ME spelling

The monophthongisation of the old diphthongs, the low vowel mergers, and the neutralisation of weak vowels produced an orthographic surplus: more potential symbols than sounds. This opened the way for two stylistic approaches to inventing spelling systems: 'economical' (choose – roughly – one symbol for each phoneme), and 'profligate' (allow for variation, even delight in it). One of the knottiest problems in interpreting early ME texts is trying to figure out what the profligate writers are doing, and whether the mass of orthographic distinctions we find match anything phonetic. What we appear to find is 'Litteral Substitution Sets' (LSSs: i.e. sets of graphs that appear to be interchangeable) for particular etymological categories, sometimes particular lexical items (see Laing, 1999; Laing & Lass, 2003). Here are some twelfth-century examples, from the *Peterborough Chronicle* (Final Continuation, Oxford, Bodleian Library, Laud Misc 636; spellings as in MS, but runic 'wynn' substituted by <w>):

(24)   OE *wǣron* 'be', pret pl: wæron 11x, uuæren 1x, wæren 1x, uueron 1x, uuaren 1x, waren 1x
            OE *wǣre* 'be', pres subj sg: uuare 1x, ware 1x
            OE *bēam* 'tree, beam': beom 1x
            OE *ēode* 'go', past: gæde1x, iæde 1x (sg), ieden 1x (pl)
            OE *eorl* 'earl': eorl 20x, æorl 1x
            OE *fēran* 'carry', past: ferde(n) 9x, feorde(n) 2x
            OE *-on*, verb past pl: -en 29x, -an 2x, -on 2x, -æn 2x, -e 1x, -i 1x, zero 1x

There are strategies for sorting out such complexity, which I will not go into here; but anybody interested in the history of English should have some idea of the apparent messiness of much of the primary material – especially as most readers will, sadly, have encountered Middle English only in sanitised and edited 'literary' versions.

2.6.2   Phonology

2.6.2.1   The vowels: MEOSL and the story of OE /ɑː/ (*bone*)

By the twelfth century OE /æː/ had raised to /ɛː/. At around 1100, then, excluding the diphthongs and the front rounded vowels if they survived, the overall shape of the monophthongal vowel system in all dialects was probably this:

(25)   iː i   u uː
            eː e   o oː
            ɛː □   □ □
            □ a   □ ɑː

The inventory is now spread over four heights rather than three (as still in most modern dialects). And, as the boxes indicate, there are now potential 'empty slots' in certain regions of the vowel space. There is of course no reason why a system has to become symmetrical, or pack its vowel space to any particular degree; but in English a number of these slots did get filled, and much of the ancient symmetry was restored, if with rather different results.

The vowel system was first reshaped by two changes, one virtually exceptionless, the other sporadic. The first was raising and rounding of OE /ɑː/ to /ɔː/ (except in the north); the second was lengthening of vowels in certain open penultimate stressed syllables, so-called Middle English Open Syllable Lengthening (MEOSL).

There are signs of the /ɑː/ > /ɔː/ change as early as the twelfth century; but it begins to stabilise – if variably – in the next. Here is a sample of OE /ɑː/ items from two thirteenth-century texts, one from the west and one from the east:

(26) (a)   *Laȝamon A* (London, British Library, MS Cotton Caligula A.ix, hand A: Worcestershire)
            OE *bān* 'bone': ban 4x, bon 2x
            OE *hlāford* 'lord': lauerd 11x, lauard 1x, læuerd 1x, louerd 1x
            OE *lāþ* 'loath': lad, lað 11x, laeð 11x, loað 1x, lod 1x, loð 1x

      (b)   *Vices and Virtues* (London, British Library, MS Stowe 34: hand A: SW Essex)
            OE *gāst* 'ghost': gast(e)- 26x, gost(e)- 11x; *gāstlice* 'ghostly, spiritual': gastlich(e) 10x, gostliche 1x
            OE *hālig* 'holy': hali(g)- 130x, holi(g)- 14x

This looks like an early stage of diffusion, typically variable and lexically specific. That is, as usual in the earlier stages of a change we cannot say that 'X has become Y', but rather that 'X is becoming Y variably in particular lexical items'. Only after the change is completed (if it ever is) can we say 'has become'. This is not what histories like to say, but such things happen even in modern standard languages. Just as one could not properly ask of *Vices and Virtues* 'what vowel/spelling does "holy" have?', one could not ask of my own dialect 'what vowel does "rather" have?' The answer in the latter case would be 'mostly [æ], less often [aː] or [ɑː]'.

Open syllable lengthening is described in the handbooks as categorical: short (non-high) vowels lengthened in stressed open penults, and the mid vowels lowered by one height. Thus OE /nɑmɑ/ 'name' > /namə/ > /naːmə/, /nosu/ 'nose' > /nozə/ > /nɔːzə/. In forms like these the final /-ə/ dropped (see below); if the final syllable was closed, it tended to remain (*naked* < *hnacod*, *beaver* < *beofor*). But MEOSL never went to completion; only a little over 50 per cent of the items that could show it actually do, and these are (with considerable statistical likelihood) ones that have lost final /-ə/. Retention of the following weak syllable militates against lengthening: note short vowels in apparent prime candidates like *camel* < *camel*, *otter* < *otor*. Lengthening of high vowels was uncommon except in the north; but a number of words show lengthening and lowering, particularly of /i/: *week* < *wicu*, *beetle* < *bitela* (ModE /iː/ here presupposes ME /eː/).

We can diagram the results of the two changes discussed here, at any point in their implementation:

(27)   Results of /ɑː/ > /ɔː/ and OSL: * = added V-type, † = lost V-type

            iː   i   u   uː
            eː   e   o   oː
            ↙   ↘
            ɛː   ɔː*
                   ↑
            aː*   ←a   ɑː†

(The lower mid vowels from OSL do not always fall in with the originals; they are still distinct in some north midland dialects.)

English now has two low vowels in front and none in back; the symmetry (in some dialects) is restored in the seventeenth and nineteenth centuries by other changes. There are also two pairs of long mid vowels.

From this point onward the connection to ModE is clearer; I will give a set of keywords for this system and the diphthongs, but in modern form, since there are so many possible ME spellings. This is based on the OE keyword list in Section 2.4.2, and once again illustrates possible mergers and splits.

(28)   *Middle English keywords*
           SHORT: /i/ *it, fill*; /e/ *bed, breast, heart*; /a/ *rat, bath, cat, arm*; /u/ *full, love, southern*; /o/ *god*
           LONG: /iː/ *bite, hide, child*; /eː/ *meet, be, week*; /ɛː/ *lead, meat, leaf*; /uː/ *house, bound*; /oː/ *food, good, flood, wood*; /ɔː/ *bone, nose*; /aː/ *name*
           DIPHTHONGS: /ai/ *day, way*; /au/ *draw, saw*; /ɛu/ *shrew*; /iu/ *rue, snow*; /ɔu/ *own, know, dough, daughter, grow, sought*

2.6.2.2   'Dropping aitches' and postvocalic /x/

At least since the late eighteenth century omission of word-initial /h/ has been a stigmatised vernacular feature. But contrary to the received wisdom, loss of /h/ is not a 'Cockney' innovation; it continues a process that had been going on since the eighth century. The real innovation is the uniform *pronunciation* of /h/ in the standards – largely a development fostered by schools and normative grammars.

Recall that OE [h] was the weak syllable-initial allophone of /x/. By the thirteenth century, many text languages indicate variable loss, if not everywhere at least in a large number of lexical items. The evidence is not only lack of <h> where it might be expected, but the opposite: <h> in positions where it could not have occurred historically, so-called 'inverse spelling'. For instance, in MS BL Cotton Otho C.XIII ('Laȝamon B'), 'arm' and 'harm' are both spelled <arm-, harm->, 'am' is spelled only <ham>, 'after' is <after, hafter>, and 'high' is <heȝe-, eȝe->. Many [h-] words on the other hand are spelled only with <h-> (e.g. 'hand'), and many vowel-initial words only with <V-> ('all'). Such distributions can be replicated in early ME texts from all regions, and this practice persists, at least in informal writing, well into the seventeenth century.

Modern native words with medial or final <gh> go back to earlier forms with a velar or palatal fricative: *through* < late OE *þruh* [θrux] (metathesised from *þurh*), *night* < *niht* [niçt]. The usual story is that postvocalic /x/ was retained throughout most of ME, and then either deleted – leaving behind a long vowel (*night, through*) – or became /f/ (*rough* < *rūh*, *dwarf* < *dwearh*). The earliest <f> spellings are from c.1300, and not always in words that have retained it: aside from *dwerf* 'dwarf', *thurf* 'through' is also attested, and the variant *dafter* for *daughter* was still current in the early eighteenth century. But the picture even in early ME was more variable and complex than is usually assumed. Consider

these spellings of OE -*ht* words in the output of one thirteenth-century scribe –
Hand A of Cambridge, Trinity College B.14.39 (323). (In the examples below
<-s-> does not mean [s], but [x] or [ç]; this is a ME device based on the fact that
in French – which these scribes also wrote – [s] before [t] became [x/ç], later [h];
some English writers adopted <s> as a possible representation of the reflex of
OE /x/ in this position as well.)

(29)   'bright': brist(e) 6x, brithe 1x, brit 3x
            'brought': brout(e) 15x, brot 1x, broutte 1x
            'bought': bousten 1x, bocðthe 1x, boute 1x
            'light': list(e) 12x
            'might' (n): mist(e) 8x, miththe 1x
            'night': nist(e) 4x, nict 1x, nicst 2x
            'right': rist 20x, ricst 1x
            'wight': viit 1x, viste 1x, vichit 1x, wist 2x

Despite the complexity, it is clear that there are at least two variant types: one
with some fricative before the /t/, and one without. (The forms in <th> may
indicate [θ], but this is uncertain.) Some words show one type only (e.g. 'night',
'brought'); others show both. And most interestingly, in a poem in this manuscript,
the scribe has a quadruple rhyme on 'bright': 'might': 'wight': 'night', spelled *brit*:
mist: *vichit*: *nicst*. The spellings suggest that he is acknowledging the presence
of variation in his readership, and saying as it were that it doesn't matter much
whether you pronounce a fricative or not (or perhaps, if you do, which one) –
as long as you use the same variant type for all four words (cf. Laing & Lass,
2003). This is not an eccentric idea: a modern non-rhotic English poet rhyming
fort: *sport* is implicitly making the same kind of allowance if he expects to be
read by Scots or rhotic Americans; on the contrary, a rhyme *sport*: *sought* forces a
pronunciation, and will feel like a non-rhyme to these same readers. This variation
in /-xC/ words persists into the seventeenth century.

2.6.2.3   Loss of final -*e*

Deletion of final weak vowels (complete by the end of the fourteenth
century) was the culmination of a tendency stretching back to Proto-Germanic: the
OE third-person verb endings -*eþ*, -*aþ* go back to *-*i-θi*, -*a-nθi* (cf. Sanskrit -*e-ti*,
-*a-nti*). The first environment for loss is in hiatus (two vowels back-to-back): there
are a few OE attestations like *sægdic* 'said I' < *sægde ic*. By the 1180s metrical
practice shows this to be common. In the *Ormulum* (c.1180), a marvellous source
of evidence because of its obsessively regular versification, weak final -*e* deletes
regularly before another vowel (or <h>, suggesting initial [h]-dropping). Thus
sun-e and mon-e (OE *sunn-e, mōn-a*) and *sone ongann* 'soon began' (OE *sōn-a*)
scan [/ x / x] and [/ x /] respectively (/ = strong syllable, x = weak). The -*e* in
sun-e and *son-e* must be deleted.

By the late fourteenth century, final weak -*e* was most likely gone in ordinary
speech (except in proper names like *Cleopatre, Athene*). But it was available for

poetry, as we can see from careful versifiers like Chaucer. Here are examples from *Troilus and Criseyde* illustrating three options: total retention, partial retention and total deletion. In these examples pronounced final *-e* is represented as *-ë*, and deleted *-e* as *-(e)*:

(30) (a)   Han felt that lov-*ë* dorst-*ë* yow disples-*ë* (27)
      (b)   O blynd-*ë* world, O blynd-*(e)* entencioun (211)
      (c)   Among this-*(e)* other-*(e)* folk was Criseyda (169)

Since many final *-e* were vowels that had triggered MEOSL, their phonological loss made available a new diacritic for indicating vowel length in writing. Given *name* /naːm/ < /naːmə/, etc., length could be marked with a 'silent' final <e>, even in originally monosyllabic words like *wrote* < *wrāt*. Similarly, after degemination, pre-cluster shortening allowed double consonant graphs to be diacritics for shortness: *otter, hammer* < OE *otor, hamor*.

2.6.2.4   Stress

The *cóntroversy* or *contróversy* about how to pronounce this word, as well as British *rotáte* vs American *rótate*, are remnants of a complex pattern of variability. The heyday of the conflict was the period from about 1600 to 1780, when both codifiers of the emerging standard and speakers in general were struggling with the relics of a complex history. But the seeds were already present in Middle English, as we can see from this Chaucerian line:

(31)   In *dívers* arts and in *divérse* figures (CT 2:1460)

Such doublets were available to later poets as well (here Shakespeare):

(32)   The *Réuennew* whereof shall furnish vs (*Richard II*, I.iv.46)
          My manors, Rents, *Reuénues*, I forgoe (*Richard II*, IV.i.212)

Two stress systems coexist, one old and one new. To understand the later developments, we must go back to Old English. Let us imagine accentuation as a kind of 'scanning' procedure that inspects a word – either from the beginning or the end – looking for certain specified syllables to make prominent. Recall that OE stress was assigned by the Germanic Stress Rule (GSR), which counts from the *left-hand* word-edge, and stresses the first syllable of the *lexical root*, ignoring prefixes (except special ones defined as stress-bearing). Examples (major lexical categories like N, V, A have brackets at each end; affixes have only one bracket; ⇒ marks the 'start' of the scan):

(33)   *input*   *stress*
          ⇒[#[_Nhand]]   [#[_Nhánd]]
          ⇒[#ge-[_Ahend]-e] 'at hand'   [#ge-[_Ahénd]-e]

Items with stressable prefixes and compounds are treated the same way: the rule scans the leftmost element first and assigns primary stress; then repeats the procedure for the right-hand element and assigns secondary stress (* marks a stressable prefix):

(34)   *input*   *stress*
➤[#wiþ-[$_V$sac-]-an] 'to contend'   [#wiþ-[$_V$sác-]-an]
➤[#*wiþer-[$_V$sac-]-a] 'adversary'   [#wíþer-[$_V$sàc-]-a]
➤[#[$_N$ hand] ➤[$_N$ belle]] 'hand-bell'   [#[$_N$ hánd] [$_N$ bèlle]]

This system, then, is 'left-handed', sensitive to morphology, and insensitive to syllable structure.

Starting in the eleventh century, increasing numbers of Romance and Graeco-Latin loanwords began to enter English. At first right-strong forms tended to be accented according to the old Germanic pattern (L *candéla* > OE *cándel*); but over time increasing numbers were imported with their original accentuation, which was of the Romance type, as it is now called. This is quite different from the Germanic, since (at least in its most elaborate form) it takes syllable weight or quantity into account. A syllable is heavy (in older literature 'long') if its rhyme (nuclear vowel plus any following material) consists of a long vowel, a diphthong, or a short vowel + two or more consonants; otherwise it is light ('short': this is a somewhat controversial definition, based on a particular syllabification; see Lass, 1992).

Romance accentuation (the Romance Stress Rule, or RSR) counts from the *right-hand* word-edge, and selects the syllable to be stressed as follows (orthographic representations: ‾ = heavy, ˘ = light; examples from the General Prologue to the *Canterbury Tales*):

(35) (a)   Stress the final syllable if it is heavy or the only syllable; ignore the final consonant:
             input   *stress*
             lic̄ōur#] ◂   licóur#]
             swich#] ◂   swích#]

     (b)   If the final syllable is
             light, stress the
             penult if it is heavy
             or the only other
             syllable:
             input   *stress*
             ĕnḡēndred#] ◂   engéndred#]
             chapĕl#] ◂   chápel#]

     (c)   If the penult is light, stress the antepenult regardless of weight:
             input   *stress*
             Zĕphĭrŭs#] ◂   Zéphirus#]
             pārdŏnĕr#] ◂   párdoner#]

In contrast to the GSR, the RSR is right-handed, insensitive to morphology, and sensitive to syllable weight. It also incorporates an ancient Indo-European constraint, the 'three-syllable rule': the main word accent may not be any further back than the antepenult.

One reason the RSR pattern was so easily adopted is that its output would often be indistinguishable from that of the GSR. Romance *Zéphirus*, *párdoner* and native *brétherhed*, *néighebor* would have the same accentuation under either system, as would Romance *en-géndred*, *chápel* and native *bi-gýnne*, *príketh*. Where different accentuations would be produced, both were often available; in the first Chaucer example given above, *dívers* and *divérse* show respectively Germanic and Romance treatments of the same word (as it happens a Romance loan). The Germanic/Romance interaction, with new complications, reappears in Section 2.7.6.

2.6.3   ME morphology

2.6.3.1   The story-line

The story of English inflectional morphology from about 1100 is one of steady attrition. Its outcome, for both noun and verb, is restriction to one 'prototypical' category for each: number and tense respectively. The concordial categories vanish: gender and case in the noun and all inflection in the adjective, marking of the verb for person and number of the subject (except in one marginal case).

2.6.3.2   The morphology/phonology interaction

Since languages are more or less 'seamless' rather than tightly 'modular', any structural component may interact with any other. A classic case is the relation between sound change and morphological restructuring. Here is a simplified version of how they interact. Consider the paradigm of an OE *a*-stem masculine noun, *stān* 'stone':

(36)

	sg	pl
nom	stān	stān-as
gen	stān-es	stān-a
dat	stān-e	stān-um
acc	stān	stān-as

Now recall two late OE/early ME changes: final /m/ > /n/ and unstressed vowels collapse in /-e/. Just these alone, with no actual morphological changes, would produce this paradigm:

(37)

	sg	pl
nom	stān	stān-es
gen	stān-es	stān e
dat	stān-e	stān-en
acc	stān	stān-es

The dative singular and genitive plural have merged, as have the genitive singular and the nominative/accusative plural. The dative plural is now identical with the oblique forms of weak nouns: all the old -*an* endings have become -*en*, including the dative plural. Is phonological change driving morphological change, or is a change in morphological type allowing the phonological changes to take place? The most likely answer is both, simultaneously. Still, I will tell the story mainly in morphological terms, because those are the surface appearances of interest.

2.6.3.3   The noun phrase: gender, case and number

In some OE nouns, 'grammatical' and 'natural' or 'semantic' gender agreed: *mann* was masculine, *fǣmne* 'virgin, bride' feminine, *hūs* 'house' neuter. In others there was clear disagreement: *wīf* 'woman' was neuter. In the majority gender was arbitrary, since the semantic notions of 'femininity' or 'masculinity' were inapplicable: masc *stān* 'stone', fem *hild* 'battle'. In addition, nouns could have the historically 'wrong' gender, or more than one gender even in the same text: in the tenth-century *Lindisfarne Gospels*, for example, *endung* 'ending' appears as masculine (abstract nouns in -*ung* are historically feminine, as they remain in German), and *stān* is both masculine and neuter.

There was also a steadily increasing tendency for semantic gender to override grammatical, particularly in human nouns. From a late tenth-century text (*Elene*, 223):

(38)   Wæs sōna gearo *wīf* [n] . . . swā *hire* [f] weoruda helm beboden haefde
         'the *woman* [n] was immediately ready, as the protector of troops [=God]
         had commanded *her* [f]'

By the eleventh century, OE certainly still had grammatical gender (nouns belonged – if not uniquely – to concord classes); but referring personal pronouns in particular tended to adopt sexual reference with human antecedents.

An OE noun in isolation is rarely recognisable as belonging to a particular gender: e.g. a termination in -*u* could mean feminine ō-stem (*gief-u* 'gift'), masculine *u*-stem (*sun-u* 'son'), or neuter plural (*scip-u* 'ships'). But with certain other markers (e.g. an *s*-genitive which in 'classical' OE at least excludes feminine), or in the presence of marked determiners or anaphoric pronouns, the identifications are relatively unambiguous. This is still largely true in many thirteenth-century ME texts. The scribe known as the 'Worcester Tremulous Scribe' (*Worcester Fragments*, MS Worcester Cathedral Library 174), shows a typical 'transition' system. The original three genders are mostly retained, and explicit concord allows identification; yet we can see the beginnings of the later system. Consider, for instance, the italicised forms in the following:

(39) (a)   *þt soul-e* hus 'the soul's house'
     (b)   seiþ *þeo* soule soriliche to *hire* licame 'the soul says sorrowfully to her body'
     (c)   saeiþ *þe* soule soriliche to *hire* licame

In (39a), the *e*-genitive marks *soule* as feminine, as the determiner *þt* (a crossed thorn in the MS = *þæt*) marks *hus* as neuter (the original OE genders). In (b), the determiner *þeo*, while not an OE form, does suggest feminine (cf. *hēo, sēo*), which is confirmed by the anaphoric pronoun *hire*. In (c) the determiner is the genderless *þe*, but again *hire* says 'feminine'.

When he marks gender, the Tremulous Scribe fairly regularly shows what would be 'expected'. But of course there are many nouns that as far as *we* can tell could be any gender: they occur in the plural, with no determiners, have no referring pronouns, and/or are marked with the uninformative *þe*. The increasing incidence of *þe* (which already appears as a variant of masculine nominative singular *se* in some ninth-century texts) marks the attrition of both the gender and case systems.

Loss of gender follows a characteristic regional path throughout the ME period. Almost everything new begins in the north and percolates down through the east midlands. The southwest midlands and the southeast remain the most conservative; as late as the 1340s there are still some traces of gender in Kent.

The loss of case marking goes along with the restructuring of noun declension. In the end there is a nearly complete takeover by the masculine *a*-stem type (recall that by the twelfth century this has -(*e*)*s* in the genitive and nominative/accusative plural), with competition from the *n*-stems (plural -*en*). The ideal narrative would compare two stages of the same regional type; but given the available materials I will compromise, and sketch the main features of two not strictly comparable sources, one from the twelfth and one from the fourteenth century. The first is the *Ormulum* (Lincolnshire, c.1180); the second is a 'consensus' of the best Chaucer MSS. While the latter do not of course tell us 'what Chaucer wrote', they are a fair sample of late fourteenth- to early fifteenth-century London English.

In the *Ormulum*, most plurals, regardless of case, are in -*ess* (Orm doubled consonant graphs after short vowels). This is so regardless of the original type: *as*-plurals (*clut-ess* 'clouts'), feminine *e*-plurals (*sinn-ess*) and neuter zero plurals (*word-ess*). The original types however remain as variants (*sinn-e, word*). Replacement of the dative plural by an unmarked 'general plural' can be seen in *amang Godspelless word-ess*, and of the genitive plural in *menn-ess* 'of men'. A few vocalic genitive plurals remain, sometimes varying with forms in -*ess*: *neddr-e/neddr-ess streon* 'generation of vipers' (OE *nǣddr-a*).

The genitive singular is almost always in -*ess*, except for a few feminines like *sawl-e* (as in genitive plural). The dative singular has become a general 'prepositional case' in -*e*: *o lifft-e* 'in the air', *þurh trowwþ-e* 'through truth', but also *o þe lifft, till þatt tun* 'to that town'. The -*e* responds to metrical and environmental constraints: it is available when a syllable is needed.

By the end of the next century, except for some minor relic types like zero and umlaut plurals, the declensional variety and case and gender specificity of earliest ME are gone. There are now two noun cases, genitive and 'common case', no inflection of the article, and only minimal adjective inflection. Virtually all nouns have gone over to the *s*-genitive and plural, except for weak nouns that retain -*en* (these increase for a while in some regions but then recede).

Chaucer looks much more 'modern' than Orm. The dominant plural is -(e)s, with -e deleted after vowel-final stems, and often in polysyllables: *book-es, soul-es, tree-s, herte-s, argument(e)s*. Loss of final -e (except in a few cases described below) rules out e-plurals. A number of nouns were attracted into the weak class, so that not only did original *n*-plurals like *oxe-n, eye-n* remain, but there were *n*-variants for original *s*-plurals (*shoo-n/-s* 'shoes') and *s*-variants for original *n*-plurals (*bee-s/bee-n* 'bees') and zero-plurals as well (*hors-es/hors*).

The genitive singular is usually in -s, though a few zero genitives occur, either from historical feminine e-genitives (*his lady grace*) or original zero (*my fader soule*). The dative singular has virtually disappeared; post-prepositional -e occurs mainly as an option at line-ends (*fro yer to yeer-e*). So except for some relics of old non-s genitives and dative singular -e, and some different assignments of nouns to declension classes, late fourteenth-century London English has virtually the same noun morphology as its modern descendants.

Recall that in OE there were two adjective inflections: an 'informative' strong declension marking case, gender and number, and a more generalised weak declension. During later ME the strong/weak opposition decayed, along with loss of case and gender marking on the article. For most of the period there is just a simple opposition: inflected adjective in -e vs uninflected. This is variable as early as the twelfth century: Orm has *þat haffeþþaȝȝ* ['aye'] *god wille/þat hafeþþ god-e wille*. By the fourteenth century inflection was responsive only to definiteness and number. In Chaucerian usage -e usually occurred after definite determiners (*the cold-e steele*), vocatives (*O fals-e mordrour*), and in attributive plurals, whether pre- or postnominal (*the long-e nyghtes, shoures sot-e* ['sweet']). Zero forms occur in singular predicate adjectives (*it was old*), after indefinite determiners (*a good wyf*), and when there are no determiners. By the fourteenth century this alternation was restricted mostly to monosyllabic adjectives; longer ones were endingless everywhere.

2.6.3.4   The personal pronoun

This is the only nominal that retains some inflection not only for number but case and gender. The OE pronoun was inflected for three numbers, four cases, and gender only in the third-person singular; like the noun, it had only one (non-gendered) plural. During ME the dual was lost; dative and accusative merged in a single form; new *she* and similar forms replaced *hēo*; and a new third person plural in *th-* gradually replaced the old *h*-forms.

The OE personal pronoun distinguished dative and accusative singular for all three genders: (*him/hine, him/hit, hēo/hī(e)*). In early ME the masculine accusative was still retained in the west, but not in the (usually more advanced) east: the *Peterborough Chronicle* in the twelfth century has already merged the two under the old dative:

(40) (a)   te folc *him* underfeng 'the folk received *him*' (direct object: accusative)
    (b)   abuten *him* 'about *him*' (prepositional object: dative)

while later SWML languages like that of the Tremulous Scribe (thirteenth century) still make the distinction:

(41) (a)   for deaþ *hine* haueþ 'for death has *him*' (direct object: accusative)
      (b)   mid/from *him* 'with/from *him*' (prepositional object: dative)

The usual explanation for the emergence of *she* is 'avoidance of ambiguity'. Even in OE the feminine nominative singular pronoun *hēo* was not maximally distinct from the all-gender nominative/accusative plural, and where /eːo/ and /eː/ merged it would fall together with masculine *hē*. Such 'functional' considerations are always problematical, and in this case parochial: many languages (e.g. Finnish, Zulu) get along perfectly well with only one genderless third-person pronoun. So whatever the reason for its emergence, we cannot say that *she* was a 'forced choice'. And indeed there is a long manuscript tradition (particularly in the west) in which pronoun ambiguity is quite acceptable. It is always instructive to look at what manuscripts actually have; here are two early inventories (reference is to textual semantic gender, not historical grammatical, as function is what concerns us here):

(42)   *Worcester Tremulous Scribe*
              (a) fem nom sg: heo 9x
              (b) neut nom sg: hit 86x; he 57x; heo 10x
              (c) masc nom sg: he 145x
              (d) nom pl: heo 158x; he 7x; ho 1x; hoe 1x

              Trinity 323, hand A
              (a) fem nom sg: heo 19x; he 2x; hoe 2x; ho 1x; ha 2x
              (b) neut nom sg: hit 10x; hid 1x; it 7x; he 1x; heo 1x; ho 1x
              (c) masc nom sg: he 148x; heo 9x
              (d) nom pl: heo 38x; he 16x; ha 4x; a 4x; hoe 4x; ho 1x; it 1x

These writers apparently did not care very much what forms their pronouns had, or whether one form appeared in all categories. Others had different preoccupations, and as these happen to be eastern and part of the lineage of Modern English, they are more relevant for us – though given the data above we have to understand their choices differently. Here is the same material from the first forty folios of *Genesis & Exodus* (Cambridge, Corpus Christi College 444, Essex, early fourteenth century):

(43) (a)   fem nom sg: ghe 56x; gge 1x; ge 1x; che 1x; sge 1x; sche 1x; she 1
      (b)   neut nom sg: it 72x; he 2x; et 1x; t 1x
      (c)   masc nom sg: he 400x
      (d)   nom pl: he 87x; it 8x; ðei 1x

This scribe is clearly interested in keeping the feminine separate, but appears uninterested in distinguishing the masculine nominative singular from the plural, though there is one instance of the new *th-* type. Such data supports what I like to think of as one of the Great Laws of language history: *no particular development is ever necessary*.

But still *she* was invented, and although we are not sure why (if that is even an askable question), we can ask how. That puzzle has not yet been solved to everybody's satisfaction. The sources invoked are normally either the feminine determiner *sēo* or the nominative singular pronoun *hēo*. Both are difficult but not impossible. The story is extremely complex and technical, but in outline the two accounts go like this:

(a)   *sēo*. Transfer of syllabicity from the second to the first element ('falling' to 'rising' diphthong; an acute marks the syllabic element): [séo] > [seó]. Then reduction of the non-syllabic [e] to [j], and lengthening of the [o] (to avoid a stressed open monosyllable with a short vowel): [seó] > [sjoː], and palatalisation of the [sj] cluster, giving [ʃoː]. This makes phonetic sense, but leaves us with the wrong vowel for the south (though it does account for the usual northern *scho*). The [eː] would have to be an analogical transfer from *hē*, which is plausible, since it produces a rhyming pair.

(b)   *hēo*. This invokes the 'Shetland theory', a development parallel to that of *Shetland* < OScand *Hjaltland*. The scenario is the same as (a) to begin with: [héo] > [heó] > [hjoː]. Then [hj] > [ç] (plausible: many ModE dialects have [ç] for /hj/ in words like *hue, human*). We then need a further change [ç] > [ʃ] (which is attested elsewhere in Germanic). In those areas of England where the Scandinavian influence was strongest, the 'Shetland' change shows up not only in place-names, but in ordinary lexical items like (*rose-*)*hip* < OE *hēope* and *heap* < OE *hēap* as [ʃuːp]. This goes along with [ʃuː] for 'she' in some of the same areas. We do need the same analogical transfer as in (a), to get the right vowel, but the source in a personal pronoun rather than a determiner, and the place-name and lexical backup are added support.

There is also a chronological problem with both of these accounts: *she*-types first appear (sparingly) in the mid twelfth century, but the original OE diphthongs had presumably monophthongised in the eleventh. This would require a rather long subterranean existence for the new form. Whatever the facts of the matter, it seems likely that *hēo* or *sēo* or both are somehow involved. And both accounts require an extra, purely morphological operation to get the right vowel. This seems like a lot of work for one pronoun; I reserve judgement, but have nothing better to offer. (The best treatment of this complicated matter, which I have skimped here, is Britton, 1991.)

The story of the plural pronoun is simpler. The modern paradigm *they/their/them* is odd: an entire grammatical subsystem borrowed from another language. These come from Scandinavian *þeir* (nom) / *þeirra* (gen) / *þeim* (dat). This system was not, however, borrowed all at once; it took at least 400 years for the new paradigm to be established in the dialect complex that gave rise to the modern standards.

The earliest northern texts (which are later than those from other regions) show the entire Scandinavian paradigm. Elsewhere there is a gradual southward movement, apparently one form at a time. Most early texts are extremely variable, but we can abstract a general three-phase story. The nominative enters the non-northern systems first, followed by the genitive, with the oblique case last. The nominative is established in the SEML by the middle of the fourteenth century; the others follow, variably as usual. On the basis of a conflated group of texts from the east midlands, we can sketch the history this way:

(44)

	c.1380	c.1440	c.1480
nom	þei	þei	they
gen	her(e)	her(e) ~ ther	their
obl	hem	hem	hem ~ them

(The sources are the Chaucerian consensus, *The Book of Margery Kempe*, and the prologues and epilogues of Caxton; in variation the first form is the commoner.) *Them* was finally stabilised in the first decade of the sixteenth century.

By the end of the ME period, then, the personal pronoun system in the London area would have looked like this (using modern spellings for identification):

(45)

The late ME 1, 2 person pronouns

	1 person		2 person	
	sg	*pl*	*sg*	*pl*
nom	I	we	thou	ye
gen	my/mine	our(s)	thy/thine	your(s)
obl	me	us	thee	you

The late ME 3 person pronoun

	masc sg	*neut sg*	*fem sg*	*pl all genders*
nom	he	hit	she	they
gen	his	his	her(s)	their(s)
obl	him	him	her	hem/them

Hers, ours, yours, theirs appeared in the north during the thirteenth century, and in the south by the later fourteenth. The *-s* is presumably analogically extended from the noun genitive. The *n*-less forms *my*, *thy* first appeared variably when the following word began with a consonant (cf. ModE *a/an*); but up through the sixteenth century both could appear in all environments.

2.6.3.5   Verb morphology: introduction

Number is now the prototype noun inflection; that for the verb is tense. The only other regular inflection is *-s* for the present third-person singular. OE, on the other hand, marked two tenses (past and present), three moods (indicative vs subjunctive vs imperative), three persons and two numbers. So there could in principle have been 26 distinct forms for any verb: 3 persons x 2 numbers x 2 tenses for indicative and subjunctive = 24, plus imperative singular and plural. But because of the loss of person marking in the plural and other historical developments, the maximum is actually 11. Various changes had produced considerable homophony within the paradigm, and the only material available was strong-verb vowel alternations: *-e*, *-(e)st*, *-eþ*, *-aþ*, *-on*, *-en* and zero. And of course after the 'transition' changes, *-eþ/-aþ* merged in *-eþ*, and *-on/-en* in *-en*, so besides zero ME has (schematically) only the strong-verb alternations, *-e*, *-st* and *-n*. None of the endings could be the source of the present third-person singular in *-s*, whose origin will be discussed later (Sections 2.6.3.7, 2.7.7.5).

2.6.3.6   The verb: tense marking

Even though the most radical changes in the ME verb involved number concord, a great deal happened to both strong and weak tense marking. The original weak verb suffix was probably a reduced form of the verb 'do', connected to the verb root by a 'thematic vowel' *-i-*, followed by person/number inflections. By late West Germanic we could represent it schematically as *-i-d-pers.no*, e.g. 1 sg *-i-d-a* > eighth-century runic *-i-d-æ* > OE *-(e)-d-e*. The thematic vowel was generally retained after light roots, and deleted after heavy ones: so OE class I weak *ner-e-de* 'he saved' vs *dēm-de* 'he judged'. Such verbs are called respectively 'thematic' and 'athematic'. Class II weak verbs, for complex historical reasons, were all thematic regardless of root type: the theme in the past was *-o-*, hence *luf-o-de* 'he loved'. Since in late OE weak vowels had fallen together, the *-e-de/-o-de* distinction disappeared: by ME times there are essentially two weak verb types, thematic and athematic; I will call them Type I and Type II pasts:

(46)

		infinitive	past 1 sg	past participle
	Type I	deem-en	deem-d-e	(y-)deem-d
		seek-en	souȝ-t-e	(y-)souȝ-t
	Type II	ner(-i)-en	ner-e-d-e	(y-)ner-e-d
		luv(-i)-en	luv-e-d-e	(y-)luv-e-d

These generalised patterns were, like everything else, not as clear as one might wish. In later ME, given the instability of final *-e*, the type I/type II contrast eventually becomes a matter of whether the (potential) *-e-* comes after a past suffix (type I) or before (type II), or whether the past participle ending is syllabic (type II) or non-syllabic (type I).

All possibilities are found throughout the period, at least in verse (our only source for this information, since <e> is often written where not etymologically justified, and you cannot count syllables in prose texts). We do certainly find maximal type II trisyllables, as in the thirteenth-century *Poema morale* (London, Lambeth Palace Library 487):

(47)   þa þe *luueden* [/xx] unright & ufel lif leden
        'those who loved unrighteousness and led (an) evil life'

By late ME increasing *e*-deletion ensures that monosyllabic verbs rarely have pasts longer than two syllables, and more commonly and increasingly only one. Here are some typical examples of variation in both type I and type II verbs, from Chaucer's General Prologue (scansion of the italiciscd examples in following brackets):

(48)   Type I   (a) Another nonne with hire *hadde* [/ x] she (163)
                      (b) This illke worthy knyght *hadde* [x] been also (64)
            Type II   (a) So hote he *loved* [/ x] that by nyghtertale (97)
                      (b) Wel *loved* [/] he by the morwe a sop in wyn (334)

The (b)-forms eventually triumphed; the modern allomorphy is purely phonological and non-historical, though thematic types remained through the seventeenth century.

With the strong verbs we are concerned not with suffixes, but the distribution of root vowels ('grades') in the various tense/number forms. Recall that the OE strong verb had four 'principal parts': I repeat some examples of the first five classes here for reference:

(49)
		present	*pret sg*	*pret pl*	*past part*
I	'bite'	wrīt-an	wrāt	writ-on	-writ-en
II	'creep'	crēop-an	crēap	crup-on	-crop-en
III	'find'	find-an	fand	fund-on	-fund-en
IV	'bear'	ber-an	bær	bǣr-on	-boren
V	'break'	brec-an	bræc	brǣc-on	-brecen

These alternations were affected by early changes, in particular homorganic lengthening and OSL: by the thirteenth century 'find' would have long vowels throughout (hence ModE *found* < *fund*), and 'bear' would have a long vowel in present, past singular and past participle, as would 'break' – again witnessed by the modern forms.

There are three main tendencies at work in the ME restructuring: reduction of the number of grades per verb; 'hybridisation' or class mixing; and shifting partly or wholly to weak. Many modern strong verbs show the latter two: e.g. *break*, *speak* with the past and past participle vowel of the 'bear' class, 'mixed' verbs with weak past and strong participle like *swell/swelled/swollen*, and original strong verbs that have become weak like *creep/crept*.

Change in the strong verb seems to have been driven by grade reduction. Increasingly throughout the ME period, the strong verbs adopted a new constraint: 'no more than three grades per verb'. This resulted in a loss of the singular/plural contrast as signalled by root vowels. There were two major strategies: merging past singular/plural under the vowel of the singular (ModE *rode*: OE sg *rād*, pl *ridon*), or under the vowel of the past participle (ModE *found*: OE sg *fand*, pp *-funden*). These mergers (and covariation between them and the original patterns) begin in the thirteenth century and increase over time. By the 1470s Caxton has no singular/plural distinction in any strong past. The story of the strong verb gains further momentum in the early modern period; I will return to this in Section 2.7.7.3.

2.6.3.7   The verb: person and number

Recall that the OE verb in 'classical' varieties had two plural markings: present -*aþ* and past indicative -*on* and subjunctive -*en*. With the late vowel collapses, these would become -*eþ* and -*en*, the first homophonous with the present third singular, the second with the infinitive marker. In the singular, first-person -*e* was bound to be unstable, but second-person singular -(*e*)*st* and third-person singular -(*e*)*þ* were (relatively) protected by the final consonants. But given the variation and instability in early ME, we might expect some major restructuring of verb inflection. The two categories subject to the greatest change were the plural and – much later – the present third singular.

For the rest of the story to make sense, we must note that there was another type of OE verb inflection, very different from the 'classical' one illustrated earlier. Some Old Northumbrian (perhaps Scandinavian-influenced) texts show a quite different present system:

(50)   *sg*   *pl*
    1 -o, -e   -es, -as
    2 -as   -es, -as
    3 -es, as -es, as

For second and third singular and all plurals, then, there was a northern form in -*s* available from earliest OE; we will see later how it migrated south (Section 2.7.7.4).

In early texts, the present and past plurals were typically still distinct, but with some variation. During the thirteenth century the present/past ending distinction gradually erodes, and each region adopts a single plural marker, either -(*e*)*n* or -(*e*)*þ* or the two in variation (-(*e*)*þ* is a southern type, gradually replaced in the London area by the midland -(*e*)*n*).

Historically what counts is presence vs absence of plural marking, not the particular marker used. A series of eastern texts from the twelfth to the fifteenth century will indicate the direction of change. The figures below are based on samples from *Peterborough Chronicle* (1154), Chaucer's *Treatise on the Astrolabe* (1381), *The Grocers' Ordinances* (1418) and a selection of Caxton's prologues (1470s). This sequence is of course a kind of proxy for a 'real' history: there is no claim implied that any earlier language is the ancestor of any later one, except in *type*.

(51)   *Plural marking on the verb*

	% -en	% zero
PC 1154	95	5
Astrolabe 1381	84	16
Grocers' 1418	52	48
Caxton Prol 1473	28	72

By the late fourteenth century, the London area had a stable and simplified conjugation:

(52)
	present		past weak		past strong	
	sg	pl	sg	pl	sg	pl
1	-(e)	-e(n)	-(e)	-e(n)	-Ø	-e(n)
2	-(e)st	-e(n)	-(e)st	-e(n)	-(est)	-e(n)
3	-(e)th	-e(n)	-(e)	-e(n)	-Ø	-e(n)

Number marking continues to decrease, and is finally lost in the early sixteenth century, with one short-lived exception, a new plural in -(e)s (Section 2.7.7.4).

During the ME period the northern present third singular in -(e)s begins to move south, and shows an interesting sociolinguistic complexity. For fourteenth-century Londoners it can be a northern stereotype: Chaucer uses it for comic purposes in the Reeve's Tale, by having his northern clerks say *gaa-s* instead of *goo-th*, etc. (Northern vowels are also part of the stereotype.) But -(e)s was also available for neutral uses. In early works (*Book of the Duchess*, ?1370), Chaucer uses it to rhyme with noun plurals:

(53)   And I wol give him al that fall-*es*
          To a chambre, and al hys hall-*es* (275–6)

The overtaking of -*th* by -*s* belongs to a later period (Section 2.7.7.4); but it was beginning to spread in the fourteenth and fifteenth centuries as an option. Some writers use it freely, others hardly at all.

2.6.3.8 The verb 'to be'

For reasons of space I will treat only the most complex and frequent of the OE 'anomalous' verbs, 'to be'; for the others see *Cambridge History of the English Language*, volumes 1 and 2 (Hogg, 1992; Lass, 1992) or any standard history.

Recall the set of paradigms making up the OE verb 'to be' (21). The tiny ModE remnant shows that this structure was dismantled at some point; but dismantling anything so complex and disorderly, itself a contingent survival of old fragments, is not likely to be very orderly. And indeed the early stages show considerable redeployment and variation. Here for instance is what we find in the language of hand D in Trinity College 323 (a final <d> in his scribal dialect may represent either /t/ or /θ/):

(54)   infinitive: ben 9x, be 1x
          pres 2 sg: ard 1x, best 1x
          pres 3 sg: (h)is 59x, bed 1x
          pres 3 pl: arren 1x, ben 1x, senden (< sindon) 1x

Similar variation in both stem-choice and endings is shown in Digby 86:

(55)   pres 2 sg: art 35x, best 1x
           pres 3 sg: (h)is 197x, beþ 3x

The numbers indicate where the system is heading; but there is considerable flux well into the next century. By the late fourteenth century it had begun to stabilise in the SEML into a paradigm that was still variable but considerably less prodigal:

(56)   PRESENT   PAST
                   ind   *subj*   *ind*   *subj*
       1   am   be   was   be
       2   art   be   were   be
       3   is   be   was   be
       pl   be(n)/are(n) be(n)   were(n)   were(n)

Throughout ME the indicative *be*-plural is far commoner than *are*. It is not clear what controls the variation, but there seems a slight preference for *be* in subordinate and negative clauses. Except for plural *be* and second singular *art*, the paradigm by the fifteenth century is the modern one.

2.6.3.9   The infinitive and participles

The Germanic infinitive is historically a neuter deverbal noun; OE *-an*, ME *-en* reflect the reduction of an old chain of suffixes (the Germanic ancestor is **-an-a-m* < IE **-on-o-m*). Under the general regime of weakening unstressed syllables, especially when they carried little syntactic information, the infinitive suffix reduced and eventually vanished. The same texts as were used in (51) tell this story up to the late fifteenth century:

(57)   Infinitive marking
                              % -en % zero
           PC 1154   100   0
           Astrolabe 1381   44   56
           Grocers' 1418   25   75
           Caxton Prol 1473   2   98

Note that the loss of endings is morphologically conditioned; though the eventual result is similar, the figures and trajectory here are quite different from those for the phonologically identical verb plural *-en*.

In ModE the gerund (verbal noun) and present participle are identical: 'I like drink-*ing*' (gerund), 'I am drink-*ing*' (participle). In OE they were not: while *-ing* (~ *-ung*) was a common abstract noun suffix, the present participle ended in *-ende* < **-and-i*. It is not clear how the merger came about, but one element was the development of a new southern participle ending *-inde*, which spread into the midlands by the thirteenth century. One might say loosely that it is 'not very far' from *-inde* to *-inge*; whatever the motivation, the variation patterns in the earliest SWML texts show *-ing* encroaching on the range of the participle. Here is a sample from three scribal languages (two in one MS), showing one conservative and two variably innovative patterns:

(58)   Cotton Caligula A.ix, (Laʒamon A), hand A: -inde 5x, -iende 1x
              Cotton Otho C.XIII (Laʒamon B): -ende 2x, -inde 2x, -ing(g)e 2x
              Cotton Caligula A.ix, (Laʒamon A), hand B: -ende 1x, -inde 1x, -inge 1x

There is still variation in the fourteenth century. The Chaucerian consensus has
-ing(e), while the contemporary Gower prefers -ende, except if a rhyme on
-ing(e) is needed. Some more southerly varieties have exclusive -inde. The -nd-
type disappears during the fifteenth century.

The past participle was originally a deverbal adjective, formed with one of the
two IE suffix chains *o-to-/*o-no-. The former was generalised in Germanic to the
weak verb, the latter to the strong. In ME the weak participle retained (as it still
does) its final -d or -t; the strong participle was more variable, and over the
period more and more variation appears, with -en/-e/-Ø often appearing in
the same text. The major transformations in the past participle (as in all parts of
the strong verb) occurred in the sixteenth to eighteenth centuries.

2.7   Early Modern and Modern English, c.1450–1800

2.7.1   Introduction

The period from about 1550 allows a new kind of historiography, particularly in phonology. For the first time we have extensive native grammatical
description, both phonetic and morphosyntactic, as well as sociolinguistic commentary. The phonetic description is controversial and often difficult; but the best
of it is so good that we feel for the first time (I think without delusion) that we
have a sense of what English might have sounded like. My exposition will be
based mainly on a selection of these sources, though for morphology I will also
use the standard range of textual materials.

2.7.2   Phonology: the Great Vowel Shift

Here is what we get if we line up the late ME long monophthongs and
their rather idealised late nineteenth-century standard reflexes:

(59)   iː—bite—ai
              eː—meet—⌐iː
              ɛː—meat—⌐/
              aː—name—eː
              uː—house—au
              oː—food—uː
              ɔː—bone—oː

By the 1890s, some scholars had noted that this apparently random set of developments had a striking conceptual geometry. Each non-high long vowel raises,
and the two high ones, which 'have no place to raise to', diphthongise. This can

be visually represented in the famous diagram that appears in virtually every textbook on the history of English:

(60)   The Great Vowel Shift

$$
\begin{array}{c}
\text{iː uː} \\
\text{ai} \nearrow \uparrow \uparrow \nwarrow \text{au} \\
\text{eː oː} \\
\uparrow \uparrow \\
\text{ɛː ɔː} \\
\uparrow \\
\text{aː}
\end{array}
$$

This icon is traditionally called the Great Vowel Shift (GVS). For close to a century it has been pivotal to treatments of post-ME phonology. It also marks a separation of the trajectories of the long and short vowels. If the GVS affected only the long vowels, it is clear why the members of the alternations produced by the early ME quantitative changes (Section 2.5.2.1) have drifted so far apart phonetically (e.g. why we have /kiːp/ vs /kɛpt/ rather than /keːp/ vs /kept/, etc.). The apparently less systematic changes of the short vowels will be treated separately (Sections 2.7.4.1 and 2.7.4.3).

The GVS as presented here, and as typically described in histories of English, appears to be an *event*: a chain-like transformation of the whole long vowel system. But it is not an 'event' in the usual sense; it is a *result*. The changes are spread over more than two centuries, and there are at least two distinct subshifts. The first (fifteenth to sixteenth century, though with stirrings as early as the thirteenth) involves the high and high mid vowels; the second (late seventeenth century) the low mid and low vowels. (There is an enormous controversial literature on the GVS; I simply present my own position here, since I lack the space to detail even the outlines of a century of debate. For summaries see Stockwell & Minkova, 1988; Lass, 1988, 1997: ch. 1, 1999.)

But if the GVS is a kind of 'musical chairs' effort, with the vowels following each other around a notional 'vowel space', the collapse of ME /eː/ and /ɛː/ in /iː/ breaks the pattern. Though to be fair, a tiny scatter of /ɛː/ words stay at expected /eː/ or thereabouts in southern English (*break*, *yea*, *steak*, *great*, *drain*), and the merger is much weaker in many Irish dialects.

There is another difficulty, not so obvious at first: the standard diagram proposes a change /iː, uː/ > /ai, au/. Dialect-internal changes this large do not generally happen. In southern English however the modern values were not reached until the nineteenth century. To clarify, I first interpolate the situation in the mid-sixteenth century, as described by the English phonetician John Hart in *An Orthographie* (1569), perhaps the most important phonetic source for that period (see the next section):

(61)   ME   1569   19th c.

          bite   iː____   ɛi____   ai
          meet   eː____   iː⟍   iː
          meat   ɛː____   ɛː⟋

name   aː____   aː____   eː
house uː____   ɔu____   au
food   oː____   uː____   uː
bone   ɔː____   ɔː____   oː

Not only have *meat* and *meet* not merged; the lower mid vowels and /aː/ have not shifted at all. I now interpolate two further stages of development, exemplified by John Wallis' *Grammatica linguae Anglicanae* (1653) and Christopher Cooper's *The English Teacher* (1687):

(62)		ME	1569	1653	1687	19th c.
	bite	iː____	ɛi____	əi____	ʌi____	aiː bite
	meet	eː____	iː____	iː____	iː___	iː meet, meat
	break, meat	ɛː____	ɛː____	eː____	eː___	
	name	aː____	aː____	ɛː____	eː___	eː name, break
	house	uː____	ɔuː____	əu____	ʌu____	auː house
	food	oː____	uː____	uː____	uː____	uː food
	bone	ɔː____	ɔː____	oː____	oː____	oː bone

So 'the GVS' is really a diagrammatic summary of two temporally extended processes: early raising of the high mid vowels with diphthongisation of the high ones, and later raising of the low mid and low vowels. Then a second raising of ME /ɛː/ leads to merger with /eː/, hence modern /iː/; but since this does not go to completion, it also leads to a split in ME /ɛː/, which produces some merger with ME /aː/, and later with ME /ai/ (*day*).

This highlights an important conflict between the nature of history and the preferences of historians: *apparent historical patternedness and directionality are typically accidental*. They are results of the coming together over time of processes that have no particular 'conceptual' relation.

2.7.3   The mid-sixteenth-century state of play: John Hart's testimony

Until perhaps the end of the nineteenth century, and then only rather broadly, there is no agreed-on standard English phonology. Grammarians argue about what varieties of English should be taken as 'the best'; but the varieties on close examination are themselves corpora of variants, often – in the same geographical and social environments – quite different, even in matters as basic as what rhymes with what. In the following sections I will treat my authorities (the sixteenth- to nineteenth-century grammarians) more or less as I did the individual early ME scribal languages. Each is a personal sample of a possible type among a welter of variants; with hindsight we can see that some died out, others survived, and still others contain a mixture of doomed and successful features.

Let us take John Hart as our first witness:

(63)   John Hart's vowels (1569)
        i: i   u u:
        ε: ε   ɔ ɔ:
        a: a
        εi ui ɔi iu εu au ɔu

(64)   *Keywords*
        SHORT: /i/ *it, fill*; /ε/ *bed, breast*; /a/ *rat, bath, arm*; /u/ *full, love, southern*;
            /ɔ/ *god*
        LONG: /i:/ *meet, be, week*; /ε:/ *lead, meat, leaf, day*; /u:/ *food, good, flood,*
            wood; /ɔ:/ *bone, nose, own, know, dough, daughter, grow, sought*; /a:/
            name
        DIPHTHONGS: /εi/ *bite, hide, child*; /ɔi/ *joy*; /ui/ *poison*; /au/ *law, all*; /εu/
            dew; /iu/ *due, flute*; /εu/ *dew*; /ɔu/*out, bound*

Note that there has as yet been no qualitative split between any of the long/short vowel pairs. (This is controversial: see Section 2.7.4.1.)

(65)   John Hart's consonants

Labial	Dental	Alveolar	Palatal	Velar	Glottal
p, b	t, d		tʃ,dʒ	k, g	h
f, v	θ, ð	s, z	ʃ		
m	n				
		l, r			
w			j		

(66)   *Keywords* (relevant consonants in boldface)
        STOPS: /p/ *path*; /b/ *bath*; /t/ *tell*; /tʃ/ *chin*; /dʒ/ *edge, joy*; /k/ *kin*; /g/ *gold*
        FRICATIVES: /f/*father*; /v/ *virgin*; /θ/ *thigh*; /ð/ *thy*; /s/ *sing*; /z/ *zodiac*; /ʃ/
            ship; /h/ *house, night*
        NASALS: /m/ *man*; /n/ *nose*
        LIQUIDS: /r/ *rat, for* 'for'; /l/ *love, all*
        SEMIVOWELS:/w/ *water*; /j/ *yoke*

I replace /x/ with /h/ to indicate that [x] does not appear in this dialect, and that there is now a distinctive glottal place of articulation, rather than a symmetrical fricative system with the velar slot filled. For Hart the postvocalic consonant in 'night' (which he writes <neiht>) is the same as the initial one in 'hand'.

2.7.4   English vowel phonology, c.1550–1800

2.7.4.1   ME /i/ (*bit*), /u/ (*put, cut*) and shortened /o:/ (*good, flood*)

In Section 2.7.3 I showed Hart's reflexes of ME /i, u/ as qualitatively identical to his long /i:, u:/. Hart says this explicitly: in his transcriptions he subpuncts the long member of each pair: 'when the vowell shal be longer *in the same sound* . . . I vse a pricke vnder ech' [my emphasis]. Since he makes no exception for short <i, u>, I assume that pairs like *did/teeth, book/do* had [i/i:], [u/u:], not as in ModE [ɪ/i:], [ʊ/u:]. This is not a widely held view; the majority opinion is that Hart must have been 'misled ' by his knowledge of Latin, where *i, ī* and *u, ū* were assumed to differ only in length, and projected this model onto the quite different English state of affairs. But Hart's agenda was *phonetically* (distinctly not 'phonemically') based spelling reform, and he had a remarkably acute ear for quite non-Latinate distinctions. He even insisted on distinguishing [ð] and [θ], which no English spelling system has ever done, and reported aspiration in voiceless stops. In most particulars his ear was so good that I see no reason not to take him at his word. (For the controversy see Lass, 1989, vs Minkova & Stockwell, 1990, and Lass, 1999: 3.4.1.3.)

The native phonetic tradition bears this out. Virtually all sixteenth- and earlier seventeenth-century grammarians (as late as Wallis, 1653) give *beet/bit, pool/pull* as pure length pairs. Cooper (1687) is our first modern-looking witness: *win* has a short version of the *wean* vowel /eː/, and *pull* a short version of *hope* [oː]. While he does not describe centralisation, he makes it clear that these vowels are not high (as they are still often mistakenly described) but mid. I read the evidence as saying that lowering and centralisation do not date to Old or Middle English as the handbooks assume, but only to the seventeenth century.

Southern (types of) ModE dialects have one more short vowel than ME: both older /ʊ/ and new /ʌ/ are possible reflexes of ME /u/ (*put: cut*). This split first appears in the 1640s. Richard Hodges (*The English Primrose*, 1644) distinguishes the vowel in *wool, pull* from that in *son, us*, and takes the first as the short version of the vowel in *pool*. Hodges does not describe the new *son* vowel, but Wallis does, if unclearly; he calls it '*u* obscurum', and it appears to be mid and centralised, and perhaps weakly rounded – but in any case distinct from the *pool* and *pull* vowels. Three decades on, Cooper's vowel is opener and unrounded. It is customary to represent the higher values like Wallis' as [ə], and the lower ones like Cooper's as [ʌ]; but neither of these symbols is really precise. The first good description of this vowel comes in the late eighteenth century, in Abraham Tucker's *Vocal Sound* (1773). Tucker describes a 'straitning made at the throat by drawing back the root of the tongue'; he also notes that if you 'slide your finger under your chin' while making this vowel, 'you will feel the finger pushed downwards, the gullet seeming to swell, occasioned by the tongue crowding in upon it'. This vowel is the same as his 'schwa': it occurs in both syllables of *London, covered*. The description matches the /ʌ/ and certain unstressed vowels of a rather conservative kind of current RP.

ME /u/ intersects the story of ME /oː/. The latter was subject to shortening at least twice during the eModE period: early shortenings merge with the lowered split of ME /u/ and have /ʌ/ (*blood, glove*); late ones merge with unlowered ME /u/ and have /ʊ/ (*foot, book*).

2.7.4.2   /a/ > [æ] (*cat*)

If we discount later influences of the southern standards, [æ] for ME /a/ occurs 'natively' only south of a line from north Norfolk to Staffordshire, and is commoner in the east than the west. The midlands, the north, Scotland and

Wales have nothing higher than [a] except as importations. All the extraterritorial Englishes except some Irish varieties have [æ] or something higher. So [æ] is a southern development, with secondary spread due to London prestige.

Raised /a/ is sporadically noted in the early seventeenth century, but does not become the norm until mid-century. For Wallis ME /a/ is a 'palatal' vowel; the middle of the tongue is raised so that speakers 'compress the air in the palate' ('aerem in Palato comprimant'). For Hart nearly a century earlier this vowel is made 'with wyde opening the mouth, as when a man yauneth'.

Wallis has the same quality long for ME /aː/ (*bate*, *pale*); so the two original low vowels are still qualitatively matched, but raised. Thirty years later Cooper calls this vowel '*a* lingual'; it is 'formed by the middle of the Tongue a little rais'd to the hollow of the Palate', and is distinct from '*e* lingual' (= ME /aː/ in *tale*), which has the tongue 'more rais'd'. The two are different heights, and short *e* lingual is the value of ME /e/, i.e. [ɛ]. Wallis and Cooper then are describing something between [ɛ] and [a], and we can date the stabilisation of this [æ] to about the 1650s.

2.7.4.3   /ɔ/ > /ɒ/ (*pot*)

By the mid-seventeenth century ME /o/ had lowered to [ɒ]. It is Wallis' lowest 'guttural' (= back) vowel. For Cooper it 'hath the most open and full sound of all'. Lowering began no later than the 1650s, and was established by the end of the century.

In the conservative (or radical) version I advocate, the story of the short vowels from 1400–1690 is:

(67)

HIGH	i u	i u	i u	
HIGH-MID	e o			ɪ ʊ
LOW-MID		ɛ ɔ	ɛ	ɛ ʌ
LOW	a	a	æ ɒ	æ ɒ
	1400	1550	1650	1690

2.7.4.4   Monophthongisation and merger: *daze, days, seas; no, know*

I choose different keywords here as a mnemonic for a complex group of changes. The precursors of the modern standards are heterogeneous and variable. The ModE reflexes of the ME lower long vowels and /ai, ɔu/ show an apparently simple pattern, involving partial or complete merger:

(68)

	ME	ModE
seas	ɛː	iː
days	ai	eɪ
daze	aː	eɪ
know	ɔu	əʊ
no	ɔː	əʊ

During the sixteenth and seventeenth centuries, however, at least three different and not always regular patterns coexisted in the southern proto-standard (not infrequently in the same speaker). Hart generally has /ɛː/ for ME /ai, ɛː/, /ɔː/ for

ME /ɔː/ and /ɔu/ ~ /ɔː/ for ME /ɔu/. He also has two 'advanced' ME /ɛː/ items, *read* and *leave* with /iː/, presupposing earlier raising to /eː/ (see below). The younger Alexander Gil (b. 1564) criticises both monophthongisations half a century later (*Logonomia Anglica*, 1619), which suggests that Hart was exceedingly 'modern' for his time (or, in Gil's interpretation, following the wrong models).

Until at least the 1620s, and in some cases up to the end of the century, the patterns available for these categories were:

(69)   Type 1 (Hart): {*daze* /aː/} vs {*days, seas* /ɛː/}
         Type 2 ('general' London): {*daze, days* /ɛː/} vs {*seas* /eː/ ~ /iː/}
         Type 3 ('standard' London): {*daze* /aː/} vs {*days* /ai/} vs {*seas* /ɛː/}

(70)   Type 1 {Hart – advanced): {*no, know* /ɔː/}
         Type 2 (Gil – conservative): {*no* /ɔː/} vs {*know* /ɔu/}

The partially merged (69, type 2) and the merged (70, type 2) have survived; the others have been deselected (see Lass, 1999: 3.4.2.1 for details).

2.7.4.5   The long mid vowels and /aː/: the *meet/meat* merger

By the last quarter of the seventeenth century the pictorial GVS (60) is complete except for minor details. ME /ɛː, ɔː/ have raised to /eː, oː/, and ME /aː/ has raised to /ɛː/ and then to /eː/ by the 1680s. There is still extensive variability and no 'codification', but the collection of languages does show an overall shape. Here is a tabular summary of the main developments of the long nuclei to c.1650:

(71)

	ME	1550	1650
bite	iː	ɛi	əi/ʌi
meet	eː	iː	iː
meat	ɛː	ɛː	eː
mate	aː	aː	aː/ɛː
day	ai	ai/ɛː	eː
out	uː	ɔu	əu/ʌu
boot	oː	uː	uː
law	au	au	ɒː
know	ɔu	ɔu/ɔː	oː
no	ɔː	ɔː	oː

(It looks as if the vowels of *out* and *know* had merged in the sixteenth century; they did not, but it is unclear what the distinction was. Hart seems to suggest that the first element of the *know* diphthong was longer. At any rate the two categories do not fall together anywhere, and the first element of *out* unrounds quite early.)

ME /ɛː/ (*meat*) and /eː/ (*meet*) have now merged in /iː/. This began around the 1650s, and took another century to complete. For some the merger is already an option in the sixteenth century (as in two words in Hart). In the 1590s Shakespeare (*Com. Err.* II.i.20–1) rhymes *these/seas* (ME /eː, ɛː/) almost certainly on /iː/; but nearly two decades later (*Henry VIII* III. i. 9–10) he can still rhyme *play/sea* (ME /ai, ɛː/), most likely on /ɛː/ or /eː/. A whole speech community and its history can coexist in one speaker.

In the late 1680s Cooper has mostly /eː/ for ME /ɛː/, keeping *meat* separate from *meet*. But a decade later the anonymous *Writing Scholar's Companion* (1695) reports complete merger in /iː/. In the early eighteenth century Pope has both old-style unmerged rhymes on /eː/ (*weak/take*, *obey/tea*), and merged new-style ones on /iː/ (*see/flea*, *ease/these*). This continued till about the 1760s.

2.7.4.6   ME /iu, ɛu/: the *due/dew* merger and some later developments

By late ME there were two front diphthongs in /-u/: /iu/ (*spew*, *due*) and /ɛu/ (*dew*, *beauty*: the first of each pair is native, the second French). Hart writes <bliu> 'blue' and <deu> 'dew', and the distinction is still visible a century later (Hodges, 1644). Wallis is the first source to show large-scale merger in /iu/, and it is apparently complete thirty years on (Cooper). Shortly afterwards, the [i] in many varieties is desyllabified to [j], and the [u] lengthens: [dɛu] > [diu] > [djuː].

In effect this introduces a new onset type, /Cj-/. Since the eighteenth century what we can call *j*-dropping has been common where the preceding consonant is /r, l, s/; except in some East Anglian dialects it remains after labials and velars (*music*, *cute*). Dropping begins in /rj-/(*rue*, *true*), and is still variable until the 1780s. Deletion after /l-/ also begins during the eighteenth century, especially in clusters: *blue*, *glue*, etc. lose /j/ quite early. Loss also begins after /s/ (*sue*), though less commonly. After /t, d, n/ it is uniformly stigmatised: for Walker (1791) *noo*, *doo* for *new*, *due* are 'corrupt' Londonisms. This deletion has never caught on in the British standards, though it is now an American stereotype (inaccurate: many eastern and southern US dialects still distinguish *do* and *dew*).

2.7.4.7   ME /oi, ui/ and /iː/: the *loin/line* instability

The diphthongs /oi/ (*joy*, *choice*) and /ui/ (*join*, *poison*), though usually spelled alike in ME, were nevertheless kept apart – if not always according to etymology – until well into the eighteenth century. Hart regularly writes <oi> for /oi/ and <ui> for /ui/, and has an occasional third value written <uei> = [wɛi] in a few words like the Dutch loan *buoy*. Hodges (1644) still retains two sets: one apparently has [ɒi] and the other [wɛi] (*boy*, *choice*, *joy* vs *boil*, *coin*, *point*). Wallis has [ɒi] in *boys*, *noise*, *toys*, and – probably – [əi] in *boil*, *oil*, *toil*; but he notes that the latter set can also have [ɒi]. And [əi] is Wallis' usual reflex for ME /iː/, so there is a partial merger which we can exemplify by *loin* and *line*.

Most of Cooper's <oi> words of whatever source have [ʌi] (thus merging with ME /iː/), except for a specified list, including *oil* and *boil*, which have [ɒi]. Yet later in his book he lists *bile/boil*, *I'le/isle/oil* as homophones in [ʌi]. This is not a 'contradiction', but a typical state for a variable: when Cooper was writing the homophone list one might say that the merger 'happened to surface', and just *was* the state of his language – for the moment. There is no puzzling 'reversal of merger'. The merged and unmerged states coexist in the same speaker: he toggles between two languages.

The unstable partial merger persists until the late eighteenth century. Mather Flint (*Prononciation de la langue angloise*, 1740) has [ɒɪ] in *boy, destroy, oil* but [aɪ] in *joint, point, voice* (= *vice*) – and both in *employ*. Forty years later Robert Nares (*Elements of orthoepy*, 1784) gives [ɒɪ] in *boil, join, poison*. By the end of the century the merger was in retreat, if still acceptable; by the next century spellings like *bile, jine* were provincial stereotypes, and the standard dialects had restored [ɒɪ].

2.7.4.8   Lengthening I: new /æː/ (*far, path, plant*), /ɒː/ (*horn, off*)

The long nuclei at c.1650 were:

(72)   iː meet   uː food   iu due, dew
        eː meat   oː bone   ʌu out, ʌi bite
        ɛː name, day   ɒː bought, ɒi boy

The modern southern standards are poorer by one contrast: *meat*, etc. have merged with *meet* or *mate*. They are also richer by at least five others: long monophthongs /ɑː/ (*far, pass*), /ɛː/ (*hurt, heard*) and centring diphthongs /ɪə/ (*fear*), /ɛə/ (*fair*), /ʊə/ (*poor*). The last four derive mainly from changes before /r/ and loss of /r/ (Section 2.7.4.9); /ɑː/, while partly of this origin, has important additional sources.

ModE /ɑː/ mostly continues lengthened and quality-shifted seventeenth-century /æ/; lowering to [aː] took place during the eighteenth century, and retraction during the later nineteenth. Lengthening occurred before /r/ (*far*), voiceless fricatives except /ʃ/ (*chaff, path, grass*) and irregularly before /ns, nt/ (*dance, plant*). Other minor sources include sporadic lengthenings, as in *father, rather*, and certain doublets of ME /au/ forms (*half, palm*). This lengthening is not normally treated unitarily in the handbooks; in 1990 I christened it 'Lengthening I' to give it an identity and distinguish it from the later lengthening of /æ/ before voiced stops and nasals (*bag, hand*), which is obviously 'Lengthening II' (see Section 2.8.2.2). This produces yet another ME /a/ reflex, [æː].

Lengthening I first produces a new [æː], later [aː]. It also affects ME /o/ in the same environments (before /r/ in *horn*, before voiceless fricatives in *off, cloth, loss*); these, however, merge with ME /au/ (*all, law*) in /ɒː/. Nowadays, lengthened ME /o/ before voiceless fricatives has largely ceded to /ɒ/, though some conservative varieties still have /ɔː/. Both long and short versions of *off, cloth*, etc. have coexisted since the late seventeenth century; the 'restoration of /ɒ/' is not a reversed merger, but a prestige-shift in a set of coexisting variants, as with *meet/meat, line/loin* (Section 2.8.2.1).

The first good witness is Cooper (1687), who has:

(73)   ME /a/   ME /o/
        [æ] path, pass, bar, car   [ɒ] loss, off
        [æː] passed, cast, gasp, barge, dart   [ɒː] lost, frost, horn

Lengthening at this stage is favoured by a following cluster; there is no quality-shift. By the 1740s there is some lowering of lengthened /æ/, notably before /r/.

Flint (1740) has [æ] in *chaff*, [æː] ~ [aː] in *bath, castle, half*, and [aː] only in *art, dart, part*.

It is hard to find two eighteenth-century sources unanimous about which words have the new vowel. By the 1780s its distribution for one type of speaker (but see below) is very close to modern, though there are still some lexical differences. Nares (1784) has 'open *A*' [aː] in *after, ask, ass* (now short), and *plant, advance, calm, palm* (on the last group see below). Data on ME /o/ is sparser: he has 'broad *A*' [ɒː] in *off, cross, cloth*, as opposed to 'short *o*' [ɒ] in *moss, dross*.

But Nares' rather modern-looking pattern is only one of many. There is a curious see-saw development: from about 1680–1780 the lengthened vowels expand; at 1780–90 a reaction sets in. John Walker (*A Critical Pronouncing Dictionary*, 1791), perhaps the most influential of the late eighteenth-century normative lexicographers, has [aː] always before /r/ in monosyllables (*car*), and <l> + labial (*balm, calf*). It was, he says, formerly commoner in *dance, glass*, etc., but is receding. To pronounce the <a> in *after, plant* 'as long as in *half, calf*, &c. borders on vulgarity'.

This likely reflects a more extreme quality-shift in London and neighbouring provincial vernaculars – especially before /r/. In reaction, anything but [æ] (or perhaps [æː]) was non-standard or 'vulgar'. But the more general lengthening persisted, and was finally adopted.

Lengthened ME /o/ was also stigmatised; Walker says that just as it 'would be gross to a degree' to have the same vowel in *castle* as in *palm*, so 'it would be equally exceptionable' to pronounce *moss, frost* as if they were spelled *mawse, frawst*. A century earlier Cooper had simply noted a fact about vowel length; a half century on Flint noted a fact about length and quality; now the neutral fact has developed a social value. Presumably the change became salient enough to attract evaluation only in the later eighteenth century, when the lowering was identified by at least some writers with more advanced (hence 'vulgar') dialects.

2.7.4.9   Vowels before liquids: /r, l/ and the *nurse* merger

Since OE times syllable-final /l/ has usually been dark (roughly [u]-coloured). This vowel-colouring could be extracted to the left, diphthongising preceding vowels, particularly [a, o]. By late ME most if not all dialects would have had [auɫ] for *all* and [jɔuɫk] for *yolk*. These fall together with existing [au, ɔu] (*law, know*), and end up with sixteenth-century [au, ɔu], and by later changes [ɒː, oː] (so ModE *all/law* and *yolk/know*).

The story of /r/ involves both vowel insertion and quality changes. Some fifteenth-century spellings like *hyar, hyer* 'here', *desyar* 'desire' suggest [ə] insertion before /r/. This is still variably spelled: *flower, briar*, but *flour, fire*. Hart has <-er> in *fire, dear, here*, and Cooper's homophone lists include *hire = higher*. Nares in 1784 remarks that *hour, power* are 'discretionally disyllabic'.

Vowels before /r/ deserve a monograph; its effects are complex and unpredictable. Beginning in the thirteenth century we find sporadic lowering of /e/ > /a/, which gains momentum in the sixteenth. Queen Elizabeth I writes *clark, hart*, *starre* (all with ME /e/); this change also yields doublets like the American vs British pronunciations of *clerk* (and of course the name *Clark*). Lowered variants, first with [æ], then with [æː > aː], are stable in Germanic words like *heart*, *dark*, but in others (e.g. *mercy*, *heard*, *verdict*) persist only until about 1800, when they become, as deselected variants so often do, vulgar or rural stereotypes.

The developments of both the short and long vowels before /r/ (whether later lost or not) are complex; here I will treat only one development, because of its major effect on most later vowel systems. This is now usually called the *nurse* merger (after Wells, 1982); it can best be illustrated by lining up the reflexes of ME /VrC/ sequences in three increasingly innovative dialect types:

(74)

	ME	Scots	Eastern US	London
bird	irC	ɪrC	ə(ː)rC	ɜːC
earth	erC	ɛrC	ə(ː)rC	ɜːC
word	urC	ʌrC	ə(ː)rC	ɜːC

During the late seventeenth to eighteenth centuries, ME /ir, ur/ merge in /ur/, and are then joined by /er/. Cooper has /er/ intact, but remarks that many words with the sound *ur* are written *ir*: *bird*, *virgin* have the same vowel as *scourge*, *adjourn*. By the end of the eighteenth century we find either etymologically inconsistent splits or total merger: Thomas Sheridan (*A General Dictionary of the English Language*, 1780) has [ɛ] in *birth*, *chirp* and [ʌ] in *fir*, *fur*. Nares (1784) is the first writer showing the change complete: 'vergin, virgin, and vurgin would be pronounced alike'.

By about 1800 the collapse is complete in England, usually to a vowel of the same quality as that of *bud*. Most writers do not mention lengthening, but it must have occurred before deletion of /r/, or *bird* and *bud* would be homophones. This new vowel, call it [ʌː], gradually moves away from *bud*, and raises and often rounds.

2.7.5 English consonant phonology, c.1550–1800

2.7.5.1 Loss of postvocalic /r/

All English dialects have /r/, but not with the same distribution. *Rhotic* dialects allow it in all syllable positions, e.g. *red*, *very*, *star(t)*. *Non-rhotic* dialects have /r/ only before vowels, i.e. in the first two but not the last. But a word-final /r/ may 'surface' if the following word begins with a vowel: /fɒː/ *far*, /ɔːf/ *off*, but /fɒːr ɔːf/ *far off* ('linking *r*'). In some varieties, etymologically or orthographically unwarranted /r/ may also appear as a hiatus-breaker after mid and low vowels, e.g. in *law and order* /lɔːr ænd ɔːdə/ ('intrusive *r*').

Scotland, Ireland, SW England, a portion of west lancashire, and most of the US and Canada are rhotic; the rest of England, parts of the US eastern seaboard and Gulf coast, South Africa, Australia and most of New Zealand are non-rhotic. So loss of /r/ is relatively late and geographically restricted. It is also gradual and complex.

This is in fact the second episode of /r/-loss. The first is sporadic, without lengthening, and starts around 1300. Typical relics are *ass* 'arse' (US, SW England) < OE *ears, bass* (fish) < OE *bærs*. These scattered survivors represent something once more widespread, as attested by occasional spellings from the fifteenth to eighteenth centuries, like *cadenall* 'cardinal', *passons* 'persons', *hash* 'harsh'. From the late seventeenth century there are inverse spellings suggesting loss in unstressed syllables: e.g. *operer* 'opera', *Bavarior* 'Bavaria' (for citations see Lass, 1999).

Though there is evidence for /r/-loss from the fourteenth century on, it is not common enough for phoneticians to notice it for another three centuries or so. In the seventeenth century /r/ was intact in all positions, though for some speakers it had apparently begun to weaken after vowels. John Wallis in the 1650s describes what appears to be a retroflex trill in all positions; three decades later Cooper shows no change.

But there was a concurrent line of development, apparent a decade before Wallis: Ben Jonson in his *English Grammar* of 1640 remarks that /r/ 'is sounded firme in the beginning of the words, and more liquid in the middle, and ends'. Presumably the 'firme' realisation is a trill; the other is probably an approximant or weak tap.

Half a century later, some speakers show a change: Mather Flint in 1740 observes that preconsonantal /r/ in some words is weakened, almost mute ('fort adouci, presque muet'). But, like his Lengthening I (see above), this is lexically restricted. Three decades later, Abraham Tucker (1773) tells us that /r/ is lost in *partial, servant, word* and 'wherever retained . . . you scarce hear a single reverberation of the tongue'. It is now apparently further weakened, but still only lost in some words.

And another two decades on, now 150 years after Jonson and a bit over a century after Cooper, John Walker (1791) says that 'the *r* in *lard, bard* . . . is pronounced so much in the throat as to be little more than the middle or Italian *a*, lengthened into *baa, baad* . . .' But he also claims that 'this letter is never silent'. This is suggestive; you do not have to say that something never happens unless it commonly does. And sure enough, Walker then adds (disapprovingly) that in London postvocalic /r/ 'is sometimes entirely sunk'. We can now finally talk seriously about /r/-loss: it is salient enough to attract a social valuation.

The virtual end of the story comes in the later nineteenth century. A. J. Ellis (b. 1814), arguably the greatest nineteenth-century English phonetician besides Sweet, notes (*Early English Pronunciation* pt IV, 1874) that in general postvocalic /r/ is not pronounced, but after non-low vowels is realised as [ə]. There is, however, 'a liberty, *seldom* [my emphasis] exercised unless a vowel follows to add the trilled (r)'. That is, postvocalic /r/ still exists, but is rare; and linking /r/ is (as now) a 'liberty', not an obligatory sandhi rule. So about two centuries after Cooper, and nearly two and a half after Jonson, there are still traces of postvocalic /r/, both in its original form and as some kind of weak vowel, though the received standard could be said to be (mostly) non-rhotic.

2.7.5.2   Palatals and palatalisation

The only Germanic palatal was *j; Old English added [tʃ, dʒ] < *k before front vowels (cinn 'chin' < *kinni), *g before *j (mycg 'midge' < *mugg-ja), and [ʃ] < *sk (fisc 'fish' < *fisk). The incidence of /tʃ, dʒ/ increased during ME through French borrowings; some of these had initial /dʒ/, so its distribution became parallel to that of the others (e.g. chase, joy). During the early Modern English period there was a second palatalisation, of dentals rather than velars, which also produced a new fricative /ʒ/, completing the modern inventory.

Dental palatalisation first manifests in the fifteenth century, but is established only in the seventeenth. The results are new [ʃ, tʃ, dʒ] < [s, t, d] in weak syllables before [i, j] (cautious, Christian, soldier); some [ʃ] also come from initial /sj-/ (sure, sugar); and – variably as still in ModE – [tʃ, dʒ] < initial [tj, dj] (tune, due). In the seventeenth century palatalisation of [zj] produces [ʒ] (vision).

The first indications of [sj] > [ʃ] are fifteenth-century spellings like sesschy-onys, oblygashons. The sixteenth century still shows variation: Hart writes <-si-> for -tion, -sion, while Mulcaster (1582) has <-sh->. By the mid-seventeenth century, the change is nearly complete: Hodges has [ʃ] in -(a)tion, -cian and most -sion words (but see below). For many speakers, palatalisation of /t, d/ lags behind that of /s, z/: Hodges has [tj] in Christian and [dj] in fraudulent (as some still do).

Hodges is the first writer to describe [ʒ], which he calls 'zhee'; it occurs (as is still the case) largely in -si- derivatives of Latin stems in -d. Thus -sion has [ʒ] in circumcision (L circumcid-io-); cf. [ʃ] where the Latin stem is in -s (passion < L pass-io-).

There is still hesitation in the 1780s; Nares notes [dʒ] in grandeur, soldier, but is uncertain if 'it is a pronunciation of which we ought to approve'. But he accepts [tʃ] in bestial, celestial and, unlike any ModE variety, also in courtier, frontier. He also gives [ʃ] in nauseate, Persian, issue, and [ʒ] not only in expected evasion, azure, but also in roseate. Modern varieties would generally have slightly different patterns: the unpalatalised form is commoner in nauseate, roseate, issue (at least in Britain) and azure. As usual, both conservative and innovating lineages leave traces in the final disposition of a lexical class.

2.7.5.3   The story of /x/

As we have seen (Section 2.6.2.2) there are at least two ME treatments of old /-VxC/ rhymes. The commonest is retention of /x/ as [x] after back vowels (bought) and [ç] after front (night). Another option is loss, probably with compensatory lengthening. Retained [x] (but not [ç]) can become [f] (dwarf, laugh). It is likely that [h] existed as a weakened variant of /-x/ in ME too, but our first hard evidence is Hart's 1569 description of the medial consonant in night as <h>, which 'hath no sound but as you wold blowe to warme your handes'. Nonetheless the younger Alexander Gil (1619) is more archaic: he uses different symbols for initial and postvocalic historical /x/, <h> vs <ħ>. Spenser already shows complete loss in the 1590s (he rhymes night and knight, both with historical /-xt/ with *quite, spite*, which have French /iːt/ – though he or his typesetters unsurprisingly spell them *quight, spight*). Postvocalic /x/ that has not become [f] is gone by the 1660s, and the only relic is initial [h-].

As we saw in Section 2.6.2.2, 'dropping aitches' was already established in OE and ME; it continued to be so until the later seventeenth century, and did not become a salient social variable until the mid-eighteenth century. Before that, the situation in all varieties, including the London standard, seems to have been what we find now in most non-Scots mainland vernaculars: initial [h-] is at least relatively less common than zero. But by the 1790s both omission of orthographic <h> and hypercorrect insertion were becoming stigmatised in London, and [h-] was eventually restored, one of the most successful efforts known of institution-alised spelling-pronunciation.

2.7.6   Stress

Throughout the early Modern English period, both the Germanic and Romance stress patterns expand, in different ways for different speakers. Both GSR and RSR are now more 'general models' than 'rules'; the formal constraints loosen while variability increases. From the sixteenth century Romance vocabulary is increasingly treated as if it were Germanic, but with a simplification: the prefix/root distinction is often not observed, and words can be initial-stressed, whether or not they contain prefixes at the left or environments at the right that would fit the Romance pattern. Below are some examples, covering a period of over a century. Note that some of these have survived as the usual forms, others have not: in accentuation more than anywhere else one gets the impression of a large-scale lottery.

(75)   Peter Levins, *Manipulus vocabulorum* (1570): délectable, éxcusable, súggestion, dístribute
Christopher Cooper, *The English Teacher* (1687): ácademy, áccessory, ánniversary, nécessary
John Kirkby, *A New English Grammar* (1746): ácceptable, áccessory, córruptible
Robert Nares, *Elements of Orthoepy* (1784): phlégmatic, tráverse, víbrate, ábsolute, ággrandize

On the other hand, many heavy finals which are now not stressed tended to attract stress in a 'hyper-Romance' pattern:

(76)   Levins (1570): parént, precépt, expért, manifést, stubbórne
Cooper (1687): colléague, advertíse, complaisánce
Nares (1784): alcóve, bombást, expért, pretéxt, salíne, recogníse

Beginning in the sixteenth century, parts of the Romance lexicon become increasingly sensitive to morphology, and a new sub-pattern develops: nouns tend to attract initial stress, and their cognate verbs final stress, producing the appearance of Germanic/Romance pairs with the same root: *óbject/objéct, súbject/subjéct,* etc. Such forms are attested throughout the period, and the pattern remains stable but marginal. The 'problem' of how to stress polysyllables has not been solved, and there is no likelihood that it will be. English still, as in ME times, has two competing stress systems.

2.7.7   English morphology, c.1550–1800

2.7.7.1   Nouns and adjectives

The sweeping restructuring that characterised Middle English was largely complete by the end of the sixteenth century. What remains to be told, except for two major developments in the pronoun and verb systems, seems rather a set of minor tweakings.

By late Middle English the noun (except for genitive) was no longer case marked, and the former plethora of declensions had mostly been levelled under the *a*-stem pattern (-*s* in plural and genitive). The basic paradigm was, as now:

(77)

	sg	pl
'common' case	-Ø	-(e)s
genitive	-(e)s	-(e)s

Differences from the modern picture appear to be mainly in distributional frequency. There were more weak -*n* plurals: original *n*-stems like *eyen* remain through the sixteenth century. Some zero or *s*-plural nouns develop *n*-forms: *housen, shoon, horsen*. But except for the 'poetical' *kine* these are marginal by the mid-seventeenth century. Zero plurals were also commoner: the old ones like *deer, sheep* remain, and there are a few new ones like *fish* (OE *fisc-as*).

The adjective had become indeclinable by the sixteenth century, though we still find occasional attributive plurals, like Queen Elizabeth's *clirrist-z days* 'clearest-pl days'. The main change was regularisation of comparison. In OE and ME for the most part regular adjectival comparison was by suffix: the type *green/greener/greenest* belongs to Proto-Germanic. In later ME a periphrastic comparison began to appear, using *more* and *most* + adj.

ModE usually apportions suffixal and periphrastic comparison according to the length of the adjective: monosyllabic bases take -*er*/-*est*. Suffixed participles, however, even if monosyllabic, must take periphrasis: *more loved*, **loved-er*. Disyllables prefer periphrasis, but can often be suffixed: *hairy/hairier* ~ *more hairy*; though some derivational markers require periphrasis (**green-isher*, **grievous-er*). Trisyllabic and longer adjectives do not suffix: hence the comic effect of Alice's 'curiouser and curiouser'.

But usage was nowhere near this regular until the eighteenth century. Both textual evidence and grammarians' comments up to then show periphrasis and suffixation as simple alternatives: in the Epistle to his *Orthographie* (1569) Hart writes *easilier, more brief* beside *more substantiallye, greater*, and this variation persists until the end of the seventeenth century without comment. By the first decade of the eighteenth century the modern restrictions are already emerging, and there is a detailed discussion of what is or is not allowed in the grammar prefacing Dr Johnson's *Dictionary* (1755). But even then usage is not fixed: Johnson notes that 'all adjectives may be compared by *more* and *most*, even if they have comparatives and superlatives regularly formed [i.e. by suffix]'. But suffixation is 'commonly' used for monosyllables, whereas polysyllables 'are seldom compared otherwise than by *more* and *most*'.

2.7.7.2   The personal pronouns

After ME two major changes affected the pronoun system. One was simple: *it* developed a new genitive, *its*. The other was lengthy, complicated and still not fully understood – the singular *thou/thy/thee* paradigm was lost and *you* took on nominative and oblique functions for both numbers, while the old genitive plural *your* came to serve as both singular and plural.

The OE genitive of *hit* 'it', like that of *hē*, was *his*. The new *its* appears to be based on a grammatical analogy: *its* = *it* + (gen) -*s*. If -*s* is simply the non-feminine genitive ending, this is a natural interpretation. The new form was manufactured out of old materials in a conceptually elementary way. *Its* first appears in the later sixteenth century; the earliest examples given by the *OED* are from the translator and lexicographer John Florio, e.g. 'for *its* owne sake' (1598). We take first written attestations as *de facto* birthdays, even though of course a form like this (as opposed to a learned or technical term) must have existed in speech for some time before first being written. *Its* is not mentioned by grammarians until the 1630s, and until well into the seventeenth century seems to have been thought unsuitable for high style. The conservative Authorised Version of the Bible (1611) has only *his*, but Wallis gives only *its* in 1653.

Indo-European languages typically have a number opposition throughout the pronoun system. If English had developed as expected, it should have a second-person singular paradigm **thou/thine/thee*, matching *you/your/you*, parallel to the other two persons. But ModE is asymmetrical: while first and third persons retain number, second person has only one set of forms for singular/plural. This is odd in two ways: lack of number in only one person, and the fact that the surviving form even in the nominative is an old oblique (*you* < OE dat/acc pl *ēow*).

The beginnings of this appear by the late thirteenth century. Here are two early examples (Cambridge Corpus Christi College 444, Genesis and Exodus: Norfolk, MS early fourteenth century; this scribe consistently spells initial /j/ as <g> in the OE style):

(78)   Quo seide *ðe* dat *gu* were naked
          'who told *thee* that *you* were naked'

          Til *gu* bea-s eft in-to erðe cumen
          'till *you* be-pres.2.sg again into earth come'

(Note the singular concord in the second example; instances of this occur throughout the sixteenth century.) Singular use of the second-person plural is probably derived from French courtly practice (based on Latin conventions). That accounts for plural in singular address, but not for non-nominative in subject function: we would expect *ye* < OE nom pl *gē*.

During ME *you* begins to generalise as the 'unmarked' pronoun of address for both numbers in upper-class and courtly registers. At the same time *thou* (apparently normal lower-class usage) begins to develop special senses like intimacy (if used reciprocally) or contempt (if non-reciprocally). By Chaucer's time *you* was well on the way to becoming neutral, and *thou* 'marked'.

By the middle of the fifteenth century there was an explicit association of *thou* with intimacy and 'equality'. This passage from Bokenham's *Life of St Elizabeth* is worth quoting in full (emphasis mine):

(79)   And so wele she groundyd was in loulynesse [= humility]
         That she nolde suffryn in no maner wyse
         Hyr maydyns hyr clepen lady nere maystresse
         Nere, whan she cam, ageyn hyr for to ryse,
         As among jentelys yt ys te guise,
         Nere in þe plurere nounbyr speken hyr to,
         But oonly in þe synggulere, she hem dede devyse,
         As soveryns to subjectys be won to do.

This neatly encapsulates the status function of *thou*: reciprocal use implies social equality, and non-reciprocal use ('as soveryns to subjectys') implies asymmetry of power. English at first appears to be on the way to developing an 'intimate' vs 'polite' system like that of German or French (*du*/*Sie*, *tu*/*vous*), where pronouns of address encode complex and stable rules for indicating status, power and solidarity. But what actually evolved was loose, unstable and pragmatically more subtle. The originally upper-class reciprocal *you* became the universal default, and *thou* was reserved for two special functions: marking (permanent or temporary) asymmetrical relationships, and as a general indicator of heightened emotional tone (positive or negative), intimacy, etc. But its use was also variably influenced by register, personal relationships, topic and other factors unconnected with status or power.

By the end of the seventeenth century, the grammarians reserve *thou* for special 'affective' uses: Cooper in his *Grammatica linguae Anglicanae* (1685) says it is used in ordinary speech only 'emphatically, contemptuously or caressingly' ('emphaticè, fastidiosè, vel blandè'). But there is another important and interesting dimension, related but distinct, which emerges from a study of one type of text where personal interaction (and hence address) is patent: private letters, particularly to intimates like children or spouses.

Most pre-seventeenth-century correspondence is rather formal; but starting in the 1620s we get increasing numbers of intimate and personal letters preserved, which suggest how complex the second-person pronoun system becomes in its late stages. At first the usage may appear paradoxical: consider for instance this letter from Thomas Knyvett to his wife in 1620:

(80)   Sweet Harte I have sent by this bearer fourteen woodcockes and a brace of
            feasants . . . If *you* will, *you* may send them to my Lady Knyvett [his
            mother] . . . I came home on Friday nighte betimes sumwhat wery, but am
            very wel and doe hope to se *the* this weeke . . . so my deerest affection to
            thyselfe; I . . . rest, *Thy* deerest Loving Husband Thomas Knyvett

While *thou* is the pronoun of normal address, there is a shift to *you* when the
addressee's mother-in-law is mentioned. This might look like a joke, but there is
a serious and interesting point involved. Here is a similar case, Henry Oxinden
to his wife, at about the same time (1622):

(81)   I did write to *thee* by the Friday post . . . My mind is with *thee* howsoever I
            am forced to be absent from *Thee*. I see *thy* care and vigilance and thank
            Thee . . . I have spoken with Sir Tho: Peyton twice and find him in such
            passions as I have no manner of hopes of his assistance; he doth me twice
            as much hurt as good; some bodie hath incensed Him very much against
            me, *you* may guesse who hath done it, the partie being not far from *you*.
            Wherby *you* may the lesse wonder of the Indifferent Ladie's not giveing
            you a better answer . . . I am at more expence than *you* can imagine . . . I
            read *thy* letters over and over, for in them I see *thee* as well as I can . . . In
            extreme hast I rest *Thine* inexpressibly . . .

At this point the *thou/you* contrast has, for many speakers, become a deictic
one: *you* is distal (distant from the speaker), *thou* proximal (speaker-oriented
or speaker/addressee-dyad oriented). *Thou* is used when the topic is within the
'charmed circle' of a relationship, and restricted to an immediate, factual present.
You is triggered (for regular *thou* users) by mention *inter alia* of mothers-in-law
(archetypal 'outsiders'), strangers, business matters, social superiors, and unreal
conditions (verbs of guessing, imagining, conjecture). But by the end of the
seventeenth century non-users appear to outnumber users, and by the eighteenth
thou is not an option in ordinary speech, though it remains in special registers
like poetry and prayer.

2.7.7.3   Pruning luxuriance: 'anomalous verbs'

By late ME, the maximal strong verb paradigm had three grades (past
plural had been lost). There are four main evolutionary options then for any verb
(aside from the option of becoming weak):

(82)   Pattern 1: Historically expected vowel-grades: *sing/sang/have sung*
            Pattern 2: Historical past pl or pp grade generalised to both past and pp:
                sing/sung/have sung
            Pattern 3: Historical past sg grade generalised to past and pp:
                sing/sang/have sang
            Pattern 4 ('crossover'): historical past vowel in pp and vice versa:
                sing/sung/have sang

All are well attested in the sixteenth to eighteenth centuries, though not uniformly
for any individual verb or verb class in any given speaker's language; all except

pattern 4 survive for at least some verbs in the modern standards (pattern 4 is especially common in some vernaculars of seventeenth- to eighteenth-century origin, e.g. in the southern US).

One of the signatures of a standard language is supposed to be 'codification': development of an 'authorised' or 'received' form with minimal variation. But if this occurs it often does so only quite late (see further Section 5.2.6). The concept of a standard was commonplace in English from the sixteenth century; but the pruning away of variation and establishment of norms did not begin in earnest until the middle of the eighteenth. This is particularly clear in the development of the strong verb (and grammarians' commentary, which from this period on is as much part of the story as the forms themselves). I will tell the story through the testimony of five seventeenth- to eighteenth-century grammarians who produced extensive lists of verb forms. For the purposes of a morphological history, these are roughly equivalent to the form inventories of individual manuscripts I used as evidence for the discussion of early Middle English variation and change. (The discussion in this section is based largely on Lass, 1994.)

(i) John Wallis (*Grammatica linguae Anglicanae*, 1653) devotes a chapter to 'anomalous' verbs – those that do not take the dental suffix (strong verbs and a few others). He notes first that the participial -*en* marker is variable: *written, bitten, chidden, broken* and *writ, bit, chid, broke* appear more or less at random ('promiscue efferentur'); he gives no status labels.

Wallis reports immense variability, and not only in the past participle. In a section on 'special anomalies', he discusses nasal stems like *win, spin, drink* (OE class III), and others like *come, stick, run*. He notes that *u* appears in the past as well as past participle: *spun, drunk*, etc. (pattern 2). But many verbs also have pasts in *a*: *wan, began, sang, drank*. Some have -*en* in the past participle (*drunken, bounden*), and most have a weak or 'irregular' form ('forma analogia') as well: *spinned, swimmed*. So a verb like *swim* could have the paradigms *swim/swam/swum, swim/swum/swum, swim/swimmed/swimmed* (or presumably any combination).

Another group has the old past vowel for both past and past participle: *take, drive, get* have past/participial *took, drove, got* (pattern 3). These may also retain the old participial vowel, with or without -*en*: *taken, driven*, etc. Other verbs also have *a* or *o* in the past: *bore/bare, spoke/spake, got/gat*.

(ii) Christopher Cooper, *Grammatica linguae Anglicanae* (1685). Wallis does not name the variety he is describing; Cooper defines his subject as the language one speaks if educated in the south, where the purest and most correct usage is the norm ('purissima & emendata loquendi consuetudo norma est'). Unlike Wallis he has a codifying agenda; without written rules rather than mere oral learning the language will quickly change and disappear ('fluctuare et citò evanescere certum est'). But despite his occasional normative posturing, he does not appear to suppress the variability in his data.

Cooper's description is rather more elaborate than Wallis', but we will be concerned with only a few classes. One is verbs that belong to his 'first conjugation', and typically have pasts in *-ed*. But a special subset also have widely used alter-native forms: there are two types of these, one historically weak but 'irregular' (*beseech-ed/besought, teach-ed/taught, catch't/caught*), the other strong verbs, mainly from OE class III. Here we find not only strong variants, but typically more than one, as in Wallis. So *shine-'d/shon, sting-ed/stung/stang*. He appears to consider these verbs 'basically' weak, but with one or more strong variants; he prefers the *u*-pasts (a preference Wallis did not express), but notes the existence of *a* in *span, shrank* and some others, which he thinks are better avoided.

Cooper's first conjugation is not only preferentially weak, but also lacks par-ticipial *-en*; his second conjugation, even more a mixed bag than the first, may or may not have *-en*, and at least one member also has a weak variant. Among the paradigms he gives are these (in this discussion he notes only the past participle, but the past can be deduced from a past participle either by dropping the suffix or just taking it as it is):

(83)   *present*   *pp*
         bid   bid-den/bade
         bind   bound-en
         chide   chid-en/chode
         rise   ris-en/rose
         speak   spok-en/spake
         strive   striv-en/strove/strave

A final group has neither *-en* endings nor weak forms, though some have only one past, others two: *fling/flung, find/found*; but *swim/swum* ∼ *swam*.

(iii) John Kirkby, *A New English Grammar* (1746). Sixty years on, the picture does not appear very different. Kirkby gives paradigms for a number of strong verbs, without comment on preference. These verbs are simply 'out of the common order' (i.e. not weak). Here are some of Kirkby's paradigms:

(84)   *past*   *pp*
       bear   bore/bare   bore/born
       drive   drove/drave   drove/driven
       shrink   shrunk/shrank/shrinked   shrunk/shrinked
       sing   sung/sang   sung
       write   wrote/writ   wrote/writ/written

So far it looks as if just about nothing has happened during the century since Wallis. But as usual history is not straightforward. Three decades before Kirkby we see a dawning dislike of formal luxuriance; the attempt to 'ascertain' and 'fix' the language had already begun in the reign of Queen Anne. I turn now to perhaps the earliest detailed attempt at ideological standardisation in a grammar of English.

(iv) James Greenwood, *An Essay Towards a Practical English Grammar* (1711). Greenwood's verb paradigms are much sparer than those of Wallis, Cooper or Kirkby. While he does list alternant past and past participle for some verbs, he almost always describes one of the (usually only two) forms as 'not proper or usual'. Greenwood's listings are interesting; most of the forms he dislikes are in fact the historically expected ones. Like many grammarians before the late eighteenth century, he tends to prefer old past plural or participial vowels for pasts. Here the dispreferred forms are marked with a following asterisk:

(85)

	past	*pp*
bear	bore, bare*	born
break	broke, breake*	broken
drink	drunk, drank*	drunk
sing	sung, sang*	sung
win	won, wan*	won
write	writ, wrote	written

A serious problem for the historian of this period now emerges: how do we distinguish reporting of usage from the filtering of data through preference? The answer is that we can, but only with difficulty; there are cues in the writer's attitudes. The more normative he appears to be, the more likely the amount of variation actually present in the community is being underreported. On the other hand, given the richness of Kirkby's data and the poverty of Greenwood's three decades earlier, it is equally likely that we are dealing with quite different languages. But we see in Greenwood's attitudes (if not unequivocally in his forms) the beginning of what was later to become a programme of active purging of variation, which through the schools and other pressures apparently did act to reduce the available pool of forms.

(v) Robert Lowth, *A Short Introduction to English Grammar* (1762). Lowth discusses a great variety of 'irregular' verbs in some detail. For most he allows only one past and/or participial form; for others he gives a pair. Text-internal evidence suggests that he lists alternatives in order of preference; in (86) I separate these forms by commas:

(86)

	past	*pp*
bear	bare, bore	born
break	brake, broke	broken
sing	sang, sung	sung
win	won	won
write	wrote	written

Lowth has more or less the modern paradigms. But his desire to normalise and prune and reorganise according to 'analogy' loses to usage in a few cases: each verb (almost) has its own history. And not all these histories are complete (or likely to be completed); at least two of the class III verbs (*sink, shrink*) still have both *a*-and *u*-pasts (though only *u*-participles). The picture is rather like that for stress alternants (e.g. *cóntroversy* vs *contróversy*): there is a relic core of variability at the heart of the most 'codified' varieties.

2.7.7.4 Northern visitors: the *-s* ending in the third singular and plural

Aside from the reorganisation of 'anomalous' and strong verbs, the last major development in the verb system is the replacement of the old present third

singular *-th* ending by *-s*. The post-fifteenth-century evolution is built on two
basic paradigm types:

(87)   *EML type*   *Southern type*
       1   -Ø   -Ø
       2   -st   -st
       3   -th/-s   -th
       pl   -s/-n/-Ø   -th/-Ø

The third singular *-s* is originally northern (see Sections 2.6.3.7 and 5.3.3). By
the fifteenth century, according to the *Linguistic Atlas of Late Mediaeval English
(LALME)* (dot map 645), *-s* endings occur thickly in the north as expected, are
common in Lincolnshire and north Norfolk, and occur in a few WML clusters
as far south as Worcestershire and Gloucestershire (indeed the LAEME corpus
shows a scatter in the SWML as early as the thirteenth century). The basic drift
over time seems to be north to south, with *-s* entering London and later diffusing
outward.

The modern results suggest a simple story: second-person singular keeps its
original *-st* where it remains, the old third-person singular *-th* 'is replaced by' *-s*,
and plural marking vanishes. We have already seen that things do not happen this
way except by hindsight. The shift took a long time to complete, and (see below)
it is not clear after a certain point that a *-th* form in a text actually means what it
says. The story of the plural is also rather complex. (For quantitative and other
details see Nevalainen & Raumolin-Brunberg, 2000.)

I begin with the singular. There is a gradual increase in *-s* in the fifteenth
century, and an apparent explosion in the sixteenth to seventeenth centuries. By
about 1600 *-s* is the norm in ordinary discourse. In Shakespeare, *-s* occurs mainly
in verse, for metrical purposes, as in:

(88)   With her that *hateth* [/x] thee and *hates* [/] vs all (*2 Henry VI* II.iv.52)

Doth, *hath* are exceptions, and persist with *-th* long after other verbs uniformly
have *-s*.

But a given language may show considerable variation, even without metrical
constraint. Here is a not atypical example, from Queen Elizabeth's translation of
Boethius:

(89)   He that seek-*ith* riches by shunning penury, nothing car-*ith* for powre, he
         chos-*ith* rather to be meane & base, and withdrawe-*s* him from many
         naturall delytes . . . But that waye, he ha-*th* not ynogh, who leue-*s* to haue,
         & greue-*s* in woe, whom neerenes ouerthrowe-*s* & obscurenes hyde-*s*. He
         that only desyre-*s* to be able, he throe-*s* away riches, despis-*ith* pleasures,
         nought esteem-*s* honour nor glory that powre want-*ith*.

A sample of 200 present-tense third-person singular verb forms from this text
gives the following picture (percentages rounded up: Lass, 1999: 3.8.4.2):

(90)

	ALL VERBS		HAVE		DO		OTHERS	
	-th	-s	-th	-s	-th	-s	-th	-s
N	66	144	10	1	16	0	55	118
%	32	69	91	9	100	0	32	68

As expected, lexical identity is one of the controllers of the diffusion of change (and frequency may be involved as well): *do* and *have* behave differently from the rest. A similar distribution persists into the next century: Donne's sermon preached at Lincoln's Inn in 1618 *overall* has 89 per cent -*s* vs 11 per cent -*th*, but 100 per cent -*th* for *have* and 78 per cent -*th* for *do*.

These figures are what we would expect in a change of this kind; but there may be a kind of temporal skewing. It seems most likely that the distribution of spellings reflects an older situation, as it so often does. There is an important passage in Richard Hodges' *Special Help to Orthography* (1643) that deserves quoting in full, along with an extract from his homophone lists:

(91)   (a) . . . wee use to write thus, *leadeth* it, *maketh* it . . . &c Yet in our ordinary speech . . . we say *leads* it, *makes* it . . . Therefore, whensoever *eth*, cometh in the end of any word, wee may pronounce it sometimes as *s* and sometimes like *z*, as in . . . *bolteth* it and *boldeth* it, which are commonly pronoun'ct, as if they were written thus, *bolts* it, *bolds* it . . .

      (b) cox, coks, cocketh; clause, claweth, claws; courses, courseth, corpses; fleas, fleaeth, flayeth; Mr *Knox*, he knocketh, many knocks; reasons, reasoneth, raisins

(The homophone list illustrates some other properties of seventeenth-century pronunciation as well, e.g. incomplete *meet/meat* merger.)

By around 1500 plural marking is lost in the past, but still occurs in the present. Given the inputs in (87), the options were zero vs suffix, and among the suffixes a 'choice' of -*th*, -*n* or -*s*. Southern -*th* is attested sporadically into the eighteenth century; the midland -*n* becomes a poetical archaism after 1550, and probably does not reflect a genuine feature of the spoken language.

The -*s* plural marker, like the singular, is originally northern, but is relatively short-lived in the south. It first appears in the north midlands in the fourteenth century (McIntosh, 1983), and moves considerably further south in the fifteenth (*LALME*, dot maps 652–3). It is quite common in the London region by the sixteenth century, but disappears during the seventeenth. This -*s* is not usually a generalised present plural marker: it is largely constrained by the 'Northern present tense rule' (NPTR: see Schendl, 2000). In its later form (still current in Scotland and northern England) it is:

(92)   *ending*   *condition*

      -Ø   if subject is a personal pronoun immediately to the left of the verb: e.g. 'they *eat*'

      -s   elsewhere: e.g. 'the men *eat-s*', 'they *eat* and *drink-s*'

The NPTR was never fully generalised in the southern standards, but it was extremely common for a while, and quite characteristic, if in a slightly looser form, in the language of Queen Elizabeth, Beaumont & Fletcher and Shakespeare, to name three well-known users (examples from Schendl):

(93)   *Queen Elizabeth*: for wicked men *giue-s* this good turn to dignitie, that they *spot* them with their own infection

   Beaumont & Fletcher: Poets, when they *rage, Turn-s* gods to men

   Shakespeare: The people *knowe-s* it, And *have* now receiv'd his accusations

2.8   Plus ça change . . . The persistence of disorder

2.8.1   Preliminary note

As we approach the present our ability to construct good narrative history declines. There are two reasons for this. First, it happens contingently that very little of large-scale structural import seems to be going on in the areas this chapter is concerned with. Second, and equally important, we have too much data, too wide a spread of well-attested and well-studied varieties, to make the kind of generalisations that were fairly simple, if a bit dodgy, for Old and Middle English.

It only becomes apparent after a long engagement with the history of the language that the quality and quantity of our data-base shifts massively over time. And the less we know, the clearer the picture.

2.8.2   Progress, regress, stasis and undecidability

2.8.2.1   The evolution of Lengthening I

Lengthening of ME /a, o/ in *pass, off*, etc. (Section 2.7.4.8) was first noted in the 1680s simply as a fact about southern English; for nearly a century is was apparently just that. But by the 1790s it was subject to prescriptive judgement – i.e. it had become a sociolinguistic variable. Both this normativism and the phonological and lexical variation that prompted it persist into the next century and well beyond.

The first good nineteenth-century discussion is by A. J. Ellis (1874: 1148). He cites among other sources a dictionary of the 1840s, which gives prescriptions for ME /a/ exactly like Walker's: [a:] only before <r, rC, lC>: *bar, calm, half*, but [æ] in the other Lengthening I environments, e.g. before voiceless fricatives and some nasal clusters (*chaff, pass, dance*). Ellis' own pronunciation (he was born in 1814) however seems much more modern, as does that of many other 'educated speakers'. The norm appears to be [a:] in all Lengthening I words; but there are variants, including unlengthened [æ], even before /r/, and sometimes lengthened but unshifted [æ:].

Avoidance of lengthened and lowered [æ] is tied up with the earlier lengthening and quality-shift before /r/; Ellis remarks that some speakers (especially female) avoid [aː] through 'fear . . . that if they said (aask), (laaf), they would be accused of the vulgarity of inserting an *r*'(in the nineteenth century phonetic transcriptions were customarily put in round brackets; doubling indicates length). But in summary (or acknowledgement of the mess), Ellis says:

> the words vary so much from mouth to mouth that *any* pronunciation would do; and short (a) would probably hit a mean to which no one would object. In a performance of *King John*, I heard Mrs Charles Kean speak of '(kæːæf) skin', with great emphasis, and Mr Alfred Wigan immediately repeated it as '(kaaf) skin', with equal distinctness.

He also gives anecdotal but interesting observations of individual speakers, whose social position indicates the sort of accents one might expect them to have: an Oxbridge professor has [aː] in *class*, [æː] ~ [aː] in *classes*, and [æ] ~ [aː] in *dance*; an army officer has [æ] ~ [aː] in *staff*, and the whole range [æ] ~ [a] ~ [aː] in *class*.

Ellis says explicitly that he is attempting to describe a 'received' standard; but he does not have a 'reducing' agenda; he finds his received variety so variable that only a 'generic' pronunciation can be specified. There is so much variation that we have to be 'content with a rather indefinite degree of approximation'. He sees, unlike many grammarians before, contemporary with and after him, no principled conflict between variability and 'standardness'. This stance makes him a particularly valuable witness: he is under no pressure to under-report variation.

Ellis has little to say about lengthened ME /o/; most forms that 'ought' to have it do, and it is not as variable as ME /a/. But at roughly the same time, Henry Sweet (1877) has a short vowel in *cloth, cross, soft*, though it may lengthen before *th, s, f* to the vowel of *broad, more*: a perfect illustration of Ellis' general point. He also allows for shortening in *glass, aunt*. Thus for Sweet's corner of RP-shire, lengthening of /o/ already appears somewhat recessive, though no social judgements attach to the two values.

It is only as we approach the 1930s that something like the modern picture appears: Ida Ward (1929) describes more or less the current pattern of ME /a/ reflexes, but lengthened ME /o/ (except before historical /r/) shows a more complex picture. In *cross, off, soft*, a short vowel 'probably . . . is used by the majority', though 'many educated speakers' have a long vowel. She thinks that the long vowel 'is dying out gradually'; 'educated speakers who use [ɔː] at the present day are mainly middle-aged, or conservative'. She also observes an element of lexical specificity associated with sociolinguistic judgements: *moss, boss, scoff* rarely have a long vowel, and in *toff* it is 'considered Cockney'. Some speakers, she notes, have a long vowel in *cross* but a short one in *toss*. The two lengthenings have clearly parted company by the 1920s, with the short variants of ME /o/ largely re-generalized from some other lineage; the long ones remain in older speakers and as lexical fossils.

At the present time, the southern standard situation is more or less as follows. Both ME /a/ and /o/ are uniformly long before historical /r/. For ME /a/ length and quality shift is the norm, but there is still an undiffused remnant: fluctuation between [æ] and [ɑː] in *chaff, Basque, masque* (but not *mask*!), *plastic, Glasgow, transport* and some others. As for ME /o/, Wells (1982) notes that as of 1980, lengthened pre-fricative ME /o/ is 'a laughable archaism of "affected" or aristocratic' speech. In England in general (but not in South Africa, for instance), [ɒ] has become the norm.

This is really a very complicated and unsatisfactory history if one wants clear and unidirectional narrative (though by now I hope the reader has given up). The lengthening and quality shift of ME /a/ spreads and recedes and then spreads again; lengthening of ME /o/ spreads and recedes, and shows no signs of spreading again. What starts out as a unitary process eventually splits into two independent lineages, with one eventually 'received' and the other stigmatised to the point of disappearance.

2.8.2.2   Lengthening II

Superficially, the change I call Lengthening II can be stated this way: /æ/ > [æː] before voiced stops, voiced fricatives and nasals except [ŋ]. This is a somewhat enigmatic change; we do not know when or where it began. The first mentions (as a marginal phenomenon in RP) come from around World War I (see MacMahon, 1998), but it must be much older than that, given its geographical distribution and cross-varietal idiosyncrasies. Lengthening II occurs in the speech of any living English speaker born and brought up south of the Wash, and in Australasian, South African and east coast varieties of American English; that is, it is a southern process. There is a 'core' change, a canonical pattern which all speakers appear to show:

(94)

æ	cap	cat	back	batch			hang		
æː	cab	cad	bag	badge	jazz	salve		ham	man

But what surrounds this core is distinctly odd. The more detailed picture is not what 'structuralist' views of change and systems would lead us to expect; but it is characteristic of what close study of variation in actual texts tends to show. It sums up the spirit of this chapter to finish it with a change whose origins are obscure, and whose status is undecidable. Is it in progress? Has it partially diffused and then aborted? Is it even just one change? The apparent chaos of some aspects of early Middle and early Modern English is not restricted to 'then': we still have it now, in our 'codified' standards, and it ought to be central to the way we do history.

The lack of mention even in the writings of phoneticians as good as Ellis and Sweet makes one wonder if the change really manifested even in the nineteenth century; I would normally take the view that if Ellis and Sweet do not mention something, it was not there. But not only is this change found in all southern British regional and extraterritorial dialects (which ought to suggest a *pre*-nineteenth-century origin); nearly the same lexical and grammatical irregularities – all of them failures of lengthening where it would be expected – occur in dialects of widely differing regional provenance. In some the exceptions are marginal; in others they are extensive enough to generate a new contrast. The internal shapes of and differences among systems showing Lengthening II provide an object lesson in the complexities of linguistic innovation, and the correlation I have been stressing between diversity in time and space. Here are some selected examples from three speakers: modern RP (b. 1950s), New York City standard (b. 1930s) and Cape Town standard (b. 1970s). In this display expected long [æː] are unmarked, and unexpected short [æ] ('failures' of lengthening) have a following*:

(95)

	RP	NYC	CT
can (aux)	æː	æ*	æ*
can (N)	æː	æː	æː
cannon	æ*	æ*	æ*
has	æː	æ*	æ*
had	æː	æ*	æ*
Hadley	æ*	æ*	æ*
ham	æː	æː	æ*
hammy	æ*	æː	æ*
Samuel	æ*	æː	æ*
Pamela	æ*	æ*	æ*
rabbit	æ*	æ*	æ*
haggard	æ*	æ*	æ*
cadge	æ*	æ*	æ*
badger	æ*	æ*	æ*

The first thing to note is that the RP distribution is rather different from the other two: while New York and Cape Town have categorical failure of lengthening in auxiliary or potentially auxiliary verbs (*can, have*), RP treats them like (nearly) any other lexical items. The syllable rhyme in *can*, whatever its part of speech, is what triggers the change. In this sense RP is simpler than the two others. This lack of grammatical conditioning also suggests that the change is older there: it is typical for sound changes to be morphosyntactically and lexically conditioned in their early stages, and to generalise later.

We can also observe an unsurprising but not fully realised further conditioning: the likelihood of lengthening failing increases with syllable number (short vowels in *Pamela, rabbit*). This appears to reflect a well-known general English 'preference' for isochrony at word level: there seems to be a kind of 'ideal' length for a word, so that the more syllables there are the shorter each is likely to be. But this is only a tendency: lengthening fails in monosyllables as well, both across all varieties (*cadge*) and only in certain ones (*ham*).

This is just a single example of the kind of living historicity that characterises human languages, whether 'standardised' or not. Languages – regardless of the ideologies that surround them – are spoken in real time by real humans, and the closer we get to the level of utterance, the more multistrandedness and stratigraphic complexity we find. The fact that only certain aspects of a language will be in flux at a certain time is what makes description possible; the certainty that at least some will be is what makes history possible. The confluence of the two is what makes the task of linguistic historiography both fascinating and eternally frustrating and productive of unease. And this is the way any intellectually respectable undertaking ought to be.

3 Syntax

Olga Fischer and Wim van der Wurff

3.1   Introduction

This chapter presents an outline history of English syntax. The main changes will be discussed and – where possible – something will be said about the factors that played a role in the changes, and about the effects of individual changes elsewhere. In its earliest stages English was a heavily inflected language with a relatively free word order and a lexical base of mainly Germanic words, rather like modern German today. A host of changes over the centuries has made it into what it is today: a language with a morphology and syntax radically different from that of German. The main causes of these changes, briefly touched upon in Chapter 1, are the rapid loss of inflections brought about both by internal, phonological weakening and by intense contact with other languages after the Viking and Norman invasions and perhaps from the continuing presence of a Celtic substratum. This chapter will document the ways in which these factors have led to a radical transformation of English syntax.

In doing so, we will be able to draw on the considerable volume of earlier work on English syntax. However, rather than going for breadth of coverage, we will try for representativeness of material in terms of importance and interest. This chapter contains full discussion of the major developments and a selection of further changes that we think are illuminating and/or intriguing, but there are inevitably many other changes that we could not include: our apologies for omitting these changes and to the scholars who have identified and written about them. We focus on syntactic change in the common core of English, for reasons of both space and availability of materials (though we have allowed ourselves one or two digressions on non-standard developments). In the discussion of individual changes, we try to reflect the current state of scholarship, so that various kinds of approach are represented. Nevertheless, we have attempted at all points to tell a coherent story rather than present an inventory of what has been said and written. At regular points in this story, we alert the reader to the fact that particular changes have not been adequately explained or even described yet – a sobering but also encouraging message, because on the one hand it forces us to recognise that progress in this field can be tantalisingly slow, while on the other hand it entails that all is not cut-and-dried and that there is still plenty to discover and explain.

Our own view is that further studies are most likely to produce answers if they combine detailed philological work (or full consideration of relevant existing work of this type) with the use of theoretical tools. Although this chapter is based on the results of research accumulated over the years rather than on a completely new investigation of the field, such a combined empirical–theoretical approach is a line of recent enquiry that we think will lead to further interesting findings in the years to come.

We have adopted as a working principle the idea that changes first need to be described and only then explained. The result is a chapter in which description is preponderant; nevertheless, we also show for many changes what kinds of explanations have been advanced and where they are still absent. The best and most detailed explanatory work on English historical syntax so far has been structural in nature, in the sense that the rise and decline of syntactic constructions have been ascribed to specific structural properties of the language at the time concerned. This, however, is no doubt partly a result of the scarcity or relative inaccessibility of other types of empirical information for large periods of the history of English. The reader should therefore keep in mind that we present a picture of the subject that in many places is oversimplified, and not only because we have had to cram over a thousand years' worth of changes in English speech and writing into a single chapter.

The basic method of presentation is simple: we first deal with the composition of the noun phrase (Section 3.2) and the verbal group (Section 3.3), and then move on to discuss the way these can be combined to form sentences, which contain clausal constituents (Section 3.4) arranged in a certain order (Section 3.5). Discussion of more complex phenomena, such as relative clauses, complementation, other types of subordinate clause, and also negation and interrogation, can be found in whatever section the phenomenon is most relevant to. Other topics have been included where they fitted in most conveniently; where necessary, cross-references are given to help readers find their way to specific subjects.

Further help is provided by Table 3.1 below, which contains a summary of the material dealt with in this chapter. It is organised as follows: in the first column, a list of the changes discussed in the chapter is found. They are ordered in the same way as the sections are, i.e. elements within the noun phrase are given first, followed by the four systems (mood, tense etc.) that play a role in the verbal phrase etc. The next three columns in each row show the overall changes that each construction has undergone in the three main periods of the history of English. The last column indicates where the relevant discussion can be found.

3.2   Internal syntax of the noun phrase

Noun phrases (NPs) can occur in various positions within the clausal unit depending on whether they function as subject, as object (direct or indirect), as complement, or as part of an adverbial or prepositional phrase. These positions

Table 3.1 *The main syntactic changes*

Changes in:	Old English	Middle English	Modern English	section
case form and function:				
genitive	genitive case only, various functions	genitive case for subjective/poss. *of*-phrase elsewhere	same	3.2.2; 3.4.2
determiners:				
system	articles present in embryo-form, system developing	articles used for presentational and referential functions	also in use in predicative and generic contexts	3.2.2
double det.	present	rare	absent	3.2.2
quantifiers:				
position of	relatively free	more restricted	fairly fixed	3.2.3
adjectives:				
position	both pre- and postnominal	mainly prenominal	prenominal with some lexical exceptions	3.2.4
form/function	strong/weak forms, functionally distinct	remnants of strong/weak forms; not functional	one form only	3.2.4
as head	fully operative	reduced; introduction of *one*	restricted to generic reference/idiomatic	3.2.1
'stacking' of	not possible	possible	possible	3.2.4
adjectival or relative clause	relative: *se, se þe, þe* subject rel.	introd.: *þæt*, wh-relative (exc. *who*), zero obj. rel.	*who* relative introduced	3.2.4
adj. + to-inf.	only active infinitives	active and passive inf.	mainly active inf.	3.2.4
aspect-system:				
use of perfect	embryonic	more frequent; in competition with 'past'	perfect and 'past' grammaticalised in different functions	3.3.2
form of perfect	*be/have* (past part. sometimes declined)	*be/have*; *have* becomes more frequent	mainly *have*	3.3.2
use and form of progressive	*be + -ende*; no clear function	*be + -ing*, infrequent, more aspectual	frequent, grammaticalising	3.3.2

(cont.)

Table 3.1 (cont.)

Changes in:	Old English	Middle English	Modern English	section
tense system:				
'present'	used for present tense, progressive, future	used for present tense and progr.; (future tense develops)	becomes restricted to 'timeless' and 'reporting' uses	3.3.1
'past'	used for past tense, (plu)perfect, past progr.	still used also for past progr. and perfect; new: modal past	restricted in function by grammaticalisation of perfect and progr.	3.3.1; 3.3.2; 3.3.2; 3.3.3
mood system:				
expressed by	subjunctive, modal verbs (epistemic advbs)	mainly modal verbs (+ develop. quasi-modals); modal past tense	same + development of new modal expressions	3.3.3
category of core modals	verbs (with exception features)	verbs (with exception features)	auxiliaries (with verbal features)	3.3.3
voice system:				
passive form	*beon/weorðan* + (infl.) past part.	*be* + uninfl. past part.	same; new GET passive	3.3.5
indirect pass.	absent	developing	(fully) present	3.4.4
prep. pass.	absent	developing	(fully) present	3.4.4
pass. infin.	only after modal verbs	after full verbs, with some nouns and adject.	same	3.4.5
negative system	*ne*+verb (other negator)	(*ne*)+verb+*not*; *not*+verb	Aux+*not*+verb; (verb+*not*)	3.3.6
interrog. system	inversion: VS	inversion: VS	Aux SV	3.3.6
DO *as operator*	absent	infrequent, not grammaticalised	becoming fully grammaticalised	3.3.6
subject:				
position filled	some pro-drop possible; dummy subjects not compulsory	pro-drop rare; dummy subjects become the norm	pro-drop highly marked stylistically; dummy subj. obligat.	3.4.1
clauses	absent	*that*-clauses and infinitival clauses	new: *for* NP *to* V clauses	3.4.5

subjectless/ impersonal constructions	common	subject position becomes obligatorily filled	extinct (some lexicalised expressions)	3.4.3
position with respect to V	both S(. . .)V and VS	S(. . .)V; VS becomes restricted to yes/no quest.	only S(adv)V; VS >Aux SV	3.5.2; 3.3.6
object:				
clauses	mainly finite *þæt*-cl., also *zero/to*-infinitive	stark increase in infinitival cl.	introduction of a.c.i. and *for* NP *to* V cl.	3.4.5; 3.5.6
position with respect to V	VO and OV	VO; OV becomes restricted	VO everywhere	3.5.3
position IO –DO	both orders; pronominal IO–DO preferred	nominal IO–DO the norm, introduction of DO *for; to* IO	IO/DO with full NPs; pronominal DO/IO predominates	3.5.4; 3.5.3
clitic pronouns	syntactic clitics	clitics disappearing	clitics absent	3.5.2; 3.5.3
adverbs:				
position	fairly free	more restricted	further restricted	3.5.5
clauses	use of correlatives + different word orders	distinct conjunctions; word order mainly SVO	all word order SVO (exc. some conditional clauses)	3.4.5
phrasal verbs	position of particle: both pre- and postverbal	great increase; position: postverbal	same	3.5.5
preposition stranding	only with pronouns (incl R-pronouns: *þær etc.*) and relative *þe*	no longer with pronouns, but new with prep. passives, interrog. and other relative clauses	no longer after R-pronouns (*there* etc.) except in fixed expressions	3.5.6

Table 3.2 *Element order within the NP in PDE*

Predeterminer	Determiner	Postdeterminer	Premodifier	Modifier	**Head**	Postmodifier
all both half	articles demonstrative, possessive, interrogative and relative pronouns, quantifiers, genitives	other quantifiers, numerals	adverbials adjectives	adjectives, adjuncts[*]	**Noun, Pronoun**	prep. phrase (some adj.) (quantifiers?) relative clause

[*] 'adjuncts' here refers to the use of nouns as modifiers (attributive nouns), as in 'a stone wall', and to denominal adjectives, as in 'Chomskyan linguistics', 'criminal law'.

are subject to rules which allow for synchronic variation, as well as to diachronic change. In PDE, the place of most clausal constituents is pretty much fixed. Changes in the position of NPs will be discussed in Section 3.5. Here we will be concerned only with the internal order of the elements within the NP.

Just as there are functional slots within the clause, there are similar slots within the NP itself. The central element within the NP is the head noun. When the head is a common noun, it may be accompanied by a number of modifying elements (with a pronoun head there are usually no modifiers, but see below). When these elements accompany the noun, they usually occur in a specific fixed order in PDE, as shown in Table 3.2.

As far as the order of the slots is concerned, there has been very little change in English, i.e. the above functional slots have always been there. What has sometimes changed is the categorial content of these slots, and the possible combinations of slots that have been allowed at the various stages. In what follows, we will look at the different formal categories that could occupy the slots and note changes in the way a slot is filled, 'combinatorial' changes and changes in the forms of these categories. We will see that it is not always so easy to distinguish between the various categories: adverbs, for instance, could look like adjectives (and still can in some cases); adjectives could be freely used as nouns; adjuncts and adjectives were not always easy to distinguish; quantifiers shared certain features with adjectives, etc. We will also sometimes point to features which do not strictly concern the internal make-up of the noun phrase, but which are relevant to the category in question or which have undergone considerable change.

3.2.1   The head of the noun phrase

The head of the NP is usually a common noun, but it can also be a name or a pronoun; the latter are mostly used by themselves, with all other functional slots left empty. Syntactically, there have been few changes here. Most of the changes that the noun has undergone concern losses, such as the loss of case endings and the loss of gender, and these are of a morphological nature (see Chapter 2). These morphological changes, however, have had repercussions on the syntax. The loss of case, for instance, meant that in certain constructions the functional role that the head nouns play in the clause (e.g. that of subject, or indirect object) had to be expressed by other means, such as a preposition or a fixed position (see further Sections 3.4 and 3.5). The loss of gender caused changes in the anaphorical or referential system (see Chapter 2) and further morphological changes.

Personal and indefinite pronouns can function by themselves as heads, while other pronouns, such as relatives, interrogatives and demonstratives, can be either head or determiner of a nominal head.

Personal pronouns occasionally occur with a modifier, as in *poor old me, us girls* and *he in the corner*. In such usages, they are in fact similar to referential nouns. Denison (1998: 106ff.), from whom these examples have been taken, notes an interesting diachronic change in these forms when they function as subject or subject complement: the older nominative form in such combinations comes to be replaced by the oblique form. This is a late ModE development, which affects not only modified pronouns (compare the earlier example in (1a) with the later one in (1b)), but also personal pronouns used independently (see (2) – third person lags well behind first) or used as a subject (complement) not occurring in the usual subject position (see (3)).

(1) a.   That poor I must write helter-skelter (1832 Gaskell, *Letters* 2, p. 2)
     b.   The miserable little me to be taken up and loved after tearing myself to
           pieces (1879 Meredith, *Egoist* xlviii.606)

(2) a.   'Not *she*,' said the Psammead a little crossly. (1906 Nesbit, *Amulet* viii, 146)
     b.   'Not *me!*' was Gerald's unhesitating rejoinder. (1907 Nesbit, *Enchanted
           Castle* I, 26)

(3) a.   The children were as white as he (1906 Nesbit, *Amulet* v.83)
     b.   for they are quite as well educated as me (1816 Austen, *Emma* I.iv.31)
                                 (spoken by the 'vulgar' Harriet Smith)

The change is quite recent: in the nineteenth century the oblique forms were still considered vulgar, but now they are normal even in educated speech. For some speakers they are still a source of uncertainty, especially when coordinated, as in *X and me/myself/I*.

When adjectives were still declined (in OE), showing case, number and gender, we frequently come across adjectives used substantively, as (4) shows.

(4) a   he gehælde untrume on ðæs Hælendes naman, blinde and deafe
          always he healed infirm in the Saviour's name, blind and deaf
          'he healed sick people in the name of the Saviour, blind as well as deaf'
                                                    (*ÆLS* (Mark)45)

These adjectives could be used generically to refer to the whole group, as in PDE (*the Dutch, the poor*), but they could also be used to refer to a specific group, person or thing, as in (4). This is now possible only with a small relic group of participial adjectives: *the accused*, *my beloved*, etc. With the loss of inflections in the ME period, this 'specific' usage became more infrequent. It survived for a while, especially in poetry, but by the end of the eModE period it had all but disappeared. For specific reference, the numeral *one* came to be used as a prop-word with adjectives from eModE onwards. This numeral had been developing into an indefinite (personal) pronoun in the ME period meaning both 'a certain' as well as being used non-specifically, in the sense of 'someone' (e.g. *þare cam on and seruede* 'there came (some)one and served', *Sleg*(Ld)227: 282). Later in the fifteenth century, perhaps under the influence of Old French *on*, it also develops into a generic pronoun used, at first at least, in subject function, where it replaces the OE indefinite pronoun *man*. At the same time, also in ME, it begins to be used as an anaphoric pronoun, replacing an earlier NP. This probably led to an extension from personal 'one' to general 'one', and hence to the prop-word 'one' as we now have it, used with adjectives, thus filling the gap that had come into existence after the loss of adjectival endings.

3.2.2   Determiners

The most common determiner in PDE is the article (definite *the* and indefinite *a(n)*). It is therefore perhaps rather surprising that in the very earliest stages of English there was no article at all. When a language develops an article system through a process called grammaticalisation, it usually does so using a limited number of sources, e.g. definite articles from demonstrative pronouns, indefinite articles from the numeral 'one' or sometimes from a quantifier (e.g. *sum* in OE; see (5b)). There is also a more or less fixed path of development: the article first appears in positions in which the NP is presentational or referential, i.e. plays some role in the further discourse (see (5)), while it is slower to develop when the NP functions predicatively, as in (6), or generically, as in (7), and slower still when the NP is in the scope of a modal or a negative element, as in (8).

(5) a.   Đa   wæs hwæþere an man rihtwis   ætforan gode. se   wæs noe   gehaten.
         then was still   a man righteous before God who was Noah called
         'Still, there was then a man, righteous in the eyes of God, called Noah'

                                                             (OE, *ÆCHom* I, 1.185.181)

    b.   ... &   þa   sæt   þær   sum blind man   be   ðam wege:
         ... and then sat   there a   blind man   by   the   way
         '... and there by the wayside sat a blind man'   (*ÆCHom* I, 258.11)

(6) a.   ... þat it is meruaylle ...
         '... that it is a miracle ...'   (lME, *Mandeville* (Tit) 104.17)

    b.   ... that were a greet merveille   (lME, Chaucer *Boece* IV, p. 1 1150–5)

(7) a.   Brutus nom Ignogen, & into scipe lædde ... heo wunden up seiles
         'Brutus took Ignogen, and led [her] into [the] ship (on board) ... they hoisted [the] sails'   (eME, *Brut* (Clg) 551–3)

    b.   Philotetes anon the sayle up droughe
         'Philotetes at once drew up the sail'   (Chaucer *LGW*, 1459)

(8)   For 'of a thousand men,' seith Salomon, 'I foond o good man, but certes, of
          alle wommen, good womman foond I nevere.'
          'For among one thousand men,' Solomon says, 'I found one good man, but
          certainly among all women, I never found [a] good woman.'
                                                    (lME, Chaucer *CT* VII, 1055)

In OE, therefore, (in)definiteness could still be expressed without articles. The
standard way to express it was by means of weak and strong forms of the adjective
(see Chapter 2 for the forms), although a demonstrative pronoun functioning as
a kind of article occurred already in early OE prose to indicate definiteness, in
combination with the weak form of the adjective. Thus in (5), the adjectives
rihtwis and *blind* introducing indefinite NPs are strong and article-less, while in
(9), the definite NPs are preceded by both a demonstrative and a weak adjective
(*unspedigan, rican*):

(9)   Caseras he geceas ac þeah he geendebyrde þone unspedigan fiscere ætforan
          þam rican casere
          'emperors he chose and yet he ranked the unwealthy fisherman before the
          rich emperor'   (*ÆCHom* I, 38 508.34)

In ME, indefinite presentative *an* (as in OE (5a)) becomes truly separate from
the numeral *an*, in that a formal distinction develops between the two. The OE
numeral *ān* develops regularly into ME *oon*, while the vowel in the article is
reduced to short [a], and the word loses the final nasal when the next word begins
with a consonant. This phonetic development is linked to the fact that the form
an encroaches both on the territory of the zero article (see (7)–(9) above), as
well as on the other indefinite marker *sum*, thus becoming more frequent and
bleached of its original meaning (as typically happens in grammaticalisation).
Sum itself became specialised in ME, occurring mainly with plurals and nouns
used generically, which remains its use in PDE.

   The use of articles is somewhat variable in geographical names, names of
diseases and body parts. In OE, ME and eModE, it was still usual for river-names
to be article-less (*yn Tempse* 'in the Thames'). With body parts OE usually had
no article. Thus the phrase *mid heafde* 'with one's head' lacks an article; in fact,
there is only one instance of a phrase containing *heaf(o)d* with an article in the
whole of the OE corpus, i.e. in: *ge scylan wyrcan rode tacen upp on þæm heafde*
'you must make the sign of the cross on the head' (*ÆLet* 3 (Wulfstan) 2 6). From
ME onwards the definite article (and later also a possessive pronoun) is the more
usual option: *And with his fest he smoot* ['hit'] *me on the heed* (Chaucer *WBProl*,
795).

   The deictic system too changed rapidly in the early ME period, with the simple
(distal) demonstrative (OE *se, seo, þæt,* pl *þa*) developing into the invariant article
þe 'the' (*þat* also continued to be used for a while, especially before the quantifiers
oon 'one' and *oþer* 'other', still surviving in some northern dialects as *the toon*
and *the tother*). The OE proximate demonstrative (*þes, þis, þeos,* pl *þas*) kept

its function. In ME we find proximate *þes(e)/þis(e)* at first used indiscriminately in the singular and the plural; later the plural generally is written with an <e> at the end, and the singular without <e>, to distinguish them. At first, we also find another proximate, *þos* (with the regular phonetic development of [aː] to [ɔː]), but since this form was rather similar to distal *þo* (the regular development of OE *þa*), these forms soon became ambiguous (also because the *-s* tended to be misanalysed as a plural marker). The two forms therefore collapsed, and *þos* became the new distal plural form (for its adoption, see also Section 2.2). In the meantime, the article system had developed invariant *þe*, so that *þat* could keep or resume its distal singular function.

Other common determiners, which occur all through the history of English, are possessive and genitive phrases, interrogative, indefinite and relative pronouns, and quantifiers (as in '*his*' or '*Tom's* daughter', '*which* daughter did you meet?', 'you can take *what* book you like', 'the woman, *whose* daughter . . .', '*some* passers-by' respectively – the determiner-relative *whose* is in fact also a genitive phrase). Syntactically, not much has changed concerning the possessive, interrogative and indefinite determiners; for changes in their forms, see Chapter 2. Quite categorial changes, however, have taken place in the relatives, which are dealt with in Section 3.2.4

Most genitive phrases in PDE are functionally similar to possessive pronouns, but this was not always so. There are two main developments to be noted in the use of the genitive phrase, a formal and a functional one, closely linked. Formally, the genitive case in nominal phrases gradually lost ground to a prepositional phrase with *of*. Mustanoja (1960: 75) shows how the *of*-phrase rose rapidly from barely 1 per cent of all genitives in the nominal phrase in OE, to roughly 85 per cent in late ME. There was a revival, however, of the *s*-genitive after ME; see below. The new *of*-construction itself is probably native (cf. similar developments in other Germanic languages) but may have been aided by the French *de*-phrase. The real 'culprit' in the loss of the inflectional genitive was of course the general loss of inflections that marked the ME period. The genitive, although one of the 'stronger' case forms, gradually became eroded, so that of all the variant OE forms (with inflections in *-an*, *-es*, *-e*, *-a*, *-ena*, depending on type of declension, gender and number) only an analogical *-(e)s* form remained, doing duty for both singular and plural. It is possible that a zero type of genitive survived in phrases like *mother tongue* (OE *Bæde þu forþi þinre modor spræce* 'suppress therefore your mother tongue', *ÆLS* (Julian and Basilissa) 3.5 353), although it is probable that such phrases were looked upon as compounds already in OE (see further Chapter 4).

In the course of the ME period the *-(e)s* form itself stops behaving like a true case ending. First of all the genitive NP became fixed in prenominal position, and postposition disappeared (cf. OE *heretoga þæs folces* 'leader of the people' (*ÆCHom* I, 12 (Pref) 531.1) versus *þæs folces ealdor* 'the people's lord' (*Mald* 202)). Secondly, the close link between noun and case inflection became loosened, so that by the beginning of the ME period we begin to come across the so-called group genitive. While in OE both name and rank would have to be inflected (*þe Eadweardes cynges fullra leafe* 'by Edward's king's full permission', *Ch* 1478 24), in ME the genitive would simply follow the last noun in the group (*þe laferrd Cristess karrte* 'the Lord Christ's chariot', *Orm* 56). In later ME the inflection could also be added to a descriptive PP following the head noun, as in *the god of slepes heyr* (Chaucer *BD* 168), thereby loosening the link between case and head noun even further. Later still, even *of*-phrases referring to origin became part of the 'group', so that late ME *the kyng Priamus sone of Troye* (Chaucer *T&C* I, 2) turned into *the king of Spaines armadas* (Camberlain 94) in eModE. This construction became the norm in the sixteenth century; the last examples of the earlier one (the so-called split genitive, with one part before the head noun and the remainder after it) are found in the second half of the seventeenth century.

A third formal change concerns the appearance of the separate word (*h*)*is* for the suffix -(*e*)*s*, as in *Of Seth, ðe was adam is sune* 'Of Seth, who was Adam's son' (*Gen&Ex* (A) 493). This has often been interpreted as the replacement of the genitive case ending by a possessive pronoun, which then developed into a syntactic clitic (cf. Janda, 1980), which in turn made possible the development of the group genitive discussed above (a syntactic clitic has a freer position than an inflectional ending, which must be tied to its head). Allen (1997), however, shows that this scenario is unlikely, since clear versions of the possessive pronoun (i.e. examples with *her* and *their*, which unlike (*h*)*is* are not ambiguous) only appear in the late sixteenth century. It is much more likely that (*h*)*is* was at first simply a variant of the inflectional ending, which by the end of the fourteenth century developed into an invariant clitic making the group genitive possible, and that this clitic was later occasionally misanalysed as a possessive pronoun, an analysis which never took a firm hold in English.

There were also functional changes. The genitive in OE could express a wide range of meanings, but in ME the use of the s-genitive became more and more restricted to the possessive and the subjective function, as in *Alfred's book* and *the newspaper's attack on* . . . respectively, while objective and partitive genitives became rare. Thus the OE objective genitive *saula neriend* 'souls' saviour' (*KtPs* 16) was replaced in ME by *the saviour of souls*, and the partitive *husa selest* 'houses' best' (*Beo* 144) became *the best of houses*. It is quite likely that this functional change is related to the fixation of the position of the genitive, while the general change in basic word order from OV to VO (see Section 3.5) may simultaneously have influenced the development. In possessive and subjective genitives, the genitive NP can be said to have a subject relation to the head noun, either as possessor or as agent, and the order GEN–head noun therefore fits in well with the predominant SV order of both OE (predominant in main clauses) and ME. In the case of the objective genitive, however, the order GEN–head noun (as in *saula neriend*) became less natural when the OV order (which in OE was still a regular order in subordinate finite and non-finite clauses) had changed to VO in the ME period.

Rosenbach et al. (2000) have noted that there is a revival of the s-genitive after 1400. This is related to the narrowing of its use outlined above. Once this new system has come into being, it becomes the norm for the synthetic genitive to occur with all human possessors. Discourse factors also play a role in the choice; thus when the human possessor is topical, the incidence of *s*-genitives is noticeably higher than when the possessor is not topical. In this way, after a quite general loss, the *s*-genitive slowly rehabilitates itself in a clearly defined niche. We will see below that discourse or information structure requirements also play a role in syntactic (word order) changes involving adjectives.

In PDE the determiner slot can only be filled by one element. This was not the case in OE, where we find combinations of possessive and demonstrative pronouns, and also genitive phrases and demonstratives, as in *on Godes þa gehal-godan cyricean* (*HomU* 20 (*BlHom* 10)(66)) 'in God's the hallowed church', and *se heora arwyrða bisceop* 'the their venerable bishop' (LS 25 (MichaelMor) 88). Examples are still found in early ME but soon die out in common usage (cf. Rissanen, 1999: 206; Denison, 1998: 115). The reason is presumably that most genitive phrases (especially pronominal ones such as *his* and *hiera*) came to be treated as definite determiners; having a genitive as well as a demonstrative would therefore be tantamount to expressing definiteness twice. This development must therefore be seen as part of a larger development in which an explicit determiner system developed in ME. Note that in PDE we can still have a combination of an article with a genitive, as in *the plane's flight was smooth* and in phrases like *these nice women's clothes*. In the former, the article is part of the genitive phrase and does not directly modify the head noun, while in the latter *women's* is a modifier rather than a determiner.

3.2.3   Pre- and postdeterminers

The predeterminer category is the least clearly defined slot in the noun phrase. The elements that can occur there, mainly quantifiers, very often also occur in other slots, e.g. *such* would be a predeterminer in *such a to-do*, a determiner in 'such people' and a postdeterminer in *another such holiday*. Likewise *all* and *both* function as predeterminers in *all/both the girls*, but more or less the same meaning is also conveyed by the expressions *all/both girls* (with *all* and *both* as determiners), and *all/both of the girls* (with *all* and *both* as pronominals), and even *the girls (. . .) all/both*. Quantifiers, in fact, are generally mobile, both as regards position and function: they may function as pronominals (indefinite pronouns) as well as semi-adverbials (*all soaked he was*) and peripheral modifiers (*she was all gentleness*). It is not surprising therefore that they occur in many of the slots given in Table 3.2 above.

The quantifiers that can occur before the determiner are fairly restricted in PDE (only *all*, *both* and *half* occur here). In ME (with some instances already occurring in OE) other quantifiers were found there too, such as *each* (OE *ælc an hagelstan* 'each a hailstone' *HomU* 36 (Nap 45) 51, ME *þurh out vch a toune, Horn* (Hrl) 218); *some* (OE *sume þa englas* 'some the angels', *ÆCHom* I, 7 236.147, ME *some þe messagers, Glo. Chron. A* (Clg) 2718); *(m)any* (ME *ony the other eyght*, Caxton's Preface, Vinaver, 1967: cxii,6); and in ME *all* and *both* could be combined (*alboth this thynges*, *Yonge S. Secr*.207.37–8). There seems to be an increasingly general tendency to insert *of* between a quantifier and the definite article. In PDE it is the rule with *some* and *any*, which are used without *of* in the OE/ME examples above. The beginning of this development is already visible in OE, where the noun following *sume* could be either in the same case as *sume* (*sume þa englas*, above) or in the genitive (*sume þara synna* 'some of-the sins', *Res* A3.25, 76). The new *of*-form is found already in ME after *some* and *any*, but has become current only much more recently with *all* and *both* (Denison, 1998: 117 notes that the *of*-less construction was still the most usual one in the nineteenth century). In OE the quantifiers could still occur in almost any slot, so we could have *some the men ate . . .* , *the men some ate . . .* , and also *the men ate some. . . .* When the number of slots decreased, probably due to the general fixation of word order in ME, some of these quantifiers or their positions disappeared (e.g. *the men some* was lost but not *the men all*) while others became reanalysed (e.g. in *some the men*, the word *some* came to be seen as an indefinite pronoun and, consequently *of* was added*)*.

Other elements that can occur before an *in*definite article, apart from quantifiers such as *each* (in OE/ME, see above), *such* and *many*, are the indefinite pronouns *what* and *which*. This usage with both quantifiers and wh-elements seems to have started in earnest in early ME, with only one or two examples found in OE (e.g. *hwylc an scep* 'which a sheep', *HomU* 42 (Nap 52) 12) and *swylc an litel cicel* 'such a little cake', *PeriD* 20.13.30). Rissanen (1967: 252) states that the separation of predeterminer and noun makes the whole phrase more emphatic. A similar kind of emphasis can be noted in constructions that also first appear in ME, of the type *so hardy a here* 'so brave an army' (*Gawain* 59). Again it is the development of the article system in ME that makes those constructions possible.

Postdeterminers in PDE are essentially also quantifiers, including ordinal and cardinal numerals, as in *the many girls*, *the two girls* and *the second girl*. Not many changes have occurred here except that again the floating possibilities of quantifiers and numerals have been reduced. In ME the group of postdetermin-ers was somewhat larger, e.g. *both* could still occur here too, as in *his boþe armes* (*Gawain* 582). Concerning position, the numerals and *other*, which are now restricted to postdeterminer position, could still occur as predeterminer in OE and ME (*oþre twegen þa fæmnan*, 'other two the women', *Mart* 5 (Kotzor) Se 16, A.17), especially before a superlative: OE *twa þa halegestan fæmnan* 'two the holiest women' (*Mart* 5 (Kotzor) My 1, A.11), ME *þre þe beste iles* 'three the best islands' (*Glo. Chron. A.* (Clg) 34). These 'predeterminer' constructions were replaced by *of*-constructions, just as happened with *some* and *any* discussed above. Again it should be noted that in OE we find both a genitive after these numerals and a case form that shows concord with the numeral. With the loss of cases, these now caseless forms went on to exist for a while until they came to be replaced by *of*-constructions.

3.2.4   Modifiers

Adjectives are the prototypical modifiers. Adjectives are also one of the most difficult categories to classify, since they share many characteristics of either nouns or verbs. Adjectives, being less well-established as a category, are a more likely target for change. Adjectives in English have two distinct functions: they can be predicative (as in *the rhythm is important*) or attributive (as in *contemporary poetry*). In the former case they are closer to the verbal end of the continuum, because together with the copula verb they form the verbal phrase, and in the latter case they may (but need not) be closer to the nominal end of the cline. There are various formal means of distinguishing between these two functions: it may be done by position, by intonation or stress, or by inflection. In the history of English, there have been important changes in these formal means, which will be the main topic of discussion here.

From a discourse point of view predicative adjectives are often salient because they convey 'new' rather than 'given' information. It has been noted in discourse and in typological studies that the more salient exponents of a category tend to be more clearly or more explicitly marked (cf. Hopper and Thompson, 1984; Thompson, 1988); we will see below that this is indeed the case with certain adjectives, but that the ways in which they have been marked have changed in the history of English.

Attributive adjectives may be either salient or non-salient. When they are salient, as is often the case with an attributive adjective in an indefinite NP (because an indefinite NP is likely to convey new information), they have some stress in PDE, but when they are non-salient the head noun receives the main stress; compare *She chose herself a rèd drèss* with *She spilled juice on her red drèss*. In the first case we are talking about a dress which has the important property of being red; in the second case we are dealing with a *particular* dress – which happens to be red. In other words, salience or new information in adjectives in PDE can be conveyed by position (predicative adjectives follow the noun) or by the stress pattern within the NP, when position is not variable. In some cases in PDE the salience of an attributive adjective can be conveyed by position too, but these are rare; compare prenominal *The present class structure is based . . .* with postnominal *. . . to allow the people present to jive*. In the first example the adjective indicates what *kind* of class structure is the topic of the discourse; it qualifies the head noun. In the second example 'present' separates one group of people from another; it distinguishes between two groups, but does not qualify the 'group' itself. We will now look at what kinds of changes have occurred in the ways the different types of adjective are marked.

More work needs to be done on the status of the adjective in OE and ME, which has been meagerly investigated so far, but some distinctive features are emerging. The most notable differences between the OE and ModE/PDE systems (with ME as a period of transition) are: (i) loss of inflections (including the strong/weak distinction); (ii) different use of position; (iii) clearer differentiation between nominal and verbal uses of adjectives; and (iv) the development of 'stacking'.

In OE the non-salient/salient distinction was made mainly morphologically, in that predicative adjectives and adjectives in indefinite NPs were practically without exception strong, whereas definite NPs as a rule had weak adjectives (usually accompanied by a demonstrative article – an article system to distinguish definiteness was beginning to develop in OE; see Section 3.2.2). There are some exceptions to this rule, but, interestingly enough, most of these can be understood from a discourse point of view. For instance, in vocative phrases like *leofan men* 'dear men' and *ælmihtiga god* 'almighty God', adjectives are always declined weak, in spite of the fact that there is no definite determiner present. Referentially, however, these adjectives are part of the 'name' of the person addressed; they do not contain 'new' information, and are therefore non-salient, hence the weak form. The case is similar with comparative forms: they are weak even when used predicatively. This again is because they are inherently referential: they always refer back to a 'given' entity (i.e. the positive form of the adjective).

Secondly, the position of the adjective was variable in OE (some remnants of this can still be seen in ME). Position was used syntactically to distinguish between strong and weak forms, and hence between salient/non-referential and non-salient/referential adjectives. Thus only strong adjectives could occur in post-nominal position, either straight after the NP or as part of the predicate, and these adjectives always conveyed 'new' or extra information. Bolinger (1972) has written on how the linear geometry of elements imposes certain relationships on those elements. Using this (essentially iconic) insight, he shows that pre- and postnominal adjectival positions are meaningful in many languages (e.g. Spanish, Italian, Modern Greek). When an adjective comes first in a linear sequence (i.e. precedes its head), it determines to some extent how the next element is going to be interpreted. When the adjective follows the noun, it no longer has the possibility of 'changing' the noun, since it can only add to what is known already. Thus in *genim þa reade netlan ufewearde* 'take then red nettles at-the-top' (OE, *Lch* 2.8.1.6), the prenominal adjective identifies the nettles as a specific type of nettle, i.e. the red-nettle, whereas the postnominal adjective, *ufewearde*, indicates which part of the nettles is needed, i.e. the top part, which is only an accidental circumstance of those nettles at the moment of speaking. In *nym betonican swa grene* 'take betony still green' (*PeriD* 63.45.24), it is not the 'green-betony' (as a different species) that must be used, but betony that is still green, i.e. fresh. It is for the same reason that referentially empty nouns like *auht, ælc wiht, sum ðing* 'anything, anyone, some thing' always take an adjective postnominally in OE, as in phrases like *sum ðing digele* 'something secret' (sometimes in the genitive, *auht godes* 'anything good'). This is because nouns without a referential function cannot be changed in quality by an adjective. In PDE, these differences are no longer expressed by position. Instead, position is more or less fixed (with the exception of a small number of adjectives like *present* discussed above). The only adjectives that can still be postnominal are a number of well-defined groups such as those following indefinites (*something good*, etc.), some idiomatic 'French' (often quasi-legal) expressions (*The Princess Royal, heir apparent*, etc.), and adjectives that cannot be used attributively because they are too verbal or adverbial, such as *no person alive, the people involved, the music played* (all three groups can in fact be seen as historical relics, with the first and the third group still obeying the adjectival rules of OE). In other words, with the increasing fixity of word order in the course of ME, the more frequent adjective position (i.e. the prenominal one) became the rule for both the restrictive and the non-restrictive function. Thus linear iconicity got replaced by phonological iconicity, i.e. stress has become the main distinguishing factor.

The OE strong adjectives were predicative in nature, as we have seen, and it is not surprising, therefore, that these strong adjectives were closer to the verbal end of the cline. We see then that some of the OE postnominal adjectives are now more easily translated adverbially or with an adverbial clause than adjectivally, as with *ufewearde* in the example above, and *unsynnigne* and *lifigende* in (10):

(10) a.   gif mon twyhyndne   mon unsynnigne mid hloðe ofslea
           if   one   twohundred man innocent   with troop kill
           'if a man worth two hundred shillings is killed when innocent
           by a troop of robbers'   (*LawAf* 1.29)

     b.   gif hwa   his rihtæwe   lifigende forlæte and on oðran wife
           if   anyone his lawful-wife living   leave   and an other woman

           on unriht   **gewifige**
           unlawfully takes
           'if anyone leaves his lawfully married wife, while she is still alive, and
           takes another woman unlawfully'   (*LawNorthu.* 64)

Adjectives derived from verbs (participles) and adverbs (e.g. *ufewearde* and other adjectives ending in *-weard*) occur more frequently in postnominal position than other adjectives, and the same is true for negative adjectives, as in (10a). Negation is typically an attribute of the predicate, rather than of the nominal group; consequently it has its position usually close to the verb. Likewise, negative adjectives generally tend to be predicative, rather than attributive. Thus when we want to convey that something is not large, we do not normally speak of an *unlarge* or *non-large* object. Another striking fact suggesting there is something verbal about strong adjectives and something nominal about weak adjectives is the total absence of intensifying adverbs like *swiþe* 'very' preceding weak adjectives, and their high frequency before strong ones. Thus a phrase like *the very old man* does not occur in OE (the equivalents of *a very old man* and *he is very old*, on the other hand, are frequent) and only begins to appear from the fifteenth century onwards. In a similar way one does not find prepositional phrases or infinitives associated with a weak adjective in OE. In PDE we can talk about *an easy dictionary to use*, and even *this easy-to-use dictionary*, but in OE this was out of the question. There, we only find the type *a dictionary easy to use* and even more frequently a predicative phrase, as in (11).

(11)

| se | x | niht | mona | he | is | god | to | standanne | mid | æðelum | mannum | & . . . |

se   x   niht   mona he is god   to standanne mid æðelum mannum & . . .
the 10th night's moon, he is good to stand   with noble   men   and . . .
'The tenth day after the new moon, is a good day to mix with noble men and . . .'

(Prog 6.9(Foerst)10)

Similarly we may now find temporal adverbs and even prepositional phrases fronted together with the adjective, as in *the still warm milk*, *this normally timid child*, *this by no means irresponsible action*, etc. In other words, in the course of time, the adjectival category has become so closely associated with prenominal position that even where the adjective phrase is clearly predicative or salient, front position is preferred.

In addition, the positional options that existed for adjectives in OE were exploited to accommodate multiple adjectives inside one NP, which was necessary because they could not be stacked. We saw that weak adjectives are closer to the nominal part of the cline, and indeed they seem in certain respects to behave more like nouns than adjectives, forming as it were a compound together with the noun. This would explain why *the very old man* does not occur in OE, just as in PDE we would not be able to say *the very greybeard* when referring to an old man rather than a beard. Similarly, it was not possible to build sequences like *a dirty old man*, where *dirty* modifies *old man* rather than *man*. When we wish to express in PDE that a man is dirty as well as old, we would normally reverse the 'natural' order of adjectives into *an old, dirty man*, and add an intonation break (here represented by the comma). It seems to be the case that in OE each adjective had the same level with respect to the noun; there was no hierarchy in which one adjective modified the remainder of the NP. It was therefore virtually impossible to put one adjective after another in a row (for some exceptions, see Fischer, 2000). Instead, the adjectives would be separated by *and*, or very often one adjective would precede and one follow the noun. The latter generally only happened when the adjectives were strong, as in *gyldenne wingeard trumlicne and fæstlicne* 'golden vineyard durable and firm' (*Alex.*1 107). When the adjectives were weak, postnominal position could only be used if the demonstrative was repeated, creating as it were an extra NP, as in *þæs swetan wætres and þæs ferscan* 'of the sweet water and the fresh' (*Alex.*1 338).

Apart from adjectives as modifiers, we also have modifying nouns, which in Table 3.2 we termed adjuncts. Adjuncts as a rule stand closest to the noun, following the other modifying adjectives, as in *a warm black leather coat*. When there are two adjuncts, the most 'nouny' one stands closest to the noun, e.g. in *a leather dog collar*, where *leather* comes first because it is more adjectival than *dog*, falling into a class which also contains true (albeit denominal) adjectives such as *woollen*, *golden*, etc. Such noun modifiers together with their head noun can be premodified by adjectives in PDE, just as adjectives with their head noun can be premodified by adjectives; they cannot be premodified by adverbs, because they are noun-like (cf. **a very leather collar*). We saw above that in OE weak adjectives behave very much like adjuncts in that they too cannot be modified by adverbs.

The fate of the pre- and postmodifiers is closely linked to that of the modifiers. We have seen that adverbial premodifiers first occurred only with predicative or attributive non-restrictive adjectives, and that they only began to occur with restrictive attributives once adjective position became fixed in ME. The fixing of adjective position and the loss of the weak/strong distinction must also have led to a string of adjectives without the linking word *and* becoming common, and an adverbial modifier becoming possible with formerly weak adjectives. Both facts together would almost naturally lead to a situation in which an adjective in a string could begin to modify the next adjective plus head noun, just as an adverb before an adjective could. It is difficult to determine when exactly this possibility became available, but that it did is clear from a development in which formerly descriptive adjectives like *nice* or *horrid* develop into value adjectives, which cannot modify a noun but only an adjective, as in *We need a good fast car*, where *good* clearly modifies *fast* or *fast car*, not *car*. Adamson (2000) has shown that to trace such a development one would first have to ascertain when an adjective like *horrid* starts being used in a row with another adjective, and secondly when *horrid*-adjectives begin to be predominantly placed in left-most position. No answers to these questions are available as yet, but it is clear from the complete corpus of Chaucerian (late ME) texts that such a development with the now classic value adjectives *horrible/horrid* and *nice* had not yet taken place. *Nice* in Chaucer occurs only by itself. *Horrible* occurs by itself 28 times; 9 times there is another adjective. Of these latter cases, 2 instances show the use of *and* (*horrible and strong prison*, *KnT* 1451); one instance has the adjectives draped around the noun (*sodeyn deth horrible*, *FrlT* 1010); 5 have two consecutive adjectives. Of these 5, however, one has *horrible* not in leftmost position (*this false horrible boke*, *RR* 7132), in three more *horrible* is likely to be descriptive because the other adjectives describe feelings of horror too (*swollen, disordinate, dedly*), while the last double adjective construction, *horrible grete synnes*, is more likely to be descriptive too, because it is followed by *or smale* (*ParsT* 960). In other words there is no evidence yet in Chaucer of the adjectives having become premodifiers.

There are both finite and non-finite clausal postmodifiers. No changes of note occurred in the non-finite ones, i.e. already in OE a head noun could be followed by an infinitival or a present participle construction:

(12) a.   Ic hæbbe mete to etenne þone   þe ge   nyton.
           I have   food to eat   which   you not-know
           'I have food to eat which you know nothing about.'   (*ÆHom* 5.71)

     b.   . . . ac him   losode an   sceap þa ða se frumsceapena man
           . . . but to-him lost   one sheep when the first-created man

           adam   syngiende forleas neorxenawanges bigwiste
           Adam sinning   lost   of-paradise   food
           '. . . but one sheep went missing on him when Adam, the first created man,
           sinning, lost the food of paradise'   (*ÆCHom* I, 372.25)

The typical finite postmodifier is the relative clause. There were many changes here, mainly in the form of the element that served to introduce the clause. In PDE we distinguish two types of relative clause, the so-called restrictive and non-restrictive ones, which differ in meaning in that the first narrows down the referent of the head noun, whereas the second gives extra information about the head noun. Formally, they are distinguished in that with the latter there is a clear intonation break (in writing indicated by the use of a comma), which is absent in the former. Another formal difference is that the relative pronoun *that* is only employed with restrictive clauses, at least in standard English, while *who* and *which* can be used with either (at least in BrE). In OE we have no clear formal criteria to distinguish them, although there is a tendency for the relative particle *þe* to occur mainly in restrictive clauses. The following elements functioned as relatives in OE: the demonstrative pronoun series *se, seo, þæt*, the undeclined particle *þe* and a combination of the two, see (13):

(13) a.   he wolde adræfan anne æþeling   se   was Cyneheard haten
        he would drive-out a   nobleman who was Cyneheard called
        'He wanted to drive away a nobleman who was called Cyneheard.'
                                (ChronA (Plummer) 755.6)

     b.   þu geearnast ... þone stede þe   se deofol of   afeoll
          you earn ...   the   place which the devil from fell
          þurh   ungehyrsumnesse.
          through disobedience
          'You will deserve the place which the devil fell out of through his
          disobedience'.   (ÆCHom I, 181.79)

     c.   Se wolde niman his magan to wife þæs cyninges dohtor.   seo
          that wanted take   his relative to wife the king's   daughter, who
          ðe wæs to abbudissan gehadod.
             was to abbess   ordained
          'That one wanted to marry his relative, the king's daughter, who had been
          ordained abbess.'   (ÆCHom II, 277.152)

Relative clauses may have had their origin in paratactic clauses (cf. Section 3.1). It is not difficult to see, for instance, how type (13a), with a demonstrative pronoun (*se was*), may have developed out of a main (coordinate) clause:

(14)   þa sæde heo þam brydguman þæt heo gesawe engel of heofenum,
          then said she to-the bridegroom that she saw   angel of heavens,
          ond se   wolde hyne slean
          and that would him kill
          myd færdeaðe,   gif he hyre æfre onhryne myd unclænre lufon.
          with sudden-death, if he her   ever touched with unclean   love
          'Then she said to the bridegroom that she had seen an angel from heaven,
          who would kill him swiftly, if he ever touched her in an unclean way.'
                         (Mart 2.1 (Herzfeld-Kotzor)no. 22 A7)

Indeed, in cases like (13a), where a demonstrative pronoun by itself functions as a relative and where there is no clear indication of coordinateness as there is in (14), it is not clear whether the relative clause is subordinate or paratactic.

Relative clauses which take a demonstrative pronoun as head as well as a particle, as in (13c), may have developed from an appositive construction, whereby the demonstrative originally was part of the main clause, as can be seen in a number of cases where the demonstrative pronoun bears the case form of the antecedent in the main clause rather than the case form of the function it reflects in the subordinate clause. Thus in (13c) the demonstrative *seo* has nominative case because it functions as subject of the relative clause, while in (15) the demonstrative *þara* is in the genitive plural, like its antecedent *ealra*, in spite of the fact that it functions as subject in the relative clause:

(15)
& þu scealt wesan ealra bysen   þara   þe ðurh   þe on ðinne god gelyfað.
and you must be   of-all example of-those who through you in your   god believe
'and you must set the example for all who through you believe in God'

(LS 4 (Christoph)57)

Another type of relative that is appositional in nature is the non-introduced relative clause:

(16)
Seo   mægð   asprang of   noes   yltstan suna wæs gehaten sem.
This maiden sprang from Noah's   eldest son, was   called   sem
'This maiden was the offspring of Noah's eldest son, (who was) called Sem.'

(*ÆCHom* I, 186.222)

This was the main type of zero-relative clause possible in OE. A zero relative where the relative element functions as any kind of object in the subordinate clause, as in *This is the book Ø I came to pick up*, first occurs in the ME period and only becomes common in ModE.

The greatest change in the ME period is the introduction of the wh-relative. In OE wh-pronouns were used as interrogatives and generalising, indefinite pronouns, but never as relatives. The introduction of wh-relatives is partly a natural development, but its use may also be due to the collapse of the OE relative system. *þe* went out of use (probably because it was phonetically weak and identical to the new, undeclined, definite article) in the early part of the ME period – a little later in the south – and was replaced by *that*, as the only left-over of the original demonstrative pronoun series *se, seo, þæt*. The use of wh-relatives ((*the*) *which* (*that*), *whom, whose*) dates from the beginning of the ME period, but became really frequent only in the early ModE period. The earliest instances are with *whom* and *whose*, possibly because, unlike *that*, they could indicate case. The development of interrogative into relative pronouns is natural when one considers their use in indirect questions such as *He wanted to know who did this*, where the interrogative could be said to function as an indefinite ('the one who') or generalising ('whoever') pronoun. Already in OE, interrogatives like *hwa, hwæt* and *hwilc* were used as indefinites (sometimes indeed called 'free relatives'), as in (17a), and they frequently occurred in indirect questions of the type mentioned above, as in (17b):

(17) a.   Ealle we sind gelice ætforan gode. buton hwa oðerne mid godum
            All   we   are   equal before   god   except who other   with good

            weorcum forþeo.
            works   oppresses
            'We are all equal in the eyes of God except the one who oppresses another
            with good works'   (*ÆCHom* I, 326.44)

     b.   þa   cwæð hi   to þan deofle: Ic wat   hwæt þu   þæncst
          then said   she to the devil: I   know what you think
                             (*LS* 14 (MargaretCCCC 303)14.4)

For the 'free relative' to develop into a 'true' or strict relative, an antecedent is required, which in the free relative is missing (or one could say 'included'). The instance in (18), from early ME, shows how this could come about:

(18)   wham mai he luue treweliche hwa ne luues his broðer
        'whom can he love truly who(ever) does not love his brother'
                            (*Wooing Lord* 275.18)

Here, *hwa* can be interpreted as a 'free relative', but at the same time it could be a strict relative referring to *he*, because *he* also has general reference.

The earliest instances of wh-relatives are mainly found in non-restrictive clauses, and tend to be preceded by a preposition. Since the general relative particle *that* could not take a preposition in front of it, this is perhaps not surprising. By the fifteenth century, *whose*, *whom* and *which* are frequent, but interestingly enough not *who*. The reason for this may be the fact mentioned above, i.e. *who* as a nominative form had no need of a preposition, and therefore this function could as easily be expressed by the usual form *that*, which was common with both animate and inanimate antecedents all through the ME period and far beyond. Another possible factor was the original meaning of the wh-relative. As an indefinite pronoun or free relative, it occurred mainly in subject position; *who* may therefore have been too strongly generalising to function as a mere relative. It is interesting to note in this respect that this 'lag of *who*' is also noticeable in German and Dutch, which even today do not allow nominative *who* (i.e. *wer* and *wie* respectively) to occur as a relative, while both *wer* and *wie are* used as free relatives.

3.3   The verbal group

      The rapid loss of inflections in the ME period had a far greater impact on the constitution of the verb phrase (here used in its narrow sense, as comprising the verbal elements only) than it had on the noun phrase. Thus finite verbs gradually lost their person and number inflections (except for the third-person singular), which according to some linguists has had further repercussions on word order (e.g Roberts, 1993; for discussion of this issue see Lightfoot, 1997; Warner, 1997; this volume, Section 5.3). Secondly some of the functions that were originally expressed synthetically (e.g. 'mood' by subjunctive endings, 'aspect' by the presence or absence of affixes such as *ge-*, *be-* and *a-*) needed to be re-expressed, usually by means of a periphrastic construction. Once periphrastic constructions had entered, others followed in their wake, often clarifying forms that had served a double purpose, such as the present tense form in OE, which was used to refer both to the present and the future. In many cases these periphrastic constructions had already arisen in OE as 'exploratory expressions' (Harris and Campbell, 1995: 72–5) – syntagms which may arise due to a wish for emphasis or clarity, mistakes in the application of grammatical rules, etc., and may or may not become part of the grammar through a process of grammaticalisation. This is indeed what we see happening in English. A number of exploratory expressions are around in OE to mark more clearly or expressively the functions that have so far been mainly expressed by mood, aspect or tense affixes. The eventual loss of these affixes is partly the result of phonetic attrition and pidginisation (see Chapter 1), but no doubt was accelerated by the availability of such 'exploratory expressions'. As is usual in grammaticalisation, we at first see competition among the new periphrastic forms to fill a specific function, later followed by the selection of one of the competing forms, and then its further grammaticalisation (in the form of bleaching of referential meaning, and phonetic reduction), after which the whole cycle may start again. As an example, consider what happened to the OE subjunctive towards the end of the OE period. The original OE synthetic subjunctive forms became opaque (because of syncretism with indicative forms), and already existing 'modal' verbs (often termed 'pre-modals', because they lacked many of the properties associated with the PDE modals), such as *cunnan* 'can', **sculan* 'shall' and *magan* 'may', began to take their place. These then gradually lost their full-verb (lexical) meanings and became restricted to deontic, dynamic and epistemic uses. As a consequence, they lost some of their verbal character-istics (infinitival, participial and 'pure' tense forms), which in turn led to a new cycle, i.e. the introduction of what are often called 'quasi-modal' verbs, such as *have to*, *be able to*, etc., to fill the syntactic gaps that the core modals had left.

In the following subsections, we will look at the main verbal categories of tense, aspect, mood and voice and describe the extensive changes that have taken place in these areas. One separate section will be devoted to one of the most remarkable developments in English, the grammaticalisation of the verb *do* to an empty operator, which was in many ways a result of the rise of so many new periphrastic constructions. A final section will deal with the ever-increasing array of auxiliaries within the verb phrase, and the relation between them, represented by strict ordering principles that developed in the course of time.

3.3.1   Tense

'Tense' is a grammatical term referring to specific verbal forms (inflectional or periphrastic) which have a relation with the notional idea of 'time'. This relation is not direct and inflexible, i.e. it is not the case that a past-tense form necessarily refers to a past-time event:

(19)   Mrs Edwina Currie claimed that many pensioners were well-off ... 'We are
            in the age of the "woopy" the well-off old person and it is about time we all
            recognised that fact ...'   (1988 *Daily Tel.* 23 Apr.1–2, *OED* s.v. 'woopy')

In (19) the past-tense *recognised* refers to the future. At the same time, it seems clear why a *past* tense is used in this clause. There is a subjective relation with past time in the speaker's mind in that in her opinion this fact should have been recognised *long ago*. This use of the past tense is a new development in ME; in OE a present subjunctive form would have been used instead, as in example (20).

(20)   Iohannes: cum   to me tima is þæt ðu   mid þinum gebroðrum
            John,   come to me time is that you with your   brothers

            wistfullige   on minum gebeorscipe.
            feast [PRES.SUBJ] in my   banquet
            'John, come to me, it is about time that you and your brothers attended one
            of my feasts.'   (*ÆCHom* I, 4 214.246)

This shows that the past tense in PDE in these examples expresses modality, rather than time. More about this modal use of the past tense will be found in Section 3.3.3; here we will concentrate on the more transparent relations between tense and time.

It is convenient to distinguish three time zones, past, present and future, and, in PDE, three more or less corresponding tenses. The past and present tense (e.g. *we went*, *we go*) are expressed morphologically. The future tense (*we will go*) is a much later development and grammatically far less fixed; it is expressed periphrastically with the help of auxiliaries such as *shall/will*. (Indeed most modern grammars of English call *we will go* a modal construction and reserve the label 'tense' for the purely inflectional present/past distinction.) Future time is of course the least certain, i.e. the least factual, of the three time zones, and it is therefore not surprising that a modal colouring (one of possibility, necessity or intention) comes to the fore in the use of the 'future tense' auxiliaries *will* and *shall*, which originally expressed intention and obligation.

When we turn to the earliest documents of English, we find that there were only two tenses, past and present. These were used more or less in the same way as in PDE in that the present tense was used to refer to the here and now, and also to timeless truths or situations (including habitual actions), while the past tense was employed to express any event that belonged to the past, including events for which we would now use a perfect or pluperfect (see (21a)). In addition the present tense was also the form normally used to refer to future time, (21b), and to past time that extends up to the moment of speaking, (21c), where PDE would prefer a perfect (but cf. Irish English, which still uses a present here, as do most Germanic languages).

(21) a. siððan hie   hie   geliornodon, hie hie   wendon <ealla> ... on
          after   they them learned   they them turned all   in
          hiora agen geðiode.
          their own language
          'after they *had* studied them they translated them all into their own
          language'   (*CPLet*Wærf 46)

     b. Ic arise of   deaðe on ðæm þriddan dæge
          I arise from death on the   third   day
          'I *will* arise from the dead on the third day'   (*ÆCHom* I, 10 (259.27))

     c. Efne   min wif is for manegum wintrum untrum, þam   wæs
          indeed my wife is for many   winters ill   for-that was
          ælc læcecræft wiðerræde oð   þis.
          each remedy   adverse   until this
          'Indeed my wife *has been* ill for many years and until now no remedy was
          (has been?) effective.'   (*ÆLS* (Apollinaris)41)

It could be said that grammatical tense forms are redundant because the time at which an action takes place is usually clear from the context. As we can see from the examples in (21), it is the adverbials or conjunctions (*siððan, on ðæm þriddan dæge, for manegum wintrum*) that help us to place an event in time. In English the choice between a past- or present-tense form has always been obligatory (later in ME, a perfect tense was added as another 'past'; note, however, that the perfect is in many ways aspectual too; more about this in Section 3.3.2); in other words one or the other has to surface in each utterance. This has not been the case, however, with the future tense.

In OE there was no future tense, as noted above, and even in PDE its use is not always obligatory. A present tense can be used, in many contexts, such as a temporal clause referring to the future (*When you [*will] go out, please close the door*) or when the future is seen as more or less definite or planned (*The train leaves at six*). What we see, then, in the development of English future markers is that **sculan* and *willan* are reinterpreted first from original dynamic and/or deontic modals, probably through some kind of pragmatic inferencing or double modal marking, into more general future markers expressing possibility or strong likelihood. Traugott (1992: 196) gives an example such as:

(22) Ic *sceal* eac *niede* þara   monegena gewinna geswigian
       I must also needs of-those many   battles be silent
       'I must (shall?) also necessarily be silent about all those battles'
                                                  (*Or* 5 2.115.29)

in which necessity is, as it were, doubly expressed, which allows the modal of 'obligation' *sceal* to become bleached into a 'weaker' future modal. Such

examples show that the modal meaning was already weakening and needed rein-
forcement by adverbials such as *niede*. Next, they come to be used in contexts
where future reference may need reinforcing, thus backgrounding the original
modality even further. The last stage would be complete grammaticalisation of
the future-tense marker. This stage has not been fully reached in PDE, but there
has been a steady increase over time in the contexts requiring future marking.
In PDE the use of the present tense is virtually restricted to clauses which are
already clearly marked as future by other means, e.g. we find the present used in
conditional clauses where the main clause has a future tense, or when the future
event is seen as or considered to be pretty definite. Thus, in the following example
from Chaucer, there is no future marking in spite of the fact that the hoped-for
kisses are rather unlikely: *For after this I hope ther cometh more* (*MillT* 3725). In
PDE some marker would be common here, either as 'I hope that more *will come*'
or 'that more *are coming*' (for this use of the progressive, see Section 3.3.2). In
example (23b) below, the same main verb *hope* is followed by a future tense,
because the verb *be* expresses a state, and it would be odd to express a state which
cannot yet be.

In written OE documents the periphrastic auxiliaries **sculan* and *willan* are
not really used as a pure tense form. Early 'pure' examples are difficult to spot,
however, because even in later uses of the two verbs the original modal meanings
may still shine through. In ME, for instance, *will* is more frequent in the first
person than *shall*, because with the first person intention or volition is more likely
to be present than obligation, while *shall* occurs far more frequently in the second
and third persons, expressing ordained events, commands and instructions, i.e.
things which are not normally willed by the subject of the clause him/herself, but
see further Sections 5.2.7, 5.3.3. Clear examples of ongoing grammaticalisation
are only provided when the subject is inanimate, i.e. cannot itself exert 'will'
or 'necessity' (23a), or when the activity expressed must be the opposite of the
subject's intentions (23b):

(23) a.   . . . that, but ye helpe, it will his bane be
            '. . . that, unless you help, it will be his death'   (Chaucer, *T&C* II, 320)

    b.   Our maunciple I hope he wil be deed
            'Our manciple, I expect he will be dead soon'   (Chaucer, *ReevT*)

Such examples only begin to show up with any frequency in ME.

Other markers of future tense also develop in the course of time, again showing
a lack of grammatical fixity; grammaticalisation is continuous here, as it were. In
late ME we see the development of *be about to* and *be going to*:

(24)
a. I was aboute to wedde a wyf, allas!   (Chaucer, *WBT* 166; Mustanoja, 1960: 354)
b. thys onhappy sowle . . . was goyng to be brought into helle for the synne and onleful
   [unlawful] lustys of her body (Monk of Evesham 43; Mustanoja, 1960: 592)

The meanings are not, of course, the same: *be about to* expresses incipient
action and has retained this rather precise meaning over the centuries, not

grammaticalising further into a general future marker. The case is different with *be going to*, which has indeed become a very general future marker in PDE, more and more bleached of its earlier concrete locative/directional meaning and in the twentieth century reduced phonetically to *gonna*.

Although present and past tense are often linked to present and past time, this is not necessarily so, as we saw with the subjective use of the past in (19) above. The past can also be used in present-tense contexts to refer to a hypothetical situation, as in *I wish I was very rich*, and in conditional clauses. We have a similar case with the present, which is sometimes used in a past-tense context, the so-called 'historical present'. There is some consensus that a true historical present does not yet occur in OE (see the discussion in Mitchell, 1985: §§623–30). It is, indeed, remarkable that instances of the historical present in Latin texts are consistently rendered by pasts in OE translations from Latin. In PDE, the historical present is frequently used in story-telling, to make a narrative more immediate and lively. This is then another case of a subjective use of a tense form: the event is presented as present because that is how it appears in the speaker's experience of it. In a similar way we could explain occasional instances of the perfect in present-day British (25a) and Australian English (25b), occurring next to past tenses all referring to the same past event:

(25) a.   'The lightning *has struck* the tree and *shot* down the trunk. One of the women *had* her back to the tree trunk, and the lightning *has gone* down her back, *ripped* open her shirt and *come* out through her feet,' the officer said. (1999 *The Guardian* p. 4, 24 Sept.; reference from Denison, 2000b)

     b.   . . . a guy in Mexico, he *said* [. . .] 'I reckon we should go to the zoo, but we shouldn't go there when it's open, we should go there when it's night time [. . .].' And so he *'s jumped* the fence with a few friends, and *went* over to the lion enclosure and he *'s dropped* his mobile phone into the lion enclosure. [. . .] Now the funny thing is [. . .] that he just *jumped* the fence, *went* into the lion enclosure to get his phone, he *'s walked* up to his phone and the phone *has started* ringing . . . .   (Triple J Radio Sydney, 22 March 2000, reference from Engel & Ritz, 2000: 134)

The use of the perfect here makes the experience more vivid and more relevant. We find a similar mixture between past and 'historical' present in late ME texts when the historical present first seems to make headway:

(26)   And to the tre she *goth* a ful good pas, | For love *made* hire so hardy in this cas, | And by the welle adoun she *gan hyre dresse*. | Allas, Than *cometh* a wilde lyonesse | Out of the wode, withoute more arest, | With blody mouth, of strangelynge of a best, | To drynken of the welle there as she *sat*. | And whan that Tisbe *hadde espyed* that, | She *rist* hire up, with a ful drery herte, | And in a cave with dredful fot she *sterte*   (Chaucer, *LGW* 802–11)

The present in (26), like the perfect in (25), makes the narrative more lively. However, the switch from past to present tense may also serve another function: Wolfson (1979) has argued that its function is to organise discourse into segments, to signal a break in the text or a change in perspective. In (26) the foregrounded, plot-advancing actions are in the present tense (*goth*, *cometh*, *rist*) and they also mark a change of perspective from Thisbe to the lion and back again. The past tenses (*made*, *sat*, *hadde espyed*), on the other hand, provide descriptive or back-grounded details. The same may be true of the past/perfect switch in (25b). Note that the past tenses in (25b) serve to set the scene, or are descriptive, providing background, while the perfects are important for the story line, advancing the plot. It has been argued (cf. Brinton, 1996: 71 and *passim*) that the construction with *gan* (*gan dresse* in (26)) often had a similar function in ME: like the historical present it was a foregrounding device. The past tense *sterte* may seem somewhat remarkable here because it could be argued to be part of the foregrounding as well. However, as very often in Chaucer, a past tense rounds off a series of activities (in the present): once Thisbe has 'rushed' (*sterte*) into the cave, she stays there, glad to be out of danger. In other words, this result (Thisbe safe in the cave) is seen as part of the description, a new stable state as it were.

3.3.2   Aspect

Aspect and tense are not always easy to distinguish in PDE. Verbal forms such as the perfect and the progressive play a part in an aspectual system (conveying completed activity and activity in progress or of limited duration, respectively), but they also function in the system of tense, with the perfect being used for past events (albeit usually with 'current relevance') and the progressive for future reference. Aspect in English is more difficult to define than tense for there have been more changes in this area, both as far as form is concerned and in content or function. Modern present and past tenses are directly derived from the OE synthetic tenses, whereas the progressive and perfect are later, periphrastic developments, which like most periphrastic constructions are less fixed in their meaning, i.e. less grammaticalised. The differences between OE and PDE in the way the *be* + *ing* form and *have* + past participle were used are quite considerable.

The OE precursor of the progressive was but rarely used, at least in the extant documents. It consisted of a form of *beon* or *wesan* (sometimes *weorðan* 'become') and the present participle in *-ende*. It has been suggested that another, similar construction with a verbal noun rather than a participle, the *beon on huntunge* type (in later English *he was in/on/an/ahunting*, etc.), was also used in the spoken language in the OE period, but the evidence we have from the written documents does not really support this idea. Nevertheless, the idea of a possible colloquial origin is understandable given the fact that in other Germanic languages, such as Dutch and German, a similar construction with a preposition and a verbal noun is used. First of all, a combination of *be* and the verbal noun in *-ung* is itself very rare, with only two suspect instances in the *Dictionary of Old English* (*DOE*) corpus, and so unlikely to be the origin of the modern progressive: we would have expected such nominal constructions to be much more frequent even in the written documents for it to grammaticalise into an aspectual marker. Yet recent investigations into the presence of a Celtic substratum in English suggest that the modern progressive may be a direct development of the gerund rather than the result of a phonetic change involving the present participle. See Filppula et al. (2002b), Poppe (2002) and White (2002).

Next to the possible variation in form, it should also be noted that the function of the *be + -ende* form was different in OE. It is often found with verbs that typically wouldn't occur in the progressive in PDE, i.e. verbs that are inherently durative, such as *wunian* 'dwell', *libban* 'live', *growan* 'grow', e.g. (27a), and when found with activity verbs, it is much more common in the past than in the present, with the sense of duration shading into one of habit or a characteristic, (27b) (for this more adjectival sense of the present participle, see also below). Strang (1970: 350–1) also notes a special sense occurring in the OE progressive with adverbials of time: in (27c) it is used for limited duration but with the connotation of persistence, of 'not giving up'; see also Poppe (2002: 241) who notes that this meaning of the progressive is also present in Middle Irish and may therefore also be due to a Celtic substratum:

(27) a. Hwæt ða   se halga wer benedictus wæs ðeonde   on witegunge. swa
        what, then the holy man Benedict   was prospering in prophecy   so
        þæt he ðurh   godes gast mihte towearde ðing   cyðan
        that he through god's spirit could future   things make-known
        'Indeed, Saint Benedict then was very successful in his divination so that by
        divine inspiration he could foretell the future'   (*ÆCHom* II, 11 98.219)

    b. Ða   cwæð Tyberius: Eala, swyðe   wæs ic gewylnigende þæt ic
       then said   Tiberius, lo,   strongly was I desiring   that I
       hyne geseon wolde.
       him see   would
       'Then Tiberius said, "Lo, my desire to see him was very strong".'
                                                            (*VSal* 1 (Cross)33.1)

    c. ... he wæs heriende &   feohtende fiftig wintra, oð he hæfde
       ... he was attacking and fighting   fifty winters till he had
       ealle Asiam on his geweald genyd
       all   Asia in his power   compelled
       '... he kept on attacking and fighting for fifty years until he had compelled
       all of Asia into his dominion'   (*Or* 1 2.21.25, taken from Strang, 1970: 351)

This function/meaning of the progressive remains more or less unchanged in the ME period, and it is only when its frequency rises considerably in the course of the eModE period that it begins to function as part of an aspectual *system* (indicating primarily 'limited duration'), as it still does nowadays. Its use is at first still optional, and the construction becomes fully grammaticalised (i.e. obligatory in contexts describing limited duration) only in the late ModE period.

Other questions that need to be asked with respect to the progressive concern its formal development and the reason why it became an obligatory part of the verbal system of English in the form that it did. Comparing the English development with that in Dutch and German above, it is not too speculative to suggest that there may have been two or three deeper causes. One is the early loss of inflections in English (in contrast to Dutch and German), which led to an early grammaticalisation of periphrastic constructions to replace those losses, which in turn led to a certain accommodation of such structures in the grammar of English. A second cause may well have been the falling together in ME of the verbal noun in *-ung* > ME *-ing* and the present participle in *-ende* > ME *-ing*, thus increasing the frequency of the ending. A possible third cause could be the fact that the *-ing* form also began to replace the bare infinitive in the ME and eModE period (see above and Fischer, 1997 for *formal* confusion between infinitive and participle), thereby enhancing the *verbal* nature of the gerund/participle, making it easier for the construction to enter the verbal system and, of course, again increasing its frequency.

Formally, in other words, the ground was being prepared for grammaticalisation of the progressive. Functionally too the development is understandable. First of all there was a gap, so to speak, in the aspectual system. In OE there were still remnants of what could be seen as a morphological–lexical system of aspect. Many verbs occurred both in their bare forms and in forms preceded by a prefix. These prefixes often indicated aspect: e.g. *a-*, *be-*, *ge-*, *of-*, etc. changed a verb from durative into perfective (*sendan/asendan* 'send/dispatch'; *bugan/bebugan* 'bow/surround'; *ridan/geridan* 'ride/occupy'; *giefan/ofgiefan* 'give/give up'), while *on-* and sometimes *in-* would make the verb inchoative (*bærnan/onbærnan* 'burn/incite'; *lyhtan/inlyhtan* 'light/enlighten'). In the general loss of affixes, these prefixes were largely lost too, and if preserved they became fully lexicalised. In such a situation, it is not at all unlikely that new productive means were looked for to express aspect, and that certain 'exploratory expressions' (see Section 3.3.3) were being pressed into service to fill some of the gaps. Indeed, we see the development of periphrastic aspect marking not just in the rise of progressive and perfect forms, but also in the rise of inchoative markers such as OE *-ginnan* / ME *gan* (see also Section 3.3.4), which came to be used to indicate the beginning of an action. For other aspectual periphrastic constructions (egressive, iterative, habitual, continuative, etc.) arising in the OE and ME period, consult Brinton (1988). There were also other means available to fill the gaps left by the loss of the prefixed verbs. Thus we see a strong growth of verb–particle combinations in eME (see Hiltunen, 1983), replacing *ofgiefan* with *give up* etc., and a replacement of native prefixes by French ones (cf. '*en*lighten', '*in*cite', above).

When we look at the progressive form and the path of development, it is easy to see how an aspectual function could arise out of it. The present participle in *-ende* was used in three different types of construction in OE. It was used predicatively together with *be* in an adjectival function, (28a,b); it was used as an appositive participle, (28c); and, again predicatively, as an agentive nominal, (28d); and it had a more clearly verbal function in (28e):

(28) a. Næs   him   cild   gemæne: for þan ðe elisabeð wæs untymende
        not-was them child in-common because Elizabeth was unteeming
        'they did not have a child together because Elizabeth was barren'

        (*ÆCHom* I, 25 379.7)

   b. Ða   ðry   englas gelicere beorhtnysse scinende wæron.
      those three angels like   brightness shining   were
      'Those three angels were bright in their splendour'

        (*ÆCHom* II, 22 191.30)

   c. Þa   wæron hyrdas   on ðam earde   waciende ofer heora eowde
      then were shepherds in that region waking   over their flock
      'there were shepherds then in that region guarding their flock'

        (*ÆCHom* I, 2 190.21)

   d. Ne beswice eower nan   oðerne on cypinge, forþon ... God his
      not deceive of-you none other in trading, because ... God of-it
      bið   wrecend.
      will-be avenger
      'No one of you should deceive another in business because God will avenge it.'

        (*ThCap* 1 (Sauer) 35.373.8)

   e. ... hit God siþþan longsumlice wrecende wæs ...
      ... it God then   long   avenging was ...
      '... and God avenged this [on him and his family] for a long time'

        (*Or* 2 1.35.30)

It is clear from these examples that the dividing line between adjective/noun and verbal element is very thin. Contrast, for instance, the (a)–(b) and the (d)–(e) examples: in (28a,d) the present participle is hardly verbal, because it is used together with the essentially adjectival prefix *un-* (in (28a)) or governs a genitive (*his* in (28d)) rather than an accusative (cf. *hit* in (28e)). In all these cases we have the verb *be* appearing either as a copula or an existential verb together with the present participle. In OE, these two elements were often separated by other constituents, but in ME they increasingly occurred next to one another (see Section 3.5 for full discussion of the relevant changes in word order). The resulting adjacency of *be* and the participle is another step towards further grammaticalisation, because it is easier with juxtaposed elements for the construction to be interpreted as a unit. Once it was a unit, it could become part of the verbal system. As far as semantic content is concerned, it is clear that the sense of *be* + *-ende* was not necessarily one of limited duration. However, when the participle in ME became more verbal – the reasons for which we noted above – the adjectives and nouns in *-ende* lost ground (as indeed they already had with the general loss of native affixes after the OE period), and the construction lost the connotation of unlimited duration it had had in such cases in OE.

The development of the progressive into a future marker, as in *We are leaving at six*, is a later one (though cf. Visser, 1963–73: §1830). It becomes common only in the eModE period but is first restricted to verbs of motion (cf. the rise of the *to be going to* construction, mentioned in Section 3.3.4). Later, other activity verbs are found here too. It is quite clear that the progressive is only used when it denotes activities that can be planned or arranged beforehand (hence its restriction to dynamic verbs). Even in PDE it cannot be used in a future sense with verbs like *rain* or *like* (**Tomorrow it is raining, *I am sure he is liking it*). The use of the progressive form here is again subjective (cf. the subjective use of tense noted in Section 3.3.3) in that the speaker already visualises the beginning of the activity that is going to take place.

The periphrastic perfect form, *have* + past participle, and the preterite can both refer to past time in PDE, but they highlight an activity differently. The use of the preterite indicates that the speaker sees the activity as firmly belonging to a particular moment in the past, whereas the perfect may be used for a past activity somehow linked to the present, or, to put it differently, *not* linked to a *specific* moment in the past. It is this reference to a certain 'duration' (i.e. of something from the past 'lasting' into the present) that links the perfect to the aspect system, but quite clearly, the perfect also plays a role in the PDE tense system. This difference between perfect and preterite has become more firmly fixed in PDE, so that a past time indicator (e.g. an adverbial expressing a *specific* moment) does not normally co-occur with a present perfect form (but see also the discussion of (25)), although this rule is very much a rule of standard *written* English. In spoken and non-standard English the distinction between the use of the past tense and the perfect is not nearly so clearcut; see Miller (2004). In the Modern English period, when the perfect was still finding its own niche, so to speak, this distinction was not yet so sharply drawn, so that one could come across examples such as:

(29) a.   I have delivered it an hour since (Shakespeare, *All's Well that Ends Well*)

b.   The Englishman . . . has murdered young Halbert . . . yesterday
morning (Galsworthy, *In Chancery*)
(both examples taken from Elsness, 1997: 250)

In other words the preterite and the perfect were variants for a while within the tense system (though no doubt the variation was governed by certain semantic or pragmatic principles – whose nature still awaits full investigation).

When we consider the rise of the perfect, we note again a slow grammaticalisation process virtually from OE to PDE. During this time there have been formal as well as semantic shifts in the construction itself (which are closely interlinked) and a corresponding shift in the contexts in which it occurs. Important formal changes are the loss of inflection, a change in word order and the gradual narrowing to only one auxiliary of the perfect, i.e. *have*:

(30)
a. Loca nu;   þin   agen geleafa þe   hæfþ gehæledne.
   look now your own faith   you has   healed
   'Look how your own faith has healed you.'   (*HomS* 8 (BlHom 2)24)

b. Gif he ær hæfþ attor   gedruncen ne biþ   him ahte þe wyrs.
   if   he ere has   poison drunk   not will-be him aught the worse
   'If he has drunk poison before, he will not be any the worse.'   (*Lch* II (3)43.1.3)

c. Miltsa   þinum folce,   þeah   hit gesyngod hæbbe
   show-mercy to-your people, though it   sinned   have
   'have pity on your people although they have sinned'   (*Exod* 32.7)

d. Þiss ic witegode on eorðe, and nu   hit is gecumen to us
   this I   predicted on earth, and now it is come   to us
   'I predicted this to happen on earth and now it has come to us'   (*Nic* (C)202)

Typical OE perfects have the following features: the past participle may still be declined like an adjective (e.g. *gehæledne* in (30a)), the object of the verb may precede the past participle (as in (30b)), and the auxiliary may be *be* rather than *have*, (30d). Now inflections are already being lost in the OE period, the object–verb order lingers on until the early ModE period and is still the norm in dialects such as Irish English, while the *be* forms are found with mutative verbs till late in the nineteenth century, with some relics left even in PDE. The general decline of this kind of variation leads to a gradual increase in the grammaticalisation of the perfect and to clearer functions for both preterite and perfect.

The semantic shift has two sides. First of all, the verb *have* loses its weak possessive meaning, and begins to occur with non-animate subjects and with intransitive verbs (this stage has already been reached in OE, witness (30a,c)), that is, it collocates with sentence elements that cannot be arguments or complements of a verb referring to possession. Secondly, whereas perfect *have* had at first only *present* time reference expressing completion (in OE), it gradually became part of the tense system, referring to an activity that started in the past and was linked to the present moment. From the ME period onwards, the perfect started to compete with the preterite. At first the distribution between the two forms is uneven and also still undefined, the preterite still dominating in contexts where we would now use the perfect, and *vice versa*.

It is interesting to compare the grammaticalisation of the perfect in English with the same process in other Germanic languages. In all languages of the Germanic branch the initial development is the same: the occurrence of a form of *be/have* and a past participle, and its use both temporally and aspectually. With the narrowing of its function, the paths begin to diverge, however. In English, and in Swedish, *be* disappears and the structure itself develops more and more into an aspectual marker. In Dutch and German, on the other hand, both *be* and *have* remain, and the structure becomes part of the tense system. In some German dialects (e.g. Swiss German) the perfect has even replaced the preterite completely as a tense marker. It is interesting to note that in PDE (especially in American English), the perfect now seems to be regressing, i.e. losing ground to the preterite. Elsness (1997: 359) attributes this development to two factors:

> (i) in informal, spoken English the present perfect auxiliary *have* usually appears in a highly reduced form; and (ii) with the vast majority of verbs in Modern English, including all regular verbs, the form of the past participle is identical with that of the preterite, in both speech and writing.

Whether the decreasing frequency of the perfect is due to this lack of distinctness is a matter that needs further investigation (one wonders why, if this is a factor, it is the perfect that decreases, and not the preterite). It could also be the case that the stronger presence of an aspect system in English (as compared to e.g. German and Dutch, which do not have a grammaticalised progressive or durative construction) has led to this development. Elsness notes on the same page:

> More and more, the present perfect seems to be developing into a verb form used above all in references to situations which not only are located within a period which extends up to the deictic zero-point, *but which themselves extend up to that point* [emphasis added].

In other words, the link with a definite past that existed in the ME and ModE periods has become further reduced in PDE.

Before we leave the perfect, two smaller points need to be addressed. First of all, why did the periphrastic perfect develop at all? We think that its origin in OE can be linked, yet again, with affixal losses, in particular with the loss of the prefix *ge-*, which indicated perfectivity in OE. *Ge-* was used both as a near-compulsory inflectional element in the past participle of verbs (reduced to *y-* in southern ME and to zero in the north) and as a derivational prefix in verbs to distinguish (lexically) perfective from durative verbs (this use did not survive the OE period; for examples, see (30) above). However, it should also be stressed that the development of a perfect from a possessive verb like *have* is quite a natural grammaticalisation path, occurring independently in many other languages.

The other point concerns the loss of the *be* auxiliary in the perfect. In OE the rule was for intransitive verbs (especially mutatives) to form the perfect with *be*, and for transitive verbs to be collocated with *have* (this goes back to the original meanings of *have* and *be* as possessive and existential verbs respectively; see above). In ME, *have* gradually extends its domain within the perfect structure, for which McWhorter (2002: 236–8, 258) sees Scandinavian influence, pointing to the fact that Old Norse, Modern Icelandic and Swedish use a cognate of *have* with both transitive and intransitive verbs, and use *be* as a resultative with only a very small number of intransitive verbs. We certainly witness a strengthening in the 'division of tasks' between the two auxiliaries: *have* comes to be associated more and more with activity and *be* with state. Thus we see that the *be* perfect collocates especially with adverbs of time or place (indicating result or state; see (31a)), while the *have* perfect is preferred with adverbs of manner or degree, which highlight the activity of the verb, irrespective of whether the verb is transitive or intransitive, (31b):

(31) a.   Be wel avysed on that ilke nyght | That we ben entred *into shippes bord*, | That noon of us ne speke nat a word (Chaucer, *MillT* 3584–6)

     b.   For ye han entred into myn hous *by violence* (Chaucer, *Melibee* 1812)

Due to the loss of the subjunctive (see Section 3.3.3), the verb *have* also comes to be used more and more often in hypothetical contexts, in contrast to *be*, presumably because in hypothetical contexts the emphasis would be on the activity rather than on the resultative state, because that state is never in fact reached. This again reduces the 'intransitive' domain of *be*. Thus in (32a) *have* is used rather than *be* because the context is one of 'irrealis', in contrast to (32b), where we have a factual situation:

(32) a.   He wende have cropen by his felawe John, | And by the millere in he creep anon   (Chaucer, *MillT* 4259–60)

   b.   noot I for-why ne how/ That jalousie, allas . . . | Thus causeles is cropen into yow   (Chaucer, *T&C* III, 1009–11)

For similar reasons *have* is more frequent in iterative and durative contexts. Frequency is a crucial factor in grammaticalisation processes, so it is not surprising that slowly *have* gains on *be*.

At the same time, there are formal and functional factors that account for the decrease of *be*. The combination of *be* + past participle was functionally at a disadvantage because it was ambiguous: it was also used for the passive construction. Thus a phrase like *she was returned* could mean 'she had returned' as well as 'she had been returned'. In addition, the common abbreviation of both *has* and *is* to *'s* led to a further falling-together of the *be* and *have* verbs, under the more frequent perfect auxiliary *have*. The decline of *be* follows the typical S-curve: it is a slow but steady one in ME and early ModE. It picks up speed in Late ModE and comes to a climax in the nineteenth century, which witnesses a dramatic drop in the frequency of *be*.

3.3.3   Mood

Mood as a formal category is typically connected with the verb. Mood inflections on the verb are used to express the attitude of the speaker towards the factual content of a proposition. Thus in OE the indicative mood is commonly used in the context of an objective, factual report and is the rule in most constructions that do not involve grammatical dependence. The subjunctive is a subjective expression and is found especially in volitional, conjectural and hypothetical contexts, which are, as it were, one step removed from the situation as fact, from our purely socio-physical experience of the world. In OE the subjunctive occurs most frequently in dependent clauses, following a main clause which introduces modality lexically. In other words, the subjunctive is not (or no longer) a primary marker of modality: it has grammaticalised. Main clauses, where modality needed a stronger expression, already usually contained a modal verb in OE; a mere subjunctive inflection on the main verb did not suffice. In some cases the grammaticalisation of OE subjunctives has gone so far that the subjunctive form has become semantically meaningless. Thus when a subordinate clause depends on another subordinate clause, the subjunctive is the rule when the first clause has a subjunctive. We also often find an 'empty' subjunctive in indirect speech:

(33)   Wulfstan sæde þæt he gefore of   Hæðum, þæt he wære on
            Wulfstan said that he went from Hedeby, that he was in

            Truso   on syfan dagum &   nihtum
            Drusno in seven days   and nights

            þæt þæt scip wæs ealne weg yrnende under segle.
            that that ship was all   way running under sail
            'Wulfstan said that he departed from Hedeby, that he reached Drusno in
            seven days and nights, and that the ship was running under full sail all
            the way.'   (Or 1 1.16.21; Traugott, 1992: 240)

In (33) it is clear that the subjunctive is semantically empty since in the first two
reported clauses a subjunctive is used (*gefore*, *wære*), while in the third there is
an indicative (*wæs*).

The subjunctive and the modal verbs could be used to express three types of
modality in OE, usually referred to as deontic, dynamic and epistemic modality.
Deontic modality is connected with the issuing of directives and is concerned with
the speaker's wishes and intentions in relation to the addressee, thus involving
such notions as permission and obligation. Dynamic modality is related to the
ability and disposition of the speaker or subject, or to the possibilities open to
him/her. Together they are often referred to as 'root' modality, to distinguish them
from epistemic modality, which is quite different and is usually a later linguistic
development. Epistemic modality is concerned with the truth of the proposition,
expressing a speaker's belief or opinion concerning a situation. The examples in
(34)–(36) illustrate the three types of modality: deontic, dynamic and epistemic,
respectively. The (a) examples show the use of the subjunctive mood in dependent
clauses following a primary (lexical) modal marker in the main clause (italicised),
while the (b) examples use a modal verb as a primary marker in an independent
clause. The (b) examples of (34) and (35) are also given to indicate that the
dynamic and deontic use of the modals in main clauses is well established in
OE. This is not true for the epistemic use of modals, so that examples like (36b)
are in fact quite rare. Usually the text needs an additional lexical marker such
as *wenunga*, *eaþe* 'probably', 'possibly', 'easily'. It is interesting that instead of
an epistemic modal verb we do find a subjunctive used even in the main clause
in OE, as (36c) illustrates. It is likely that here the subjunctive lasted longer
because the modal auxilaries had not yet developed a clear epistemic function
in OE.

(34)
a. And micel is *nydþearf* manna gehwilcum þæt he Godes lage gime[SUBJ]
   and much is need   of-men each   that he God's law heed
   'And it is necessary for each man that he should heed God's law.'   (*WHom* 20.2 26)

b. Þa   ðe   bet   cunnon and magon. *sceolon* gyman oðra   manna.
   those who better can   and may   must   heed of-other men
   'Those who have more abilities should take care of other men.'
                                                      (*ÆCHom* II, 15 159.311)

(35)

a. þæt hit nan *wundor* nys,   þæt se halga cynincg untrumnysse gehæle[SUBJ]
   that it no wonder not-is that the holy king illnesses heal

   nu he on heofonum leofað
   now he in heavens lives
   'that it is no wonder that the holy king can heal sickness now that he lives in heaven'
(ÆLS (Oswald)272)

b. . . . ac he ne *mæg* nænne gehælan. þe   god sylf ær   geuntrumode.
   . . . but he not can none heal,   whom god self before made-sick
   ' . . . but he cannot heal anyone who had been made sick by God himself'
(ÆCHom I (Pref)175.81)

(36) a. Ne bið \<his\> lof   na ðy læsse, ac is *wen*   þæt hit
      not is his   praise not the less, but is probable that it

      sie[SUBJ] þy mare;
      be   the more
      'His praise will not be the less, but may be greater.'   (*Bo* 40.138.19)

   b. Eastewerd hit [se mor]   mæg bion syxtig mila   brad oþþe
      eastwards it [the waste land] can be   sixty of-miles broad or

      hwene   brædre
      somewhat broader
      'Towards the east it may be sixty miles wide or a little wider.'   (*Or* 1 1.15.26)

   c. . . . he gymde þy læs his agenra þearfa &   *wenunga* hine sylfne
      . . . he heeded the less his own   needs and probably him self

        forlete[SUBJ]
        neglected
        ' . . . he cared about his own needs less and less and probably neglected
        himself'   (*GD* 2 (C)3.106.10)

It is clear from these examples that mood can be expressed in many different ways. The marking may be primarily lexical, i.e. by means of full verbs, 'hedges' (e.g. phrases like *I guess, I think*), adverbs, idiomatic expressions, etc. One step down the ladder of grammaticalisation would be the use of modal auxiliaries, while the subjunctive is an even further grammaticalised form.

As far as the expression of mood in the history of English is concerned, we see two main shifts, both involving the modal verbs. First of all, there is the replacement of (subjunctive) inflections by periphrastic (modal) constructions. In grammaticalisation terms, this is the beginning of a new cycle, in that a bleached inflection becomes replaced by a new, more expressive modal verb. We see this already happening in subordinate clauses in later OE. Where, before, a subjunctive was sufficient to express mood (as shown in the (a) examples above), we more and more see the insertion of a modal verb in that position, often itself in the subjunctive. Compare the instances in (37) with a modal verb, to (34a) and (35a), which still have only a subjunctive inflection on the finite verb:

(37) a. Forþon   us is nydþearf, þæt þa mynstru   of   þære stowe *moten*[SUBJ]
       therefore us is need   that the monasteries from that   place must

       beon gecyrrede to oþre stowe.
       be   changed to other place
       'it is necessary therefore that the monasteries will be moved from that place to
       another'   (*GD* 2 (C)5.112.24)

    b. se Hælend cwæð to him,   gelyfe gyt þæt ic inc   *mæg* gehælan
      the Saviour said   to them, believe yet that I you-two can   heal
      'the Saviour said to them, do you believe me now that I can heal both of you?'
                                 (*Mt* (WSCp) 9.28)

This development was possible because modals were already fully employed in main clauses. The development was also necessary. In OE the verb had different forms for the following moods: indicative, imperative and subjunctive (see Chapter 2). However, already in OE not all endings were distinctive: there was no distinction between indicative and subjunctive in the past tense of strong verbs in the second-person singular, nor in the past tense of weak verbs in the first- and third-person singular. Distinctiveness decreased further in ME, where all -*e*, -*on*, -*en* endings fell together under -*e*, thus obliterating many earlier differences between indicative and subjunctive forms. In PDE practically all these endings have disappeared: only the stem form is left and one single inflection to mark the third-person singular present indicative, i.e. -*s*. The imperative is now distinguished only by its front position and the fact that usually no subject is present; the form itself does not differ from the indicative form (or rather the stem) in PDE. The PDE subjunctive has been reduced to a few relics like *were* (*If I were you*) and the occasional use of the stem form in subordinate clauses such as *It is necessary that every member* **inform** *himself of these rules*, and in main clauses (In its optative function) in set expressions like *Heaven forbid that . . .*

The second important shift concerns the modal verb itself. When it slowly grammaticalised into an auxiliary through replacing the subjunctive, it also began to enter the epistemic or discourse domain, taking the place of earlier *lexical* markers of epistemic modality. Thus whereas in OE it was usual to employ adverbs and predicative phrases such as *wenunga, eaþe, wen is þæt* '(it is) possible, probable', or verbal constructions such as *me þynceþ* 'me seems', to indicate epistemic modality, the modals begin to play a much larger role here in later English. In fact, this development has led to some modals becoming virtually restricted to the epistemic domain. Thus the form *might*, which used to have dynamic and deontic meanings (i.e. it expressed ability and – later – permission), is now (almost) exclusively used as an epistemic modal, so that *He might come a bit later* can only be understood as the description of a possibility, but not ability or permission; in its wake, an utterance like *He may come a bit later*, with the modal *may*, is now also gradually losing its permission sense, especially in American English.

Finally, one other development must be noted here, that of the so-called modal preterite. In OE it was usual to employ a past-tense subjunctive in hypothetical constructions, both in present and past-time contexts:

(38)   Witodlice næfde   godes gelaðung paulum to lareowe: gif se
        truly   not-had god's church   Paul   as teacher if the

        halga martyr stephanus swa ne   bæde.
        holy martyr Stephen   so   not asked
        'God's church would not have had St Paul as teacher, if the holy martyr
        Stephen had not asked for this.'   (*ÆCHom* I, 3 202.113)

In ME this preterite subjunctive was often replaced by a periphrastic construction
with a modal verb, but the old subjunctive form itself, which had now fallen in
with the preterite indicative, remained in use too, and served *by itself* as a modal
marker especially in present-tense contexts:

(39)   But soore wepte she if oon of hem were[SUBJ] deed, | Or if men smoot
        [INDIC] it with a yerde smerte
        'But she would weep sorely if one of them died or if someone hit it smartly
        with a stick.'   (Chaucer, *GProl.* 148–9)

Since past-tense indicative modal verbs were also used in such hypothetical situations in OE, the past tense of modals acquired a similar role, as we can see
from the translation of ME *wepte* into PDE *would weep*, and the past tense of
modal verbs gradually lost their 'pure' past-time reference; for details, see below.
When the hypothetical situation was placed in a past-tense context, the pluperfect
came to be used with the same modal colouring; this was a new development
in ME:

(40)   I dar wel seyn, if she *hadde been* a mous, | And he a cat, he wolde hire
        hente anon
        'I dare say, if she had been a mouse, and he a cat, he would have caught her
        at once.'   (Chaucer, *MillT* 3346–7)

Note again, that PDE would use a (plu)perfect in both main and subordinate
clause, whereas in ME the past modal *wolde* alone could still function there.

3.3.4   The story of the modals

In the previous section, we have looked at changes in the way mood
was expressed in English, especially the relation between subjunctive and modal
verbs, but we have not yet considered the modal verbs themselves and the changes
that took place there. The 'modal story' is particularly interesting because the
original modal verbs have changed much more radically in English than in any
of its sister languages. In English the modals have developed into what Warner
(1993: 49ff.) has called 'anaphorical islands', i.e. they show an 'independent
"word-like" status', with non-transparent morphology, in contrast to full verbs
which have transparent morphological inflections of person and tense. The modals
in other Germanic languages, on the other hand, have retained most of their verbal
features. Additionally, the story is of theoretical interest because it has been used to

support a generative linguistic view of change whereby certain grammar changes may have been 'radical', i.e. the idea that seemingly unrelated changes on the surface may be related to one, deeper and more abstract change in the base. Such evidence is important, since it may not only tell us more about how syntactic change takes place but may also serve as empirical evidence for the existence of such an abstract rule system, particularly for the degree of abstractness of this system; more generally, it may tell us more about the role the theory of grammar plays in change.

The idea of a radical change was first proposed by David Lightfoot (1974, 1979), who saw the modals as a paradigm case. His groundbreaking work has been followed by others but has also led to reactions from linguists who believed that the change was gradual rather than radical (notably Warner, 1983, 1993; Plank, 1984). Lightfoot's story briefly is as follows. In OE and ME the core modals *willan*, **sculan*, *magan*, **motan* and *cunnan* behaved like any other verb, and there is no reason to assume that they belonged to a special category, set apart from the category Verb (see Section 3.2.4). The descendants of these modals in PDE, *will*, *shall*, *may*, *must* and *can*, on the other hand, are no longer verbs but must be considered to belong to a separate category, namely Aux(iliary). Thus the pre-modals (as Lightfoot terms them) could occur in positions where they now no longer occur: they could be used in both finite and non-finite position, they could be found on their own with a direct object NP or complement clause, and they could be combined with another modal. The examples in (41) from OE and ME illustrate this:

(41) a. *as infinitive*
         To conne deye is to haue in all tymes his herte redy (ME, Warner, 1993:
         199, Caxton *The Arte and Crafte to knowe Well to Dye* 2)

     b. *two modals combined*
         &   hwu muge we þone weig cunnen?
         and how may   we the   way can
         'And how can we know the way?'   (OE, *Jn* (Warn 30)14.5)

     c. *as present participle*
         Se ðe bið butan   willan besmiten oððe se ðe willende on slæpe
         He who is without will   defiled or   who willing in sleep

         gefyrenað, singe <XXIV> sealma.
         fornicates, sing 24   psalms
         'Whoever is defiled against his will or who, willingly, fornicates in his
         sleep, let him sing twenty-four psalms'   (OE, *Conf* 1.1(Spindler) 46)

     d. *as past participle*
         Wee wolden han gon toward tho trees full gladly, ʒif wee had might
         (ME, Visser §2042, Mandeville 196, 34)

     e. *with an object*
         He cwæð þæt he sceolde him hundteontig mittan hwætes.
         He said that he owed   him (a) hundred bushels of-wheat
                                              (OE, *ÆHom* 17 26)

f.   *with a clause*
Leof cynehlaford, ic wille, þæt þu beo æt minum gebeorscipe
dear liege-lord, I will that you be at my   banquet
'Dear lord, I would like you to be present at my banquet'
(OE, *ÆHomM* 14 (Ass 8) 185)

In the course of the OE and ME periods a number of 'unrelated' changes took place
that isolated the pre-modals from the other verbs (cf. Lightfoot, 1979: 101–9):

(42)
(i)   the pre-modals lost the ability to take direct objects
(ii)   the pre-modals were the only preterite-present verbs left; all others of this class were lost
(iii) the past-tense forms of the pre-modals no longer signal past-time reference
(iv)   the pre-modals alone take a bare infinitive; all other verbs start taking *to*-infinitives

These changes are believed to be unrelated because they are accidental (especially
(ii) and (iv), which concern the behaviour of verbs other than the pre-modals)
and/or because they do not happen at the same time. The changes had a common effect, however, in that they resulted in the isolation of the pre-modals: they
became 'identifiable as a unique class' (Lightfoot, 1979: 109). The evidence for
this category change is to be found in the fact that the pre-modals now underwent a second phase of changes, which *were* related and which did take place
simultaneously (Lightfoot, 1979: 110):

(43) (i)   the old pre-modals could no longer appear in infinitival constructions
      (ii)   the old pre-modals could no longer occur as present participles
      (iii)   the old pre-modals could no longer occur as past participles
      (iv)   the old pre-modals could no longer occur in combination (except in some
              dialects, such as Modern Scots)

The simultaneity of these changes, according to Lightfoot, provides evidence
that a deep, radical change must have taken place in the abstract system, which
dissolved the verbal status of the pre-modals (i.e. they became a new category,
that of Auxiliary) and thus forced the four characteristics given in (43) upon them.
The simultaneity, therefore, is crucial.

   There are a number of problems with this story. First of all, all the characteristics
given in (43) involve losses, and such negative evidence is very difficult to date.
The evidence would have been more convincing if, due to the category change to
Aux, the modals began to occur in *new* constructions, but this is not the case. Also
note that the first change under (42), the loss of direct objects after pre-modals,
is really on a par with the changes under (43). It too involves a feature that would
be the result of a category change from Verb to Aux. Since losses are difficult to
spot in time, (42i) could as easily have been placed under the changes of (43).
Indeed, examples of modals with a direct object are found quite late, i.e. after
1500, the time of the purported change. Visser (§§551, 557–8) notes examples
with *can* until 1652, with *may* until 1597 and with *will* until 1862. Another aspect
that remains hidden under the notion of 'losses' is the interesting fact that (43)

mostly involves ME losses and not OE ones: the use of infinitive forms and of past and present participles was actually more frequent in ME than in OE. With a story of loss, one would expect the frequencies to be the other way around. The paucity of these forms in OE may be due to a lack of data, although that is unlikely (see Plank, 1984: 314), but the new forms in ME may also be due to changes taking place elsewhere: for example, the occurrence of two modals in combination is found mainly with *shall* and begins to occur only after *shall* has developed into a future-tense auxiliary (see Visser §§1685, 2134). Warner (1993: 101) also notes that the pre-modals became more verbal rather than less in ME, with *shall*, *can* and *may* developing full verb inflectional endings such as third-person -*eþ* in both the singular and the plural in southern texts, and the occurrence of certain non-finite forms that had not been attested in OE (see also below).

Another aspect that has been questioned is whether the changes in (42) are really unrelated and accidental. If we start from the assumption, as many linguists do, that already in OE the pre-modals were set apart from other verbs as a group (see Warner 1993: 152, 97ff.), then the changes under (42) can easily be seen as related. We saw above that in OE the past-tense modals could be used to express present-time modality, so in that respect they differed from 'normal' verbs. As to verbal complementation, (42iv), not much changes here. In OE there was only a restricted class of verbs that could take a bare infinitive. This class comprised the modals, verbs of physical perception ('see', 'hear') and causatives (OE *lætan*, *biddan*, *hatan*). With a few exceptions (i.e. there were some verbs that could take both bare and *to*-infinitives: e.g. *þencan* 'think' in OE, and in ME also *helpen*, *maken*), all other verbs took only *to*-infinitival complements. There is no evidence that the *to*-infinitive encroached on the domain of the bare infinitive in ME. It is true that the *to*-infinitive became much more frequent in ME, but this is due to the fact that it started replacing *that*-clauses, the distribution of the bare infinitive itself remaining relatively unaffected in ME (Los, 2005). As to the loss of all other preterite-present verbs, (42ii), Harris & Campbell write (1995: 179): 'But if auxiliary variants of the modal verbs already existed, it was the entire class of preterite-present verbs that was lost, and it was no accident.' Indeed, if the pre-modals were already looked upon as a subgroup in OE, then this very fact may have pushed the other preterite-present verbs out of the system. Harris & Campbell suggest that the modals in OE fell into two homophonous categories, one an auxiliary and the other a fully lexical verb. The OE examples given in (41) in fact illustrate this well: thus the infinitive *cunnen* (41b), the present participle *willende* (41c), *sceolde* with a direct object (41e), and *wille* with a object clause (41f) are all examples of the pre-modals used with full referential meaning, i.e. without deontic or dynamic modality. When the modals began to play a more important and frequent role in the ME period due to the loss of the subjunctive, it was the homophonous lexical pre-modals that began to die out, while the truly modal pre-modals developed further, at first still maintaining their verbal status, but gradually developing into more independent 'word-like' elements.

It is interesting to observe that the ME increase in the infinitival and participial forms of the pre-modals may have been connected with the development of periphrastic constructions to express the future and the perfect (see Sections 3.3.1 and 3.3.2). The pre-modals (which were, after all, auxiliary-like too) were caught up in this, forming combinations with the auxiliaries of tense and aspect (just as they had combined with the auxiliaries of the passive in OE), and we see constructions such as *shall may* and *have mought* occurring. The subsequent disappearance of these infinitival and participial forms presumably has to do with the fact that they were awkward to begin with (as we have seen, they were rare to non-existent in OE), and with the fact that the homophonous lexical modals, which could have given support to these non-finite forms, had become truly separated from their sisters (indeed they all eventually became obsolescent). Another problem may well have been that the modals' tense forms were already used in OE as modality markers, i.e. they were not strict members of the tense system. This non-tense characteristic became reinforced in ME with the loss of the subjunctive and the subsequent rise of indicative past-tense modal markers to take their place (see Section 3.3.3). In other words, the modals did not sit well in a system of tense or aspect, and this made the combination with perfect *have* and future *shall* difficult. Finally, the order of the auxiliary verbs presumably plays a role in this development as well, as suggested by Warner (1993); we will look at this in more detail in Section 3.3.7.

Because of the loss of tense distinctions in the modals, we begin to witness the rise of periphrastic modals or 'exploratory expressions' to indicate the sense of ability and obligation in the past. These same expressions could then easily spread to other non-finite positions, which in turn may have aided the disappearance of non-finite modal forms.

(44) a. For certes, by no force ne by no meede [bribe], | Hym thoughte, he was not able for to speede [be successful]   (Chaucer, *Phys.T* 133–4)

b. By wey of kynde [nature], ye oghten to been able | To have pite of folk that be in peyne.   (Chaucer, *Mars* 282–3)

c. As she was bown to goon the wey forth right | Toward the gardyn ther as she had hight [promised]   (Chaucer, *Frk.T* 1503–4)

d. . . . that thow art bounde to shewen hym al the remenaunt of thy sinnes (Chaucer, *Pars.T* 1007)

Next to *to be able to* and *to be bound to*, there are other expressions in use early (*to have power/might, to be to*). The emergence of today's regular periphrastic constructions such as *have (got) to* and *be compelled to* is somewhat later. It is interesting to observe too that these periphrastic modals, like their predecessors the pre-modals, follow more or less the same path. They are first used dynamically and deontically, while epistemic use is always later. *Have to*, for instance, developed into a deontic modal at the beginning of the eModE period, but its epistemic use (as in *It has to be true that . . .*) is quite recent. Similarly, there is a tendency for these periphrastic modals to lose their non-finite forms, just as their predecessors did. *Have got* (now often reduced to *got*), for instance, is finite only, and so are *had/'d rather* and *(had/'d) better*. Instances with non-finite *be to* now sound distinctly archaic:

(45) a. You will be to visit me in prison with a basket of provisions
          (Austen, *Mansfield Park* I.xiv.135; Denison, 1998: 174)

     b. N.B. No snuff being to be had in the village she made us some.
          (Keats, *Letters* 78 p. 189 (20 Jul.); Denison, 1998: 174)

To sum up, the evidence for assuming that there was only one homogeneous verbal category in OE, which included the pre-modals, as suggested by Lightfoot, is not all that strong. It is not the case that the pre-modals developed more and more exception features in the OE and ME period; they were exceptional within the category of verbs to start with but retained their verbal status, certainly still in ME. After the ME period they became isolated more and more, losing the trappings of full verbs in the process, but this happened slowly and not in the same way for each pre-modal. It may be that the pre-modals have become so opaque as verbs that they should be considered a different category, i.e. Aux, but the problem is that it is hard if not impossible to pinpoint when such a change could have taken place. It is clear that within the verbal class there is a continuum running from full verbs to auxiliary-like verbs, where all the different features (verbal and less-than-verbal) available are distributed unevenly across the original pre-modals, other modals and other auxiliary-like verbs such as perfect *have*, passive *be*, *do* etc.

In some varieties of English, there is evidence that the modals have undergone further development after reaching their auxiliary-like status. In Southern American English and Scottish English, combinations of two modals can be found, as in the examples in (28); see further Chapter 7:

(46) a. I thought you said we might could get some candy.
     b. If we had known, we may still could have done it.
     c. He will can do it.

These combinations are first attested in the period 1750–1850. They are therefore not likely to be direct continuations of the pattern in (41b), *hwu muge we þone weig cunnen?* 'how may we the way can', i.e. 'how can we know the way?', which disappeared after the ME period (and in which the second modal always had a clearly infinitival form). Rather, the double modals in (46) seem to represent an innovation, which may find its origin in a reinterpretation from modal to (epistemic) adverb. This would mean that in each example there is a sequence Adverb–Modal (or Modal–Adverb), making these sentences quite unexceptional apart from the specific form that the adverb takes. Some support for this analysis comes from interrogative and negative clauses with 'double modals', as in (47a, b), and an admittedly very rare type with a 'modal' and a form of *do*, as in (47c):

(47) a.   Could you might possibly use a teller machine?
     b.   They might not could have gone over the state line to get her.
     c.   Could be he may didn't want to come.

All three sentences could be viewed as featuring a regular auxiliary together with a modal-derived adverb (*might, could* and *may* in (47), respectively), for which perhaps the term 'post-modal' might be appropriate. The distribution of sentences like (47) fits in well with this analysis of double modals: they have been found to be frequent especially in face-to-face conversation, where they typically have a hedging, politely suggestive and non-intrusive sense. It is not surprising to see that in these contexts, politeness is reinforced by the use of an extra hedging marker in the form of a post-modal. Whatever the precise nature of the construction (and its possible further spread, or loss, in the years to come), it is certainly interesting to see that well-known historical changes in the syntax of English, such as the large-scale developments that have affected the modals, do not simply stop once the stage of Modern English has been reached; on the contrary, they continue to play themselves out and thereby make themselves available for much more detailed investigation than we can ever hope to achieve for aspects of the change completed at earlier periods.

3.3.5   Voice

From earliest times English has made use of a periphrastic construction to express the passive, the original (medio-)passive inflectional endings of Germanic having been lost at a prehistoric stage. The only remnant of this old system in OE is seen in the verb *hatan*. The meaning of this verb in OE was 'to call' (next to some other meanings such as 'promise', 'command'), and medio-passive forms such as sg *hatte*/pl *hatton*, '(s)he was called/they were called', were in use till the beginning of the ME period. Due to its exceptional position within the system of voice, these forms were eventually lost, aided no doubt by the availability of the Old Norse loanword *kalla* 'to call', which, used in the periphrastic passive, replaced it. In German and Dutch, the medio-passive form remained but acquired a new, active-looking infinitive – *heissen/heten* 'to be called' – which, as it were, lexicalised the passive meaning. Such a development also took place in ME when a new verb *highten* 'to be called' developed, but this was short-lived.

The OE periphrastic passive was formed with *weorþan* and *beon/wesan*. It is tempting to assume that *weorþan* functioned like its Modern German and Dutch counterparts *werden* and *worden* in denoting process rather than state, but there is no firm or conclusive evidence to be found in the OE documents. Presumably *weorþan*, used elsewhere in OE in the sense of 'become' rather than 'be', may have indicated process rather than result at first, but in many OE writers no difference is made in the passive construction between *weorþan* on the one hand and *beon/wesan* on the other. It is possible to read 'process' into the *weorþan* instances in (48) and 'resultant state' into the *wæs*-construction, but it is difficult to be certain:

(48)

On þæm feorþan geare his   rices   he gefeaht wiþ Gotan, &   gefliemed
In the   fourth   year of-his kingdom he fought with Goths, and put-to-flight

wearð, &   bedrifen on   anne tun, &   þær   wearð on anum huse
was   and pursued into a   town and there was   in a   house

forbærned.   þær   wæs swiþe ryht dom   geendad þæt hie   þone
burned-to-death. There was very just sentence ended   that they that-one

woroldlice forbærndon   þe   hie   þohte bærnan on ecnesse.
worldly   burned-to-death who them thought burn in eternity

'In the fourth year of his reign, he fought against the Goths, and was put to flight and got
trapped in a village, and there was burned to death in a house. A very just sentence was
carried out there in that they burned to death the person who intended letting them burn
in eternity.'   (*Or* 6 34.153.14; Traugott, 1992: 199)

Presumably, because the difference in meaning between *weorþan* and *beon/wesan*
became indistinct in OE, a tendency arose to use only the *beon/wesan* form, which
was the most frequent form; by the late ME period *weorþan* was no longer used.

The changes taking place in the periphrastic passive are typical of a grammaticalisation process. At first we see the use of full or, in this case, copula verbs
like *beon* or *weorþan* combined with a past participle that is used adjectivally.
At this stage the verbs in question still must have had their own, lexical meanings (i.e. expressing 'state' and 'process' respectively). Evidence that the past
participles were adjectival can be found in the fact that in OE there are traces of
declined past participles. In the *Orosius* (the text used in (48)), we still find both,
but apparently without any difference in meaning: compare *ii æþelingas wurdon
afliemed of Sciþþium* (*Or* Head 1.10) with *wurdon twegen æþelingas afliemde
of Sciþþian* (*Or* 1 10.29.14), 'two princes got/were banished from Scythia'. The
past participles and the copula verbs next come to be looked upon as part of a
new passive construction through their increasingly frequent use and the almost
complete absence of an inflectional passive. Consequently both elements lose
their independent status as adjectives (through loss of adjectival trappings) and
verbs (meanings becoming bleached), respectively. While the initial 'exploratory'
periphrastic passives still show many variants, it is usual at the end of the grammaticalisation chain for just one variant to survive; in this case that is the verb
be. The choice of *be* as the passive auxiliary, and the loss of *weorþan*, must have
led to the exploration of new ways to express the difference between process and
result. The first instances of a new process passive with *get* are encountered in
the seventeenth century and have become very popular since then. Other process
verbs used are *fall* and *become*, and new resultative verbs are *remain*, *stay*.

Alongside changes taking place in the verbal part of the passive construction,
there are a number of very interesting developments in the types of construction
in which passives could occur. In OE only the direct object of a transitive verb
could fill the subject position in a passive construction. In ME this position could
also be filled by indirect and prepositional objects. This development will be

discussed in Sections 3.4.4 and 3.5.6. Secondly, in OE there was a very limited use of passive infinitives, which are only found after modal verbs. In all other constructions where we now use a passive infinitive, an active form of the infinitive was used instead (often called the 'passival infinitive'). This development is further discussed in Section 3.4.5.

3.3.6   Rise of *do*

A major feature of English is the obligatory use of *do* in negative and interrogative sentences when there is no other auxiliary present. In these cases *do* is used as an empty 'operator', that is, it is a purely grammatical element without any referential meaning. Operator *do* is the end result of a grammaticalisation process that started in the ME period. As is usual in such a situation, grammaticalised *do* developed out of full-verb *do*. In what follows, we will look at what full-verb uses of *do* may have been the source of the operator and, secondly, we will sketch what the causes may have been that led to the rather idiosyncratic grammaticalisation of *do* in English. For the possibility that the rise of *do* was connected with the presence of a Celtic substratum, see Klemola (2002).

There are a number of candidates for the origin of operator *do*. Full verb uses of *do* usually cited are causative *do*, anticipative *do* and substitute *do*. All three uses already occurred in the OE period, and are indeed common usages in all other West Germanic languages:

(49)   . . . and deþ hi   sittan, and he gæþ sylf and hym þenað.
          . . . and does them sit,   and he goes self and them serves
          '. . . and makes them sit down, and goes himself and serves them'
                                                              (*ÆHom* 26.1 8)

(50)   . . . ac utan   don swa us þearf is, gelæstan hit georne.
          . . . but let-us do as   us need is, perform   it carefully
          '. . . but let us do as we should, i.e. carry it out with care'
                                                              (*WHom* 8c 125)

(51)   and hit þær forbærnð   þæt mancyn, swa hit her   ær   dyde.
          and it there burns-to-death that people, as it here before did
          'and it will burn those people to death, as it has done here before'
                                                              (*HomU* 35.1 (Nap 43) 9)

Note that as candidates for the origin of empty *do*, (49)–(51) each have their advantages and drawbacks. Causative *do*, (49), shows the required syntactic pattern in that it is immediately followed by an infinitive, but with the notion of 'causation' this *do* seems less than ideal, because the loss or bleaching of causation should result in a different sense in the context. It should also be noted that the more usual causatives in this construction in OE were *biddan* and *lætan*, and that *do* only becomes frequent here in ME. The meaning change is less of an obstacle, however, when we consider that causation is often implicit in transitive verbs, i.e. many verbs (e.g. *break*, *build*) can be both causative and non-causative, depending on context. Thus a causative *do* combined with such verbs could be 'equivocal', i.e. *do* could be read as either a causative or an empty verb. Many such cases are found in ME, where causative *do* with an infinitive was itself also more frequent:

(52)   A noble churche heo dude a-rere
         a noble church   she did   raise
         'She built a noble church / she had a noble church built'
                    (*Sleg.* (Ld) 4.118; Fischer, 1992: 271)

Here the context makes clear that the subject was not likely to do the building herself, and we see that in PDE too both a straight transitive verb and a causative construction can be used. Such a situation enables the ME language user to read *do* as empty of meaning.

The anticipative and substitute uses of *do* in (50) and (51), respectively, are perhaps better candidates from a semantic point of view because here *do* is practically empty of content already. They function as a kind of prop to the main verb, so that in the context they take on the meaning of the main verb. Syntactically, however, they are less appropriate because with anticipative *do* the infinitive does not immediately follow, while with substitute *do*, the matrix verb precedes and is not even infinitival.

We are still somewhat in the dark as to what constructions provided the origin or what factors were most crucial to the development. It should be stressed that general verbs like *do* are a frequent source for grammaticalisation developments in any language: *do*, in other words, is always around to be used when necessary. It has been noticed, for instance, that in many languages causative *do* comes to express perfective aspect because it is natural, when something needs to be done, that one concentrates on the resultant state. Denison (1985) indeed suggests that 'perfective' *do* may have been an intermediate stage between causative *do* and operator *do*. Another factor that may have aided the rise of empty *do* in ME is the large influx of French loanwords. Such new verbs can be difficult to fit into the native inflectional system, and a way of avoiding a hybrid form (a French word with an English past tense in *-ed* or a present in *-est* or *-es/-eth*) would be to use a form of the all-purpose verb *do* plus an infinitive (a strategy for incorporating loan verbs that is in fact found in several other languages). Once *do* has become more common, it may also begin to be used more frequently with other infinitives, possibly for phonotactic reasons (e.g. when a cluster of consonants – *thou imaginedst* – can be avoided this way), for reasons of rhyme and meter, for emphasis, for clarity (to disambiguate verbs like *set, put* which have the same form in present and past), etc. All these factors have been mentioned and investigated in the vast amount of literature on *do*, and no doubt they all played some role.

Whatever caused the initial spread of *do* in late ME, it is clear that after this initial period we see a very steep rise of empty *do* in the second half of the sixteenth century in all types of clause: affirmative, interrogative and negative. This very sudden increase, and the later quite rapid decline of *do* in affirmative clauses in the seventeenth century, cannot quite be explained by the simple continuation of the factors mentioned above. Most linguists believe that there must have been other macro-causes for this rather special development. Three major factors have been mentioned: (i) the rise of periphrastic constructions elsewhere (in the tense, aspect, mood and voice systems); (ii) the increasing fixity of word order as SVO; and (iii) changes in the position of the adverbial.

Concerning the first, it seems likely that this may have influenced the initial increase but it cannot really be held responsible for the sudden decrease in affirmative *do* in the seventeenth century. It is possible that other periphrastic constructions (such as the progressive) became available in affirmative clauses to take over some of the uses affirmative *do* had been put to, but more likely it was combination with the other two factors that triggered the demise of affirmative *do*.

The fixation of word order has to do with the loss of the so-called verb-second rule; more will be said about that in Section 3.5. What is crucial for us here is that in OE the verb could appear in different positions in the clause. By the late ME period, however, it had become the rule for the lexical verb to immediately precede the object, i.e. the language was firmly VO, and for the subject to be positioned before the verb, i.e. the language was SV. In questions without an auxiliary, however, the direct adjacency of lexical verb and object and the order subject–verb would be disturbed. Thus compare declarative (53) with interrogative (54):

(53)   He knew the danger (subject–verb–object)

(54)   Knew he the danger? (verb–subject–object)

Inversion of S and V in sentences like (54) was a grammatical marker with a semantic function, i.e. it made a clause interrogative. Of course, intonation by itself could do the job (as it does in many languages and to some extent in English too), but the availability of *do* made it possible to have a finite verb in initial position, indicating the interrogative nature of the clause, while at the same time keeping the main verb fixed between S and O, in accordance with the VO nature of the language.

(55)   Did he know the danger? (subject–verb–object)

Evidence supporting this idea is the fact that *do* was first more frequent in yes/no questions (this may have been further assisted by the fact that only yes/no questions use verbal tags containing *do*), and only later became more current in other types of question which possessed an additional interrogative marker such as a wh-element. Thus in the early stages we would have the use of *do* in sentences like (55), where *do* 'helps' to keep both S and O close to the matrix verb, whereas *do* was less necessary in sentences like *What said he* and *When came he*, where there was an interrogative marker in the form of the wh-element and where, in addition, there was no object that had to be positioned next to the verb, due to wh-movement and an intransitive matrix verb, respectively.

For very similar reasons, inversion of S and V after adverbials and other initial elements (in sentences like *Then went these people to the town*) was lost around this time too. Here, too, *do* could have been selected in order to keep the inverted order (as it indeed did after negative elements like *only*), but very little was lost here semantically – in contrast to the interrogatives – and so the more usual solution was to give up the inversion. This was moreover helped by the fact that personal pronouns already appeared here in the position *before* the finite verb (i.e. the usual order was *Then they went to the town*), due to their clitic nature (see further Sections 3.5.2 and 3.5.3). Now that all subjects were no longer inverted, the cliticisation of pronouns was abandoned too.

Fixed word order, in other words, played an influential role in generalising already available *do* in questions. Denison (1993: 467) suggests that the increase of semi-lexicalised units, such as *take place*, *pay heed to*, *call out*, etc., may also have been influential in the increase of *do*, because again *do* would serve here to keep the idiom together in questions and negatives.

The spread of *do* in negatives is slightly more complicated. Besides fixed word order, a role is played by the general tendency for the negative element (*ne* in OE and later) to occur before the finite verb. *Not*, in the form of *naht*, *noht*, *nawiht* etc., first came to be used in OE as a reinforcer placed after the verb, creating a multiple negative as in *Ne derode Iobe naht þæs deofles costnung* 'not harmed Job not the devil's temptation' (*ÆCHom* II, 262.61). Gradually the use of a second negative increased, so that in ME two negatives became the rule. This paved the way for the loss of *ne*. *Not* then took over as a single negative, but still at first in its old position – thus no longer in the preferred position. It is not surprising, therefore, that we begin to see some variation in the placement of *not*, both in its 'old' postverbal position (cf. *cowde not*, *dredeþ not* in (56a,c)), and before the verb (*not herd*, *not repente* in (56a,b)):

(56) a. I seyd I cowde not tellyn that I not herd
                    (*Paston Letters* 705.51–2; Ukaji, 1992: 454)
      b. I not repente me of my late disguise
                    (Jonson, *Volpone* II.iv.27; Ukaji, 1992: 454)
      c. þise maner of pepull dredeþ not God ne noon seynte in heven
                    (*ME Sermons* 69.13–14; Jack, 1978: 66)

Both constructions were found unsatisfactory: postverbal *not* was not in the natural position for the negative with respect to the verb and separated the verb from its complement in clauses without an auxiliary, as in (56c), while preverbal *not* separated the main verb from the subject. Ellegård (1953: 194ff.) also notes that there was a general tendency in the fifteenth and sixteenth centuries for 'light adverbs' to move to preverbal position. This caused *not*, after the loss of *ne*, 'to stand out as an exception'. (56a) also shows that the position of *not* after an auxiliary (*cowde*) was better placed for ultimate success because the intimate connection between the negative and the main verb (*tellyn*) was not disturbed, while the subject was still next to the verbal part that carried the INFL (tense, number) characteristics. As Denison (1993: 467) writes, the order Aux *not* Verb was also probably the most frequently occurring pattern (cf. factor (i) above concerning the general rise of periphrastic constructions), so it cannot come as a surprise that this order became the preferred one in negative sentences and thus, as it were, forced *do* into the negative clause pattern.

Empirical evidence for the idea that the awkward place of adverbial *not* played a role can be found in Ellegård (1953: 195), who notes that the use of *do* in negative sentences is consistently higher with transitive verbs than with intransitive verbs, thus stressing the importance of the need to keep main verb and object together. Secondly, there are a number of verbs that resist pre-placement of *not* and take longer to accept the *do*-periphrasis. This group consists of verbs such as *say*, *think*, *hope*, *know*, *doubt*, *trow*, *woot*, *fear*, etc. It is precisely this group of verbs with which negatives typically can have two different scopes: the scope can be over the matrix verb or just its complement. In most instances in which these verbs are used, however, the scope of the negative will be the complement rather than the verb itself, which means that the position of *not after* the verb is more appropriate for these verbs. Note that in tag expressions like *I hope not*, *I think not*, where the negative clearly concerns the content of the hoping and thinking, and not the absence of the mental action itself, postverbal placement of *not* is still the rule.

3.3.7   Internal structure of the Aux phrase

We have already seen that a large number of new periphrastic constructions developed in the ME period and beyond, to express tense, mood and aspect distinctions that had formerly been part of the inflectional form of the verb. Two points need to be discussed in connection with these new auxiliaries, namely the diachronic order in which they develop and occur combined with each other, and the linear sequencing of these auxiliaries at each synchronic stage. The more grammaticalised these auxiliaries became, the more strict we would expect their ordering principles to be (grammatical items are usually strictly bound in the syntax of the clause, which is much less true for fully referential lexical items). This expectation is fully borne out in the case of the grammatical markers in the verbal group; in fact, the developments here ultimately resulted in one of the most orderly and systematic areas of English syntax. Denison (2000a) provides a very useful overview of the earliest occurrence of various combinations of auxiliaries (see Table 3.3). Table 3.3 makes clear that the modals were the first to find a firm position in the auxiliary system; already in OE they freely combine with the passive auxiliary (*It can be* sung, not shown in Denison's table), with perfect *have* (*He must have sung it*) and with progressive *be* (*He will be singing it*), even though the latter two were only just developing. This is presumably because from the very beginning the modals were followed by infinitives, and it was only a small step from a full verb infinitive to an auxiliary-like infinitive. The combinations of other auxiliaries was in each case later because they first had to develop firm auxiliary status before they could be combined with verbs that they had never before been combined with. For instance, *have* was in OE only found with a past participle of a full, transitive verb. Only when *have* had lost its independent

Table 3.3 *Combinations of auxiliaries in the verbal group (adapted from Denison, 2000a: 139)*

Pattern	Date:	first pair	second pair	three auxiliaries
Modal + Perfect + Progr. + V (*he will have been singing it*)		OE	a.1325	?a.1425
Modal + Perfect +Passive *be* + V (*it will have been sung*)		OE	c.1180	c.1300
Perfect + Progr. + Passive *be* + V (*it has been being sung*)		a.1325	1772	1886/1929
Modal + Progr. + Passive *be* + V (*it will be being sung*)		OE	1772	1915
Modal + Perfect + Passive GET + V (*it will have gotten sung*)		OE	1832	1950–
Modal + Progr. + Passive GET + V (*it will be getting sung*)		OE	1819	PDE
Perfect + Progr. + Passive GET + V (*it has been getting sung*)		a.1325	1819	PDE

status did it come to occur in combinations with passive *be* (*It has been sung*) and progressive *be* (*He has been singing it*) (all in ME). The combinations of passive and progressive *be* are all late (rows 3 and 4 in Table 3.3), much later than even the four-verb combinations that did not result in double *be* (the first two in Table 3.3). It is very likely that the awkwardness of double *be* played a role in this. There is a natural tendency in language to avoid repetition of grammatical forms in immediate succession. Presumably the two *be*'s first had to grammaticalise into *separate* lexical items (see also below) before they could co-occur.

Warner (1993) emphasises that the combinatory possibilities of the auxiliaries is very much constrained by the category and subcategorisation properties that each auxiliary has. For instance, modals must be followed by an infinitival form. Because the modals do not possess an infinitival form, they cannot occur consecutively to another modal. This then forbids combinations of modals syntactically in standard English even though semantically they make perfect sense (as the occurrence of 'double modals' in American and Scottish English shows; see Section 3.3.3 above). Likewise, because modals do not have participial forms, they cannot occur *after* perfect *have* and progressive *be*, which are subcategorised for a past and present participle, respectively. In other words, in English the modal must occupy the first slot in the VP. The case with perfect *have* is slightly different. Unlike the modals, it possesses an infinitival form, but like the modals it lacks a participle (note that the present participle of perfect *have* may occur in non-finite clauses). Consequently, perfect *have* can occur after a modal, but it cannot occur after passive or progressive *be* because both of these are subcategorised for a participle. Warner thus shows that the ordering constraints are formal rather than semantic, as follows:

(57)   Finite – infinitive – past participle – progressive participle – passive participle

These developments also show that an essential aspect of the grammaticalisation of the auxiliaries was their moving away from the original full verbs they developed from. We saw this with the modals in Section 3.3.4. The core modals lost their non-finite forms in the course of their development into auxiliaries. Likewise the *full* verb *have* still possesses a past participle *had* and a present participle *having*; perfect *have*, however, has neither, at least in finite clauses. It is the loss of such forms in the course of grammaticalisation, which, as it were, led automatically to the formal position that the auxiliaries acquire in the order given in (57), which can be described lexically as follows:

(58)   modal – perfect *have* – progressive *be* – passive *be* – main verb

Warner (1993) shows that the obsolescence of certain constructions can be squared with this scenario of lexicalisation via grammaticalisation. Thus before *is to* had grammaticalised into a 'true' modal, having only a finite form like other modals, it could still occur in a position which is not available to modals according to the schemes in (57)–(58). The examples given in (45) above show this. In (45a) modal *be to* itself follows a modal, while in (45b) it still occurs in a non-finite form. As long as the progressive was not fully grammaticalised, the progressive auxiliary could still occur in all non-finite forms, just like the verb it derived from. Once it had got fitted into the order of (58), it became subject to its restrictions. Thus we still have a past participle of progressive *be*: *he has been playing the piano*, because the progressive slot occurs after the perfect slot. However, since neither the modal slot nor perfect *have* require a form *being*, this form was lost for progressive *be*.

3.4   Clausal constituents

3.4.1   Subjects

Throughout its history, English has had a stable system of grammatical functions in active clauses that contain an agent expression: the agent of the clause functions as the subject, the theme or affected entity functions as the direct object, and the recipient or experiencer as the indirect object, while other roles, such as instrument or source, have adjunct status. In (59) we give two present-day examples in which notional roles and grammatical functions are linked in this way. Sentences of this type have existed since the earliest records of the language (although there have of course been changes in case marking and word order; see Sections 3.2 and 3.5).

(59) a.   They had promised   him   a large sum of money.
          AGENT   RECIPIENT   THEME
     b.   He had borrowed   some books   from the library   with his friend's library card
          AGENT   THEME   SOURCE   INSTRUMENT

However, even within the basic clause type illustrated in (59), certain variations and alternations are possible, and these have seen several changes in the types of elements that can function as specific clausal constituents. As far as subjects arc concerned, the principal changes have to do with empty subjects and dummy subjects.

First, let us look at empty subjects, as in PDE (60) and (61). We use the symbol Ø to mark the empty subjects.

(60)   Ø seems he is not coming back.

(61)   Unfortunately, however, when Ø came to pour out tea Ø realised Ø did not
            have any milk or sugar (Helen Fielding, 'Bridget Jones's Diary', *Daily
            Telegraph*, 2/5/1998, p. 24)

The sentence in (60) illustrates omission of an *it* which has no referential meaning but would be present just to fill the subject slot in clauses containing a subordinate argument clause; we will use the label 'null dummy subject' for this phenomenon. The sentence in (61) is different, since the empty subject position has to be interpreted as *I*, a meaningful pronoun. In PDE, the distribution of these two types of empty subjects is not exactly the same: *it*-omission as in (60) appears to be characteristic of informal speech, while pronoun omission of the type seen in (61) (for which the term *pro*-drop is sometimes used) is typical of diary style (see Haegeman, 1997).

Null dummy subjects are plentifully attested in OE texts; an example is (62). The corresponding example in (63) makes clear that use of an overt *it/hit* dummy subject was also possible.

(62)   nis   me earfeðe to geþolianne þeodnes   willan
            not io me difficult to endure   lord-GEN will-ACC
            'It is not difficult for me to endure the Lord's will.'   (*Guth* A,B 1065)

(63)   hit bið swiðe unieðe ægðer to donne
            it is very   difficult either to do
            'It is very difficult to do either.'   (*CP* 46.355.19)

In ME texts both null and overt dummy subjects continue to exist side by side; an example with a null dummy subject from this period can be seen in (64).

(64)   himm   wass lihht to lokenn himm   fra   þeyre laþe wiless
            for-him was   easy to keep   himself from   their evil wiles
            'It was easy for him to protect himself against their evil wiles.'
                                                        (*Orm* 10316)

After 1500, however, only the variant with overt dummy *it* survives in the written record (and therefore becomes correspondingly more frequent). Some suggestions have been made about the possible causes of this development (increased fixity of subject–verb order being one of them; compare Section 3.5.2), but the existence of informal spoken examples like (60) in PDE must make us hesitate to declare null dummy subjects dead and buried by 1500. Rather, the development appears to have been from general use of null dummies in OE to restricted use in PDE.

The history of *pro*-drop in English, as in sentence (61), presents us with a somewhat similar picture. The usual account of the development holds that *pro*-drop was possible (but not very frequent) in OE, and disappeared well before the present time. An OE example of the phenomenon is given in (65):

(65)   ... Ø wolde   on ðam westene   wæstmes tilian
         ... Ø wanted in the wasteland crop   grow
         '. . . he wanted to grow a crop in the wasteland.'   (*ÆCHom* II, 10.86.176)

In this case, the existence of PDE sentences like (61) forms glaring counter-evidence to the idea that this option was lost from the language. Again, the development seems to have been from somewhat wider (but not very frequent) use in OE to very restricted use in PDE. A factor that seems to have played a role in OE is person features: first and second pronouns are omitted less often than third-person ones; the example in (65) is typical in this respect. Another context promoting *pro*-drop appears to have been a sequence of clauses with identical subjects; the example in (65) is actually also an instance of this, since it is preceded by the sentence *Se halga ða het him bringan sæd* 'The saint then ordered seed to be brought to him.'

There are also cases in OE where the omitted subject is identical to a non-subject in an earlier clause or where the omitted subject (or its overt referent) is inside a subordinate clause. The example in (66), where the empty subject is understood to refer back to the dative *him* in the preceding clause, instantiates both of these possibilities:

(66)   ah hie a   motan mid him gefeon, þær   Ø leofað &
         but they ever may   with him rejoice where Ø lives and

         rixað a   buton ende
         rules ever without end
         'But they may rejoice with him for ever, where he lives and rules for ever
         without end.'   (*HomU* 18 (Bl Hom 1) 188)

Pronoun omission of this type continues throughout the ME period and is still sometimes found in the sixteenth century, but then disappears from written texts.

A final context for *pro*-drop that we mention here is the use of a second-person singular verb in -(*e*)*st*, which sometimes – perhaps because of the distinctiveness of the verbal ending – lacks the subject pronoun *thou* (see Chapter 2 for the morphology of these forms). We saw above that *pro*-drop of a second-person pronoun is somewhat rare in OE; but it is not unusual in ME and it continues in early ModE, until the pronoun *thou* and the associated verbal form cease to be used altogether. A Shakespearian example is given in (67):

(67)   Hast thou neuer an eie in thy heade? Canst Ø not heare?
                           (*1 Henry IV* II.i.26)

Overall, then, *pro*-drop in the history of English goes from infrequent use to even more infrequent use. Moreover, at each stage of the language it tends to occur only in a few specific contexts; some broad continuities and discontinuities in the types of contexts can be observed, but much more detailed empirical investigation is still needed to make visible their precise nature and also their stylistic distribution.

Besides the use of *it* as a dummy subject, the word *there* can also be found as a dummy or expletive subject in PDE existential sentences, i.e. in intransitive clauses with an indefinite logical subject, as in example (68):

(68)   There is an apple on the table.

This usage goes back to OE times, but at that period the *there*-construction was only one of several competing variants (and a rather minor variant to begin with). Thus in the relevant sentence types the use of *there*, (69a), alternated with the use of *hit*, (69b), and the absence of a dummy subject, (69c):

(69)
a. ... þæt þær nære   buton twegen dælas: Asia &   þæt oþer Europe
   ... that there not-were but   two   parts Asia and the other Europe
   '. . . that there were only two parts: Asia, and the other one, Europe'   (*Or* 1 1.8.11)

b. Is hit lytel tweo ðæt ðæs   wæterscipes   welsprynge is on hefonrice
   is it little doubt that the-GEN watercourse-GEN spring   is in heaven
   'There is little doubt that the spring of the watercourse is in heaven.'   (*CPEp* 6)
c. Sum rice man wæs
   some rich man was
   'There was a rich man.'   (*ÆCHom* I, 23 366.44)

It is during the ME period that these other variants fall out of use, and the PDE situation establishes itself, so that use of expletive *there* becomes the rule in any intransitive clause with an indefinite logical subject.

While on subjects, we may also note a relatively minor change in the form of subject predicatives, which nevertheless has given rise to a great deal of heated prescriptive comment. It is seen in sentences like (70):

(70) a.   The person responsible is he.
      b.   The person responsible is him.

In earlier English, the form of the pronoun in this sentence type would always be the nominative, i.e. *I/we/he/she/they*, in accordance with the principle of case agreement. In OE this principle meant that not only pronouns but also ordinary noun phrases would take the nominative form when used as a subject complement, as can be seen in (71a). A further instance of the operation of the same principle in OE can be seen in (71b), where there is case agreement between the object and the object predicative.

(71) a.   þæt he   wære soð witega
            that he-NOM was true prophet-NOM
            'that he was a true prophet'   (*ÆCHom* I, 12 280.141)

b.   we sceolon ... healdan þone   broþerlican   bend unforodne
      we must   keep   the-ACC brotherly-ACC bond unbroken-ACC
      'we must keep the brotherly bond unbroken'   (*ÆCHom* I, 19 327.47)

With the decline of the case system in the ME period, case agreement lost much of its scope, and was essentially reduced to operating only in sentences with a personal pronoun functioning as a subject predicative, which agreed with the subject in taking the nominative form, as in (70a). However, this isolated fact soon yielded to other pressures: after the adoption of fixed verb–complement order (see Section 3.5.3 for details), there came an increasing tendency to mark the predicative with objective case. The first examples of this kind are attested in the sixteenth century; a Shakespearian example is *Oh, the dogge is me, and I am my selfe* (*Two Gentlemen of Verona* II.iii.18). In the following centuries, this sentence type becomes very common. That the older form as in (70a) has managed to survive at all is in fact surprising; prescriptive condemnation of (70b) may have played some role here (compare also the case changes noted in Section 3.3.2).

3.4.2   Objects

Objects have undergone a number of changes in their nature and marking. To begin with, the loss of case distinctions had an effect on the marking of the direct object. In OE, the canonical case for direct objects was the accusative, but some verbs governed a dative object and some a genitive one. Examples are given in (72):

(72) a.   He sende þone halgan gast to eorþan.
        'He sent the Holy Ghost (ACC) to the earth.' (*ÆCHom* I, 22 360.168)

     b.   he wolde gehelpan ... þearfum   and wannhalum
         he wanted to help   poor-DAT and sick-DAT
         'He wanted to help the poor and the sick.' (*ÆLS* (Oswald) 272)

     c.   Uton for þi   brucan þæs   fyrstes   þe us god forgeaf
         let-us for that enjoy   the-GEN time-GEN that us God gave
         'Let's therefore enjoy the time that God has given us.' (*ÆCHom* I, 40 530.186)

The choice of case form may have a semantic correlate, with the accusative marking complete and direct affectedness of the object, the dative a kind of incomplete or indirect affectedness, and the genitive some sort of partitive meaning. In particular for verbs that show variation in the case form of their object, some kind of semantic differentiation seems plausible. The OE pair in (73), for example, may express antagonistic action in (73a) and a less directly oppositional action in (73b). On this whole issue, see Plank (1983) and Fischer & van der Leek (1987).

(73) a.   and ða   folgode   feorhgeniðlan
        and then followed deadly-foes-ACC
        'and then he pursued his deadly foes'   (*Beo* 2928)

b.   Him   folgiað fuglas scyne
        him-DAT follow birds fair
        'Fair birds will follow him.'   (*Phoe* 591)

However, the difference is not always clear-cut, and for many verbs allowing only one case option, the specific form taken was probably to a large extent conventional rather than semantically motivated (though the respective roles of convention and semantic motivation need not have been the same for all verbs or verb classes; Mitchell, 1985: §1082 gives a convenient overview of the meaning classes that verbs governing the dative and genitive tend to fall into). Whatever the exact system in OE may have been, the disappearance of the formal accusative–dative distinction in all nouns and pronouns after the OE period meant that contrasts as in (73a,b) could no longer be made. Instead, it became the rule for any object to have the objective form (i.e. the base form of any ordinary noun and the object form of the personal pronoun).

From the early ME period onwards, there was also an increase in the use of verb–preposition–complement collocations where OE might have had a verb–object collocation. Thus the OE verb *ofsendan*, seen in (74), has disappeared from the language, but its function has been taken over by the prepositional verb *send for*.

(74)   &   ofsænde se   cyng Godwine eorl
         and   sent-for the-NOM king Godwin earl
         'and the king sent for Earl Godwin'   (*Chron* E(Plummer)1048.35)

In ModE, this development has continued to the point where there are systematic pairs like *hit/stab/poke* versus *hit at/stab at/poke at* or *live/feed/subsist* versus *live on/feed on/subsist on*. These modern pairs often express distinctions that were made in OE by means of prefixation to the verb (thus OE *geotan* means 'to pour (sth.)', but *begeotan* means 'to pour (sth.) over (sth./sb.)'; see also Chapter 4). In addition, the language has many loanwords from Romance, which helped to express meanings that might have been expressed differently – or not at all – in OE; see also Chapter 4. The changes in this area are therefore most profitably viewed as consisting in a shift in general methods of meaning-making rather than the replacement of individual forms by others.

Another long-term development in meaning-making involving the object concerns the use of 'light-verb combinations' like *take a look, do a somersault, make an attempt* and *have lunch*, where the meaning of the combination appears to be located primarily in the (usually indefinite) object noun phrase rather than in the verb. Some combinations like this are attested in OE (e.g. *andan habban* 'have envy', *rest habban* 'take rest' and *blod lætan* 'let blood'); more appear in ME, also with nouns preceded by the indefinite article, such as *take a nap, make a leap* (see the data in Iglesias-Rábade, 2001 and Moralejo-Gárate, 2001); and, from 1500, there is a further steady increase in the types and tokens of these collocations. Their high frequency in PDE is therefore the result of a gradual process stretching over more than a thousand years.

We saw above that after the OE period the direct object came to be uniformly marked as objective. The loss of the accusative–dative distinction also had an effect on the marking of the indirect object. In OE, this constituent was always in the dative, as in (75), but from ME onwards it had objective case, as in (76), making it formally indistinguishable from the direct object:

(75)   & sealde ðam fixum sund & ðam fugelum fliht
           'And gave the fishes sea and the birds flight'   (*ÆCHom* I, 1 182.106)

(76)   Wolle we sullen Iosep þis chapmen þat here come?
           'Shall we sell Joseph to these merchants that have come here?
                                   (*Jacob & Joseph* 118)

Perhaps as a reaction to this reduction in overt marking, another option developed for the indirect object: the *to*-phrase, as in (77):

(77)   Betir is that Y ȝyue hir to thee than to another man.
           'It is better if I give her to you than to another man.'   (Wycliff Gen. 29.19)

A few instances of this option are found in late OE texts, and in the course of the ME period it becomes a fully productive alternative to the bare indirect object. Whether there was any difference in meaning between the two options at this time is difficult to say: a great deal of effort has been spent on the 'dative' alternation in PDE (see, for example, Thompson, 1995, Pesetsky, 1995, and Davidse, 1996), but so far there has been little work on this question for historical stages of the language.

3.4.3   Impersonal constructions

We have seen that changes affecting the subject as such and the object as such have been unspectacular. However, when it comes to alternations involving subjects and objects together, there have been major changes. Losses have mainly affected the class of constructions usually labelled impersonal (discussed here), while the gains have been in the passive (discussed in the next section).

In OE, there was a well-developed system of grammatical marking for verbs expressing various kinds of sensation and emotion, i.e. verbs with meanings like 'be ashamed', 'regret', 'be hungry', 'like', 'detest', etc. (sometimes called 'psych' verbs, bringing out their shared concern with psychological states). Concentrating on verbs involving an experiencer and a source (or cause) of the relevant sensation/emotion, we can summarise the grammatical patterns in OE as in (78):

(78) a.   EXPERIENCER   SOURCE
           nominative   genitive/PP

     b.   SOURCE   EXPERIENCER
           nominative   dative/accusative

     c.   EXPERIENCER   SOURCE
           dative/accusative genitive/PP

The alternation between experiencer-as-subject and source-as-subject is in itself remarkable enough; it is complemented by a third pattern which has no overt subject at all, and oblique marking of both experiencer and source. Example sentences with the impersonal verb *ofhreowan* 'pity/repent' are given in (79a–c).

(79) a. se   mæssepreost þæs   mannes   ofhreow
          the-NOM mass-priest   the-GEN man-GEN pitied
          'The priest felt pity for the man.'   (*ÆLS* (Oswald) 262)

     b. Ða ofhreow þam   munuce   þæs hreoflian mægenleaste
          then pitied   the-DAT monk-DAT the leper's   feebleness-NOM
          'Then the monk felt pity for the leper's feebleness.' (*ÆCHom* I, 23 369.139)

     c. him   ofhreow þæs   mannes
          him-DAT pitied   the-GEN man-GEN
          'He felt pity for the man.'   (*ÆCHom* I, 13 281.12)

Not all OE impersonal verbs occur in all three constructions, and some verbs show a clear preference for one or the other pattern, but these differences appear to be lexical rather than grammatical.

In cases where the EXPERIENCER is in the dative and the SOURCE is itself a clause, dummy *hit* sometimes fills the subject slot (compare Section 3.4.1), as shown in (80), although the empty subject variant as in (81) is much more usual.

(80)   hit ne gerist nanum   ricum   cynincge þæt. . .
          it not befits no-DAT powerful-DAT king-DAT that
          'It does not befit any powerful king to . . .'   (*ÆLS* (Augurius)257)

(81)   Ne gedafenað biscope   þæt . . .
          not befits   bishop-DAT that
          'It does not befit a bishop to . . .'   (*ÆCHom* II, 10 81.14)

What happened to this OE system of impersonal verbs? In ME, the system survives but shows signs of a slow loss of productivity. Several of the relevant OE verbs were lost from the language, including those in (80) and (81), and the remainder tend to become restricted to one or the other pattern, with other lexical items, often from French (e.g. *please*), filling the gaps. Nevertheless, the three patterns of (78) remain (though without any formal distinction between accusative and dative, and without genitive marking of any arguments), and there are some new additions to the class of impersonal verbs. These include some instances of the native English modals *ought* and *must*, as in (82), but also loans from French, such as *marvel* in (83):

(82)   us must worschepyn hym
          'We must worship him.'   (*Dives and Pauper* I 206.34)

(83)   me marvaylyyth mychil why God ӡeuyth wyckyd men swych power
          me marvels   much   why God gives   wicked men such   power
          'I wonder a lot why God gives wicked men such power.'
                                                                (*Dives and Pauper* I.1 336.2)

By the end of the ME period, however, the patterns of (78) cannot be said to be characteristic of the class of impersonals any more. The empty subject option (78c) was lost from the language altogether (compare Section 3.4.1 above) and individual verbs had mostly become restricted to the pattern of either (78a) or (78b).

One of the reasons for the ultimate demise of the system of grammatical marking for impersonals may be the influx of French loanwords, which might have 'impersonal' meanings but resist full-scale integration in the system of impersonal syntax, thus introducing all kinds of exceptional behaviour into this verbal class. Other causes may also have played a role. Thus it has repeatedly been suggested that instances of (78b) with a preposed experiencer could have been reanalysed as instances of (78a), with the experiencer functioning as subject. The standard (but invented) example given to illustrate this is (84):

(84) a.   þam cyninge   licodon   þa   peran (OE)
           the   king-DAT liked-PLUR the pears-NOM

     b.   the king liked the pears (ME)

In (84a) the phrase *þam cyninge* is unambiguously recognisable as a dative, and the verb *licodon* is clearly plural, showing that the plural noun *peran* is the subject of the clause. In (84b), however, the relevant formal markers have disappeared and the sentence would therefore be liable to reanalysis, whereby *the king* would become subject (in accordance with the increasing fixity of subject–verb word order) and *the pears* object. It has been objected that the very frequent sentence-type *Him liked pears*, where the case of the experiencer is unambiguously objective, would be counterevidence to such a reanalysis, but this observation itself has been countered by arguments to the effect that preposed dative experiencers had several subject properties anyway, even in OE (see especially Allen, 1995).

3.4.4   Passive

The passive has undergone considerable development in the history of English. Some of the relevant changes were discussed in the section on the verbal group (Section 3.3.3). Here, we deal with changes in the realisation of the arguments of the passive verb in a finite clause. We shall first distinguish three types of passive in PDE, as shown in (85):

(85) a.   He was arrested.   direct passive
     b.   He was given a reprimand.   indirect passive
     c.   This was frowned upon.   prepositional passive

The labels in (85) reflect the status that the passive subject would have in the corresponding active clause: direct object in (85a) (*they arrested him*), indirect object in (85b) (*they gave him a reprimand*) and object of a preposition in (85c) (*they frowned upon this*). Of these three types, only the first goes back to OE times; the other two came into existence in the ME period. The indirect passive is first found towards the end of the fourteenth century; an example is (86):

(86)   whan he was gyvyn the gre be my lorde kynge Arthure
        'When he was given the prize by my lord King Arthur'
                    (Malory, *Morte Darthur* 699.19)

Its rise has been attributed to the coalescence of the dative and the accusative, which would have the effect of making the indirect object of an active clause formally indistinguishable from the direct object: both would have the same objective case. Hence, this explanation runs, the indirect object of an active clause would be just as eligible as a direct object to become the subject of a passive clause.

Another account of the change focuses on passive clauses already in existence. Compare the OE example in (87) with the similar ME one in (88).

(87)
Dæm   scipmannum is beboden ... þæt ... hig Gode þone teoðan dæl agyfen
the-DAT traders-DAT is ordered that   they God the   tenth part give
'The farmers are ordered to give a tenth part to God.'   (ThCap 1 (Sauer) 35.375.12)

(88)
eche   bischop ... is ordeyned ... that he offre ʒiftis and sacrifices for synnes
every bishop   is ordered   that he offer gifts and sacrifices for sins
'Every bishop is ordered to offer gifts and sacrifices to atone for sins.'
                                                            (Wyclif, Hebr 5.1)

In OE (87) the initial NP is clearly marked as a dative and the clause has an empty subject, just like the example in (62). In ME (88), however, the initial NP would have become liable to reanalysis as a subject (a reinterpretation analogous to that in (84)), since it had lost its case marking and occupied the canonical subject position.

A problem for both these two scenarios is that the indirect passive only starts appearing some two centuries after the loss of case marking on common nouns. It has been pointed out that a closer chronological fit can be obtained by linking its appearance with the solidification of word order to verb – indirect object – direct object, which took place in the fourteenth century (for details, see Section 3.5.4). If we assume that passive is sensitive to linear order (i.e. only NPs systematically adjacent to the verb can be passivised), then it could have been this word-order change that triggered the rise of the new indirect passive.

A fact that is left unexplained in the above accounts (and there are several versions around of the three sketched here) is the extreme slowness of the spread of the indirect passive. Only a handful of clear examples have been found in fifteenth-century texts, and several run-of-the-mill PDE instances were still considered odd (or characteristic of careless usage) in the early twentieth century. It therefore appears that lexical factors have played a major role in the development, with certain verbs accepting the new construction long before others.

Prepositional passives as in (85c) are somewhat older than indirect passives: they start appearing around 1200. In their rise, a crucial role is played by the change in word order from object–verb to verb–object, and their history is therefore dealt with in Section 3.5.6.

To set off against these gains in the possibilities for passive formation, there is one type that existed in OE but disappeared early in the ME period. This is the passive of a verb that did not take an accusative object. We saw in (72b) that *help* was such a verb; a passive with it is given in (89):

(89)   and wæs ða   geholpen ðam   unscyldigum huse
         and was then helped   the-DAT innocent-DAT house-DAT
         'and then the innocent house was helped'   (*ÆCHom* II, 39.1 293.178)

Here, the passive has an empty subject, and the only argument of the verb is the object – marked by dative case, just as in the active (72b). Another OE passive with an empty subject can be seen in (90), where the object of the passive verb is a clause.

(90)   Næs   nanum men forgifen þæt he moste habban ... his agen
         not-was no   man granted that he might have   his own

         fulluht buton Iohanne anum.
         baptism but   John   alone
         'It was granted to no one to perform his own baptism except to John.'
                                            (*ÆCHom* II, 3 25.206)

Sometimes, the subject position in such sentences is filled by dummy *hit/it* in OE, and this becomes the norm in ME (compare the discussion of other empty subject constructions in Sections 3.4.1 and 3.4.3 above).

We also briefly mention here a phenomenon that is somewhat similar in effect to the passive as far as meaning is concerned. It consists in the suppression of the agent argument of a verb and conversion of its direct object to subject status, but without the attendant introduction of a passive auxiliary. In studies of PDE, the construction is sometimes called the 'middle' or 'medio-passive'; an example is given in (91):

(91)   This car drives like a dream.

In PDE, the middle use of verbs is different from the simple active use in typically requiring either a manner adverbial or a modal. This type of alternation is already found in early ModE, but it becomes really frequent only in texts from the last two hundred years. The causes of its rise in popularity, and the pathway that it has followed, still need to be fully investigated. The development is no doubt connected with the fact that, throughout the history of English, individual verbs have sometimes allowed both transitive and intransitive uses; examples are the verbs *grow* (*the potatoes grew/they grew potatoes*), *heal* (*the wound healed fast/he healed the wound*) and many others. The overall result of the increase of all these alternations is that the subject position in English has come to be associated with a wide variety of notional roles. The subject was strongly associated in OE active clauses with the notional role of agent (except in one of the variants of the well-defined impersonal system) and in passive clauses with the role of theme, but at later stages subjects of an active clause can be theme or experiencer instead of agent, while in passives the only role they cannot bear is that of agent.

3.4.5   Subordinate clauses

So far we have looked mainly at clausal constituents consisting of NPs. However, it is also possible for a clausal constituent to take the form of a subordinate clause, and in this section we will discuss some of the historical developments in this area of grammar. We will start with *that*-clauses, next deal with infinitive and -*ing*-clauses, and finally say something about (non-finite) adverbial clauses.

As far as *that*-clauses are concerned, their three main uses in PDE are the following:

(92)   That he agreed was a big surprise. (subject)

(93)   The problem is that he doesn't listen. (subject predicative)

(94)   I didn't realise that it was so terrible. (complement to verb)

That-clauses clearly functioning as a subject, as in (92), are first found in the late ME period. The reasons for their non-occurrence in OE and early ME are not entirely clear but may have something to do with the fact that they involve a rather 'difficult' type of embedding as far as processing is concerned. In fact, even today (especially in the spoken language), the preferred option would be to use the dummy subject *it* and have the subordinate clause in extraposed position, as in (95) (cf. Biber et al., 1999: 676):

(95)   It was a big surprise that he agreed.

This option also existed in OE; see the example in (80). Besides, until the fifteenth century we also find in written texts the variant in which *it* is absent and the subject is therefore empty, as in (81) and (90). As noted in Section 3.4.1, this variant is still found in present-day colloquial spoken English, highlighting the need to be careful in pronouncing any specific construction dead and buried at a particular time.

Sentences as in (93) and (94), with a *that*-clause functioning as a subject predicative and as a direct object (or complement to the verb, to use the more general and usual label), have existed throughout the history of the language. They are frequent in PDE and, if anything, even more frequent in earlier English. Omission of the word *that*, very common in more informal registers in PDE, is less usual until c.1500. In the early examples, the complement clause itself often has a further subordinate clause in initial position, as in (96), where omission of *that* may be due to a desire to avoid a sequence of two subordinators (*that if*):

(96)   Hwæt ic wat,   gif ure godo ænige mihte hæfdon, þonne woldan
        indeed I know if our gods any   power had   then   would

        hie me ma   fultumian.
        they me more help
        'Indeed, I know (that), if our gods had any power, they would help me more.'
                                                              (Bede 2 10.134.18)

Just like *that*-clauses, infinitival clauses can be used as subject, subject predicative, or complement to a verb, as in (97a,b,c); an important further use is as complement to an adjective, as in (97d):

(97) a.   To agree straightaway would be a mistake.
     b.   Their plan was to get it all over and done with this week.
     c.   They wanted to leave as soon as possible.
     d.   These texts are hard to decipher.

In discussing the history of these constructions, which basically involves the external syntax of infinitive clauses, we shall also pay some attention to their internal syntax: unlike *that*-clauses, infinitive clauses differ from main clauses in several major respects having to do with their own clausal constituents and, closely associated with them, the nature of the verbal group.

A first thing to note is that in all four uses shown in (97), the infinitival clause lacks an overt subject. This was the only option for infinitival clauses until the late ME period. At that time, however, overt subjects started appearing, first in the form of a bare noun phrase (*Him to agree would be a surprise*, or even *He to agree would be a surprise*), but later (also) introduced by the preposition *for* (*For him to agree would be a surprise*). The origins of this innovation lie in changes in word order, and we therefore postpone fuller discussion until Section 3.5.6.

Infinitivals functioning as subject predicative or as complement to a verb or adjective (see (97b–d)) are found from the earliest records of the language. The pattern in (97a), however, is not: just like *that*-clauses (and probably for the same reasons), infinitival clauses unambiguously functioning as subjects are not attested until the later ME period. Instead, a variant with a dummy or empty subject was used, in which the infinitival clause was in extraposed position; examples can be seen in (62) and (63).

Predicative infinitives of the type exemplified in (97b) are rare until the late ME period, but those of the type seen in (98) are frequent from the earliest texts onwards:

(98)   hit nis   no   to forseone
        it   is-not not to despise
        'It is not to be despised.'   (*Bo* 24.56.2)

What is special here is that, notionally, the matrix subject is interpreted as the object of the lexical verb in the infinitival clause (i.e. despising it would be wrong), making the construction similar in meaning to regular passive clauses; a label sometimes given to this construction is 'modal passive'. In OE, the construction always featured an infinitive that was active in form, as in (98). In PDE, use of the active infinitive is restricted to a few lexicalised expressions, such as *This house is to let* and *You are to blame*; in all other cases, the infinitive has the passive form, as in (99):

(99)   This work is to be done as soon as possible.

The modern form of the construction, with *to be* followed by the past participle, first appears in the ME period; initially, it is only found with the direct passive, i.e. in sentences like (99), but soon the infinitival prepositional passive, (100), also starts being used, probably as an extension of the finite prepositional passive.

(100)   The whiche hevene . . . nys nat . . . to be wondryd upon
                  'Which heaven is not to be marvelled at.'   (Chaucer, *Boece* III Prose 8, 784)

The use of the active infinitive form, however, persists in this construction. It is common throughout the ME period and sporadic instances can be found until c.1900. One such late example is given in (101):

(101)   The wet and the cold were now to reckon with. (1902 H. James, *Wings of the Dove* (Scribner's 1937), II.IX.ii.261)

The passive *to*-infinitive, which eventually replaced the active form still seen in (101), was a verbal form that did not exist in OE at all. It first appears in the ME period, not only in the so-called modal passive of (98)–(99) above but also in other constructions. An early example of its use is (102):

(102)   he till hiss Fader wass | Offredd forr uss o   rode, | All als he
                  he to   his   father was   offered   for us   on cross all   as   he

                  wære an lamb to ben | Offredd
                  were a lamb to be   offered
                  'He was offered to his Father for us on the cross, just as if He was a lamb to be offered.'   (*Orm* 12644–7)

Its rise has been linked to a developing preference in ME for interpreting a pre-verbal NP as the subject, as a result of the developing predominance of SVO word order (see Section 3.5.3). In cases like (98) such an interpretation is manifestly impossible, hence the use of a passive infinitive came to be favoured here. The result was a more explicit marking of grammatical functions. This may have been particularly welcome because of the rise of another construction with a *to*-infinitive following a form of *be*, which can be seen in (103):

(103)   You are to follow all instructions carefully.

Here the matrix subject is interpreted as also functioning as notional subject of the infinitival verb. The roots of this construction lie in OE sentences with the present participle *tocumende* (of the prefixed verb *tocuman*), which at some point was reinterpreted as the infinitive of the verb *cuman* (*He wæs tocumende* > *he wæs to cumenne*). In ME, other verbs also start being used in this frame, which means that the construction of (103) is born. This in turn would lead to systematic ambiguity of sentences of the type X *is to* V, where X might have to be interpreted either as the subject of V (as in (103)) or the object of V (as in modal passives like (98)). In actual use, meaning and context would no doubt resolve the ambiguity in many cases, but adoption of the passive *to*-infinitive for the object interpretation eliminated it altogether.

The infinitive used as complement to a verb, as in PDE (97c), can be found throughout the history of the language. In (104) we give examples from OE, ME and early ModE:

(104) a. ne   þe   nan neodþearf ne lærde   to wyrcanne þæt þæt ðu   worhtest
          nor you no   need   not taught to do   that that you did
          'Nor did any need teach you to do what you did.'   (*Bo* 33.79.16)

    b. Godde we scullen bihaten,   ure   sunnen to beten
       God   we must   promise   our   sins   to atone-for
       'We must promise God to atone for our sins.'   (Layamon, *Brut*(Clg) 9180)

    c. they forbore to assist it with their purses (Drake, *An Essay Concerning the Necessity of Equal Taxes* 949 (1702))

Note that in (104a), the object of the matrix verb, *þe*, is also understood to function as the subject of the infinitive (i.e. the sentence has object control), while in (104b,c) it is the matrix subject that is so interpreted (subject control). Both types have existed since OE times.

While infinitival complement clauses have been a stable feature of the grammar of English for a very long time, some changes have affected them. A first change concerns the form of the infinitive. In PDE, the bare infinitive has a rather restricted range of occurrence: apart from its use after modal auxiliaries (see Section 3.3.4), it is only frequent after verbs of sense perception and causation, as in (105):

(105) a.   We saw him come in.
     b.   They made us work harder.

In earlier English, the bare infinitive had somewhat wider use, since it regularly occurred after verbs with other meanings as well; OE and ME examples are given in (106) and (107):

(106)   Đa   sona   he nydde his leorningcnihtas on scyp stigan.
         then immediately he forced his disciples   on ship climb
         'Then straightaway he forced his disciples to go on board.'
                                                 (*Mk*(WSCp) 6.45)

(107)   Who . . . hath suffred aprochen to this sike man thise comune strompetis?
         'Who has permitted these common strumpets to come near this sick man?'
                                                 (Chaucer, *Bo.* 1.pr1.47)

Some individual verbs allowed both options; the choice between the two infinitives often appears to depend on the degree of 'directness' of the relation between matrix verb and infinitive, with the bare infinitive being favoured in cases where the two verbs have a shared time domain and there is direct logical entailment. Thus in (106) and (107) the boarding and coming are understood to be co-temporal with and directly dependent on the forcing and permitting respectively, promoting the use of the bare infinitive. In (104a,b), however, the two verbs appear to each have their own time domains, hence the use of the *to*-infinitive.

After the ME period, the bare infinitive becomes more restricted in its use, eventually reaching the PDE situation sketched above. There were various reasons for this. One was its formal indistinctiveness: the bare-infinitive suffix -(*i*)*an* underwent a process of erosion, first making it coalesce with the subjunctive plural ending in -*en*, and later making it disappear altogether (for details, see Chapter 2). Another reason may have been the emergence of the -*ing*-form (see below), which replaced the original present participle in -*ende*. The -*ende* participle competed with the bare infinitive after perception verbs, and the new -*ing*-form may have spread from there, replacing some bare infinitives. In sharp contrast to the bare infinitive, the *to*-infinitive becomes more and more frequent after the OE period. In particular, it becomes common after many verbs that earlier had regularly taken a *that*-clause. This shift appears to be connected with the decline of the subjunctive: when this form started coalescing with the indicative, the *to*-infinitive provided a means to continue marking indirectness and/or non-factuality of the complement clause. This development starts in the OE period (Los, 2005 shows that its effects can already be seen by comparing earlier and later versions of one and the same OE text) and continues in ME. The overall outcome is that, by the early ModE period, the *to*-infinitive with complement function has become vastly more common than it had been in OE.

Another infinitival context which has existed since OE times but has under-gone several changes over the centuries is that of complement to an adjective, exemplified in PDE (97d). Two main types can be distinguished; OE examples can be seen in (108) and (109); the translations given show that both types still exist:

(108)   ic eom gearo to gecyrrenne to munuclicere drohtnunge
          'I am ready to turn to monastic life.'   (*ÆCHom* I, 35 484.251)

(109)   ðis me is hefi   to donne
          this me is heavy to do
          'This is hard to do for me.'   (*Mart* 5 (Kotzor) Se 16, A.14)

The type in (108), sometimes called the *eager-to-please* construction, shows subject control: the matrix subject is also interpreted as functioning as subject of the infinitive. The type in (109), often called the *easy-to-please* construction, is different: the matrix subject corresponds to the object of the infinitive (compare the modal passive discussed above), while the subject of the infinitive is controlled by an NP in the dative, if there is one. Another construction in which *easy*-adjectives have been used from the earliest texts onwards can be seen in (62) and (63); here the infinitival clause has an overt object and the matrix clause has an empty or dummy subject: (*It*) *is hard for me to do this*. In all these sentence types, the rule has always been the use of the *to*-infinitive rather than the bare infinitive.

The *eager-to-please* construction has been remarkably stable throughout the history of the language, but the *easy-to-please* construction has undergone a number of changes. From around 1400, two slightly more complex variants of the construction are found: one has a preposition in the infinitival clause, as in (110), and another has a passive infinitive, as in (111):

(110)   þei fond it good and esy to dele wiþ also
          'They found it good and easy to deal with also.'   (a.1400(a1325) *Cursor*
          (LD and Trin-C) 16557)

(111)   þe blak of þe yȝe . . . is hardest to be helid and I-cured
          'The black of the eye is hardest to heal and cure.
                                                        (a.1398 Trevisa Barth 42a/b)

This development is the same as that of the modal passive (compare (101) and (99), respectively) and some degree of mutual influence seems likely. However, this mutual influence was apparently not strong enough to maintain the similarity of the two constructions: while the modal passive came to favour the use of a passive infinitive, eventually giving up the active infinitive altogether, the *easy-to-please* construction retained the active infinitive and eventually abandoned the use of the passive infinitive. A late example of *easy-to-please* with the passive infinitive is given in (112).

(112)   books which are rather difficult to be procured, from having been privately
          published (1850 Gaskell, *Letters* 74, p. 122)

The reason for this difference in development may be that after adjectives and nouns the need for a passive infinitive in PDE is less strong than after verbs, because verbs require their argument positions to be filled (lexically or by means of a silent element), whereas adjectives and nouns (see also the example in (102), where the infinitive depends on a noun) are freer in this respect. Note also that in clauses such as (109), the subject *ðis* can be said to have not only an object relation with the verb *donne* but also, at some level of analysis, a thematic subject relation with the adjective *hefi*. This 'double allegiance' does not exist in cases such as (99) and (102). With adjectives, passive infinitives are generally only used in PDE when an active infinitive may lead to ambiguity, as in the case of *likely* or *fit*, cf. *you are not fit to be seen* vs *you are not fit to serve*. Another adjective which has retained the option of using a passive infinitive is *ready*. Thus the well-known ambiguity of (113) can be avoided by using the variant in (114):

(113)   The lamb is ready to eat.

(114)   The lamb is ready to be eaten.

Other adjectives still allowing the passive infinitive tend to be like *ready* in that they can occur in both the *easy-to-please* construction (where the matrix subject is understood to be interpretable as the object of the infinitive) and the *eager-to-please* construction (where it is to be interpreted as the subject of the infinitive). In fact, the desire to avoid ambiguity may also have been one of the factors responsible for the ME introduction of the passive option in this construction in the first place. For the specific example in (111) we may note firstly that both *heal* and *cure* were verbs that could be used either transitively or intransitively, and secondly that in ME the adjective *hard* could also be used in the meaning 'slow', as in *His eres waxes deef, and hard to here* 'His ears grow deaf and slow to hear' (a.1425 (a.1400) *PConsc.* 782). As a result, a sentence like (115) might be ambiguous, and the variant in (111) might be resorted to.

(115)   The black of the eye is hardest to heal
         a. 'The black of the eye is most difficult to make better.'
         b. 'The black of the eye is slowest to get better.'

The third type of subordinate clause that we discuss is headed by an *-ing*-participle. We shall first consider its use as a complement to V, since this ties in with the use of the *to*-infinitive as a complement, which we have just dealt with. A PDE example is (116):

(116)   He avoided mentioning the incident.

Nowadays, the situation is that some verbs can only take a clausal complement with an *-ing*-form (*avoid* is one of these), others allow either an *-ing*-form or a *to*-infinitive, in some cases with a difference in meaning (as in *I remembered posting it* vs *I remembered to post it*) and yet other verbs only allow the *to*-infinitive (*he promised to be in time*).

The use of *-ing*-complements dates back to the ME period, but it is not yet frequent at that time; an example is (117):

(117)   he oughte forto forbere bothe inward and outward preising and preying and
         worschiping, dispreising and disworschiping
         'He ought to refrain from both inward and outward praising and praying
         and worshiping, and also dispraising and disrespecting.'
                                        (Pecock, *Rule Crysten Religion* 56.4 (1443))

In this and other ME examples, the *-ing*-form as a rule behaves like a nominal form, taking an adjectival modifier and either no object or one introduced by the preposition *of*. It is only in the early ModE period that it regularly shows verbal behaviour, taking adverbial modifiers and being followed by a bare NP object, as in (118):

(118)   In as much haste as I am, I cannot forebear giving one example. (Dryden, *A
         Parallel between Painting and Poetry* 331)

Both (117) and (118) feature the matrix verb *forbear*, and this is no coincidence: the rise of *-ing*-complements follows a path of lexical diffusion, with verbs of negative import such as *avoid, escape* and *forbear* leading the way. The example may have been set by another group of verbs with negative import, i.e. *defend, keep* and *let* (all basically meaning 'prevent'), which occurred in the frame 'prevent sb. from V-ing' (i.e. with V-*ing* following a preposition) already in ME. This early association with negative meaning must also be the reason why the *ing*-form came to be used in examples like *I could not help noticing* and why it is frequent in the eighteenth century after verbs like *decline, fail* and *refuse* (which, however, have since reverted to use of the infinitive; cf. also example (104c)).

Use of the *ing*-form in PDE is of course not restricted to verb complements. In fact, constructions headed by an *ing*-form can be found occupying all positions that an ordinary NP can occupy; see the examples in (119):

(119) a.   The finding of the body was a crucial breakthrough.   (subject)
       b.   His only interest in life is making money.   (predicative)
       c.   He regretted having to leave so early.   (object/complement to V)
       d.   He was offended at being passed over.   (object of P)

The traditional label for the *-ing*-forms in (119a–d) is the gerund. As can be seen, the gerund comes in two basic types: its internal syntax can be either nominal (as shown by the presence of an object introduced by *of* and the presence of an article in (119a)) or verbal (see the presence of a bare NP object in (119b), the complementation by a *to*-infinitive in (119c), and the presence of the passive auxiliary in (119d)). The nominal gerund is less frequent in PDE than the verbal gerund, but historically it is the older type.

The gerund's ultimate origin is to be found in OE nouns ending with the derivational suffix *-ing/-ung*, such as *huntung* 'hunting' and *binding* 'binding'. In OE, these nouns are often used without any dependents, but when *with* dependents, their syntax is entirely nominal: they take a genitive 'subject' (as in *mine halsunge* 'my entreaty/my begging' *PPs* 142.1), a genitive 'object' (as in *æfter his hadunga* 'after his ordination/after ordaining him', *GD Pref* and 3(C)23.225.23) and the type of modifiers, such as adjectives, that would be normal in NPs (as in *mid gelomum scotungum* 'by frequent shooting/shots', *ÆLS* (Edmund) 181). From the late ME period onwards, however, such nouns slowly start acquiring verbal characteristics. Thus they come to take a bare NP as object and an adverb as modifier, as in (120); they come to take an objective-case subject, as in (121); they allow negation by means of *not*, as in (122); and they occur in the perfect and passive, as in (123):

(120)   the coste of buyldynge them anew (More, *Utopia*, tr. Robinson; ed. Lupton)

(121)   it was true of this light contynuyng from day to daye (1536 John de Ponte, Ellis, *Original Letters* I 2, 125)

(122)   . . . humblye desyreing your excuse for her not wrighting (1629 *Barrington Family Letters* 116)

(123)   He . . . bore a great pique at Alexander, for having been preferr'd before him to the See of Alexandria (1676 Marvell, *Mr Smirke* Hivb)

The origins of this process of verbalisation may lie in genitive dependents of the *ing*-form being reinterpreted as having objective case. This could happen to nouns having no formal marking of genitive, as in ME *after is fader buriinge* (*Gloucester Chron.* 7859) 'after his father's burying/after burying his father'. Here *fader*, originally an endingless genitive singular (see Section 2.6.3.3), could be taken to be an objective form, entailing verbal status for the form *buriinge*. In the case of singular nouns, this structural ambiguity would exist only for those items which happened to have endingless genitives; in the case of plural nouns, the ambiguity would be more widespread, since the genitive plural was not systematically marked by a designated ending in ME; see further Jack (1988).

From the beginning, verbalisation is most pronounced in gerunds functioning as complement to a preposition, as in all of (120)–(123). This, in fact, is the syntactic context that is favoured by gerunds of all types: different studies have found frequencies of 30 to 80 per cent of gerunds with this function, the figures increasing from ME to early ModE times. The reason for this lopsided distributional pattern of the gerund probably lies in the impossibility of complementing a preposition with an infinitive (cf. **I was surprised at him to say this*) – the gerund provided a convenient method for nevertheless having a clausal complement in this position (*I was surprised at him saying this*).

During the process of verbalisation, nominal use of the gerund continued to be possible (see (124)), and there also arose certain types of mixed nominal–verbal gerunds, as in (125), where the adverb *quickly* would be appropriate to a verbal gerund, while the object introduced by the preposition *of* suggests a nominal gerund.

(124)   He gave five hundred pounds for the walling of that towne (Ph. Holland, *Camden's Britain* II 194)

(125)   The quickly doing of it is the grace (Jonson, *Alchemist* (Everym.) IV, ii, p. 62)

In PDE (see Quirk et al., 1985: §§15.12, 15.14), it is still possible to have a verbal gerund with a genitive subject (*I was surprised at John's leaving so early*) and with the determiners *no* (*There is no denying it*) and, somewhat marginally, *this* (*This telling tales has to stop*), but in all other cases the gerund has polarised into a purely verbal and a purely nominal type; the last mixed examples like (125) are from around 1900. The causes of the polarisation are probably to be sought in the influence of two related forms/constructions, both of which showed an enormous increase in frequency in the period 1600–1900: on the one hand, there was the *ing*-form used in the progressive (see Section 3.3.2), which was entirely verbal and might pull the gerund in the same direction; on the other hand, there was a host of deverbal abstract nouns like *blockage, appraisal, deterrence, colonisation* and *fulfilment* (see Chapter 4), which would exert nominal pressure on (and to some extent replace) the gerund. As a result, hybrid forms like (125) gave way to purely nominal or verbal gerunds.

Finally, we briefly discuss some changes in non-finite adverbial clauses. Some examples in PDE are given in (126):

(126) a.   He did it to annoy us.
      b.   All things told, it would be better not to do it.
      c.   Tears filling his eyes, he told her what had happened.

The first type, a *to*-infinitival clause expressing purpose, is already found in OE. An example is:

(127)   he   ne   com   na   to demenne mancynn ...   ac   to gehælenne
          he   not came not to judge   mankind   but to heal
          'He came not to judge mankind but to redeem them.'
                                                  (*ÆCHom* I, 22 359.132)

This usage continues uninterrupted to the present day, but in the course of the centuries some variants developed that re-emphasise the notion of purpose, suggesting that the simple *to*-infinitive – which had become very common in other uses, as shown above – was sometimes felt to be insufficiently expressive of purposive meaning. In early ME, perhaps helped by Scandinavian influence (Kytö & Danchev, 2001), the marker *for to* starts being used; this persists into the early ModE period, as in (128):

(128)   sith ['since'] almightie God the father would gyue hys moste dearely
          beloued sonne vnto suche an horrible death onely for to quenche and to
          extincte sinne (Fisher 398)

However, in ME already *for to* soon develops into a general infinitive marker, losing its purposive character in the process; see, for example, its use after the modal verb *ought* in (117). In the seventeenth century, renewed marking of purpose was achieved by the introduction of *in order to*, as in (129); a more recent form can be seen in *We told them in advance so as to avoid any misunderstanding*.

(129)   T'is said hee and his family comes up to London upon Wedensday next, in
          order to go into Kent.   (H. Oxinden 277)

In PDE, other types of non-finite adverbial, as in (126b,c), are found especially in quite formal written registers, but in early ModE they seem to be used somewhat more generally. Their origins probably lie in influence from Latin (which has various types of absolutive constructions); examples can already be found in OE and ME texts.

In early ModE, a non-finite adverbial clause is sometimes preceded by a preposition which specifies more explicitly the nature of the adverbial modification, as in (130):

(130)   Wherupon the duke sent him a lettre of defiaunce, and called Paulmer, who
          after denial made of his declaracion was let goe.   (Edward VI, *Diary*
          354, 1550–2)

This usage has disappeared again, except when the preposition is *with*, as in (131); this has developed into a very common construction, which is not restricted to formal types of writing. If we also consider examples with the preposition *without*, as in (132), we are at the borderline between gerunds and non-finite adverbials:

(131)   'You don't mean to say you took 'em down, rings and all, with him lying there?' said Joe. (Dickens, *Christmas Carol* iv.63)

(132)   and she could be burned to a crisp without anybody knowing it (*Brown Corpus* Belles Lettres P02:87)

3.5   Word order

3.5.1   Introduction

To begin the discussion of changes in word order, it may be useful to take a run-of-the-mill sentence in OE and compare it with its present-day English counterpart. This will show up some of the main differences between the earliest and latest stages of the language, for which we shall present fuller descriptions, analyses and explanations below. Consider, then, the following OE sentence:

(133)   ða   se Wisdom ða   ðis leoð swiðe lustbærlice &   gesceadwislice
         when the wisdom then this song very   pleasantly and wisely

         asungen hæfde, ða   hæfde ic ða   giet hwylchwugu gemynd on
         sung   had   then had   I   then still what-little   memory in

         minum mode ðære   unrotnesse þe   ic <ær>   hæfde
         my   mind of-the sadness   that I   before had

         'When Wisdom had sung this song so pleasantly and wisely, I still
         remembered some of the sadness that I used to feel.'   (Bo 36.103.23)

Here the subordinate clause *ða se Wisdom . . . asungen hæfde* has the entire verbal group in final position, where it follows the direct object *ðis leoð*. In the main clause, the finite verb *hæfde* occupies the second position of the clause, immediately following the word *ða*. Also note that the direct object of the subordinate clause is separated from the infinitive by the adverbial *swiðe lustbærlice & gesceadwislice*. In grammatical terminology, we would say that the subordinate clause has verb-final order, while the main clause has inversion, or verb-second (to be precise, the finite element of the verbal group comes after the first constituent, whatever its function may be). A comparison with the present-day English translation shows that verb-final order and verb-second have basically disappeared from the language. Furthermore, the direct object and the verb can no longer be separated but must be adjacent. Given these clear differences, it is natural to wonder about questions like: when did these changes take place? how did they take place? and why did they take place? These and similar questions will be addressed in the following subsections, not only for the changes observable in

(133) but also for other changes in the order of sentence elements that have taken place in the history of English.

3.5.2   Developments in the order of subject and verb

We saw in (133) that in OE main clauses the finite verb can occupy the second position of the clause, where it may precede the subject. Another example of this phenomenon (which is usually referred to as the verb-second rule, or simply verb-second or even V2) is given in (134):

(134)   On twam þingum hæfde God þæs mannes saule gegodod
         in two   things   had God the man's soul endowed
         'With two things God had endowed man's soul'   (ÆCHom I, 1 184.161)

Example (134) also has a non-finite verb, *gegodod*, which appears in clause-final position; the finite and non-finite verbs in this sentence form what is sometimes called a brace construction.

A widely accepted analysis of such OE verb-second sentences, originally developed for Modern Dutch and German, is to say that the initial element (*on twam þingum* in (134)) is in a special topic-slot at the left boundary of the clause, and that it somehow attracts the finite verb into a position to its immediate right (see den Besten, 1977; van Kemenade, 1987). Any non-finite verb remains where it was. The abstract structure of verb-second sentences would therefore be as in (135):

(135)   [TOPIC V$_{finite}$ [SUBJECT rest of clause]]

This analysis is attractive because it directly expresses the similarity between declarative main clauses, as in (133)–(134), and wh-interrogatives such as (136):

(136)   Hwæt witst þu . . . us?
         what blame you   us
         'Why do you reproach us?'   (Bo 7.19.11)

Clauses like this have of course retained inversion up to the present day. In OE, they could be regarded as special cases of the structure in (135), with the wh-element taking the place of the TOPIC.

Subordinate clauses generally do not have verb-second in OE, as illustrated in (133) and also (137):

(137)   sona swa ic þe ærest on þisse unrotnesse geseah
         soon as I you first in this sadness   saw
         'As soon as I first saw you in this state of unhappiness'   (Bo 5.11.2)

Instead of second position, the verb here occupies clause-final position (as does the non-finite verb in the verb-second sentence (134)), and it has therefore been suggested that OE, just like Modern Dutch and German, basically has verb-final order, except that in main clauses the finite verb moves to second position. The reason for this movement may lie in a requirement that the relevant position be occupied by some element; in subordinate clauses it is the subordinating conjunction (*sona swa* in (137)), but in main clauses the finite verb is called upon to fill the slot. Although this analysis may seem quite neat and tidy, the pattern as described here is far from exceptionless. For one thing, it is easy to find OE main clauses that do not have verb-second, as (138)–(140) show:

(138)   nu   ealle ðas   þing   sind mid anum naman genemnode gesceaft.
          now   all   these things are with one   name named   creature
          'Now, all these things are called with one name: creature.'

                                                        (*ÆCHom* I, 20 335.19)

(139)   Ðillice word   Maria heold aræfniende   on hyre heortan
          such   words Mary kept   ponderingly in her   heart
          'Such words Mary kept and pondered in her heart.'   (*ÆCHom* I, 2 197.214)

(140)   Forð on   we sceolan mid ealle mod &   mægene to Gode gecyrran
          Therefore we must   with all   mind and power to God   turn
          'Therefore we must turn to God with all our mind and power.'

                                                        (*HomU*19 (BlHom 8) 26)

The initial elements *nu, ðyllice word* and *forðon* appear to be in topic position, but they fail to attract the finite verb into second position. Such a 'failure' of verb-second is common when the initial element is a disjunct or sentence adverbial, as in (138), but it also occurs with initial elements that are fully integrated clause constituents, as in (139), and is particularly frequent when the subject of the clause is a pronoun, as in (140). To account for cases like (138) and (139), it appears that we have to say that verb-second is simply optional. It can take place, but does not have to. For cases like (140), a somewhat stronger analysis is possible, which makes use of the well-established fact that, in many languages, personal pronouns participate in special word-order patterns (for the – quite complex – details of OE pronominal position, viewed in this light, see van Kemenade, 1987 and Pintzuk, 1998).

There is yet more that is distinctive in the OE rule of verb-second. While verb-second in general appears to be optional and is rare with pronominal subjects, there is at least one context in which it virtually always applies. This is in clauses starting with the adverb *þa* 'then', as in the main clause of (133) and in (141):

(141)   þa   eodon hie   ut
          then went   they out
          'Then they went out.'   (*ChronA* (Plummer) 894.83)

Why the adverb *þa*, which is a very frequent word in OE, should have this effect is not very clear. Moreover, there are some other initial adverbs, such as *þonne* 'then' and *her* 'here', that also trigger verb-second with pronouns quite regularly (though less often than *þa*). Descriptively, there seems to be a sort of continuum, ranging from the absolute verb-second trigger *þa* at one end to a non-verb-second triggering group of disjuncts at the other, but there may be too much variability in the texts (perhaps reflecting differences that cannot be fully recovered) to establish its exact form and nature.

This, then, is the situation in OE. In declarative main clauses, verb-second is frequent; it is rare when the subject is a personal pronoun; but it is categorical, even with pronouns, when the clause starts with the adverb *þa* 'then'. Interrogative main clauses always have inversion. After the OE period the scope of inversion slowly decreases, though not in a monotonic fashion: throughout the centuries, it is preserved in interrogatives (though the use of an auxiliary becomes obligatory in the course of the early ModE period; see Section 3.3.6), but it becomes gradually rarer in declarative clauses, except when these are introduced by some negative or restrictive element or when they have a presentative function. Moreover, there are some late medieval texts which show an increase in the use of inversion compared with OE.

In ME prose, verb-second is still frequent, especially following an initial adverbial, but personal pronouns seem to retain their resistance to inversion in most texts. (142) is an example with non-inversion of a pronominal subject:

(142)   bi þis 3e mahen seon ant witen . . .
          'by this you may see and know . . .'   (early 13th c., *SWard*. 263.23)

In some northern texts of the thirteenth century, the situation is somewhat different, in that verb-second applies in declarative clauses quite consistently, whatever the function of the initial element or the nature of the subject. An example from the early thirteenth-century text *The Rule of St Benet* is given in (143):

(143)   Oþir labur   sal   þai   do
          other labour shall they do
          'They must do other labour.'   *(Ben.Rule(1)* (Lnsd) 33.20)

In these dialects, pronominal subjects appear to have lost their clitic status and were subsequently treated like any other subject, i.e. they became eligible for inversion. Significantly, as Kroch & Taylor (1997) show, the relevant texts are from the area in which there was heavy influence from Scandinavian, which has consistent verb-second and no clitic pronouns.

After 1500, a decline in the use of verb-second can be observed which finds its culmination in the seventeenth century, when only those patterns of inversion that are still possible in present-day English continue to be regularly used. This concerns clauses with an initial negative or restrictive element, and various clause types with initial *there* or a locative phrase and an intransitive verb signifying (dis)appearance or some related notion, as in the following early ModE examples:

(144)   never will I go aboard another fleet (1709, Delarivier Manley, *The New Atalantis* 10, 2)

(145)   Seldom have you seen anie Poet possessed with avarice (1594, Thomas Nash, *The Unfortunate Traveller* 44, 25)

(146)   In this place begins that fruitful and plentiful Country which was call'd the
             Vale of Esham (1726, Daniel Defoe, *Tour of Great Britain* 441, 6)

In general terms, instances of these patterns can be regarded as survivals of an earlier verb-second stage of the language (though, as shown by Nevalainen, 1997, before the eighteenth century, sentences like (144) and (145) sometimes lacked verb-second).

As for the causes of the decline and loss of verb-second in most contexts, there are several factors that appear to have played a role in this, though their exact contribution and interaction remain to be established to everybody's satisfaction. One factor that has often been cited is language contact. This could have taken the form of influence from French and Scandinavian, either directly (from French, in which inversion was being lost in the Middle Ages) or indirectly (where speakers in a contact situation might evolve a grammar without any inversion at all, rather than retaining this rule together with its individual language-specific intricacies). A problem for this idea is the fact that it does not straightforwardly account for the continued use of verb-second, which we saw persisted into the seventeenth century. Another factor that has been investigated is the role of de-cliticisation of personal pronouns (see Lightfoot, 1999, for a summary of this work). If at some point, and for some independent reason, preverbal pronominal subjects, as in (140), came to be interpreted as just ordinary subjects, instead of special clitics, this would have the effect of enormously increasing the number of inversion-less clauses (already attested in sentences like (138) and (139)) and this could have set in motion a process leading to the loss of inversion except in some well-defined grammatical contexts. Such a reinterpretation may in fact have been triggered by a situation of language contact arising from increased mobility of a population that was somewhat linguistically differentiated due to earlier immigrations. Thus speakers of Scandinavian-influenced varieties might not have had clitic pronouns in their grammar (i.e. they would produce orders as in (143)), and they might therefore reinterpret clauses in southern varieties which had clitic subject pronouns (i.e. (142)) as simply being clauses with the order subject–verb, without any inversion. In a situation of close contact involving large groups of speakers (which is attested for late medieval and early modern London), this could easily lead to the development by language learners of grammars lacking inversion.

3.5.3 Developments in the order of object and verb

In the discussion above we suggested that in OE verbs are usually in clause-final position, but that a finite verb is moved to second position in main clauses, i.e. the language could be labelled as being 'OV with V2'. We also saw that there are several complications to this simple picture that need to be taken into account. One further complication is the fact that some main clauses have OV order. This is not a frequent pattern, but it is sometimes found when the object is a personal pronoun, as in example (147):

(147)   Ic hit gemunde   gio
             I it remembered formerly
             'I used to remember it.'   (*Bo* 5.13.2)

Given the distinctive behaviour of subject pronouns in OE, as discussed above, it is not entirely surprising to find object pronouns also occupying a special position (even though this particular word order is a minor one).

Another complication is that in both main and subordinate clauses in OE, the direct object sometimes follows a verb that cannot have undergone verb-second. This is a well-attested pattern with full NP objects, as in example (148), and it is found in a few examples with a pronominal object, as in (149):

(148)   þæt he nolde   niman mancyn neadunga of   ðam deofle
             that he not-would take   mankind forcibly from the   devil
             'That he would not have taken mankind forcibly from the devil'
                                                    (*ÆCHom* I, 14.1 296.167)

(149)   He nolde   genyman us neadunge of deofles anwealde
             he not-wanted take   us forcibly of devil's power
             'He would not forcibly take us from the devil's power.'
                                                    (*ÆCHom* I, 1 188.272)

As in the case of verb-second, it is clear that OE OV order too is not exceptionless. Examples of what was to become the regular order in later English, i.e. VO, already existed at this stage of the language. When it comes to the analysis of these early instances of VO order, there are basically two schools of thought. By some, such as van Kemenade (1987), these sentences are thought to be due to an operation of extraposition, which can move an object from preverbal to clause-final position (some support for this can be found in the language of the OE poem *Beowulf*, in which such VO orders tend to have a metrical break between verb and object). Others, such as Pintzuk (1998), believe that these cases simply show that (late) OE allowed VO order in addition to OV order, perhaps with some kind of competition existing between the two variants. Initially, VO order may have been due to extraposition, but later it developed into a regular word-order option. It is certainly the case that VO order becomes more frequent in the course of the OE period, though the development is very gradual and can look somewhat erratic if one compares only single texts.

After the OE period, the use of OV order continues as a productive option for all kinds of objects (with pronominal ones predominating in some but not all texts) until c.1400. A fourteenth-century example is given in (150):

(150)   I may my persone and myn hous so kepen and deffenden.
             'I can keep and defend myself and my house in such a way.'
                                                    (Chaucer, *Melibee* 1334)

However, the frequency of OV clauses undergoes a slow but steady decline in the ME period, with northern texts leading the development. In prose texts written after 1400, OV order also comes to be structurally restricted, continuing to occur at any frequency only in a few grammatical environments. Chief among these is the pattern with an auxiliary and a negated object, as in (151); see Moerenhout & van der Wurff (2000).

(151)   and sche seyd nay, be here feyth sche wuld no more days ʒeve ʒw þer-jn
             'and she said, "No", by her faith she would give you no more time in this
             matter' (*Paston Letters* 128.13–14)

After the middle of the sixteenth century, all instances of OV order cease to occur in prose, except as relics of an earlier era, in the form of quotations, proverbs and fixed expressions like (152):

(152)   He that mischief hatches, mischief catches.

In poetry, OV order continues to be used productively much longer: until the beginning of the twentieth century all kinds of examples of OV, not just ones like (151), are regularly found there. An example of OV and one of verb-second in nineteenth-century verse are given in (153) and (154):

(153)   He who would build his fame up high, / The rule and plummet must apply
             (1834, Walter Savage Landor, 'To Wordsworth' 37–38)

(154)   Here will I sit and wait (1853, Matthew Arnold, 'The Scholar-Gypsy' 16)

Having seen how OV was lost and VO established itself as the canonical word order, we can now inquire into the causes of this development. Since the change from OV to VO order, in English but also other languages, has attracted the attention of many linguists, there is no shortage of proposed explanations. As in the case of verb-second, language contact has also been held responsible for the decline of OV order, whether by direct influence from French (though for this hypothesis, the loss of preverbal pronominal objects in English is a problem, as is the fact that OV survives more tenaciously in ME southern texts than in northern texts) or by more indirect influence from Scandinavian (with a situation of bilingualism or perhaps even pidginisation said to promote the use of VO order; see Weerman, 1993; Kroch & Taylor, 2000). A different line of approach, pursued by Colman (1988a), Ogura (2001) and others, has focused on the possible effect of heavy processing costs of embedded clauses in an OV language, where – in theory at least – complicated sentences like (155) could occur:

(155)   This is the cat that the rat that the malt that in the house that Jack built lay
             ate killed.

Another recurrent theme in accounts of the change is the loss of case distinctions, as discussed in Chapter 2. When the syntactic function of an NP could no longer be read off its case endings, word order came to be the sole formal marker of subjects and direct objects, and it has been suggested that they came to be distinguished more clearly by increased use of the SVO pattern, which was common in the language anyway, in both main and subordinate clauses. There are many variations on this theme, depending on the particular theory of case and word order that the writer adopts (a modern generative version can be found in Roberts, 1997); all of them face the problem that the consistent use of SOV order is in principle also sufficient to distinguish the subject from the verb. That such a system can work efficiently in practice is proved by the case of Modern Dutch, which has no more case marking than present-day English and still gets by fine with OV order. However, it is true that Modern Dutch has much less variability in word-order patterning than OE, so perhaps the loss of case should be viewed as triggering greater consistency in word order, whether this is OV or VO, rather than triggering a change towards SVO order. An important role may also be played by the presence of verbal inflections: in Old and early Middle English (as in Dutch), there is still in most cases a systematic distinction between singular and plural in verbal endings, and in many sentences this will aid in determining subject and object. Further aid comes from the fact that subjects typically represent given information, which means that they often take the form of a personal pronoun, and it is exactly these forms that have preserved case distinctions up to the present day. If we also take into account the considerable help of contextual, pragmatic and semantic factors in the task of decoding clauses, it is clear that it is a simplification to view the loss of case as having led to rampant ambiguity of subject and object status of NPs, for which the use of consistent SVO order needed to be employed as a repair strategy.

3.5.4   Developments in the order of direct objects and indirect objects

In standard present-day English, the position of the indirect object is rigidly fixed: if it is expressed in the form of a bare NP, it must immediately follow the verb and precede the direct object. No reordering of these elements is allowed, even in cases where the indirect object is very long and might be thought to fit in more comfortably at the end of the clause, in conformity with the principle of end weight. An example with verb–IO–DO order is given in (156), while reordering leading to ungrammaticality is exemplified in (157):

(156)   We have decided to give all the competitors a small prize.

(157)   *We have decided to give a small prize all the many young competitors that have put so much time and energy into preparing themselves for this tournament.

If a *to*-phrase or a *for*-phrase is used instead of an indirect object, the prepositional phrase normally follows the DO, as in (158):

(158)   We have decided to give a prize to everybody.

As in the previous two sections, the history of indirect object constructions shows a somewhat wider range of word-order options in OE gradually developing into the more restricted range of present-day English.

One of the options existing in OE was the order direct object–indirect object, which was about as frequent as the reverse order. Examples of both orders are given in (159) and (160):

(159)   ðonne he nyle   ða bisne (DO) oðrum(IO) eowian
             when he not-wants the example   others   show

             ða   he mid ryhte eowian sceal
             that he properly show   must
             'When he does not want to set the example to others that he properly ought
             to set'   (*CP* 59.449.29)

(160)   &   noldon   Iuliuse (IO) nænne weorþscipe (DO) don
             and not-wanted Iulius   no   worship   do
             'and did not want to worship Iulius'   (*Or* 5 10.124.9)

If one of the objects is pronominal (this is usually the indirect object), it nearly always precedes the nominal object, which is another example of pronouns favouring positions early in the clause. When there are two pronominal objects, the predominant order is for the direct object to come first, as in (161):

(161)   þu   hit (DO) him (IO) of   þinum handum sealdest
             you it   him   from your   hands   gave
             'you gave it to him with your own hands'   (LS 34 (Seven Sleepers) 607)

As the above three examples show, the indirect object is often preverbal, in accordance with the OV character of OE.

The pattern in (161) continues as the most frequent order in ME when both objects are pronominal, and so does the pattern IO–DO when only the indirect object is pronominal, of which we give an ME example in (162):

(162)   leafdi do me are
             lady   do me mercy
             'Lady, have mercy on me'   (*AW* 26.3)

The pair in (159) and (160), however, undergoes change: the order DO–IO (with both objects being NPs) is still found in early ME, as in (163), but then goes into a serious decline and disappears by the mid-fourteenth century.

(163)   deð hearm (DO) moni ancre (IO)
             does harm   many anchoress
             'does harm to many an anchoress'   (*AW* 62.21)

The loss of sentences like (163) has been accounted for by an appeal to the loss of dative and accusative inflections and the consequent need to distinguish the two objects by means of more rigid word order, with the order IO–DO becoming fixed because this was the usual order when the IO was a pronoun, as in the very frequent pattern of (162). However, this fails to account for the fact that sentences like (163) continued to be used long after the inflectional distinction between dative and accusative had worn away. Another reason for the loss of (163) may have been increasing competition from the indirect object expressed by a *to*-phrase (see Section 3.4.2), which nearly always followed the direct object.

In both (162) and (163) the indirect object follows the verb, and this is not accidental: in the ME period as a whole, indirect objects preceding the verb are very rare. In fact, so few examples of preverbal indirect objects have been found that it is difficult to say whether their decline follows more or less the same route as that of preverbal direct objects, as sketched in the previous section. This rarity may be partly due to an overall decrease in the number of clauses with an indirect object, which has been noted in ME texts and attributed to the loss of a large number of OE ditransitive verbs from the lexicon of the language (compare Chapter 4).

After the ME period, there is only one further change to be observed in the ordering of objects. When both objects are pronominal, the predominant order in Old and ME was DO–IO (*I gave it him*, as in (161)); this pattern still exists (see Biber et al., 1999: 929) but seems to have been overtaken in frequency by the reverse order IO–DO (*I gave him it*) at some point during the nineteenth century, in the south of England at least. It could be hypothesised that there is a preference for the IO–DO pattern due the obligatory use of this order when both objects are NPs, but this would be a rather imprecise idea that cannot explain the robust survival of DO–IO order with pronouns during all those centuries that NP objects have consistently had IO–DO order.

3.5.5   Developments in the position of particles and adverbs

While a great deal is known about the history of subject, verb and object placement in English sentences, less attention has so far been paid to the position of other sentence elements and the changes that have affected them. In particular the position of adverbial phrases relative to other constituents has been poorly studied, in spite of the fact that they are very frequent (Crystal, 1980 reports that nearly two-thirds of all sentences in a corpus of spoken English contain an adverbial, and they do not seem to be much less frequent in older stages of the language). One reason for this neglect may be the difficulty of establishing a positional framework for adverbials, which typically show a high degree of freedom in placement. Nevertheless, a certain amount of work has been done on some aspects of the history of adverbial positioning.

One type of adverb that has received attention is the particle found in present-day phrasal verbs like *turn up, hold out* and *take down*. These combinations go back to OE structures of the type shown in (164) and (165):

(164)   Hi   ða   upastigon
          they   then   up-went
          'Then they went up.'   (*ÆCH*om II, 18 172.95)

(165)   þa   *sticode* him mon   þa eagan *ut*
         then stuck   him people the eyes   out
         'Then they gouged out his eyes.'   (*Or* 4.5.90.13)

The forms *upastigan* and *utstician* and scores of others consist of a verb (*astigan*, *stician*) prededed by an adverb-like element (*up, ut*), which can be adjacent to the verb, as in (164), but can also occur in a non-adjacent position, as in (165); these elements are sometimes called separable prefixes, but we shall use the term particles for them, to bring out the continuity with present-day phrasal verbs.

   In OE, the position of particles at first sight appears to be relatively unconstrained: they can be found before and after the verb, in both cases with or without intervening material. Examples (164)–(167) illustrate some of the possibilities.

(166)   for ðan þe se stream berð aweg placidum
         'Because the stream carries away Placidus.'   (*ÆCHom* II, 11 95.97)

(167)   he bæd   hire, þæt heo ut of þam byrene gan sceolde
         he asked her   that she out of the stable go   should
         'He asked her to go out of the stable.'   (*GD* 1 (C) 9.69.1)

This freedom makes it look as if not much of interest can be said about particle position in OE. However, closer investigation shows that certain positions are disfavoured. For one thing, sentences with the particle in initial position, as in PDE (168a), are quite rare in OE; the few examples that have been found, such as (168b), are all from poetry.

(168) a. Up they went.
      h   Up aræmde Abraham þa
          'Up rose Abraham then.'   (Ex. 411)

Hence nearly all instances of the order [particle X V] are like (167) in having the particle in clause-medial position. Moreover, most of them feature a prepositional phrase directly following the particle, which means that they can be interpreted as actually having not a particle but a complex prepositional phrase. In (167), for example, there would be one phrase [$_{PP}$ *ut of þam byrene*], rather than a sequence of [$_{prt}$ *ut*] followed by [$_{PP}$ *of þam byrene*]. The result of such an analysis is that the order [particle X V] as such is very rare. Furthermore, it has been noted that the option [V X particle], as in (165), is somewhat rare in subordinate clauses, especially when the verb in question is non-finite.

   Recall Sections 3.5.2 and 3.5.3, where we concluded that OE verbs are basically clause-final but that finite verbs in main clauses can be fronted to second position. This could explain the rarity of the orders [V X particle] (in subordinate clauses) and [particle X V], if we assume that verb and particle form a unit out of which particles cannot readily move. Finite verb fronting would lead to the order [V X particle] in main clauses, but would not be expected in subordinate clauses, and certainly not with non-finites. The order [particle X V] is manifestly not a possible result of verb fronting either, and that is why it is highly infrequent. The position of particles in OE thus provides some confirmation for the conclusions reached in Sections 3.5.2 and 3.5.3

In early ME, there is a rapid change in the order of the particle and the verb: after 1100, the order particle–verb becomes rare, so that in the great majority of cases the particle follows the verb, in both main and subordinate clauses. An example is given in (169):

(169)   þat   he   ealle   his   castles   sculde   iiuen   up
          that   he   all   his   castles   should   give   up
          'that he should give up all his castles'   (*ChronE* (Plummer) 1140.42)

This change has been linked to the change from predominant OV to VO order, discussed in Section 3.5.3, in such a way that the verb has been taken to be no longer the final element in the predicate, but the initial element, which would lead to the order [verb X Y Z], with X, Y, Z being objects, particles, or any other constituents of the predicate. However, this link is not entirely straightforward, since other constituents continue to precede the verb fairly regularly for several centuries even though particles nearly always follow it. Sentence (169), in which the object *ealle his castles* is preverbal but the particle *up* postverbal, is a good case in point (see Section 3.5.3 for details).

A subsequent change affecting particles concerns not position but frequency: particle verbs have become enormously frequent in Modern English. This appears to a large extent to be due to an increase in combinations having a particle with metaphorical meaning (as in *let somebody down*, *take up a hobby*, etc.), which set in after the early ModE period (for descriptive data on their rise in frequency, both in types and tokens, see Claridge, 2000).

There are just a few other points that we can deal with here concerning the position of adverbs. Generally speaking, the overall historical picture is one of relative freedom in OE slowly giving way to a more constrained system of the type operative in present-day English. This development is illustrated well by the case of adverbs intervening between the object and the verb. In OE, when objects were often preverbal, a clause often had an adverb or even a longer phrase separating the object from the verb, as examples like (133) and (137) show. In ME, preverbal objects slowly become less usual, but they can still be followed by an adverbial, as in examples like (150). However, the intervening element in this type of ME sentence is usually fairly short, a restriction that is perhaps understandable for a language in which OV order was becoming more and more marked.

ME clauses with VO order also allow an adverb to intervene between the object and the verb. An example is given in (170):

(170)   he scapyd of hard & left þer hir scrippe
          'he escaped with difficulty and left her bag there' (*MKempe* A 118.15)

Use of this option declines after c.1500, but examples such as (171) – often featuring the verb *have* – show that it can still be found as late as the nineteenth century:

(171)   Accordingly, we had always wine and dessert (1851–3, Gaskell, *Cranford* iii.25)

The reason for the loss of [V adverb O] order, as in (170)–(171), has been sought in structural changes in the make-up of the clause, which are linked to the disappearance of inflectional marking on verbs, in particular the loss of the inflectional marker *-en* for plural. This idea, rather technical in its full details but clearly set out in Roberts (1993), is based on an observed similarity between ME and Modern French, which still has fairly rich verbal inflections as well as the option of using [V adverb O] order.

A special case of the [V X O] pattern is found in negative clauses without *do* or other auxiliary, where an object NP can be separated from the verb by the word *not*, as in (172) (see also Section 3.3.6):

(172)   I . . . saw not Betty (1667, Pepys, *Diary* VIII 514.2 (1 Nov.))

This pattern is found from the thirteenth century, when *not* started to be used as the regular marker of negation, until the eighteenth century, when the use of *do* had become the rule in sentences of this type. During this entire period, there is a clear split between ordinary NPs and pronouns: the former always follow *not*, as in (172), while pronouns virtually always precede *not*, as in (173):

(173)   I have it not by me, or I would copy you the exact passage. (1848, Gaskell, *Mary Barton* v.62)

Note that (173), a rather late example of this pattern, features the lexical verb *have*, which is well known for long resisting the use of *do* (and for behaving like an auxiliary also in other ways; compare (171)).

3.5.6   Consequences

After our discussion of word-order changes above, we will also consider some of their consequences. In particular, the change from predominant OV order to predominant VO order that English underwent in the Middle Ages has been associated with the development of several new constructions. These involve the rise of some new infinitival complementation patterns and the extension of preposition stranding.

A first innovation is the so-called 'accusative-plus-infinitive' or Exceptional Case Marking construction, a modern example of which is (174):

(174)   We believe this to be wrong.

This type of sentence, in which the matrix verb takes a clausal complement which itself has an overt NP subject, does not occur in OE (except in glosses to Latin texts). The first unambiguous examples are found around 1400; the fifteenth-century instances tend to occur mainly in formal texts, and even today there is something elevated about the construction in many cases. Careful assessment of a great deal of textual evidence by several scholars has led to a consensus that the construction represents a case of syntactic borrowing from Latin; but there were some prior English-internal changes that made this borrowing possible. We give an early example in (175):

(175)   she dare not aventure her money to be brought vp to London for feere of
           robbyng
           'She dare not venture her money to be brought up to London for fear of
           robbery.'   (*Paston Letters* 156, 7–10)

The rise of this construction in English can be seen as a result of the change to regular VO order. To see how this explanation works, consider the NP *her money* in (175). Thematically, it functions as the subject to the infinitival verb *to be brought vp*, but as far as case marking is concerned, it can be said to be the object of the matrix verb *venture*. However, this is only possible if verbs precede their objects. In OE, where the object regularly preceded the verb, it was impossible for the relevant NP to occupy the canonical object position of the matrix clause and at the same time the subject position of the infinitival clause. For this reason, the construction could only gain a foothold in English after the modern VO order had fully established itself, a change that, as we saw above, was nearing completion by 1400. This interpretation derives further strength from developments in the history of Dutch and German: in both languages, which are firmly OV, we can see some toying with this construction in strongly Latin-influenced texts from the Renaissance, but the construction did not spread from there and died out again.

Another infinitival construction which first arose in the late ME period, probably also as a result of the change from OV to VO order, is the so-called 'for NP-to-VP' construction, as in (176):

(176)   It will be awkward for anyone to claim their money back.
           (in the sense 'It will be awkward if anyone claims their money back.')

Here, the infinitival clause has an overt subject introduced by *for*. Again, this construction is not found in OE texts but starts being used in the fourteenth century (first with the subject taking the form of a bare NP, but from the sixteenth century onwards in the form of a PP introduced by *for*). In this case, there is little evidence for influence from Latin. Instead, its origins are probably to be sought in the following OE construction, which itself has in fact survived to this day:

(177)   Hit þuncþ monige monnum wunderlice to herenne ... hu   deofel
           it   seems many   men   miraculous to hear   how devil

           æfre þa   durstinesse hæfde
           ever the audacity   had
           'It seems miraculous to many people to hear how the devil ever had the
           audacity.'   (*HomU* 1 (Irv 5) 82)

In this sentence type, the dative NP, here *monige monnum*, is not the subject of the infinitival clause, but a kind of complement to the main clause predicate, (*þuncþ*) *wunderlic*. In (177) this dative NP precedes the adjective, while the infinitival clause follows it. At some point, however, such dative NPs came to be regularly placed after the predicative element, probably due to analogy with the newly prevailing VO order. The result would be sentences such as (178):

(178)   if it be a foul thing a man to waste his catel on wommen
          'if it is a foul thing for a man to waste his property on women'
                                        (Chaucer, *Pars.T* 848)

Since this construction now has a sequence [NP to VP], it is liable to reanalysis in such a way that the NP comes to be interpreted as the subject of the infinitive, rather than as a complement to the predicate *be a foul thing*. In the specific sentence in (178) and others, there might not be a great deal of difference in meaning between the two interpretations, thus facilitating the reanalysis. However, the new analysis led to innovative sentences like (179) in which the infinitival clause introduced by the word *as* clearly includes the bare NP *mon*, which can therefore not be a complement to the matrix element *bitter*, and must be interpreted as being the subject of the infinitival clause:

(179)   No thing ... so bitter is ... As mon for God &   heuen   blis
          no thing   so bitter is   as man for God and Heaven's bliss

          to suffre deth   with gode wille
          to suffer death with good will
          'Nothing is so bitter as when a man, for the sake of God and the bliss of heaven, suffers death with good will.'
                                        (*Stanzaic Life of Chr.*, Forster 1926: 206)

After 1500, the bare NP subject of such infinitivals comes to be introduced by *for* (and, for a while, *to*). Again, the construction – with or without an introductory preposition – did not arise in Dutch and German, where the prevailing complement–head order meant that, just as in the OE example (177), the relevant NP was not adjacent to the infinitive of the subordinate clause, thus blocking reanalysis.

A final phenomenon for which the change to VO order has been invoked as a causative factor is the extension of preposition stranding, i.e. cases in which a preposition is not immediately followed by its complement. In OE, preposition stranding occurred when the complement was a pronoun or the word *þær*, as in examples (180) and (181):

(180)   þa   wendon hi   me heora bæc to
          then turned they me their back to
          'Then they turned their backs on me.'   (*Bo* 2.8.9)

(181)   Be þæm þu   meaht ongietan ðæt þu
          by that you can   perceive that you

> þær   nane   myrhðe   on   næfdest
> there no   happiness on   had-not
> 'From that you could understand that you did not take joy in it.'
> (*Bo* 7.15.11)

Both of these cases also allow an option whereby the complement immediately precedes the preposition, as shown in (182) and (183):

(182)   and hi   ne   dorston him   fore gebiddan
        and they not dared   him   for   pray
        'And they did not dare to pray for him.'   (*ÆHom* 20. 225)

(183)   and com   æfter fyrste to ðam treowe sohte   wæstm ðæron.
        and came   after while   to the tree   looked-for   fruit   there-on

        and nænne ne gemette
        and none   not found
        'And after a while he went to the tree and looked for fruit on it, but found none.'
        (*ÆCHom* II, 30 237.72)

On the basis of an analysis proposed for Modern Dutch, which has a partly similar pattern, van Kemenade (1987) suggests that preposition stranding in OE always involves a complement being fronted through the position immediately to the left of the preposition, i.e. that the order in (182)–(183) forms the basis for that in (180)–(181). Any element that cannot occur in the order of (182)–(183), such as an ordinary NP, also cannot strand its preposition.

Some further cases of preposition stranding which existed in OE, such as relative clauses without a relative pronoun, as in (184), have been analysed as containing a kind of empty pronoun, or silent counterpart to *þær*:

(184)   þæt gewrit   þe   hit on awriten wæs
           the document that it   on written was
           'The document that it was written in'   (*Or* 6 13.141.21)

This rather limited array of stranding options was greatly extended in the ME period. Around 1200, the first few examples are found of stranding in passives; (185) is one of them:

(185)   þer   wes sorhe   to seon hire leoflich lich
           there was sorrow to see   her   lovely   body

           faren so reowliche wið
           dealt so cruelly   with
           'It was a sad sight to see her lovely body dealt with so cruelly.'
           (c.1225, *St Juliana* (Roy) 22.195)

Obviously, there cannot be an empty pronoun involved here. Instead, this sentence type could be analysed in the way present-day prepositional passives usually are, i.e. as having a combination of verb and preposition that at some level is equivalent to a transitive verb. This would make the passive in (185) comparable to ordinary passives like *the house was sold*, which are attested throughout the history of English (see Section 3.4.4). A simple structural representation of this idea is given in (186):

(186)   [V] [$_{PP}$P NP] –> [$_V$V + P] NP

This process of univerbation, at it has been called, would be unlikely to take place as long as the verb was regularly clause-final, since this would yield sentences like *he with her dealt*, in which the verb and the preposition are not adjacent and can therefore not be analysed as forming one unit. However, after the regular order had become *he dealt with her*, univerbation was free to occur. This process appears to have initially affected only verbs in which an object interpretation of the complement NP is plausible from a semantic point of view, as in the combination *fare* ('deal') *with* in (185).

From these rather simple beginnings, preposition stranding in passives slowly spread to more and more verbs (some 24 of them are attested in the prepositional passive before 1400) and more and more passive constructions. It begins to be attested in various passive infinitive constructions, as in (187), in the fourteenth century. At roughly the same time, it is extended to collocations consisting of a verb, a nominal and a preposition, as in (188), and in the sixteenth century it appears with phrasal prepositional verbs, as in (189):

(187)   how worthy it es to ben wondrid uppon
          'How worthy it is to be marvelled at.'   (Chaucer, *Bo* 4.pr1.22)

(188)   and þes oþer wordis of þis bischop ouȝte to be taken hede to
          'And these other words of this bishop ought to be taken heed of.'
                                                    (Wyclif, *Clergy HP* 369.1)

(189)   I understand there there was a servant of yours, and a kynsman of myne, was
          myschevously made away with (c.1613 (1502), *Plumpton Let.* 130 164.11)

A further area in which preposition stranding underwent a widening of possibilities was relative and interrogative clauses. OE only allowed stranding in relative clauses introduced by the complementiser *þe*, as in (184); this pattern was continued when *þe* was replaced by *that*. In early ME it also came to be used in relative clauses introduced by the new relative pronoun *which*, as in (190), and from there it appears to have spread to interrogative clauses with *which* and also *who*, as in (191):

(190)   And   getenisse men   ben   in   ebron/
          and   gigantic   men   are   in   Hebron
          Quilc men   mai   get   wundren on
          which men   may   still wonder   at
          'And there are gigantic men in Hebron, whom people may still marvel at.'
                                                    (a.1325(c.1250), *Cursor* 145)

(191)   Nuste   nan kempe whæ he sculde slæn on
          not-knew no warrior who he should strike on
          'No warrior knew who he should strike.'   (Layamon, *Brut* 27487)

Set off against these gains in preposition stranding, there are also some losses to record. The OE option of separating a personal pronoun from its preposition, as in (180), and also the order pronoun–preposition, (182), died out soon after 1200. Combinations with *there* and a non-adjacent preposition, (181), also did not survive the ME period. Much more tenacious were combinations like *therein*, *thereat* and *thereon*, as in the OE example (183). In the ME period, these expressions are frequently used as alternatives to prepositional phrases like *in it, at it* and *for it*; an example with *therewith* is given in (192):

(192)   þai toke stone, and made þerwiþ þe tour
          'They took stone and made the tower with it.'   (c.1400, *Brut* ccviii. 238)

The pattern was also extended to combinations with *here* and *where*, as in (193) and (194):

(193)   Here by þou mayst lere þat of o   dysshe þey etyn yn fere
          hereby   you may learn that of one dish   they eat in company
          'Hereby you may learn that they eat together of one dish.'
                                                (c. 1320, R. Brunne, *Medit.* 67)

(194)   Mete quorbi ðei miȝten liuen
          'Food whereby they might live.'   (c. 1250, Gen. & Ex. 573)

These combinations are also very frequent in the early ModE period. After 1800, however, they become less usual, and today they are characteristic of archaic and/or legal usage, although a number of them are still used more widely as lexicalised units (such as *therefore*, *whereabouts*, *the wherewithal* and *the why and the wherefore*). This decline might in general terms be attributed to their divergent word order (with the preposition being preceded by its complement), were it not for the fact that the pattern survived for more than four hundred years after this order had become divergent.

4   Vocabulary

Dieter Kastovsky

4.1   Introduction

4.1.1   The function of lexemes

The 'normal' native speaker of a language will probably regard sounds and words as the most basic building blocks of a language, because they are the elements which can be perceived most easily without specific training. We put sounds together to form words, and we put words together to form larger structures, i.e. sentences realised as utterances (at least that is what we think we are doing). Therefore, speakers tend to react most readily to variation and change of pronunciation and vocabulary. Words, or rather lexical items or lexemes (= dictionary entries), can be regarded as intermediate elements between the level of sounds and the level of syntactic structure. But there are some additional reasons having to do with the existence of certain types of lexemes and their function why lexemes have this bridge function between phonology, morphology, syntax and the lexicon (see Section 4.1.5. below).

Lexemes are the means by which we make direct reference to extralinguistic reality, converting our basic perception of the world around us into language. Their basic function thus is to serve as labels for segments of extralinguistic reality which a speech community finds nameworthy, so that it can talk about it in a simple and direct way. And it is only when one has such 'nameworthy' entities that one can talk about their relationship (more precisely the relationship between their referents) in terms of more complex grammatical structures such as sentences (utterances): first one has to identify something to talk about before one can talk about it, i.e. one has to know 'who is doing what to whom'. This is why lexemes are one of the most central categories in language: it is their existence that links the perception of more or less discrete extralinguistic phenomena (like bushes or trees, apes or monkeys, types of movement such as *walk*, *fly*, *swim*, manners of producing sounds such as *talk*, *shout*, *whisper*, *bark*, *meow*, *chirp*, etc.) to our perception of the world around us. On the other hand, it is often the case that the very existence of a lexeme creates a demarcation in an otherwise continuous extralinguistic referent. Thus in terms of its physical nature, the colour spectrum is continuous; linguistically it is divided into segments, whose number varies from language to language. Similarly, there is no visible dividing line between chin and cheek, but the existence of the lexemes *chin* and *cheek* forces us to make this distinction, which does not necessarily exist in all languages. In English we always make a distinction between *hand* and *arm*, *foot* and *leg*, but in Polish this distinction is optional, and normally *ręka* is used for both arm and hand, and *noga* for both foot and leg. Lexemes thus not only act as labels for referents that have an autonomous extralinguistic existence, they also create such referents by introducing distinctions that are not given *a priori* in extralinguistic reality. Even closely related languages, such as English and German, or Italian, French and Spanish, will differ considerably as to the overall structure of their vocabulary, because of the different communicative needs of the speech communities involved and the vagaries of historical development. Thus why would German want to make a distinction between the ingestion of food or drink by human beings and animals in the form of *essen* (human being) : *fressen* (animal, but extended to human beings if they behave like an animal), *trinken* (human being) : *saufen* (animals, but also human beings who overdo it with a specific type of beverage, i.e. alcohol), when English simply makes do with *eat* : *drink*; and why, at least until recently, did British English differentiate between *coach* (long-distance) and *bus* (local), when German just has *(Auto)-Bus*?

The same is true of different historical stages of one and the same language, and for English this is perhaps even more striking than for any other European language. Its vocabulary structure was transformed profoundly between the first records of English and today, so that what we find in the eighth century at the level of vocabulary is basically unrecognisable to us, and today's English would also be equally alien to someone from the eighth century, even disregarding phonological and morphological changes.

A simple example, viz. an OE Bible passage and its early Modern English and Modern English equivalents, might serve to illustrate this (the lexical differences between OE and the other periods are indicated by italics):

> *Sōþlīċe* on *þām* dagum wæs *ġeworden ġebod* fram *þām cāsere* Augusto, þæt eall *ymbehwyrft* wǣre *tōmearcod*. þēos *tōmearcodnes* wæs *ǣrest ġeworden* fram *þām dēman* Syriġe Cirīno. And ealle *hiġ ēodon* and *syndriġe fērdon* on *hyra ċeastre*.   (West Saxon translation, early eleventh century)

> And it *chaunced* in thoose dayes that ther *went oute* a *commaundment* from Auguste the *Emperour*, that all the woorlde shuld be *taxed*. And this *taxynge* was the fyrst and *executed* when Syrenius was *leftenaunt* in Syria. And every man went vnto his awne *citie* to be *taxed*.   (Early Modern English, Tyndale 1534)

> *Truely* in these days it *happened* that an *order* was *issued* by the *Emperor* Augustus that the *whole* world should be *assessed* for *taxes*. This *taxing* was the first and was *implemented* when Syrenus was *judge* in Syria. And everybody went to *their place* of birth to be *taxed*.   (Modern English, translation DK)

4.1.2   The stratification of the vocabulary

An important aspect here is the fact that the vocabulary used by a speech community exhibits a complex, multidimensional stratification. For Modern English, the following dimensions of linguistic variation have become established (cf., e.g., Quirk et al., 1985:15ff.): (a) region, (b) social group, (c) field of discourse, (d) medium, (e) attitude.

There is no reason to assume that the situation was radically different in earlier periods. We know that there had always been dialectal differences, and these were fairly great. Thus the author of the *Cursor Mundi*, a northern poem from about 1300, remarks that he had to translate a text written in Southern English into Northern English for the benefit of the northerners who were not familiar with other forms of English:

In sotherin englis was it draun,	'In Southern English was it written,
And turn it haue I till our aun	and I have turned it into our own
Langage o northrin lede	language of the Northern people,
þat can nan oiþer englis rede	who can't read any other English.'

There must certainly also always have been differences according to the field of discourse, insofar as poetic diction clearly differed from prose diction, and the same is true of technical texts such as medical, legal, religious ones, etc. But our picture of this variation is rather patchy for the earlier periods due to the restricted documentation that we have. This is true, in particular, as regards the difference between spoken and written language. Thus until the late Middle Ages we only have records of written language and the registers that go with it. This reflects a very limited degree of variation, since only a fraction of the population was literate. So we do not really know anything about the lexical variation of spoken English. It is only when private letters, court proceedings and plays begin to appear that we get a glimpse of the spoken language, too, which is at the end of the ME period, but above all from the early Modern English period onwards.

4.1.3   Lexical change

If the vocabulary of a language reflects the perception of the world by a speech community, it will have to be constantly adapted to its changing needs. Therefore, the vocabulary is as much a reflection of deep-seated cultural, intellectual and emotional interests, perhaps even of the whole *Weltbild* of a speech community, as are the texts that have been produced by its members. The systematic study of the vocabulary of a language thus is an important contribution to the understanding of the culture and civilisation of a speech community over and above the analysis of the texts in which this vocabulary is put to communicative use. And the history of the vocabulary of a speech community is a reflection of its general history, since both innovations and losses document changes in the social needs of this community arising from the pressure to adapt to changing external circumstances. The vocabulary of a language thus is also a link to the material and spiritual culture of its speakers; conversely, without knowing this material and spiritual culture one might often not know what someone is talking about. Let me illustrate this with two examples I came across during a recent stay in the US.

In a bar in New York I saw the following ad: *When was the last time you were Jägermeistered?* In order to understand this, it is not enough to know that English has an expression *to wine and dine a person* (with the passive *to be wined and dined*), which in turn is based (at least for *wine*) on the pattern *to water flowers, salt soup, butter the bread* 'provide something with x', formally parallel to the verbs *bomb, knife, stone, guillotine* 'attack, kill someone by x'. One also has to know that *Jägermeister* fits into the wining/dining scenario and not the attack scenario, i.e. that this is a German liqueur and not the name of a person or instrument. Thus, on the basis of all this (extra)linguistic knowledge, one can eventually arrive at the interpretation 'When were you last treated to a Jägermeister?' During the same trip I also learned that the *doggy-bags*, which have been an important part of American culture for many years, are now replaced by *go-boxes*, at least in some areas. Without the restaurant context and the familiar look of the bag (*go-boxes* still come in brown bags) I would probably not have been able to figure out what a *go-box* is.

Many changes in the English vocabulary are due to massive borrowing from the languages with which English came into contact in the course of its history, and this has also had far-reaching repercussions for morphology and phonology. If we take a bird's eye view of the vocabulary of Modern English, we cannot but be amazed by its overall size: estimates range between 700,000 and more than a million documented lexical items; the second edition of the *OED*, our main source for the history of the English vocabulary, contains about 616,500 lexical items according to its own estimate (*OED* 1:xxiii), but it certainly makes reference to many more via sub- and run-on entries, although, admittedly, this source also contains much that is no longer used. But it is not just the sheer size of the vocabulary, it is also its heterogeneity which is remarkable. Almost unlimited borrowing since the tenth and eleventh centuries – first from Latin, then from Scandinavian, then from French, then again from Latin and Greek, and finally from almost any language English came into contact with – is responsible for this situation. As a result of its history, English is far less resistant than any other European language to borrowing, and since the battle against the 'hard words' in the seventeenth century there has never been any serious campaign against foreign elements comparable to the government-decreed measures in France, Slovakia, or Russia, or the Germanisation movement in Germany in the first half of the twentieth century. About 70 per cent of present-day English vocabulary consists of loans, with loans from French and/or Latin (including Greek and Neo-Latin) taking up the lion's share. Just over 350 languages have contributed to this wealth (see Section 9.4). When, in contradistinction, we look at recorded OE lexemes, only about 3 per cent are loans, basically from Latin (and often not recognisable as such); the proportion of loans in the early Modern English neologism vocabulary is estimated at 40 to 50 per cent (see Scheler, 1977: 74), i.e. still much lower than today.

The following is only a small selection illustrating the range of languages that have contributed to English vocabulary (Latin, Greek and French will be left out here, because their influence will be discussed separately below): American Indian (*caucus, moose, racoon*), Arabic (*alcohol, assassin, zero*), Chinese (*ketchup, tea, wok*), Czech (*gherkin, robot, vampire*), Dutch (*brandy, cookie, landscape*), Finnish (*mink, sauna*), German (*kindergarten, sauerkraut, snorkel*), Hebrew (*cherub, jubilee*), Hindi (*bungalow, dinghy, shampoo*), Hungarian (*goulash, paprika*), Italian (*aria, balcony, lava, mafia, opera, piano, spaghetti*), Japanese (*futon, soy, sushi*), Mexican Indian (*avocado, chocolate, tomato*), Persian (*arsenic, lilac, pyjamas*), Portuguese (*buffalo, marmalade, port*), Russian (*bistro, mammoth, sputnik, vodka*), Sanskrit (*candy, indigo, jungle*), Spanish (*cafeteria, cash, cockroach, sherry, siesta*), Tahitian (*tattoo*), Tamil (*catamaran, cheroot, mango*), Tongan (*taboo*), Turkish (*caftan, coffee, scarlet, yoghurt*), Yiddish (*bagel, glitzy, kosher, kugel, schmaltz(y), schlep, schmooze, yenta*); see Hughes (2000: 365ff.).

As a consequence especially of the borrowings from French, Latin and Greek, the morphophonemic and word-formation systems of Modern English are also heterogeneous, because they involve different strata, i.e. a native and a non-native one. This is most conspicuous if we look at lexical families which are based on a common meaning. In languages such as German, and for that matter OE, there are usually etymological, formal-morphological ties between the members of such families, i.e. the members are derived by word-formation processes from a common basis – the vocabulary is 'associated'. In Modern English, on the other hand, the vocabulary is often 'dissociated', because semantically related words are unrelated etymologically; cf. the following English and German examples:

(1)   gall   : bilious   Galle : gallig
            mouth : oral   Mund : mündlich
            eye   : oculist, ophthalmologist   Auge : Augenarzt
            father : paternal/fatherly   Vater : väterlich
            moon   : lunar vehicle   Mond : Mondfahrzeug

Thus semantic relationships within the vocabulary are much more transparent in German than they are in English. But this has not always been the case. In OE the situation was much like that in Modern High German. The vocabulary was associative, i.e. based on a systematic exploitation of native word-formation patterns, which produced extensive, transparent word families. Cf. the following selected list of compounds and derivatives related to the verbs *gan/gangan* 'to go', which is fairly typical of the overall situation in OE (notice the many Romance equivalents in the glosses, replacing the original Germanic lexemes):

(2) *gān/gangan* 'go, come, move, proceed; depart; happen'

  gang, masc. 'going, journey; track, footprint; passage, way; privy; steps,
    platform'; *ċiriċ-gang* 'churchgoing', *ears-gang* 'excrement', *forliġ-gang*
    'adultery, lit. going to adultery', *hin-gang* 'a going hence, death',
    hlāf-gang 'a going to eat bread = communion', etc., etc.

  gang-ern, gang-pytt, gang-setl, gang-stōl, gang-tūn 'privy, toilet, i.e. some
    place to which one goes', *gang-dæġ* 'Rogation Day', *gange-wifre*
    'spider, lit. a going weaver', etc.

  genġe n. 'troops, company'

  -genġe, fem. in *niht-genġe* 'hyena, i.e. an animal that prowls at night'

  -genġa, masc. in *ān-genġa* 'a solitary goer', *æfter-genġa* 'one who follows',
    hinder-genġa 'one that goes backwards, a crab', *hūsel-genġa* 'one who
    goes to the Lord's supper', *sǣ-genġa* 'sea-goer, sailor; ship', etc., etc.

  genġe adj. 'prevailing, going, effectual, agreeable'

  -genġel, masc. in *æfter-genġel* 'successor', cf. also *æfter-genġan*, wk vb, to
    go behind'

  genġan, wk vb 'to go', *æfter-genġness* 'succession, posterity'

  ā-gān 'go, go by, pass, pass into possession, occur, befall, come forth'

  be-gān/be-gangan 'go over, go to, visit; cultivate; surround; honour,
    worship', *be-gang/bī-gang* 'practice, worship', *be-genġ/bī-genġa* masc.
    'inhabitant, cultivator' with numerous compounds, *be-genġe*, n. 'practice,
    worship', *bī-genġere* 'worker, worshipper', *bī-genġestre*, fem. 'hand
    maiden, attendant, worshipper', *be-gangness* 'calendae, celebration'; and
    many other combinations with the prefixes/prepositions/adverbs *fore,
    forþ, in, niþer, of, ofer, on, oþ-, tō, þurh, under, ūp, ūt, wiþ, ymb-*

Another aspect reflecting the thoroughly Germanic character of OE vocabulary
is the preservation of Indo-European ablaut alternations not only as part of the
morphology of the strong verbs (e.g. *wrītan : wrāt : writon : ġewriten* 'write', cf.
ModE *write : wrote : written*) but also in related nouns and adjectives:

(3) *drincan: drinc* 'drink, drinking', *gedrinca* one who drinks with another',
    drincere 'drinker', *drenċ* 'drink, drinking', *drenċan* 'give to drink',
    drenċ-hūs 'drinking-house', *druncen* 'drunkenness', *druncennis*
    'drunkenness', *druncnian* 'be, get drunk', *druncning* 'drinking', *drynċ*
    'drink, potion, drinking'

Almost all of these nouns and adjectives were lost in ME, however, apart from
a few survivors such as *song, writ, breach, drunk*, unlike the other Germanic
languages, where these nouns and adjectives are still part of the core vocabulary.
We will therefore have to tackle the question of why such a substantial part of the
core vocabulary was lost, and what it was replaced by.

4.1.4   Lexical structures

The traditional view of language is that its grammar is systematic, structured, rule-governed and therefore predictive, i.e. it allows for

generalisations. Its lexicon, on the other hand, is often regarded as unsystematic, not subject to any rules or generalisations; cf. Bloomfield (1935: 274): 'The lexicon of a language is an appendix of the grammar, a list of basic irregularities', a quotation which is repeated almost verbatim in Chomsky (1965: 142). But this view is not really appropriate; cf., e.g., Aitchison (1987: 7): 'Words are not just stacked higgledy-piggledy into our minds – they are organised into an intricate, interlocking system.' Without understanding this intricate system, we also cannot make sense of the historical development of the vocabulary of a language.

There are basically two types of structure, viz. purely semantic ones based on meaning relations, and formal-morphological ones based on morphosemantic relations. Both intersect with each other, and both are also affected by the borrowing processes mentioned above.

Semantic structures are based on the fact that lexical items sharing a basic meaning are organised in terms of semantic relationships characterising lexical fields (cf. Coseriu, 1973; Coseriu & Geckeler, 1981; Cruse, 1986, 2000; Kastovsky, 1982; Lipka, 2002; Lyons, 1977: 230–335). Typical examples are lexical relations such as hyponymy, antonymy, complementarity and others:

(4) a.   hyponymy: *flower : tulip, rose, daffodil, crocus, snowdrop*, etc.
    b.   antonymy: *big : small, long : short, giant : dwarf, love : hate*
    c.   complementarity: *married : single, male : female, man : woman*
    d.   reversativity: *open : close, tie : untie, arm : disarm*

In hyponymy, there is one general term to which some more specific terms are subordinated. Their number may be open-ended. Antonymy characterises the relationship between two lexical items which refer to the greater or lesser presence of a given property, i.e. the items are gradable and there is a neither-nor area between them (e.g. *this box is bigger than that box, this is neither big nor small*) Complementaries are not gradable and divide a common semantic area into two mutually exclusive semantic domains (e.g. someone is either married or single, there is nothing in between). Reversatives denote the undoing of a state that may or may not have come about by a previous action.

Assume you have a structure that consists of *x* lexemes dividing up a lexical space such as 'come into a place: get out of a place', as in OE *incuman* or *ingangan* and *lǣfan, ūtgangan*. Then a number of lexemes such as *enter, arrive, depart, exit* are added by borrowing. Obviously this changes the structural make-up of the respective lexical fields by introducing additional semantic distinctions (much along the lines of German *essen : fressen* as against English *eat*). Thus, as a result of the massive borrowings, lexical fields in English are rather large and complex, with subtle stylistic and register differentiations, and it is unfortunate that not too many synchronic, let alone historical, studies exist of this phenomenon.

Formal-morphological structures in the lexicon are the result of word-formation processes. The delimitation rests on the distinction between simple and complex lexical items; cf.

(5)   *author, butcher, carpenter, architect* (= simple) : *writ-er, build-er,*
        violin-ist, post-man (= complex); *empty, full, busy* (simple) : *air-less,*
        crowd-ed, ston-y (= complex)

Simple lexical items reflect the primary categorisation of extralinguistic reality
in a language. Complex lexical items represent a supplementary, derived categorisation, which operates on the basis of this primary categorisation and adds
further categorisations according to the needs of the speech community. Both
levels interact with each other, i.e. word-formation patterns take up the structure
of lexical fields and can be described in terms of the same semantic relations as
simple lexical items; cf.

(6) a.   hyponymy: *tree : oak tree, pear tree, cherry tree, apple tree,* etc.
    b.   antonymy: *kind : unkind, friendly : unfriendly*
    c.   complementarity: *true : untrue, loyal : disloyal*

Complex lexical items therefore fill gaps in lexical fields: a certain notion exists but
has no expression in the form of a simple lexical item, and when a communicative
need calls for its lexical realisation, an appropriate word-formation process (or
borrowing) is activated.

4.1.5   Principles of word formation

        Besides borrowing, word formation, i.e. the combining of already
existing elements to form new lexical items, is thus another way of enriching the
vocabulary. Such new, derived lexemes have the advantage that their meanings
can be derived from the meanings of the constituents and the patterns that underlie
the formations, because these patterns are also present in other complex lexical
items. No language would be able to function properly without such patterns.
Just think of numbers: it would be impossible to memorise all numbers from
1 to *1,334,566,778* or even higher, if they were arbitrary names. This is why
language has means to create transparent names such as *one billion three hundred
and thirty-four million five hundred and sixty-six thousand seven hundred and
seventy-eight.*

   Borrowing and word formation have co-operated in the history of English,
because many Modern English word-formation patterns are the result of borrowing, e.g. *arrive : arrival, consult : consultant, employ : employee, post : postal,
bake : bakery* (here only the suffix is borrowed), *history : historic : historicity,
militarise : demilitarise, pilot : co-pilot, entangle : disentangle,* etc., etc.

   As stated above, the basic function of all lexical items is naming, and
word-formation processes also create names; cf. instances such as *hamburger,
cheeseburger, beefburger, alligator-burger,* or *Watergate, Irangate, nannygate*
(referring to President Clinton's problem in 1992 of finding an attorney general
who had not illegally employed an immigrant household help) and, last but not
least, Clinton's *zippergate.* But word formation is also involved in another equally
important function, viz. what might be called syntactic recategorisation, since it

has syntactic properties. Here, a complex lexical item takes up the previous context and repeats it – almost like a pronoun – in nominal, adjectival or verbal form:

(7) a.   'So you simply can't **change history** using stasis?' . . . 'No. . . . One small boy . . . is hardly going to be a **history-changer** because we've brought him forward to our era.' (Isaac Asimov & Robert Silverberg, *Child of Time*, 1992)

   b.   A few thought they had noticed someone **resembling** the man in the picture. I wasted two days tracking one of the supposed **resemblers**, and found no **resemblance** at all. (Robert Silverberg, *Up the Line*, 1969/1975)

   c.   . . . do we assume that the **stone-chucker, wire-stretcher, composite letter-writer, dumper of green lady** and **telephonist** are one and the same person and that this person is also the **murderer** of Miss Cost? . . . Miss Pride . . . is convinced that the **ringer-up** was Miss Cost. (Ngaio Marsh, *Dead Water*, 1964, summing up the previous events of the novel)

   d.   If you want **shares in Rolls-Royce** apply now! . . . A Public Application Form for **Rolls Royce shares** appears in this newspaper. (Newspaper ad, *The Times*)

   e.   It's **blood** on his hands. His hands **get covered with blood**, not visible to anyone else, and he goes and washes them . . . He wouldn't give his name and didn't mention **bloody** hands. (Rex Stout, *Please Pass the Guilt*, 1973)

   f.   Finally, he put the juice in **bottles. Bottled** juice was easier to store.

Such formations are often used for information condensation, text cohesion, pronominalisation. As a result, the contents of a previous sentence can be easily modified without a clumsy syntactic construction. The most frequent type of recategorisation are nominalisations. These are closely related to relative and complement clauses; cf.

(8) a.   I know someone of whom it is alleged that he has discovered how one can travel through time.

   b.   I know someone allegedly having / alleged to have discovered travel through time.

   c.   I know an alleged discoverer of time-travel.

These formations are basically interpretable by referring to functions such as Subject, Object, Adverbial (sometimes called 'argument structure') or syntactic-semantic functions, such as Agent, Patient (Theme), Locative, etc. (sometimes called 'thematic roles', echoing Fillmore's (1968) deep-structure cases or roles). Thus a *history-changer* is 'someone who (Subject/Agent) changes history (Object/Patient = Theme)' and *to bottle* means 'put into bottles' (Adverbial Complement/Locative). Here we have a close parallelism between syntax and word formation, although the nature of this relationship is controversial.

Such formations provide a problem for the lexicographer, and for someone who wants to describe the history of the vocabulary, too, because it is questionable whether all such formations, whose meaning is fully predictable, should and actually would be listed in a dictionary like the *OED*, our primary source for the history of the English vocabulary. And in fact very often such formations are not included, or included only unsystematically (cf. Kastovsky, 2000). This means that we do not really know what formations actually existed at a certain time, unless we go to large text corpora. This is also the reason why it is impossible to give accurate numbers as to the size of a vocabulary, because with productive patterns such as those involved in (7) it is always possible for a speaker to come up with a new formation at any time. And this makes the vocabulary of a language in principle non-finite. But languages certainly differ in the extent to which they make use of this possibility, and they also change the extent to which they do this over time. Thus OE was more prone to using such processes, whereas Modern English very often relies on borrowing, especially when it comes to the naming function.

The basic principle of word formation is comparison, i.e. 'to see a thing identical with another already existing and at the same time different from it' (Marchand, 1969: 1). This principle is the reason why word formations typically exhibit a binary structure, consisting of a determinant (dt, modifier) and a determinatum (dm, head). This kind of structure is usually called 'syntagma' (cf. Marchand, 1969, and Kastovsky, 1999). Cf. the following examples:

(9)   determinant / determinatum   determinant / determinatum
         (modifier) / (head)   (modifier) / (head)
         rope   / *dancer*   *writ*   / *er*
         cave   / *man*   *clear*   / *ing/ance*
         ex   / *husband*   *bak*   / *ery*
         pre   / *cook*   *fl(a)ut*   / *ist*
         re   / *write*   *civil*   / *ise*
         over   / *zealous*   *beauti*   / *fy*
         un   / *kind*   *fear*   / *less*

The sequence of dt and dm is language-specific. The Germanic languages are generally characterised by a dt/dm sequence within word formation syntagmas, whereas syntactic structures also allow the reversed sequence. The Romance languages, on the other hand, allow both dt/dm and dm/dt structures in word formation; cf. (10), where the dm is underlined:

(10) a.   F *chant-eur*, Sp. *cant-ador* 'singer', F *im-possible*, It. *im-possibile*
     b.   F *chemin de fer* 'railway', *barbe-bleu*, It. *Barba blu*, 'bluebeard',
           F *tire-bouchon*, Sp. *saca-corchos* 'corkscrew'

Constituent order in complex lexical items thus is language-specific, not universal. Assuming that English, like all Germanic languages, has a general dt/dm sequence, an assumption that seems justified on typological and quantitative grounds, we still have to explain certain patterns that seem to violate this principle. This raises questions about the demarcation of word formation from syntax and the incorporation of syntactic constructions, i.e. phrases, into the lexicon, which is also of historical interest.

Compare:

(11)   *cónsul(s) géneral, héir(s) appárent, létters pátent, cóurt mártial(s)*

consisting of a noun and an adjective in that order, which deviates from the regular order adjective/noun both in compounds and syntactic groups, e.g. *blackbird, general store, Black Sea*, etc., i.e. it has a dm/dt sequence. The explanation in this case is simple: the pattern was borrowed from French, which allows this order (cf. *barbe-bleu* in (10b) above). The pattern entered English in ME and belongs to legal or semi-legal jargon; only a few instances are part of the general vocabulary, and it has not really become productive in English; see also Section 3.2.4. There are two other loan patterns with the reversed dm/dt order, viz. personal names, e.g. *Fitzherbert* (<Anglo-Norman *fitz* 'son' *de Herbert*), *MacArthur* 'son of Arthur' (Gaelic-Scottish). Again, these patterns have not become productive.

Instances such as (12) also pose problems for the posited general dt/dm sequence in English word formation:

(12) a.   *father-in-law*, *jack-in-the-box*, *jack-of-all-trades*, *man-in-the-street*
     b.   *come in*, *go out*

They illustrate a further means of extending the vocabulary not mentioned so far.

From a lexicological point of view, we would like to treat these cases as lexical items, and since they clearly are complex, they should be regarded as results of word-formation processes. But they exhibit certain anomalies not found in the typical word-formation patterns. Thus they do not conform to the regular dt/dm order but exhibit a dm/dt order. This order reflects the order NP + PP, typical of syntactic constructions, which have to be kept separate from word formations proper. Additionally, the formations in (12a) contain syntactic markers like prepositions or articles very uncommon in word formations:

(13)   *church-going* vs *going to church*, *brain-surgery* vs *surgery of the brain*
         wf   syntax   wf   syntax

And also compare (12b) with formations like *income, incoming, outgoing (mail)*, where the particle (preposition/adverb) is preposed rather than postposed.

On the basis of these structural properties, it would seem to be justified to treat formations like (12) as syntactic constructions rather than as word formations in the strict sense. Nevertheless, such formations are usually listed in dictionaries, i.e. they have been accorded the status of lexical items. This means that complex lexical items not only arise from word-formation processes but also through the lexicalisation of syntactic phrases, which adopt a special meaning and are then treated as lexical wholes, although they preserve their original syntactic properties. Moreover, it should be added that with nominal compounds the delimitation between word formations and syntactic constructions is also problematic, because they also consist of independent lexemes. Thus fore-stressed instances such as *hóuse-dòor, stéam-bòat*, etc. are usually recognised as compounds, whereas the status of level-stressed formations (with an end-stressed variant), such as *góld wátch* ~ *gòld wátch, gláss cáse* ~ *glàss cáse*, etc. is controversial. Marchand (1969: 20ff.) treats them as syntactic groups, Bauer (1983: 102–12) as compounds just like the fore-stressed combinations. On the other hand, everybody seems to agree that level-stressed *dáncing gírl* ~ *dàncing gírl* 'girl who is dancing', or *bláck bírd* ~ *blàck bírd* are syntactic groups, whereas fore-stressed *dáncing gìrl, bláckbìrd* are always treated as compounds, probably because there always seems to be a semantic difference between the two types of construction, which is not always true of N + N-compounds, cf. *íce créam* and *íce crèam*, which have the same meaning. A similar problem arises with formations such as *begínner's lúck*, which look like regular syntactic groups consisting of a preposed genitive + N and also have the stress pattern associated with syntactic constructions. But in this case the compound interpretation is obvious: *incredible beginner's luck* cannot be paraphrased as 'luck of an incredible beginner'; the adjective clearly modifies the determinatum *luck*, unlike *beautiful singer's voice*, which allows both 'voice of a beautiful singer' and 'beautiful voice of a singer' (cf. Marchand, 1969: 27–8, 65–9). This is why the *-s* in *beginner's luck* and similar instances should not be treated as a genitive morpheme, but rather as a so-called 'linking element' (*Fugenelement*), as in G *Ankunftszeit* 'time of arrival', *Frauenkirche* 'church of Our Lady'.

Lexicalisation of such syntactic phrases is thus a further means of extending the vocabulary, which may in fact go very far and extend to fully idiomatised phrases such as *kick the bucket, red herring, pull one's leg*, etc. This kind of lexicalisation and idiomatisation is also relevant to word formations. Once a formation has been accepted into the general vocabulary, it is subject to changes of meaning just like any simple lexeme. Thus OE *hāliġdæġ* was indeed a 'holy day', but *holiday* no longer is, and even though blackboards where originally and legitimately called *blackboards*, the change in colour of the referents (now usually green) has created some degree of idiomatisation, and the most recent exemplars are therefore justifiably called *whiteboards*. All these processes have of course been at work throughout the history of English.

The morphological status of the constituents dt and dm as either words or bound morphemes (affixes) results in a subdivision of word formation into two basic sub-categories. If both constituents are actual or potential lexemes, we speak of compounds, as in *bird/cage, girl/friend, letter/writer, writing/table, racehorse/owner, colour/blind, home/sick, home/made*, etc. If one of the two constituents is a bound morpheme which is not the representation of a lexeme, we speak of affixation or derivation, with a subdivision into prefixation (the bound morpheme occurs before the lexeme representation), e.g. *counter/propaganda, dis/believe, in/justice, re/write*, and suffixation (the bound morpheme occurs to the right of the lexeme representation), e.g. *arriv/al, king/dom, champion/ship; feather/ed, hope/ful, atom/ic, whit/ish; dark/en, legal/ise.*

A further possibility of creating new lexemes is converting a lexeme belonging to one word class into a member of a different word class, e.g. *bridge* sb > *bridge* vb, *cheat* vb > *cheat* sb (BrE), or *clean* adj > *clean* vb. For this, the term 'conversion' is widely used, but it is problematic, because it obscures the fact that the difference in word-class affiliation is regularly accompanied by a meaning difference, i.e. that this involves more than just a shift of word-class affiliation. Moreover, this meaning difference matches the type of semantic contrasts we find with suffixation; cf.:

(14) a.   *cheat* vb : *cheat* sb = *write* vb : *writ/er* sb ('someone who vb')
     b.   *stop* vb : *stop* sb = *land* vb : *land/ing* sb ('place where one vb')
     c.   *cash* sb : *cash* vb = *atom* sb : *atom/ise* vb ('to convert into sb')
     d.   *clean* adj : *clean* vb = *legal* adj : *legal/ise* vb ('cause to become adj')

Obviously, the same semantic content, i.e. 'someone who V-s (habitually, professionally)' in (14a), 'place where one V-s' in (14b), 'convert into N' in (14c), and 'cause to become Adj' in (14d) can be expressed both by suffixes and conversions. From this it follows that conversions are regular derivatives like normal suffixations, except that they exhibit a morphological peculiarity: the deriving suffix is not expressed overtly.

In order to express this parallelism between suffixal derivatives and conversions, the latter have been interpreted as 'zero derivatives' by some linguists, e.g. Marchand (1969: 359–89), i.e. as word formation syntagmas where the determinatum is a zero morpheme, in order to preserve the binary structure of word formations; zero morphemes indicate a functional position which is not filled by a formal exponent. This analysis is somewhat controversial, and whether one accepts zero derivation or not is a matter of theoretical orientation (from a historical point of view it makes sense, however, since the zero element always replaces an originally overt morpheme, usually a stem formative; cf. Kastovsky, 1980, 1996). Alternatively, one might also call this process 'affixless derivation'. The main point is that this process, in view of its semantic properties, should be recognised as a sub-category of derivation, and not merely as a shift of word class.

It is sometimes claimed that this type of word formation is restricted to Modern English or is particularly characteristic of Modern English, but in fact it also exists in OE with its fully-fledged inflectional system:

(15) a.   *cum-an* 'to come': *cum-Ø-a* 'one who comes, a guest'; *ġief-an* 'to give': *ġief-Ø-u* 'what is given, gift'; *hunt-an* 'to hunt': *hunt-Ø* 'hunting': *hunt-Ø-a* 'hunter'
     b.   *beorht* 'bright': *beorht-Ø-ian* 'to make bright'; *ār* 'honour': *ār-Ø-ian* 'to honour'; *munuc* 'monk': *munuc-Ø-ian* 'to make into a monk'

Assuming that there is a strict functional delimitation between inflection (the derivation of word forms of lexemes) and word formation (the creation of new lexemes), the endings -*a*, -*u* in (15a), and -*ian* in (15b) have to be regarded as part of the inflectional system (see Section 2.4.5.1) and thus do not have any derivational function but mark grammatical functions such as case/number or infinitive/person/number. Formations such as *cuma, ġiefu, beorhtian* thus lack a derivational affix just like their Modern English equivalents, except that this is somewhat obscured by the pervasive presence of inflectional endings with grammatical functions.

In view of the important typological changes in the history of English word formation, a few remarks as to typological properties of morphology might be appropriate, which primarily relate to the structure of inflection. Here we can distinguish two types, viz. word-based and stem-based morphology. In the first type, there is one unmarked form in an inflectional paradigm which can function as a word in a sentence without any inflectional ending, e.g. Modern English *cat*, *cat-s*; *kiss*, *kiss-es*, *kiss-ed*, *kiss-ing*. The form without inflectional ending acts as input to the inflectional and derivational processes, which is why we can speak of word-based morphology. In the second case, the inflectional paradigm does not contain any form without an inflectional ending which can function as base form, as, e.g., in OE verbal paradigms such as *luf-ian*, *luf-ie*, *luf-iaþ*, *luf-od-e*, *ġe-luf-od*, or nominal paradigms such as *cum-a*, *cum-an*, *cum-ena*, *cum-um*; *tal-u*, *tal-e*, *tal-a*, *tal-um*. Thus when we cut off the inflectional endings we are left with a lexeme representation like *luf-* or *tal-*, which cannot occur on its own as a word. Such a lexeme representation is called a stem, which is why we speak of stem-based morphology in this case. This notion can be extended to instances such as Modern English *scient-ist*, *dramat-ist*, *astro-naut*, *tele-gram*, where *scient-* (cf. *science*), *dramat-* (cf. *drama*), *astro-*, *-naut*, *tele-*, *-gram* do not occur as independent words, but only in combination with other morphological elements. They therefore have to be regarded as stems. This distinction is historically very important, since in OE we had a mixture of stem- and word-based morphology, which gradually developed towards a purely word-based morphology in ME. At the same time, borrowing from languages with stem-based morphology, such as French, Latin or Greek, introduced a new type of stem-based morphology into word formation, which, however, is restricted to the non-native part of the vocabulary and has again created a typologically heterogeneous system, although of a different nature: now the distinction marks the delimitation of a native vs a non-native word-formation stratum. The same is true of morphophonemic/allomorphic alternations. These were pervasive in OE, but were gradually lost in ME and were replaced by a non-alternating morphological system. Alternations in inflections such as *keep* ∼ *kept*, *drink* ∼ *drank* ∼ *drunk*, *mouse* ∼ *mice*, *foot* ∼ *feet* characterise these forms as belonging to the class of irregular verbs and nouns. Similarly, native or nativised word-formation patterns do not exhibit alternations of the base, so that alternating formations such as *sane* ∼ *sanity*, *hístory* ∼ *históric* ∼ *historícity*, *Japán* ∼ *Jàpanése* are marked as belonging to the non-native stratum.

The synchronic delimitation between compounding and affixation is not always clear-cut because of change: constituents of compounds may gradually change to affixal status, e.g. Modern English *out-* in *outbid* 'bid higher than an opponent'; *under-* in *underestimate* 'estimate below a fixed norm' (see Marchand, 1969: 96–100), where the particle has lost its original locative meaning; or *-like* in *manlike*, *boldlike*; *-monger* (< OE *mang-ere* 'merchant' < *mangian* 'to sell') in *fishmonger*, *warmonger*; *-wise* in *anti-clockwise*, *moneywise*, *weatherwise*, which Marchand (1969: 356) calls 'semi-suffixes'. This is due to the fact that a constituent of a compound may be used for forming a whole series of combinations, which may result in a semantic bleaching of its meaning. Eventually, even a change of grammatical category might happen, as is the case with *-wise*, where from a purely morphological point of view the formations look like nominal compounds, but they function as adverbs. This kind of phenomenon can be regarded as an instance of grammaticalisation. Thus the Modern English adverbial suffix *-ly* continues OE *-līċ-e* as in *blind-līċ-e* 'blindly', which in turn contains the adjective-forming suffix *-līċ*, but this in fact was originally a noun, viz. *līċ* 'body, form'. The origin of this type of formation thus is some nominal construction 'in x's form', just as with the Modern English *-wise*-derivatives. Similarly, some Modern English suffixes like *-dom*, *-hood* can be traced back to full words in OE, whose status as second members in complex lexemes was ambivalent. The noun *dōm* originally meant 'judgement', but in derivatives such as *martyrdōm* 'martyrdom', *frēodōm* 'freedom' it adopted the meaning 'state, condition, fact of being', which is also the meaning of Modern English *-dom*, e.g. *dukedom, stardom, freedom*. A similar development can be assumed for *hād* 'state, condition, rank, order', as in *abbud-hād* 'rank of an abbot', *ċild-hād* 'childhood'.

One more domain of word formation has to be mentioned as contributing to the extension and modification of the vocabulary, less rule-governed than the processes discussed so far, although some of the categories involved have become very important since the early twentieth century: phonetic symbolism (onomatopoeia), clipping, blending and word manufacturing; see Marchand (1969: 397–454).

Phonetic symbolism uses the possibility of language to imitate sounds either directly or indirectly, sometimes associating some metaphorical interpretation with the sounds in question, e.g. extending sound to the representation of movement. Examples are *puff, pop, splash, swish, chitchat, zig-zag, pitter-patter, hocus-pocus, mumbo-jumbo*. Many of these formations are primarily part of spoken language, which is why a historical account of the development of these formations is rather difficult, but at least some formations must already be of OE origin, and many are attested from late ME and early Modern English.

Clipping consists in the reduction of a word to one of its syllabic parts, e.g. *ad* < *advertisement, exam* < *examination, flu* < *influenza, lab* < *laboratory, plane* < *airplane*. This process seems to be particularly popular with designations of persons, especially first names (see also Section 6.3.8), often in combination with the emotive suffix *-ie*, e.g. *Al, Alfie* < *Alfred, Andy* < *Andrew, Archie* < *Archibald, Aussie* < *Australian, commie* < *communist, Debby* < *Deborah, Fred(die)* < *Frederick, granny* < *grandmother, looney* < *lunatic*.

Clipping is primarily a modern phenomenon, but examples can already be found in early Modern English, e.g. *coz* < *cousin* (1559), *gent* < *gentleman* (1564); seventeenth-century examples are *van* < *vanguard, brandy* < *brandywine* (a Dutch loan), *wig* < *periwig*; eighteenth-century formations are *brig* < *brigantine*, *gin* < *geneva*, *spec* < *speculation*. That century was especially fond of this process; cf. Swift's remark in his *Introduction to Polite Conversation* (quoted in Jespersen, 1942: 29.41):

> The only Invention of late Years, which hath any way contributed towards Politeness in Discourse, is that of abbreviating or reducing Words of many Syllables into one, by lopping off the rest . . . Pozz for Positive, Mobb for Mobile, Phizz for Physiognomy, Rep for Reputation, Plenipo for Plenipotentiary, Incog for Incognito, Hyppo or Hippo for Hypocondriacks, Bam for Bamboozle, and Bamboozle for God knows what.

And it would seem that this fashion has been revived again today.

Blending is a combination of clipping and compounding, i.e. two lexemes are clipped and then combined into one unit, e.g. *smoke* + *fog* > *smog*, *motor* + *hotel* > *motel*, *breakfast* + *lunch* > *brunch*. This process is moderately productive today, though the results more often than not are rather short-lived.

Rather important today is word manufacturing, which consists of two subcategories, acronyms ('letter words') and fully arbitrary creations. Both play an important role especially in the naming of technical products and their marketing in terms of brand names. Acronyms are usually based on initial letters of names for organisations, processes, gadgets, etc. The letters are either pronounced separately, as in *EU* < *European Union*, *UN* < *United Nations*, or the combination is pronounced like a regular word, as in *Aids* < *acquired immune deficiency syndrome, laser* (1960) < *light amplification by the stimulated emission of radiation, radar* (1941) < *radio detection and ranging, snafu* < *situation normal, all fouled/fucked up*, and many others. Arbitrary creations play an important role in brand names, e.g. *Kodak, Viagra, Xerox*, etc.

In the preceding section, word formations were classified in terms of the morphological properties of their constituents. But there is another possibility, which is based on the function of the constituents. This again results in two basic categories, viz. expansions and derivations, which intersect with the above classification (cf. Marchand, 1969: 11). This classification uses the criterion of whether the head can stand for the whole combination or not, which can be represented by the two formulas AB = B (expansion) and AB ≠ B (derivation). With compounds like *house/door*, *rattle/snake*, *colour/blind*, the head can stand for the whole combination, i.e. a *house-door* is a *door*, a *rattlesnake* is a *snake*, etc. The same is true of prefixations: a *co-author* is a kind of *author*, *hyper-active* is a kind of *active*, and *re-write* is a kind of *write*. They thus satisfy the formula AB = B and are expansions. Formations such as *sleep-er*, *pott-er*, *ston-y*, *atom-ise* do not satisfy this formula, since the head cannot stand for the whole combination, because it is a bound morpheme, which transposes the determinant into another word class or semantic category. They therefore qualify as derivatives. This criterion has consequences for the classification of formations which look like compounds but do not satisfy the AB = B criterion: a *paleface* is not a *face*, a *pickpocket* is not a *pocket*, and *barefoot* is not a *foot*. Such formations have been called *bahuvrihi*-compounds, exocentric compounds or pseudo-compounds (see Kastovsky, 2002b) and are treated by Marchand (1969: 380ff.) as containing a zero morpheme as determinatum, i.e. as derivatives from phrases. I will follow this analysis, although there are alternatives for some of them, e.g. treating them as instances of metonymy.

A similar problem exists with the analysis of prefixal verbs like *delouse, disarm, unbutton*, where the second part is a noun. It has been argued, therefore, that in this case the prefix acts as head and changes the word class, which, however, goes against the general constituent order of the Germanic languages. Such instances should therefore be treated as a combination of prefixation and zero derivation, cf. the parallelism between *to bone/Ø a chicken* 'remove the bones' (a simple zero derivative) and *to delouse/Ø a person* 'remove the lice' (combination of zero derivation and prefixation).

4.1.6   Change of meaning

We have to add one more way in which the vocabulary can change (and expand), viz. meaning change. This can take various forms: meanings can be widened or narrowed, ameliorated or get a pejorative tinge. Thus an existing lexeme can adopt an additional meaning by borrowing it from a lexeme of another language, which has at least partly the same meaning. Thus the OE lexeme *cniht* 'boy, servant' took on the additional meaning of Lat. *discipulus* 'disciple of Christ'; in ME it adopted the meanings 'male military servant of a person of high rank, a man raised to honorary military rank by a monarch, ranking below a baron', probably in connection with the introduction of the Norman feudal system, and acted as an equivalent of Fr. *chevalier*; in late ME it finally developed the Modern English meaning 'a man awarded a title by a sovereign in recognition of personal merit, ranking below a baronet, and entitled to be styled *Sir*' (*ShOED*). Another example is the OE lexeme *synn* 'injury, enmity, feud', which adopted the additional meaning 'sin, crime' from Lat. *peccatum*, since it was usually used to translate the latter and therefore also moved from the purely legal to the religious sphere. Note that eventually the original legal meaning 'crime, injury' was lost (it was replaced by Romance equivalents, since the legal language in the ME period was at least partly French), and only the religious meaning survived.

Another possibility is the translation of the meaning of a foreign expression by means of native material without borrowing the lexical item itself. This phenomenon is extremely frequent in OE, where it is preferred to direct borrowing. In principle we can distinguish two types, which, however, can not always be neatly separated: (a) the translation is a direct, morpheme-by-morpheme imitation of the foreign original (a 'loan translation'), as in Ælfric's attempt to create an Anglo-Saxon grammatical terminology on the basis of the Latin original in his eleventh-century *Grammar and Vocabulary*, e.g. *dæl-nimend* 'something taking part' for *participium*, *forsetnys* 'that which is put before' for *praepositio*, *betwuxaworpennys, betwuxaleġednys* 'that which is thrown or placed between' for *interiectio, getācnung* (< *tācnian* 'mark, signify' < *tācen* 'sign') for *significatio*; (b) the translation is relatively free and does not follow the morphological structure of the original (= 'loan creation'), e.g. *þæs naman spelġend* 'substitute for the name' for *pronomen, fāg-wyrm* 'variegated reptile' for *basiliscus*. Semantic loans and loan translations or loan creations are of course rather difficult to identify, except if one deals with translations. This is why there are hardly any systematic investigations of this phenomenon, but for OE see Gneuss (1955).

In other cases, the original meaning of a lexeme is extended by applying it to new referents. Thus *current* originally only referred to the movement of water, but after the invention of electricity, it also adopted the meaning 'flow of electric energy'; and *mouse*, originally a lexeme referring to an agile little animal, adopted the additional meaning of a computer gadget in connection with the development of personal computers.

Other examples illustrating different kinds of changes are the pairs *bird : fowl, dog : hound*. In OE, the general term was *fugol*, with the meaning 'bird', whereas *brid* or *bird* meant 'young bird, chicken'; in Modern English the originally more specific term has become the general term *bird*, whereas *fowl* has become more specific, referring only to particular subspecies. The same holds for the other pair. OE *hund* was the general term, whereas *docga*, which is only attested in a few quotations, must have referred to some more specific breed. But during the ME period, *dog* gradually developed the Modern English general meaning, while *hound* came to be restricted to hunting dogs. Another example is *knave*. OE *knafa* simply meant 'boy', but in ME this acquired a negative connotation and today is equivalent to 'rogue' except in card games. The OE compound *hūs-wīf* 'housewife' ended up as Modern English *hussy* and was therefore replaced by the more recent new formation *housewife*.

Another factor playing an important part in meaning changes is taboo, when a lexeme may refer not only to an innocuous referent but also, at least in some specific instances, to referents which are unmentionable in everyday conversation. This is why in American English *cock* is generally replaced by *rooster* (British English seems to be less prudish in this case), and lexemes like *erection, ejaculation* tend more and more to be avoided because of their sexual overtones. A similar fate happened to *gay*, which until the 1960s just meant 'jolly', then adopted the additional meaning 'homosexual', and this meaning eventually took over so that *gay* can no longer be used in its original meaning.

4.2   Old English

4.2.1   Introduction

What we conveniently call OE covers a span of about 500–600 years. In view of the differences between 1450 and today – roughly the same span – it is obvious that OE must also have undergone substantial changes during its time. But what we can say about OE is based on limited evidence, both temporally and locally, in terms of registers and text-types, which are relatively restricted (prose, mainly religious-didactic, legal or medical and poetry). What we can say with certainty, however, is that the language spoken by the Anglo-Saxons was a typically 'Germanic' language: its vocabulary contains only very few loans, see above. It also has many other structural characteristics which Modern German has preserved, e.g. the relatively clear distinction between strong and weak verbs, and the whole range of ablaut nouns and adjectives related to strong verbs (see (3) above).

Due to the nature of the sources that have come down to us, what we have in the way of vocabulary – roughly 23,000 to 24,000 lexical items according to Scheler (1977), according to Hughes (2000: 86) some 40,000 words, probably a slight exaggeration – represents a fairly restricted spectrum. Any general conclusions as to its structure and organisation will therefore have to be drawn with due care. Nevertheless, the sample will still contain a substantial number of items that belong to the 'common core of the language' (Quirk et al., 1985: 16). Consequently, general conclusions as to certain structural properties, e.g. the domain of word formation, the structure of semantic fields, the attitude towards borrowing, etc., are not without a sufficiently large empirical basis (see Kastovsky, 1992).

One conspicuous feature of OE vocabulary is the existence of large lexical families tied together by means of word formation; see Section 4.1.3. This is also reflected by the behaviour with regard to borrowing, especially when translating Latin texts. The translator would usually coin an Anglo-Saxon word rather than just borrow the Latin word if the OE vernacular did not have an obvious equivalent, i.e. he would resort to loan translations and loan creations. In this respect, OE is diametrically opposed to early Modern English, where borrowing was the normal process. The attitude towards borrowing only changed towards the end of the OE period in the wake of the Benedictine Reform, when direct, unadapted loans became more frequent, paving the way for the later developments.

Another conspicuous feature is primarily due to the fact that a high proportion of the material preserved consists of poetic texts, which are characterised by a special style and vocabulary choice. One of the main artistic devices of poetry was lexical variation, the expression of the same concept by a set of different lexemes occurring next to each other. Thus there are certain areas in the vocabulary that abound in near-synonyms or perhaps even complete synonyms, where it is not always possible to establish clear meaning differences between these lexemes.

4.2.2   The stratification of the vocabulary

Let us begin with diatopic variation. Traditionally, one distinguishes four dialect areas in the OE period, Northumbrian, Mercian, West Saxon and Kentish; see further Section 7.2. OE dialectology was originally based primarily on phonological criteria, but more recently an OE word geography has developed investigating the dialectal (and also chronological) distribution of the vocabulary, which provides additional criteria for localising manuscripts (see Gneuss, 1972; Hofstetter, 1987; Schabram, 1965; Wenisch, 1979). Most of this work is concerned with the difference between West Saxon and especially its emerging written standard, on the one hand, and Anglian, on the other; it reveals rather marked and conscious lexical choices, especially on the part of the West Saxon authors connected with Æþelwold's Winchester school like Ælfric, one of the most prolific writers around 1000. This diatopic variation intersects with a diachronic difference, because King Alfred's ninth-century prose, though based on the language of his capital, Winchester, but influenced by Anglian sources, also differs markedly in its vocabulary from the vocabulary of the late ninth and the eleventh centuries belonging to the same area. A good illustration of this variation is found in Schabram's (1965) study of the lexical field *superbia* 'pride, haughtiness'. There are four lexical families with numerous derivatives (41 items all in all) based on the following central lexemes: *ofer-hyġd-, ofer-mōd-, mōdiġ-, prūt-/prūd-*, all meaning 'pride' or 'proud'. But there is a clear dialectal split: the *ofer-hyġd-* family is restricted to Anglian, while the other three families are only found in West Saxon and Kentish. But there is also a diachronic split: *ofer-mōd-* dominates in early West Saxon, *mōdiġ-* is introduced in connection with the translation of the Benedictine Rule and begins to dominate from c.1000, but does not replace *ofer-mōd-* completely, and from c.950 onwards the French *prūt-/prūd-* family enters the scene, which is the only one that survived into Modern English. Other specifically Anglian lexemes (with their West Saxon equivalents in parentheses) are *in (on)* 'in', *nemne, nymþe (būton)* 'unless, except', *ġen, ġeona (ġiet)* 'yet'; *alan (fēdan)* 'feed', *bebyċgan (sellan)* 'sell', *bisene (blind)* 'blind', *cluċġe (bell)* 'bell' (see Kastovsky, 1992: 342–51). There is also an interesting difference in the distribution of the suffixes *-estre* (West Saxon) and *-iċġe* (Anglian) for the formation of female agent nouns. Thus *byrdiċġe* 'embroideress', *dryiċġe* 'sorceress', *huntiċġe* 'huntress' only occur in Anglian texts, whereas *bepæcestre* 'whore', *berþestre* 'female carrier', *hearpestre* 'female harper', *huntiġestre* 'huntress' are only found in West Saxon texts. But there is a substantial core of the vocabulary that is shared by all dialects.

Diaphasic variation is difficult to assess in view of the nature of the OE texts. The only attempt at representing spoken language is Ælfric's *Colloquy*, a Latin didactic text with an interlinear gloss, from which we may gather that *ēalā* glosses 'oh, lo, alas', which would seem to belong to spoken language. Thus variation with regard to social group, medium and attitude is absent. There have been some attempts to discover colloquialisms in riddles, and it has been suggested that *wamb* 'womb', *neb* 'nose', *þyrel* 'hole', *steort* 'tail', all possibly with obscene connotations and absent in other types of poetry, as well as the meaning 'lust' of *wlonc* and *gal*, might have been colloquial. But such conclusions must remain tentative.

At the more formal level we notice remarkable differences between poetry and prose, and even within these categories, e.g. between heroic and Christian poetry, or between didactic, legal or scientific prose (see especially Godden, 1992). There are basically three categories of lexemes: (1) those that are common OE and occur both in prose and poetry, e.g. *blōd* 'blood', *heofon* 'heaven', *hūs* 'house', *man* 'man'; (2) those that only or predominantly occur in poetry, e.g. *beorn, freca, hæleþ, rinc, seċġ* 'hero, warrior, man', *brego, eodor, fengel, ræswa, þengel* 'prince, king', *ides* 'woman, queen'; (3) those that only or predominantly occur in prose, e.g. *abbod* 'abbot', *borg* 'surety', *eġe* 'fright', *hopa* 'hope', derived nouns in *-ere*, verbs in *-lǣcan*, loan translations, later loans from Latin, etc. (see Stanley, 1971). Of these categories, the group of poetic lexemes has attracted the greatest attention, especially in connection with the poetic device of variation, i.e. the use of different lexemes side by side for the same concept, as in the following passage from Beowulf:

	Ic þæs wine Deniga,
	I that the lord of the Danes,
frean Scyldinga	frinan wille
the ruler of the Scyldings	ask will
beaga bryttan	swa þu bena eart
of rings the giver	as thou petitioner art
þeoden mærne	ymb þinne sið
the prince famous	concerning thy travel (visit)

'I shall ask the lord of the Danes, the ruler of the Scyldings, giver of rings, as you make petition, ask the famous prince concerning your visit . . .'

Here, *wine Deniga, frean Scyldinga, beaga bryttan, þeoden mærne* all refer to King Hrothgar but describe him from different points of view and attribute different properties to him. This poetical device requires a large number of synonyms, and especially with the simple lexemes it is not always clear whether there is a meaning difference between them or not, whereas with complex lexemes, because of their morphosemantic transparency, meaning differences can be more easily ascertained. Examples of such densely populated lexical fields are expressions for 'man' and 'warrior' (*beorn, guma, hæleþ, rinc, seċġ; man, wiga*), 'battle' (*gūþ, hild, beadu; wiġ*), or 'heart', 'mind' (*sefa, ferhþ, hyġ; mōd*). The lexical items before the semicolon are predominantly or exclusively used in poetry, while those after the semicolon are of general currency.

Another phenomenon widespread in poetry is the metaphorical use of simple or complex lexemes with clearly different meanings for the same extralinguistic referent. Such lexemes are called 'kennings', a term borrowed from Old Norse and Icelandic poetry. Thus a lord or king will not only be referred to by *frēa* 'ruler, lord', or *cyning* 'king', but also by epithets such as *burg-āgend* 'city-owner', *bēag-ġifa* 'ring-giver', *ēðel-weard* 'lord of the realm', etc. And the sea is not just called *sǣ, ġeofon, heafu, mere, lagu* or just *wæter*, but also *fām* 'foam', *wǣġ* 'wave', or *hryċġ* 'back, ridge', as well as *ār-ġebland* 'waveblend, surge', *strēam-ġewinn* 'strife of waters', *hwæl-weġ* 'whale-way', *seolh-bæþ* 'seal-bath', etc. And ship is not just referred to as *sċip* but also as *brim-wudu* 'water-wood', *ċeol* 'keel', *hringed-stefa* 'ship having a ringed prow', *mere-hūs* 'sea-house', *sǣ-genġa* 'sea-traveller', *sǣ-hengest, sund-hengest* 'see-steed', *wǣġ-flota* 'see-floater', *ȳþ-mearh* 'wave-horse'. Again the importance of word formation is obvious here, since very often we find compounds or derivatives which are fully transparent or at least used metaphorically without losing their transparency completely (as, e.g., *flota* 'something which floats = ship', *sǣ-genġa* 'sea-goer = ship', and the metaphorical *brim-wudu, wǣġ-hengest*, etc.). Thus in the 3,182 lines of *Beowulf* we find 903 distinct substantival compounds, of which 518 only occur in this poem, and 578 are found only once in it. For a more detailed description see Kastovsky (1992: 352ff.).

4.2.3   Foreign influence

For Old English, Latin is the dominant source of influence. Usually three periods of Latin influence are distinguished (see Serjeantson, 1935: 1ff.; Baugh & Cable, 1978: 75): (1) continental borrowing; (2) borrowing during the settlement period ('Latin through Celtic transmission', Baugh & Cable, 1978: 79); (3) borrowings in connection with the Christianisation of the Anglo-Saxons after c.600/650 and the rise of Anglo-Saxon civilisation and learning, with the Benedictine Reform in the late ninth and the tenth centuries as a crucial dividing line separating this third period into two sub-periods. Before this reform, Latin words were usually integrated more or less completely into the linguistic system, so that they were not really recognisable as loans, e.g. *antefnere* 'gradual' < *antiphonaria, tropere* 'troper' (book containing tropes) < *troparium, (p)salter(e)* 'psalter' < *psalterium, ċīese* 'cheese' < *caseus, pytt* 'hole, well' < *puteus, turnian* 'turn' < *turnare, fersian* 'versify' < *versus*. Moreover, borrowing during this period seems to have primarily happened at an oral level and more often than not from Vulgar rather than Classical Latin, which is also indicated by the fact that the Latin source had undergone some sound change, e.g. *copor* 'copper' < VLat. *coprum* < *cuprum, peru* 'pear' < VLat. *perum* < *pirum*. But during and after the Benedictine Reform, lexemes were very often borrowed without any attempt at adaptation, for instance keeping their Latin inflectional endings, e.g. *circulus, zodiacus, firmamentum, terminus* (Ælfric), *sacramentor(i)um, antiphonaria*. This suggests that these words were borrowed through the written rather than the oral medium and from Classical Latin. Sometimes this leads to doublets, where an early loan is matched or replaced by a later, learned one, e.g. *ċelċ/caliċ* 'cup', *cliroc/clēriċ* 'clerk', *ċellendre/coryandre* 'coriander', *leahtriċ/lactuca* 'lettuce', *lǣden/latin* 'Latin'.

There had been contacts between the Germanic tribes and the Latin-speaking peoples since the days of Julius Caesar, with more and more Germanic tribesmen joining the Roman military forces. It is therefore not surprising that quite a few lexemes referring to everyday objects in use in camp and town, or to plants and animals hitherto unknown, made their way into the vocabulary of the Germanic tribes the Romans came in contact with. It is estimated that about 170 lexemes recorded in OE were borrowed during the continental period (see Serjeantson, 1935: 271–7; Williams, 1975: 57). Examples are:

Plants: *box* 'box-tree' < *buxum*, *ċiris* 'cherry' < *ceresia*, *plante* 'pant' < *planta*, *wīn* 'wine' < *vinum*

Animals: *catt(e)* 'cat' < *cattus*, *elpend/ylpend* 'elephant' < *elephant-*, *pēa/pāwa* 'peacock' < *pavo*

Food: *butere* 'butter' < *butyrum*, *ċiese* 'cheese' < *caseus*, *must* 'must, new wine' < *mustum*

Household items: *bytt* 'bottle' < *bottis*, *ċetel* 'kettle' < *catillus*, *cupp(e)* 'cup' < *cuppa*, *disċ* 'plate, dish' < *discus*, *mylen* 'mill' < *molinis, -a*

Dress, etc.: *belt* 'belt' < *balteus*, *sacc* 'sack' < **saccium*, 'bag', *side* 'silk' < VLat. *seda* < *seta*

Buildings, building material, etc.: *ċeaster* 'city' < *castra*, *cyċene* 'kitchen' < *coquina*, *port* 'gate, door' < *porta*, *port* 'harbour' < *portus*, *tiġle* 'tile, brick' < *tegula*, *weall* 'wall' < *vallum*

Military, legal, geographical etc. terms: *camp* 'field, battle' < *campus* (with *campian* 'to fight', *cempa* 'fighter'), *diht* 'saying, direction' < *dictum*, *sċrīfan* 'allot, decree' < *scribere*

Trade, etc.: *ċēap* 'goods, market', *ċēapian/ċīepan* 'buy' < *caupo* 'inn-keeper, wine-seller', *mangere* 'trader', *mīl* 'mile' < *mille (passum)*, *pund* 'pound' < *pondo*

Religion: *abbud* 'abbot' < *abbat-em*, *mæsse* 'mass' < *missa*, *munuc* 'monk' < *monachus*, *mynster* 'minster' < *monasterium*, *predician* 'preach' < *praedicare*, *sċōl* 'school' < *scola*

The source of the loans of the second period, which is usually identified with the settlement period after c.450 until the Christianisation of the Anglo-Saxons towards the end of the sixth century, was also mainly Vulgar and not Classical Latin. There is no agreement as to whether the loans attributed to this period were borrowed directly from Latin (if it was still a kind of official language; see Jackson, 1953: ch. 3; Strang, 1970: 390) or via Celtic transmission, if Latin was no longer in use as a spoken medium (see Baugh & Cable, 1978: 80). It is rather difficult to separate these loans from the continental loans, and there is no agreement about individual cases, but the following seem to be generally accepted as belonging to this period: *eced* 'vinegar' < *acetum*, *forca* 'fork' < *furca*, *lǣden* 'Latin; a language' < *latinus*, *lent* 'lentil' < *lent-em*, *munt* 'mountain' < *mont-em*, *mūr* 'wall' < *murus*, *oele* 'oil' < *oleum*, *seġn* 'sign' < *signum*, *torr* 'tower' < *turris*, *truht* 'trout' < *tructa*.

In the third period, the type of loans gradually changed, because the church became the dominant vehicle for their introduction. Moreover, especially from the ninth century onwards, loans came more and more from Classical Latin, and partly through the written language. Loans coming in during the late tenth and the eleventh centuries in connection with the Benedictine Reform probably never entered the spoken register at all and remained confined to the written language. Thus the introduction of the Benedictine Reform at the end of the tenth century was a crucial dividing line as to the type of borrowing. It marks the beginning of a preference for borrowing rather than loan translation, and at the same time the beginning of borrowing without an attempt to adapt the loans to the native morphological (and phonological) patterns, thus paving the way for the subsequent development in Middle and early Modern English.

During the first part of this period, loans were still adapted to a certain degree, e.g. *alter* 'altar' < *altar*, *(a)postol* 'apostle' < *apostolus*, *bēte* 'beetroot' < *beta*, *(e)pistol* 'letter' < *epistola, fenester* 'window' < *fenestra, mæsse* 'mass' < *missa, offrian* 'sacrifice' < *offerre*.

During the second part of this period, roughly 150 additional Latin loans are attested, many of which were scarcely integrated into the native system. Loans of this period mainly fill gaps relevant to the concerns of the educated people dealing with religion and other scholarly concerns. Examples of borrowing attributed to this third period are:

Religion: *acolitus* 'acolyte', *apostata* 'apostate', *crēda* 'creed, belief', *discīpul* 'disciple' < *discipulus, paradīs* 'paradise' <*paradisus*

Books and learning: *bibliopēce* 'library' < *bibliotheca, capitol(a)* 'chapter' < *capitulum, declīnian* 'decline' < *declinare, nōtere* 'notary' < *notarius, punct* 'point' < *punctum*

Astronomy: *comēta* 'comet' (but also glossed as *feaxede steorra* 'haired star', a loan creation)

Food, vessels, etc.: *ampulle* 'flask', *press* 'wine-press' < *pressa, scutel* 'dish, scuttle' < *scutula*

Plants: *berbēne* 'verbena', *cēder* 'cedar', *cucumer* 'cucumber' < *cucumer, organe* 'marjoram' < *origanum, peonie* 'peony' < *paeonia, perwince* 'periwinkle', *salfie* 'sage' < *salvia*

Animals: *aspide* 'asp, viper' < *aspida, basilisca* 'basilisk' (also glossed as *feah-wyrm*) < *basiliscus, cancer* 'crab', *lēo* 'lion'

Medical terms: *mamma* 'breast', *plaster* 'plaster' < *emplastrum, scrōfel* 'scrofula' < *scrofula, temprian* 'to mix, mingle' < *temperare*

As earlier, the overwhelming majority of the loans are nouns; adjectives and verbs are relatively rare, but we do find denominal adjectives and denominal verbs derived from these nouns coined on the basis of OE word-formation patterns, which shows that these loanwords were integrated to a certain degree into the vocabulary.

Considering the impact that Roman culture and Christianisation had on the way of thinking and on the material culture of the Anglo-Saxons, the number of Latin loans is remarkably small, in particular if we compare it to the number of loans in ME and early Modern English. The main reason seems to have been the versatility with which the native vocabulary could be used in order to render a foreign concept. We still lack a full-scale investigation of semantic loans, loan translations and loan creations for the OE period. It would seem that these processes were all-pervasive and far outweigh the loans discussed here (cf. Kroesch, 1929;

Gneuss, 1955, 1972, 1985). But loans are much easier to recognise. Nevertheless, semantic borrowings and loan translations can sometimes be identified. Thus semantic borrowing certainly played a role in the following examples: *þrōwung* 'suffering' > 'Christ's Passion' < *passio, tunge* 'tongue' > 'language' < *lingua, hierde* 'shepherd' > 'pastor, guardian of the soul' < *pastor, god* 'heathen deity (with plural)' > *God* 'God' < *deus, dryhten* 'ruler, king' > 'Lord God' < *Dominus, rōd* 'rod, pole' > 'cross, rood' < *crux*.

The following are examples of loan translations: *blētsung-bōc* 'book of blessings' < *liber benedictionum, godspell-boc* 'gospel book' < *liber evangelii* (compounds); *efen-herian* 'praise together' < *col-laudare, eft-gān* 'go back' < *re-gredi, forþ-cyþan* 'announce' < *e-nuntiare, un-sċeðð-end-e* 'innocent, harmless' < *in-noc-en-s* (prefixations); *bisċeop-hād* 'office of bishop, episcopate' < *episcop-atus, ġe-āgn-iendlīċ* 'possessive' < *possess-ivus, hæl-end* 'Saviour' < *Salvator, þrē-ness* 'trinity' < *trinitas, ān-horn, ān-hyrne* 'unicorn' / 'having one horn' < *unicornis, unicornuus, lytel-mōd, wāc-mōd* 'having little courage' < *pusillanimus* (suffixations, zero derivations).

Loan renditions, i.e. somewhat less direct translations, are illustrated by the following examples: *ġe-hūs-sċipe* lit. 'houseship' = 'family, race' < *domus, fela-sprec-ol-ness* lit. 'much-speakingness' = 'loquacity' < *loquacitas, milc-dēo-nd, milc-sūc-end* 'suckling, i.e. someone who sucks milk' < *lact-ans, reste-dæġ* 'day of rest' < *sabbatum*.

The second major influence on OE vocabulary is due to the Scandinavian settlement in the Danelaw, an area north of a line roughly between Chester and London occupied by Danish and Norwegian settlers from the ninth till the twelfth century, when they were finally anglicised, i.e. gave up their Scandinavian language; see further Sections 1.3 and 6.5.6. The intensity of the Scandinavian influence on all parts of the vocabulary as well as its temporal deployment needs some explanation. In OE we only find about 150 loans, mainly technical terms for ships, money, legal institutions, warfare, etc., but in ME there are several thousand (Hansen, 1984: 63), especially in western and northern manuscripts, of which between 400 and 900 (Hansen, 1984: 60; Geipel, 1971: 70) have survived in standard English, and a further 600 or more in the dialects. And these include numerous everyday words: nouns such as *band, bank, birth, egg, fellow, gift, kettle, knife, leg, loan, root, score, scrap, sister, skill, skin, sky, slaughter, snare, steak, window*; adjectives such as *ill, loose, low, odd, scant, tight, weak*; and verbs such as *call, cast, clip, crave, crawl, die, gasp, get, give, glitter, lift, raise, rake, scare, scowl, sprint, take, thrive, thrust*. Furthermore, the phrasal verb type *come on, make up* seems to be due to Scandinavian influence (Poussa, 1982: 73) or was at least strengthened by a parallel Scandinavian pattern (Hiltunen, 1983: 42–4). Moreover, not only lexical items were borrowed, but also form words such as the pronouns *they, them, their, both, same*, or the prepositions *till, fro* (in *to and fro*), *though*. This kind of borrowing points to a language contact situation in Old English, an issue which is discussed in Section 1.3 and Chapter 3, *passim*.

The relatively low number of loans in the earlier period is typical of a cultural clash, where words denoting referents unknown to one language are borrowed by the other, especially when this is the language of the rulers, as was the case in the Danelaw. But after 1066, the situation must have changed drastically, because from then on many everyday lexemes were borrowed. The most plausible explanation for this is language death with concomitant language shift: the Scandinavian-speaking population was gradually switching to English with concomitant loss of bilingualism. This is corroborated by what happened to French in late ME: there, too, the major borrowing of everyday vocabulary coincides with the switch of the French-speaking population to English, during which they took along a considerable part of their native vocabulary. We are thus faced with two different contact situations with different effects on the language. The early Scandinavian loans were mainly adopted by bilingual, and possibly also monolingual, speakers for whom English was the basic language and Scandinavian was the language of the overlords. The ME loans, on the other hand, are primarily, although certainly not exclusively, due to speakers of Scandinavian descent and their switch from Danish/Norwegian to English.

On account of the genetic relationship between Scandinavian and OE there is a considerable overlap in core vocabulary. It is therefore necessary to establish some criteria that allow us to distinguish Scandinavian loans from native lexical items. Fairly safe criteria are phonological differences resulting from different phonological developments in the two languages. The most noticeable feature is the lack of palatalisation and assibilation of velar stops in front of originally front vowels and of initial /sk/, i.e. the pre-OE and OE changes /g/ > /j/ (*ġiefan*), /k/ > /tʃ/ (*ċild*), /gg/ > /ddʒ/ (*seċġan*), /kk/ > /ttʃ/ (*streċċan*), /sk/ > /ʃ/ (*sċyrte*). On the basis of this criterion, the following examples are clearly Scandinavian replacements of originally OE words, which had a palatal glide instead of the stop: *again, begin, dike* (vs *ditch* < OE *dīċ*), *gate, give, gear, get, guest, kettle, scant, score, scrub, skill, skin, skirt* (vs *shirt* <OE *sċyrte*), *sky*. Another safe criterion is the development of Germanic /ai/, which in OE became /ɑː/ = ModE /əʊ/, while in Scandinavian it became /ei/ or /eː/ = ModE /eɪ/, cf. the pairs *no/nay, whole/hale, lord/laird*.

The earliest Scandinavian loans appear in the Treaty of Wedmore between Alfred and Guthrum (886), viz. *healfmearc* 'half a mark' and *līesing* 'freedman'. More can be found in the *Anglo-Saxon Chronicle*, especially in the D and E manuscripts from York and Peterborough, in some of Æthelred's laws, in vocabularies, in the Lindisfarne and Rushworth Gospels and in the Durham Ritual. The following small selection taken from Peters (1981a, b), the most comprehensive investigation of the loans of this period, illustrates the main semantic domains.

Seafaring terms: *æsċ* 'warship' (semantic loan; cf. ON *askr* 'ash, small ship', as the usual term for the Scandinavian boats), *cnearr* 'small ship', *hā* 'oar-hole', *hæfene* 'haven, port', *lænding* 'landing-site', *healdan* 'proceed, steer' (semantic loan; cf. ON *halda skipi* 'to hold in a certain direction' vs OE *healdan* 'hold'), *æsċ-here* 'Viking army' (lit. 'ship-army').

Legal terms: *cost* 'terms, condition', *fēo-laga* 'fellow, partner', *for-mǣl/for-mǣl* 'negotiation, treaty', *grið* 'truce, sanctuary', *lagu* 'law' (first restricting OE *ǣ* to 'spiritual law', and then replacing it altogether) together with numerous compounds (partly native, partly loan translations), e.g. *lah-breca* 'law-breaker', *ūt-laga* 'outlaw', *nīþing* 'outlaw', *sac* 'guilty', *sac-lēas* 'innocent' (loan translation of ON *sac-laus*), *seht* 'settlement', *un-seht* 'discord', *wrang* 'wrong'; *bōnd, būnda, hūs-bōnda* 'householder, husbandman', *þrǣll* 'slave'; *eorl* 'nobleman, chief', also as semantic loan replacing OE *ealdor-man* (OE *eorl* 'warrior, free man').

War terms: *bryniġe* 'mail-shirt', *cnīf* 'knife', *fēsian, fȳsian* 'put to flight, banish', *genġe* 'troop', *lið* 'host, fleet', *rǣdan on* 'attack'.

Measures: *mans-lot* 'the amount of land allotted to the head of the family', *marc* 'mark, half a pound', *ōra* 'Danish coin', *oxan-gang* 'eighth of a plough-land, hide', *scoru* 'score'.

Other semantic areas: *afol* 'power', *becc* 'brook, beck', *carl* 'man', *lǣst* 'fault, sin', *loft* 'air' (cf. *aloft*), *mǣl* 'speech', *rōt* 'root', *sala* 'sale', *scinn* 'skin, fur', *sneare* 'snare', *toft* 'homestead', *þrēding* 'third part of a county', *wǣpen-ġetǣc* 'district'; partial loan translations: *brȳd-hlōp* 'ceremony of conducting a bride to her new home, wedding', *land(es)-mann* 'native', *rǣdes-mann* 'counsellor, steward', *ġe-crōcod* 'crooked', *dearf* 'bold' (with derivatives *dearflīċ* 'bold, presumptuous', *dearfsċipe* 'boldness'), *gold-wreċċen* 'covered with gold' (loan translation of ON *gull-rekinn* 'prosper'), *ġe-eggian* 'to egg on', *hittan* 'hit', *tacan* 'take'.

There are some other languages which contributed to Old English vocabulary, although in a rather limited way, viz. Celtic, Continental Germanic and French.

The most puzzling phenomenon is the role of Celtic. When one people conquers another and subsequently the two peoples mix by intermarriage, the resulting contact situation normally has important linguistic consequences. Usually, one of the two languages, either that of the conquerors or that of the conquered people, will eventually prevail. In any case, the result will always be an interaction of the two languages with substantial changes in whichever language eventually surfaces as the 'winner'. This was the case with Latin and Celtic in France, where the Celtic substratum substantially modified Latin (with a substantial admixture of Germanic later on), but Latin remained the foundation of what eventually became French. The same is true of the interaction between the Anglo-Saxon dialects and the dialects spoken by the Scandinavian invaders in the tenth and eleventh centuries, as well as the influence French exerted on English after the Norman invasion. A similar development would be expected after the gradual take-over of Britain by the Germanic tribes in the fifth and sixth centuries. It seems that the Celts were by no means completely exterminated by the invaders, as the place-name evidence shows, although many Celts fled to the west and the north, where a Celtic-speaking population survives today in Wales and Scotland. There is a whole cluster of Celtic place-names in the northeastern part of Dorsetshire, and there is also evidence that Celtic must have lingered on in Northumbria because of certain loans found only in Northumbrian texts, e.g. *bratt* 'cloak', *carr* 'rock', *lūh* 'lake'. Moreover, it is not unlikely that Celts were held as slaves by the conquerors, and certainly many of the Anglo-Saxons married Celtic women. Thus, at least in parts of England, contact between the two peoples must have been fairly intimate and must have persisted over several generations. Nevertheless, the traces Celtic has left on the Anglo-Saxon dialects are minimal. This is also true of loans, with the exception of place-names. The following items have been identified as Celtic loans in OE: *rīce* 'rule, empire', *ambeht* 'servant, service, office', possibly via Latin *ambactus* (these might be continental loans); *binn* 'bin', *bannoc* 'a bit, piece (of a cake or loaf)', *gafeluc* 'a small spear', *dunn* 'dun, dark-coloured, grey' (as modifier of *tunecan* 'tunic' and *stān* 'stone'), *broc* 'badger', *assen* 'ass' (< Lat. *asinus*); place-name elements, which also occur as independent lexical items: *torr* 'rock, rocky peak, hill', *cumb* 'deep valley' (e.g. *Ilfracombe*), *funta* 'Spring' (< Lat. *font-em*) (e.g. *Chalfont*). Loans probably borrowed from the Irish missionaries are *drȳ* 'magician' < OIr. *drui* (pl *druid*), from which a feminine *drȳeġġe* 'female magician' was derived by means of a native suffix, *cross* (vs native *rōd*). Thus, except for place-names, the Celts have left few traces in OE vocabulary.

There had also been contacts with the continent, especially with the Frisians and the Saxons. It is assumed that *īegland* 'island' is of Frisian origin, and the following lexical items, occurring partly in translations of Saxon originals, e.g. *Heliand, Genesis B*, are attributed to Saxon influence: *gāl, gālsċipe* 'proud, pride' (semantic loan), *hearra* 'lord, master', *macian, ġemacian* 'make', *suht* 'illness', *wǣr* 'true'.

Since the religious revival in the late tenth and the eleventh centuries had its starting point in France, and since Edward the Confessor brought French friends to England when he came to the throne in 1042, we also find a few French loans in pre-conquest manuscripts. The most noticeable is the *prūd* 'proud' family with the derivatives *prūtlīċ(e)* 'proud(ly)', *prȳto/prȳte, prȳtsċipe, prūtness* 'pride' and numerous compounds, which encroach on the indigenous *overmōd, mōdig* territory. Especially remarkable is the analogical transfer of the alternation /uː ~ yː/ (cf. *fūl* 'foul' ~ *fȳlþ* 'filth'), originally due to *i*-umlaut, but at that stage purely morphologically conditioned, which indicates that it must still have been productive at least sporadically. Other loans found in the mid and late eleventh century, especially in the *Anglo-Saxon Chronicle* between 1048 and 1100, are *sot* 'foolish', *bacun* 'bacon', *cancelere* 'chancellor', *capun* 'capon', *castel* 'castle', *prisun* 'prison', *servian* 'serve', *serfice* 'service', *tumbere* 'dancer'.

4.2.4   Word formation

Word formation was the most important means of expanding OE vocabulary, both in terms of its indigenous needs in poetry and the requirements imposed by the translation of Latin texts into the vernacular. Thus all major categories of word formation – compounding, prefixation, suffixation including zero derivation – were highly productive.

One striking property of OE word formation is its pervasive stem allomorphy. This is a residue of a number of sound changes the language had undergone, leaving their traces in the morphology in the form of morphophonemic/allomorphic alternations (for a more detailed treatment of this area, see Dressler, 1985). It was only during the ME period that the principle of stem invariancy for regular inflection and native word formation characteristic of Modern English took over, leading to many analogical non-alternating formations. This is especially noticeable with nouns and adjectives exhibiting ablaut alternations; see (3) in Section 4.1.3. above.

The major alternations characteristic of OE morphology apart from ablaut are due to the following sound changes:

i-umlaut (*i*-mutation): *full* ∼ *fyllan* < **full-j-an* 'fill', *curon* (: *ċēosan*) ∼ *cyre* (also involving Verner's Law) 'choice', *gram* ∼ *gremman* 'enrage', *trum* ∼ *trymþ* 'firmness'

consonant gemination: *gram* ∼ *gremman*, *wefan* ∼ *webba* 'weaver', *sagu* ∼ *seċġan* 'saying'

palatalisation + assibilation: *ċēosan* ∼ *curon, cyre, lugon* ∼ *lyġen* 'lie', *brecan, brucon* ∼ *bryċe* 'breach', *gangan* ∼ *genġa* 'goer', *acan* ∼ *eċe* 'ache'

Anglo-Frisian Brightening/*a*-Restoration: /æ/ ∼ /a/: *faran* ∼ *fær* 'journey', *grafan* ∼ *græf* 'style for writing', *græft* 'carved object', *bacan* ∼ *ġebæċ* 'baking'

Originally, these alternations had been phonologically conditioned, but due to the loss of the conditioning factors they were no longer predictable in OE and have to be treated as morphologically conditioned. Also, their distribution is far from systematic, and one and the same derivational pattern may have forms with and without the respective alternation, e.g. *stāniġ* ∼ *stǣniġ* 'stony', *þorniht* ∼ *þyrniht* 'thorny', etc. This unsystematicity was no doubt one of the major reasons why stem variancy was replaced by basic stem invariancy in ME in connection with the generalisation of word-based morphology.

There is also suprasegmental alternation, where certain prefixes are unstressed or receive only a secondary stress when they occur in verbs, but have a full stress when they occur in nouns; this stress alternation may also be accompanied by a segmental alternation, e.g. *à-wéorpan* 'throw away' ∼ *ǽ-wỳrp* 'what is thrown away', *òn-sácan* 'contest' ∼ *ánd-sæc* 'denial', *ánd-sàca* 'adversary', besides homological *òn-sǽc*. The alternation goes back to the proto-Germanic period, when word stress came to be fixed on the first syllable. At this stage, there were already prefixed nouns, whose prefixes were stressed, but the verbal prefixes were a later development, and therefore with them the stress remained on the verbal base. It is not unlikely that this alternation is at least one of the factors that contributed to the establishment of the Modern English stress alternation *conflíct* vb

~ *cónflict* sb, *permít* vb ~ *pérmit* sb, *recórd* vb ~ *récord* sb, etc. in connection with the integration of French and Latin verb/noun pairs in late ME and early Modern English.

Compounds consist of two or more lexical items, but in the latter case the formations are usually analysable on a binary basis, cf. *dēofol-ġyld/hūs* 'heathen temple = house where devil-tribute is given', *gōd-spell/bodung* 'gospel preaching'. There are substantival, adjectival and verbal compounds. The latter are restricted to instances with adverbs and prepositions as first members, e.g. *forþ-faran* 'depart', *ofer-leċġan* 'overlay, place over', *under-leċġan* 'underlay'. Verbs such as *cyne-helm(ian)* 'crown', *grist-bit(ian)* 'gnash the teeth' are derivatives from nominal compounds (*cyne-helm* 'crown', *grist-bite* 'gnashing') and not verbal compounds.

The delimitation of compounds from other types of combinations is sometimes problematic. Adj + N compounds are easily recognisable because the adjective is not inflected, cf. *hēah-englas* 'archangels', *wild-dēora* 'wild beasts' as against *hēane englas, wilde dēor*, where the adjective is inflected and marks the construction as syntactic. In combinations of the apparent structure N + Genitive + N, such as *Sunn-an-dæġ* 'Sunday', *cyning-es-wyrt* 'marjoram, lit. king's root', *dæġ-es-ēage* 'daisy, lit. day's eye', which correspond to Modern English formations like *beginner's luck* (see Section 4.1.5 above), the whole NP has to be checked as to whether any of the determining elements can refer to the determinant or not. If the determiner *þǣre* and the adjective *sweartan* refer to the determinatum *helle*, as in *þǣre sweartan helle grundes* 'the bottom of this black hell', we have a syntactic group, whereas with *se eġesfullīca dōmesdæġe* 'the terrible doomsday', where both the determiner *se* and the adjective *eġesfullīca* refer to the determinatum *dæġe*, we have a compound. In such cases elements such as *-es* have to be regarded as linking elements; the same is true of vocalic elements in compounds such as *hild-e-calla* 'war-herald', *gold-e-frætwe* 'gold ornament', *yrf-e-weard* 'heir'.

The delimitation of compounding from prefixation and suffixation is fuzzy. Thus *cyne-* 'royal' as in *cyne-ġild* 'king's compensation' only occurs as a determinant and might therefore be regarded as a prefix. On the other hand, it seems to be in complementary distribution with *cyning*, which hardly ever occurs as a first member of compounds. Moreover, there are formations such as *cyne-līċ* 'royal', where the second part is a suffix, but combinations of prefixes and suffixes do not occur; *cyne* must therefore be interpreted as an allomorph of *cyning* (but on the way to becoming a prefix). On the other hand, nominal *-dōm, -hād, -rǣden* or adjectival *-fæst, -ful(l), -lēas* seem to have already reached suffixal status.

Another problem is formations such as *bǣr-fōt* 'barefoot', *riht-heort* 'righteous = having a right heart', *yfel-wille* 'malevolent = having an evil intent', *ān-hyrne* 'having one horn', *ān-horn* 'unicorn = something having one horn' (see also Section 4.1.5 above). Here, the overt second constituent is a noun, but the formations function either as adjectives or in a different semantic category as the noun; thus *ān-horn* does not refer to a horn but an animal. Such formations have traditionally been called *bahuvrihi* or exocentric compounds; see Section 4.1.5 above and Kastovsky (2002b) for discussion.

Since the superficial morphological structure of such formations did not agree with their function, they were often re-formed either by changing the inflectional class, usually to the weak declension, cf. *ān-horn-a, bunden-stefn-a* 'ship with an ornamented prow', as against *stefn*, or by adding an explicit derivational suffix, e.g. *clifer-fēt-e* 'cloven-footed' (*-e* < *-j-a*), *ēaþ-mōd-iġ, ēaþ-mōd-līċ* 'humble = having a low mood' besides *ēaþ-mōd*. Eventually this suffixal type of formation prevailed for adjectives (e.g. *long-legged, blue-eyed*, etc.), whereas with nouns the exocentric type *paleface, hunchback*, etc. won out.

4.2.4.1   Noun compounds
N (stem) + N
This type represents the most frequent compound pattern and has been productive throughout the history of English. The relationship between the two immediate constituents, determinant and determinatum, can be reduced to three basic types, viz. additive, copulative and rectional.

The additive type consists of the coordination of two nouns, which are treated as a group, and is only represented by two examples from poetry, viz. *āþum-swerian* 'son-in-law and father-in-law', *suhtor-(ġe)fædran* 'nephew and uncle'. This might also be interpreted as a zero derivative based on a phrase 'entity = Ø consisting of X +Y'. It was probably unproductive in OE, but modern additive formations such as *Austria-Hungary* 'political body consisting of both Austria and Hungary', *north-east* 'directed towards both north and east' also admit of such an analysis rather than following the standard AB = B compound schema. In such combinations neither constituent dominates and the basic idea is that the referent really is a combination of the properties of both parts.

Copulative compounds can be paraphrased by a construction containing the copula *be*, e.g. *eofor-swīn* 'pig (*swīn*) which is a boar (*eofor*)', *frēa-wine* 'friend (*wine*) who is a lord (*frēa*)'. There are two subgroups, viz. attributive and subsumptive compounds, and both types survive into Modern English (cf. the glosses). In attributive compounds the dt attributes a specific property to the dm; in subsumptive compounds the dt denotes a subclass of the dm.

Attributive compounds are typically represented by sex-denoting formations or names of the offspring of animals, as well as names of professions, e.g. *cniht-ċild* 'male child', *cū-cealf* 'heifer-calf', *wīf-mann* 'woman'; the reverse order occurs in *ass-mȳre* 'mare (female) which is an ass = she-ass', *gāt-bucca* 'buck which is a goat = billy-goat'. The latter formations have the same semantic structure as sex-denoting suffixal derivatives like *gyd-en* 'goddess = female who is a god', *drȳ-iċġe* 'female who is a *drȳ* (magician) = sorceress', i.e. the dm denotes the sex, the dt the species.

With subsumptive compounds the following possibilities exist:

(a)   The dt denotes a concept with which the dm is compared: *col-māse* 'coal-tit', *spere-wyrt* 'spearwort'.

(b)   The dt denotes the species, the dm the genus proximum: *ceder-bēam* 'cedar', *ċiris-bēam* 'cherry-tree', *marman-stān* 'marble (stone)'.

(c)   Both constituents denote different aspects of the same thing: *were-wulf* 'a being which is both a wolf and a man', *ealdor-bisċeop, bisċeop-ealdor* 'chief and bishop'.

(d)   The meaning of the dt is already contained more or less in the dm (pleonastic compounds): *eorþ-stede, eorþ-weġ* 'earth-place', *lagu-strēam, mere-strēam* 'ocean-water = sea'.

(e)   The two constituents are practically synonymous (tautologous compounds): *æht-ġesteald, æht-ġestrēon* 'possessions-possessions', *ǣled-fyȳ* 'fire-fire', *holt-wudu, wudu-holt* 'wood-wood'. These basically only occur in poetry.

Rectional compounds are best defined negatively as compounds that do not allow a copulative paraphrase. Morphologically, we can distinguish two subcategories, viz. pure nominal compounds (N + N), and compounds that contain a deverbal dm, such as *ber-end* 'carrier', *fall-ung* 'falling'. With the latter, the dt represents an argument (Subject/Agent, Object/Theme, Adverbial/Locative, Instrument, Temporal, etc.) of the verb, and the suffix also either represents an argument, or the semantic categories 'Act(ion), Fact, State'. These patterns continue into Modern English, and a number of new ones were added through borrowing (see Kastovsky, 1985, 1986). Semantically speaking, both verbal and non-verbal compounds can express the same kinds of relationship.

1. Compounds with a deverbal dm:

(a)   The dm is an agent noun, the dt denotes the Goal/Object (*blōd-lǣtere* 'blood-letter', *helm-berend* 'helm-bearer', *frēols-ġifa* 'giver of freedom'), Place (*eorþ-būend* 'earth-dweller', *sǣ-genġa* 'sea-traveller, sea-goer = sailor'), Instrument (*gār-wīgend* 'spear-fighter', *fugel-wīġlere* 'diviner by birds'), or Time (*mete-rǣdere* 'monk reading at meals', *nihte-gale* 'night-singer = nightingale', *niht-genġa* 'night-goer = goblin') of the action. According to Burnley (1992: 442), none of these survived into ME, so that the corresponding ME formations occurring from the thirteenth century onwards, such as *wæi-witere* 'guide', *money-maker, good-doer, lawmaker, householder*, look like 'a fresh beginning', but I doubt this. In view of the parallel with action nouns as second members, the pattern probably never lost its productivity.

(b)   The dm is an action noun, the dt denotes the Subject/Agent (*eorþ-beofung* 'earthquake'), Object/Goal (*wæter-fyrhtness* 'fear of water', *āþ-swerung*), Place, etc. (*land-firding* 'military operation on land', *ċiriċ-gang* 'church-going', *wǣġ-faru* 'passage through the sea', *ǣfen-rǣ;ding* 'evening-reading', *niht-feormung* 'hospitality for the night') of the action.

2. N + N compounds without a verbal constituent:

(a)   The dm is an Agent, the dt an Object, Place, etc.: *brōþor-bana* 'brother-killer', *dure-weard* 'door-warden'; *sǣ-fisċ* 'seafish', *here-flȳma* 'army-fleer = deserter'; *eċġ-bana* 'sword-killer'; *niht-hrǣfn* 'night-raven', *niht-weard* 'night-guardian'.

(b)   The dm represents an Object/Goal, the dt an Agent, Material, Place, etc. connected with this Object: *bēo-brēad* 'honey = bread produced by bees', *smiþ-belġ* 'bellows'; *bed-strēaw* 'bedstraw'; *ǣfen-steorra* 'evening-star'; *rǣd-hors* 'riding-horse', *blētsing-boc* 'blessing-book, benedictional', *rǣding-bōc* 'reading-book' (note that these are regular N + N formations, where *blētsing, rǣding* have to be regarded as deverbal nouns, in contradistinction to Modern English *swimming pool, writing-table*, where the first part can be interpreted as a participle; the latter are an innovation of ME).

(c)   The determinatum is part of the determinant: *bord-rima* 'edge of a plank', *cawel-stela* 'cabbage-stem', *hearpe-streng* 'harpstring'.

(d)   The dm represents a place to which the dt is related as object or action: *sealt-fæt* 'salt-vessel (-cellar)', *bēor-sele* 'beer-hall', *drenċ-hūs* 'drink(ing)-house', *melċing-fæt* 'milkpail'.

(e)   The dm represents an instrument, the dt an object or action: *brēost-beorg* 'breastplate', *fisċ-nett* 'fishnet'; *snid-īsen* 'cutting-iron', *brǣding-panne* 'frying-pan'.

(f)   The dm represents a time, the dt an action related to it: *hærfest-mōnaþ* 'harvest-month', *sǣd-tīma* 'sowing-time', *clǣnsung-dæġ* 'day for purging'.

(g)   The determinant functions as intensifier and has partially or totally lost its literal meaning: *firen-þearf* 'dire distress', *firen-synn* 'great sin' (*firen* = 'sin, crime'), *mæġen-fultum* 'great help' (*mæġen* = 'strength, power'), *þēod-bealu* 'great calamity' (*þēod* = 'people, nation').

There are also some compounds consisting of three lexemes: *eafor-hēafod/seġn* 'boar-head banner', *god-spell/bodung* 'gospel preaching' (compound determinant); *bisċeop/hēafod-līn* 'bishop's head ornament', *niht/butor-flēoge* 'night butterfly, moth' (compound determinatum). Compounds with more than three lexemes do not seem to exist. All these types still exist in Modern English and will therefore not be exemplified again in the sections on Middle and early Modern English.

N + linking element + N

Compounds such as *dōm-es-dæġ* 'doomsday', *Sunn-an-dæġ* 'Sunday' are equiv alent to Modern English *craftsman, driver's seat, beginner's luck*, where *-es-* and

-an- function as linking elements and not as inflectional markers, although historically they may have had this function in syntactic groups. A similar analysis seems to be required for *rest-e-dæġ* 'rest day', *hell-e-cwalu* (besides *hell-cwalu*) 'pains of hell', where the intermediate vowel could be interpreted either as a genitive, a linking element or as the stem-formative of the determinant; again, the interpretation as a linking element seems to be the best option. The following semantic patterns belong to this type:

(a)   days of the week: *Sunn-an-dæġ, Mōnan-dæġ*, and some analogical formations, e.g. *ġebyr-e-tīd* 'time of birth', *sunn-an-setl-gong* 'sunset', *ūht-(an-)tīd* 'time of dawn, twilight'

(b)   person-denoting nouns: *cynn-es-mann* 'kinsman', *land-es-mann* 'native', *æht-e-mann* 'farmer', *gāt-a-hyrde* 'goatherd', *ox-an-hyrde* 'oxherd'

(c)   place-names: *cyn(ing)-es-tūn* > Kingston

(d)   plant-names: *dæġ-es-ēage* 'daisy', *henn-e-belle* 'henbane', *ox-an-slyppe* 'oxlip' (these might also be interpreted as *bahuvrihi* compounds)

(e)   others without specific semantic characteristics: *bog-en-streng* 'bowstring', *tunn-e-botm* 'bottom of a cask', *nunn-(an-)mynster* 'convent'. Many of these are only found in late texts.

As in Modern English, the semantic range of this type of compounding is much more restricted than that of the regular N + N compounds.

Adj + N

With Adj + N compounds, the relationship between the determinatum and the determinant is that of attribution. Examples of this fairly productive pattern are *cwic-seolfor* 'living silver = mercury', *efen-niht* 'equinox', *eald-fæder* 'ancestor', *gylden-bēag* 'golden crown', *sūr-meolc* 'sour milk'. The pattern also continues into Modern English. It was also very productive with *bahuvrihis* of the type *heard-heort* 'hard-hearted'; see Section 4.2.4.7.

V + N

The pattern V(erbal stem) + N, as in Modern English *bakehouse*, OE *bæc-hūs*, was a recent development in the Germanic languages. It resulted from compounds such as *delf-īsen* 'digging-iron = spade', where the determinant originally was a deverbal noun (*delf* 'digging'), which was formally identical with the verbal stem *delf-*. This led to a reinterpretation of the first constituent as a verbal stem, although for a while (and probably still in OE) many such formations may have been ambiguous between an N + N and a V + N interpretation. This type came to rival an older nominal pattern, 'Verbal substantive in *-ing/-ung* + N', e.g. *brēding-panne* 'frying-pan'. In ME these verbal nouns in *-ing/-ung* merged with the participles ending in *-ende*, creating an ambivalent *-ing*-form. This could be interpreted as nominal, as, e.g., in *the writing of letters takes time*, or as verbal, as in *writing letters takes time*. Consequently, a formation like Modern English *writing-table* is also ambivalent: *writing* can be analysed as a verbal noun, cf. 'table for writing', or as a participle relating to the paraphrase 'table on which one can write'. More often than not the pattern can today be simply interpreted as a morphological rival of a simple V + N compound.

The major semantic types are: V + Subject/Agent (*spyre-mann* 'tracker', *wīġ-mann* 'fighting man = warrior'); V + Object/Goal (*feald-e-stōl* 'folding-stool', *tyrn-ġeat* 'turn-stile'); V + Locative (*bæc-hūs* 'bake-house'; *ete-land* 'eating land = pasture'); V + Instrumental (*bærn-īsen* 'branding iron', *hwete-stān* 'whetstone'); V + Temporal (*reste-dæġ* 'rest day'); V + Cause (*fielle-sēocness, fielle-wærc* 'sickness that makes one fall = epilepsy', *spīw-drenċ* 'emetic').

Second participle + N
This pattern is relatively weak and is mainly represented by *bahuvrihis* of the type *wunden-feax* 'with twisted mane'. Regular compounds are *brōden-mǣl, sċeaden-mǣl, wunden-mǣl* 'damascened sword', *næġled-cnearr* 'nail-fastened vessel', *eten-lǣs* 'pasture'.

Adverb + N
There are many compounds of this type, where the adverb combines with an independent primary or derived noun, e.g. *ofer-ealdorman* 'chief officer', *ofer-biterness* 'excessive bitterness', or where the combination can also be considered a derivative from a verbal compound, e.g. *ofer-lēorness* 'transgression' < *ofer-lēoran* 'transgress'. It is therefore not always possible to provide an unambiguous analysis.

Typical formations are *æt-ēaca* 'to-adding = addition', *ān-būend* 'one living alone = hermit', *fore-brēost* 'chest', *forþ-fæder* 'forefather', *in-flǣsċness* 'incarnation', *mid-ġesīþ* 'fellow traveller', *ofer-lufu* 'too great love', *under-cyning* 'underking', *wiþer-steall* 'resistance'.

4.2.4.2   Compound adjectives
N + Adj
Basically, the same semantic types as in Modern English occur:

(a)   The dt can be regarded as a complement of the adjective: *ēag-sȳne* 'visible to the eye', *ellen-rōf* 'famed for strength', *hand-tam* 'tamed by hand', *dēofol-sēoc* 'possessed by the devil'.

(b)   The dm is compared to an implicit property of the dt; the comparison can be bleached to mere intensification: *blōd-rēad* 'blood-red', *huniġ-swēte* 'sweet as honey', *hete-grim* 'fierce', *reġn-heard* 'very hard' (*reġn* 'rain, showers of rain').

(c)   The dm functions as an attribute of the dt, probably going back to a reversed *bahuvrihi* (cf. Carr, 1939: 260, 341): *sēoc-mōd* 'having a sick heart' (*bahuvrihi*) > *mōd-sēoc* 'sick with regard to the heart, heartsick' (reversed *bahuvrihi*), *ferþ-wērig* 'soul-weary', *mōd-glæd* 'glad at heart'.

Adj + Adj
The following relations occur:

(a)   additive (*nearu-fāh* 'difficult and hostile', *earm-ćearig* 'poor and sorrowful')

(b)   subordinative (*brūn-basu* 'brownish-purple', *heard-sǣlig* 'unhappy')

(c)   intensifying/downtoning (*eal-mihtig* 'all-mighty', *fela-gēomor* 'very sad', *efen-eald* 'of equal age', *stǣr-blind* 'stoneblind', *healf-dǣd* 'half-dead')

(d)   dt functions as goal of the dm (*clǣn-georne* 'clean-prone', *ellor-fūs* 'ready to depart')

(e)   dt functions as manner adverb with a deverbal adjective (*dēop-þancol* 'deep-thinking', *fela-specol* 'much-speaking = talkative', *hearm-cwidol* 'evil-speaking')

N/Adv (Adj) + first participle
Most of these formations are kennings; in their inflected forms they are not always distinguishable from synthetic agent nouns of the type *land-būend(e)* 'one who lives in the land' / 'living in the land', and we often find doublets (cf. Kärre, 1915: 7ff.; Carr, 1939: 211ff.). The first part functions as Subject (*hunig-flōwende* 'flowing with honey', *blōd-iernende* 'blood-running'), Object (*ealo-drincende* 'beer-drinking', *sweord-berende* 'sword-bearing'), Locative (*benć-sittende* 'sitting on the bench', *sǣ-līþende* 'sea-faring'), Instrumental (*rond-wīgende* 'fighting with a shield', *sweord-wīgende* 'fighting with a sword'), Adverb (*ān-būende* 'dwelling alone', *fūl-stinćende* 'foul-smelling'). These patterns still exist in Modern English.

N/Adv (Adj) + second participle
Again, the determinant functions as an argument of the underlying verb, i.e. as Subject (*ćeorl-boren* 'low-born', *hunger-biten* 'bitten by hunger'), Instrumental (*hand-locen* 'joined by hand', *wīn-druncen* 'drunken with wine'), Locative (*ǣht-boren* 'born in bondage', *hēofon-cenned* 'heaven-born'), Manner (*ǣwum-boren* 'legally born', *wundor-agrǣfen* 'wonderously engraved'; this relation does not exist in Modern English), Adjective/Adverb (*æþel-boren* 'of noble birth', *full-rīpod* 'fully riped = mature', *healf-brocen* 'half-broken').

Adverb/Particle + Adj/Participle
This type can be illustrated by the following examples: *æfter-writen* 'written afterwards', *ǣr-nemned* 'afore-mentioned', *eft-boren* 'born again', *fore-cweden* 'aforesaid', *forþ-snotor* 'very wise', *in-gemynde* 'well-remembered', *ofer-froren* 'frozen over', *ofer-ćeald* 'excessively cold', *þurh-lǣred* 'thoroughly learned', *wiþer-mēde* 'antagonistic'.

4.2.4.3   Compound verbs

In OE verbal compounds were mostly restricted to combinations with adverbs or prepositions as dts. These occurred in two patterns, viz. as 'inseparable' and 'separable' compounds. With the former, the adverbial or prepositional particle always occurred before the verb in all syntactic environments and could not be interrupted by any material, cf. the infinitive *tō ofer-feohtanne* 'conquer', or *hē for-cōm* 'he came before'. This property makes the respective formations similar to prefixations, and the semantics corroborate this: the particles more often than not have a non-literal meaning. With the separable pattern, the particle could be separated from the verb, cf. the infinitive *forþ tō brenganne* 'bring forth', and could also occur after the verb, e.g. *brenganne forþ.* The separable pattern is the antecedent of the Modern English phrasal verbs *come in, go out, eat up*, etc., with the particle in postverbal position and very often keeping its basic locative meaning. The type *out-do, over-bid, under-cut*, on the other hand, continuing the Old English inseparable type, has undergone semantic modification, adopting a non-literal meaning. For OE, the distinction between the two patterns is not always clear (cf. Hiltunen, 1983: 25ff.), and I will not make any attempt in the following very limited set of examples to separate the two patterns; nor will there be any attempt to distinguish between phrasal adverbs, prepositional adverbs and prepositions.

Some of the most important particles are: *æfter* 'after' (*æfter-folgian* 'succeed'), *æt* 'at' (*æt-bēon* 'be present'), *aweġ/onweġ* 'away' (*aweġ-gān* 'go away'), *be* 'around' (*be-būgan* 'flow around'), *fore* 'before' (*fore-sittan* 'preside'), *forþ* 'forth' (*forþ-beran* 'bring forth'), *full* 'completely' (*full-fremman* 'fulfil'), *ġeond* 'completely' (*ġeond-drincan* 'drink excessively'), *in(n)* 'in' (*in-faran* 'go in'), *ofer* 'over, too much' (*ofer-faran* 'go over', *ofer-dōn* 'overdo'), *tō* 'to; apart' (*tō-clīfan* 'cleave to', *tō-beran* 'carry off'), *þurh* 'through' (*þurh-sēon* 'see through'), *under* 'under' (*under-delfan* 'dig under'), *ūp* 'up' (*ūp-gān* 'go up'), *ūt* 'out' (*ūt-gān* 'go out'), *wiþer* 'against' (*wiþer-standan* 'withstand').

There are two further patterns which should be mentioned. The first is illustrated by *cyne-helmian* 'crown', *riht-wīsan* 'justify', *nīd-niman* 'take by force'. These are derivations from nominal compounds, i.e. *cynehelm* 'crown', *riht-wīs* 'justifiable', or back-derivations (*nīd-niman < nīd-nimung* 'commit *nīd-nimung*'). The other pattern is illustrated by *ellen-campian* 'campaign vigorously', *ġe-cwealm-bǣran* 'torture to death', *ġe-þanc-metian* 'deliberate', *morgen-wacian* 'rise early', *wēa-cwānian* 'lament'. The status of this pattern is less clear, since there does not seem to exist a corresponding nominal basis. This may be due to fragmentary evidence, but it might also indicate a sporadic attempt at verbal composition, which seems to be developing in Modern English, cf. verbs like *cold-rinse, warm-iron, chain-drink*, etc.

Prefixes are functionally equivalent to an adjective when they modify a noun (e.g. *sin-* in *sin-drēam* 'everlasting joy'), equivalent to an adverb when they modify an adjective (e.g. *sin-ċeald* 'perpetually cold') or a verb (e.g. *mis-cweþan* 'speak ill'), or equivalent to a preposition (e.g. *ǣ-felle* 'without skin'). In the latter case prefixation is combined with (affixless) derivation, since a change in word class is involved; these formations might therefore be regarded as negative *bahuvrihis* involving both prefixation and zero derivation; see Kastovsky (2002b).

At the end of the tenth century, the system of the OE verbal prefixes was in a state of advanced decay, both semantically and formally, and many prefix combinations had lost their transparency: it was no longer possible to associate a consistent meaning with a given prefix such as *a-/ā-, ġe-,* or *oþ-*; very often the verbal base and the prefixed form seem to have had the same meaning (cf. Horgan, 1980; Hiltunen, 1983). Thus in subsequent copies of one and the same text prefixes are often omitted, added to the base form, or exchanged for other prefixes, but without any apparent semantic effect. This decaying system was therefore an easy victim to inroads from two domains: the replacement by semantically more clearly defined Romance prefixes in the course of ME borrowing, and the strengthening and eventual dominance of the phrasal verbs of the type *go out, eat up, let in,* etc. In view of this, I will restrict the exemplification of OE prefixation to types which are still relevant in Modern English, and those which had a certain quantitative significance in OE.

The prefix *a-/æ-* (not surviving into Modern English) is relatively frequent, but how much meaning it actually contributed is not clear: cf. pairs like *bacan/a-bacan* 'bake', *beran/a-beran* 'bear', where there does not seem to be any semantic difference; but sometimes it seems to mean 'out', e.g. *a-berstan* 'burst out', *a-cleopian* 'call out', and sometimes it seems to be intensifying, e.g. *a-bēatan* 'beat to pieces'. It has a stressed allomorph *ǽ-* in deverbal nouns like *ǽ-cȳrf* 'wood-choppings', *ǽ-rist* 'rising, resurrection'.

The prefix *ánd-* (not surviving) was the stressed (nominal) variant of the unstressed verbal prefix *on-*; the original meaning had been 'against', but was partly obscured, e.g. *and-cwiss* 'answer' (cf. *on-cweþan* 'to answer'), *and-ġiet* 'understanding' (cf. *on-ġietan* 'to understand').

The status of *be-/bī-* (surviving only to a limited extent) is not always quite clear, and some instances might be treated also as representing a preposition. The following, however, seem to be clear cases of prefixation with specific functions: (a) transitivisation: *be-feohtan* 'take by fighting', *be-sprenġan* 'besprinkle'; (b) intensification: *be-brecan* 'break to pieces', *be-gnīdan* 'rub thoroughly'; (c) no specific meaning: *be-bēodan* 'offer, announce', *be-ċēapian* 'sell'. It also occurs in deverbal nouns such as *be-clypping* 'embrace', *be-frīġnung* 'inquiry'. In independent nominal formations the prefix is *bī-*, e.g. *bī-fylċe* 'neighbouring people', *bī-genġ(e)* 'worship, practice'.

For- (not surviving as a productive prefix) occurs with verbs and deverbal nouns as well as with adjectives. The following meanings occur: 'loss, destruction' (*for-berstan* 'burst asunder', *for-dōn* 'destroy'), intensification, perfectivity (*for-bærnan* 'burn up', *for-bītan* 'bite through', *for-heard* 'very hard', *for-maniġ* 'very many'), but often also without any specific meaning (*for-bēodan* 'forbid', *for-ġiefan* 'forgive').

One of the most frequent prefixes was *ġe-*, which, however, did not survive the Middle English period, just like *ġe-* in its function as a co-marker of the past participle; it occurred with verbs, adjectives and nouns, where it had different functions.

Verbal *ġe-*, when it can still be attributed a recognisable meaning, denotes 'perfectivity, result', often also transitivising an intransitive verb, e.g. *ġe-ǣrnan* 'gain by running', *ġe-āscian* 'learn by asking'. But many instances do not seem to exhibit a semantic difference between the simplex and the prefixation, e.g. *(ġe)-ādlian* 'be, become ill', *(ġe-)ǣmtiġian* 'to empty', or the meaning difference between the simplex and the prefixation is idiosyncratic, e.g. *standan* 'to stand': *ġe-standan* 'endure, last', *weorþan* 'be worthy': *ġe-weorþan* 'agree'.

Related to this is an adjectival-participial meaning 'provided with', which may or may not involve an intermediate verb form; in some instances there is no explicit derivative suffix, i.e. the formation should be interpreted as a zero derivative accompanied by a prefix (*ġe-bird(-e)* 'bearded', *ġe-frǣġ(-e)* 'known (by asking)'), but in others there is a suffix (*ġe-clād-ed* 'clothed', *ġe-glōf-ed* 'gloved'); in some other instances, the meaning is 'associativity', as with some nouns (*ġe-feder-en* 'having the same fathers', *ġe-mōd-Ø* 'of one mind').

With nouns other than direct derivatives from *ġe-*verbs, two related meanings occur: 'collectivity' and 'associativity'. The first refers to a collectivity of persons or objects, e.g. *ġe-genġ* 'body of fellow-travellers', *ġe-brōþor* 'brethren', or a repetitive action, e.g. *ġe-beorc* 'barking'. The second indicates that the subject performs some overt or implied action in conjunction with somebody else (often a translation of Lat. *con-*), e.g. *ġe-fara* 'one who travels with another', *ġe-bedda* 'one who lies in bed with another'.

Mis- (surviving with the help of French *mes-*) had the meaning 'bad, badly', and occurs with verbs (*mis-cweþan* 'speak ill', *mis-dōn* 'do evil'), nouns (*mis-ġe-hyġd* 'evil thought', *mis-(ġe)widere* 'bad weather') and participial adjectives (*mis-boren* 'abortive').

Another frequent prefix is *un-*, which survived in all of its functions. Its basic meaning comprises negativity ('not, opposite'), primarily producing complementaries and antonyms with adjectives and corresponding adjectival nouns, e.g. *un-æþele* 'of low birth', *un-berende* 'unbearable, unfruitful', *un-brād* 'narrow', but also with primary nouns, cf. *un-ār* 'dishonour', *un-friþ* 'enmity'. From this basic meaning, a pejorative meaning seems to have developed, viz. 'bad(ly), excessively', e.g. *un-forht* 'very afraid', *un-lagu* 'bad law, injustice'. With verbal bases, the prefix has reversative force, denoting the undoing of the result of a pre-action, e.g. *un-bindan* 'unbind', *un-dōn* 'undo'. The other meanings (privative and ablative) current in Modern English (e.g. privative *behead, defrost, stone*; ablative *deplane, disbar, unsaddle*) did not exist in Old English and were added later under French and Latin influence in connection with the adoption of the prefixes *de-* and *dis-* (see Kastovsky, 2002a).

Most of the Old English prefixes did not survive, and the Modern English prefix system is basically the result of later borrowing from French, Latin and Greek.

In contradistinction to prefixes, suffixes may cause morphophonemic alterna-tions, especially due to *i*-mutation and related phenomena such as gemination and palatalisation. But even though these alternations seem to have preserved some productivity until late Old English, the originally morphophonemic sta-tus of this alternation had changed to a purely allomorphic one, because in all instances the conditioning phonological factor had been lost. It is therefore not surprising that in late Old English we find more and more instances where an alternating derivative is replaced by a non-alternating one, and in Middle English this homological principle eventually prevails, at least in the native Germanic vocabulary.

The reason for this development is the progressive weakening and eventual loss of final unstressed syllables. This also had consequences for a number of word-formation patterns which had originally contained a suffix. This suffix was lost and the patterns in question shifted to affixless (i.e. zero) derivation. This holds for deadjectival and denominal weak verbs as well as for certain deverbal and deadjectival nouns. Thus the original structure of weak verbs was stem (base) + derivational affix (= stem formative) + inflection proper (tense, person + number); cf. class 1 (Inf. **trum + j + an*, Pret. **trum + i + d + a*), class 2 (Inf. **luf + oːj + an*, Pret. **luf + oː + d + a*). The alternating elements /j ∼ i/ and /oːj ∼ oː/ are referred to as stem formatives, indicating a particular inflectional class, but at the same time having the function of derivational suffixes, i.e. they do double duty: at this early (Germanic and pre-Old English) stage, inflection and derivation overlap (see Kastovsky, 1996). These structures represent the situation reconstructed for the fifth century (see Hogg, 1992b: 157–8, 160) and are still morphologically fully transparent. But with the loss of /i, j/ or its reduction to /e/ (cf. OE *trymm-an, trym-ed-e*) and the reduction of /oːj ∼ oː/ to /i, a, o/ (cf. OE *luf-ian, luf-ast, luf-od-e*), this transparency was lost. These changes eliminated the overt stem formative/derivational suffix, whose surviving reflexes became an integral part of the inflectional endings, e.g. **trum + i + d + a > trym + ed + e, *luf + oː + d + a > luf + od + e*. The patterns in question now have to be reinterpreted as affixless derivations, because the inflectional endings did not have any derivational function: inflection and word formation became completely separated.

Similar developments happened with deverbal nouns such as *lyġe < *lug + i + Ø* (: *lēog + an*) or deadjectival nouns such as *hǣte < *hāt + i + Ø*, where -*i*-was originally both a stem formative and a derivational suffix, but subsequently lost this function. These patterns also shifted to zero derivation, probably in the pre-Old English or the earliest Old English period.

4.2.4.4   Nominal suffixes

The principal nominal suffixes are *-dōm, -en, -end, -ere, -estre, -hād, -inċel, -ing, -ling, -ness, -sċipe, -þ(o)/-t, -ung/-ing, -wist*.

Suffixes determine gender affiliation. Some suffixes, e.g. *-dōm, -en, -estre, -hād, -ling, -ness, -ing/-ung*, are gender-invariant, others, e.g. *-end, -ere*, belong to more than one gender.

The suffix -*dōm* (Modern English -*dom*) goes back to the noun *dōm* 'judgement', but this meaning is no longer present, so that -*dōm* has to be regarded at least as a suffixoid, if not a real suffix. It derives denominal and deadjectival abstract nouns with the meanings 'state, condition, fact of being, action of', e.g. denominal *cāserdōm* 'empire', *campdōm* 'contest', *martyrdōm* 'martyrdom'; deadjectival *frēodōm* 'freedom', *wīsdōm* 'wisdom'.

With the suffix -*en* (not surviving) there are two semantic patterns, both deriving feminine nouns. The first is the counterpart of German -*in* (*Herrin, Lehrerin*) deriving feminines from nouns denoting male beings (an extremely restricted pattern in Modern English; see Kastovsky & Dalton-Puffer, 2002), e.g. *fyxen* 'vixen', *gyden* 'goddess', *mynecen* 'nun'. The second pattern produces abstract and concrete deverbal and denominal derivatives. Action nouns: *sīen* f. 'sight', *swefen* n. 'sleep, dream'; object/result: *fæsten* f. 'fortress', *sellen* f. 'gift'; instrumental nouns: *fæsten* n. 'fastener'; locative nouns: *hengen* f. 'rack, cross', *byrġen* f., n. 'grave'.

One of the most productive suffixes is -*end*, which primarily forms Agent nouns and is a rival of -*ere*. The latter remained the major Agent-noun-forming suffix in Modern English, whereas -*end* was lost in Middle English. Agent nouns (*biddend* 'petitioner', *hǣlend* 'Saviour', *lǣrend* 'teacher', *dǣl-nimend* 'participle'), Object nouns (*ġehæftend* 'prisoner'), instrumental nouns ((*ġe-*)*bīcniend* 'forefinger') are strong masculines. There are also some feminine action nouns, e.g. *nīd-nimend* 'taking by force', *blinnend* 'rest, ceasing'.

The suffix -*ere* also forms primarily masculine Agent nouns, but other semantic categories also occur. It was originally denominal (e.g. *sċipere* 'sailor', *sċō(h)ere* 'shoemaker'), but was subsequently extended to deverbal derivation with the same semantic categories that are covered by -*end*: *leornere* 'pupil', *sċeāwere* 'mirror', *pūnere* 'pestle', *word-samnere* 'catalogue' (all masculine), as well as the neuter Action noun (*dirne-*)*ġeliġere* 'adultery'.

In contradistinction to Modern English (or German), Old English had a suffix deriving female Agent nouns directly from verbs or nouns, viz. -*estre*, which did not presuppose a male agent to which it could be added (cf. *steward* > *stewardess, Lehrer* > *Lehrerin*). Deverbal derivatives are *hlēapestre* 'female dancer', *tæppestre* 'female tavern-keeper', *wæsċestre* 'washer'; denominal derivatives are *byrþestre* 'female carrier', *fiþelestre* 'female fiddler'. This situation provided the possibility of minimal pairs such as *bæcere: bæcestre* 'male/female baker', etc. The female reference of -*estre* was lost in Middle English, so that Modern English -*ster*-nouns like *gangster, roadster, speedster* are no longer gender-specific and -*er* has also become gender-neutral.

The status of -*hād* is comparable to that of -*dōm*. It originally goes back to the noun *hād* 'state, rank, position, character', which frequently occurred as a determinatum in compounds. But in this capacity it underwent semantic bleaching, so that at least in late Old English it had reached the status of a suffixoid, developing into a real suffix in Middle English, which its Modern English counterpart -*hood*/-*head* certainly is. Examples are: *abbudhād* 'rank of an abbot', *camphād* 'warfare', *ċildhād* 'childhood'.

English has never been very productive in the domain of diminutives. For Old English, only one suffix is recorded, neuter -inċel (not surviving), as in bōginċel 'small bough', hūsinċel 'little house', sċipinċel 'little ship'.

The suffix -ing, still active in Modern English, forms masculine nouns denoting 'proceeding or derived from N/Adj/V', often also with a patronymic function, e.g. Sċylding 'descendant of the Scylds', wīcing 'pirate'; æþeling 'son of a noble', ierming 'poor wretch'; fōstring 'fosterchild', līsing 'free man'.

The suffix -ling is related to -ing and resulted from a reanalysis of derivatives such as æþeling, etc., where the stem-final consonant was mistakenly also associated as the initial consonant of the suffix. This resulted in formations such as dēorling 'favourite', ġeongling 'youngling', fōstorling 'fosterchild'.

One of the most productive suffixes to derive feminine Action and State nouns (but also other semantic patterns) from adjectives and verbs is -ness. Typical deadjectival formations are æþelness 'nobility', beorhtness 'brightness', bitterness 'bitterness'. Deverbal formations can be based on the present or the past participle, but also on the simple verb stem, which is no longer possible in Modern English. Sometimes we find doublets and even triplets without any meaning difference. Action nouns are brecness 'breach', costness 'temptation', astandendness 'continuance', ġebētendness 'emendation', ūparisenness 'resurrection', cirredness 'turning'; blinness/ablinnendness 'cessation', forġifness/forġifennes 'forgiveness', lēorness/lēorendness/lēoredness 'departure, passing away', alīsness/alīsendness/alīsedness 'redemption'. Object/result nouns are onbærnness 'incense', an-/insetness 'ordinance, regulation', āgendness 'property', aleġedness 'interjection', foreset(ed)ness 'preposition'. Instrumental and locative nouns are fēdness 'nourishment', ġereordness 'food', smireness 'ointment', wuneness 'dwelling', behȳdedness 'secret place'. There may well have been a diachronic development with derivation from the infinitive stem having been the earlier preference, being gradually superseded by derivation from the participles.

The very productive suffix -sċipe forms masculine abstract nouns with the meanings 'state, act, fact' (bodsċipe 'message', frēondsċipe 'friendship', lēodsċipe 'nation, people').

The suffix family -þ(o)/-t derives feminine deadjectival abstract nouns (with and without umlaut), e.g. fȳlþ 'filth', hīehþ(o) 'height'; a particular strong group is derived from adjectives with the suffix -lēas, e.g. lārlēast/lārlīest 'ignorance', līflēast 'lack of life = death'.

The suffix alternants -ung/-ing derive feminine deverbal nouns from both strong and weak verbs; -ung primarily occurs with weak class 2 verbs, and -ing elsewhere, although this originally relatively clear-cut complementary distribution is no longer fully observed in late Old English. The surviving form, both for verbal nouns, gerunds (and eventually also present participles) is -ing. The typical semantic patterns are Action nouns (binding 'binding', huntung 'hunting'); Agent nouns (gaderung 'gathering, assembly', (ġe)mēting 'meeting, assembly'); Object/Result nouns (beorning 'incense', āgnung 'possessions'); Instrumental nouns (*lācnung* 'medicine', *wering* 'dam'); Locative nouns (*cȳping* 'market', *wunung* 'dwelling').

The survival rate of the Old English nominal suffixes was clearly higher than that of the prefixes, although there were quite a number of casualties, too, and later on a considerable influx of French and Latin suffixes competing with the native suffixes.

4.2.4.5   Adjectival suffixes

The following adjectival suffixes are of major importance for Old English: *-bǣre*, *-cund*, *-ed(e)/-od(e)*, *-en*, *-feald*, *-full*, *-iġ*, *-isċ*, *-lēas*, *-līċ*, *-sum*, *-weard*, most of which survived into Modern English.

The status of *-bǣre* (related to *beran* 'carry', not surviving) is not quite clear, but it seems that it had reached the status of a suffixoid (if not of a full-fledged suffix) rather than still being the second member of a compound. The meaning is 'productive of, having', e.g. *æppelbǣre* 'apple-bearing', *ātorbǣre* 'poisonous', *cornbǣre* 'corn-bearing'.

The suffix *-cund* (not surviving) produces denominal and deadjectival adjectives meaning 'of the nature of, originating from'; cf. denominal *engelcund* 'angelic', *gāstcund* 'spiritual', *godcund* 'divine'; deadjectival *æþelcund* 'of noble birth', *innancund* 'internal', *ȳfelcund* 'evil'.

The suffix alternants *-ed(e)/-od(e)* are related to the weak past participle endings (just as Modern English *-ed* in *bearded*), meaning 'provided with'. The bases are simple or compound nouns, the latter resulting in extended *bahuvrihi* compounds, e.g. *fēower-fōte, fēower-fēte* > *fēower-fōtede* 'four-footed'. We thus find many *bahuvrihi* and extended *bahuvrihi* doublets. Other meanings are 'resembling, having the character of', e.g. *a-ġimmed* 'set with gems', *ān-hyrned* 'having one horn', *fēower-hwēolod* 'four-wheeled'.

The suffix *-en* derives denominal adjectives with the meanings 'made of, consisting of, characterised by'. Older formations have *i*-umlaut, more recent ones do not: *æsċen* 'made of ash-wood', *ċēoslen* 'gravelly', *hyrnen* 'made of horn'.

The suffix *-feald* is used to form adjectives with the meaning '-fold' from numerals and quantifiers, e.g. *ānfeald* 'single', *maniġfeald* 'manifold'.

The suffix *-ful* 'having, being', still very productive today, derives adjectives from nouns, adjectives, and occasionally from verbs, e.g. denominal *andġietful* 'intelligent', *bealoful* 'wicked'; deadjectival *earmful* 'wretched, miserable', *ġeornful* 'eager'; deverbal *hyspful* 'contumelious, ridiculous'.

The very productive suffix *-iġ* (Modern English *-y*) produces denominal, deadjectival and deverbal adjectives meaning 'characterised by, having', many of which are extended *bahuvrihis*. This is a rival of *-līċ*, so that we find many *-iġ/-līċ* doublets. Examples are: *ādliġ* 'sick', *blissiġ* 'joyful', *blōdiġ* 'bloody' (denominal); *untrymiġ* 'infirm', *ġesyndiġ* 'sound' (deadjectival); *ċēorlġ* 'querulous', *ġefyndiġ* 'inventive, capable' (deverbal).

The very productive suffix -*isċ* 'being like, having the character of' forms denominal adjectives with and without *i*-umlaut, e.g. *ċeorlisċ* 'of a churl, common', *ċildisċ* 'childish', *denisċ* 'Danish', *englisċ* 'English', *sċyttisċ* 'Scottish'.

The negative counterpart of -*ful* is -*lēas* 'lack of', e.g. *bismerlēas* 'blameless', *blōdlēas* 'bloodless', *brōþorlēas* 'brotherless', etc.

The suffix -*līċ* 'being, characterised by, having' (= Modern English -*ly*) is a rival of -*iġ*. Denominal formations are *ǣlmeslīċ* 'charitable, depending on alms', *ċildlīċ* 'childish'; deadjectival formations are *ǣþellīċ* 'noble', *dēoplīċ* 'deep'; deverbal formations are *ċīeplīċ* 'for sale', *(ġe-)cwēmlīċ* 'pleasing, satisfying'.

The suffix -*sum* 'being, characterised by' derives denominal (*friþsum* 'peaceful', *ġelēafsum* 'believing', *ġedeorfsum* 'troublesome'), deadjectival (*ānsum* 'whole', *fremsum* 'beneficial', *ġenyhtsum* 'abundant') and deverbal ((*ġe-)hīersum* 'obedient', *healdsum* 'careful') adjectives.

The suffix -*weard* '-wards' occurs in *æfterweard* 'following', *heononweard* 'going hence', *norþ(e)weard* 'northwards' and similar formations.

4.2.4.6   Verbal suffixes

Verbal derivation is typically affixless. The four overt suffixes -*ett(an)*, -*lǣċ(an)*, -*n(ian)* and -*s(ian)* were not very productive and not always fully semantically transparent. The only one surviving into Modern English with increased productivity in Middle English is -*n(ian)*.

-*ett(an)* seems to have frequentative or intensifying meaning, and occurs with nominal (*bōtettan* 'repair', *sārettan* 'lament'), and adjectival (*āgnettan* 'appropriate, usurp', *hālettan* 'greet'), but primarily with verbal bases (*bliċettan* 'glitter, quiver', *dropettan* 'drop, drip', *hlēapettan* 'leap up').

-*lǣċ(an)* forms deadjectival verbs with the meanings 'be, become' (*dyrstlǣċan* 'dare', *ġe-ānlǣċan* 'make one, join', *rihtlǣċan* 'put right') and denominal verbs meaning 'produce, become' (*ǣfenlǣċan* 'become evening', *loflǣċan* 'promise', *sumorlǣċan* 'become summer').

The suffix -*n(ian)*, according to Marchand (1969: 271), resulted from a reanalysis of zero-derived verbs such as *fægen-ian* > *fæge-n-ian*, *open-ian* > *ope-n-ian*, but it might also be assumed that it continues Germanic class 4 weak verbs, which had an -*n*-formative, e.g. Gothic *full-n-an*. Old English formations are *beorhtnian* 'glorify', *lācnian* 'heal', *þrēatnian* 'threaten'.

The suffix -*s(ian)* derives deadjectival and denominal verbs, e.g. *ċildsian* 'be childish', *mētsian* 'feed', *blīþsian* 'make glad', *clǣnsian* 'make clean, cleanse'.

4.2.4.7   Zero derivation

The bases for the assumption of zero or affixless derivation are the distinction between inflectional and derivational morphology and expansion and derivation (see Section 4.1.5). Until the earliest Old English period, inflection and derivation had not been separated completely, because the verbal and nominal stem formatives had a function in both domains. But with their loss or integration into the stem or the inflectional endings, the respective patterns changed to affixless (zero) derivation. It should also be pointed out that ablaut alternations had no derivational function. Moreover, although the lexical items involved in these ablaut patterns belong to the core vocabulary, the patterns themselves were probably no longer productive. The distinction between expansion and derivation mentioned above is responsible for treating *bahuvrihis* like *ān-horn* as zero derivatives.

4.2.4.8   Nominal derivatives

Deverbal nouns exhibit the full semantic range typical of this category, although Action and Agent nouns dominate. All genders are represented, and most inflectional classes within them. A considerable number of derivatives are affected by *i*-umlaut. There is no strict correlation between semantic category, gender, inflectional class and ablaut grade, but some preferences reflecting earlier regularities are discernible. Thus agent nouns tend to be masculine and to have reduced grade and masculine action nouns frequently have a full-grade base, while neuter ones often go with the reduced grade. Derivation is made both from strong and weak verbs. Derivatives related to strong verbs seem to have originally been root-based like the strong verbs themselves, developing their stem-based status in the Germanic period. Weak verbs, on the other hand, originally were typically denominal, deadjectival and deverbal. But in the course of time, in many instances the direction of derivation came to be reversed in analogy with other patterns, which happened throughout the history of English. Thus, from a semantic point of view, it is more natural for an Action or Agent noun to be derived from a verb (e.g. *gnorn* 'affliction, sorrow' < *gnornian* 'grieve, be sad', *peddle* > *peddler* ModE) than for a verb to be derived from a primary Action or Agent noun (e.g. *gnorn* > *gnornian, pedlar/peddler* > *peddle* eModE). Consequently, the 'unnatural' direction of derivation was replaced by the more 'natural' one (see also Kastovsky, 1968: 93ff.).

Strong masculine action nouns from strong and weak verbs are *drepe* 'slaying', *cyme* 'coming', *bælċ* 'belch', *drenċ* 'drowning'; weak masculines are *steorfa* 'mortality', *sċeapa* 'harm', *hopa* 'hope'; strong feminines are *faru* 'journey, going', *ġiefu/ġiefe* 'gift, favour', *lufu* 'love'; weak feminines are *birċe* 'barking', *feohte* 'fight', *ġiċċe* 'itch'; strong neuters are *beorc* 'barking', *berst* 'eruption', *ġebirġ* 'tasting', *ġeċīd* 'strife'.

Strong masculine agent nouns are *gang, genġ* 'a company, gang', *wæter-ġyte* 'Aquarius', *ġe-nēat* 'one who enjoys with another'; weak masculines are *āga* 'owner', *cuma* 'comer, guest', *hunta* 'hunter'. For a fairly complete listing of these zero derivatives, see Kastovsky (1968).

Deadjectival nouns are typically strong feminines with the meanings 'quality, fact, state of being', usually having *i*-umlaut, e.g. *bieldu* 'boldness', *birhtu* 'brightness', *ċieldu* 'cold'.

Denominal nouns are *bahuvrihi* compounds with the meaning 'someone, something having N', e.g. *ān-horn/Ø* 'animal having one horn = unicorn'. In Old English, this nominal type was much weaker than the adjectival type, which (with the exception of *barefoot*) was lost, with the nominal type taking over. Many formations are loan translations from Latin, often denoting plants or animals. The most frequent patterns are Adj + N, Num + N. Sometimes the overt second part changes its morphological behaviour in the combination, e.g. *lēaf* 'leaf' (strong neuter) vs *fīf-lēafe* 'quinquefolium' (weak feminine), besides *fīf-lēaf* (with the preservation of the morphological properties of the second part). Further examples are *ān-horn/ān-horn-a/ān-hyrn-e* 'unicorn', *belced-swēora* 'one having a swollen neck', *bunden-stefn-a* 'ship with an ornamented prow', *hyrned-nebb-a* 'horny-beaked bird, eagle'.

4.2.4.9   Adjectival derivatives

Affixless deverbal adjectives related to strong verbs are in the majority; they may or may not have *i*-umlaut and they very often occur as second members of compounds. Their meaning is usually 'prone to do, doing, being V-ed', e.g. *swiċe* 'deceitful', *ēaþ-fynde* 'easy to find', *cwēme* 'pleasant, agreeable'.

The numerous simple and complex zero-derived denominal adjectives meaning 'having, being like' either have a masculine nominative singular ending in *-e* (e.g. *fielde* 'fieldlike', *ān-bīeme* 'made of one trunk', *ān-ēage* 'one-eyed') or have no ending (e.g. *bær-fōt* 'barefoot', *lang-mōd* 'patient', *blanden-feax* 'grey-haired'). Many of these have affixal doublets, and it is this latter formative type which survives into Modern English.

4.2.4.10   Verbal derivation

Affixless derivation was the major source of new verbs in Old English. The results are weak verbs, but only the derivation of class 2 weak verbs from nouns, adjectives and adverbs (type *beorht* > *beorhtian* 'be, make bright', *wuldor* > *wuldrian* 'glorify') was fully productive in Old English, whereas the derivation of class 1 weak verbs involving *i*-umlaut (type *full* > *fyllan* 'fill', *scrūd* > *sċryd* 'clothe') was certainly productive as long as *i*-umlaut was fully transparent, but it must have lost its productivity in early Old English. As a consequence, many class 1 verbs joined class 2, so there are numerous doublets. Most of the semantic types found in Modern English (see Marchand, 1969: 365–71) are already attested in Old English.

Typical denominal verbs denote 'be, act like, become' (*ambehtan* 'minister, serve', *dagian* 'dawn'), 'provide with, add' (*ārian* 'give honour to', *frēfran* 'comfort'), but also the opposite, i.e. 'remove' (*hēafdian* 'behead'), 'produce' (*blēdan* 'bleed', *blōstmian* 'blossom'), 'make into' (*hēapian* 'heap', *munucian* 'make into a monk'), 'perform' (*cræftan* 'perform a craft', *cossian* 'kiss'), 'put into, go to' (*gryndan* 'come to the ground, set', *hæftan* 'imprison', *hūsian* 'house').

Deadjectival verbs have two possible meanings, viz. 'be, become' and 'make'. Many derivatives have both meanings, e.g. *byldan* 'make bold', *blōdiġian* 'make bloody', *brædan* 'broaden', *dēopian* 'become, make deep'.

4.2.4.11 Adverbs

The formation of adverbs is a borderline case between word formation and inflection. Since adverbs are regarded as a separate part of speech, their derivation from adjectives and nouns involves a change of word class, which is by definition a derivational process. But this process does not add any additional semantic feature, which is typically the case in derivation proper.

The most frequent deadjectival suffix is *-e* (e.g. *dēope* 'deeply', *ġeorne* 'eagerly'). If the adjective itself ends in *-e*, adjective and adverb are homonymous, e.g. *blīþe* 'joyful(ly)', *milde* 'mild(ly)'. From the many adjectives ending in *-līċ* and their adverbial form *-līċe* (e.g. *mōdiġlīċe* 'proudly', *sārlīċe* 'grievously') a new complex suffix *-līċe* was created and used to directly form adverbs not only from adjectives not ending in *-līċe* (e.g. *blindlīċe* 'blindly', *holdlīċe* 'graciously'), but also from nouns (e.g. *frīondlīċe* 'in a friendly manner', *eornostlīċe* 'earnestly'). After the loss of final *-e* in late Old English and early Middle English, this suffix develops into the standard means of forming adverbs, i.e. it is the antecedent of Modern English *-ly*.

Other adverb-forming suffixes are *-inga/-linga/-unga/-lunga* (*ednīwunga* 'anew', *grundlinga/grundlunga* 'to the ground, completely', *nēad(l)inga/nēadlunga* 'by force'). Furthermore, denominal adverbs can also be formed by using an inflectional form of the noun, e.g. the masculine genitive singular in *-es* (e.g. *dæġes* 'daily', *selfwilles* 'voluntarily') or the dative plural (*dæġtīdum* 'by day', *ġēardagum* 'formerly', *dropmǣlum* 'drop by drop', etc).

4.2.4.12 The typological status of Old English word formation

This typological characterisation is based on several intersecting parameters, such as the morphological status of the input to and the output of the word-formation processes, the order of the dt and dm, the frequency, regulating, conditioning and functioning of morphophonemic/allomorphic alternations, and the number of derivational levels.

Old English is in a stage of transition from stem-based to word-based inflection and derivation. The verb system is stem-based, and it is only towards the end of the Old English period and during the Middle English period that with the loss of the infinitive ending the verb develops an unmarked base form, which can function as a word, i.e. shifts from stem-based to word-based inflection and derivation. The nominal system is heterogeneous in this respect. Weak nouns (*gum+a*, *tung+e*) as well as strong feminines (*luf+u*) are stem-based, whereas strong masculines (*cyning*) and neuters (*word*) as well as adjectives (*gōd*) have an unmarked nominative/accusative singular, i.e. they have word-based inflection and derivation. Again, with the progressive loss of inflectional endings this type will eventually prevail.

Major changes took place in the morphophonemic system. The Indo-European ablaut system had gradually become more and more opaque during the Germanic and pre-Old English period, due to a number of sound changes, leading to the progressive breaking-up of the ablaut classes of the strong verbs. This also gradually resulted in a dissociation between the strong verbs and the related ablaut nouns and adjectives, which were, with the exception of a few relics such as *batch, drove, song, writ* and some additional dialectal forms, almost completely lost during Middle English. A contributing factor was probably also the generalisation of word-based derivation, which had as its input the unmarked base form. The other morphophonemic alternations, though originally transparent, in the course of the (pre-)Old English period lost their conditioning factors and shifted from phonological to (unpredictable) morphological conditioning. The most important of the alternations was unquestionably *i*-umlaut, which not only lost its conditioning factor, but, due to progressive unrounding, also its phonetic transparency. At the end of the Old English period, probably accelerated by the various lengthening and shortening processes affecting the vowel system, this morphophonemic/allomorphic system must have broken down completely. The subsequent restructuring in Middle English, little investigated so far, established homological, i.e. alternation-free, derivation as the dominant principle of word formation, which it still is in Modern English in the native and nativised patterns. It is only in non-native Romance and Neo-Latin patterns that we have alternations today, e.g. *sane* ~ *sanity, divine* ~ *divinity, Japán* ~ *Japanése*, etc. Thus, whereas in Old English we have only one derivational level, viz. derivation on a native basis, Modern English operates at both a native and a non-native level, whose boundaries are not neatly delimited. This duality is the result of the massive borrowing from French and Neo-Latin in the Middle English and early Modern English periods, as we will see below.

4.3   Middle English

4.3.1   Introduction

As explained in Chapter 1, the linguistic situation at the end of the twelfth century was rather complex, both socially and geographically. In fact, we find four different linguistic strata.

First of all, there are monolingual native speakers of English (usually members of the lower social ranks), speaking local dialects with no supra-regional standard; the emergent West Saxon written standard was petering out during the twelfth century. A second geographically but also socially distinct group lived in the former Danelaw area, where we still have to reckon with partial Scandinavian–English bilingualism in the eleventh and early twelfth centuries. This bilingualism, however, must have rapidly decreased in favour of English monolingualism due to the changed political situation. The result was the loss of Scandinavian as a means of communication (language death) with massive borrowing of basic vocabulary. A third group consisted of those who mainly or exclusively used French (Anglo-Norman) in oral communication, usually members of the nobility, including the royal family. But towards the end of the twelfth century, more and more members of this class began to also learn English, probably resulting in considerable bilingualism. At the same time we witness an increase of French among members of the middle class, especially with traders and craftsmen in towns. Fourthly, it should not be forgotten that Latin had remained in use as the language of the church and of scholarship (where it was also used as a spoken medium), and of public records.

Thus at the beginning of the thirteenth century we are confronted with a rather complex sociolinguistic situation. There were people who spoke only French and many more who spoke only English. There were likewise a considerable number who were genuinely bilingual as well as those who had some understanding of two languages while speaking only one. Thus Henry II (1154–89) understood English but did not speak it, whereas his wife, Eleanor of Aquitaine, did not understand English at all and always needed an interpreter. Had this situation continued, England might well have developed into a bilingual country, but important political changes at the end of the twelfth century brought about the re-establishment of English as the dominant – and eventually only – language in England. The crucial change was the loss of Normandy to the French crown by King John as a result of his politically unwise marriage to Isabel of Angoulême. The nobility had to make a choice with regard to their allegiance either to the king of England or the king of France, with the concomitant loss of their property in France or England, respectively.

There was one phenomenon which delayed the demise of French for some time, namely the cultural dominance of France and French. At this time France was commonly regarded as representing chivalrous society in its most polished form, and French literature was regarded highly at most courts in Europe and was often translated or imitated in the vernacular. This was also enhanced by the fame of the University of Paris as the centre of medieval scholarship. Thus the position of French gradually changed in the thirteenth century. The upper classes continued to speak French, but primarily due to social custom, administrative convention and for prestige reasons, rather than necessity. At the same time, English more and more gained ground, and by the middle of the thirteenth century had become the language of everyday business even among the upper classes. This is the period when we observe the largest number of French loans entering the English vocabulary, especially those belonging to everyday language such as *action, age, city, country, hour, mountain, noise, flower, people, piece, power, reason, river, tailor, use, waste; able, active, brief, calm, certain, common, cruel, double, eager, easy, faint, firm, frail, honest, jolly, large, mean, moist, natural, nice, plain, poor, pure, real, safe, secret, solid, sure, tender, usual; advance, advise, aim, allow, arrive, catch, change, chase, conceal, count, cover, defeat, desire, destroy, enjoy, enter, err, flatter, form, grant, join, marry, mount, obey, pass, please, push, quit, receive, refuse, remember, reply, rob, save, serve, strangle, strive, suppose, tempt, tremble, wait,* etc. The reason for the demise of French is the same as in the case of Scandinavian: language death. The French language lost ground, speakers switched to English, but brought a lot of their vocabulary with them. By the end of the thirteenth century, French was no longer a native language for many and had to be taught systematically. As a result, we now find French manuals with English glosses, i.e. language-teaching material; an example is the treatise written by Walter of Bibbesworth to teach children French – how to speak and how to reply: 'Which every gentleman ought to know' – in the middle of the thirteenth century.

Another aspect detrimental to French in England was its provincial linguistic status. It had originated as the language of the Normans coming to England, which was a regional variety. At the time of the Norman Conquest there had basically been four French dialects, viz. Norman, Picard (northeast France), Burgundian (east) and Central French (Paris and Ile-de-France), which enjoyed a certain local prestige. But in the thirteenth century, Paris and its dialect became dominant and the Anglo-Norman dialect spoken in England came to be regarded as very provincial. Thus, even if French remained the first language with some speakers in England, it would be regarded as odd by the real French, and made 'real', i.e. Parisian, French even more of a foreign language. This is also reflected by the changing source of French loans, as we will see below. Another factor contributing to the establishment of English as the primary spoken language was the general demographic development and the rise of a substantial middle class.

All this shows that for about at least 300 years English had been subject to continuous foreign influence, primarily from French, but also to a certain extent from Latin. While the Scandinavian influence had not really changed the character of the vocabulary, the influence of French and Latin was much more pervasive, since it also had repercussions for the phonological and morphological system of the language, apart from merely adding to the number of lexical items with the result of introducing numerous quasi-synonyms (partly semantically, partly just stylistically differentiated). This made lexical fields more complex than they had been in Old English; cf. the following examples: *rise : mount : ascend, ask : question : interrogate, goodness : virtue : probity, fire : flame : conflagration, fear : terror : trepidation, holy : sacred : consecrated, hearty : cordial, stench : smell : aroma : odour : perfume : fragrance, might : power, ask : demand, shun : avoid, seethe : boil, shut : close, wish : desire.* On the other hand, many of these loans replaced older words, e.g. *ēam > uncle, æþele > noble, dryhten > lord, lēod > people, dēma / dēman / dōm > judge / judgement* (vs *doom / deem*), *sċyldiġ > guilty, here > army, cempa > warrior, sibb > peace, ādl > disease, ieldo > age, lyft > air, earm > poor, andettan > confess, dihtan > compose, beorgan > protect, herian > praise, lēan / lēanian > reward, belīfan > remain.*

There were two further factors that shaped the history of the English language: the emergence of a standard language in the late fouteenth and fifteenth centuries and the later introduction of printing. Both factors contributed to a gradual differentiation between the standard language and local dialects, which gradually became regarded as inferior.

4.3.2   Borrowing

4.3.2.1   Scandinavian

As has already been mentioned, the majority of the Scandinavian loans make their appearance in Middle English. To these belong many everyday words such as *anger, bag, cake, dirt, flat, fog, husband, leg, neck, silver, skin, sky, smile, Thursday, window*; *happy, ill, low, odd*; *raise, seem, take, want*, etc. In some instances borrowing resulted in doublets, e.g. *skirt* vs *shirt*, *dike* vs *ditch*, *scrub* vs *shrub*, but in many other pairs only one pair member survived the Middle English period, e.g. *give* vs *yive*, *gate* vs *yate*. Especially remarkable is the fact that function words were also borrowed, e.g. the personal pronouns *they, their, them*, but also *both, same, against, though*. Many more loans survived in the English dialects spoken in the original settlement areas of the Scandinavians but have been lost in the emerging standard; for further details see Burnley (1992: 414–23).

4.3.2.2   French

French loans were adopted in two stages from two different varieties of French, with the dividing line around 1250. During the first period, the borrowings are less numerous and are more likely to exhibit peculiarities of Norman and Anglo-Norman in their phonology. Moreover, the roughly 900 words borrowed during this period are such that the lower classes would become familiar with them through contact with a French-speaking nobility, e.g. *baron, noble, dame, servant, messenger, feast, minstrel, juggler*, i.e. they reflect the 'superiority' of the French culture. In the period after 1250, the pattern changed: now words were introduced by those who so far had spoken French but now turned to English as their normal, everyday spoken language. This introduced many words related to government and administration, but also words drawn from the domains of fashion, food, social life, art, learning and medicine, and other domains of everyday life. Moreover, the source was now Central French, which had had a different phonological development. This occasionally also led to doublets. The following are examples of the more important differences (the first represents the Norman or Anglo-Norman form, the second the Central French one): /k/ vs /tʃ/ (*catch* vs *chase*), /w/ vs /g/ (*wile* vs *guile*, *warrant* vs *guarantee*, *warden* vs *guardian*), /e, ei/ vs /oi/ (*convey* vs *convoy*).

Typical examples representing the areas mentioned above are:

1.   Government and administration: *authority, court, crown, government, majesty, reign, state*; *alliance, parliament, treaty*; *record, revenue, tax*; *exile, rebel, traitor, treason, liberty, office*; *chancellor, constable, governor, mayor, treasure*; *count, duke, madam, mistress, page, peer, prince, peasant, slave*; *administer, govern, oppress, usurp*; *royal*

2.   Ecclesiastical words: *clergy, clerk, confession, lesson, prayer, religion, sacrament, sermon, theology*; *cardinal, chaplain, dean, hermit, parson, vicar, abbey, convent, image, incense, miracle, priory*;

creator, saviour, saint, trinity, virgin; charity, damnation, devotion, faith, mercy, mystery, obedience, piety, pity, reverence, temptation, virtue; devout, divine, solemn; adore, anoint, chant, confess, convert, ordain, pray, preach, repent, sacrifice

3.   Law: *bar, crime, justice, judgement, plea, suit; attorney, defendant, judge, jury, plaintiff, felon; complaint, petition, evidence, proof, bail, verdict, sentence, award, fine, punishment; prison, jail; adultery, arson, fraud, libel, perjury, slander; executor, heir, legacy, property, tenant; accuse, acquit, arrest, blame, condem, plead, pardon, sue, seize; innocent, just*

4.   Fashion, meals, social life: *boots, dress, cloak, coat, collar, fashion, garment, gown, robe, veil, button, embroidery, garter, lace; adorn, embellish; beaver, ermine, fur, sable, satin; blue, brown, saffron, scarlet, vermilion, tawny; jewel, ornament, ivory; crystal, diamond, emerald, ruby, pearl; appetite, dinner, feast, supper, taste; mackerel, oyster, perch, salmon, sole; beef, pork, mutton, poultry, veal, venison; bacon, loin, sausage; biscuit, cream, gravy, sugar, toast, lettuce, salad; almonds, cherry, date, fig, grape, lemon, orange, peach; clove, herb, mustard, nutmeg, spice, thyme, vinegar; blanch, boil, fry, grate, roast, stew*

All in all, around 10,000 French words were introduced into English during the Middle English period, of which about 75 per cent are still in current use.

4.3.2.3   Latin

Latin, as the language of the church, scholarship, and partly of law, normally acted only as a written source. Typical loans from these areas are: *diocese, psalm, requiem, redemptor, allegory, cause, contradiction, desk, scribe; explicit, formal, major, minor; client, conviction, executor, memorandum, prosecute, proviso, testify, legitimate.* Others belonging to more general domains are: *adjacent, conspiracy, contempt, custody, distract, frustrate, genius, history, immune, include, incredible, individual, inferior, infinite, intellect, interrupt, lunatic, magnify, mechanical, moderate, necessary, nervous, notary, picture, polite, popular, prevent, project, promote, quiet, rational, reject, script(ure), secular, solar, spacious, subordinate, subscribe, substitute, summary, suppress, tributary, ulcer.*

4.3.3   Word formation

Middle English is the starting point of a development which resulted in a restructuring of the English word-formation system by borrowing from French and Latin, and which was intensified in early Modern English. This led to a system with two derivational strata, a native and a foreign one, which, however, partially overlap. The former is word-based and base-invariant, whereas the latter is at least partly stem-based and exhibits morphophonemic alternations of the base (see Kastovsky, 1994). Thus with *-able* we find besides word-based *allow-able, understand-able* also stem-based *charit-able, navig-able* (besides *navigat-able*), *cultiv-able* (besides *cultivat-able*). The alternations *-ate* ~ *-acy*, as in *pirate* ~ *pira-cy, obstinate* ~ *obstina-cy, -ant* ~ *-ancy*, as in *sergeant* ~ *sergean-cy, innocent* ~ *innocen-cy*, were adopted in Middle English from French. Other examples are *edify* ~ *edific-ation, rectify* ~ *rectific-ation, astrology* ~ *astrolog-er*, etc.

The origin of these non-native patterns was the borrowing of individual lexical items which had already been derivationally related in the source languages, e.g. *allow* ~ *disallow, arm* ~ *disarm, chain* ~ *enchain, enter* ~ *re-enter, establish* ~ *restablish*; *accept* ~ *acceptable, blame* ~ *blamable, arrive* ~ *arrival, suppose* ~ *supposal, accept* ~ *acceptance, endure* ~ *endurance, excellent* ~ *excellency, sufficient* ~ *sufficiency, edify* ~ *edification, organise* ~ *organisation, assign* ~ *assignee, grant* ~ *grantee, rob* ~ *robbery*, etc. Once a number of such pairs had been borrowed, a derivational relationship could also be established in English, from which it could then be extended to new formations not necessarily having a parallel in the source language, probably first by individual analogical formations, until the pattern finally became productive on a larger scale (see Kastovsky, 1986). Traditionally, it has been assumed that non-native, especially French patterns had become productive fairly early. However, in a corpus-based study of nominal suffixes Dalton-Puffer (1996) has argued that the Romance suffixes had not really become productive in Middle English. Hybrid formations containing a Germanic base and a Romance affix, such as *spekable, knowable, bondage, aldermanrie, outlawery, hunteresse, worshippour* and a few others (Dalton-Puffer, 1996: 221), which might be indicative of beginning productivity, are according to her due to direct analogy; only with *-able* 'we must indeed be observing a budding derivational rule for deverbal adjectives' (Dalton-Puffer, 1996: 221). Burnley (1992: 447 ff.) seems to favour late Middle English as the starting point, especially for prefixation. Here, additional studies are necessary, especially since Middle English word formation in general is a rather under-researched area. Following this line of argument, the real productivity of many Romance and Latin derivational patterns only started during the late Middle and early Modern English period, when apparently a critical mass of borrowings and analogical formations had accumulated to get the derivational processes going (see also Nevalainen, 1999: 378ff.). Dalton-Puffer's study only covers nominal derivations. In view of the number of prefixes and suffixes entering the English language in Middle English according to Marchand (1969) and as listed below, the increase of productivity must have been gradual and certainly differed from affix to affix.

Another aspect, already discussed with regard to phonology in general in Section 2.6.2.4, is the impact of this borrowing process on the morphophonemic system of derivational patterns. Originally, lexical items had their stress on the first syllable except for certain prefixed verbs, and stress assignment was from left to right independent of syllable weight. The loans from French and Latin had a different prosodic structure, viz. non-initial, partly movable stress. Here, stress assignment operates from right to left, taking into account syllable weight. Stress could therefore be placed on the final (*licóur*), penultimate (*engéndred*) or antepenultimate (*párdoner*) syllable, depending on weight distribution, with considerable variation. This automatically led to movable stress in derivationally related patterns, especially since suffixes could bear stress themselves (*emplóy* ~ *employée*, *Japán* ~ *Japanése*) or determine the position of stress (*history* ~ *históric* ~ *historícity*, *admíre* ~ *ádmirable/admírable*). This affected the English phonological system profoundly, since stress position additionally led to phonological alternations between full vowels in stressed and schwa in unstressed position. It must therefore be assumed that Middle English (as well as Modern English) operates with two competing stress systems, the continuation of the original Germanic one and the new Romance one (see also Dalton-Puffer, 2002, where she investigates variation between these stress patterns, as in *ádmirable/admírable*, etc., proving that both patterns are equally relevant and in competition).

Moreover, alternations originally due to stress assignment were affected by shortening processes in connection with the number of syllables involved, e.g. *sǣn* ~ *sǽnity*, *divīn* ~ *divínity*, etc., which after the Great Vowel Shift also led to segmental alternations such as /sein/ ~ /sænɪti/, /dɪvaɪn/ ~ /dɪvɪnɪti/. Whether such alternations (dubbed Trisyllabic Laxing in Chomsky & Halle, 1968) have really become productive in English is questionable (cf. Minkova & Stockwell, 1998). On the other hand, the alternation called Velar Softening, i.e. the alternation between a velar stop and a palatal or alveolar fricative or affricate, as in *historic* ~ *historicity*, *magic* ~ *magician*, *concept* ~ *conceptual*, etc., certainly is productive, although tied to the respective non-native suffixes and therefore morphologically-lexically conditioned.

Thus the borrowing process not only changed the overall phonological system of English, especially with regard to stress alternations and concomitant segmental alternations, but also the morphophonemic system of derivational morphology, establishing two derivational levels.

A third aspect is the loss of patterns. Thus a number of OE suffixes were lost, e.g. the Agent noun suffix *-end*, the adjectival suffixes *-bǣre,-ende*, all verbal suffixes with the exception of *-en*, which made room for Romance *-ate*, *-ify* and *-ise*. Even more significant is the almost complete loss of the OE verbal prefixes. This paved the way for the large-scale adoption of the Romance and Latin prefixes (see the list in Section 4.3.3.2), which also filled a number of semantic gaps, such as ablative verbs of the type *dislodge* (1450), *displace* (1551), which had no Old English counterparts and which may have caused the extension of privative *un-* as in *unsaddle* 'remove the saddle' to ablative *un-* as in *unsaddle* 'remove the rider from the saddle' (see Kastovsky, 2002b: 106ff.; Nevalainen, 1999: 378ff.).

One further important development is the almost complete loss of the ablaut nouns and adjectives, which in Old English had been part of the core vocabulary. Why German preserved these derivatives and English lost them requires an explanation, although this can only be speculative. It would seem that this development is connected with the general restructuring of the morphological system of English. English had more and more shifted towards a word-based morphology both in inflection and in derivation, with a progressive loss of morphophonemic alternations, whereas German had preserved stem-based morphology to a much greater extent. Also, the preservation of umlaut as a productive process in German (even though only morphologically conditioned) made ablaut alternations more acceptable. The loss of ablaut nouns is thus in all probability triggered by the reorientation towards a word-based English morphological system in Middle English, which favoured non-alternating derivations. The introduction of morphophonemic alternations in non-native derivation can therefore be seen as a consequence of the reintroduction of stem-based morphology.

4.3.3.1   Compounding

With the exception of a few instances, the OE patterns continued and partly extended their semantic range or were reinterpreted morphologically. But there were also a number of new patterns, which emerged partly as a native development, partly as the result of foreign influence.

In OE, the pattern *brǣding-panne* 'frying-pan' was an N + N combination, since the suffixes *-ing/-ung* derived verbal nouns. In ME, *-ing*-formations gradually adopted participial (and gerundial) functions, which in the fourteenth century resulted in the reinterpretation of such formations along the lines of the V + N pattern *whet-stone*, i.e. as a verbal nexus combination, of which it became a morphological rival, i.e. the *-ing*-form functioned as a verbal predicate: *brǣding-panne* 'pan for frying' > 'pan in which one can fry'.

The pattern N + deverbal Agent noun (e.g. OE *blōd-lǣtere* 'blood-letter') got a new boost as of the fourteenth century and has remained strong ever since.

New is the sex-denoting type *he-lamb*, *she-ass*, which begins to appear in the thirteenth century, and in the fourteenth century we find the first instances of the type *Tom Fool*, *tomcat*.

A further innovation is the level-stressed N + N compound type *stóne wáll*, whose origin still needs closer investigation. In OE, nominal compounds were always forestressed (as they are in German), with stress reduction of the second member, the dm. The new type has no reduction of the stress on the second member, but for rhythmic reasons may reduce the stress on the first member, i.e. *stóne wáll* ~ *stòne wáll*. As to the status of the two types of compounds, see Section 4.1.5 above.

With adjective compounds, the majority of the OE patterns continued and increased their productivity (cf. Marchand, 1969: 84–95). But there are also a few new types. Thus the type *icy-cold* seems to have arisen in the fourteenth century, the earliest formations being *red-hot*, *lukewarm*, *wordly-wise*, *light green* from the fourteenth and fifteenth centuries. The type *heart-breaking*, *ocean-going* also arose in Middle English in connection with *-ing* developing participial function, replacing the Old English type *hunig-flōwende*, *land-būende*, and has subsequently become extremely productive until today. The same is true of the type *moss-grown*, *moth-eaten*, which existed in Old English, but increased its productivity considerably during Middle English and is still very much alive. Finally, another type developing in this period is *high-born*, where the participial dm is modified by an adjective which historically at least partly goes back to an adverb, e.g. *new-born*, *new-clad*, *dead-born*, *new-sown* from the fourteenth century; real productivity, however, starts in the second half of the sixteenth century.

Compound verbs of the type *outbid* (*outlive*, *outride*), *override* (*overreach*, *oversleep*), *underbid* (*undervalue*, *underrate*), where the dt has a metaphorical meaning 'do in excess' or 'below the expected limit', continuing the locative particles with originally a literal meaning, appear in the fifteenth and sixteenth centuries and have preserved a moderate productivity till today, whereas their literal counterparts have become unproductive. A replacement for the latter is phrasal verbs such as *go out*, *come in*, *put up*. This type starts to be generalised in the fourteenth century and is more or less established in the fifteenth century (with some fluctuation).

4.3.3.2   Prefixation

The Old English prefixes *be-*, *fore-*, *mis-*, *un-* and a few others continued to be productive in Middle English, but most of the other verbal ones lost their productivity and also their morphosemantic transparency. This paved the way for borrowing from French and Latin. How far these prefixes had already become productive in Middle English is difficult to judge, since it is not always possible to decide whether the derivationally related forms were independent borrowings or already English formations using a non-native or even nativised pattern. The following prefixes make their appearance in Middle English, often filling semantic gaps in the English derivational system: *arch-* (*arch-dean*, *arch*-priest), *co-* (*co-executor*, *co-inheritor*, *co-heir*), *counter-* (*counterpoise*, *counter-guard*, *counterplea*), *dis-* (*discharge*, *disobey*, fourteenth century; *dishonest*, *disloyal*, fourteenth–fifteenth centuries), *en-* (*embow*, *ennoble*, *enlighten*, fifteenth century), *in-* (*incomprehensible*, *infinite*, fourteenth and fifteenth centuries), *inter-* (*interchange*, *interspace*, fourteenth and fifteenth centuries), *mis-*, fusing with French *mes-* (*misdo*, *misapply*, *misconceive*), *non-* (*non-age*, *non-payment*, fourteenth century), *re-* (*re-enter*, *re-establish*, fifteenth century), *vice-* (*viceadmiral*, *vice-consul*, fifteenth and sixteenth centuries).

4.3.3.3   Suffixation

Here we witness a greater continuity than with prefixes, but there are also many new, foreign patterns, and some old ones which died out.

Among the suffixes adopted in Middle English, whether just as part of the borrowing process or already with incipient productivity, are *-able* (*acceptable*, *blamable*, *desirable*, loans from French; *believable*, *eatable*, *unknowable*, *unthinkable*, English coinings with a native basis); *-acy* ∼ *-ate* (*prelacy* ∼ *prelate*, *advocacy* ~ *advocate, delicacy* ~ *delicate*, fourteenth century); *-age* (*baron-age, bondage, leekage, peerage*, fourteenth and fifteenth centuries); *-al* (*arrival, supposal*, fourteenth-century loans; *acquittal, refusal, removal*, fifteenth century, probably English formations); *-al* (*poetical, analytical, grammatical*, fourteenth and fifteenth centuries as an extension of *-ic*; the rivalry of *-ic* and *-ical* still exists); *-ance/-ence* (*acceptance, attendance, entrance, resemblance*, French loans from the fourteenth and fifteenth centuries; *utterance, furtherance*, native coinages, fifteenth century); *-ancy/-ency* ~ *-ant/-ent* (*sergeancy, innocency, excellency, sufficiency*, fourteenth and fifteenth centuries); *-ation*, correlating with verbal *-ate, -ify, -ise* (*accumulation, accusation, creation, intimation, moderation, restoration; edification, justifaction; canonisation, moralisation*, fourteenth and fifteenth centuries, but the pattern becomes really active as of the sixteenth century); *-ee* (*donee/donor, lessee/lessor* as loans in the fifteenth century restricted to legal language, extended as deverbal passive nouns beyond the legal system in the fifteenth century, e.g. *assignee, grantee, appellee*); *-ery* (*ancestry, robbery, sophistry, tenantry,* French loans, thirteenth and fourteenth centuries; *archery, beggary, buggary, husbandry, mastery*, English coinages, fourteenth and fifteenth centuries); *-ess* (*adulteress, countess, patroness*, loans; *dwelleress, huntress, shepherdess, teacheress*, English formations, fourteenth and fifteenth centuries); *-ity* (*actuality, fatality, liberality*, fourteenth and fifteenth centuries); *-ise* (*canonise, solemnise, moralise*, loans, fifteenth century; *bastardise, equalise, popularise*, English formations, sixteenth century); *-ment* (*achievement, adornment, judgment*, loans, thirteenth century; *chastisement, incresement, endowment, annulment*, English, fourteenth and fifteenth centuries); *-ous* (*poisonous, villainous, gluttonous, superfluous*, fourteenth and fifteenth centuries).

4.3.3.4   Zero derivation

Again, the Old English patterns continue, but due to the progressive loss of inflectional endings and the shift towards word-based morphology, the status as zero derivatives becomes more obvious, although there is no change in terms of the derivational category as such.

There are a few changes, however. Thus the adjectival *bahuvrihis* of the type *barefoot* were generally replaced by extended formations of the type *long-legged*, whereas the OE substantival type (*paleface*), which had been in the minority, continued and gradually increased its productivity, perhaps in connection with the rise of the *pickpocket* type (see Marchand, 1969: 388). This latter pattern appeared in the early fourteenth century and is instanced by *cutpurse, pinchpenny, spillbread*, etc., possibly influenced by the French pattern *coupe-gorge, tire-bouchon*. But since German has a similar pattern with names, cf. *Fürchtegott, Habedank*, etc., the origin might be native spoken language, from where it was introduced into written language under French influence. Again, this needs further investigation on the basis of corpus-based material; here, the investigation of religious plays might also be useful.

4.4   Early Modern English

4.4.1   Introduction

The individual character of early Modern English was recognised only in the second half of the twentieth century; see Görlach (1994) and Kastovsky (1994). The beginning of the period is usually associated with the introduction of printing by Caxton in 1476, its end in the second half of the seventeenth century with the end of the Stuart period and the accession of William of Orange to the throne (1689). The period thus starts out in the late Middle Ages, and includes the Renaissance, the Reformation and the Age of Enlightenment, i.e. periods of important cultural, political and intellectual upheavals. It also marks the rise of a written and spoken standard, it sees a substantial growth of literacy throughout the population, and the vernacular was extended to practically all contexts of speech and writing, i.e. also to the sciences, especially in the latter half of the eighteenth century.

These developments had one major consequence: we witness the greatest expansion of the vocabulary in the history of the English language, especially in the domain of learned and technical vocabulary, both through borrowing (primarily from Latin) and through word formation (with new Latin and French patterns, but also those having emerged in Middle English, becoming productive in English). The most typical example is Shakespeare, who is credited with around 1,700 neologisms or first attestations.

It is also during this period that the first dictionaries appear. The first are bilingual Latin–English dictionaries, followed by bilingual English–French dictionaries, e.g. Palsgrave (1530) *Lesclarcissement de la langue francoyse*, and also multilingual ones. The first monolingual English dictionaries were published in the early seventeenth century, primarily providing glosses for the increasing stock of learned vocabulary, so-called 'hard words', but gradually they were expanded and also included ordinary everyday usage. The greatest milestone in this development was Samuel Johnson's (1755) dictionary, which served as a model for dictionary makers throughout many generations, until work on the *OED* started in the nineteenth century.

At the beginning of the period, neither orthography nor patterns of word formations were tightly regulated. Both domains were gradually regulated only towards the end of the eighteenth century (see Chapter 5). In word formation we therefore often find rivalling forms having the same meaning. Subsequently, these were either subjected to semantic diversification, or only one of the rivalling forms survived, cf. *frequency/frequentness, immaturity/immatureness, immediacy/immediateness, light/lighten/enlighten, length/lengthen/enlength, disthronize/disthrone /dethrone/unthrone /dethronize*. The best tool for the investigation of the tremendous increase of the vocabulary is the *Chronological English Dictionary* (*CED*; Finkenstaedt, Leisi & Wolff, 1970), whose entries are based on the first attestations quoted in the *Shorter OED*, although there is a need for redating in view of more recent research.

The extensive borrowing from Latin and French brings about an increased dissociation of the vocabulary, i.e. fewer and fewer semantically related words are also formally morphologically related on the basis of transparent word-formation patterns. This increased and partly exaggerated borrowing also starts the controversy about 'hard words' or 'inkhorn terms', i.e. learned words that average people without a classical education would not understand. It is this controversy and the problems underlying it which prompt the appearance of monolingual dictionaries, at the beginning just in the form of lists, e.g. Cawdrey (1604), who in the preface gives the following reason for the book. It was, he says,

> gathered for the benefit & helpe of Ladies, Gentlewomen, or any other vnskilfull persons, Wherby they may the more easily and better vunderstand many hard English wordes, which they shall heare or read in Scriptures, Sermons, or elswhere, and also be made able to vse the same aptly themselues.

The inkhorn controversy was also commemorated in Shakespeare's *Love's Labours Lost* by the pedant Holofernes, and later on in the eighteenth century by Mrs Malaprop in Sheridan's *The Rivals*, hence the term 'malapropism'. At the same time we also witness a considerable loss of old vocabulary, which, however, is less easy to document, and, in the second half of seventeenth century, also the loss of many neologisms. This is especially due to the systematic weeding-out of doublets as a symptom of the progressive and conscious regularisation of the language.

During the whole eModE period borrowing was the most frequent way of enrichment and word formation was less prominent. In the eighteenth century, however, the tide is beginning to turn, and word formation becomes more important than borrowing, probably because the forcign word-formation patterns had become sufficiently established to really become productive within the English vocabulary. The main reasons for borrowing were the expanding functions of the standard language from a means for regular everyday communication to technical usage in law, religion, medicine, science, etc., and a growing fashion that favoured learned words.

4.4.2   Borrowing

4.4.2.1   Latin

Latin was the dominant source of borrowed lexis in eModE. Between 1560 and 1670 well over half of the loanwords attested in the *CED* come from Latin, the peak period being 1610–24. These were mainly bookish lexical items, but quite a few also became part of the general vocabulary. The morphological integration of the loans into the English morphological system primarily resulted in the loss of verbal inflections of the borrowed items. But sometimes some Latin features were preserved, e.g. plural forms such as *fungus: fungi, cactus: cacti/cactuses*.

The following provide some examples in chronological order:

1.   1476–1599: *dismiss, instruct, inspector, hostile, permit, popular, pro-
        duce, cadaver, genius, junior, fungus, folio, area, exit, peninsula,
        abdomen, circus, axis, vacuum, genus, medium, species, caesura,
        corona, innuendo, interregnum, omen, militia, radius, sinus, virus*

2.   1600–99: *premium, equilibrium, spectrum, census, vertebra, tenet,
        squalor, agenda, veto, formula, crux, focus, data, copula, album,
        larva, complex, vortex, pallor, pendulum, nebula, rabies, minimum,
        serum, calculus, stimulus, lumbago, status, antenna*

3.   1700–76: *nucleus, inertia, locus, propaganda, alibi, auditorium, ulti-
        matum, maximum, colloquial, cellulose, decorator, insomnia, tenta-
        cle, fauna, bonus*

4.4.2.2   French

At the beginning of the eModE period, French loans were more frequent than Latin loans, which was certainly an aftermath of the ME integration of
French into English. Gradually French influence receded in favour of Latin, but
in the latter half of the seventeenth century we notice a marked increase of French
influence due to the improved relations between France and England. The reasons
were the restoration of the monarchy and the rising cultural prestige of France
and with it French (cf. the importance of Louis XIV and his court at Versailles).
This increased French influence was often criticised at the time, because it was
regarded as overdone, but in the late eighteenth century such influence gradually
lessened – again for political reasons: the French Revolution was far from popular
in England.

The integration of French loans was slightly more difficult than that of Latin
loans because of certain adaptations that segmental sound structures had to
undergo, since there were no direct equivalents in English. Thus there was a
general replacement of nasalised vowels by a vowel + nasal sequence (as in
envelope), or the replacement of final /e/ by /ei/ (as in *ballet, valet*). The source of
these loans was primarily the emerging French standard of the area around Paris,
although some provincial loans are also recorded.

Examples (chronologically ordered beginning with the late fifteenth century):

1.   fifteenth–sixteenth centuries: *domicile, industry, consume, elegant,
        decision, intuition, trophy, pioneer, pilot, colonel, indigo, vase, vogue,
        genteel, scene, machine, grotesque, moustache*

2.   seventeenth century: *brigade, platoon, envoy, repartee, liaison, naive,
        class, rapport, beau, verve, role, soup, cabaret, memoirs, champagne,
        ballet, pool, denim, attic, mousseline, vinaigrette*

3.   eighteenth century: *casserole, croquette, ragout, liqueur, critique,
        précis, brochure, civilisation, envelope, salon, bouquet, police,
        glacier, picnic, etiquette, dentist, souvenir, regime*

4.   loan translations: *at your service, do me the favour, to make/pay a visit,
        by occasion, in detail, in favour of, in the last resort, in particular, to
        the contrary*

4.4.2.3   Greek

Many Greek loans entered English via Latin, e.g. *alphabet, drama, dilemma, catastrophe, archive, programme, electric, camera, anaesthesia*. But there are also quite a few direct loans during this period, due to the increased interest in Antiquity in the Renaissance and Enlightenment periods, e.g. *crisis, hegemony, pathos, praxis, hypothesis, epiglottis, meteorology, psyche, cosmos, elastic, euphemism, narcosis, phlox, monotony, philander*.

4.4.2.4   Italian

In Tudor times there were direct trade connections with Italy through the Flemish trade conducted with Venice; moreover private travel to Italy became fashionable (in the course of the Grand Tour of the continent). Typical borrowings of this period are *artichoke, parmesan, regatta, frigate, traffic, ballot, bankrupt, carnival, sonnet, lottery, duel, arcade, stanza, motto, manage, garb, umbrella, gala, firm, volcano, granite, lava, malaria, influenza, cupola, fresco, stucco, villa, concerto, falsetto, opera, oratorio, sonata, solo, tempo, trombone, soprano, aria, pianoforte*.

4.4.2.5   Spanish

During the first part of the eModE period there were increased contacts with Spain, primarily due to the personal connections of Queen Mary, but also via trade, which introduced a number of Spanish loans, and through Spanish also loans from overseas: *cask, anchovy, sherry, cargo, renegade, booby, creole, desperado, armada, embargo, flotilla, tornado, sombrero, guitar, siesta, marinade, cigar; cannibal, negro, maize, potato, alligator, tobacco, banana, vanilla, avocado, barbecue, tortilla*.

4.4.2.6   Other languages

One important source during this period was Dutch. Trading relations, shipbuilding, but also painting (notably the 'Dutch masters' such as Rembrandt) played an important role here, hence *easel, sketch, landscape, hose, scone, dock, dollar, yacht, wagon, snuff, filibuster, split, rant, cruise, brandy, tea, smuggle, drill, skate, hustle, schooner, cookie, yankee, mangle*.

Other European and non-European languages were also involved, e.g. Portuguese (*apricot, flamingo, molasses, mango, mandarin, guinea, tank, pagoda, teak, veranda*); Celtic (*whisky, bog, brat, trousers, galore, glen, plaid, slogan, flannel*); non-European (*horde, caftan, jackal, yoghurt, pasha, turban, shah, bazaar, caravan, parsee, typhoon, curry, coolie, toddy, guru, cot, pundit, bungalow, jungle, bamboo, ketchup, soy, mikado, wigwam, racoon, opossum, moccasin, moose, skunk, tomahawk, caucus, jaguar*). The latter are certainly due to the expansion of the British empire in connection with the beginning colonisation of overseas countries.

4.4.3   Word formation

As has already been pointed out, it was during the early Modern English period that non-native word-formation patterns finally gained a real foothold in English and began to compete seriously with the native patterns. This is in line with the general explosion in the size of the vocabulary thanks to nearly unconstrained borrowing, which in turn provided many more analysable examples on the basis of which new formations could be produced that had no counterpart in the source languages. In the present context, a more detailed discussion of this process is impossible. What we can say, however, is that the Middle English loan patterns mentioned above were strengthened, and if they had not already been productive on a limited scale they now finally became productive, with some more affixes added to the already existing stock. This of course also affected the overall structure of the word-formation system, because this development introduced increased competition between patterns (see Kastovsky, 1985). This competition not only concerned the rivalry between native affixes (*fore-, mid-, un-; -dom, -ed, -en, -er, -ful, -hood, -ing, -ish, -less, -let, -like, -ling, -ness, -ship*, zero) and non-native affixes (*ante-, circum-, dis-, extra-, in-, inter-, non-, post-, pre-, re-, sub-, super-, trans-; -able, -acy, -age, -al, -an, -ance, -ancy, -ant, -arian, -ate, -ation, -ee, -eer, -ery, -ese, -ic, -ical, -ician, -ify, -ise, -ism, -ist, -ment, -ory, -ous, -ure*), but also between the non-native affixes themselves. Thus, to give just one example, Old English had had only one productive negative prefix, viz. *un-*, as in *un-wīs*. In Middle and early Modern English four competing non-native prefixes were added: *a-, dis-, in-, non-*, which now competed with *un-* and among themselves. This situation in fact persists till today and, despite the work of Aronoff (1980), Anshen & Aronoff (1988), Baayen (1989), Plag (1999), Riddle (1985) and some others, is still in need of a more thorough investigation, especially as regards the gradually emerging semantic and distributional restrictions. In early Modern English we often find rivalling forms from one and the same basis, e.g. *frequency ~ frequentness, immaturity ~ immatureness, immediacy ~ immediateness*; *light/Ø ~ lighten ~ enlighten*; *disthronise ~ disthrone/Ø ~ dethrone/Ø ~ dethronise ~ unthrone/Ø*. Eventually one of the forms survived, whereas the others were discarded, or else some semantic differentiation took place. Again, the rivalry of these competing patterns and their sorting-out in the eighteenth and nineteenth centuries are in need of further empirical investigation, especially with regard to their distribution among text types and the influence of prescriptive grammar.

Another consequence of this development is the consolidation of the non-native level of word formation with its morphophonemic alternations and stem-based properties. There was great variation during this period, some of which still persists, and a more systematic investigation of the rise, implementation and systematisation of these patterns is still needed.

4.4.3.1   Compounding

In general, the compound types described in the sections above continued to be productive. But there were also changes. Thus there seems to have been a revival of the copulative compounds in literary language of the type *giant-dwarf, king-cardinal, master-mistress, sober-sad, pale-dull* (Shakespeare), from where they made their way into technical language in the seventeenth century, e.g. *hydraulo-pneumatical, anatomic-chirurgical*. Another revival, beginning in the sixteenth century, is the type *all-seer, all-creator, self-seeker, all-affecting, all-knowing, self-boasting, self-giving*. Another innovation is the adjectival type *Anglo-Norman, concavo-convex, medical-physical*, which is partly non-native.

4.4.3.2   Prefixation

It was during this period that the majority of the foreign prefixes still productive today became productive on a larger scale or entered the language, although hybrid formations (non-native prefix + native base) seem to have been relatively constrained. A comprehensive survey is not possible here, but certain sense groups might be quoted in the following, based on Marchand (1969: 140–208) and Nevalainen (1999: 379–91).

Negative prefixes

un- had originally been the only native suffix in this domain, expressing complementary and contrary opposition with adjectives and nouns:

  (a) adjectives: *unfit, ungodly, uncommon, uncomfortable, unfashionable, un-English, uncritical, unbecoming, undeserving, uncome-at-able, unheard-of, uncared-for; unboundless, uncomfortless, unhelpless* (the latter from the sixteenth and seventeenth centuries, now unacceptable)
  (b) nouns: *uncharity, ungratitude, unsuccess, unintelligence, unsatisfaction, unconcern*

non- originated in Law Latin and Law French; later it was extended beyond the legal domain: *non-ability, non-appearance, non-performance, non-resident, non-user, non-knowledge, non-truth; non-harmonious, non-graduated, non-preaching*

in- (French and Latin) is basically restricted to non-native bases; it also exhibits morphophonemic alternation (assimilation): *inanimate, inextinguishable, inseparate, illegal, illegitimate, irresponsible; incivility, incompetence, inhospitality, inutility*

dis- (French and Latin): *discontent, dispassionate, disadvantageous, dissimilar, disharmonious, discontinuous, disrespectful; distrust, disorder, disfavour, disregard*

a- (Greek): *atheological, asymbolic, apsychical, asymmetric*

Reversative and privative prefixes

un- is the only native prefix in this domain:

  (a) reversative: *unbewitch, unbless, unconsecrate, undress, unfreeze, unmarry* (sixteenth century), *unblock, unlink, unmount, uncanonise, undignify, uncoil, unhitch, unlay, unstow*

(b) privative/ablative: *unballast, unburden, uncloak, unfrock, unman, unnerve* ('remove object'); *unbosom, uncage, unhinge, unhook, unkennel* ('remove from place')

dis- (French and Latin):

(a) reversative: *disentangle, dishearten, discompose, disappear, disestablisih, disinfect, disunite, disassociate, discanonise, disarrange, disconnect, disqualify*

(b) privative/ablative: *disburden, discloud, dismast, dismerit, dispriviledge, disrank, distune* ('remove object'); *displace, dishouse, discase, disbar* ('remove from place')

de- (French and Latin) becomes productive only in the eighteenth century, gradually restricting *dis*-formations: *debark, demast, deobstruct, detomb, dethrone, detruth*

Locative prefixes

a-(native, < *on*): *ajar, atilt, adrift, agape, astride, aflame, ahorseback, ashore, a-tiptoe*

fore- (native): *forename, forecourt, forehand, foregound, forearm, foreshore*

mid- (native)*: mid-channel, mid-earth, mid-finger, mid-ship*

inter- (French, Latin): *interlink, intermix, intermarry, interlock, intertwine; interspeech, intermark; interlunar, interstellar, intermundane*

sub- (Latin): *sub-constable, sub-head, sub-treasurer, sub-officer, subcommittee, subspecies; sub-coastal, sublingual, subspinal; sublet*

super- (Latin): *superstructure, superimposition; superordinate, superterranean*

trans- (Latin): *transnature, transdialect; translocation; transsubstantial, translunary*

Temporal prefixes

fore- (native): *foreappoint, forbear, foreshadow, forebode, foreact, foregame, forenight*

mid- (native): *midnoon, midnight, mid-week, mid-season*

ante- (Latin): *antediluvian, ante-theme, antedate, ante-noon*

post- (Latin): *post-date, post-eternity, post-date* (vb); *post-exist, postmeridian, post-deluvian*

pre- (Latin): *preconceive, pre-elect, precontract, prejudge, premeditate, preequipment, predisposition, pre-existence, prearrangement*

re- (French, Latin): *reassume, reconsider, reinforce, re-examine, reappear, recast, refill*

Prefixes denoting opposition and support ('attitudinal prefixes')

anti- (Latin): *antipope, anticlimax, antimonarchical, antipapal, antifebrile, anticatarrhal*

counter- (French): *counterbalance, counterpart, counterplea, counterplot*
co- (French, Latin): *coheir, co-defendant, co-juror, co-agency, co-existence, co-articulate, co-work, co-extensive, co-infinite*
pro- (Latin): *pro-rector, pro-vice-chancellor*

Pejorative prefixes

mal- (French): *maladministration, malconduct*
mis- (native and French *mes-*): *misapply, mishandle*; *misfortune, miscarriage, misconduct*
pseudo- (Greek): *pseudo-Catholic, pseudo-politician*

Intensifying prefixes

arch- (Greek, Latin): *archbishop*
hyper- (Greek): *hyper-prophetical, hyper-magnetic*
proto- (Latin): *protoplot, protodevil, protorebel*
sub- (Latin): *sub-red, sub-angelical, sub-rustic*

Quantitative prefixes

bi- (Latin): *bicapited, bicapsular, biforked, bilobed*
demi- (French): *demigod, demi-lion, demicannon, demi-quaver*
multi- (Latin): *multivarious, multicapsular*

4.4.3.3   Suffixation

With suffixation the pattern is similar: the majority of the early Modern English suffixes are of non-native origin, although they perhaps were not as productive as the native ones. At least some of them already made their appearance in Middle English, but started to become productive on a larger scale only in the early Modern English period. In the following I will concentrate on borrowed suffixes, since the patterns characterising the surviving native suffixes have already been illustrated above.

Noun-forming suffixes

-acy (French and Latin, deadjectival and denominal abstract nouns): *accuracy, illiteracy, intimacy, curacy, piracy, magistracy*
-age (French, abstract and collective denominal and deverbal nouns; result, location): *baronetage, orphanage, leafage, mileage, parsonage, vicarage; anchorage, drainage, leakage, postage, storage, sweepage*
-al (French, deverbal abstract nouns): *approval, bestowal, carousal, denial, disposal, proposal, recital, removal, renewal, survival*
-an/-ian (French and Latin, denominal and deadjectival nouns and adjectives): *Cantabrigian, Chaucerian, Devonian, Etonian, Norwegian, Oxonian*
-ance/-ence (French, deverbal abstract nouns): *admittance, appliance, bearance, clearance, convergence, emergence, guidance, reliance, remittance*

-ancy/-ency (French, deadjectival and denominal abstract nouns): *agency, brilliancy, consistency, deceny, deficiency, efficiency, redundancy, tendency, vacancy*

-ant/-ent (French and Latin, personal and instrumental nouns): *absorbent, attendant, claimant, defendant, dependant, illuminant, solvent*

-arian (Latin, denominal nouns and adjectives): *sectarian, septuagenarian, Trinitarian*

-ate (Latin, abstract nouns): *episcopate, electorate, patriarchate, tribunate, triumvirate*

-ation (French, Latin, abstract nouns): *amplification, beautification, identification, authorisation, formalisation, affiliation, education, flirtation, intimidation, starvation*

-ee (French, personal passive nouns): *debtee, donee, grantee, mortgagee, payee, trustee*

-eer (French, personal nouns): *privateer, pamphleteer, sonneteer* (mainly derogatory)

-ery (French, abstract and collective nouns, location): *bigotry, brewery, fishery, foolery, ironmongery, peasantry, printery, rivalry, slavery, soldiery, swannery*

-ese (Italian, denominal nouns and adjectives): *Genoese, Milanese, Siamese*

-ess (French, female nouns): *actress, ambassadress, farmeress, heiress, murderess, poetess*

-ician (French, personal nouns): *dialectician, geometrician, mechanician, politician*

-ism (Latin and French, abstract nouns): *anglicism, criticism, modernism, Protestantism, truism, witticism*

-ist (Latin and French, personal nouns and adjectives): *bigamist, duellist, egotist, flutist, non-conformist, novelist* 'innovator', *tobacconist* 'one addicted to tobacco'

-ity (French and Latin, deadjectival abstract nouns): *brutality, capability, compatibility, eccentricity, elasticity, oddity, regularity, similarity*

-let (French, diminutive): *droplet, ringlet, streamlet, townlet, winglet*

-ment (French, abstract and concrete nouns): *abasement, amusement, astonishment, commitment, equipment, fulfilment, management, retirement, statement, treatment*

-ure (French, abstract nouns): *closure, erasure, exposure, pressure*

-y/-ie (Scottish, hypocoristic): *brownie, Charlie, daddy, granny, hubby, jockey, kitty, laddie*

Adjective-forming suffixes

Here, native suffixes have maintained their position and are fairly productive:
-ed (*roofed, spirited, pig-headed*), *-en* (*earthen, milken*), *-ful* (*deceitful, hopeful*),
-ish (*Cornish, Jewish, bookish, modish*), *-less* (*honourless, seamless, stateless*),

-like (?semi-suffix, *bishoplike, godlike*), *-ly* (*cowardly, orderly*), *-some* (*awesome, quarrelsome, tiresome*), *-y* (*creamy, nutty, silky*). Non-native suffixes becoming productive during this period are:

-able (French, mainly deverbal): *advisable, answerable, eatable, drinkable, per-ishable, unbreakable, unconsumable; come-at-able, get-at-able; actionable, fashionable, sizeable*

-al (*-ial, -ical, -orial, -ual*): *global, horizontal, dictatorial, professional, logical, rhetorical, whimsical, accentual, conceptual* (all basically Latin-based)

-ary (Latin): *cautionary, complementary, fragmentary, revolutionary*

-ate (Latin and French): *affectionate, compassionate, opinionate*

-esque (French): *carnivalesque, picturesque*

-ic (French): *Celtic, democratic, Germanic, Miltonic, operatic, parasitic, prob-lematic*

-ive (French and Latin): *amusive, conducive, depressive, preventive, sportive*

-ous (French): *analogous, burdenous, hazardous, ostentatious, poisonous, thunderous*

Verb-forming suffixes

-ate (Latin): *capacitate, fabricate, facilitate*

-ify (French and Latin): *beautify, countrify, fishify, Frenchify, monkeyfy, speechify, uglify*

-ise (French and Latin): *apologise, bastardise, fertilise, popularise, satirise, womanise*

Other types of formation

Zero derivation continues in early Modern English in all domains and sense groups discussed above, including derivation from loans.

Deverbal nouns: *contest, grasp, push, scream; award, brew, convert, produce, stew; cheat, pry, sneak; bend, dip, lounge; goggles, rattle; spring*

Denominal verbs: *bottle, channel, garrison, pocket; gun, net, trumpet; com-motion, gesture, paraphrase, serenade; brick, glove, mask; bundle, group, pulp; butcher, mother, nurse, usher*

Deadjectival verbs: *dirty, empty, numb, obscure; idle, mute, shy, swift*

Other types such as acronyms, reduplication, clipping and blending, which are of great importance in Modern English, begin to show up in this period. Thus the acronyms *a.m.* 'ante meridian', MA 'Master of Arts', are recorded from the eighteenth century. *Clap-trap, hocus-pocus, shilly-shally, tittle-tattle, pooh-pooh, yap-yap* are also recorded from this period. Clippings like *miss* < *mistress, cute* < *acute, wig* < *periwig; brandy* < *brandywine, chap* < *chapman, gent* < *gentleman, hack* < *hackney, van* < *vanguard* are also found for the first time in this period. Recorded blends from this period are *twirl* < *twist* + *whirl, blotch* < *blot* + *botch, dumfound* < *dumb* + *confound*.

4.5   Modern English

4.5.1   Introduction

In the late eighteenth century the developments sketched above continued. The vocabulary grew steadily due to language contact and the expansion of English around the globe, until it became the international language it is today. Also, extralinguistic requirements such as technical and scientific discoveries made themselves felt especially in word formation, and the introduction of many Latin and Neo-Latin affixes contributed to this development. With the rapid technical and scientific developments in the twentieth century, the size of the vocabulary grew even more rapidly. Furthermore, the development of what has come to be called 'Englishes' (cf. Görlach, 1991, 1995, 1998, 2002 and Rissanen et al., 1992) – i.e. varieties of English in the US, Canada, Australia, New Zealand, South Africa, Central Africa, India, etc. – has resulted in a remarkable diversification of 'English'. This has also led to the publication of dictionaries for these varieties, e.g. *The Australian National Dictionary* (1988), Cassidy & Le Page (1980) for Jamaican English, or Branford (1987) for South African English, to mention only a few. Nevertheless, as Algeo (1998: 61) rightly argues, there is still a basic homogeneity despite these regional differences, which allows us to speak of 'the English language' in general, although admittedly with a certain amount of national/regional variation; see also Chapter 9.

The growth pattern of the vocabulary is difficult to assess precisely because of the unreliability of the sources on which the estimates are based (Algeo, 1998: 61ff.). The major source for such estimates is the *Oxford English Dictionary* (1st edition, 1884–1933, with Supplements; 2nd edition 1989; 3rd edition online, 2001–), and its derivative, the *Shorter Oxford English Dictionary*, which in turn served as the basis for Finkenstaedt et al. (1970), the most comprehensive survey of the growth of the English vocabulary. This in turn was the input to Finkenstaedt et al. (1973), a statistical survey of the vocabulary growth over the centuries. There is one basic problem with these data, however, namely documentation: the problem is what sources were used by the dictionary compilers, on which the information on first recordings of lexical items is based. Unfortunately, this is most uneven, and therefore quite a number of re-datings had to be made for the earlier periods (cf. Schäfer, 1980). For the period in question it seems that documentation is also particularly uneven. Thus, according to Finkenstaedt et al. (1970, 1973), of the lexical items added to the English vocabulary after 1776, '51 per cent were coined in the mid-nineteenth century (1826–75), and only 4 per cent in the early twentieth century' (Finkenstaedt et al., 1970). This ratio is most implausible and probably just reflects the lack of relevant data in the source material, the first edition of the *OED*. First of all, the sources of the *OED* are primarily literary and therefore neglect other genres, especially scientific literature, newspapers, etc. Also, the sources are primarily based on British English not on American texts (some of the American sources were lost or disregarded). This means that the discontinuities in the growth of the vocabulary (a peak in the seventeenth century, a slump in the eighteenth century, and a rise again after that) are an artefact of the documentation available. Therefore, on the whole, despite the ups and downs, we might – in view of the present-day situation – assume a fairly steady increase of the vocabulary growth during this period, fed by the usual sources, borrowing and word formation, rather than the up-and-down development suggested in Finkenstaedt et al. (1973). But in order to substantiate this, we would need other sources than the *OED*.

4.5.2   Borrowing

At the beginning of the Modern English period, it would seem that the classical languages (Latin and Greek) were still the major source of loans, but in the nineteenth and twentieth centuries the spectrum substantially widened. While the classical languages remained prominent, especially in scientific and technical terminology, although in this respect rather through word formation than direct borrowing, languages like French and Spanish, and more exotic languages like Indian, Arabic, Japanese, Chinese, etc. (see Section 4.1.3 above) became more and more important.

Perhaps the most important source apart from the classical languages is French, the reason being the proximity of France with regard to the British Isles and its role as the first foreign language taught at school. Moreover, there had always been a certain cultural prominence in fields such as *couture* and *cuisine*, the fine arts and entertainment, which provided loans such as *aperitif, art deco, blouse, charade, courgette, lingerie, menu, nuance, premiere, résumé, repertoire, restaurant, sorbet, soufflé, suède*, but also from other domains, such as *chauffeur, espionage, fuselage, garage, hangar, limousine, morgue, ravine*.

The prominent position of Spanish is partly due to its influence on American English because of the substantial (and growing) Spanish-speaking population, from where lexical items such as *bonanza, cafeteria* (and its derivatives *luncheteria, washeteria*, etc.), *canyon, lasso, mustang, ranch, rodeo* migrated to other varieties of English.

Italian contributed *confetti, fiasco, intermezzo, spaghetti, studio, vendetta*; whilst from Arabic we have *razzia, safari*; of Indian origin are *cashmere, chutney, khaki, loot, pyjamas*; from Japanese we have *geisha, harakiri, tycoon*; and from Australia we have *boomerang, koala, outback*.

But it was not only overseas varieties that contributed to the expansion of the vocabulary; there were also regional sources, especially Scots (see Görlach, 1999:102f.), due in part to the popularity of Sir Walter Scott's novels, from where words such as *awesome, blackmail, brownie, cosy, glamour, glint, guffaw, kith, raid, winsome* made it into standard English.

4.5.3   Word formation

With compounding, the established patterns continued, producing many new combinations due to the increasing demand of new designations for new referents. The following extremely selective examples are first documented from this period:

N + N: *air miles, aircraft, barman, border-land, congressman, couch potato, fingerprint, frogman, home page, lifestyle, lipstick, mountain bike, policeman, rifle-range, soap opera, speed camera, sword-opera*

Ns + N: *bailsman, clansman, oarsman, plainsman*

Adj + N: *blackboard, hardware, mobile home, software, tightrope*

V-*ing* + N: *adding machine, sewing machine, swimming pool*

V + N: *helpline, hushmoney, payload, pushboat, thinktank*

N + V-*er*: *baby-sitter, cash-dispenser, dog-sitter, house-sitter*

N + V-*ing*: *road-pricing, desktop publishing*

N + V/Ø: *bellhop, hairdo, jetlag, nightfall, shoeblack, soda jerk*

N + Adj: *air-sick, car-sick, class-conscious, colour-fast, duty-free, kiss-proof, nation-wide*

Adj + Adj: *Anglo-French, Anglo-American, German-Jewish, phonetic-semantic, Swedish-American*

N + V+-*ed*: *airborne, communist infiltrated, factory packed, government owned*

A structural innovation is the apparent shift of backderived verbs of the type *proofread* < *proofreading, stage-manage* < *stagemanager* to compound status, which originally could not, for semantic reasons, be analysed as compounds ('read proofs', 'manage the stage') but as 'do proofreading', 'act as stage-manager'. This is due to the proliferation of such formations, often without a nominal base. Thus we now find *to chain-drink, half-close, half-rise, consumer-test, handwash, coldrinse, shortspin, warmiron*. Many of these formations are part of technical jargon, but quite a few have made it into the general vocabulary, where they act as models for further formations.

Another development is the increase of combinations with classical stems, sometimes referred to as 'combining forms' (cf. *OED*; Stein, 1978). In fact, these should be interpreted as stem-compounds, i.e. compounds whose constituents are stems rather than words: *anthropomorph, astrometry, astronaut, autocrat, auto-erotism, automobile, biology, bioscope, biosphere, cosmonaut, demography, ecology, photography, photosynthesis, telegraph, telepathy, telephone, television, fluoroscope, stethoscope, telescope*.

The already existing prefixes continued and increased their productivity. But, supported by the needs of scientific terminology, quite a number of new prefixes made their appearance during this period and became productive, e.g. *ante-* (*anteroom, ante-orbital*), *auto-* (*autobiography, auto-infectant*), *di-* (*dipetalous, dioxide*), *epi-* (*epibasal, epidermis*), *hypo-* (*hypodermic, hypo-acid*), *intra-* (*intra-abdominal, intra-state (traffic)*), *meta-* (*meta-arthritic, meta-theory*), *micro-* (*micro-bacillus, micro-cosmos*), *neo-* (*Neo-Platonism, Neo-Cambrian*), *per-* (*perchloride, percloric*), *poly-* (*polychromatic, polygrooved (rifle)*), *pro-* (*pro-ethnic, pro-British*), *retro-* (*retro-act, retro-buccal*), *semi-* (*semi-fluid, semi-ape*).

With suffixes, we do not find so many innovations, the most noticeable being *-ate* (*acetate, citrate*), *-ine* (*bovine, chlorine, fluorine*). Thus the number of borrowed prefixes by far outnumbers the number of borrowed suffixes. Here an investigation of the development of the scientific and technical nomenclature is still pending, especially since there had also been uncertainties with regard to the development of this kind of terminology.

Apart from these more conventional means of word formation there are three others, which became extremely productive in the late nineteenth but especially during the twentieth century: clipping, blending and acronyms (cf. Section 4.1.5 above).

Clipping as such is not a new process, but in Modern English it seems to have gained great popularity. We can distinguish three types:

(a)   Back-clippings, i.e. the first part of the word is retained: *ad(vertisement), bike (bicycle), brill(iant), cable(gram), co-op(erative association), co-ed(ucational female student), doc(tor), grad(uate), fax (facsimile), memo(randum), Met(ropolitan Opera), mike (microphone), prefab(ricate house), sarge (sergeant), Tech(nological Institute), vet(erinary)*. Also frequent are clippings of names, e.g. *Al(fred)*; see further Section 6.3.8. Sometimes, a hypocoristic suffix is added, as in *Alfie, Aussie, bookie, commie, Jerry, movie, telly.*

(b)   Fore-clippings, i.e. the latter part of the word is retained: *(air)plane, (auto)bus, (Ara)Bella, (Her)Bert(ie), (rac)coon, (tele)phone, (uni)varsity, (violin)cello, Web (World Wide Web)*; *Sandie (Alexander), Trixy (Beatrice).*

(c)   Back- + fore-clipping, i.e. the middle of the word is retained: *(in)flu(enza), (de)tec(tive), (E)Liz(abeth), (re)fridge(rator), (San) Fr(anc)isco.*

Blending and clipping compounds (cf. Pound, 1914) also became more and more popular in the nineteenth and, especially, the twentieth centuries. Genuine blends are instances where both parts lose part of their phonological substance, e.g. the classical examples *brunch (breakfast + lunch), motel (motor (car) + hotel), smog (smoke + fog)*, and also Lewis Carroll's imaginative creations such as *slithy (slimy + lithe), chortle (chuckle + snort)*; others are *electro(exe)cution, info(rmation enter)tainment, positron (positive electron), sitcom (situation comedy), stagflation (stagnation + inflation)*.

In clipping compounds, a clipped lexical item is combined with a regular lexical item (the delimitation from blending is not always quite clear): *Amer(ican)indian, cam(era)(re)corder, cell(ular tele)phone, Clint(ec)onomics, cyber(net)café, cyberpunk, eco(logically)friendly, e-(lectronic)mail, Eur(ope)asia, Eurovision, guestimate (guess + estimate), mini disc, mis(sing)per(son), paratrooper (parachutist trooper), worka(lco)holic.*

With acronyms, a process which has also become increasingly popular over the last decades (cf. Crowley & Thomas, 1973)), the first letters of a string of words are put together to form an abbreviated form of this string. There are two options: either the letters are pronounced separately, or they form a phonological string that can be pronounced as if it were a normal word. For want of a convenient designation we might perhaps call these 'letter acronyms' and 'word acronyms'.

Letter acronyms of the last years are: *asap (as soon as possible), ATM (automatic teller machine), BSE (bovine spongiform encephalopathy), CD (compact disc), DJ (disk jockey), DVD (digital video disc), EC (European Community), EU (European Union), HIV (human immunodeficiency virus), PC (personal computer, political correctness), VAT (value added tax)*, which by some speakers is, however, also treated as a word acronym.

Word acronyms are: *Aids (acquired immune deficiency syndrome), BASIC (Beginners' All-purpose Symbolic Instruction Code), Care (Cooperative for American Remittances to Europe), dink(y) (double income, no kids), LAN (local area network), NATO (North Atlantic Treaty Organisation), PIN (personal identification number), SALT (Strategic Arms Limitation Talks), WASP (white Anglo-Saxon protestant), yuppie (young urban/upwardly mobile professional (people) + -ie).*

4.6   Conclusion

Packing the history of the expanding vocabulary of a language like English into less than a hundred pages is difficult, if not impossible. Therefore, all that could be done in this chapter was to highlight and exemplify some of the most conspicuous aspects. One was the gradual internationalisation of the language through borrowing from languages such as Latin, Scandinavian, French, Greek and many others. As a result, the Modern English vocabulary is less Germanic than foreign, at least as far as the lexical types go – in terms of lexical tokens, however, it still is basically Germanic, because the most frequent token instances come from this source. As a consequence, the originally homogeneous Germanic word-formation system was changed into a dual system with overlapping native and non-native patterns having different properties with regard to their morphological, morphophonemic and phonological structure. The study of the vocabulary is as much a mirror of the internal developments of the language as it is a reflection of the external history in terms of political and cultural changes, language contact and language conflict, and one of the major objectives of this chapter was to illustrate this close interrelationship between the external and internal history of a language in the domain of its vocabulary.

5   Standardisation

Terttu Nevalainen and Ingrid Tieken-Boon van Ostade

5.1   Introduction

If William the Conqueror had not invaded England in the year 1066, standard English would have looked completely different today. Not only would the enormous French component in the English vocabulary have been considerably smaller, the standard language would in all likelihood have had its origin in a different dialect as well. While present-day standard English derives primarily from the east midland dialects, as the end product of a process which began after the age of Chaucer, a standardisation process was already going on well before that time, in the tenth century. This process affected the West Saxon dialect, with Winchester as its main cultural centre. The Norman Conquest, which introduced French as the language of the government and of administration alongside Latin as the language of the church, brought this situation to an abrupt end. English effectively ceased to be a written language, with the *Peterborough Chronicle* one of the very few witnesses to what proved to be a futile attempt to keep the medium alive. With the exception of some local pockets where the English literary tradition continued unbroken, English was consequently reduced to a spoken medium.

The earliest standardisation attempts, which go back as far as the reign of King Alfred (b. 849–901) and even beyond, aimed at making English – or rather West Saxon – the official language, to be used as the medium of teaching and of scholarship. While previously these functions had been the sole domain of Latin, the adoption of West Saxon as the language of writing suggests that this vernacular was beginning to emancipate itself from Latin. By the tenth century West Saxon was losing its regional function, and it was developing into a supraregional dialect, which is one of the main characteristics of a standard language. Furthermore, by being used as a written language, West Saxon gained in prestige, another important development in a standardisation process. But before this process could continue any further, the West Saxon linguistic hegemony came to an end around the middle of the eleventh century.

The importance of the role played by Latin goes back to the introduction of Christianity in England at the end of the sixth century, when the Anglo-Saxons were confronted not only with a new language but also with a new medium: Latin as the language – the written language – of the church. While theirs had been an oral culture – Anglo-Saxon runes cannot really be seen as a written code because they were used only in restricted circumstances – the church had a long tradition of Latin writing, and this new medium introduced itself in England along with the new religion. In sociolinguistic terms this meant that Anglo-Saxon England became a diglossic society, in that one language came to be used in one set of circumstances, i.e. Latin as the language of religion, scholarship and education, while another language, English, was used in an entirely different set of circumstances, namely in all those contexts in which Latin was not used. In other words, Latin became the High language and English, in its many different dialects, the Low language. Other High functions of a language are its use as the language of the law and of literature. Interestingly, the Anglo-Saxon kings were apparently very quick to discover the advantages of the new medium, for already in the early seventh century, King Ine of Wessex had his law code put into writing. He and his council must have realised that writing down the laws of the country was a better guarantee of their preservation than the former custom, characteristic of oral societies, of handing them down in memorised form. Yet, at the same time, we see in this process the beginnings of the emancipation of the vernacular language, an early effect of the elaboration of function which the West Saxon dialect underwent by adopting at least one of the functions of a High language. It is clear that kings and governments play an important role in guaranteeing the success of such a process, by imposing the new code as it were from above, just as, earlier, the new religion had been imposed from above as well. As such, we have here a clear case of what is known in sociolinguistics as 'change from above', or conscious change. Another High domain of the vernacular during the Anglo-Saxon period would have been its use for literature, but it is unfortunate that the main body of Old English literature has come down to us only in the form of tenth-century manuscripts. Because most of the poetry has an oral basis, we do not know how much of it was written down prior to that time. It may well be that, in contrast to the laws, its preservation was regarded as of less political consequence, so that the need to record works of literature did not present itself. Poetry and laws simply belonged to completely different linguistic modes.

This diglossic situation was complicated by the coming of the Normans in 1066, when the High functions of the English language which had evolved were suddenly taken over by French. Because the situation as regards Latin did not change – Latin continued to be primarily the language of religion, scholarship and education – we now have what might be referred to as a triglossic situation, with English once more reduced to a Low language, and the High functions of the language shared by Latin and French. At the same time, a social distinction was introduced within the spoken medium, in that the Low language was used by the common people while one of the High languages, French, became the language of the aristocracy. The use of the other High language, Latin, at first remained strictly defined as the medium of the church, though eventually it would be adopted for administrative purposes as well. In between the two extremes, of French and Latin on the one hand and English on the other, there was a lot of French–English bilingualism, due to the fact that there were large numbers of people who were in contact with both ends of the social scale. Examples of such people must have been parish priests, merchants, country stewards and wet-nurses, but someone like Chaucer was probably bilingual too. It is interesting to see that the functional division of the three languages in use in England after the Norman Conquest neatly corresponds to the traditional medieval division of society into the three estates: those who normally fought used French, those who worked, English, and those who prayed, Latin. In present-day diglossic societies, there is likewise a social split between speakers of either language, in that the more fluent they are in the High language, the more opportunities they will have to be involved in the domains in which the High language is used. In the Middle Ages, however, education was primarily in the hands of the church; consequently, it did not really function yet as a means available to those who wished to advance in society – unlike in most western societies today. This situation begins to change when, in the fifteenth century, the rising middle ranks of society demanded an educational system of their own, a type of school, which came to be called the 'petty school' after the French word *petit*, where they could send their sons – not, of course, their daughters – to be educated for the merchant trade rather than for the church. But by then the traditional division of medieval society had already come to an end.

In order to understand what happened during the later Middle English period when the English language was once more subjected to a standardisation process, it is helpful to look at the developments in terms of the discussion of standardisation by Lesley and James Milroy in their book *Authority in Language* (1991). The Milroys define standardisation as the suppression of optional variability in language, observing that 'the various stages that are usually involved in the development of a standard language may be described as the consequence of a need for uniformity that is felt by influential portions of society at a given time' (1991: 27). In the implementation of this development, they identify several stages: selection, acceptance, diffusion, maintenance, elaboration of function, codification and prescription. By applying these stages to the various standardisation processes that can be identified in the history of English, it will be possible to see why and when one process ceased to be effective while another continued further or was even brought to a conclusion – or nearly so, because it will be shown that it is an illusion to think that a language can ever reach full standardisation. This approach is useful when considering large-scale processes, such as those operating during the time of King Alfred and in the tenth century, as well as during the Chaucerian age and afterwards, but also in the case of individual attempts, such as those by Orm (c.1180) with regard to spelling, William Barnes (1801–86), who aimed at giving equal status to his native Dorset dialect as that of standard English, and Noah Webster (1758–1843), who developed what might be called a standardisation programme for American English. To explain the operation of the process, we will apply the various stages as distinguished by the Milroys to the one process which is still ongoing today, i.e. standard English. In doing so, we are adopting an approach which is primarily based on the perspective of standardisation as a change from above, that was both consciously implemented and consciously adopted. In this approach, the production and dissemination of official documents plays an important role, as well as that of private documents such as letters. Currently, new insights are being developed into the role played by other text types in the standardisation process, such as medical treatises. As a result, more and more data are becoming available which, we expect, will interestingly complement the picture we will attempt to present in this chapter.

5.2   The rise and development of standard English

5.2.1   Selection

When Henry V (1413–22) was campaigning in France, he wrote his letters home in English. This fact is significant for two reasons. Firstly, it shows that French, which had been the language of the aristocracy in England since the coming of the Normans, had lost its former prestige. This loss of prestige had set in when King John lost Normandy in 1204, and it was further accelerated by the Hundred Years' War (1337–1453), when French came to be seen as the language of the enemy country. Consequently, we can identify a rise in English nationalism, and the English aristocracy abandoned French in favour of English. During this period the largest number of French loanwords entered the English language (see the statistics quoted by Baugh & Cable, 2002: 178, note; see also Culpeper & Clapham, 1996). Secondly, while the rise of standard English is associated with the chancery, the country's independent administrative office (see Section 5.2.2), Chancery English has a precursor in the form of English used by Henry V's Signet Office, the king's private secretariat which travelled with him on his foreign campaigns. It is significant that the selection of the variety which was to develop into what is generally referred to as the Chancery Standard originated with the king and his secretariat: the implementation of a standard variety can only be successful when it has institutional support.

Institutional support can take the form of a king imposing on his subjects a particular decision which has linguistic implications, such as the adoption of Christianity in the sixth century, or of an Act of Parliament being passed involving a new language policy, as in the case of the formal adoption of sex-indefinite *he* in 1850 (Bodine, 1975: 136). We have already encountered an earlier example in the adoption of West Saxon for the Laws of King Ine, though the case of Henry V possibly reflects not so much a decision made by an enlightened monarch and his council as political and practical motives: by writing in English, Henry first and foremost identified himself as an Englishman at war with France, while at the same time seeking to curry favour with the English-speaking merchants, who might be prevailed upon to finance his campaigns.

The variety used by Henry V's Signet Office, and hence *selected* in Milroyan terms, was that spoken in the east midland area. Arguments usually given to explain this development are that this dialect was spoken by the largest number of people, that the east midland area was agriculturally rich, that it contained the seat of government and administration as well as the two universities Oxford and Cambridge, that it contained good ports and that it was close to the chief archiepiscopal see, Canterbury (see, for example, Lass, 1987: 65–7). In other words, what qualified this dialect as a possible standard was the fact that the area in which it was spoken was connected with all the domains of a High language: government and administration, education and learning, and the church. In addition, it was used and understood by many speakers from a large, affluent area. One of Lass's criteria for a dialect to develop into a standard language is that it must be a 'high-prestige dialect in which the nation's business is conducted' (1987: 61). As the language of the court, and with parliament and the port of London as the centres of national and international business, the East Midland dialect qualified as no other. As for the use as the language 'in which serious (or any) literature is normally written', another of Lass's criteria, the fact that popular poets such as Chaucer and Gower had written in English – though differing in a number of ways from the dialect which eventually developed into standard English – must have contributed to the rise in status of the vernacular vis-à-vis that of French and Latin.

The Chancery variety was only one of four incipient standards identified by Samuels (1963), the other three being the Wycliffite variety, Chaucer's dialect and the Greater London variety as shown in the Auchinleck MS. That none of the others was *selected* instead of the Chancery variety has indeed partly to do with lack of institutional support. Literary varieties such as the dialect of Chaucer and that of the Auchinleck MS which included, among other texts, a copy of *Kyng Alysaunder*, must have been seen as rather more ephemeral modes. As for the Wycliffite variety, widespread though it was, it was used as part of what was largely an underground movement and for that very reason never stood a chance of gaining official sanction.

5.2.2   Acceptance

Early Chancery English, the variety of English used by the chancery, the office responsible for the production of official documents issued by the king and the government, shows much resemblance to London English, particularly as found in the Guildhall Letter Books (Fisher, 1996: 63). The adoption of this variety as its medium in the 1420s may have been influenced by the factors listed above, possibly reinforced by the fact that English had been used by Henry V's Signet Office, too – even if 'the English of Henry's signet letters bears a closer resemblance to the English of the later Chancery documents than the Chancery documents of his time' (Heikkonen, 1996:115). We see in this the continuation of earlier practice, and therefore the *acceptance* of practice already current. In adopting this variety, the chancery had to convert a spoken dialect into a written form. For a long time, the history of standard English is, indeed, a history of standard *written* English; the beginnings of the standardisation process of the spoken language can be primarily located in the eighteenth century. In *The Emergence of Standard English* (1996), Fisher notes that what was developed by the chancery clerks was in effect an artificial system. What these men strove after was uniformity in handwriting as well as in language, and during their apprenticeship chancery scribes were trained to acquire such uniformity. According to Fisher, the chancery was 'a compact, disciplined, hierarchical body of civil servants' (1996: 43); it is only in such an environment that an attempt at normalisation – an important element in any standardisation process – would have had any chance of success. Again, we see the significance of institutional support, or in this case imposition from above, as an essential ingredient in the process. Such a development could only have taken place in a hierarchical organisation like the chancery.

There are many aspects of present-day English spelling which we owe to the chancery, such as the spelling <gh> for the velar which was still pronounced at the end of the Middle English period in words like *light* and *knight*, and <ig> in the word *reign*. Similarly, the <d> ending (rather than <t>) in the past tense and past participle forms of weak verbs was regularised by the chancery, and there were a number of preferred spellings, such as *I* for the first-person singular, and the forms *which*, *should*, *such*, *much*, *but* and *ask*. Even so, Fisher writes, the influence was greater on morphology than on spelling, and he mentions the second-person singular always being *ye/you*, the third-person plural regularly being *they*, *them* and *their* and the reflexive pronoun ending in *self/selves*. Other preferred forms are *those* as the plural of *that* (instead of *tho*), the adverb ending in *-ly* instead of *-liche*, the absence of present plural *-n* in verbs, and past participles ending in *-n*. Participles with the prefix *y-* as in *ydo* 'done' are not found. As for syntax, Fisher notes that the chancery preferred postverbal negation to preverbal negation, as in *they that be noght able* instead of *they that ne be able* (Fisher, 1996: 49–51); see also Section 3.3.6.

5.2.3   Diffusion

Being 'the agency that produced most of the official proclamations and parliamentary records' (Fisher, 1996: 39), the chancery was naturally instrumental in the *diffusion* of the written code that had been adopted. This worked in two ways. In the first place, the chancery at that time represented the only official body which attempted to produce a relatively uniform writing system. As such it at once filled a gap and set an example to local administrative centres which were brought into contact with chancery documents. The chancery written form consequently came to be widely imitated. Secondly, many of the chancery clerks came from the north, according to Fisher (1996: 51). This may have been part of the general wave of immigration from the north in the fifteenth century, which brought many people to the capital in search of work. The chancery must have been one of the institutions offering good prospects for boys with a certain amount of education who did not wish to pursue a career in the church, the more so in the light of the new developments with respect to the adoption of uniform writing systems in administrative centres elsewhere in the country. It is perhaps not too far-fetched to suppose that young men were even sent to train with the chancery. The chancery itself, however, had far more apprenticeships than jobs for clerks, so many trained apprentices returned to their homes to find employment there, taking their accomplishments with them. These men would have been immensely respected for their knowledge and skills at writing, which in turn invested the work they produced with a kind of 'correctness', a stamp of official approval, in the eyes of the local authorities. Thus, on the one hand it was the chancery itself which was responsible for spreading its writing system, while on the other hand it was also the people that had been trained as clerks, and who had been attracted to the chancery as an institution offering apprenticeships, who helped in the further diffusion of the writing system.

5.2.4   Maintenance

About fifty years after the chancery adopted the East Midland dialect as its written medium, in the year 1476, the printing press was introduced into England by the merchant William Caxton (c.1421–91). Caxton spent thirty years (or so he claims) on the continent, where he had learnt about movable type. This greatly speeded up the process of book production, both in comparison with manuscript production and with the printing of pages from wooden blocks. Caxton, who had previously been involved in the lucrative trade in luxury goods, which included manuscripts, soon realised the economic prospects of the new invention, and he decided to become a publisher himself. First he learned the trade in Cologne (1471), and then set up a book-selling business in Bruges, where about three years later he published the first book ever printed in English, the *History of Troy* (1473–4). He moved to England, possibly assisted financially by his patron Earl Rivers, the brother-in-law of the king. Caxton set up his printing press in Westminster, close to parliament, from which he hoped to attract clients with money to spend, and he made the very shrewd decision to publish books in the vernacular only. The remarkable foresight which inspired this decision is shown by the failure of nearly contemporary attempts to set up printing presses in Oxford and St Albans (Blake, 1987). These printers published in Latin, hoping to find a place on the academic market, but Latin books were already easily available through trade with the Continent, and the ventures were soon given up.

That language was an important issue to Caxton appears from a number of comments in his prologues to the books he printed. In the prologue to the *Eneydos* (1490), for example, he writes as follows:

> And certaynly our langage now used varyeth ferre from that whiche was used an spoken whan I was borne, for we Englysshemen ben borne under the domynacyon of the mone whiche is never stedfaste but ever waverynge: wexynge one season, and waneth & dyscreaseth another season. And that comyn Englysshe that is spoken in one shyre varyeth from another. In so

> moche that in my dayes happened that certayn marchauntes were in a shippe in Tamyse for to have sayled over the see into Zelande. And for lacke of wynde thai taryed atte forlond and wente to lande for to refreshe them. And one of theym named Sheffelde, a mercer, cam into an hows and axed for mete and specially he axyd after egges. And the goode wife answered that she coude speke no Frenshe. And the marchaunt was angry for he also coude speke no Frenshe, but wolde have hadde egges; and she understode hym not. And thenne at laste another sayd that he wolde have eyren; then the good wyf sayd that she understod hym wel. Loo! what sholde a man in thyse dayes now wryte, 'egges' or 'eyren'? Certaynly it is harde to playse every man bycause of dyversite & chaunge of langage. For in these days every man that is in ony reputacyon in his countre wyll utter his commynycacyon and maters in suche maners & termes that few men shall understonde theym.   (Blake, 1973: 79–80)

However, Caxton's concerns expressed here are not linguistic, as is often thought, but economic: as a merchant he wanted to sell books which last a long time, linguistically speaking, and which can be read by as large a reading public as possible. In other words, he was seeking a relatively stable language variety that could serve a supraregional function to speakers of different dialects. 'And thus between playn, rude, & curyous, I stande abasshed,' he wrote. He solved the problem as follows:

> And for as moche as this present booke is not for a rude, uplondyssh man to laboure therin ne rede it, but onely for a clerke & a noble gentylman that feleth and understondeth in faytes of armes, in love & in noble chyvalrye, therfor in a meane betwene bothe I have reduced and translated this sayd booke in to our Englysshe not ouer rode ne curyous, but in suche termes as shall be understanden by Goddys grace accordynge to my copye.   (Blake, 1973: 80)

In other words, he translated his book into the variety used by his intended audience, educated people and those belonging to the higher regions of society.

But in his choice of language variety Caxton was not as free as he himself appears to have thought. In view both of his intended audience and of his economic motives – to sell as many copies of the book as possible – it would have been unwise for him to have selected a variety different from that already in use by the chancery. By the time he set up his printing press, the most widely accepted written variety already was the dialect into which he translated his books. This was the variety in use by the literate section of society, which also constituted his own intended audience. What Caxton did, then, was no more than *maintain* a selection which had already been made in the early decades of the century, but what is interesting about the passages quoted here are the reasons he gave for doing so. These reasons demonstrate that by the end of the fifteenth century economic motivations contributed significantly to earlier linguistic and political ones in the standardisation process of the language.

5.2.5   Elaboration of function

Caxton is often regarded as a linguistic innovator because there are many words in today's vocabulary which were first recorded in his writings. Some examples are *abandon* (n[1]), *abase*, *abolish*, *absorb* and *abstractive* (see the *Oxford English Dictionary*, *OED* online). The first two were first attested in his *Jason* (c.1477) and the latter three in the *Eneydos* (1490). Not all of Caxton's innovations were permanent additions to the English language: of the words listed here, only the words *abandon*, *abolish* and *absorb* are still current today. At the same time, Caxton has been accused of being a poor translator: he appears to have taken too little time to look for English equivalents for the words he translated. Some examples are *fauell* 'fallow' from French *favel*, and *tattle*, now meaning 'prattle, tatter', from Middle Flemish *tatelen*. And indeed, the concordance to his own prose (compiled by Mizobata, 1990) shows that about half the words in his vocabulary occur only once, and that many of them are words like *bienfayttes*, *ospytal* and *reprehendat*, which are direct transpositions from French or Latin into English. But Caxton was not alone in translating his texts in this way: other translators worked similarly (Elliott, 1974: 153 ff.; Hellinga & Hellinga, 1984). For one thing, many Latinate or Romance words may have lent greater prestige to a text, giving it a learned character. At the same time, it may often have been an easy option for a translator to adapt the form of a word slightly to give it an English appearance; after all, there were already many such words in the English language. But one important factor must have been that the English language simply lacked the equivalent terms for many French concepts. Functionally speaking, English still did not match up to Latin or French as a High language: Caxton's decision to print his books in the vernacular acted as a strong impetus in bringing this about. Consequently, the *functions* of the English language were being *elaborated* at the expense of French and Latin, but the English language needed to adapt accordingly.

With Caxton the extension of the vocabulary was very likely largely an unconscious process; during the next two centuries, *elaborating the functions* of the language becomes a more conscious one, affecting not only vocabulary but also spelling and style. It might be argued that during this period a certain amount of linguistic experimentation was going on. In his study of early Modern English, Barber (1997: 53–70) distinguishes three movements which were concerned with the expansion of the English vocabulary: the Neologisers, the Purists and the Archaisers. The first movement was responsible for introducing many loanwords into the language simply by adopting them from Latin and Greek. Some examples are *education*, *frugality* and *persist*, but also *adjuvate* 'to assist or aid', *compendious* 'profitable' and *obtestate* 'to beseech'. The other two movements turned to the English language itself, drawing on existing processes of word formation, as in the case of the Purists, or trying to revive old words. Examples of words coined by the Purists are *biwordes* 'parables', *wasching* 'baptism', *moond* 'lunatic' and *witcraft* 'logic'. The Archaisers, of whom the poet Spenser was the main exponent, revived archaic words like *algate* 'always', *sicker* 'certainly' and *yode* 'went'. That none of these words became permanent additions to the English language indicates the marginal nature of the latter two movements, yet they did serve an important function, i.e. to keep the Neologisers in check. For word borrowing soon led to excess, and the English language was in danger of being flooded with words which could only be understood by people with a classical education. That the use of the words *compendious* (third sense) and *obtestate* is illustrated in the *OED* by early seventeenth-century dictionary entries as quotations suggests that these words, and many like them, were not in common use. The excessive use of Latinate loanwords soon came to be ridiculed, and the words were referred to as 'ynkhorne termes', words 'that smelled of the inkpot'. The character of Holofernes, the pedant in Shakespeare's *Love's Labour's Lost*, illustrates the controversy at its best when he utters the following speech:

> He draweth out the thred of his verbositie, finer than the staple of his argument. I abhor such phanaticall phantasims, such insociable and poynt deuise companions, such rackers of ortagriphie, as to speake dout fine, when he should say doubt; det, when he shold pronounce debt; d e b t, not det: he clepeth a Calf, Caufe: halfe, haufe: neighbour *vocatur* nebour; neigh abreuiated ne: this is abhominable, which he would call abhominable: it insinuateth me of infamie: *ne inteligis domine*, to make franticke, lunaticke? (First Folio, Act V, scene i)

Infamie should probably be read as *insanie*, in which case the gloss provided by Holofernes for *to insinuate of insanie*, 'to make franticke, lunaticke', makes sense.

Holofernes not only illustrates the 'inkhorne controversy' but also what Scragg (1974) refers to as the etymologising movement. *Debt* and *doubt* (v) were spelled with a <b> in the sixteenth century as a result of Latin influence on the spelling. Though the words had been borrowed from French as *dette* and *doute*, they came to be reinterpreted as having had their origin in Latin *debitum* and *dubitare*. While the spelling of these words was permanently affected, their pronunciation was not, despite Holofernes' injunction that the <b> should be pronounced. Words which underwent the same treatment are *salmon*, from French *saumon* but Latin *salmo*, and *victuals*, from French *vitaille* but Latin *victualia*. The other words mentioned by Holofernes, *calf*, *half*, *neighbour* as well as *abominable*, belong to two different categories: while Holofernes' comment suggests a discrepancy between the pronunciation and the spelling of *-alf* and *neigh-* due to a change in pronunciation which occurred after the spelling of these words had already become more or less fixed, the spelling of *abominable* as *abhominable* represents a popular but mistaken etymology. Many scholars at the time believed that the word derived from the Latin *ab homine* (from *homo*) instead of *ab omine* (from *omen*). The spelling with <h> occurs eighteen times in *Love's Labours Lost*, which indicates that the compositor of the text had failed to see the intended pun in the above passage. The effect of the pun evidently depended on the actor. At times, the etymologising movement produced unetymological spellings, such as the words *scissors* and *scythe*, which are not related to Latin *scindere* 'cut' but to *cisorium* 'cutting instrument', and *island*, which derives from the native English *ieʒlond* rather than Latin *insula*, Old French *ile*, *isle*. The new spellings led to a phenomenon known as 'spelling pronunciation', a process according to which the pronunciation of a word is affected by its changed spelling. Examples are *adventure* (French *aventure*, Latin *adventura*) and *apothecary* (Middle English *apotecarie*, while the Greek word has <th>). The phenomenon was on the one hand influenced by a popular conviction at the time among spelling reformers and pedants like Holofernes that all letters in a word should be pronounced; at the same time, it would occur in words that were of low frequency, when people had as it were forgotten the original pronunciation of a word. A modern candidate for the process would be the word *victuals*, which is so rare that its original pronunciation, /vɪtlz/, may be in danger of being forgotten.

Scragg argues that the etymologising movement was the result of the introduction of large numbers of loanwords in English from the classical languages due to the revival of learning during the Renaissance. In the context of the standardisation process which was going on, however, we may reinterpret the movement as an effort on the part of scholars and other writers to give greater status to the language: by showing through the spelling that English words were related to their Latin and Greek counterparts, the high status of these languages might rub off on English. In this we can see a clear attempt at *elaborating the function* of English. That the attempts to raise the status of English in this way were not uncontroversial is clear from Shakespeare's parody in Holofernes of the spelling reformer Mulcaster.

Another way in which attempts were made to make English more suitable to take the place of Latin was in the field of style. Gordon (1966), gives an overview of the different styles of writing he identified for the early modern period. Many of these styles were modelled on classical authors, such as Cicero, Tacitus and Seneca, while from these styles others evolved, what he refers to as 'the loose and free' and the Baroque. In analysing seventeenth-century prose we can see writers experimenting with these styles, trying to suit the Latin-based medium to the English language. By modern standards these attempts were not always successful, and it is easy to ridicule contemporary efforts to write scholarly prose in single sentences consisting of three hundred words or so. The attempts, however, were serious, and the three-hundred-word sentence referred to here was, according to Gordon, 'for [Milton] the proper way in which English prose should be written' (1966: 107). As with the experiments with the vocabulary of English, there were also attempts to explore the possibilities of the native language, and Gordon reports on 'the persistent pressure of speech-based prose on prose of more obvious literary pretensions' (1966: 120). At the same time, specific registers developed, such as the language of science and medical prose (see Taavitsainen & Pahta, 1997, and Section 5.3.5). It was with the foundation of the Royal Society in 1660 that the advantages of this native prose style won out; it became the prescribed style of the Society. As Thomas Sprat wrote in his *History of the Royal Society* (1667):

> They have therefore been most rigorous in putting in execution the only
> Remedy, that can be found for this *extravagance*: and that has been, a constant
> Resolution, to reject all the amplifications, digressions, and swellings of style:
> to return back to the primitive purity, and shortness, when men deliver'd so
> many *things*, almost in an equal number of *words*. They have exacted from all
> their members, a close, naked, natural way of speaking; positive expressions;
> clear senses; a native easiness; bringing all things as near the Mathematical
> plainness, as they can: and preferring the language of Artizans, Countrymen,
> and Merchants, before that, of Wits, or Scholars. (as quoted in Gordon, 1966:
> 127)

It is interesting to notice that here, too, we have an example of the importance of institutional support by which a particular change can be put into effect. As a result, we first see an awareness of a distinction between literary and scientific styles of writing.

Significantly, the *elaboration of function* stage in the standardisation process affected the English language at various levels, those of vocabulary, spelling and style of writing. Only at the stylistic level do we see any imposition from above; the attempts at expanding the vocabulary took place largely at the level of the individual writer, and they led to violent public debate resulting in what we now look upon as the inkhorn controversy. As far as spelling changes are concerned, although there was no official body advocating a particular series of changes, the role of the seventeenth-century printers may be taken as equivalent to some extent. The standardisation of English spelling, or rather its 'stabilisation' as Scragg calls it, was more or less completed by the end of the century, that is to say in formal, printed texts. The medium of the private letter remained unaffected for some time to come (see Section 5.3.3), though the effect of education on the part of the letter writer was most apparent. Syntax is an area which similarly underwent a lot of influence from Latin (see e.g. Johnson, 1944; Sørensen, 1957). Van der Wurff (1989), for example, argues that constructions of the type *It is my will, the which if thou respect,/ Show a fair presence and put off these frowns* (Shakespeare, *Romeo and Juliet*, I.v.75f.) arose out of a need to imitate similar sentences in Latin. Such sentences were primarily attested between the sixteenth and the nineteenth centuries, and they appear to have functioned, along with other 'Latinate features such as loan-words, extensive rhetoric, syntactic complexity and references to the classical world', as markers of stylistic formality (van der Wurff, 1989: 141). It is striking that at all four levels at which the *elaboration of function* stage had its effect it was to Latin that speakers and writers of English turned as their model, despite the fact that the language was emancipating itself from Latin. But then Latin was the only example available.

5.2.6   Codification

Latin also provided an important point of reference in the next stage of the standardisation process, *codification*. When applied to a linguistic standardisation process, codification involves the laying down of rules for the language in grammars and dictionaries which would serve as authoritative handbooks for its speakers. In several countries this phase was in the hands of an official body, an academy, such as the Accademia della Crusca (founded in 1582) in Italy, the Académie Française (1635) in France and the Academia Real (1713) in Spain. Though there were frequent calls for an academy in England, too, by well-known men of letters such as Dryden, Defoe, Swift and Addison, an English Academy never came about. In the abortive attempts at founding an English Academy we can also see the importance of institutional support in a standardisation process: an early project, according to Baugh & Cable (2002: 264), 'died with James I', and as for the early decades of the eighteenth century, when renewed attempts were made, it seems that especially Swift's *Proposal for Correcting, Improving, and Ascertaining the English Tongue* (1712) had the support of the Queen. Baugh & Cable (2002: 268) quote an opponent of the idea, the Whig John Oldmixon, as saying that:

> It is well known . . . that if the Queen had lived a year or two longer, this proposal would, in all probability, have taken effect. For the Lord Treasurer had already nominated several persons without distinction of quality or party, who were to compose a society for the purposes mentioned by the author; and resolved to use his credit with her Majesty, that a fund should be applied to support the expence of a large room, where the society should meet, and for other incidents. But this scheme fell to the ground, partly by the dissensions among the great men at court; but chiefly by the lamented death of that glorious princess.

Despite the fact that no official body came into being which would have been responsible for the production of an authoritative grammar and dictionary, such works came into being of their own accord. The first dictionaries were direct products of the previous stage in the standardisation process, as so many unfamiliar words had come into the language that dictionaries were needed to explain them to the common user, even to those who were fairly well educated. Consequently, the early dictionaries were 'hard word dictionaries', which, unlike users' dictionaries today, did not list the common everyday words of the language. The decision to include all words in the language must be attributed to Nathan Bailey at the beginning of the eighteenth century, whose *Dictionarium Britannicum* (1730) was used as a source by Johnson for his *Dictionary of the English Language* (1755). Johnson's dictionary was so popular that it came to function as a standard reference work. In an argument with his printer Robert Dodsley over the spelling of the word *bull* 'papal edict', Robert Lowth (1710–87), author of one of the most influential grammars of English produced in the eighteenth century (see Section 5.2.8), for instance, refers to the authority which Johnson's dictionary had as little as two years after its appearance:

> Observe, that I spell *Bulle* always with an *e* at the end, as being more regular & agreable to the geniology, & also to distinguish it from that other word

of the same sound wch. has been the source of so many puns upon this. You will tell me that practice & custom are against me, & make an appeal to Johnson's Dictionary, &c. Regardless, I think I am right, & believe I could give authorities: but if you contest y^e^. matter, I submit. (ed. Tierney, 1988: 304)

The early English grammars were bilingual grammars, for Frenchmen wanting to learn English and for Englishmen wanting to learn French. The first grammar of English proper was written by Bullokar. It was published in 1586, and for the next seventy years or so several more grammars were written, some in English (by Ben Jonson, for example), others in Latin. All early grammarians primarily resorted to Latin grammar to provide them with a model, describing the grammar of English as if it had eight parts of speech, three tenses, two moods and six persons. There was, again, no other model available. English grammar was not at first considered an object worthy of study for its own sake. Joshua Poole, for example, whose *English Accidence* was published in 1646, presented his grammar as 'a short, plaine, and easie way, for the more speedy attaining the Latin tongue, by the helpe of the English'. It is not until Wallis published his *Grammatica Linguae Anglicanae* in 1653 that grammarians, though sparingly at first, began to have an eye for characteristics peculiar to English grammar itself. At first, English was treated like Latin, and the early grammarians therefore only paid attention to its morphology. What is more, the eighteenth-century grammarians saw it as their aim to 'reduce the language to rule . . . to refine it . . . and to fix it permanently in the desired form' (Baugh & Cable, 2002: 257). Only gradually – and this is a process which took place around the middle of the eighteenth century – did they come to realise that it was an illusion to think that a living language could forever be fixed. In this respect, they began to recognise an important difference between English and Latin. Subsequently, it was noticed that in a language which was poor in morphology, syntax was far more important, and the amount of space in a grammar devoted to syntax steadily grew from just over eight pages in Greenwood's grammar (1711) to sixty pages in the one by Lowth (1762).

5.2.7   Prescription

Lowth's *Short Introduction to the English Language* (1762) marks the beginning of the next stage in the standardisation process, the *prescription* stage. The grammar distinguishes itself from others produced around the same time in that in the footnotes to its section on syntax it provides an inventory of grammatical errors made by more or less contemporary authors as well as by those whose language was often upheld as representing the norm of good usage. Even 'our best Authors . . . have sometimes fallen into mistakes', Lowth wrote in his preface, and a grammar such as his own would be needed to remedy the defects he identified. Lowth, and others after him, presented his reading public with a norm of correct English. In formulating this norm, many eighteenth-century grammarians relied upon the codification attempts of their predecessors; a good example is Lindley Murray, who based much of his grammar (first published in 1795 and many times reprinted) on the one by Lowth, for reasons explained in his introduction:

> When the number and variety of English Grammars already published . . . are considered, little can be expected from a new compilation, besides a careful selection of the most useful matter, and some degree of improvement in the mode of adapting it to the understanding, and the gradual progress of learners. In these respects something, perhaps, may yet be done, for the ease and advantage of young persons. (Murray, 1795: iii)

And a compilation is what Murray provided, to the extent even that he was accused of plagiarism – upon which he at once corrected his failure to specify his sources. While Lowth's grammar may be regarded as the epitome of normative grammar writing, Murray has been called the 'father of English grammar': the enormous number of reprints of the grammar, in England and America as well as in other countries, suggests that his grammar came to be looked upon as a handbook of English grammar. That his grammar was translated into many different languages – French, German, Dutch, Swedish, Spanish, Russian and Japanese (Alston, 1965: 96) – indicates that it also provided an important tool in learning English as a foreign language. Though it was not the first of its nature (Lowth's grammar, for example, had been translated into German in 1790), Murray's grammar may be taken to mark the beginnings of the spread of English as a world language, used by speakers who did not already have English as their mother tongue.

According to Milroy & Milroy (1991: 69), the *prescriptive* stage in the standardisation process has not been very successful, particularly when applied to speech. A comparison between present-day handbooks of usage and eighteenth-century grammars shows that modern writers are still largely concerned with the same issues as their eighteenth-century predecessors: whether it should be *different to, different from* or *different than*; whether it should be *it is me* or *it is I, taller than me* or *taller than I* and whether a sentence should be allowed to end with a preposition (cf. Ilson, 1985; Fowler, 1965). People even write to the media to expose a particular grammatical error made by a public speaker or writer; Milroy & Milroy refer to this practice as the 'complaint tradition', which arose as a consequence of a belief in the existence of a standard language which is invariable and the use of which is prescribed in the media as well as other formal contexts. These issues have even come to form a kind of set list of items which are constantly invoked by purists, but it is interesting to note that there is little difference between those which were commented on by eighteenth-century writers on language, such as Baker (1770), and those of today, such as Simon (1980). Such writers fail to see that language has to remain variable in order to be able to respond to all kinds of changes as a result of developments in technology, culture and global communication generally. To think that language could be fixed in the same way as, say, the metre or shoe sizes or video systems is an illusion. Even so, many speakers believe in the existence of a fixed linguistic norm which should be taught in schools and used in formal situations – a belief which Milroy & Milroy refer to as an 'ideology', an elitist point of view according to which education and social background are the backbones of society. Consequently, many speakers are shocked by what they perceive as the decline of the standard, which is attributed to a general decline in standards, particularly moral ones. What they are in fact reacting against is the constant adaptation of language to new developments, such as a greater tolerance of norms – linguistic and otherwise – other than those upheld by speakers of standard English. And the standard is responding to such changing attitudes, so that we can see a greater tolerance for forms of speech formerly banned with great zeal by schoolmasters and other language guardians. A survey conducted by Mittins et al. (1970) among schoolteachers, professional writers, administrators, doctors, clergymen and lawyers showed that even in the late 1960s a construction like *I will be twenty-one tomorrow* (instead of the historically more 'correct' form with *I shall*; see Tieken-Boon van Ostade, 1985) had reached an acceptance level of 56 per cent. In this day and age, students are indeed no longer obliged to use *I shall* in their essays.

5.2.8   Conclusion

According to some, there is no such thing as a standard language. And indeed, according to a strict interpretation of the word, to think that complete standardisation can be achieved is an illusion. Even so, to many people the notion of 'a standard language' is very real indeed, just as much as their concern at an apparent decline in norms of behaviour. While greater tolerance of non-standard dialects has led to a discussion of whether standard English still remains the appropriate medium of education, it would increase social disadvantages if this use of the standard were to be abolished altogether. As Shuman (1985: 317) points out, students 'need to be taught about levels of usage and about appropriateness rather than about "correctness" and "incorrectness"'. To do so would allow non-standard speakers to remain loyal to their native dialect while at the same time offering them a maximum of opportunities at learning to function in contexts which, rightly or wrongly, require ability in the standard.

The standardisation process, though described here chronologically, was not a straightforward process. It proceeded in fits and starts, mainly due to the fact that it was not a consciously monitored development, unlike the standardisation process taking place, for example, in Indonesia since the end of the Second World War or in the Basque Country since the late 1960s. The fits and starts of an unmonitored standardisation process, as in the case of English, are due to competing local standards and conscious standardisation attempts. At the same time, we must reckon with influential speakers or groups of speakers whose language was considered so important by those around them as to act as a norm independent of that of the incipient standards. One example is Dr Johnson, whose rather archaic usage of periphrastic *do* in the second half of the eighteenth century was copied by speakers who consequently deviated consciously from the general direction in which *do* was heading. Rissanen (1999b), moreover, has found that the first Acts of Parliament which were written in English in the 1480s reflect the language of the chancery but still show a large degree of variation. This suggests that the primary aim of standardisation, the suppression of optional variability in language, was not achieved all at once. This is a topic that we shall return to in Section 5.3, below.

What the standardisation process has in fact led to is the creation of a relatively focussed variety of the English language which is used as the written medium and as a medium felt to be appropriate to formal contexts. That this variety had its basis in the East Midland dialect is a matter of historical and geographical accident. If English kings had continued to travel around the country, or if they had settled their court elsewhere in the country, another Middle English dialect might well have been selected. And if the Norman Conquest had not happened, this would quite possibly have been West Saxon.

5.3   A general and focussed language?

5.3.1   Introduction

In the previous sections we looked at the process of standardisation from an institutional perspective. Institutions such as the chancery had a leading role to play in setting linguistic models for others to follow. But the existence of such norm-setters did not mean a wholesale adoption of these norms by other institutions, let alone by the language community as a whole. Chancery forms were not followed, for instance, by the scribes copying the manuscripts of Chaucer's *Canterbury Tales* in the fifteenth century, who continued to use the 'colourless' written language, a dialectal mixture of non-chancery forms, that had been well established in late Middle English. Even by the last quarter of the fifteenth century, these scribes had not adopted chancery forms for common items like *these*, *their*, *given* and *through* (Smith, 1996: 73–5). Although these Chaucer manuscripts show considerable variation in usage, they were written in a levelled dialect which shows no particular dialectal distinctiveness.

The chancery documents, too, contain a range of variation both in spelling and in morphology, alongside their preferred or majority forms discussed in Section 5.2.2. Spelling was the less regular of the two. Fisher (1996: 50) mentions that variation between non-distinctive pairs like *i/y*, *u/v*, *u/w*, *ou/ow*, and the presence or absence of final *-e*, could vary from word to word. It is obvious that even recognised institutional norms were far from fixed at the time. To explore this matter further, we shall adopt the term *focussing*, which is used by sociolinguists to refer to a high level of agreement in a language community as to what does and what does not constitute 'the language' at a given time (Trudgill, 1986: 86). Language communities differ considerably as to how much variation is tolerated in a given domain of language use and, conversely, how fixed the norms are to which speakers and writers are expected to adhere. In late medieval England these norms were clearly more diffuse than today.

To put the standardisation processes on a more concrete footing we also need to assess how and to what extent local and regional norms were replaced by supralocal ones in the course of time. *Supralocalisation* is here used as an umbrella term to refer to the geographical diffusion of linguistic features beyond their region of origin. When supralocalisation takes place, it typically results in dialect levelling, loss of marked and/or rare elements. In this respect it achieves the chief goal of standardisation, to reduce the amount of permissible variation. However, and this should be stressed, many processes of supralocalisation in English, both today and in the past, have been induced naturally by dialect contacts without any conscious effort towards producing an official standard language. This was already the case with the 'colourless regional language' of late Middle English. In the early modern period, non-localisable dialects were called the 'usual', 'customary' or 'common' language by contemporaries. In his *Logonomia Anglica* (1619), Alexander Gil combined regional and register criteria when dividing the dialects of England into 'the general, the Northern, the Southern, the Eastern, the Western, and the Poetic'. His 'general' dialect is specifically identified as the language of 'persons of genteel character and cultured upbringing' (1619 [1972], vol. 2: 102, 104]). What Gil had in mind were the sociolects spoken by the wealthier sections of the population, particularly in the region around the capital.

As noted by J. Milroy (1994: 20), standardisation is often facilitated by the prior development of suitable supralocal norms, being, as it were, superimposed upon them. But as standardisation is a long-term process and involves centres of focussing that themselves are liable to be modified with time – for instance, as a result of migration and changes in dialect input – the norms that are codified as standard combine features from supralocal and focussed usages of various origins. In many respects, standard English therefore constitutes a composite dialect. The chancery forms of *such* and *their* are now part of standard English, not the levelled regional forms *swich* and *hir* found in the majority of the *Canterbury Tales* texts. *Their*, however, is not a native southern dialect form, but a northern one. The preferred chancery forms themselves are representative of various dialects. There are two explanations for this: the language spoken in London at the time was based on the southern dialect as modified by immigrants – as discussed in Section 5.2.2, many chancery clerks came from the northern counties – and the new official language was itself an amalgam of earlier written norms (Fisher, 1996: 50–1). Our aim here is to outline some of the major processes of supralocalisation and focussing that have shaped the norms of standard English at various levels of the language from the early Modern English period until the present day.

Standardisation presupposes focussing, but the relation between the two is not a simple one. It continues to be regionally and chronologically complicated by the fact that English is what Romaine (1998: 27) calls a 'pluricentric' language, 'one whose norms are focussed in different local centres, capitals, centres of economy, publishing, education and political power'. Some aspects of the language were generalised throughout the country, and later on globally, becoming part of the standard language in all registers, in both speech and writing. This is, however, not the case with all aspects, but 'competing magnets of prestige' – to use a phrase coined by Smith (1996: 65) – continue to exert their influence to varying degrees in many areas of standard language use. To see how non-localisable norms actually became a codified part of standard English as we know it today, it is useful to consider spelling, grammar, vocabulary and pronunciation separately, because they showed different degrees of focussing when the various stages of standardisation were being implemented.

Looking at processes of standardisation on these various linguistic levels, we find the regularisation of public spellings at the focussed end at an early stage. Printing-house practices were largely fixed in the course of the seventeenth century. Grammatical features, too, were focussed, but not to the same degree in the early Modern English period. A distinctive element in the history of standard English grammar is register-specific focussing: written registers typically come at the focussed end, with fixed norms, while many spoken registers, casual conversation in particular, allow more variation. Finally, despite the many references to a common southern usage in the sixteenth century, the national pronunciation norm (variously referred to as RP or Received Pronunciation, Oxford English, the Queen's English or BBC English) reached the more focussed end of the scale in England only in the late eighteenth and early nineteenth centuries. Spelling reforms had been advocated already in the sixteenth century by John Hart and other orthoepists because of the discrepancy between spelling and pronunciation at the time. As a result of the early fixing of spelling as opposed to the much greater diffuseness of pronunciation, the two have drifted even further apart since then.

5.3.2   Spelling

When Caxton set up his printing press in Westminster in 1476, he was confronted with a spelling system that was characterised by a great amount of variability. However, rather than attempting to do something about it, as might perhaps be expected of a printer and as others did after him, his compositors made use of the abundance of spelling variants which appeared to be available to them, in order to be able to justify the lines. Thus, in the *Concordance to Caxton's Own Prose* (Mizobata, 1990) we find *do* alongside *doo*, *don* alongside *done*, *doon* and *doone*, and depending on the amount of space needed, the compositor could select any of the variants. What is more, the early compositors, Wynkyn de Worde and Richard Pynson, were foreigners, and they could not be expected to direct a variable spelling system towards greater regularity. So, though around the end of the Middle Ages manuscript spelling had reached a fair amount of consistency and regularity, the introduction of printing in England at first made spelling considerably worse (Scragg, 1974: 64). With the next generation of printers the situation improved to a certain extent: Aronoff (1987) has shown that after he took over

Caxton's printing business, Wynkyn de Worde appears to have adopted a kind of style sheet for spelling, containing rules such as 'The inflectional suffixes are spelled *es, eth, ed,* except after sonorant consonants (*r, n, l*), where there is no *e*' (1987: 95). Unfortunately, the style sheet itself has not survived, and the spelling rules drawn up by Aronoff are reconstructions based on the available spelling evidence.

Although it is a much debated point whether we owe the regulation of English spelling to the printers or the sixteenth-century spelling reformers (cf. Scragg, 1974 as against Carney, 1994), there is increasing evidence of the important role played by the early printers in the development of English spelling (Salmon, 1989 and Caon, 2002). By the middle of the seventeenth century in any case, printing-house practice had reached a high degree of uniformity in spelling. Private writing, however, continued to show much more variation, but it is a kind of variation that shows a certain degree of regularity in its own right, to such an extent even that Osselton (1963 and 1984a) distinguishes between two spelling systems for the eighteenth century, a public and a private one. The public spelling system was that found in the printed texts of the time, which, apart from a few differences such as *emperour, mirrour* and *superiour* (Osselton, 1963: 269), was identical to that of present-day English, while the private spelling system allowed for spellings like Boswell's *beautyfull* and *agreable* (Tieken-Boon van Ostade, 1996a). Private spelling as such eventually disappeared, and by the early nineteenth century spelling forms such as those found in Boswell's private writings are rare and should perhaps be interpreted as mistakes rather than variants. Any random check of the British National Corpus will show the extent to which even educated writers today continue to be baffled by such seemingly illogical spelling distinctions as those between *its* and *it's*.

At all times, spelling was one of the areas of language use that closely corresponded to the writer's level of literacy. In the Middle English period writing was a professional skill, and a male preserve at that. Women's general level of literacy was much lower then but also throughout the early Modern English period (Nevalainen & Raumolin-Brunberg, 2003: 42), down to the middle of the nineteenth century, when the educational opportunities for women increased significantly (Raftery, 1997). Although considerable sections of the population may have possessed rudimentary reading skills during the late Middle Ages, this was not true for writing, which was taught separately from reading. According to research based on signatures, no more than one-third of the male population in England around 1600 was able to both read and write (Cressy, 1980); the figures for women were considerably lower. Margaret Paston (1420?–84), for example, could read but not write, while Lady Brilliana Harley (1600?–43), the third wife of Sir Robert Harley, who is described as 'a woman of intelligence and culture', uses a 'spelling system [which] is rather inconsistent and idiosyncratic, confusing standard forms with the writer's own phonetic spellings' (Burnley, 1992: 255–6). Though lack of education is obviously linked to a writer's gender, it would be dangerous to link poor spelling ability to the sex of the writer alone: Queen

Elizabeth had received an excellent education, and her spelling is equal to that of any educated male writer of her time. In her letters, too, Sarah Fielding (1710–68) spells as well as or perhaps even better than her brother Henry (Tieken-Boon van Ostade, 1998), but then she was a learned woman, despite the fact that she had not enjoyed the kind of formal education normally reserved for men at the time.

All through the late Middle English and early Modern periods there were pronounced regional and social differences in the ability to write and to spell, and much higher percentages of full literacy have been noted for the London region as well as among the highest social ranks – though even here there are exceptions, as in the case of the Clift family, a poor, lower-working-class family from Cornwall, whose members quite exceptionally kept in touch with each other by letter. There is no question about the basic literacy of most of the individual family members, though their spelling is very poor. Even before the youngest member of the family, William (1775–1849), went to London to take up an apprenticeship there, his language comes very close to standard English, and whatever dialectal traits still remained in his language were lost soon after his arrival in the capital (Austin, 1994). In his letters, moreover, there are very few traces of the private spelling system in use at the time, which suggests that he was much influenced in his writing by a self-imposed reading programme.

5.3.3   Grammar

By definition, all dialects of a given language are expected to bear a close structural resemblance to each other. Standard English, too, shares most of its grammar with non-standard varieties of English. It does, however, have a number of basic grammatical features that make it different from most regional and social varieties of English around the world. Trudgill (1999a: 125–6) gives a list of eight such features. Four of them concern the morphology and syntax of the verb phrase, three are pronominal, and one has to do with negation. Trudgill's list will be presented below. The list is, of course, not exhaustive, but it provides a selection of the fixed, codified features of standard English grammar. Some of the processes of focussing and supralocalisation from which they resulted in the early Modern period will be discussed later on in this section. The section will finish with the present day, and look at some less strictly focalised areas of standard English grammar.

The modern standard English verb phrase is characterised by the unusual marking of the third-person singular in the present tense: *he goes* vs *I go*. Many other varieties either use zero (*I go, you go, he go*) or mark all persons (*I goes, you goes, he goes*). Standard English also has irregular forms of the verb *to be* both in the present (*am, is, are*) and the past (*was, were*). Many other varieties have only one form for the present (e.g. *I be, you be*) and one for the past (*I were, you were*). Similarly with other irregular verbs, standard English has different forms for the past and the perfect, which is accompanied with the auxiliary *have* (*I saw* vs *I have seen*). In many non-standard varieties, the tense distinction is often carried by the auxiliary (*I seen* vs *I have seen*). By contrast, no distinction is made in standard English between the (tensed) forms of the auxiliary *do* and the main verb *do*, whereas modal auxiliaries are distinguished from full lexical verbs. Regional dialects typically differentiate between the present-tense forms of the auxiliary (*I do*, *he do*) and of the main verb (*I does*, *he does*), and similarly between the past-tense forms of the auxiliary (*did*) and the main verb (*done*; e.g. *You done it, did you?*).

The pronominal features that make standard English different from other varieties include the lack of distinction between the second-person singular and plural forms of personal pronouns; *you* is used for both in the standard. In many traditional dialects either the older distinction between *thou* and *you* is maintained or new number distinctions have developed (e.g. *you* vs *youse* or *y'all*). The standard English demonstrative pronoun system has similarly lost a distinction: what is left is a two-way contrast between *this* (close to the speaker) and *that* (away from the speaker). A three-way contrast is maintained in many regional varieties, which make a further distinction between *that* (close to the listener) and *yon* (away from both speaker and listener). Finally, standard English is less regular than many non-standard varieties in that its reflexive pronouns are derived from two different sources. Forms like *myself* are based on possessive pronouns, and forms like *himself* on objective pronouns. Many regional dialects regularly employ the possessive forms (e.g. *myself, hisself, theirselves*).

One of the socially most marked features on Trudgill's list (1999a: 125) is the fact that standard English grammar lacks multiple negation (or negative concord), and so does not allow sentences like *I don't want none*. Single negation followed by non-assertive indefinites is the only possible alternative in the standard: *I don't want any*. Most non-standard varieties of English around the world permit multiple negation, as do many European standard languages, such as Italian and Greek.

It is probably true to say that where new linguistic norms are being established in a language community, the issue will be as complex as the sociolinguistic situation in the community. Recent corpus-based research on early Modern English indicates that the grammatical characteristics of standard English outlined above were typically the result of competing processes of supralocalisation, most of which can be traced to times well before the period of normative grammar in the eighteenth century. Many of the features that supralocalised in the early Modern English period did not have any direct institutional support in their initial stages in the way that public spellings, for instance, did. Neither was institutional support necessarily a guarantee for a feature eventually being codified as part of standard English grammar. This point will be illustrated with the rivalry between the third-person-singular endings -(*e*)*s* and -(*e*)*th*. Standardisation may therefore be superimposed on supralocal usages established prior to codification, as suggested by J. Milroy (1994: 20).

The rise of many of the future standard features can be traced to densely populated areas. A case in point is the population of London with its variable input of immigrants from different parts of the country in the late Middle and early Modern English periods. In the fourteenth and fifteenth centuries, London gained a large number of inhabitants from the midlands. But in the fifteenth and early sixteenth centuries, the capital also attracted a sizeable number of immigrants from the northern counties. Sixty per cent of London apprentices, for instance, are estimated to have come from the north in the last decade of the fifteenth century, and nearly 50 per cent in the middle of the sixteenth century. Of all the apprentices migrating to London from England and Wales, the corresponding figures for the midlands were 10 and 20 per cent for these two periods, respectively (Wareing, 1980: 243). The effects of regional mobility and dialect contact can be seen in the grammatical features that were supralocalised throughout the country in the fifteenth and sixteenth centuries.

Despite such centres of focussing as the chancery and the printing press, it is evident that a number of those grammatical features which had begun to gain ground in London in the fifteenth century or earlier did not originate in the south. Present-day standard English has forms such as the plural *are* of the verb *be* and the third-person-singular -(*e*)*s* in the present indicative that go back to northern dialects. The forms current in chancery manuscripts and books printed in London in the fifteenth century were the traditional southern plural form *be* and third-person -(*e*)*th*. However, even these two features travelled different paths: the supralocalisation of *are* looks like a case of regular dialect diffusion that progressed over the centuries from north to south – a process suggested by the Middle English data charted in *A Linguistic Atlas of Late Mediaeval English* (*LALME*; McIntosh et al., 1986). The *Corpus of Early English Correspondence* (*CEEC*) indicates that *are* plurals were more frequent in East Anglia, for instance, than in London for the better part of the sixteenth century, but that they were generalised in the capital, too, in the latter half of the century (Nevalainen, 2000: 348). As is commonly the case with language change in progress, both the incoming and recessive forms may be used by one and the same person in the same context, as is shown by John Johnson, a London merchant, writing to his wife Sabine Johnson in 1545 (the variant forms are marked in boldface):

> All your menservauntes have bene of counsaill with hym, for they **be** of no les opynion, declaring that your breid is not good ynoghe for dogges, and drincke so evill that they cannot drinck it, but **ar** fayn when they go into the towne to drincke to their dynnars.   (John Johnson; *CEEC*, JOHNSON, 250)

By contrast, the third-person suffix -(*e*)*s* looks more like a case of 'dialect-hopping'. In the *LALME* sources, which cover the period up to 1450, it had not quite reached the central midlands. In the latter half of the fifteenth century the suffix, however, shows up in personal letters in London – well before it appears in East Anglia. It is noteworthy that the early users of -(*e*)*s* in London are mostly merchants, mobile people with many weak ties within the community and outside it. Moreover, when -(*e*)*s* began to diffuse throughout the country, as the *CEEC* data suggest, in the latter half of the sixteenth century, the process was headed by the City of London, while the high administrators and other representatives of the royal court were slower to adopt it (Nevalainen, 2000: 349–52). This had been the case with *are* as well. Evidence like this suggests that the processes did not proceed from the higher social ranks to the lower in the south but rather the other way around. Before the processes were completed, mixed usage was the rule even in the highest ranks, as is illustrated by a letter written by Queen Elizabeth I to King James VI of Scotland in 1585:

> . . . he **knoweth** not the prise of my bloude, wiche shuld be spild by bloudy hande of a murtherar, wiche some of your nere-a-kin did graunt. A sore question, you may suppose, but no other act than suche as I am assured he **knowes,** and therfor I hope he wyl not dare deny you a truthe;   (Queen Elizabeth I; *CEEC*, ROYAL 1, 11)

These findings agree with what we see in such conservative written sources as the 1611 King James Bible and the 1662 version of the Book of Common Prayer. In both texts, -(*e*)*th* continues to be the norm in the third-person singular, while *be* and *are* both appear in the present indicative plural, though *are* predominates (Nevalainen, 1987). It is also interesting to note that *are* was even more frequent in passages that were specifically intended for oral delivery. Both books constituted staple reading at the time, both privately, at home, and publicly, in church. We shall therefore have to reckon with the influence of variable norms even in elements of the core grammar in early Modern English. Consequently, it is possible to observe contending forces in supralocalisation: those from above, originating from various institutional centres of focussing such as the chancery, the church and the printing press, and those from below, operating through everyday spoken interaction and often emanating from less literate speakers. Although *are* and -(*e*)*s* were resisted by influences from above, change from below eventually won the day in both cases.

However, the outcome of the competing forces described here would not necessarily have been predictable at the time. With both -(*e*)*s* and *are*, the processes of supralocalisation were two-way streets between the north and the south: not only were the two new features percolating south, but the southern features -(*e*)*th* and *be* were spreading northwards. This is what one might expect of forms that were part of chancery usage and were adopted by Caxton in his printed books. The southern -(*e*)*th*, for instance, could be employed by educated northerners in the sixteenth century when writing to more distant correspondents – presumably in recognition of the southern norm – and -(*e*)*s* when writing to their immediate family. The choice of variant may therefore be interpreted as a register indicator for a northerner in the sixteenth century. Despite its appearance in London in the late fifteenth century, to many educated southerners, by contrast, -(*e*)*s* does not seem to have presented a major alternative even in the family circle until the second half of the sixteenth century.

When talking about change from below, we should not forget that a third option, the zero form (*he go*), was also available at the time. It was, however, relatively infrequent in the correspondence data, suggesting that it was not a viable alternative for the section of the language community that could write at the time (around 20 per cent of the entire population c.1550 and around 30 per cent c.1650, but with a large amount of regional variation throughout the period; Cressy, 1980). However, some writers could display a three-way contrast in the third-person singular in certain areas of the country. In 1626 Lady Katherine Paston used all three, -(e)s, -(e)th and zero, in the letter to her son cited below. She was a native of East Anglia, where the zero form has been preserved in the local dialect to the present day. Katherine Paston also uses the traditional second-person-singular pronoun *thou* when addressing her fourteen-year-old son. *You* had, however, replaced *thou* in most contexts even within the immediate family as early as the sixteenth century, as is suggested by John Johnson's letter to his wife cited above. Again we find that neither the regional use of *thou* nor its prominence in the language of the Authorised Version of the Bible served as models for the evolving supralocal usages.

> . . . thy father **remembers** his loue to the and **take** thy wrightinge to him very kindly: thy brother **remember** his louingest loue to the . . . I had thought to haue written to mr Roberts this time. but this sudene Iornye of this mesinger **affordethe** me not so much time (Lady Katherine Paston; *CEEC*, PASTONK, 90).

While both *are* and -(e)s spread from north to south, research on the letter corpus suggests that most grammatical features that made their way to the supralocal *Gemeinsprache* during the sixteenth and seventeenth centuries diffused from the capital region to the rest of the country. As noted above, London led the process in the last phase of the diffusion of -(e)s in the latter half of the sixteenth century. In a survey of four localities, viz. north, East Anglia, London (the City) and the court, this also appears to have been the case with the personal pronoun form *you* replacing *ye* in the subject function and the replacement of multiple negation (*not + nobody, nothing, never*) with single negation followed by non-assertive indefinites (*not + anybody, anything, ever*; Nevalainen, 2000: 353–6). The diffusion of *you* proved to be extremely rapid: it first gained momentum in London in the first decades of the sixteenth century and was completed by the end of the century in all four localities. Multiple negation was also disappearing rapidly in the first half of the sixteenth century but took a much longer time than *you*, and the process was not fully completed even by the first half of the eighteenth century (Tieken-Boon van Ostade, 1982: 285, note).

These results do not, however, mean that simple generalisations could be made about London English in these two cases either. The use of *you* as subject diffused in a similar fashion in both London 'proper' and the royal court, and found its way to most regional varieties in England (*ye* is attested only in parts of Northumberland in the *Survey of English Dialects*; Orton et al., 1998). By contrast, a significant difference emerged in the disappearance of multiple negation between the two London localities, i.e. basically between the City and Westminster. It was the court with its professional administrators that took the lead in the process. The letter sources suggest that the rest of London did not catch up with the court until towards the end of the sixteenth century. A passage from a letter composed in 1523 by Thomas Cromwell, the king's chief minister, is cited below showing the pattern of negation that was later to be codified as part of standard English. It may be contrasted with a passage from the correspondence of Sabine Johnson, a London merchant's wife, writing to her husband in 1545. The divergent evidence on the spread of *you* and on the loss of multiple negation supports the view that, in the early Modern English period, supralocal processes did emanate both 'from above' and 'from below', in terms of social status as well as social awareness.

> . . . and wher as I accordinglye haue not in lyke wise remembrid and rescribid it hath bene for that I haue **not** hade **anything** to wryt of to your aduauncement.   (Thomas Cromwell; *CEEC*, CROMWELL I, 313)

> Har answar was that she wold **not** set har myend to **no** man tell she was delyvered and choirched [churched], and than as God shall provyde for har;   (Sabine Johnson; *CEEC*, JOHNSON, 396)

The processes described above were very effective in that they all resulted in morpheme substitutions in the general supralocal variety and, when codified as part of the standard language, became part of a system with no variation in form: standard English retains only one form in the third-person-singular present indicative, one second-person pronoun in the subject position, and so on. As noted in Section 5.2.7, language standardisation is, however, never implemented with the same rigour as the standardisation of weights and measures. Even today, after the codification of standard English in grammar books and dictionaries, a fair amount of variability is allowed in the non-localisable standard. There are, for instance, as many as three relative markers for expressing the object relation with non-human nouns, *that*, *which* and zero: *the book that/which/Ø I bought*. They all go back to Middle English, or even earlier, but underwent some modifications in early Modern English, which include the 'dehumanisation' of *which* as relative, i.e. the restriction of *which* to non-human antecedents (cf. the Lord's Prayer in the 1611 Bible: *Our father which art in heauen*). Similarly, indefinite pronouns with human reference come in two series in standard English, with both *-one* and *-body* (*Anyone/anybody home?*). The *-man* series was eliminated in the early Modern English period; what remains of it are a few fixed expressions such as *no-man's-land* (Raumolin-Brunberg, 1998). Standard English also marks future time by several auxiliaries and semi-auxiliaries such as *shall, will, be going to* and its variant form *gonna*. The roots of *be going to* (as in *I'm going to go there tomorrow*) can be traced to late Middle English, but the semi-auxiliary did not gain ground until the seventeenth century (Rissanen, 1999a: 223).

Which variant is chosen in each case largely depends on register, the way language is used in different situational contexts. A comparison of spoken and written registers will show that the relative pronoun *which* is more typical of writing than of speech, while the opposite is the case with *that* and the zero relativiser. Similarly, forms in *-body* are preferred in speech to those in *-one*, and *be going to* and *will* to *shall*. The zero relativiser, *-body* pronouns and *be going to* all go back to earlier oral and speech-like registers and have retained these connotations up to the present day. But regional variation also appears in the use of these forms. In American English *will* is regularly used as a future auxiliary with *I* and *we* (Quirk et al., 1985: 227–8). As noted in Section 5.2.7, it has become acceptable in most kinds of British English, too, but *shall* used to be the prescribed form until the last quarter of the twentieth century. Corpus studies also indicate that *be going to* is more frequent in American than in British English in both fiction and conversation; American English similarly prefers pronouns in *-body* to those in *-one*, and *that* to *which* in restrictive relative clauses even in written contexts (Biber et al., 1999: 353, 487–8, 616). In sum, in these cases the more colloquial forms are more common in American than in British English.

We also find that there are forms and structures that are acceptable in speech but not allowed in most kinds of writing. They include the use of the interrogative subject pronoun *who* as an object form (***who** did you talk to*? vs ***whom** did you talk to*?). This use of *who* as an object form has spread throughout the English-speaking world and is no longer confined to casual conversation (Biber et al., 1999: 214–15). Probably due to the fact that it has had a bad press with prescriptivists, it is one of those casual spoken-language features that was never generalised in writing. Although it is commonly attested in early Modern English, for instance, in Shakespeare (*O Lord sir*, ***who** do you meane*? in *1 Henry* IV, II.iv), it was probably too slow in spreading high and far enough before codification set in (Schneider, 1992). But there are signs suggesting that the status of *who* may be slowly changing. It is accepted as 'legitimate modern practice' in influential works like *The New Fowler's Modern English Usage* (Burchfield, 1996: 848), which is critically concerned only with those cases in which the objective form *whom* is ungrammatically used for the subjective *who* (*. . . far more hostile to Diana **whom** she believes betrayed the Prince of Wales*; *Independent Mag.*, 1993).

Although the object *who* may be more acceptable to normative grammarians and educated speakers now than it was in the past, there are a number of grammatical features in conversational language along the standard vs non-standard line that continue to divide speaker reactions. Spoken norms are, however, not only less focussed than written standard norms, but they have also become an object of extensive linguistic research much more recently. One thing that appears from the descriptive grammars of present-day usage based on electronic corpora is that many non-standard spoken-language features, too, have supralocalised world-wide. Some of the ways in which the grammar of written standard English may differ from casual conversation will be discussed below. The illustrations are all drawn from the *Longman Grammar of Spoken and Written English* (*LGSWE*; Biber et al., 1999). The differences are both morphological and syntactic.

A set of features specific to casual conversation can be found in pronominal forms and verbal inflections. They coincide in subject–verb concord. In order

Table 5.1 *Concord patterns in conversation (from Biber et al.,*
1999: 191)

Standard form	Non-standard (NS) form	% of use of NS form
I was	*I were*	c.5
you were	*you was*	c.10
she was	*she were*	c.10
they were	*they was*	c.5
I say	*I says*	c.50
you say	*you says*	less than 2
he doesn't	*he don't*	c.40
they don't	*they doesn't*	less than 2

to see that the grammar of conversation often displays variants not admitted in writing, we may consider the findings reported in *LGSWE* on the use of standard and vernacular concord patterns. They are based on a corpus of roughly four million words of British English and two and a half million words of American English (Biber et al., 1999: 25, 29). Table 5.1 presents the distribution of some typical concord patterns across the conversational data, all recorded after 1980.

Some of the findings may be explained by the fact that the corpus also includes some children and teenagers, whose language may not be as close to the standard as middle-aged people's usage. *I says* and *he don't* are, however, so frequent that they call for further comment. *LGSWE* classifies forms like this as parts of larger chunks where individual elements are not independently chosen. Although not mainstream variants in the past, both forms can be traced to earlier English, and are frequent in present-day regional varieties (Cheshire et al., 1993: 79–81; Trudgill, 1999a: 125–6). Shared by non-standard and standard speakers alike, some casual speech features may therefore have wider distribution globally than their written standard equivalents. Partly for this reason some writers on the topic prefer to talk about 'general English', which excludes obvious local and regional dialects but has a wider distribution than standard English in that it accommodates spoken language and more or less stigmatised grammatical forms such as *he don't* (Gramley, 2001: 2–3).

Biber's chunking explanation appears particularly appropriate in the case of colloquial contractions like *there's*, *here's* and *where's* followed by plural subjects. The *LGSWE* database provides examples like: *Gary*, **there's** *apples if you want one*; **here's** *your shoes*; **where's** *your tapes*? In fact, *there's* preceding a plural subject occurs more frequently in casual conversation than *there* followed by a plural verb. That we have a continuum here that crosses the boundary between speech and writing can be seen with singular forms of *be* followed by coordinated noun phrases. Where a singular noun phrase immediately follows the verb, singular concord is in fact the more frequent choice with coordinated phrases in both speech and writing (*When he left an hour later* **there was** *no shrug and not* *much of a smile*; Biber et al., 1999: 186). Two factors seem to be at work here: the proximity of a singular noun to the verb and the fact that the subject position in the clause is occupied by the 'singular'-looking existential *there*. Again we are not dealing with present-day innovations but a feature that has a long history in the spoken medium from the Middle English period onwards (Jespersen, [1914] 1961: 181–3; Dekeyser, 1975: 164–8; Fischer, 1992: 364–7; Cheshire et al., 1993: 70).

Two conclusions may be drawn from these data on standard and non-standard grammar. It appears to be the case that, as J. K. Chambers (1995: 241–2) suggests, when a standard variety differs from other varieties, the difference lies both in the quantity and in the quality of variation. Non-standard varieties and the less focussed areas of the standard have variation where the focussed standard core allows none. Table 5.1 illustrates this by displaying two expressions in casual speech for cases of concord that are limited to only one in the written standard. The table also suggests that high-frequency standard variants are typically the historical ones. They attest to the relative conservatism and resistance to change of the focussed core of the standard language and often reflect the grammar of English at the time when it was codified. However, many casual features labelled as non-standard, too, have a long history and wide distribution in the English-speaking world. Which of them are going to be accepted as part of the standard written usage in the future depends on the stringency with which normative views are upheld. If the reception of the *New Fowler* is anything to go by (Morton, 1998: 323), new 'legitimate modern practices' may have brighter prospects in Britain than in the United States.

5.3.4   Vocabulary

As discussed in Section 5.2, standard English vocabulary was codified in dictionaries in the course of the seventeenth and eighteenth centuries. But as the vocabulary of a living language is open-ended, and may be freely augmented, its codification will always remain incomplete: no dictionary can be expected to include all the possible words of a language at a given time. Dictionary makers may even choose to omit parts of the vocabulary of what might be considered the standard language. In his preface to *A Dictionary of the English Language* (1755) Samuel Johnson claimed that he had not included any quotations from his contemporaries, but illustrated his entries with 'the writers before the restoration'. Although this is not quite true – Johnson does cite contemporaries, particularly Samuel Richardson and himself (Keast, 1957) – he regarded the late sixteenth and seventeenth centuries as a golden age, 'the wells of English undefiled' (Preface, fol. C^r), from which the literary language had later degenerated under the influence of French.

The Oxford English Dictionary (*OED*) similarly prioritises the literary language. Although it aims at charting not only the origins but also the use of English vocabulary, it is based on written sources – a situation unavoidable in a dictionary working on historical principles, but one that necessarily leads to omission of a large portion of colloquial vocabulary. In fact, some Anglo-Saxonisms that do appear in writing were omitted from the first edition of the *OED* because they were deemed too delicate for its Victorian readership (Finegan, 1998: 562). Any restrictions in the usage of words are marked by a set of status and field indicators. These labels show if a word or a sense is restricted to a particular geographical area (e.g. Australia, North America, Scotland), to a register or style (e.g. colloquial, poetic, slang) or to a branch of knowledge or field of activity (e.g. heraldry, law, zoology). English dialect vocabulary was, however, largely omitted from the first edition of the *OED*, because there was a simultaneous project with the specific aim of producing *The English Dialect Dictionary* (Wright, 1898–1905).

As the second edition of the *OED* was published as recently as 1989, one might expect it to embrace a late twentieth-century view of what counts as standard English vocabulary worldwide. The historical bias of the *OED* was, however, carried through to the second edition, and to the *New Shorter Oxford English Dictionary*, in that usages restricted to English English were typically not singled out but were subsumed under the common core of the English language. Despite the current large-scale revision the *OED* is undergoing at the present time, much of this will still be apparent in the dictionary's online edition, which still predominantly only shows RP pronunciations. That the English-speaking world is to a significant extent lexically divided by a common language is, however, evidenced by the fact that all the major national varieties of English today possess dictionaries of their own. Despite the impressive *OED* coverage of regional variation in Englishes around the world, there is to date no single, comprehensive lexical repository of world Englishes, not even first-language varieties, let alone the new Englishes discussed by Crystal in this volume.

While there are relatively few absolute grammatical and spelling differences between the British and American written standards, lexical variation is noticeable. It has to do with institutional differences in fields such as politics, banking, legal systems, the armed forces and sports, with local customs, folklore, flora and fauna, everyday slang and historical choices between variant forms. David Grote's dictionary *British English for American Readers*, for example, contains nearly 6,500 entries. A large number of these words appear in both varieties but differ in their denotations or connotations, or both. So in British English *joint* ordinarily means 'roast meat, especially for Sunday lunch' (not marijuana), *junction* is 'intersection', *junior school* refers to 'the older section of a primary school' and *public school* means 'private school' (Crystal, 1995: 306).

Thinking of the global coverage of standard English, the greatest lexical uniformity can be found in two different domains of language use. The first, the *common core*, literally constitutes the foundations of the standard. It largely goes back to the Anglo-Saxon heritage of English and consists of frequent everyday vocabulary used in all registers, in speech and writing alike (Gordon, 1966: 3). It includes names of everyday objects and actions, the commoner adjectives, verbs and adverbs, terms of family and social relationships, and central grammatical function words (pronouns, prepositions, articles and auxiliary verbs). The ten most frequent word occurrences in a million-word corpus of standard present-day British English are all grammatical: *the*, *of*, *and*, *to*, *a*, *in*, *that*, *is*, *was* and *it* (Hofland & Johansson, 1982). The top ten most frequent word forms in the early Modern English section (1500–1710) of the *Helsinki Corpus of English Texts* and of Caxton's own prose (Mizobata, 1990: 601) contain *I* but not *was* (or *it* in the case of Caxton, whose list contains *as* and *for* instead); the rest are the same as in the present-day corpus. These words are all Proto-Germanic in origin.

In the course of time, the core vocabulary has absorbed a number of loanwords, but according to some estimates, roughly 50 per cent of the core vocabulary items of English remains Germanic (Scheler, 1977: 73). The dozen most frequent lexical verbs in the *LGSWE* corpus are, in order of frequency: *say*, *get*, *go*, *know*, *think*, *see*, *make*, *come*, *take*, *want*, *give* and *mean* (Biber et al., 1999: 373). They all go back to the native Old English stock except for *take*, which is a Scandinavian loanword in late Old English, and *want*, another word of Scandinavian origin, first attested in Middle English (the initial /g/ in *give* may similarly be attributed to Scandinavian influence in Middle English). The registers drawing heavily on the common core, enriched with their international register-specific lexis, include those of the news media. The written standard English that appears in newspapers all over the world can easily be read without immediately suggesting its country of origin.

Other areas to show a high degree of shared lexis and continued elaboration of function are found in the many professional specialisations where English is used for special purposes (ESP). At the focussed end of ESP come the nomenclatures of various branches of science and technology. Their special terminologies date from different historical periods. While the common core vocabulary goes back to times before any documented national or international standards, specialist terms were increasingly recorded in monolingual glossaries and dictionaries in the early Modern English period. Schäfer (1989) shows that well over a hundred such publications appeared in the period 1475–1640 alone. These early fields of lexical focussing include a large variety of specialisations, including architecture, classics, cosmography, fencing, geography, grammar, heraldry, herbals, law, mathematics, poetry, rhetoric, and weights and measures. The terms defined in these works are typically not regionally localisable. Specialist terms figure prominently in seventeenth-century hard-word dictionaries, as in Thomas Blount's *Glossographia* (1656) and Elisha Coles' *An English Dictionary* (1676). By the end of the century, the basic terms in fields such as anatomy and mathematics had already been established. Most of them were borrowed from Latin, still the language of international scholarship at the time.

Most scientific terminologies, however, came into being only after this first wave of lexical codification in the sixteenth and seventeenth centuries. What these early works had managed to do was to regulate to a large extent the morphological shape and spelling of the lexical items they covered. But they could not fix their meanings. Where a word continued in technical use, its meaning was bound to reflect advances in science, technology and scholarship (Nevalainen, 1999: 435–54). This was, of course, also the case with more recent technical terminology.

One of the many scientific terms to come into English in the seventeenth century was *electricity*. In his *Dictionary* (1755), Dr Johnson glosses it as 'a property in some bodies, whereby, when rubbed so as to grow warm, they draw little bits of paper, or such like substances, to them'. His comment on the gloss is worth quoting because it reveals the ongoing changes in the extension of the term:

> Such was the account given a few years ago of electricity; but the industry of the present age, first excited by the experiments of *Gray*, has discovered in electricity a multitude of philosophical wonders. Bodies electrified by a sphere of glass, turned nimbly round, not only emit flame, but may be fitted with such a quantity of the electrical vapour, as, if discharged at once upon a human body, would endanger life. The force of this vapour has hitherto appeared instantaneous, persons at both ends of a long chain seeming to be struck at once. The philosophers are now endeavouring to intercept the strokes of lightning.   (*A Dictionary of the English Language*, 1755, s.v. *electricity*)

Johnson's *philosophers* in this context refers to 'men deep in knowledge, either moral or natural'. In his time *philosophy* was still the general term used of human knowledge of all kinds, including 'the course of sciences read in the schools'. *Science* itself came to English from Old French in the fourteenth century in the broad sense of '(certain) knowledge', which persisted into early Modern English. *Science* was also used for acquaintance with or mastery of any department of learning. In his dictionary of 'hard words', *A Table Alphabeticall*, Robert Cawdrey (1604) simply defines it as 'knowledge, or skill'. In early Modern English *the seven liberal sciences* was used to refer to 'the seven liberal arts' of the *Trivium* (Grammar, Logic, Rhetoric) and the *Quadrivium* (Arithmetic, Music, Geometry, Astronomy). The modern, narrower sense was introduced in the eighteenth century:

> The word science, is usually applied to a whole body of regular or methodical observations or propositions [. . .] concerning any subject of speculation.
> (*OED*, s.v. *science*; 1725, Watts, *Logic* II.ii.§9)

The more specialised sense of 'natural and physical science' did not appear until the latter half of the nineteenth century, thus reflecting the increasing separation of the physical from the mental in the field of human learning (Nevalainen, 1999: 435–6). An unprecedented number of specialist dictionaries appeared in the nineteenth century, when the Industrial Revolution, and new discoveries in natural sciences, medicine and philology, all gave rise to new terminologies to be recorded and standardised. More than two hundred specialist dictionaries and glossaries were published, as well as over thirty encyclopaedias. A similar upsurge in dictionaries and other reference works would next be seen in the 1980s (Crystal, 1995: 82).

In the nineteenth century, a number of new science names were established, including *biology* (1802), *palaeontology* (1838), *ethnology* (1842), *gynaecology* (1847), *histology* (1847), *embryology* (1859) and *ecology* (1866) (Savory, 1967: 89–90). Novel concepts were introduced in many fields, particularly in biology, chemistry, geology, medicine and physics. A large variety of new words had to be coined to meet the new needs – further examples of focussing and continuing elaboration of the standard. Many of these words were borrowed from Latin and Greek, or coined using Latin and Greek elements, thus increasing the number of what are called Neo-Latin/Greek Internationalisms – or NGIs, as Görlach (1999) calls them – in English. The Greek elements that can now freely combine to form technical terms include both prefixed elements such as *apo-*, *auto-*, *bio-*, *di-*, *dia-*, *eco-*, *hetero-*, *neo-*, *poly-*, *tele-*, *thermo-* and *xeno-*, and suffixal ones such as *-cracy*, *-gamy*, *-graph(y)*, *-logy*, *-meter*, *-nomy*, *-pathy*, *-phoby*, *-phone* and *-scope* (Görlach, 1999: 111–12).

The consequences of augmenting the technical and scientific lexis of the English language by systematic introduction of neo-classical and other Latinate elements were twofold. As Görlach (1999: 114–15) notes, the stock of these words is international, and they are widely intelligible across language boundaries. They have therefore significantly increased the transparency of English worldwide, and greatly enhanced its role as an international lingua franca of science and technology. The inevitable downside of neo-classical coinages and extensive borrowing is that they make English vocabulary less transparent and intelligible to native speakers, and are hence instrumental in raising a 'language bar' between the educated and uneducated. The sharp contrast between a largely Germanic common core and non-native special-register lexis amounts to a dual lexicon – or 'double tongue', as Adamson (1989) calls it – causing linguistic insecurity and problems of acquisition. They are reflected in a wide variety of vocabulary-related activities ranging from spelling bees to courses in vocabulary building in school curricula, and continue to guarantee the popularity of usage guides. Large portions of these guides are devoted to lexical matters – from 'elegant variation' and 'superfluous words' to the famous 'pairs and snares', *contemptuous* and *contemptible*, *deprecate* and *depreciate*, *masterful* and *masterly*, etc. (Fowler, 1926).

5.3.5   Registers

As was shown in Sections 5.3.3 and 5.3.4, standard English grammar and vocabulary both have a common core but may vary according to register. We have also seen that there have been a number of centres of focussing to promote linguistic standardisation in particular registers. One of the first to have a supralocal impact on register-specific language was no doubt the king's chancery in the fifteenth century (see Section 5.2.1). It is nevertheless arguable whether chancery writings served as immediate stylistic models in genres other than official documents. The most influential of these documents were the Acts of Parliament, the first one being issued in English in 1483.

The Statutes of the Realm are characterised by compactness and precision of expression. In the fifteenth and sixteenth centuries these characteristics were reflected in linguistic features such as participial adjectives with anaphoric reference (*the (afore)mentioned, the (afore)said*), compound adverbs (*herewith, thereof*), and compound noun-phrase determiners (***this his*** *realm,* ***any our*** *grant*). The requirement of precision gave rise to new clausal links such as *except* and *provided (that)* based on French and Latin models. Some of these features continue as the hallmark of legalese today (*the said, herewith*), while others have become obsolete in all registers (*this his*). Others still, typically conjunctions like *except* and *provided that*, spread to other registers – but not without native competition from less formal contexts of use. One of the competitors of *except* was *unless*, which surpassed it as a conjunction in most contexts in the seventeenth century (Rissanen, 1999b: 200 and 2000: 126–7).

In the course of the last four or five hundred years, the functional elaboration of standard English has been marked by the proliferation of genre-specific styles. One way to weigh their similarities and differences is to consider particular individual linguistic features of these styles, as was done above with statutory language. A more complex task is to compare the various paths of development undergone by whole genres across time. This kind of reconstruction can be based on the idea that there are sets of functionally related linguistic features which co-occur in a genre at any given time. It has been established by quantitative methods, for instance, that face-to-face conversations and personal letters today typically show high frequencies of features expressing personal involvement, including first- and second-person pronouns, private verbs (e.g. *think, know*), *that*-deletion, present-tense verbs, contractions (*it's, won't*), hedges (*maybe, sort of*), emphatics and amplifiers (*really, totally*). By contrast, academic texts, such as scientific research articles, exhibit few involvement markers. They focus on information and display features such as high frequencies of nouns, prepositions, attributive adjectives, long words and varied lexis (Biber, 1988, 1995).

Register comparisons based on bundles of linguistic features show several contextual dimensions reflected in linguistic variation in different kinds of speech and writing in present-day English. Comparisons carried out with historical material from the early Modern English period onwards also reveal trends of diachronic register evolution along these dimensions. Apart from involved as opposed to informational production, they include situation-dependent as opposed to elaborated reference, and non-impersonal vs impersonal style. The three dimensions all distinguish between stereotypically oral (conversational) registers and stereotypically literate (written expository) registers. Biber & Finegan (1997) discuss how such popular written registers as essays and fiction largely develop in a more oral direction along these three dimensions between 1650 and 1990 in both British and American English. By contrast, such specialist expository registers as legal, medical and other scientific writings reveal a consistent trend towards the more literate end of these dimensions: they all show varying tendencies of increasingly informational production, elaborated reference and impersonal style (see also Biber et al., 1994).

Some aspects of this generic specialisation may be illustrated by two scientific texts, both describing experiments which deal with electricity, an expanding field of research referred to in Section 5.3.4 above. The first passage comes from the first book on electricity to appear in the English language. It was published in 1675 by Robert Boyle (1627–91), an Anglo-Irish chemist and founding member of the Royal Society.

EXPER. I

ANd first, having with a very mild heat slowly evaporated about a fourth part of good Turpentine, I found, that the remaining body would not, when cold, continue a Liquor, but harden'd into a transparent Gum almost like Amber, which, as I look'd for, proved Electrical.

EXPER. II

SEcondly, by mixing two such liquid Bodies as *Petroleum* and strong Spirit of Nitre in a certain proportion, and then distilling them till there remained a dry mass, I obtain'd a brittle substance as black as Jet; and whose Superficies (where it was contiguous to the Retort) was glossie like that Mineral when polished; and as I expected I found it also to resemble Jet, in being endowed with an Electrical Faculty.   (Robert Boyle, *Experiments and Notes about the Mechanical Origine or Production of Electricity*, 1675: 21–2)

The second extract is taken from *An Elementary Treatise on Electricity* by James Clerk Maxwell (1831–79), the Scottish physicist and developer of the theory of electromagnetism. The treatise, based on his earlier, more extensive exposition, was published posthumously in 1881.

Electric phenomena of Tourmaline

141.] Certain crystals of tourmaline and of other minerals possess what might be called Electric Polarity. Suppose a crystal of tourmaline to be at a uniform temperature, and apparently free from electrification on its surface. Let its temperature be now raised, the crystal remaining insulated. One end will be found positively and the other end negatively electrified. Let the surface be deprived of this apparent electrification by means of a flame or otherwise; then if the crystal be made still hotter, electrification of the same kind as before will appear, but if the crystal be cooled the end which was positive when the crystal was heated will become negative. (James Clerk Maxwell, *An Elementary Treatise on Electricity*, 2nd edition, 1888: 117)

As both texts have few time and place adverbials or adverbs in general, they do not rely on the external context for interpretation. But neither are they very elaborated in terms of reference: they contain, for instance, only a few nominalisations (e.g. *electrification* in Maxwell) and wh-relatives (**which** . . . *proved Electrical*, **whose** *Superficies* . . . , in Boyle and **which** *was positive* in Maxwell). The two texts, however, markedly differ in their use of impersonal style, which is signalled by frequent use of passives, both agentless and *by*-passives, and passive postnominal clauses. Boyle has two passive forms (*when polished*; *being endowed with*), while Maxwell's slightly shorter passage contains as many as nine (e.g. *what might be called*; *if the crystal be made still hotter*). Boyle also shows personal involvement by referring to himself both here and elsewhere in his treatise, whereas Maxwell avoids self-references. This striking movement away from an author-centred approach is well documented from the seventeenth century onwards, for instance, in the research articles published in the *Philosophical Transactions of the Royal Society of London* (Atkinson, 1996).

Generic focussing is typically accompanied by an increase in technical terminology in the various branches of science over the last couple of centuries. Present-day scientific prose shares general features such as technical taxonomies, lexical density and nominalisations. They are singled out by M. A. K. Halliday (1993: 71) as grammatical problems typical of scientific English. His list does not stop here; it also mentions interlocking definitions, syntactic ambiguity, and semantic discontinuity. Having started off with the classical models of the Renaissance and the simplicity advocated by the Royal Society, the functional elaboration of standard English has resulted in conventions in these fields that require science literacy – learning how to access these specialist genres not only in terms of content but also of the linguistic forms they typically assume in writing.

5.3.6   Pronunciation

The story of English pronunciation standards runs parallel to spelling and grammar in that, from early on, there is evidence of supralocal usages, or recommendations for such usages. Many early commentators typically focus on varieties rather than on any particular features of pronunciation. In *The Arte of English Poesie*, first published in 1589, George Puttenham advises prospective poets to follow 'the vsuall speach of the Courte, and that of London and the shires lying about London within lx. myles, and not much aboue' ([1589] 1968: 120). Puttenham's 'usual speech' refers to both social and regional focussing, as he suggests that poets should imitate 'the better brought-up sort' in London and in the home counties. Their language and pronunciation, he argues, is widely understood throughout the country. John Hart, a phonetician and orthoepist writing twenty years before Puttenham, agrees with him on the 'best speech', which Hart, too, finds is spoken in and around London and at the royal court by the learned and literate (Danielsson, 1963: 31–4).

Valuable though the orthoepists' accounts are, they do not tell us much about pronunciation differences in London and the home counties at the time. Although the present-day standard pronunciations of a large number of individual words may be traced to a variety of regional sources – probably reflecting dialect mixing in the capital region at any one time – the fact that focussing was taking place must have been of significance. The ideology of standardisation itself may have contributed to increased uniformity (Lass, 1999: 7). But there is also some evidence that the degree of focussing may not have remained at the same level in the following century. Mugglestone (2003: 14) exercises caution when interpreting some seventeenth-century pronunciation treatises:

> Nevertheless, it should not be assumed that such statements indicate the existence of a 'standard' of speech, either in terms of process or ideology, which is akin to that described, and, more importantly, prescribed in the late eighteenth and nineteenth centuries. Coles, for instance, writing in the late seventeenth century evidently feels constrained to defend his choice of the one variety of 'proper' pronunciation which he documents in his book, a situation inconceivable a century later.

Multiple centres of phonological norms continue to be a source of complaints in the eighteenth century. Thomas Sheridan (1719–88), an Irish-born actor and theatrical manager, laments the lack of uniformity in the preface to his *General Dictionary of the English Language* (1780): 'There is a great diversity of pronunciation of the same words, not only in individuals, but in whole bodies of men. That there are some adopted by the universities; some prevail at the bar, and some in the senate-house' (quoted in MacMahon, 1998: 383). The kind of variability that worried Sheridan included word-initial /h/-dropping, simplification of word-initial /wh/ to /w/ in words like *while* and *whet*, and unstressed syllables not being given their full, stressed values. To create uniformity and to 'fix' the language, Sheridan makes a strong appeal in favour of imitating the speech patterns of the court. Although the other leading London orthoepist of the time, John Walker, downplays the amount of variation in his *Critical Pronouncing Dictionary* (1791), other dictionary compilers give evidence of a large number of variant pronunciations at the time (MacMahon, 1998: 382–4).

   The term *Received Pronunciation* (RP) was first coined by the dialectologist Alexander Ellis (1869: 23), who in his *On Early English Pronunciation* defined it as the educated accent 'of the metropolis, of the court, the pulpit, and the bar'. Ellis based his accent classification on social criteria, and singled out the various public domains of language use as the centres of focussing where the standard norms were set. Although he maintains that Received Pronunciation may be heard throughout the country, he adds that those who come from the provinces are likely to retain traces of their regional accents in their pronunciation. Geographical focussing is also therefore clearly in evidence: the educated pronunciation of London and the court takes precedence over other educated accents in the country.

   It is only relatively recently that the norms of standard British (or rather English) English pronunciation were first systematically codified. Attempts were made to that effect in pronunciation dictionaries in the late eighteenth century by Walker (1791) and, in particular, Sheridan (1780). However, a more detailed codification did not become possible until the International Phonetic Alphabet (IPA) came into existence and began to be used by Henry Sweet, Daniel Jones and their fellow phoneticians in the late nineteenth and early twentieth centuries. Jones' works ran into a large number of editions, *An Outline of English Phonetics*, first published in its entirety in 1918, into as many as nine. His *English Pronouncing Dictionary* came out in 1917 and underwent a series of revisions first by Jones himself, and later by A. C. Gimson and Susan Ramsaran (14th edition, 1977). Its sixteenth edition, prepared by Peter Roach and James Hartman, came out in 2003. The most comprehensive recent work in the field is John Wells' *Longman Pronunciation Dictionary* (1990), which shows both RP and General American pronunciations.

By its very nature, pronunciation does not, however, easily lend itself to standardisation. Jones (1963: 13) himself points out in his *Outline* that he cannot offer a full and uniform description of RP. He primarily aims at describing the slower colloquial style, which he deems suitable for the use of foreign learners as well. The variation inherent in RP is similarly discussed by A. C. Gimson, whose *Introduction to the Pronunciation of English* was first published in 1962 (2nd edition, 1970). Gimson (1970: 88) distinguishes three varieties of RP: 'conservative', 'general', and 'advanced'. According to Gimson, conservative RP is used by the older generation and certain professions, general RP is typified by the pronunciation adopted by the BBC, whereas advanced RP is mainly used by young people of some exclusive social groups and in certain professional circles.

In Alan Cruttenden's revised version of Gimson (1994: 80), the chief RP varieties are labelled 'general', 'refined' and 'regional'. Refined RP is used to refer to upper-class usage, with declining numbers of speakers, while the label regional RP is based on geographical rather than social variation. Cruttenden (1994: 80–1) defends his choice of label by saying that although regional RP may sound like a contradiction in terms, it reflects the fact that there is today a far greater tolerance of dialectal variation in all walks of life (the term 'modified regional pronunciation' is used by Gimson, 1970: 87). What looked like a heightening of focussing in the first half of the twentieth century, appears to have subsided and resulted in less focalised norms. This may be due to several factors, not least the fact that one of the main centres of pronunciation focussing, the BBC, no longer exercises as strict a pronunciation policy with regard to the use of RP as it used to. Moreover, with the widening range of English-speaking mass media in the last few decades, the position of the BBC as the major trendsetter is itself undergoing change.

As suggested by Wells' pronunciation dictionary, which describes two varieties of standard English, English pronunciation standards differ significantly from grammar norms in that they are not global. Standard English grammar is compatible with a variety of accents both in Britain and globally. While about 12–15 per cent of the population of England are native speakers of standard English, perhaps 7–12 per cent speak it with some kind of regional accent. This means, as pointed out by Trudgill (1999b: 2–3), that only between 3 and 5 per cent of the population of England speak general, non-regional RP. According to some estimates, the figure is less than 3 per cent (Crystal, 1995: 365).

Other national pronunciation standards have arisen throughout the English-speaking world, including a focussed standard Scottish form of pronunciation, which has a long history (C. Jones, 1994). The former strong RP influence is also declining in more recent British-based varieties such as Australian, New Zealand and South African English. All of them have evolved a range of accents of their own from Cultivated to General and Broad. While the Cultivated or Conservative variety is still focussed on RP, the General – or Respectable, as the South African taxonomy has it – one is distinctly local. While the General varieties are not stigmatised, they may not be the obvious choice of accent, for instance, 'for the more up-market sectors of the electronic media' (Lass, 1990: 272–3; see also Trudgill & Hannah, 1994).

Because of a longer period of separation, the normative status of British pronunciation standards had begun to decline earlier in the United States. Voices started to be heard in favour of current American forms of pronunciation at the end of the eighteenth and beginning of the nineteenth centuries. 'American pronunciations' were promoted, among others, by the young lexicographer Noah Webster. But opposing views were also propagated, notably in the pronouncing dictionaries published by Joseph Worcester between 1830 and 1860. Where American pronunciations were different from British, Worcester preferred British forms, regarding them as 'better', 'more accurate' and 'more harmonious and agreeable' (Bronstein, 1990: 139). Throughout the nineteenth century, pronunciation focussing in the United States was divided between two centres: educated usage at home and in England.

Even today, there are fundamental differences between American and British English pronunciation standards. Although no longer looking to British models, American English has not developed a high degree of focussing. As there are a number of non-stigmatised regional accents used by educated speakers, Romaine (1998: 39) suggests that US English might be viewed as accentually pluricentric. Alternatively, it is possible to focus on the lack of distinctive dialect characteristics and speak about a mainstream accent associated with the levelled dialects of the northern midwest as standard. However, as shown by Dennis Preston's studies in perceptual dialectology (e.g. 1996), ordinary people can rarely agree where the *best* American English is spoken. It is easier for them to reach agreement on where and by whom the *worst* US English is spoken (by e.g. Southerners, New Yorkers, African Americans, Asians, Mexican Americans).

Pronunciation dictionaries such as Wells (1990) resort to the label *General American* (GA) to refer to the pronunciation of US speakers with no noticeable eastern or southern accent. This widely used label might suggest a fair degree of supralocalisation and extensive codification. While the former is the case, the latter is not. One of the few detailed descriptions of 'General American' is John Kenyon & Thomas Knott's *A Pronouncing Dictionary of American English* (1944, 1953), which was intended as the American counterpart to Daniel Jones' RP dictionary. Kenyon & Knott based their description on the colloquial speech of cultivated speakers of American English. The work remains, according to Bronstein (1990: 146–7), to date 'the only significantly comprehensive pronunciation lexicon for American English, despite the fact that linguistic/phonetic research over the past

40 years does render it somewhat out of date'. Although a new edition of Kenyon & Knott appeared in 1975, there is apparently no great demand for a codified version of GA.

5.3.7   Conclusion

History suggests that the two requirements set for a standard language, maximum application (generality) and minimum variation (focussing), are not likely to be met by an international language like English. These conditions are best fulfilled by the spelling system, which is the most fully standardised part of standard English: it is shared by all English-writing nations and shows the least national variation (such as the *-our/-or* variation between British and American English in words like *harbour/ harbor*). This global success of spelling standard-isation may be attributed to its continued institutional support: it is maintained by the systems of education and government and the role played by the printed word in the mass media.

On all other linguistic levels, the standard proves either less focussed or has a more limited distribution. Besides features shared by the great majority of English dialects, standard English grammar contains a codified set of features that rarely appear in other, non-standard varieties, such as the suffix *-s* in the third-person singular present indicative. Although the core grammar of standard English is fixed worldwide, the problem of fuzzy edges, however, remains: it is not always easy to tell where standard grammar ends and non-standard begins. Pressure continues to be exerted even on the codified core by colloquial usages. The *New Fowler* notes, for instance, that the old resistance to the conjunction *like* is now slowly beginning to crumble (*Gordon needs Sylvia **like** some people need to spend an hour or two every day simply staring out of the window* – P. Lively, *Moon Tiger*, 1987; Burchfield, 1996: 458). As this and many other cases indicate, the history of standard English clearly continues as a combination of processes, not as a fixed product, both in terms of levels of language and of individual linguistic elements.

The common core of English vocabulary consists of a large, mostly Germanic element shared by all speakers of English, standard and non-standard alike. The extension of the vernacular in the Modern English period to all domains of language use and to all four corners of the world has led to further lexical convergence – but also to divergence. On the one hand, the global expansion of English has been followed by growing lexical differentiation to fulfil the local needs met by national varieties. On the other hand, many international domains of language use such as the news media now further strengthen the worldwide common core. In many technical registers, the usage does not, however, build on the core. As the tradition in word coining from the Renaissance onwards has been to resort to foreign borrowing in technical and learned contexts, Latinate lexis has come to dominate them. These borrowed elements effectively reduce the number of competent native speakers in many specialised domains of standard language use.

On all levels of language, register variation emerges as one of the key factors setting limits to the codification and generalisation of language standards. While it may not be unproblematic to regulate all the various aspects of the written word, many of them are maintained and reinforced through the institutions of education and the printing press. It is harder, if not impossible, to do the same with colloquial speech. This is particularly true of pronunciation. There has never been one standard accent shared by all speakers of standard English. The current norms are further affected by the fact that national broadcasting companies such as the BBC no longer serve as the norm enforcers they used to be in the past. New local centres of pronunciation focussing also emerge. For some English speakers, Estuary English, 'a cockneyfied RP', lends the kind of prestige combined with popular acceptance that they value in their social and working lives. But even with the vastly improved communications of the electronic age, it is unlikely that an international pronunciation standard comparable to the spelling standard would see the light of day in the near future.

6 Names

Richard Coates

6.1 Theoretical preliminaries

6.1.1 The status of proper names

Names is a technical term for a subset of the nominal expressions of a language which are used for referring ('identifying or selecting in context') and, in some cases, for addressing a partner in communication. Nominal expressions are in general headed by nouns. According to one of the most ancient distinctions in linguistics, nouns may be common or proper, which has something to do with whether they denote a class or an individual (e.g. *queen* vs *Victoria*), where *individual* means a single-member set of any sort, not just a person. Much discussion has taken place about how this distinction should be refined to be both accurate and useful, for instance by addressing the obvious difficulty that a typical proper noun denoting persons may denote many separate individuals who bear it, and that common nouns may refer to individuals by being constructed into phrases (*the queen*). I will leave the concept [± proper], applied to nouns, for intuitive or educated recognition before returning to discussion of the inclusive concept of *proper names* directly. Proper nouns have no inherent semantic content, even when they are homonymous with lexical words (*Daisy, Wells*), and many, perhaps all, cultures recognise nouns whose sole function is to be proper (*Sarah, Ipswich*). Typically they have a unique intended referent in a context of utterance. Proper names are the class of such proper nouns included in the class of all expressions which have the properties of being devoid of sense and being used with the intention of achieving unique reference in context. *Onomastics* is the study of proper names, and concentrates on proper nouns; I shall confine the main subject-matter of this chapter to the institutionalised proper nouns associated with English and, in accordance with ordinary usage, I shall call them *proper names* or just *names*. Readers should note that strictly speaking these are a subset of proper names, and from time to time other members of the larger set will be discussed. There is some evidence from aphasiology and cognitive neuropsychology that institutionalised proper nouns – especially personal names – form a psychologically real class (Semenza & Zettin, 1989b; Semenza, 1997; and other papers from Semenza's team; van Lancker & Klein, 1990; the papers in Cohen & Burke, 1993; and the literature mentioned by Hanley & Kay, 1998).

Proper names are unlike other words of a language; indeed, it may be debated to what extent they really are part of the language with which they are conventionally associated. They obey the same synchronic constraints of phonology, with some marginal exceptions. Names change in ways related, though not always identical, to those applying to lexical words. Processes of reduction may be more radical in names than in corresponding lexical expressions: compare the older, defunct, pronunciation of the Northamptonshire village-name *Silverstone* /silsn/ (*PN Nth* 43) with that of the expression *silver stone* (which appears to have been the thirteenth-century name and which has nowadays been drafted in, with stress adjustment, to replace the older name form). Typically, on creation, proper names are formed of current lexical material and respect current principles of word formation. However, what invests a name with significance when it is created does not necessarily stay with it. In the roles they have to perform, names function independently of their etymological meaning and structure. County Oak (Sussex) has a name denoting a tree marking a county boundary. The oak has gone and the boundary has been moved; nevertheless the name serves perfectly well as a direct denotator of the place, and its written and spoken forms are semantically, synchronically, empty. It means only in an etymological way; it is not the sense which is transparent but its history. If I said that I lived by the pub, but that it isn't there any more, you would accuse me of not using words in their normal function; when used, concrete nouns carry a presupposition of the existence of a relevant example of what they denote. But names carry no obligation to use any lexical content they appear to have in order to do referring. Much English name study is devoted to uncovering the original meanings of proper names. Since linguistic change may have the effect of making structured names opaque, and therefore of allowing any synchronically opaque string of sounds or letters to function as a proper name, it is possible to exploit this characteristic by inventing names consisting of arbitrary material. The consequences of this important point will surface from time to time below. It has been refined into the *Onymic Default Principle*, which states that the default interpretation of any string of linguistic units is a proper name (Coates, 2005a).

This might be taken as implying that the set of lexical items is divided into words and phrases, whose elements and structure are meaningful at the moment of usage, and names, whose elements and structures are not. However, many – probably most – names are meaningful on creation or bestowal, but cease to be meaningful as time passes. At what point do they stop being meaningful? We might argue that an act of name-bestowal has as a component a formal abrogation of meaning (i.e. of sense). If I had been a Puritan in seventeenth-century England, I might have called my daughter *Charity*, and I would have done so by appropriating to my own use the word *charity* in full recognition of its meaning. On baptism, that meaning would disappear insofar as the linguistic string was used to refer to my daughter. *Charity* as a lexeme would be uncompromised if the girl turned out uncharitable; and if she did, *Charity* would be no less valid as her name.

Many names, though, especially place-names, appear to ease into existence through the wearing-down of full expressions, rather than by being bestowed. In a Berkshire charter originally drafted in about 950 CE, a boundary point was referred to as *ut on fulan Riþe* 'out to (the) foul stream' (definiteness is marked by the adjectival inflection here, not by a definite article; cf. Section 3.2.2). The stream is now called *Foudry Brook*; the first word perpetuates the ancient description. At some point it became opaque because it is opaque now. There may well have been a time when some people used this string of words in full knowledge of their etymology and used them fully meaningfully ('go to the foul stream') whilst for others they were simple indicators of a place ('go to Foulstream'). The second group were further down the road to properhood. It follows from that that properness – absence of sense – is a matter of the intention (or at any rate of some mental state) of the user at the time of utterance (Coates, 2000, 2005a, forthcoming a). A name is fully proper when no one uses it with a primary intention to convey linguistic meaning – and that may be the end of a protracted process.

This *onomastic divorce* of names from the matrix of their source language allows some linguistic processes to affect them earlier and more thoroughly than the rest of the vocabulary (Clark, 1992a: 453; Colman, 1988b, 1990). Compound names may be obscured and sound-developments may affect names radically, resulting in greater attrition than in corresponding expressions of the language. Conversely, some names are exempt from otherwise general changes; there are still traces of an otherwise lost Old English (OE) definite adjectival inflection *-an* in such names as *Stapenhill* (Staffordshire), and of a nominal dative plural *-um* in *Newsham* (Yorkshire, North Riding). These facts make name material difficult to handle when trying to study historical phonology and/or morphology and dialectology, as they may appear to disobey sound laws or be exceptional to grammatical processes; and their status as evidence for or against the operation of such changes may be problematic.

All (proper) names are morphosyntactically definite but most in English have no definite article. A theoretical account of this is offered by Longobardi (1994), who suggests that, in general, proper nouns occupy the determiner position in noun phrases 'because [they] are rigid designators' in Kripke's sense (1982: *passim*). Exceptions which do have an article range from those which are arguably not yet proper for all users, i.e. are ambiguous between proper and common readings, such as *The East Anglian Heights*, to not readily explicable exceptions, such as the hill-name *The Cheviot* (Northumberland) and the waterway-name *The Solent* (Hampshire). The synchronic opacity of these last two names is not what protects the article – compare the names for similar features *Skiddaw* (Cumberland), *Wallet* (Essex), which are equally opaque but do not have one – but it may well be retained in names with no synchronic lexically recognisable head. Other names have more or less explicitly definite sources by having the name of an individual or an expression denoting an individual (without an article) as the specifier: *St Edmundsbury* (diocese, Suffolk), *Kingston* (*passim*).

Names as onomastic items do not inflect for number. *Hale* and *Hales* must be different places, despite having etymologies which are distinct only as regards number. If they do pluralise, names do not do so in virtue of any lexical content (*three Middletons* means 'three places called *Middleton*' and not 'three middle villages'). If they are inherently plural, they do not singularise without loss of properness; *the Yorkshire moor* (as in *the Yorkshire moor on which I grew up*) is not the singular of *The Yorkshire Moors*, and *the Pennine* can only be interpreted as a jocular expression 'a definite one of the things collectively called *The Pennines*'. Some morphosyntactic changes are found most often in names; it is not uncommon for oblique case forms (usually datives functioning as locatives) to replace original nominatives, as with *Newsham* mentioned above and as with *Bury*, which is usually from *byrig*, the dative singular of *burg*, whose nominative form turns up by strict subjection to known phonological changes as *Borough*. Some OE place-names have elements in specifier position that are neither the base form of a noun nor its genitive singular.

6.1.2   Namables

What kinds of things may bear names? All cultures appear to deploy names for individual persons and for places. They may be chosen from a traditional stock, as has been the case for most of the history of English personal names, or created at the point of bestowal from current linguistic materials and therefore meaningful to the bestower, as for example with Yoruba personal names. Instances of the latter type may in all cultures drift into the former, at first through the commemoration of people previously bearing a particular name. These names, however they are acquired, are not necessarily the sole or even dominant means of referring to the individual named. For instance, Koreans all bear personal names, but their traditional conversational way of referring to an adult person or even addressing them may be by an expression (*teknonym*) meaning 'mother/father of [name of their eldest child]', and similar though less systematic phenomena can be found in English too, for example in *pro-names* (generalised non-proper names that may act as name-surrogates) such as *Mum* and *Dad*. Place-names also appear to be a universal category, and may either evolve through conversational use from expressions descriptive of the site or be created and bestowed by deliberate acts.

Personal names appear to be the prototypical names, as all humans have over-whelming interest (1) in being able to refer conversationally to other humans with the expectation of uniquely identifying them in context, and (2) in catching the attention of other humans individually. Accordingly, personal names typically have both a referential and a vocative function. Their fundamental nature is also seen in the way they are applicable to other categories of individual, for instance animals. Places gain significance because we all move and act in space, so they gain significance through the way(s) in which they fit into human perceptions of landscape, townscape and starscape, which is what governs their naming. Other categories of object may bear proper names, and the more intimately associated with human activity a type of object is, the more readily it seems able to acquire a proper name, though the systematic application of names to other categories is quite rare, and the degree of intimacy with which something is felt to be associated with human activity may vary from culture to culture.

Everyone will have noted that some objects in classes not generally bearing names are occasionally named. In my experience of literature or real life I have come across a mandolin named *Antonia*, a steam-powered dildo called *Steely Dan*, a diamond called *Koh-i-Noor*, a child's chair called *Fifi*, a bell called *Great Tom*, windmills called *Jack* and *Jill*, a dishwasher called *Oscar*, a tree called *The Major Oak*, lottery machines called *Arthur* and *Guinevere*, and a streetcar named *Desire*. Many of these are transferred from the set of primordial names: personal names. The very nature of properhood (cf. Section 6.1.1), a conversational device for promoting maximally successful individual reference in context whilst cancelling any linguistic senses or implicatures of the expressions used, means that any individual 'thing' of any category may in principle bear a proper name, so whether any of the namings in this paragraph causes surprise has to do with whether they uphold or violate cultural expectation, and not with the linguistic nature of names.

Some particular name may be traditionally associated with one category of things. But it would be simplistic to regard a name form as in itself (e.g.) a personal name. *Dr Syntax* was a character invented by the writer William Combe. His versified exploits were very popular in the early 1800s and a famous racehorse, twice winner of the Preston Gold Cup, was named after him. A pub in Preston bears the name of the horse. Items that began as place-names may become surnames and then personal names (*Shirley, Tracy, Everton*); place-names may be adaptations of names for persons (*Telford, Peterlee, Washington*). A linguistic string has a default interpretation as a proper name, but it follows from that that its intended referent-type needs to be inferred in the context of usage, which includes participants' personal experience of naming. But from the linguistic point of view a name is just a name, with limitless applicability in principle.

6.1.3   Properhood and tropes

Any proper name may come to be used as a common noun or in a common expression (*cardigan, sandwich, john, dobermann, (baked) alaska, (eau de) cologne, china*). This may happen through a trope by which an object is associated with a named individual, and by its subsequent taking-on of that individual's name; the trope is seen nakedly in *Amsterdam is the Venice of the North*, but in this case the name has not been borrowed – *Venice* has not come to have 'Amsterdam' among its meanings. In the case of wellingtons, the type of boots associated with the first Duke of Wellington came to be known as *Wellington boots* and then *wellington boots*, and by conversational omission of the generic, *wellingtons* (and latterly *wellies*). This process may be paralleled in cases where the name has been bestowed, rather than being produced conversationally, as with the common nouns denoting sizes of champagne bottle which are applications of personal names found in the Bible (1 Kings 9:28). And any common expression may court properhood by being used of unique objects such as *The Milky Way* or *The Great Barrier Reef*, being proper only if none of the possible literal inferences derivable from the expression is intended at the moment of usage, e.g. 'there exists a way which is milky' or 'the reef is a barrier' (Coates, 2000).

6.2 English onomastics

6.2.1 The discipline of English onomastics

Current onomastic work in the United Kingdom seeks to explain the linguistic origin of personal and place-names or to assess the historical significance of their distribution, and in the latter case as applied to personal names it is a tool of genealogy, and genealogical methods help refine historical-linguistic analysis. There have been small amounts of recent work on the social psychology of personal naming and nicknaming. There is sporadic work on literary onomastics (dealing with proper names for characters and locations in fictional works), but more in North America. In English-speaking countries beyond the British Isles, and indeed also in Ireland, Wales and Scotland, there is considerable interest in the heritage of names derived from languages that have been partly or totally displaced (for instance in North America and Australia), and in the cultural contexts in which naming has taken place, information about which tends to be of greater interest than in England, where the contexts of naming that generate most interest are medieval. In the words of William Bright: 'American onomatologists . . . have given greater emphasis to "the motivation of the namer" – to the "human activity" of naming.'

6.2.2 Source materials for English onomastics

The Anglo-Saxon (AS) period yields chronicles, coins and 'charters' (often writs and land grants or confirmations). *Domesday Book (DB)* may be regarded as the final collection of AS evidence and the first medieval collection. It is indispensable for many areas where it represents both the first and the last evidence for AS names, especially in the north of England. *DB* is actually a set of books, but they portray the facts of landholding immediately pre- and post-Conquest. Those responsible for carrying out the survey were Norman French speakers accustomed to writing in Latin and had little or no experience of English except for what local informants might tell them. That makes it a frustrating document; it offers many obstacles to the interpretation of the names. In addition, some of the returns of the commissioners who toured the country to establish what the Conqueror's tax-base was have been reworked. We may therefore be at several removes from an actual mention of an English name when we find it on a folio of *DB*. Spelling is a severe problem, with scribes not conversant with the orthographic practices of the AS administrative system. Names are the most information-intensive of linguistic material, with low predictability in context, and the context of collection was hardly designed to combat this problem, so we are not surprised to find a document requiring careful linguistic analysis and yielding sometimes disheartening results. Many other AS documents exist only in later, post-Conquest, copies, often in c(h)artularies (collections of transcriptions); during the Middle Ages consistency of spelling did not rank as a virtue and was probably not even conceptualised. Until the fifteenth century, documents containing names were overwhelmingly written in Latin or French, and what is by origin an English name is often presented in one or the other guise (e.g. *in civitate Scrobbensis* 901; *Saropesberia* eleventh century; *Salopie* or *Salopia* thirteenth century, all meaning '(at) Shrewsbury' (*PN Sa* I: 267–71)). Name records need analysis in the light of scribal practice and textual history.

Other AS-period evidence is in inscriptions, chronicles and confraternity books. Coin inscriptions may display kings' and moneyers' names and locations of mints. An insight into the special difficulties in interpreting this material may be had from Smart (1979) and Colman (1984: 96–108; 1992: *passim*). The *Anglo-Saxon Chronicle* contains personal names mainly of dynastic importance, and place-names which surface according to the sweep of political history – few and random except to the extent that major events happened in significant places. In the absence of an AS *DB*, the prime source for early English names is Bede's *Historia ecclesiastica gentis Anglorum*, finalised in about 731. The confraternity books of Durham and Hyde (Winchester) are lists of names of benefactors, built up incrementally (like chronicles), and giving few hints as to the social and ethnic status of the persons named.

Many documents from the medieval period are now available in reasonably user-friendly editions, but these documents may be of different interest and value according to the degree of local knowledge possessed by the drafter or copyist, and especially for place-name purposes the most locally aware documents tend to be of the greatest value. Legal and central administrative documents may perpetuate errors or archaisms; local documents may give evidence of linguistic innovation. Later the volume of documentation containing name forms increases exponentially. Sources may be public or domestic, published or unpublished, verbal or cartographic.

6.3   Personal names

6.3.1   Preliminaries

Following Clark (1992a), the term *personal name* will be used for a name bestowed on an individual as a matter of conscious choice. This concept is to be distinguished from one inherited (*patronym* or *metronym* vs *family-name (surname)*), or one applied because it is appropriate to the person, ironically or otherwise (*by-name*). The term *nickname* can be used restrictively to mean a personal name not falling into one of the other categories, for example *Tug* and *Nobby*, the once-traditional but now almost forgotten names automatically bestowed on men with the surname *Wilson* and *Clark*, respectively – bestowed because thought appropriate to the surname, not to the person. For further information see the section on Further Reading.

6.3.2   The earliest English personal names

The AS period is interesting as being the last when the linguistic material of most personal names was English. Since then, only an upsurge of Puritan naming in the sixteenth and seventeenth centuries and some special fashions in the last 200 years of the second millennium have relied significantly on English words. The earliest naming practice among the Germanic peoples was geared to the production of a large number of distinct names, because custom required a single name unique to the individual bearing it – at least ideally. The most characteristic AS names are composed of a single element, usually coinciding in form with an OE lexical word, or of two such elements, selected from partly overlapping lists, where the second relates to the sex of the bearer (not to be confused with the grammatical gender of the word). Scholars call such names *monothematic* and *dithematic* respectively; each of the elements is a *theme*. The two-element structure was the engine which generated a constant supply of new names. Originally the supply was sufficient to satisfy a society with no central records and no large groupings of people in regular interaction with each other, and which therefore could tolerate occasional duplication that might be remedied through by-naming. Later, certain combinations became favoured and therefore replicated, and this led to the emergence of other naming strategies to help achieve disambiguation of reference in context: certainly the creation of surnames in Europe, and possibly the more systematic creation of by-names, though we have no real evidence for the antiquity or otherwise of the latter as a systematic device. The best wide-ranging discussions of OE name elements are Ström (1939) and Anderson (1941), supplemented by Colman (1992: 71–125), and for an excellent culturally situated discussion see also Insley (2002).

The system is substantially the one inherited from Common West Germanic (CWGmc). In the two-element names, either element might be either an adjective or a noun, and in some instances a bound morpheme with a comparable sort of lexical meaning. A few were synchronically opaque in recorded OE. The list of first elements (*protothemes*, written *X-* below) is larger than that of second elements (*deuterothemes*, written *-x* below). The themes are not semantically random. Those which predominate have to do with group identification and loyalty (*Swæf-* 'Swabian', *þēod-* 'nation'), physical and moral prowess and its rewards (*Beald-/-beald* 'brave', *Weald-/-weald* 'power', *Beorht-/-beorht* and *Æðel-* 'noble', *Cūð-* and *-mǣr* 'famous'), the warrior life (*Hild-/-hild* and *Wīg-/ -wīg* 'battle', *-brord* and *-gār* 'spear', *Beorn-* 'warrior', *Wulf-/-wulf* 'wolf' or arguably 'warrior', *Here-/-here* 'army', *Sige-/-sige* 'victory', *Ēad-* 'prosperity, treasure') and pre-Christian religion (*Ōs-* 'deity', *Ælf-* 'elf', *Rūn-/-rūn* 'secret, mystery'). Less easy to categorise are *-stān* 'stone', *Eorp-* 'red' and *Ēast-* 'east'. Some themes appear related to more peaceful pursuits, but it is easy to see how they might fit into the conceptual framework of a culture that saw itself as a warrior people: *Rǣd-/-rǣd* 'counsel', *Burg-/-burg* 'pledge' and *Mund-/-mund* 'hand; protection', *-helm* 'protection; helmet'. *Friðu-/-frið* 'peace' might be viewed as the fruit of war, along with loot. That said, *Lēof-* 'dear' and *Wine-/-wine* 'friend' were also popular; maybe these should be understood in terms of comradeship in arms, though any such connotation is unlikely to have been permanent. The prototheme appeared in its stem form, and when the deuterotheme was inflected, male names were generally treated as *a*-stems and female ones as *ō*-stems (cf. Section 2.4.5), even where that was at variance with the morphology of the related lexical word, as with *-burg*.

Other kinds of name were known. Some ordinary lexemes standing uncompounded were used both for men (*Hengest* 'stallion', *Frōd* 'wise') and women (*Hild* 'battle', *Bēage* 'ring'). Some names are derived from other themes by suffixation, especially using the elements *-ing* (perhaps originally patronymic, e.g. *Lēofing*), *-el (Beorhtel)*, *-uc (Hwītuc)* and *-(i/e)ca (Haneca)*.

6.3.3   The impact of the Norman Conquest

Clark (1979: 13) suggests that '[i]n any homogeneous community, naming-behaviour will remain constant, except when disturbed by outside influence'. We might expect to find, therefore, that the system just described, except as disturbed by the Scandinavian settlement, would undergo rapid change around the Norman Conquest. Indeed, names of English origin declined fairly suddenly after 1066, but at different rates in different social groups (Clark, 1987a, 1987b), persisting till about 1250 only among the peasantry. Clark (1987b) explores various possibilities about the models adopted by the English for the naming of their own children after the new fashion, and notes occasional voluntary adoption of a new-style name, e.g. in adolescence as opposed to at baptism. Very few names of OE origin were preserved, the only really durable ones being of three popular saints, *Edmund, Edward* and *Cuthbert*.

The typical 'English' names of the Middle Ages and later fall mainly into two categories: French-mediated ones of CWGmc origin and French-mediated ones of customary saints. Germanic ones included *William, Robert, Richard, Gilbert, Alice, Eleanor, Rose/Rohais, Maud*, together with the Breton *Alan*; Christian names were those of biblical personages or post-biblical popular saints, including *Adam, Matthew, Bartholomew, James, Thomas, Andrew, Stephen, Nicholas, Peter/Piers, John* and its feminine *Joan, Anne, Margaret/Margery*, from the late twelfth century onwards, *Mary*, and from the fourteenth *Christopher*. Whilst the fortune of individual names ebbed and flowed in time and in place, this is the name stock for both sexes which until recently served as the canon of 'English' names. Other impacts were few; whilst the nobles played at being Knights of the Round Table, the names of the characters of the romances had little impact on their naming habits; children baptised *Arthur*, *Guenevere* and *Launcelot* appeared occasionally but *Galahad*, so far as I know, not at all, despite his unimpeachable character. The difference between this and the openness to literary and showbiz models evident since about 1550–1600 is very striking.

6.3.4   New names of the Renaissance and Reformation

The first systematic threat to this canon came in the sixteenth century (for the background to this see Wilson, 1998: chs. 9, 10). The new availability of printed books publishing the literature, mythology and scholarship of classical times offered a whole new name stock. Parents might bestow on their children names from antiquity; aristocratic parents led the way with such names as *Penelope* and *Ambrose* being used by the Essex and Warwick families respectively; others were *Cynthia*, *Diana*, *Ant(h)ony* and *Mark/Marcus* (though *Mark* might be for the evangelist). Formally, these might be either in the Latin nominative singular form (whatever the source: *Hercules*, not *Heracles*; *Theophilus* not *Theophilos*) or with anglicisation consisting of the dropping of some masculine suffixes; note that Shakespeare has *Antony* in *Antony and Cleopatra* but *Antonius* in *Julius Caesar*. In the longer term, anglicised forms dominated: *Mark*, *Claud(e)*, though their precise form might owe something to conventional modes of spelling derived from French. Only *Marcus* of male names still current retains its Latin form. In striking contrast, for females, forms of the Latin first declension have become accepted as normal, often alongside vernacularised forms: compare *Diana/Diane, Julia/Julie, Clara/Cla(i)re* and *Helena/Helen~Ellen~Elaine*; but it may well be important that some of these 'Latin' forms coincided phonologically (in England) with favoured Italian continuations or revivals of the names (e.g. *Diana, Giulia*). Since the Reformation these have gradually percolated through the English class system. A few Italian names became current in the sixteenth and seventeenth centuries, such as *Ferdinando* and *Orlando*. The latter shows the impact of vernacular literatures in England, since it is the name of Ariosto's epic hero (Italian for *Roland*), and Italian-derived literature has been responsible for the import of *Oliver, Juliet (Giulietta), Gulielma* and *Guido*.

These trends secured the position of *-a* as the mark of female names par excellence (cf. Lieberson & Mikelson, 1995), and which stimulated the popularity of many names in *-a* from a variety of sources (*Anna, Susanna, Eva, Olivia*) and in more modern times *-a* as a formative element used to create distinctively female names from male ones (*Roberta, Davina* – mainly Scottish, irregularly from *David*, which itself was more popular in medieval Scotland than in England – *Philippa* and *Georgia*).

These patterns of foreign influence over English naming can be traced unambiguously to prevailing cultural and political circumstances. Italy was the perceived source of much that was admired in the Renaissance. Spain was a source of suspicion because of its designs on the thrones of the Netherlands and of England itself, because of colonial rivalry, and because of its zealous counter-Reformation; for all its high cultural achievements during the period 1500–1700, it unsurprisingly did not offer a general model for naming practices.

Contemporary with these international currents were the first widespread appearances of Old Testament names given by religious radicals. We find *Solomon, Samuel, David, Nathaniel, Gamaliel* and *Isaac*, for example, some of which became popular whilst others did not. A further manifestation of Puritanism was the first outbreak of naming in English since the Norman Conquest. After an initial burst of religiously inspired naming in Latin (*Beata, Desiderius*), zealous reformers advised parents to give pious transparent English baptismal names to their children, such as *Much-Mercy, Increased, Sin-Deny* and *Fear-not*. This trend has been much ridiculed, but around 1600 some families gave names such as *Accepted, Thankful, Praisegod, Safe-on-High* (all male). At the extreme margin were the equally pious names recalling the fallen nature of human beings, such as *Job-rak'd-out-of-the-ashes, Fly-fornication* (wished on bastards of either sex) and the almost incredible Calvinistic *If-Christ-had-not-died-thou-hadst-been-damned* (Bardsley, 1880; sometimes cited in slightly varying forms).

Court fashion through successive dynasties was responsible for the promotion of some lasting naming trends. Elizabeth I set off single-handed the immense popularity of her own name (it replaced the Provençal form *Isabel* of the biblical original which had been popular in medieval times), whilst the vogue for European naming styles was cemented by the preference of the Stuart courts for dynastic links southwards.

6.3.5   The modern period

The eighteenth century brought the Latin renderings of some names popular from medieval times out of the archival closet to become popular in their own right, especially *Jo(h)anna* for *Joan* and *Matilda* for *Maud(e)*, and these blended effortlessly with the group in <-(i)a> from classical and other sources which was becoming a paradigm for female names.

French naming patterns of the eighteenth and nineteenth centuries showed some systematicity foreign to previous English traditions. In particular, female names could be derived from male ones by phonological and/or orthographic suffixation, favoured orthographic suffixes being the prototypical <-e>, and also <-ette/-otte> and <-ine>. Names of these types also entered English partly through the model of French naming used in the German royal house of Hanover, which acquired the English throne in 1714. To them we owe the widespread English use of such names as *Sophie* (originally Greek, but here frenchified), *Charlotte* and *Caroline*, and by other channels we have acquired *Denise, (Ni)Colette, Georgette, Suzette, Jacqueline, Christine, Thomasine* (especially in its Cornish-English form *Tamsin*), etc. Personal-name derivation works overwhelmingly in the direction male >> female in English.

The origin of some (especially female) given names, or rather their source as 'English' names, is known precisely, because they are literary inventions or adoptions by influential authors. Shakespeare was the inventor or the first populariser in England of *Juliet*, **Jessica* and *Cordelia*, Sidney of **Pamela* (though Richardson popularised it), Swift of **Vanessa*, Richardson of **Clarissa*, and Scott of *Brenda*; and **Scarlett* is due to the American author Margaret Mitchell (those marked * being inventions rather than adoptions or adaptations). Seventeenth-century literary fashion even provoked some novel morphology; the 'suffix' *-inda* was used in *Clarinda* (Spenser), *Belinda* (Pope, though he did not invent it), *Lucinda* (Steele) and such subsequent coinings as *Verinda*. A conspicuous movement in Victorian England was the promotion of abandoned names from history, especially saints' names, as a conscious rediscovery or invention and promotion of a 'British' heritage. To this movement we are indebted for *Maud(e)*, made wildly popular through the heroine of Tennyson's poem (1855). In this vein, the Oxford Movement (1833–) contributed names briefly popular, especially in High Church circles, deriving mainly from early British saints and abbots/abbesses, and scrupulously Christian English rulers, such as *Aidan, Kenelm, Alfred, Edwin, Ethel, Mildred, Hild* (usually in the Latin form *Hilda*) and the frenchified *Audrey* (i.e. St Etheldreda of Ely).

Since about 1800, there have been occasional waves of popularity in England for names that are, or are perceived as, of Scottish or Irish origin. From Scotland we have had *Duncan, Hamish, Alistair* and *Sheena*; and from Ireland, as anti-Irish prejudice finally began to evaporate in the mid-twentieth century, came *Caoimhín, Seán, Siobhán, Sinéad* or anglicised spellings of them (*Kevin, Sean/Shaun, Shevaun* and so on), usually at first indicating devotion to a media star with Gaelic forebears such as Sean Connery, Siobhán McKenna or Sinéad O'Connor, the 'Irishness' as such of the adopted name probably being of less significance than its distinctiveness and its source in the film or musical world.

The twentieth century also saw the continuing, renewed, or novel popularity of names (female especially) drawn from the Romance languages (but of whatever ultimate origin), such as *Marie, Maria, Marguerite, Corinne, Bianca, Louise, Patricia, Sylvia*. From a linguistic point of view, the most significant aspect of this trend was the cementing of particular phonological patterns as being stereotypical for female names, such as penultimate stress and final /-(i)ə/, the latter being represented orthographically by <-(i)a> (*Anna, Julia, Alexandra, Antonia, Marina, Martina, Saskia*).

The whole question of the fashion factor in driving the choice of names for children is dealt with by Lieberson & Bell (1992). Cutler, McQueen & Robinson (1990) demonstrated that current personal names have some further phonological characteristics that may be attributable to general sound symbolism. More than would be expected by chance, male names are monosyllabic, and, more than would be expected, female names are polysyllabic, non-initially stressed, and contain high front vowels in stressed position and in suffixal /-i/. The third characteristic is tentatively explained in terms of a universal tendency for [i] to symbolise smallness and therefore relative weakness.

A further trend worthy of notice is that of certain originally male names to be applied to females, and then to decline steeply in popularity (if ever truly popular) for males. This is true of, for instance, *Evelyn, Shirley, Hilary* and *Trac(e)y*, though males with these names are still found in small numbers in England. The social psychology of this process in America is discussed by Barry & Harper (1982). These scholars have also produced a series of papers dealing with the differences in linguistic attributes between male and female names, of which a sample is mentioned in the bibliography.

6.3.6   The most recent trends

In the late twentieth century, the restraining influence of the baptismal font has practically disappeared. English personal-naming practices have been blown wide open, mainly as a result of cultural currents emerging from the United States. In America, there were some practices that diverged from those in Britain; some names from these alternative traditions (even if only briefly) became popular through the influence of distinctively named Hollywood stars such as Ava Gardner and Marilyn Monroe. Female names dominated in this new climate, and many new female names entered the canon – if such there was – before 2000, whilst unambiguously new male names were quite few; conspicuously, the distinctive given names of prominent film stars and jazz and rock artists such as Rudolph Valentino, Thelonious Monk and Elvis Presley were never copied in large numbers. But the role of Nashville and Hollywood in promoting small bursts of popularity, e.g. for *Woody* (first probably from Woody [properly Woodrow Wilson] Guthrie, and then from Woody Harrelson), cannot be denied. For several briefly or currently fashionable names a showbiz or television source can be established: *Kylie, Keanu, Frazier, Chandler, Tyler.*

Tracking the progress of late-twentieth-century American given names is difficult because of their rapid turnover and the multiplicity of their sources; the ethnically varied makeup of the population has meant that especially European given names have had the opportunity to spread beyond their original communities; witness, for example, the recent popularity of such names as *André* and *Antonio* among African Americans. The moving staircase features, for example, *Tracey, Chelsea* and *Brittany* (and many spelling variants of each); these are mainly reapplied names drawn from other categories of namables. Names popular mainly in African American and Afro-Caribbean communities since around the mid-1960s have on the whole been more inventive, with whole rafts sharing phonological units that begin to look like morphological elements, though semantically empty – witness the many names in *La-* and *Sha-* like *Laverne* and *Latisha* (female) and *Shamika* (female) and *Shaquille* (male), and those in *Ma-* have had the unexpected consequence of allowing the reinterpretation of Scottish surnames in *M(a)c-* as female given names (*McKenna* and *Mackenzie* were popular in 2003). There is also much free, *ex nihilo*, creation, but Lieberson & Mikelson (1995) show that name giving in this community continues to be constrained by phonological patterns of names in the dominant community.

6.3.7 Modern English-language personal names

Much of the above is about names of a variety of origins being taken into use in English-speaking lands. There is rather little personal naming that could be called English in the sense of being formed of English lexical elements, and, as we have seen, some imported morphological patterns have had a strong impact on naming practices. There have been, however, occasional irruptions of English words used as names, and some of these have remained popular, though not systematically so. The first set was the Puritan names of the sixteenth and seventeenth centuries. The nineteenth and twentieth centuries favoured, from time to time, female names drawn from the semantic category of flower- and plant-names, possibly on the long-available model of *Rose*, which was an independent name, a pet-form of *Rosamund*, and taken to be a pet-form of *Rosalind*. In the later ninteenth and early twentieth centuries we find *Daisy, Iris, Violet* and *Ivy*, whilst the later twentieth century favoured *Poppy, Bryony, Holly* and *Fern*. A small group of names from (semi-)precious stones has been established (*Beryl, Ruby*, and more recently *Crystal, Jade* and *Amber*).

6.3.8 Evidence for pet-names (hypocoristics) from early times to the present

Pet-names (hypocoristics) have been use in English-speaking areas for as long as we have records. In the *Anglo-Saxon Chronicle*, King Cuthwulf of the West Saxons is also referred to as *Cutha*; the first element of his name has been abstracted and provided with the suffix of the weak masculine declension of OE. There is a systematic method for the formation of pet-forms from male dithematic names which is a little more elaborate, often of the type CV(C)Ca, where the third C (and the second if identical to the third) is the first consonant of the second element, e.g. *Sibba* for *Sigebeorht*. If the evidence of place-names is a reliable guide to the incidence of full-names and pet-names, either might be used in expressions referring to places.

The standard stock of the Middle Ages was also subject to patterns of pet-name formation, of which by far the most sophisticated recent study is McClure (1998). The evidence of surname formation would point to this even if there were no documentary evidence at all. Simple abbreviation to a stressed syllable and a following interlude consonant was common: *T(h)om(as), Sim(on), Ben(edict), Nic(holas)* – especially in Christian names in the narrower sense; compare the surnames *Thom(p)son, Sim(p)son, Benson* and *Nickson (Nixon)*. In Gmc names filtered through Norman French, a system operated akin to that found in OE, giving *Gibbe* for *Gilbert, Wat* for *Walter*; compare *Gibson, Watson*. In other names of this origin, simple abbreviation is found too where the base name had, or had come to have, a single intervocalic consonant: *Rob(ert)*, *Jeff(rey)/Geoff(rey)*, *Will(iam)*; compare *Robson, Jeffson, Wil(l)son*.

Some medieval male names were subject to a system of pet-name formation which has defied historical explanation. This is based on alternation of initial consonants, though no phonetic basis can be discerned. Names in <R->, i.e. *Richard/Rickard, Robert* and *Roger*, form abbreviated alternants in <H-> and <D->, and these regularly show up in originally patronymic surnames of the types *Hobson/Dobson* and *Hobbs/Dobbs* alongside *Robson* (but not *Robbs*). *Ralph* has now also been shown to have had a <D-> variant and also possibly one in <H-> (McClure, 1998: 124–30). The surnames suggest that the use of the various alternants may have had a regional basis. Most other instances of initial consonant alternation in male names (such as *Robert/Bob* and *William/Bill*) are later and phonologically different. Some female names participate in a phonologically different alternation; *Margaret* gives *Mag, Mog* and *Meg*, then *Pog* and *Peg*; *Mald/Maud* (originally; and perhaps later *Mary*; McClure, 1998: 103) gives *Mall/Moll* and then *Poll*.

Among other medieval and postmedieval hypocoristics showing phonological alternation, we see some which show an affinity with the system of OE described above. *Kit, Gib, Wat, Heb* and *Phip* for *Christopher, Gilbert, Walter, Herbert* and *Philip*, with their consonant cluster reductions and syncope, are early enough to have had an impact in surnaming. Given the known patterns of children's acquisition of phonology, it seems likely that *Kit*, at least, is an adoption by adult speakers of a juvenile pronunciation. It is uncertain whether this applies to any of the other instances. The general characteristic is that consonants relatively high on the sonority hierarchy (/r/, /l/, /w/) tend to disappear adjacent to others, along with unstressed vowels.

Another device used in pet-name formation is what has traditionally been viewed as metanalysis, where syntagms such as *mine Anne* yield *Nan* as a pet-form; this is also the source of *Nell* for *Eleanor*, *Noll* for *Oliver* and *Ned* for *Edward*, and is therefore independent of the sex of the addressee. McClure (1998: 109) plausibly suggests, however, that it is part of the system of rhyming hypocoristics discussed above, since *Nib* for *Ib* (from *Isabel*) is paralleled by *Lib* and *Tib*. From quite early in the Middle Ages, there is also evidence of suffixal hypocoristics. Most frequent is the use of elements such as *-cock, -on, -et* or *-kin*, which are appended (sometimes in pairs) to the abbreviated version of a full name where there is one or to the full name where not; evidently, this gives us a direct insight into the most popular names of the age of surnaming, since surnames provide a raft of evidence for the phenomenon. We find, for example, *Batcock* (from *Bartholomew*), *Adcock* (*Adam*), *Hickock* and *Hitchcock* (*Richard*), *Hancock* (a regional form of *John*), *Jeffcock* (*Geoffrey*) and eventually *Johncock* (first recorded late). Many of these names have undergone a variety of analogical alterations, for instance to *Badcock* and *Jeffcoat*. Names in *-kin* include *Adkin*, *Wilkin* (from *William*) and *Hodgkin* (*Roger*). Forms in *-y* or *-ie* have also been much in evidence over several centuries, and are still current (see below).

In modern times, a phonologically interesting development has affected names which, if abbreviated in a way which would yield a CVC structure, would have /r/ as the second C. Such a word-final /r/ is phonologically inadmissible in the non-rhotic accents of British English, and it has been treated in one of two ways: substitution by /l/ or by /z/, both of which share the apicality and voicedness of the historic /r/. The former tactic has been available for centuries for names applicable to both sexes, as in *Hal* for Harry (as old as Shakespeare), but the set of names treated in this way has gained recent recruits such as *Del* for Derek and *Tel* for Terence. The latter has grown up as a competitor, as in *Dez* for Derek, *Loz* for Laurence (I have also heard *Lol*, but not recently), *Baz* for Barry, *Gaz* for Gary and *Daz* for Darren; in the latter two cases there is no competing form in /l/. Female names may be affected in the same way, e.g. *Shaz* for Sharon, *Caz* for Carol(ine).

Towards the end of the twentieth century, the tide turned decisively away from pet-forms for male names that show alternation of either the initial consonant or the stressed vowel. Informal polls among people around twenty years old now show that the hypocoristics *Bill, Bob, Ned/Ted, Dick* and the like are in full retreat before *Will, Rob, Ed* and *Rick/Rich*.

Suffixal pet-forms have been found at all periods, but in modern times almost exclusively formations in /-i(:)/ suffixed to either the full form of a name (*Johnny, Janey*) or a pet-form consisting of the stressed syllable or a hypocoristic of it, the stressed syllable carrying any intervocalic consonant(s) shared with the following syllable as its coda (*Rob, Jim, Poll*; '*(Alec)sand(er)*', *(Re)bec(ca), (A)mand(a), (E)liz(abeth)*). Exceptional are *Penny* and *Cassie*, based on the written form of the initial but unstressed syllable of *Penelope* and *Cassandra*, and in the former case supported by the homophonous lexical word. This is especially widely found as a tactic for making female pet-names, and some phonological research has suggested that, for some, the suffix may now stereotypically connote femininity. Indeed, striking numbers of female basic names, with a wide variety of origins, have this shape (*Mary, Lucy, Lindsey, Sally, Sophie, Wendy, Dulcie, Daisy, Bonnie, Tracy*), whilst relatively few male ones do (though note *Barry, Gary, Henry/Harry, Jamie/Jaime*). For different reasons, therefore, both men and women may have reason to avoid it. This may account for the preference of some women to be known by a hypocoristic without /-i(:)/ where /-i(:)/ is traditional, e.g. *Jen* or *Cath* rather than *Jenny* or *Cathy*.

6.4 Surnames

6.4.1 The origin of surnames

Surnames came into use among the Norman aristocracy shortly before the Conquest. The practice was neither universal nor stable then or in the early period of Norman rule in England, though by about 1250 it was the norm in the highest social class and the knightly and other taxpaying classes. Between 1300 and 1400 the practice had spread to the urban moneyed classes, though it appears that in some towns, such as York, the lower classes might be without surnames till as late as 1600. Rural small free tenants, for whom evidence is more scant, began to acquire surnames before 1300 in the south, and the practice moved northwards, with new surnames still being formed in Lancashire as late as the sixteenth and seventeenth centuries; and this development is mirrored by that of the servile class. The adoption of surnames did not happen overnight anywhere, and our knowledge of the process is hindered by the different degrees to which social classes are represented in the record; see McKinley (1990: 5, 25–39). Women might take their husbands' surnames from about 1350 onwards, sometimes, in the southern half of England, in a genitival form where the surname was occupational; in the north, there was an alternative custom of using a name of the husband's (personal name or by-name) with *wife* to form a by-name. But there is no hard and fast pattern in the practice of female surnaming; in some areas of England the custom of adopting the husband's surname was not established till the sixteenth century, and in Welsh Wales not finally till the nineteenth (McKinley, 1990: 47–9).

Surnames are distinguishing names given to people bearing the same personal name, and many of these came to be inherited, though the system is not in fully complete operation everywhere till the 1600s. Those which have been inherited were of course the ones originally bestowed on males, for a complex of reasons involving unambiguous identification of the rightful heir. As the system developed, it is clear that legalistic causes were not the only, or even the main, stimulus to surname development. It is hard to believe that administrators were the sole creators of such names as *Grosseteste* 'big head', *Paramore* 'philanderer', *Sweetapple* or the startling (and extinct) *Clawcunte*; surely they were recording (or translating) what contemporaries called them.

6.4.2   Some problems with surname interpretation

There are many pitfalls in the study of surnames. Many occur in a wide range of different spellings. This may be important in cases of popular insistence that, for example, *Brown* and *Browne* are not the same name; which is of course true at the orthographic level synchronically, but historically misleading since they have the same origin and became fixed in particular spellings for individual families at a time when orthography had not been standardised. It is worth mentioning that some 'English' surnames are of multiple origin, and that only detailed scrutiny of a person's genealogy may be capable of determining the source in difficult cases. *Mitchell* may be a French form of *Michael* or the early ME for 'big'; *Law* may be a pet-form of *Lawrence* or a topographical name from the north country meaning 'hill'; *Hurley* may be an English place-name or it may represent the Anglo-Irish *O'Herlihy*. Some names do not have the obvious origin, and folk-etymological sports abound. *Reader* is normally 'thatcher'. *Redwood* is generally traced to the ME *rēd-wōd* 'enraged to the point of being scarlet; irascible'. *Prettyjohn* is for the mythical Christian ruler in the Orient, Prester John, made famous through Mandeville's *Travels*. Other radical and irregular changes, many analogical, have taken place. *Honeyball* and *Hannibal* are for the Old French female name *Amabel/Anabel*. *Lillicrap* means 'lily(-white) crop (i.e. head)', 'blond hair'. We cannot do justice to all these difficulties here.

6.4.3   Types of surname

From the outset, surnames have been of only four denotational types:

1. those derived from true by-names, having the form of an adjective alone or with a complement, or of a noun phrase, being descriptive of or predicable of the original bearer, such as *Reid/Read* 'red(-haired)', *Short*, *Secrett* 'discreet', *Cornish*, *Tait* (Scandinavian) 'joyful'; *Strongitharm*; *Goodfellow*, *Bairnsfather* '(alleged) father of the child'; in this category may also be included elliptical or synecdochic names such as *Whitelegg* '(having) pale legs', *Fairfax* '(having) fair or nice hair', *Godsmark* '(having a) plague-spot'. We can identify further a category of metonymic by-name surnames, such as *Christmas* or *Midwinter* (from the time of birth); and further still nouns or noun phrases lacking an article that function metaphorically to indicate personal qualities or attributes such as *Nightingale, Bull, Milsopp* 'milksop', *Gildersleeve* 'golden sleeve'. Some verb-phrase names indicating such characteristics are also found, again ranging from what amount to truthful by-names to metonymic names; these include names such as *Standaloft*, *Golightly*, *Rideout*, *Hopshort* and *Drinkwater*, and there are sentence-names (optative mood) which encode favourite expressions (often pious or impious) of the bearer, such as *Dugard* (French) 'God look after (you)', and *Godber* (sometimes) 'God be here', not to mention the imprecation *Bigod* 'by God'.

2. those derived from locations, i.e. expressions descriptive of where the original bearer lived, and therefore strictly metonymic, e.g. *Marsh, Green*, *Street*, *Newhouse*, *Townsend*, and true place-names, e.g. *Bristow* ('Bristol'), *Crawley*, *Keenlyside*, *Litherland*, *Sutton*, *Thickness*, *Darbyshire*, *Ireland*, *Sessions* ('Soissons' in Normandy); also in this general type belong prepositional phrases (usually without the article) such as *Uppiby* 'up in the village' (Scandinavian), *Atwell*, *Bysouth*, *atten Oak* and the original type represented by the French *de Lacy*, where the last word is a place-name. This type was once extremely frequent, but over the centuries the prepositions have mostly disappeared. The original surnames of the landed classes were predominantly of this type, both in Normandy and in England, and often took the form [*de/of* + place-name].

3.   those derived from family relationships, i.e. normally incorporating the original bearer's father's name, e.g. *Andrew, Andrews, Anderson*, either in its full form or a pet-form in the abbreviated (*Nickson* and *Dobson*) or suffixal state (*Wilcockson* and *Wilkinson*). More rarely they incorporate the mother's – *Marjorison, Sibson (Sibyl), Tillotson (Matilda)* – or some other relative's – *Hitchmough* (see Section 6.4.4), *Cousins*; and, more rarely still, from some relationship not mentioning the name of the ancestor, e.g. *Cookson, Masterson*, or from a non-blood relationship, perhaps usually indicating a feudal tie or other bond, e.g. *King(s)man* and maybe *Dukes, Hickman* 'Hick's (serving-) man' or *Henman* 'Henry's man'. Names such as *Andrew* or *Bishop*, with no overt expression of filiation or any other relationship, may be regarded as metonymic, i.e. expressing an unspecified association.

4.   those derived from occupational terms, e.g. *Coward* 'cow-herd', *Cartwright, Smith, Latimer* 'professional Latin-user', *Bailey* 'bailiff', *Baker, Reeve, Hayward, Collier* 'charcoal-burner', *Billiter* 'bellfounder'; and metonymic allusions to such occupations, *Wain* 'cart', *Whitbread* 'wheatbread', i.e. implying a baker of high-quality bread, *Runcie* 'nag, old horse', perhaps for one who looked after them, and the more obvious *Hogsflesh, Goodale* and *Jewell*. This category is covered in the comprehensive study by Fransson (1935). Some have dropped out of use, like *Mustardmaker* and *Dishward*, and it is not possible without genealogical investigation to say whether this is because the male line has died out or whether the name has been discarded in favour of an alternative; see further Reaney (1967).

These four categories are not as distinct as might appear at first sight; they are all in origin by-names, i.e. expressions true of the original bearer at the moment of bestowal, either directly or by metonymy. Sometimes they may be ironic inversions, i.e. deliberately false of the person on whom they have alighted, and they were sometimes perhaps applied slanderously. We cannot be sure that everyone named *Short* had a tiny ancestor, for the word might be ironically applied to a seven-footer. *Mildmay* is 'gentle maiden' – recall that all surnames were originally applied to men. As for *Halfknight* – we shall probably never know whether he held half a knight's fee, or whether he was truly or falsely a helmet short of a suit of armour.

By-names become surnames at the moment at which they are inherited, since they then attach to someone for whom they were not invented, and of whom they are not necessarily true (allowing for irony). The development of surnames was hesitant: not every by-name crystallised into a surname, and those that did were not immune from replacement after a few generations.

Much is still to be learned about the preference for different surname types by different social groups, though the monographs by McKinley and Postles make excellent attempts to identify patterns which to some extent differ regionally. The situation as currently understood is set out by McKinley (1990: 199–203); he shows that the difference in surnaming practices of different classes was relative rather than absolute.

The surname stock, once established, is not subject to much radical change. But an unexplained major development takes place principally between about 1550 and 1650, whereby surnames of a topographical kind, such as *Mill* and *Grove*, may sprout an <s>, and surnames with this <s> have in some areas become at least as frequent as their counterparts without (McKinley, 1990: 85–7).

6.4.4   The linguistic structure of surnames

Spellings of surnames can be very problematic. As we have noted, surnames with the same origin may turn up in more than one guise due to their having become locally fixed before the standardisation of spelling (*Brown/Browne*). Some may show the effect of local sound changes (*Vowles*, *Oldroyd*, *Wheat-fill*), which may have been reversed in the lexical word or source name through the influence of spelling (*Bailey* (= *bailiff*), *Lunnon* (= *London*)), whilst others show conservative spellings (notoriously such items as *Featherstonehaugh*, pronounced *Fanshaw*, where the syncopated form also exists alongside the etymological source form, and *ffitch*, where an early modern spelling using an allograph of <f> that looks like a double <f> has been preserved). In this group are also names taken from places where the general pronunciation departs from that of the local place-name, e.g. *Greenhalgh* [griːnhalʃ], [griːnhɔ(l)], from the Lancashire place whose name is pronounced [griːnə]. Others may respect current phonology more than the spelling of the corresponding lexical word does (*Clark* and *Sargeant* as compared with *clerk* and *sergeant*). A reasonably consistent spelling rule is that where a monosyllabic short-vowelled lexical item ends in a single consonant, the corresponding surname has this consonant doubled (*Squibb*, *Catt*, *Knapp*, *Starr*, *Ramm*, *Wrenn*; though we may find *Trim*, *Ham*, *Wren*, etc. where the final consonant is a nasal). The influence of spelling conventions for names of classical origin may be seen in *Bacchus* for *Backhouse* and *Rhodes* for *Roads*, which have nothing to do historically with the names they now resemble.

Folk-etymology and seemingly arbitrary change (presumably originally due to mishearing by non-local writers) abound in surnames; note *Kittermaster* (from *Kidderminster* Wo), *Thoroughgood* (from the Norse name usually spelt in England *Thurgood*), *Faircloth* (for *Fairclough*, place-name 'beautiful ravine') and *Potiphar* (Med Fr *pé de fer* 'iron foot'), showing the impact of biblical knowledge.

We can classify surnames into these categories:

1.   Descriptive surnames are usually plain adjectives (e.g. *Long*, *Hardy*, *Raggett* 'ragged', *Arliss* 'earless') or much less commonly adjectives with postmodification (e.g. *Fullalove* 'full of love', 'randy') or premodification (*Wellbeloved*); or plain nouns applied in virtue of their literal meaning (excluding here those of occupation) such as *Twinn*

or *Gemmell* 'twin' or (judgementally) *Treacher* 'cheat', or metaphor-ically such as *Frogg* or *Bull* (if the latter is not metonymic for a cattle-related occupation). NPs lacking a determiner may be literal (*Younghusband, Goodlad, Longman*) or have a metonymic applica-tion amounting to 'having (a) NP' where the NP presumably refers to what is the bearer's most distinctive trait, as with *Beard, Great-head, Proudfoot, Lovelock, Sheepshanks*; and VPs with a bare-stem verb may have the application '(he) characteristically Xs', as with *Gotobed, Startup, Standaloft, Eatwell*, or '(he) characteristically Vs (a, or his) NP', as with *Dolittle, Shakeshaft, Scattergood, Catchpole* 'chase-chicken' (i.e. someone who collected taxes in kind).

2.   Locational surnames mainly take the form of metonymic noun phrases with no overt determiner (*Green, Church, Lane, Backhouse* 'bake-house'), with A+N sequences functioning effectively as compounds if they are not actually place-names (*Greenwood, Diplock* 'deep stream'), and of course countless locational surnames are place-names used metonymically. Some French names in England are PPs where the NP is represented by a place-name (*Diaper* = *d'Ypres*; *Disney* = *d'Isigny*), though the place-name is rarely if ever one in Eng-land in surviving surnames. However, English topographical nouns in (Law) French structures are found in *Delbridge* and *Delahooke*. Fully English prepositional phrases were once found, e.g. *In the Hale*, but few survive, and most of those that do are formed with *at* and a (synchronically) undetermined noun (*Atwell, Underhill*). Traces of a determiner can be seen before a vowel-initial noun, as with *Nash* (ME *atten Asshe*). Other PP-names include *Bytheseashore* and *Bywood*. It has now been demonstrated that surnames of the suffixed shape *X-er* may mean 'man living at a/the X', as in *Waterer* (McClure, 1982). Compounds of a locational term with *man* are known, e.g. *Bridgeman, Hillman*, and with a place-name, especially from the north country, e.g. *Fentiman* 'Fenton man'.

3.   Surnames of relationship are mainly patronymic. The basic type is where the father's name was simply appended to the given name without modification. It is very striking that those OE given names which have survived to be modern surnames are almost invariably structurally plain, and the exceptions are easily categorised. In this set fall *Seabright, Livesey, Godwin, Edrich* and *Woolgar*; we return to the exceptions shortly. If it is true that such plain names are typi-cal of southern and eastern surnaming practices, then it follows that survival of OE given names was strongest in these areas, but that has not become the accepted opinion. Modified patronyms are formed either by adding *-son* (mainly northern) or *-s* (mainly western), as in *Johnson* vs *Johns*. The few OE survivals which may participate in this system are *Edward*(*-s*; rarely *-son*), *Edmund*(*-s, -son*) and

Cuthbert(*-son*; never *-s*). These are significant as the names of widely venerated pre-Conquest saints which were not supplanted in the replacement of the native stock discussed in Section 6.2. Only *Alderson* (from OE *Ealdhere*) appears to be a fairly frequent true exception. Phonology dictates that we cannot tell whether names like *Johnson* were originally [plain name + *son*] or [name in the genitive case + *son*], because ME male names in the genitive took a suffix *-(e)s*. No clear evidence for the latter possibility exists. Where the base given name is female, we can be sure it was plain, since female names did not form suffixal genitives in high ME (hence *Marjorison* 'Margery-son'). The only blood relationship expressed in surnames apart from that of son is the one expressed by the rare *-mough* in *Hitchmough* and *Watmough*. This is from ME *māʒ*, and is generally held to mean loosely 'kinsman', here the kinsman of *Hitch* (*Richard*) and *Wat* (*Walter*). No names are known to have entered this construction with a suffixal genitive, which makes it very probable that the *Johnson* type also did not. A looser usage developed where *man* could be attached to a personal name, as with *Rickman* and *Henman* for men associated with *Rickard* and *Henry*. A non-blood relationship is indicated in the defunct by-name *Milnerstepson* 'miller's stepson' (NB with a descriptive term not a personal name) and the extraordinary by-name *Johanesleman* 'John's lover', likewise defunct for obvious reasons.

We discussed earlier the immense range of hypocoristic names that were derived in the Middle Ages from a fairly small set of current given names. Surnames could, in principle, be formed from any one of these. Accordingly, taking *William* as an example, we find: *William Williamson Williams Will Willson/Willison Wills/Willis Willmot Willmots Willet Willets Willard Willie Willcock Willcockson Willcocks Wilkin Wilkinson Wilkins Wilk Wilks* with numerous spelling variants such as the dominant *Wilson* and *Wilcox*. Often the most interesting thing about these name groups is the original geographical distribution of the variants; thus for instance *Wilkinson* and *Williamson* are markedly northern English and/or Scottish, and there is a concentration of *Willmott* in Derbyshire.

We may broaden the 'relationship' category by including surnames which allude to relationships without naming. Into this category go *Milnerstepson* and the still-extant *Cookson*, both based on occupational terms, and *Wid(d)owson* and the enigmatic *Ba(i)rnsfather* 'child's father', perhaps euphemistically for 'bastard's father' in a context where bastards were few.

4.   Occupational terms are usually structurally straightforward, although many naturally end in *-er*, the agent suffix (witness the material in Fransson, 1935), or the more specific *-herd*, *-wright* and *-smith*. A common variant of the occupational type is represented by a

metonymic usage, i.e. one which alludes to the trade of the man named without mentioning it. A spice merchant might be called *Culpepper* 'gather pepper'; a baker might be called *Cakebread* or *Wafer*, though we cannot be sure whether these were his specialities or joking ways of referring to the trade he followed.

Of great linguistic and cultural interest are the occupational surnames in *-ster*, such as *Webster* 'weaver' and *Baxter* 'baker'. These originally denoted a female, and they contrast with male equivalents like *Webber, Baker*. They are the only surnames in this group to express formally the sex of the bearer, though it is clear that eventually no such contrast was observed. They were being used of men at least in the south country by 1200, but until 1400 there can be found relatively rare instances of the descent of surnames through the female line (McKinley, 1990: 47–8). It is therefore possible that *Webster* and the like were indeed originally the occupational by-names of women. But since it is very hard to suggest surnames in the other three categories which must originally denote females, the presumption must remain that ambivalent cases apply to a male. The whole question of women's by-names surviving to become inherited surnames needs more research.

6.4.5   Other languages of English surnames

During the surname-forming period the native language of some of the population was French, and French was the language of civil administration. Accordingly, some characteristically English surnames are in fact French. Latin was also used as a language of record for some purposes, e.g. the business of manorial courts, and quite rarely we have cases of what appears to be a stock surname perpetuated in Latin translation, notably *Faber* 'smith' and *Sutor* 'shoemaker'. We have already noted occasional classicising influence on the spelling of fully English names.

6.4.6   Surnaming since about 1500

Once the surname stock was established, which was done essentially by the fifteenth century, little happened to change the system. In linguistic terms, the next major development was the introduction of compounded ('double-barrelled') surnames from the eighteenth century onwards. This happened largely for legal and social reasons. A man might adopt, in addition to his own, the surname of another family as a condition of coming into an inheritance, or simply to associate himself with some social clout. Once this pattern was established, double-barrelling for its own sake became widespread. It is noticeable how many double-barrelled surnames have one of the more frequent surnames as the second element; a typical case must have been that of the Victorian painter who was born (1833) E. B. (Edward Burne) Jones and died (1898) (Sir) Edward Burne-Jones.

A major cultural, as opposed to linguistic, issue is that of the retention by women of their inherited surname on marriage. The literature of the social psychology of this phenomenon is reviewed and discussed by Duggan, Cota & Dion (1993) with a plea for further study, as done for instance by Murray (1997). It is clear that 'retaining' women are viewed stereotypically in a much different light from those who follow tradition and adopt their husband's surname. More significant formally, however, has been the introduction of new non-traditional practices. One is forming a surname on marriage by merger (e.g. *Taygan* from *Taylor* and *Regan*); according to Brightman (1994: 9), this is now done by about 2 per cent of American women, but I have no figures for men. Another is abutting the surnames of both parties or hyphenating them to form a new surname for both or for their baby (as opposed to women simply using both, generally with the married name second, as with Hillary *Rodham Clinton*), as allowed for instance by the rules for surnaming of babies in the province of Saskatchewan. More radical is adopting at random a surname which is not that of either. None of these marriage-related practices has become systematic, and some gay couples in stable relationships do similar things. All have in common, of course, the rejection of the traditional practice whereby the bride adopts her groom's surname.

An unresearched historical development involves shift of stress in surnames whose forms might with some latitude suggest a French name with a suffixal element. Established 'English' names such as *Burnett*, *Ovett*, *Mantell* and *Purcell*, which originated with initial stress, are now often pronounced with final stress. We must assume that the motivating factor is the cachet of French names, especially in the nineteenth century; few have gone so far as to completely frenchify the spelling, though I have spotted the occasional *Burnette*.

6.5   Place-names

6.5.1   Preliminaries

The key texts for the study of place-names in England are the introductory book by Cameron (1961/1996), and two specialised volumes on the relation between place-names and history (Gelling, 1997) and on the relation between place-names and topography (Gelling & Cole, 2000). There is a new comprehensive place-name dictionary by Watts (2004), complementing the former standard works by Ekwall (1960) and Mills (1998), and a dictionary of place-name elements is under way (Parsons et al., 1997–), eventually to replace the previous standard work by Smith (1956). The key data for interpretation is furnished by the county volumes of the Survey of English Place-Names (1923–) and a few published volumes or unpublished dissertations outside this series on counties which have not yet been fully surveyed (Wallenberg, 1931, 1934; Mills, 1976; Padel, 1985; Coplestone-Crow, 1989; Coates, 1989; Cameron, 1998; Watts, 2002; and the dissertations by Cullen, 1997 and Horovitz, 2005). Other major works covering particular aspects of place-name study are introduced below.

For the principal works on English-language place-naming beyond England (which all contain information on names formed in a variety of indigenous languages), see as follows: Scotland, Nicolaisen (2001); Wales, Charles (1938); the United States, Stewart (1967) and his dictionary (1970), and Ashley (2003), with many other more locally focused works; Canada, Rayburn (1997); southern Africa, Raper (1989). In Australia there is an ongoing national place-name survey which is reported on in a newsletter published from Macquarie University, called *Placenames Australia*, and there are nationwide accounts of Aboriginal, but not English, names, paralleled by Bright's important national work on Native American names (2004). The whole of Great Britain is covered by Gelling, Nicolaisen & Richards (1970) and, more dependently, by Room (2003). Note that a paragraph on American place-names by the present author has been incorporated into Chapter 8, at the end of Section 8.1. A list of abbreviations of English county-names may be found in the Appendix to this chapter.

6.5.2   The ethnic and linguistic context of English names

The oldest stratum of place-names in English speaking England is that which has survived through being taken up by English speakers from their predecessors. A significant number of river-names falls into this category (e.g. *Thames, Severn, Humber, Don*), as does a rather small but probably underestimated number of names for inhabited places, either complete (*Wigan* (L), *Carlisle* (Cu), *London* (Mx), *Crewe* (Ch)) or embedded in names that are structurally English (*Manchester* (La), *Berkshire, Breedon* (Wo), *Charnwood* (Lei), *Luton* (Bd)). On the issue of surviving pre-English names, see Coates & Breeze (2000: *passim*) and many other papers by both authors.

The English adopted little of the available heritage, on the whole, though quite a large number of the major river-names were taken up, and the Brittonic word for 'river', **aßon*, became the proper name of six English rivers. OE accepted occasional words from Latin, such as *ceaster* 'fort' and *wīc* 'place of special economic status' (Gelling, 1997: 63–86; Coates, 1999). These aside, we are left with the fact that the entire place-name stock of England is English, until it is overlain by layers of Danish and Norwegian in some areas, with some marginal contributions from Irish, some later Welsh, Medieval Latin and French.

It has been suggested, most recently by Piroth (1979), that the ancestors of the English brought certain place-names with them ready-made from their continental homeland. Most scholars think rather that English names were constructed from the resources available to the continental Saxons and other Germanic peoples, and that that is enough to explain the similarities between insular and continental names. It used to be thought that the incoming warbands of Angles and Saxons struck roots and gave English names to the places where they struck them. Scholars today have a more cautious view of the settlement process, taking account of the fact that in mid-Saxon times there was an agricultural upheaval which resulted in radical changes to the settlement pattern (Hamerow, 1991). There was an opportunity for wholesale renaming as new nucleated settlements sprang up. It is no longer possible to be sure that the familiar English names are the ones originally bestowed on the places; that this was the case remains nothing more than the default assumption.

We will begin by considering place-names as names for parts of the geographical space of England, remembering that the greater part of southeast Scotland is the northernmost region of the original English linguistic area and is to be understood as included in 'England' where necessary, and that the same applies to areas of eastern Wales. This will allow us to consider names of geographical regions, natural features both large and small, political-administrative regions, settlements considered both as inhabited places and as ecclesiastical parishes, and the microstructures of human activity such as fields and managed aspects of the landscape, archaeologically significant structures such as barrows and 'hillforts', streets and elements of townscape such as blocks and buildings. Evidence for the early forms of names for these features is unevenly distributed in time. To some extent this is controlled by the nature of the thing named; there was no significant townscape naming before the Middle Ages, and modern fields are in many parts of the country the products of eighteenth-century changes in agricultural practices (Field, 1972, 1993). There is on the whole more early evidence for the names of larger features than smaller ones, though the accident of extant records means that there is better early information for the south than the north, and areas remote from settlement tend to be late in the record; the great mountain *Helvellyn* (Cu/We) is not recorded till the sixteenth century despite having a name that could be at least 1,000 years older than that (Coates, 1988: 30–3). Allowing for these skews of the record, settlement-names, especially when they apply also to parishes, tend to hit the record early in their history, as do the names of major features, especially rivers, and those other features which may delimit boundaries, especially of the parish or what would later be called the manor. This skew results in a linguistic skew. Presumably the Britons who lived here before the English named the same range of things as their new political masters, even if they conceptualised them differently (natural features could be viewed as supernatural beings, like the river *Dee* 'the goddess'; the English observed features inhabited by divinities rather than manifesting them, like the various *Puckpool*s 'pool inhabited by a goblin'). If the evidence can be taken at face value, the English took over names for some larger features, including some settlements and districts and rivers (and the further west one goes in England the more evidence for such borrowing one finds), but they appear to have wiped clean any Brittonic microtoponymy except where we have watertight historical evidence for the survival of Welsh and Cornish into medieval times (especially Cornwall, west and southwest Herefordshire and west Shropshire, and to some extent northern Cumberland; on all this see Coates & Breeze, 2000: 1–14 *et passim*).

The kinds of places bearing Scandinavian names in the former Danelaw and the Norse settlements of the northwest are similar to those bearing English names, and the names one finds are structurally similar with the exception of the Irish-influenced so-called inversion compounds of the northwest, such as *Kirkpatrick* with the specifier second. English has borrowed a small amount of toponymic lexical material from Scandinavian and applied it beyond its original habitat (e.g. *gap* and very importantly *cross*). Irish naming is found only in association with northwestern Norse settlements and very sporadically for places holy to Irish monks. French and Latin as administrative languages and languages of record have left scattered traces in the landscape with no specially marked geographical distribution; you might come across the occasional French name anywhere, and there are too few Latin ones to evaluate their significance. A special marginal impact is represented by the small number of minor names in Cumberland bestowed by immigrant German-speaking miners (*PN Cu* III: xxxix). Very occasional names formulated in other languages are found, usually transferred from places abroad; most of these are biblical. Others represent interest in current events, such as the repeated *Gibraltar* and *Portobello*, which testify to English naval prowess in the eighteenth century. *Etruria* (St) illustrates deference to ancient Italian ceramic art by the founders of this pottery-producing community, and *Fulneck* (YWR) is a name from Silesia transferred by an immigrant Moravian Protestant community, both of these also being eighteenth-century creations (though the latter is at a place previously called *Fall Neck* (*PN YWR* III: 236), and it is clearly an example of 'providential' renaming).

6.5.3   The explanation of place-names

Speakers of any language may be interested in the place-names associated with that language, but the nature of their interest can vary quite radically. Welsh, Finnish and Maori names tend to transparency, and therefore explaining them is largely a matter of specifying the context in which they were first applied, or accounting for their distribution in space and time. English names are different. Many are very old. Even those which look and sound English may in fact have been formulated in a language which is no longer part of the repertoire of English speakers: Latin, Brittonic, Danish, Irish and French, for instance, are the sources of *Speen* (Brk), *Malvern* (Wo), *Skegby* (Nt), *Liscard* (Ch) and *Belper* (Db), respectively. This means that explaining many English names is a delicate exercise in philology, as the elements which make them up have to be identified in one of a number of languages. The tradition of writing in England stretches back more than 1,300 years, and phonetic and orthographic evolution have not always been in step with each other. In addition, there is a radical discontinuity in the written record. Before 1066, the record contains many place-names formulated in interpretable OE, the native language of most of those engaged in writing, though Latin was also a language of record. After 1066, a bureaucracy was installed where, irrespective of the writers' native language, Latin and French were the languages of record; the scribal practices adopted were in part those used for Latin, but otherwise those originally applied in the writing of French late in the first millennium. These did not sit easily with the phonology of English, and there was a period where the recorded names may be hard to interpret, i.e. to assign to known places. By the thirteenth century, those who applied the conventions were again producing passable renderings of the phonology of English names, and they often begin to show affinity with the forms current now. Until the fifteenth century, they are often still in French or Latin texts and influenced to some degree by that context, e.g. by being formed and spelt in a way suitable for declension in Latin (normally first-declension feminine – *Exonia* for Exeter, for instance, or more mechanically the twelfth-century *Stouenesbia* for Stonesby (Lei)); administrative writing in English belongs only to the period since Henry V set the tone for the use of English in chancery.

Some problems for name scholars emerge from these facts. Firstly, that of tying up OE-period and later ME-period forms of names: often the OE ones have undergone radical transformation, and it is not always obvious that the political and linguistic revolution of 1066 is solely responsible. It is now believed that the *Gislheresuuyrth* recorded in 695 is Isleworth (Mx); the second element of the personal name, *-here*, is irrecoverable from post-Conquest sources, possibly because of phonetic or morphological reduction during the late AS period. A medial *-ing-* vanishes between OE and ME in the record of *Charlbury* (O). Such may be the case, undiscoverably, with many other names that we first know only later in history. Secondly, there is the problem of understanding names which are recorded for the first time by French-using clerks. Not all English names – far from it – are recorded in OE times, and many are first known in *Domesday Book* (1086) or documents of an even later period. This may mean that the earliest intelligible forms of names of English origin may appear as late as the thirteenth century, up to 700–800 years after they were formulated. Thirdly, English itself has changed, partly under the impact of the medieval triglossia. OE words that could serve as place-name elements have been replaced by others; English noun and adjective morphology has been radically simplified; and both phonology and orthographic practice have changed. Furthermore, the recorded vocabulary of OE has been augmented by words found only in place-names and established by the techniques of comparative and internal reconstruction. For instance, a noun corresponding to the adjective *steep* has been plausibly conjectured from the shape of place-names in southern England, and backed by the existence of corresponding nouns in continental Germanic languages. A word corresponding to German *naß* 'wet' is needed for a name such as *Nateley* (Ha) ('wet wood or clearing') which is otherwise difficult to explain. Other words have been convincingly conjectured because they satisfy OE word formation; *rīmuc* 'edge' is plausible in *Ringwood* (Ha) because the word *rīma* 'rim' is recorded and because the suffix *-uc* is known in other OE topographical words, such as those which give *paddock* and *hillock*. OE words known in a particular dialectal form may be inferred in another dialect, with appropriate recalculation of the phonology; *Smethwick* (St) contains an otherwise unrecorded Anglian form of *smith, *smeoða* (genitive plural), and the known *stubb* 'tree-stump' is unable to account for some north-country names for which only an inferred **stobb* will serve.

6.5.4   English-language place-names

The most ancient layer of English place-names appears to consist mainly of names which are simply descriptive of the place named, either its physical aspect or its ownership or tenure. It is not possible to say how many names evolved from descriptive phrases of the *Newnham* 'the new estate' type and how many were deliberately created and bestowed. It is generally assumed that the former is the dominant type. This assumption is supported by the fact that the typical OE place-names are very prosaic: 'shallow ford', 'bishop's tree', 'old fort', 'churls' farm', 'Cēol's island', 'west minster', 'stone way', 'oak wood' and so on. There is nothing here resembling the types of *Miramar* or *Sans Souci*, and few examples even of evaluative names like 'beautiful X'. It is easy to imagine a Saxon traveller being directed by means of names most of which were transparent in the landscape, and quite strong claims have been made recently about the importance of names as guides on heavily used long-distance ways in the period of earliest settlement (Cole, 1990, 1992, 1993 and especially 1994; Gelling & Cole, 2000: xvi). I shall say more below about the exactitude conveyed by OE topographical terms.

The individual elements that appear in place-names are many, though the generics form a much more restricted class than the specifiers. Some of these are words that have survived to ModE relatively unscathed both phonologically and semantically (*brycg/bridge*; *ford*; *wudu/wood*; *hyll/hill*; *mōr/moor*; *stān/stone*). Others have survived but undergone significant changes in application, especially those pertaining most directly to human institutions (*hām* 'major farm estate'/ *home*; *tūn* 'farm'/*town*; *burg* 'defended place'/*borough*). Some have survived in the vocabulary of the modern dialects (*ēa* 'river', now *ee* or *eau* 'minor watercourse'; *bece*, now *batch* 'stream'). Finally, some, even the most important numerically, have disappeared altogether in their original sense, like *ofer* 'shoulder-shaped hill' and *lēah* 'woodland; woodland clearing'. Where the original application is no longer served by the original English term, modern naming will use borrowed terms, especially from French, e.g. *forest* (which has lost its original legal sense in favour of a topographical-ecological one), *village*, *river*, *mount*.

A recent significant development has been the recognition of the delicacy and precision of reference in OE topographical vocabulary (Gelling, 1984; Gelling & Cole, 2000, and supporting article literature). Whereas modern English toponymy makes do with the word *hill* and others serving as loose onomastic equivalents (often with a regional, and therefore partly geomorphological basis) such as *down*, *top*, *pike*, *law* and *fell*, OE had words that distinguished hill shape subtly and reliably (the evidence is still visible). *Ōra* and *ofer* denoted hills with a shoulder-shaped profile, whilst *hōh*, literally 'heel; hough', had a scarp-dip profile with a slight extra rise at the highest point; *dūn* was a hill with a levellish summit suitable for settlement; *hlið* was a hillside with a convex profile; the inferred term **ric* was a narrow strip of raised ground, for instance a glacial moraine; and so on. *Hyll* appears to have been a general word for elevations that were hard to categorise. Valleys could be classified with similar delicacy, as could watercourses. Other, non-topographical, elements which have received extensive philological and/or culture-historical discussion recently are *worth(y)* 'tenant farm'(Kitson, 1997), *wīc* 'dependent settlement' (Coates, 1999) and the ME lexis for the notion 'town' (Svensson, 1997).

The typical English-language place-name consists of two elements, E1 and E2. E2 is a noun serving as a generic term for a category of place. One set of E2 categories is those which are habitative or otherwise indicating the fruits of human activity, e.g. major estate, village or farm, enclosure/curtilage, defended place, church, bridge, landing-place, place of special economic status, burial-mound, as illustrated respectively by *Seaham* (Du), *Charlton* (K), *Tamworth* (St), *Peterborough* (Nth), *Pucklechurch* (Gl), *Cambridge, Rotherhithe* (Sr), *Droitwich* (Wo) and *Berwick* (Nb), and *Ludlow* (Sa). The other major set of categories is topographical, e.g. hill, valley, stream, ford, wood, moor, heath, field (= open land), head (= promontory), tree. English inhabited places very often bear by metonymy a name which was originally that of a landscape feature, or which at least referred to one, as exemplified respectively by *Ferryhill* (Du), *Rochdale* (La), *Blackburn* (La), *Oxford, Brewood* (St), *Wedmore* (So), *Blackheath* (K), *Hatfield* (YWR), *Minehead* (So) and *Coventry* (Wa).

In addition to such two-element names with a generic and a (normally preceding) specifier, there are names consisting of a stand-alone E2 (always an instance of an element found in compounds), e.g. *Ash* (Sr), *Down* (K), *Leigh* (Wo); this is a special case of the normal type which is used as if an E1 can be understood or as if one is unnecessary in the context of use. In such cases, an earlier E1 may have disappeared, as we know for certain in the cases of *Chester, Stow* (L), *Leigh* (Wo) and *Bridge* (K). In pre-Conquest documents, Stow (L) was *Marianstowe*, for instance, and Leigh (Wo) was *Beornodesleah*. A name does not necessarily require an act of political will to change it. A change of ownership might suffice, or the place might be salient through being the only one of its kind locally, therefore requiring no specifier in its name. When we consider what the original name of a place recorded only late might have been, we must allow the possibility that a first element might have been lost or substituted before records began. It is possible, for example, that Alfriston (Sx) is a relatively early *tūn*-name, but that it takes its current name from the Ælfric who held it in 1066. Further, one English name may have been entirely supplanted by another, as has happened in the case of Abingdon (Brk), whose name was apparently that of an adjacent hill, but which came to be applied to the settlement originally called (in ME) *Sevekesham* 'Seofuc's estate or hemmed-in land'.

E1 falls into a number of different categories.

(a) It may be an adjective strictly modifying E2, as in *Langstone* (Ha) 'long stone', *Newcastle* (St), *Higham* (Db) 'high farming estate', *Blackburn* (La), *Cromwell* (Nt) 'winding stream', and the frequent *Norton* 'north farm', with *uppe* adjectival in place-names like the widespread *Upton*, and with participles counting as adjectives, as with *Brokenborough* (W) 'broken barrow'.

(b) It may be a common noun forming a compound with E2, as in *Eton* (Bk) 'island farm', *Fenton* (St), *Chalkwell* (Ess), *Bristol* 'bridge place', *Gatwick* (Sr) 'goat farm', *Quy* (C) 'cow island', *Staplehurst* (K) 'post or pillar wood', *Woodbridge* (Sf), including those denoting people or categories of people, as in *Charlton* (K) 'churls' farm', *Huntingdon* (Hu) 'hunters' hill', *Canterbury* (K) 'stronghold of the people of Kent', *Normanton* (Db) 'Northmen's farm'.

(b′) It may be an earlier place-name (including river-names), of any structure, forming a compound with E2, as in *Alnwick* (Nb), *Severnstoke* (Wo), *Manchester* (La), *Launceston* (Co), *Quantoxhead* (So).

(b″) It may be a personal name, of any structure, forming a compound with E2, as in *Edgbaston* (Wa), *Godmanchester* (Hu), *Oswestry* (Sa), *Baltonsborough* (So), *Grimston* (Lei), *Edwinstowe* (Nt), *Cholsey* (Brk).

Structures of type (a) may or may not show signs of weak adjectival inflection of E1, giving evidence for the original definite article. Those that do can be assumed to have originated as fully meaningful definite expressions in running speech (as with *Foudry Brook*, Section 6.1.1 above). Those that do not may have been bestowed in a deliberate act, or at any rate may have been treated as names from their conception, rather than as fully compositional referring expressions requiring explicit definiteness in context. The difference between these types is illustrated by *at the long ridge* and *at Longridge*. The modern reflexes of such name types may be identical, but the documentary record will probably show differences in the medieval spellings. Medieval forms of the former type may show a weak inflection on the adjective, showing that the name originated in a prepositional phrase containing a definite NP, and such a trace may survive; *Newnham* (C), for instance, is '(at) the new estate', where the <-n-> represents the vestige of the dative singular after a lost definite article.

Structures of type (b) may or may not show signs of nominal inflection of E1. Those that do typically have E1 in the genitive case. These are in the great majority in type (b″), though secure instances of a bare-stem compound of a personal name and an E2 are known (*Edwalton* (Nt)) and in other instances a former attested genitive marker has disappeared (*Alwoodley* (YWR), Latin of ME period *Adelwaldesleia*), and sometimes the elements are connected by an *-ing* which is a derivational suffix but appears tantamount to a 'genitival' inflection in such names (*Chilbolton* (Ha), OE *Ceolboldingtun*). A relatively rare group of names, typified by *Altrincham* (Ch), has been identified on phonological grounds as having E1 in other case forms, typically an instrumental- or dative-locative

(Dodgson, in a series of important articles in the 1960s). These are marked by a palatal consonant at the end of E1. It may be impossible to tell without such phonological effects whether an E1 was originally in the bare-stem form or in an inflected form where the desinence has disappeared through regular phonetic attrition, as is typically the case with OE weak inflections. Type (b) structures with an inflected common noun in the genitive case as E1 include *Alresford* (Ha), *Farnsfield* (Nt), *Saddlescombe* (Sx) – cf. Tengstrand (1940). Type (b″) names with an inflected proper noun as E1 are perhaps the most typical of all English place-name types: *Branston* (Nt), *Harrietsham* (K), *Livingston* (West Lothian), *Wilmslow* (Ch), *Aldersey* (Ch).

A serious issue, which is probably unresolvable, hinges on names where it is unclear whether the first element is a personal name or a related lexical word. *Ramsbury* (W) may be 'raven's fort' or 'Hræfn's fort' (where *Hræfn* is actually the word for 'raven' used as a male personal name). A name such as *Whitchurch* (Do) may have as its first element the known male personal name *Hwīta*, which is an application of the word *hwīt* 'white', or this word itself. Scholars rarely spell out in gruesome detail the case for ambiguity in each such name. *Hræfn* is often found in names for remote and/or high places, which may prejudice one to favour the 'raven' interpretation for a name including *burg/byrig* '(hill)fort', on the basis of modern raven habitat. There are other cases far less clear-cut, and the possible ambiguity should always be borne in mind.

Somewhat harder to classify are those names in which the elements are connected by other formal means. The problem in classification comes from the fact that the same phonological material was called upon to perform more than one duty, and it is not really clear whether some usages coincided or overlapped in time, nor whether the elements involved should be classified as homonyms or as one polysemous item. Principally, this question is about *-ing*. Sometimes *-ing* was used to create nouns which denoted groups of people; then, of course, it appeared in the plural form, *-ingas*. Such names could stand alone as 'tribal' names or be used metonymically for the territories these tribal units occupied. The base of such names was usually either a (male) personal name or a pre-existing place-name. Accordingly, such names have been interpreted as 'followers of X' or 'dwellers at X'. This *-ing* is CGmc, and could be used as an expression of filiation ('son of'), though clearly the 'tribal' names require the interpretation to be a looser one than strict filiation; we might have to do with blood loyalties, or with other kinds of social ties. In the 'dwellers' application, the perceived relationship was with the locality rather than with the community. For present purposes, these names are important because they may stand as E1 in an inflected form, almost always the genitive plural, in such names as *Birmingham* (Wa) 'estate of the followers of Beorma', but occasionally a locative singular, as in *Ovingham* (Nb). They may also stand alone; the best known of these is *Hastings* (Sx).

There was also a singular use of *-ing*, where the suffix was attached directly to a lexical root to form a place-name in the singular, as with *Deeping* (L) and *Clavering* (Ess) 'clover place', and it has been argued recently (Coates, 1997b) that this singular *-ing* could occur in the plural in some names, e.g. the paired villages called (Great and Bardfield) *Saling* (Ess) (*Salinges* 1086; 'places of the sallows'). There is clear evidence that this singular suffix could attach to personal names, as with the lost **Cynewolding* (K), which makes it extraordinarily difficult to decide whether a place recorded first in ME in spellings varying between <XingeY> and <XingY> (as often happens), where *X* is a personal name, are instances of *-ingas* in its natural genitive plural form, or of *-ing* in the genitive plural or some other case, or of the connective *-ing* mentioned in relation to Chilbolton (Ha) (and if the last, whether E1 was originally case marked or not). The matter is complicated still further by the fact that *-ing* can interchange with other elements; see Smith (1956, I: 282–303).

The overwhelming majority of English names of inhabited places in England fall into one of these categories (a) and the various subtypes of (b). Apparent three-element names are usually best analysed as being two-element compounds, one element of which is itself a two-element compound, as with the repeated genitival compound *Ludgershall* (W) and the like, where E1 is believed to be a compound *lūte-gār* 'trapping spear' (Tengstrand, 1940: 219–24), and *Brockhampton* (He), where E2 is the compound *hām-tūn* 'major agricultural estate'.

Place-names as defined above may themselves be modified. A very limited number of adjectives may be used to pre-modify a name; these are pretty well restricted to the compass-point adjectives, *low(er)* and *high(er)* or synonyms of these, *inner* and *outer*, *middle*, the lexical variants *great*, *much* and *broad*, *little*, *long*, *old* and *new*, and *burnt* (ME *brent*, *brant*), and rarely a topographical term (*Fenny* Stratford (Bk)). Where such names have become official in their administrative-Latin translation, the Latin or Latin-derived element postmodifies (Rickinghall *Inferior* (Sf), Ludford *Parva* (L), Bradfield *Combust* (Sf)). Premodification by a noun in the genitive case is quite frequent (*King's* Worthy (Ha), *Bishop's* Nympton (D)), again translated with Latin postmodification (Whitchurch *Canonicorum* (Do), Rowley *Regis* (St)). Sometimes an uninflected noun denoting a characteristic building premodifies (*Steeple* Morden (C), *Castle* Cary (So)), or a church dedication may postmodify (Stanton *St John* (O), Horsham *St Faith* (Nf)). We rarely find some other kind of qualifier, but note Piddle*trenthide* (Do), which proclaims its fiscal status in Law French, 'thirty hides of land'. In the great majority of such instances, the modified place-name contrasts with another having a different qualifier (*King's* Worthy vs *Martyr* Worthy (Ha); Sutton *St Edmund* and Sutton *St James* (L)). Whether the modern name has English or Latin qualification appears to be a matter of administrative chance. Very rarely, a French modifier persists, though this was less infrequent in medieval records; two including the status or occupation of the feudal overlord are *Friern* Barnet (Hrt) and Hinton *Ampner* (Ha) ('friar' genitive pl and 'almoner', used as borrowed English words) and Ower*moigne* (Do) ('monk'), but some of this type were surnames sharing the form of an occupational term, as is certainly the case with Owermoigne. Postmodification by a surname, again indicating feudal overlordship, is frequent in some counties (Norton *Disney* (L),

Stretton *Grandison* (He), Hatfield *Peverel* (Ess), Milton *Keynes* (Bk)); sometimes such a surname premodified, and where it did so it was in the genitive, as with *Bingham's* Melcombe (Do). Some place-names are modified by a term indicating their civil status, the most frequent instance being 'market', as in the English *chipping*, which premodifies (*Chipping* Sodbury (Gl)), the Latin *forum*, which postmodifies (Blandford *Forum* (Do)) or the Anglo-Norman *market*, which may do either (*Market* Rasen (L), Downham *Market* (Nf)).

English names in Scotland may have superficially similar forms, but postspecification is strongly represented, as in Gaelic, leading to the strong suspicion that it may be a substrate effect in Scots. Whilst *Castle Cary* in Somerset is to be understood as 'the place called Cary that has a castle', *Castle Cary* (Stirlingshire) is 'the castle belonging to the Cary family', i.e. a head-first construction seen also in *Kirkcudbright*, and we also find characteristic postmodification by a PP with *of*, as in *Gatehouse of Fleet* (Kirkcudbrightshire), *Yetts o' Muckhart* (Clackmannanshire). Places sharing a frequent name such as *Kirkton* may have them distinguished by (*of* + place-name), as with the following in Angus: *Kirkton of Kingoldrum, of Glenisla, of Tealing*, and so on. A hamlet or other new development within a parish (or the equivalent) may be named in a structurally similar way, as with *Coaltown of Wemyss* in Wemyss (Fife) and *Spittal of Glenmuick* (Aberdeenshire). This construction extends also to the names of natural features; there are many streams with names of the type *Water of X*, for instance (Nicolaisen, 2001: 79–80).

6.5.5   Place-names and urban history

Street-naming (see Room, 1992) took its classic form in medieval times in London and the smaller cities like Norwich, York and Bristol. Names consisted of a generic element preceded by a modifier of exactly the same range of types that we noted earlier for major place-names plus directional names of the type (*the*, later omitted) *London Road* 'highway to London'. The generic element was usually *street* (and in formerly Danish areas the equivalent *gate*), *lane, row*, by the sixteenth century *alley* and (in Edinburgh) *wynd*, and where appropriate *market* or an equivalent or hyponym or meronym (e.g. *Poultry* 'hen market' in London and *The Shambles* 'butcher's stalls', Carlisle; *The Bull Ring*, Birmingham; *Beast Fair*, Snaith (YWR)). There was occasional metonymic use of topographical terms such as *hill*, and of the names of buildings for the streets in which they were situated (e.g. *Minories*, London, and *Whitehall*, Westminster); and the names of many other buildings, especially inns and taverns, and of the dedicatees of churches, were compounded into lasting street-names. The enormous majority of medieval street-names can be regarded as having been ecologically appropriate; their relevance to the place named was almost exceptionlessly obvious. The range of generics in towns remained practically unchanged for centuries until the addition of *road* and *way* (in non-directional names) in the modern era. Both of these are significantly absent from pre-1600 names in London, Bristol, Cambridge,

Leicester, Lincoln and Chester, with the few exceptions like *le Endelesweye* 'the endless way' in thirteenth-century Cambridge, *Posterne-Way* in Chester in 1415 and the unusual name embedded in *Sanvey Gate* in Leicester (*Sand Way*), an occasional race-track. There are no *road*s in Lincoln before *New-Road* in 1790, and few elsewhere before 1800. *Road* in urban names might be applied to a thoroughfare of unusual width, i.e. designed with riding traffic in mind, and between towns to a highway or turnpike (as with *London Road, Welford Road* and *Narborough Road* in Leicester), or a major highway whether turnpiked or not. Some later *road*s previously had other generics, as with *Knighton Road* (previously *Highway*), Leicester. From the eighteenth century, however, with the advent of urban planning, a proliferation of terms occurred, first geometrical (*crescent, square, terrace, circus*) and social-functional (*parade, drive*), and then some which reflect post-revolutionary Paris (*avenue, court, mansions, place* and ultimately *boulevard*), even where, as in the case of *avenue* 'approach', the word itself had been in English for some time without finding its way into names. As villages expanded into towns during the Industrial Revolution, fields were enclosed and eventually sold off for speculative building, field-names were deployed in street-names, and, somewhat later, rural generics like *close* and *garth* 'field' and *drove/drift* 'path for driving animals' came into use (but rarely *field* itself unless incorporated into a single word or earlier-established field-name like *Springfield*). The rural idyll of suburbia then provided *grove* (usually of course with a tree-name as specifier, *elm* and *lime* being dominant), *green, mead(s)* and *gardens* and the like; the touristic requirements of the Picturesque movement added *prospect* and (later) *view*; and non-vehicular thoroughfares might be *walk*, suggesting invigorating country hikes. In the mid-twentieth century some of the system of onomastic restraint was abandoned, and streets might be called *The X* (usually in the plural, with a final syllable of the form *-ings* very popular); *The Avenue* (passim), *The Cresta* (Grimsby (L)), *The Sidings* (Lyminge (K)), *The Moorings* (Pill (So)), *The Swallows* (Wallsend (Nb)). In such names, *X* could be but was by no means necessarily a traditional generic. *Street* itself became decidedly unfashionable and was deployed very rarely after about 1920, presumably because it had come to suggest insalubrious urban development.

Several regions or individual towns have locally distinctive street- or alley-name generics: examples include *backs* (Bristol), *batch* in various Somerset towns, *wynd* (Edinburgh and some northern English towns), *chare* (Newcastle upon Tyne and Hexham), *loke* in East Anglia and *twitten* (almost exclusively Sussex). Some stock names are also partly regionalised, like the *Fore Street* frequent in towns of the southwest of England, which often alludes to the line of a *High Street* projected beyond a city wall or boundary, as at Exeter. Other recent developments are too idiosyncratic to discuss here.

House-naming as a mass activity is a phenomenon of the nineteenth century onwards. Bestowed names fall overwhelmingly into a small number of categories: names derived from local topography; names referring to vegetation (*The Elms, Fern Villa*) in idealized conceptions of landscape such as those discussed fully by Schama (1995) (*Fernleigh, Ferndale*); transferred place-names; humorous references to the owner's name or the financial burden of ownership (*Costa Packet*, as in this instance often alluding to one of the other categories, and the famous *Cobwebs*, an acronym for 'Currently Owned By Woolwich Equitable Building Society'); other word-plays (*Rest-a-Wyle, Dunroamin*; again typically presented as if a place-name); and allusions to the history of the building (*The Old Forge*). The history and sociology of such name-giving practices (see Miles, 2000) is tied closely to general cultural history, and fashion in other spheres of human endeavour is reflected in the choice of names at particular times.

6.5.6   Place-names in languages arriving after English

Settlement by Scandinavian speakers from the later ninth century onwards has had a profound impact on the naming of certain areas of the British Isles (Fellows-Jensen, 1972, 1978, 1985). In England, Scandinavian primary place-names can be found over much of the east midlands and the north, and especially densely in Lincolnshire and Yorkshire. This evidence is the only linguistic evidence for where Scandinavians settled, apart from the vocabulary of regional dialects. It is generally believed that some areas were characteristically Danish and some Norwegian, and this can also be read off from the map, but there are references to both of these stocks outside their primary areas and it would be misleading to think rigidly in terms of ethnic zones. The onomastic impact can be seen in the use of place-name generics whose modern forms are *by* 'village, farm', *thorp(e)* 'secondary settlement, hamlet' (though this reinforces the use of a phonologically similar native English term; on some problems with *by* see Fellows-Jensen, 1992), *toft* 'farmstead, house-plot' (on which see Gammeltoft, 2003), *kirk* 'church', *wath* 'ford', *beck* 'stream', *foss/force* 'waterfall', *dale* '(major) valley' (or in minor names 'share of land', from a different Scandinavian word *deil-) and *lound/lund* 'grove'. Some of these terms were taken up into the general vocabulary of the northern and eastern dialects (see Cox, 1988 and 1990 for discussion of some key elements), and this may pose difficulties for deciding whether a name of apparently Scandinavian form really does originate in that language. *Driby* (L) has an English specifier 'dry' (compare Scandinavian *þur*-), which may suggest that the name was created by English speakers, though we cannot discount the possibility that the English word had been borrowed into the local Scandinavian; there is practically no surviving textual evidence for the Scandinavian of England. Equally, Scandinavians may have partly renamed an existing place with a name such as *Dryton. Conversely, *Austwick* (YWR) has a Scandinavian specifier 'east' and an English generic 'dependent farm'. Place-name scholars have long recognised a category of names with an English generic and a Scandinavian personal name as E1; they are normally now called Toton-hybrids after *Toton* (Nt); here, the personal name is *Tofi*, apparently inflected in Scandinavian (i.e. *Tofa*, not *Tofes), which leads to much difficulty in imagining whether these were English or Scandinavian settlements, ethnically or linguistically, and the matter could do with further research (Coates, forthcoming b).

Some English and Scandinavian words for the same notion are of course conspicuously different from each other, and it is easy to tell which has been used: for instance the English *tūn* and *ford* versus Scandinavian *bȳ* and *vað*; but other pairs are identical, such as those represented by modern *moor* and *house*. Still other pairs are distinguished phonologically, such as *stān* and **stein-* 'stone', *brād* and *breið* 'broad', *gār* and *geiri* 'triangular piece of land'. But it is not always easy to tell in what language a particular name was first formulated. It is by no means rare for places with names recorded in what appears to be an English form in *Domesday Book* and of English appearance now to have records in medieval times with elements in Scandinavian guise, and some elements, especially *church* and *kirk*, may alternate in names into early modern times (see Figure 1.6 in Chapter 1).

The question of the original language of a name is interwoven with the whole issue of how long Scandinavian continued to be spoken in England, which is far from easy to decide. The facts just mentioned could suggest that Scandinavian was spoken into the early Middle Ages, but this possibility needs to be distinguished carefully from the possibility of partly relexified dialects of English coexisting with more traditionally English ones and exchanging lexical material with them, and from that of more generally Scandinavianised dialects of English showing a range of Scandinavian substrate features. Much work still remains to be done on the contribution that onomastic evidence can make to the resolution of the issue of the survival of Scandinavian (see Coates, forthcoming b, for a brief overview, after Fellows-Jensen, 2000 and Parsons, 1997), and to the general linguistic question of language contact.

Scholars often write as if Scandinavian found in England was Old Norse (ON), the developed literary dialect of West Scandinavian. For some purposes this does little real harm, but Scandinavian this side of the North Sea has not undergone several of the sound changes that characterise ON, for instance the diphthongisation of [e] to [ja] and of [a] to [jo] under the influence of the vowel of a following syllable ([a] and [u] respectively); note ON *fjall* 'mountain' and *tjǫrn* 'mountain lake' but in England *fell* and *tarn*. There is no evidence in England for a nominative singular inflection, but there is some evidence for words in different inflectional classes than in classical ON. Place-name elements should therefore be cited in a reconstructed Anglo-Scandinavian form, as done where necessary in this section. Since there is some evidence for both East and West Scandinavian features in different regions, it would be better still to distinguish Anglo-East Scandinavian (Anglo-Danish) from Anglo-West Scandinavian (Anglo-Norwegian), the former for instance having a genitive singular in *-a* and the latter in the more conservative *-ar*, displayed most often in case marking of the E1 of compound place-names.

A characteristic feature of Anglo-West Scandinavian place-naming is the so-called inversion compounds, where the specifier follows the generic. These are especially numerous in Cumberland and adjacent counties of Scotland, where we find for instance *Kirkoswald* (Cu and Ayrshire). These respond to Irish/Manx name-syntax, and they suggest that Vikings from Man and Dublin might have used this syntax with their own Scandinavian name-elements. This possibility is borne out by the truly Celtic names in Cumberland and adjacent areas with the same syntactic form, such as *Greysouthen* (Cu) and *Crossmichael* (Dumfriesshire), and the *Torthorwald* (Dumfriesshire) which Nicolaisen (2001: 143) takes to be a Gaelic name denoting the possession of a Scandinavian man.

A recent issue has been what the distribution of Scandinavian place-names can tell us about the nature of ninth- and tenth-century settlement. The work of Cameron (1965, 1970, 1971 (1977)) demonstrates that we are not dealing with a straightforward land-grab by the victorious Danish army in the later ninth century. In Lincolnshire, at least – part of the Danish heartland – the Scandinavian-named settlements show a clear affinity with geology yielding soils of lower agricultural value (as rated by twentieth-century geographers) than those with English names. Cameron concludes that this demonstrates peaceful infill by a wave of post-hostilities immigrants rather than a rush for the best land by successful marauders. That is an appropriate conclusion provided we assume that Danes did not also take over English-named settlements without renaming them. We know that some renaming took place (*Northworthy* (Db) famously became *Derby*, a Danish military headquarters), but there is no compelling evidence against Cameron's thesis.

For a couple of centuries after the Norman Conquest many of the records of English place-names are due to scribes trained in the orthographic system for rendering Old French and in many cases ignorant of the names they were trying to render. This raises a difficult methodological problem. Since many of our place-names are not recorded before the Conquest, especially in the north of England and Scotland, we are often faced with early records which may not reliably represent names in their contemporary phonological form, and later records at variance with these which are more in tune both with the modern form of the name and with the presumable etymology. *DB* gives *Ormeresfelt* for *Dogmersfield* (Ha) and *Scache(r)torp* for *Scottlethorpe* (L), the latter so divergent as to rouse the suspicion that its E1 has been substituted. Some typical normanisms were discussed by Zachrisson (1924), still a handy checklist when used with Clark (1992c).

By far the largest group of French names consists of names for major estates giving an aesthetic judgement about the places (rare indeed in English names), and most contain AN *bel* 'beautiful': *Belper* (Db) 'beautiful retreat', *Belvoir* (Lei) 'beautiful view', *Bewdley* (Sa) 'beautiful place (or, perhaps better, 'monastery')'. Monasteries might also have pious French names: *Vaudey* (L) 'God's valley', *Gracedew* (Lei) 'thanks to God', *Dieulacres* (St) 'may God increase it'. The probability that French was the working language of some orders is revealed by the final form of the names of some Cistercian foundations such as *Rievaulx* (YNR) 'valley of the river Rye' and *Fountains* (YNR). Unique among parish-names is *Miserden* (Gl), whose early spellings reveal it to be of a type still found in the Channel Islands, *(la) Musarderie* 'place of [the family called] *Musard*'. Other French names for major places are scattered, e.g. *Mold* (Flintshire; from OFr *Mont Halt*) 'high hill' and *Pomfret* (now standardised in its latinised form *Pontefract*) (YWR) 'broken bridge'.

Words of French origin which came to be used as elements include *broyle* 'deer-park', *bruyere* 'heath', *chapel, devise(s)* 'boundary' and usually much later (from the seventeenth century onwards) *mount* 'hill' (but see further below). Sometimes Law French has left its mark on the syntax of a name (as with postposed specifiers) and on the connecting elements that form it. *Chapel en le Frith* (Db) and *Laughton en le Morthen* (YWR) are among the most striking, but prepositions and articles may remain fossilised in French (these and *Holton le Clay* (L), *Poulton le Fylde* (La)) or alternate with Latin or English elements (*Barton in the Beans* (Lei) / *in Fabis* (Nt), two names of identical origin).

In more recent times, minor names have been formed on French models. The most familiar is the eighteenth-century creation *Mount Pleasant*, now ubiquitous, but the earliest is probably the house *Mount Surrey* in Norwich, built by the Earl of Surrey in 1542, which has given rise to or encouraged the use as minor local names of many other *mount*-names with a postposed specifier, such as *Mountstephen* in Halberton (D) and *Mountsorrel* (Lei). Other elements favouring this syntax in modern times are seen in *Fort William* (Inverness-shire), an eighteenth-century name for a fort to keep the Highlanders suppressed, and the names from the period of industrialisation, *Port Talbot* (Glamorgan) and *Port Sunlight* (Ch) – contrast *Maryport* (Cu) and *Ellesmere Port* (Ch); and in the regional names *Vale of York* (Y), *Forest of Dean* (Gl) and *Isle of Purbeck* (Do), with their French generics and their phrasal postspecifiers (which, in the English instances at least, may go back to medieval documentary antecedents and may be translations of name forms found there).

6.6   Conclusion

We have looked at the theoretical issues involved in understanding what it is to be a name, and at the major categories of English names, personal names, surnames and place-names. The chapter has taken a traditional, i.e. England-centred, view of what is fundamental in English onomastics research. The historical orientation has led to concentration on philological questions of remote times, and on structures laid down before the expansion of English beyond its early boundaries. Treatment of name categories has been selective, and has followed the main lines of the most recent general research. There has been little space to cover issues that are important as regards the proportion of the technical literature that they fill, such as improved interpretations of individual place-names, and occasional debunkings, which are frequently carried by the journals *Nomina* and *Journal of the English Place-Name Society*, or refinements in the understanding of the regional and demographic sources of particular surnames. These two journals both carry substantial annual bibliographies, and there is an annual report on English onomastics in *The Year's Work in English Studies*. A major general resource for all onomastics, begun in 2005, is the new bibliographical database of the International Council of Onomastic Sciences. The Council also publishes an annual journal *Onoma*, each issue of which is devoted to a general, as opposed to a regional, theme, such as names in literature, the teaching of onomastics, or name theory (the topics for publication years 2004–6). *Onoma* and *Names*, the journal of the American Name Society, are the only truly general journals of onomastics published (at least in part) in English.

Appendix: abbreviations of English county-names

Bd	Bedfordshire	Mx	Middlesex
Bk	Buckinghamshire	Nb	Northumberland
Brk	Berkshire	Nf	Norfolk
C	Cambridgeshire	Nt	Nottinghamshire
Ch	Cheshire	Nth	Northamptonshire
Co	Cornwall	O	Oxfordshire
Cu	Cumberland	R	Rutland
D	Devon	Sa	Shropshire
Db	Derbyshire	Sf	Suffolk
Do	Dorset	So	Somerset
Du	Co. Durham	Sr	Surrey
Ess	Essex	St	Staffordshire
Gl	Gloucestershire	Sx	Sussex
Ha	Hampshire	W	Wiltshire
He	Herefordshire	Wa	Warwickshire
Hrt	Hertfordshire	We	Westmorland
Hu	Huntingdonshire	Wo	Worcestershire
K	Kent	YER	Yorkshire East Riding
L	Lincolnshire	YNR	Yorkshire North Riding
La	Lancashire	YWR	Yorkshire West Riding
Lei	Leicestershire		

7 English in Britain

Richard Hogg

7.1   Introduction

We can be certain that, for as long as the English language has been established in Britain, so dialect variation has also existed. If we examine dialect variation in present-day English, even if it is possible to assume that there is a single over-arching speech community which makes up the language which we might, for the lack of a better term and with acknowledgement of the insult thereby perpetrated on the Irish, call 'British English', there remains the problem of what we recognise as the dialects of that community. We could simply recognise the individual nations, and talk about English, Scottish, Welsh and Irish dialects. But it takes only a moment to see that that will not do. The speaker from Kent does not see his or her dialect as the same as that of someone from Newcastle, any more than speakers from Aberdeen and Glasgow think that they share a single dialect.

Suppose, however, that we were able to set out a geography of British English dialects which somehow overcame the above points. Dialects are not merely a matter of geography. For dialects vary by much more than geography. Speakers vary in age, gender, social class and, increasingly, ethnicity. So, speakers from the same geographical area must differ from each other because of their age, their gender, and other social variables. All these variations may cause difficulties for the student of present-day English. But for the historian of English they are even worse. Amongst the questions which we will have to face up to, the most basic, here, as elsewhere, concern the question of data. This question confronts historical dialectology in several forms.

Firstly, there is the issue of who our informants might be. Not only are there no recordings of informants for any period significantly before the twentieth century, but the only material we have before then is in the form of written texts. This leads to a second issue. Speakers vary not only in geography, but also in age, gender, social class and ethnicity. If we are dealing with English before the twentieth century, then ethnicity is a not a serious issue (although instances of exceptions to this can be found). But class and gender are ever present.

These present difficulties of their own in the context of written language. For, overwhelmingly, our written texts are produced by men of the upper classes. It is true that female writing can be found from the time of the *Paston Letters* in the fifteenth century (although male scribes were used by the non-literate women), but it cannot be denied that women are significantly under-represented in every period until, and including, the present. Proportionately, it may well be the case that lower-class speech, in terms of written material, is even more poorly represented than female speech. Even age causes problems. For, in every historical period, the majority of data comes from the middle-aged.

The picture I have painted above must seem depressing. But to understand the problem is, as always, half way to the solution. We do have to acknowledge the limitations of our methods and data. But we do not have to submit to them. Indeed, such limitations make the study of historical dialectology more interesting. One way in which this happens is intimately connected with the history of English dialectology itself. We should start our story with the coming of English to Britain. Note that the use of the term *English* above is one that I, and others who are not, in the sense of national identity, English, find unappealing. Yet there is no helpful alternative, even if it excludes, wrongly, many Irish dialects. I can only hope that the variations I use will be unambiguous in context.

7.2   Old English

When the Anglo-Saxons arrived in Britain, they came from a variety of Germanic tribes and the language they spoke is often described as a dialect of Germanic. Thus, for example, Prokosch (1939: 31) talks about dialect groups, and this usage is quite common in works written from a Germanic or Indo-European standpoint. It is usually held that English as a unity was transmitted to the prehistoric period of English. As the founding father of the history of English, Henry Sweet, wrote (1876: 560–1), 'What were the dialectal distinctions in English during the first few centuries of the conquest of Britain? The answer is that they were very slight.' This is a reflection of the era in which Sweet was writing. It was a time when the nation-state was pre-eminent, and in linguistics the Neogrammarian revolution was on the point of bursting forth. It is certainly true that we have very little evidence indeed about dialectal variety in English before, at the earliest, around 700, when the first vernacular texts begin to appear. And these first texts do not in themselves provide convincing evidence of substantial dialectal variety.

However, there are important theoretical objections to Sweet's view. Most writers believe in some form of the theory of linguistic uniformitarianism. This states, roughly, that whatever holds today must also have held true for the past. And since we know that dialect variation holds true today, it must therefore hold true at every time in the past history of English. In particular, there must have been dialect variation throughout the Old English period too. Of course, the emergence of dialectal varieties is gradual, and there may well be valid arguments about how to evaluate evidence of dialect variation in particular cases; see, for example the

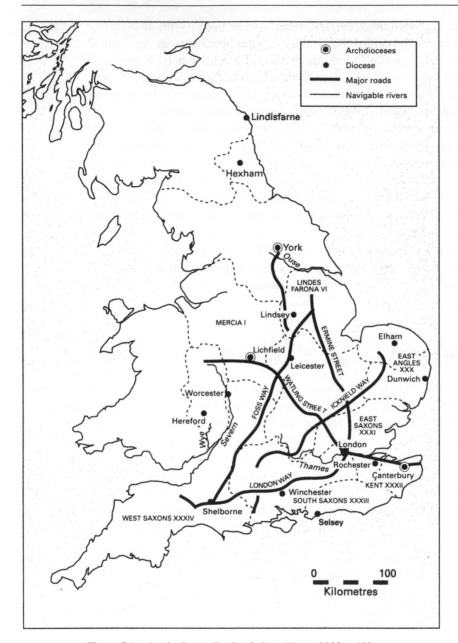

Figure 7.1   *Anglo-Saxon England (from Hogg, 1992a: 419)*

argument between DeCamp (1958) and Samuels (1971) about the origins of Old English dialects.

How, then, are Old English dialects conventionally delimited? In his *Old English Grammar* Alistair Campbell writes (1959: 4): 'In the extant Old English monuments four well-marked dialects are to be traced, *Northumbrian, Mercian, West Saxon*, and *Kentish*.' This is a standard view, although, as we shall see,

Campbell's position is actually more sophisticated than this. Nevertheless, this picture, which can already be found in Sweet's work, is substantially the one found in almost all textbooks. Once manuscripts begin to appear in substantial numbers, it gradually becomes clear that they can be assigned to one of the above four dialects on linguistic grounds alone. These grounds include the evidence of palaeography, i.e. the study of the manuscripts themselves, since such matters as letter-shapes are important and may give clues about the provenance of texts. There may also be evidence of where particular texts are located geographically, although such evidence is often insecure.

As far as the texts themselves are concerned, it turns out that the evidence is much more patchy than we could have wished for. Of all the texts available to us, the vast majority come from the eleventh century, and, if we exclude the poetry, for reasons to which we shall have to return, a very large proportion are written in a form of West Saxon. To stick to the traditional dialect areas, we can suggest that all the texts we have can be assigned to West Saxon, with the following exceptions:

Northumbrian: (a) a small number of eighth-century, mainly poetic, texts, e.g. *Cædmon's Hymn*, *Bede's Death Song*, and the runic inscription from the Ruthwell Cross; (b) an extensive group of late tenth century interlinear glosses, of which the best known are the glosses to the *Lindisfarne Gospels* and the Northumbrian part of the *Rushworth Gospels* (see immediately below).

Mercian: (a) a group of eighth- and ninth-century Latin to English glossaries, namely the *Épinal*, *Erfurt* and *Corpus Glossaries*; (b) the ninth-century gloss to the *Vespasian Psalter*; (c) the Mercian gloss to the *Rushworth Gospels*, see immediately above.

Kentish: (a) a series of charters from Kent and surrounding areas dating from throughout the ninth century; (b) some short texts and glosses to Proverbs, all from the tenth century.

In West Saxon itself, the first substantial group of texts appear just before and after 900, and these are texts associated with the court of Alfred the Great, notably the *Cura Pastoralis* (*Pastoral Care*), the first parts of the *Anglo-Saxon* (Parker) *Chronicle*, and the translation of *Orosius*. There are a number of texts in the second half of the tenth-century, but the great bulk of texts appear around 1000, when the texts of Ælfric and, a decade or so later, Wulfstan were composed, followed by much more material for the following decades until the effects of the Norman Conquest are felt.

The reason why the position is different with regard to the poetry is that almost all the poetry is contained in four manuscripts, namely the Vercelli Book, the Exeter Book, the *Beowulf* manuscript, and the Junius manuscript, all of which can be dated to around 1000. Undoubtedly many of the poetic texts were composed much earlier than this – for example a fragment of the *Dream of the Rood*, which is found in the Vercelli Book, is also found on the eighth-century runic inscription on the Ruthwell Cross, see further below. But from the point of view of dialectology the crucial factor is that all four manuscripts are written in a dialect which seems to be a mixture of West Saxon and Anglian forms without much clear linguistic evidence of their ultimate origins.

I have already alluded to questions of diachrony. Clearly, Old English dialects must have been subject to variation through time as well as through geography. Yet the picture we have painted above has ignored that issue. Diachronic change in the Old English period certainly occurred, but some aspects of such change can be contentious. We shall have to return to them later. To understand such variation, we need to tackle the question sideways. We also have to note that a complete account of Old English dialects is always going to be impossible. There are simply not enough texts: we are missing, for example, texts from an area such as East Anglia, despite the fact that it was one of the first areas settled by the English. In such cases it is possible, to some extent, to work back from the Middle English evidence, but this can only take us so far.

With these reservations in mind, let us now look in more detail at the traditional view of Old English dialectology. Historically, the emphasis has always been on questions of variation in phonology and morphology. There are good reasons why this should be so. The most obvious of these is that, in a historical period where the raw material, i.e. texts, are scanty, it is easier to concentrate on features which are relatively abundant. Syntax, in particular, requires a great deal of material before generalisations can be made. But in both phonology and morphology only a little can go a long way.

However, a more compelling reason than the accidents of contingency relates to the history of linguistics. In the upheavals of the Neogrammarian movement mentioned above, not only was diachrony privileged above synchrony, but the establishment of apparently inviolable claims about sound change (the so-called *Ausnahmslösigkeit der Lautgesetze* = exceptionlessness of sound change) equally privileged phonology over syntax. This has meant, although there are exceptions, that historical dialectology has been more interested in examining the effects of sound change than in any other element of the language.

The argument above may seem unfair. Indeed, it has to be tested by the relevant evidence. If we consider a standard view, such as presented in Campbell (1959), we find that dialectal variations are largely viewed in terms of sound change. Thus almost all writers accept the view that a fundamental dialect split occurred at the very earliest period, when West Germanic */aː/ developed to /æː/ in West Saxon but to /eː/ everywhere else. This split is often referred to as *Pogatscher's Line*, and this reflects the assumption that it deals with a dialect isogloss in Old English.

Pogatscher's Line turns out to be of particular interest. It is true that outside West Saxon the normal development of */aː/ is eventually to /eː/. However, it is not obvious that every dialect reached /eː/ by the same route. In particular, it seems quite possible that, whilst there was an early general raising to /eː/ in Anglian, the situation in Kentish was rather different. There the original forms may have been retained at least until the eighth century; see Hogg (1988). If this is so, we are dealing with differential diachronic change, rather than mere geographical variation.

This temptation to concentrate on phonological features must be resisted. There are, however, important phonological dialect variations, including, of course, Pogatscher's Line. For the perspective of the later history of English, that change is indeed important since /eː/ is the source of Anglian ME forms such as /seːd/ 'seed' where West Saxon would have given ME /sɛːd/. Not all variations have obvious consequences for later periods. For example, from quite early in Old English there is a split between southern [a] and northern [ɒ] in words such as *mann* ~ *monn* 'man'. The split is no longer found, but there is clear evidence that it did remain during the ME period and indeed it may be possible to trace the gradual disappearance of the northern form as it becomes confined to the west midlands; see Kristensson (1987), Hogg (1997).

Sometimes, the full impact of changes is not apparent until after the Old English period. For example, the important change of *i*-mutation results in /u(ː)/ and /o(ː)/ being fronted to, respectively, /y(ː)/ and /œ(ː)/. Throughout northern areas the latter is retained, but it becomes /e(ː)/ in West Saxon. Since in ME even northern forms unround, there would appear to be nothing remarkable happening. In the case of /y(ː)/, at first sight it looks even less interesting, since /y(ː)/ remains in both West Saxon and Anglian. But that ignores Kentish in both cases. There, not only does /œ(ː)/ unround, as would be expected in the south, but /y(ː)/ both unrounds and lowers to /e(ː)/. This is the source of PDE words such as *merry* from OE *myrige*.

One apparently insignificant change which is both a sign of what will happen in later centuries and a good link to morphology is the loss of final inflectional /n/ in Northumbrian. There we find infinitives such as *habba* 'have' where other dialects have *habban*. Although the change is restricted to some morphological categories, it is an early sign of a more extensive loss in ME. Northumbrian, in fact, has a wide range of morphosyntactic changes. These include: new forms of the verb *be*, such as *aron* 'they are' alongside *sint* or *sindon* found elsewhere – *aron* is clearly the antecedent of PDE *are*; the second- and third-person singular of the present tense are confused so that we find both the types *ridas* and *ridað* (also *rides* ~ *rideð*) for both 'thou ridest' and 'it rides'. The two examples we have chosen are obviously particularly important for the later history of the language. We may also note that the standard (but now archaic) second-person type *thou ridest* appears to have originated in this period in the south: even today, northern dialects prefer forms without final *-t*.

In dealing with syntactic variation, we face the major difficulty that the dominance of West Saxon material makes it difficult to distinguish between genuine dialect differences and features which are only found in West Saxon because other material is too scanty. However, one well-documented case is variation in negative contraction. In West Saxon and West Mercian contraction of the negative particle *ne* with verbs such as *habban* 'have' and *was* 'was' is very common, whereas in the north and east uncontracted forms occur in about one-third of cases.

In lexis, on the other hand, there have been extensive studies over many decades. Much of the effort here has been expended in distinguishing between Anglian and West Saxon vocabulary, but there have also been important attempts to identify the characteristics and origins of the standardised vocabulary employed, above all, by Ælfric. Studies on contrasts between West Saxon and Anglian cover not merely lexis; word formation is also relevant. For example, it can be shown that the feminine agentive suffix *-icge* (e.g. *hunticge* 'huntress') is almost always of Anglian origin, whilst *-estre* (e.g. *huntigestre*) occurs only in West Saxon.

One point has become more emphasised over the past two or three decades in lexical studies. This is the difficulty of clearly delineating texts, especially when many texts are either copies of others or our understanding of dialect boundaries is so imprecise. It is with this issue that I want to conclude this overview of Old English dialectology. Since the mid-1980s there has emerged an increasing dissatisfaction with the traditional approach to Old English dialects, although, admittedly, there has not yet been time for a new consensus to appear. There can be little doubt that the impetus for this dissatisfaction comes from recent work on Middle English, which we shall review in Section 7.3.

One problem which we have already noted is the impossibility of ever obtaining a complete picture, since we lack texts from large parts of the country. Another issue that we have touched on is the interaction of diachronic change and geography. And a further important question is the localisation of individual texts. These two last issues come together in what we can call the West Saxon problem. It has long been known that there are significant contrasts between early West Saxon, the language of Alfred and, hence, perhaps the language of Winchester roundabout 900, and late West Saxon, particularly associated with Ælfric roundabout 1000. Unfortunately, the very names appear to presuppose that the differences are diachronic. But this is difficult to square with well-known differences such as the absence of <ie> spellings in Ælfrician writings as against the frequent use of those spellings in early West Saxon; see also the more detailed and recent work by Peter Kitson using additional charter material (1992, 1993).

Because of problems such as these, I have argued elsewhere (Hogg, 1992c) that it may be more helpful to group the major texts or textual traditions by some alternative classification. The most obvious possibility is to use the known diocesan boundaries. The reason for this, of course, is that almost all our texts come from monks working in one or other monastery. Thus, instead of talking about Northumbrian, Mercian, West Saxon and Kentish, we might refer to Durham, Lichfield, Winchester and Canterbury or to the dioceses whose sees are situated in these places. In itself this is not sufficient, because it ignores other important centres such as Worcester and Rochester. It does, however, allow us to disassociate texts from pre-determined dialect groupings and also emphasise the central role of the church.

Some texts present difficulties of their own, which may only be exacerbated if they are too simply classified as one dialect rather than another. An instructive group of texts here are the 'Southumbrian' *Rushworth 2*, the 'North Mercian'

Rushworth 1 and the 'West Mercian' *Vespasian Psalter*. We know the scribes who composed the two parts of Rushworth, which is a single manuscript: *Rushworth 1* was written by Farman, a priest at 'Harawuda' (traditionally equated with Harewood in West Yorkshire) and the scribe of *Rushworth 2* was a Northumbrian called Owun. The anonymous *Psalter* was probably written at Canterbury by a Kentish scribe who faithfully copied a West Mercian original (presumably from Lichfield, one of the major diocesan centres). In addition, in *Rushworth 1* Farman uses a number of perhaps stereotyped West Saxon forms, such as *eall* 'all' rather than the Anglian *all*. As we examine all the evidence, it becomes clear that *Rushworth 2*, although closely related to the typical Northumbrian *Lindisfarne Gospels*, has a number of significant variations from the latter. Conversely, despite clear equivalences with the *Vespasian Psalter, Rushworth 1* shows important variations from *Vespasian*. In particular, although the sound change known as Second Fronting (whereby $a > æ$ and $æ > e$), and which is perhaps the canonical mark of *Vespasian*, does sometimes appear in *Rushworth 1*, it is more usually absent.

What we seem to be dealing with is a continuum. At one end there is *Lindisfarne*, at the other there is *Vespasian*. Somewhere in between these lie the two versions of *Rushworth*. In other words, we have a situation which is normal in studies of present-day dialects. There, although there may be gross differences, variation is continuous over the whole range. This is the very first point we made in this chapter and it is worth repeating. For the example we have chosen is not isolated, but is representative of a major issue for Old English dialectology. There are more sophisticated cases than this one, and, in particular, the work of Peter Kitson on Ælfric (see again Kitson, 1993), has allowed us to understand much more of the geography of the period and indeed of the relations between the major linguistic figures of the time; see also Benskin (1994).

Furthermore, thanks to some remarkable detective work by Richard Coates, it now looks most probable that the *Rushworth Gospels* were glossed, not at Harewood, which has always seemed improbable, but at Lichfield; see Coates (1997a). This implies that both *Rushworth 1* and the *Vespasian Psalter* were written at the same place, and yet they are significantly different in character. This can only be explained by supposing that the two scribes, Farmon and whoever was the scribe of *Vespasian*, had different dialects; see also Hogg (2004). But with our present state of knowledge, this merely emphasises that our knowledge of Old English dialect variation remains patchy.

7.3   Middle English

As Barbara Strang (1970: 224) stated over thirty years ago, 'ME is, *par excellence*, the dialectal phase of English, in the sense that while dialects have been spoken at all periods, it was in ME that divergent local usage was normally indicated in writing.' Even if we need to qualify that comment in certain ways, it remains usefully true. There are several reasons for this. Firstly, both in Old English (albeit only to a limited and rather complex degree) and in later periods, there were clear attempts at producing at least a written national standard language; see Chapter 5. But, as Strang states, this was not true for the Middle English period. Secondly, the relative quantity of text is far greater than for Old English, especially from the fourteenth century on. Thirdly, the variety of types of English had increased, both because of the increase in texts which are varied in type and not overwhelmingly religious and because of the variable influence of French and Scandinavian (Old Danish, Old Norse) on English. And fourthly, partly a combination of the preceding, but also a result of political shifts, we can observe the (partial) emergence of a distinct Scots language (see McClure, 1994).

Some of the difficulties when discussing Middle English dialects are exactly parallel to those found with Old English, but there are some subtle differences. Naturally we are still dealing only with written texts. However, the increase in varieties and the relative absence of standardisation means that texts were, as it were, written as they were spoken. Not exactly, of course, for it would be wrong to imply that spelling practices were simply anarchic: there is clear evidence of some regional standards, as in the so-called AB dialect of the early thirteenth-century west midlands (the best-known text in this group is the *Ancrene Wisse*); see Laing & Lass (2003). But the absence of standardisation did allow, at its extreme, Orm, a thirteenth-century monk, to devise a spelling system of his own from which we can derive considerable information.

Also in this period, we start to find comments about dialect variation. These can be indirect comments, such as Chaucer's use of northern forms for the students in *The Reeve's Tale*:

> . . . man sal taa of twa thynges
> Slyk as he fyndes, or taa slyk as he brynges

No doubt the intention was humorous, but it could hardly have worked if Chaucer's audience had been unable to understand some basic northern forms, just as today a film (leaving aside the book) such as *Trainspotting* assumes basic comprehension on the part of its audience. But a more direct comment comes from the Cornishman John of Trevisa, writing in 1385, a contemporary of Chaucer. He writes:

> Englischmen, þey3 hy hadde fram þe bygynnyng þre maner speche, Souþeron, Northeron, and Myddel speche in þe myddel of þe lond, . . . noþeles by commyxstion and mellyng, furst wiþ Danes and afterward wiþ Normans, in menye þe contray longage ys aperyed, and som vseþ strange wlaffyng, chyteryng, harryng, and garryng grisbytting.

> . . . Þerfore ht ys þat Mercii, þat buþ men of myddel Englelond, as hyt were parteners of þe endes, vnderstondeþ betre þe syde longages, Norþeron and Souþeron, þan Norþeron and Souþeron vnderstondeþ eyþer oþer.

Although, from the beginning, Englishmen had three manners of speaking.
southern, northern and, in the middle of the country, midlands speech, ... nevertheless, through intermingling and mixing, first with the Danes and afterwards with the Normans, amongst many the country language has arisen, and
some use strange stammering, chattering, snarling, and grating gnashing.

 ... therefore it is the case that the Mercians, the men of middle England,
as it were, the partners of the extremities, understand better the dialects of
either side, northern and southern, than the northern and southern dialects
understand each other.

Whatever the aesthetic validity of Trevisa's remarks, they undoubtedly contain
a truth about the dialect situation at the time. Perhaps an even more revealing
example, this time from the north, is provided by the West Yorkshire author of
Cursor Mundi:

In a writt þis ilk i fand
He-self it wroght ic vnderstand
In sotherin englis was it drawn
And turnd it haue i till our aun
Langage o northrin lede ['people']
Þat can nan oiþer englis rede

When discussing Old English dialects, we observed that the standard view
presents four fairly distinct dialects. The traditional picture of the Middle English
dialect situation has never been seen as quite so stable, but, broadly speaking,
there is some sense in talking of five regional mappings: North, East Midlands,
West Midlands, Southeast and Southwest. This picture, unfortunately, has the
illusory advantage of suggesting that there is continuity between the traditional
mapping of Old English and the later history. Thus, Northumbrian maps on to
Northern, Mercian maps on to West Midlands, and perhaps East Midlands, West
Saxon equates to Southwestern and Kentish to Southeastern.

In order to see why the continuity is illusory, it is not sufficient to repeat our
comments about traditional Old English dialectology. Rather, we have to understand the development of Middle English dialectology itself. The earliest studies
tended to be concerned with individual, or restricted groups of, texts, often determined primarily on literary grounds – this was equally true for Old English. Early
in the twentieth century the systematic study of place-names brought significant
advances to our knowledge of dialect variation. However, such material tends to
be dominantly of phonological interest, with some additional lexical material, and
hence it virtually excludes, by definition, some major features of the language.
And it may be worth observing that, in Ekwall's (1960) assessment of the value
of place-name study, he places the value of place-names for linguistic study sixth
(out of six!).

Despite the value of the work of such scholars as Ekwall, and in more recent
times, Kristensson (1967, 1987), the only large-scale attempts at dialect geography
before the 1950s were studies by Oakden (1930) and Moore, Meech & Whitehall

(1935). Although both these studies are valuable, it cannot be denied that they have considerable flaws. In particular, both surveys (and Oakden's is intended only as an introduction to Middle English alliterative verse) have a very limited scope. Nevertheless, it is instructive to examine these works, above all, perhaps, to see how the mapping of dialect features and isoglosses are correlated very closely with traditional conceptions of ME dialect boundaries. This is not surprising, given the linguistic temper of the age, and, of course, it leads to the kind of unity between OE and ME dialects about which we complained in Section 7.2.

A revolution in ME dialectology came with the publication in 1986 of *A Linguistic Atlas of Late Mediaeval English* by Angus McIntosh, Michael Samuels and Michael Benskin. *LALME* had been long in coming, having been started by McIntosh (and soon joined by Samuels) in 1952. For important early work on this project, see McIntosh (1956, 1963), Samuels (1963), whilst Benskin (1994) allows us to see how the project has advanced since then both in analysis and theory. The key element in this revolution was the adoption of the methods employed in present-day dialectology, adapted to the historical requirements.

Essentially, *LALME* attempts to provide as comprehensive a survey as possible of the material between the mid-fourteenth and mid-fifteenth centuries. In particular, *LALME* includes both non-localised literary texts and texts which had been 'translated' from one dialect area to another. This was a difficult and risky speculation, and probably would not have been possible if it had not been for the invention of the 'fit' technique. This technique proceeds from the known to the unknown. Assume that some informants (or texts) are localised independently by external methods. Each such text will reveal its forms. These forms can be plotted on maps. Then take a text which is not localised, and plot one of its forms on the maps. Every time this is done, it will be observable that the chosen form can only be placed on some areas of the map and yet remain consistent with already localised material. Then, over and over again, but one by one, forms from the chosen text are plotted on the existing maps. After a number of forms have been plotted, it will become clear that the previously unlocalised text can only come from one or two areas.

The fit technique can only work if it involves constant reiterations of the process. Furthermore, it first has to be used with texts whose provenances, although not independently fully localised, are nevertheless on other grounds thought most probably to relate to a particular area where there are a number of localised texts. It is also necessary to consider other evidence, including, for example, rhymes and alliteration. Particular attention has to be given to composite texts, where more than one scribe has been involved. McIntosh and his co-authors devote particular attention to *Mischsprachen*, texts which contain a unique combination of variant forms not otherwise found in single texts. The localisation of such texts is a major issue in *LALME*, for the identification of them is crucial to the attempt to map adequately the geographical space.

Rather than continue this exploration of methodology, it seems preferable to consider some of the consequences of *LALME* in the wider perspective. In order

Figure 7.2   *Survey points used for the* Linguistic Atlas of Late Mediaeval English *(see also Smith, 1996)*

to demonstrate the kind of results provided by *LALME*, consider some of the variant forms of 'she'. It has long been known that there were three major forms of this pronoun in ME: (1) forms directly derivable from OE *heo*; (2) a new form *sche*; (3) a new form *scho*. It was known for a long time before the publication of *LALME* that these forms appeared in different parts of the country. Broadly speaking, *heo* and related forms such as *he*, *hi* were found in the south and the west, *sche* in the south and the east midlands, and *scho* was essentially northern.

One result of *LALME* is that a far more detailed picture emerges, a picture which allows us to note local variation and establish clearer limits on the geography of particular variations. In the case of *she*, the most interesting dialect feature is the question of how *she* eventually became the usual form almost everywhere (forms derived from *heo* still survive in the west midlands). An inspection of the *LALME* maps shows us that the major centres in the north, in particular York and Durham, have 'she' forms earlier than elsewhere in the north. We can, in other words, see the spread of the new form from the east midlands to the north along patterns of trade. At a later stage the new prestige form would have spread more locally due to the importance of York and Durham.

But the spread of innovating forms was never in a single direction. Indeed, it could be argued that there were more innovations which spread in a north–south direction than vice versa. This was certainly true of, for example, the rise of *they* (in contrast to *he*, the most frequent development of Old English plural personal pronoun *hi*) and also of *are*, which began to supplant Old English *sint*. Generally speaking, and in terms of core items in the vocabulary, most of the innovations seem to have sprung from areas of the country where there had been substantial Scandinavian settlement at the time of the Danelaw. And, of course, this meant above all the eastern part of England from Northumberland as far south as, broadly speaking, Lincolnshire.

Outside the core vocabulary the picture is somewhat different, for here French influence was at least as important as any Scandinavian influence. The differences between French influence and Scandinavian influence are important for dialect variation. Yet the issue here is not one of geography. Unlike Scandinavian forms, French forms were quite well spread throughout the country. But they differ in that French loans are distributed differently in terms of variety. Such loans are found significantly more in religious and other high styles of speech.

An interesting demonstration of this is found in *Gawain and the Grene Knight*. This alliterative poem, contemporary with Chaucer, was written in the far north of Staffordshire. Here is a short extract:

> Bot Gawayne on þat *giserne* glyfte hym bysyde
> As hit com glydande adoun on glode hym to schende,
> And schranke a lytel with þe schulderes for þe scharp yrne.
> That oþer schalk wyth a schunt þe schene wythhaldeȝ,
> And þenne *repreued* he þe *prynce* with mony *prowde* wordeȝ:
> 'Þou art not Gawayn,' quod þe gome, 'þat is so goud halden,
> þat neuer arȝed for no here, by hylle ne be *vale*,
> And now þou fles for ferde er þou fele harmeȝ!
> Such *cowardise* of þat knyȝt cowþe I neuer here.
> Nawþer fyked I ne flaȝe, freke, quen þou myntest,
> Ne kest no *kauelacion*, in kyngeȝ hous Arthor.

I have italicised the French loanwords and underlined those from Scandinavian. Note how the *Gawain* poet uses the different languages to enrich the variety of his language, as in *ne kest no kauelacion*. Compare such variation with these two lines from Chaucer's *The Wife of Bath's Tale*:

> She nolde do that *vileynye* or synne
> To make hir housbonde han so foul a name

Chaucer uses far fewer Scandinavian words – although core vocabulary can be of Scandinavian origin, as is the case here with *housbonde*. But like the *Gawain* poet, he uses frequent doublets where French and English words are paired: *vileynye or synne*.

Table 7.1 *Some Middle English texts*

Date	Text	Location	Dialect
1155	*Peterborough Chronicle*	Peterborough	East Midlands
a.1200	*Ormulum*	South Lincolnshire	Northeast Midlands
1225	*Ancrene Wisse*	Herefordshire	West Midlands
a.1250	Kentish Sermons	Kent	Kentish
a.1300	*Cursor Mundi*	Durham/Yorkshire	Northeast
1340	Ayenbite of Inwit	Kent	Kentish
1375	*Gawain*	Staffordshire	Northwest Midlands
1375	Barbour's *Bruce*	Scotland	Scots
1380	Wiclif	Leicestershire	Southeast Midlands
1387	John of Trevisa	Cornwall	Southwest
1390	Chaucer	London	Southeast

A comparison of any extract from Chaucer and from the *Gawain* poet will reveal how dialectally diverse contemporary writings could be at the end of the fourteenth century. In order to elucidate the variety of writings during the ME period, Table 7.1 is a quick guide to some of the more interesting dialect texts. It is very selective, and it is no substitute for a fuller investigation of the type of material presented in a textbook such as Burrow & Turville-Petre (1992).

It should be observed that the dates give in Table 7.1 are approximate and only intended to help readers identify texts for study. Note also that many of these texts appear in various manuscripts, which may originate from different parts of the country.

7.4   A Scottish interlude

So far we have given the impression that all British dialects were located in England. This, however, is to mislead. In the case of Welsh English this is not too important, since we have little reliable information about such varieties until the twentieth century (see Thomas, 1994), and we shall leave that issue aside for the present. But the English dialects of Scotland are a quite different matter. Not only that, but the terms which can be used to describe them are often unclear. It is, therefore, useful to spend a few moments dealing with matters of history and terminology.

English-speaking settlements in what is now Scotland were first established in the second half of the sixth century – indeed the Ruthwell Cross, with its inscription from the Anglo-Saxon *Dream of the Rood*, is to be found in southwest Scotland. It is clear that from an early time English had become the dominant language in the Borders and Lothian, i.e. southeast Scotland up to Edinburgh, and possibly also in the southwest. But the Viking invasions and the English-based Norman Conquest created a complex set of linguistic and other relationships in Scotland.

At the time of the Norman Conquest the kingdom of Scotland, which was beginning to emerge, remained fundamentally Gaelic-speaking. But Gaelic was under threat from English, as a result of the Norman Conquest, the development of Anglo-Scottish commerce and, soon, the accession to the Scottish throne of native English-speaking Scots. Just as important from our point of view is the fact that the fourteenth century saw the War of Independence against the English. Therefore the growing dominance of the English language, allied with hostile relations with the English and friendlier relations with the continent, especially France, did not, at this time, lead to a subordinate variety of English in Scotland.

Sisam (1921: xx) writes: 'The literary centre swings back to the capital – now London instead of Winchester – which henceforth provides the models for authors of any pretensions throughout England and across the Scottish border.' As a description of the activities of, say, the *Gawain* poet, this seems misleading. All the more so, then, does it inadequately describe the writing of John Barbour, the fourteenth-century author of *The Bruce*. Here is a typical extract from the poem:

> Engynys alsua for till cast
> Thai ordanit and maid redy fast,
> And set ilk man syne till his ward;
> And Schir Valter, the gude Steward,
> With armyt men shuld ryde about,
> And se quhar at thar war mast dout,
> And succur thar with his menʒhe.
> And quhen thai into sic degré
> Had maid thame for thair assaling,
> On the Rude-evyn in the dawing,
> The Inglis host blew till assale.

Many of the particular features of this passage can equally be found in texts from northern English. However it is notable how many Scots features extend throughout the system. It is not simply a matter of orthography, even given spellings such as <quh-> (for English <wh>) or the use of <i> to indicate a long vowel, as in <maid> 'made'. Note, for example, the *for + till* construction. This equates to English *for + to* and might be thought to show only lexical variation. But there is a different point to be made. Although in ME the *for + to* construction was common (see Fischer, 1992), it became obsolete shortly afterwards (see Rissanen, 1999a). However it survives in present-day Scots, albeit in a semi-English form, i.e. as *firtae*. In phonology the spelling of <gude> signals the fronting and raising of ME /oː/ to /øː/ and eventually /yː/, which occurs in all northern varieties. A particular feature of the extract above is the use of the French loanword *assale*. The word exists in English too, but it is more frequent in Scots, which has many

French loans not found in English, e.g. *tassie* 'cup' < Fr. *tasse*. There are also Old English words which have been lost from English but remain in Modern Scots, here *dawing*, cf. English *dawn(ing)*.

Before we conclude this interlude it is necessary to say a few words about terminology, as I promised. It is normal to distinguish between Scots and Scottish English. Essentially Scots refers to the language which is descended from Northumbrian OE and became in the latter part of the medieval period close to becoming a language distinct from English. Scottish English refers to the anglicised form of the language which was to become dominant, partly due to the Union of the two kingdoms in 1603 but also because of the influence exerted by the Authorised Version of the Bible. To what extent devolution (1999) will switch the balance back towards Scots is a question at present unanswerable.

7.5   Early Modern English

The period from the rise of printing to the American Declaration of Independence marks the last time when English could be seen as a phenomenon solely associated with the British Isles. At the same time, it is a period which marks the transition from a state where all dialects had at best a local focus. For the great movement at this time was the quite rapid emergence of a standard language, a topic that is handled in Chapter 5. We shall therefore attempt to avoid repetition here, although it will be clear to everyone that there is such interlocking of the standard and non-standard varieties that such an attempt is doomed to failure.

The first point which has to be made is that although the amount of material available for this period appears to be substantial in comparison with previous times, this appearance of quantity belies the true state of affairs. The rise of printing and the quickening spread of education of course led to more being written (and read), but at the same time the rise of a standard language caused writing in local dialect to be stigmatised. Quite early in this period (1589) we find George Puttenham writing as follows:

> ye shall therfore take the vsuall speach of the Court, and that of London and the shires lying about London within lx. myles, and not much aboue. I say not this but that in euery shyre of England there be gentlemen and others that speake but especially write as good Southerne as we of Middlesex or Surrey do, but not the common people of euery shire . . .   (Görlach, 1991)

And at the end of the period we find Thomas Sheridan writing as follows in 1762:

> One [mode of pronunciation] is current in the city, and is called the cockney; the other at the court-end, and is called the polite pronunciation. As amongst these various dialects, one must have the preference, and become fashionable, it will of course fall to the lot of which prevails at court, the source of fashions of all kinds. All other dialects, are sure marks, of either a provincial, rustic,

> pedantic, or mechanic education; and therefore have some degree of disgrace annexed to them.   (Görlach, 1999, quoting from Wakelin, 1977)

Let us first examine the state of affairs in the mid-fifteenth century. At this time there are indeed a growing number of texts which demonstrate, if not a standard language, what the authors of *LALME* describe as a colourless variety which, although not conforming to the emerging standard, is generally devoid of localised forms (see also Smith, 1996: 73ff.). One such text is Bokenham's *Mappa Mundi*. Bokenham came from Suffolk and the text dates from just before the middle of the century. Here is a typical extract:

> . . . hit is to been vndirstondyn that, as mony dyuerys peeples as it haþe dwellers, so many hit haþe dyuersites of toungis and languagis . . . Angli, all be hit þat from the first bygynnynge, after þe thre dyuersytees of peeplis of Germayne þe which they comyn of, hadyn thre dyuersites of sowndyngis yn hure language and yn thre diuerys places, as Sowþe, Norþe, and Mydlonde, yet of commyxtioun dyvers, firste Danys and sethe with Normannys, they haue corrupte her first nativ toungis and vsyn now I ne wot what straunge and pylgryms blaberyng and cheteryng, noþyng accordynge onto here firste speche.   (From Burnley, 1992)

It is, of course, interesting to compare this extract with that from Trevisa which we discussed in Section 7.3, since this new text is from the same original source. But it is even more interesting to compare it with the material emerging from the new Chancery Standard discussed in Chapter 5. There are a variety of different features which do not appear in Chancery Standard, such as: third-person plural *-yn*, *hit* 'it', *hure* 'their', negative *ne wot*. But perhaps most obvious of all is the variation in forms: note for example the various spellings of *diversity*.

Yet if we look at another contemporary East Anglian letter, we can see the difference between a colourless variety such as Bokenham's and a localised variety. This extract is from the collection of letters written by the Norfolk *Paston Family*. It is from a letter dictated by Margaret Paston to her husband John on 19 May 1448:

> Qwhan Wymdham seyd þat Jamys xuld dy I seyd to hym þat I soposyd þat he xuld repent hym jf he schlow hym or dede to hym any bodyly harm; and he seyd nay, he xuld never repent hym ner have a ferding wurth of harm þow he kelyd ʒw and hym bothe . . . It js told me þat he xall kom to London jn hast. I pray ʒw be ware hw ʒe walkyn jf he be þere, for he js ful cursyd-hertyd and lwmysch.   (From Burnley, 1992)

The most obvious features here are the particularly East Anglian spellings, such as *qwhan* 'when', *xuld* 'should', *schlow* 'slew', but also *jf* 'if', *jn* 'in'. Yet there are other East Anglian features too, for example inflectional *-yn* and the dialect word *lwmysch* 'loutish'. Sometimes, as with *-yn*, these are identical with the colourless variety, but more often they are clearly local, and the result is for us today a text which is not immediately readable. The Paston family were well-to-do; John

Paston was a barrister at the Inner Temple, and in letters twenty or so years later, we find his sons writing in a form much closer to the Chancery Standard (letters sometimes dictated by their mother, who remained non-literate). Such a shift shows how quickly standard spelling practices were adopted.

It therefore begins to appear as if non-standard English is disappearing. But that is not a helpful view of the situation. It is true that ever since the mid-fifteenth century standardised forms of the language have come to dominate, more and more, written discourse. And conversely, non-standard written forms have become, except for particular purposes, stigmatised. The critical word here is 'written'. As we shall see later, spoken dialect variation continued to flourish. But since it became exiled from the written discourse, it becomes harder for us today to discover direct evidence for its existence, until the invention of technology such as tape-recording towards the end of the nineteenth century.

This shift away from written dialect forms can be astonishingly quick. Here, for example, is a short extract from the diary kept by Henry Machyn, a London tradesman, between 1550 and 1563:

> The xxv day of Marche, the wyche was owre lade [day,] ther was as gret justes as youe have sene at the tylt at Vestmynster; the chalengers was a Spaneard and ser Gorge Haward; and all ther men, and ther horsses trymmyd in whyt, and then cam the Kyng and a gret mene all in bluw . . . and all ther veffelers and ther fotemen . . .   (from Burnley, 1992)

Perhaps what is most obvious about such non-standard language is the extent to which it nevertheless approximates to the standard. When, therefore, Machyn (originally from southwest Yorkshire; see now Britton, 2000) writes *wyche* alongside *whyt* and, elsewhere, *what* and *where*, most early spelling reformers, such as John Hart and Alexander Gil, preserve the distinction between [hw] and [w], and the variation shown by Machyn may signal a struggle between standardised and dialect forms. Machyn also demonstrates another difficulty we face when dealing with a localised spelling system, namely the question of how to interpret certain spellings. Thus the value of the use of <v> in both *Vestminster* and *veffelers* (= *whifflers*) is obscure, and we might be misled by Dickensian overtones.

What we might call the 'underground' nature of the non-standard dialects means that for most of the early Modern English period substantial information about the structure of the dialects is rather limited. To some extent what we have to do is to interpolate; we have to pool our resources about the situation in Middle English and the situation in the present-day language in order to ascertain the likely state of affairs in the intervening period. The best source of contemporary evidence for the period comes from spelling reformers, or orthoepists, and grammarians.

Nevertheless, it is during this period that a number of dialect distinctions emerge which are highly salient in the present-day language. Most of these, because of the nature of the limited evidence, are phonological. I give below a short summary of some of these distinctions.

- Most northern English dialects of PDE lack the phoneme /ʌ/. This phoneme arose with the split of ME phoneme /ʊ/, so that standard English contrasts *foot* /fʊt/ and *strut* /strʌt/. The first direct evidence for the split comes in 1640 (for this and other phonological evidence during the period, Dobson, 1957, is essential and invaluable). Interestingly, already in 1596, Edmund Coote, the author of *The English Schoole-Master* (see Dobson, 1957: 33), had detected the split. Coote, based in Suffolk, objects to 'the barbarous speech of your country people', but for us this may be an indication of an East Anglian source for the split.

- A particularly salient variation results from the early Modern English change by which /a/ is lengthened before voiceless fricatives. This lengthening produces standard English forms such as /lɑːf/, /bɑːθ/, /pɑːst/ for *laugh*, *bath*, *past*. Although the evolution of such forms is in fact lengthy, so that the position is by no means stable even today, it is worth noting the situation here, since it was in the early Modern English period that the contrasts came to be established. The best-known dialectal variation is that almost all northern dialects have /baθ/, etc. in all these words. But there are variations too. For example, many midlands dialects show lengthening but not retraction, i.e. /baːθ/, and over many southern areas raising to /æː/ is common and can equally affect the vowel of *cat* to give /kæt/.

- In many west midlands and northwestern dialects the final /g/ in words such as *thing* is retained, i.e. /θɪŋg/ against standard /θɪŋ/. The standard loss of final /g/ is observable from the end of the sixteenth century but that appears to be the result of earlier loss in East Anglia and Essex.

- One interesting change which is to some extent a conservative throwback associated with the Great Vowel Shift is the preservation of the distinction between /iː/ and /eː/ (from ME /eː/ and /ɜː/) in *meet* and *meat*. As discussed elsewhere, in the standard language these vowels merged during the eighteenth century, but some dialects preserved the distinction. This is true of parts of the north and also of Ireland; see further below. But the distinction has been receding everywhere and may soon be lost completely.

7.6   Modern English

If the Middle English period can be described as the age of dialects, then a parallel description of the Modern English period would be as the period of dialectology. The aptness of such a description is based on many different features. And it seems appropriate to consider some of these here. The reason for this is that it is only through a discussion of the basics of the development of dialectological theory that we can hope to reach an understanding of how the attitudes to and the treatment of dialects has evolved.

Although grammarians of the seventeenth and eighteenth centuries often discuss non-standard forms, their principal reason for so doing was almost always from the vantage point of standard English and their aim to guide their readers away from social misfortune; see, for example, Mugglestone (2003). When dialect collections first appear – and perhaps the first important such collection is by John Ray in 1674 with a second edition in 1691 – the interest is primarily in vocabulary. In terms of dialect mapping, Ray classifies forms largely by county, which is a common feature of later studies too. But Ihalainen (1994) suggests that Ray probably considered there to be a north–south divide with that division roughly along a line from Bristol to the Wash, not a division which would seem sensible to later dialectologists. Ihalainen (1994) also provides a useful overview of later eighteenth- and nineteenth-century dialect collections, culminating, perhaps, in Halliwell's *Dictionary of Archaic and Provincial Words*, first published in 1847.

But, as Ihalainen also says, there was until the last quarter of the nineteenth century no serious attempt to present a coherent picture of the contemporary dialect situation. There is no single reason why the situation should have changed then, but rather a multiplicity of reasons. Clearly the ever growing urbanisation of England created an emerging polarity between standard English and local urban dialects. As Sweet (1890) writes: 'The Cockney dialect seems very ugly to an Englishman or woman because he – and still more she – lives in perpetual terror of being taken for a Cockney . . .' And many dialectologists complained about the way in which the railways were destroying local dialects, in terms rather reminiscent of Wordsworth's fears for the Lake District in the age of steam.

But there was also a purely linguistic factor involved. For this was the time of both the Neogrammarian movement, which spread out from Leipzig, and of the first systematic attempts at dialect geography, in particular the German atlas started by Georg Wenkler in 1876, almost simultaneous with the birth of Neogrammarianism. In Britain this burst of activity was evident in both the Philological Society and the English Dialect Society. Thus in 1875, Alexander Ellis, with the assistance of others, produced a classification of English dialects which remains important today; see Ellis (1875) and also Ihalainen (1994) for detailed discussion; Trudgill (1999b) offers a brief introduction to the distinctions between present-day dialects and those in the *Survey of English Dialects* (*SED*), that is, the dialect situation at the end of the nineteenth century.

In 1889 Ellis produced what is generally recognised as the first systematic survey of English dialects (Ellis, 1889). Alongside this work, there began to appear the first systematic studies on individual dialects, of which Elworthy's study of the dialect of West Somerset (1875) is a notable example. Even more interesting was the study of the dialect of Windhill in Yorkshire, published by Joseph Wright in 1892. Wright was not only a native of Windhill, a manufacturing township now

Figure 7.3   *Traditional dialect areas (Trudgill, 1999b)*

part of the Leeds–Bradford conurbation, but he was to become both Professor of Comparative Philology at Oxford and editor of the *English Dialect Dictionary* (Wright, 1898–1905). This latter work retains its interest today, not merely as a fund of information, although it is that. The production of the *EDD* was contemporary with the production of the *OED* and indeed the *EDD* was intended as an adjunct to the *OED*. As such, it attempted to replicate features of the *OED*, such as using only written citations. From our point of view today, this is unfortunate, but the temper of the times was very different from that to which we are used.

Unlike the position in Germany and France, and indeed several other continental countries, it was a remarkably long time before a full-scale dialect atlas of either England or Scotland was produced. In Britain we had to wait until 1948, when Harold Orton, of the University of Leeds, together with Eugen Dieth of

Figure 7.4   *Modern dialect areas (Trudgill, 1999b)*

Zurich, started work on the *Survey of English Dialects* (*SED*), which was eventually published in 1962–71 (Orton et al., 1962–71).

It is worth spending some time on the *SED*, since it is the essential tool for the study of traditional dialectology in Britain (although it is in fact exclusively English). The *SED* proceeded by means of directly interviewing dialect speakers from some 313 different localities in England, usually, but not always, one single informant from each locality. But these bare facts tell us very little. It is important to understand exactly what the aims of this study were, and to recall that it was only recently that mobile recording equipment had become easily available and also acceptable to untutored informants. Thus, above all, the *SED* strove to gather information about rural dialects which, it was felt, were fast disappearing under the pressures of urbanisation.

This meant that the *SED* was interested primarily in speakers who met four criteria: they had to be non-mobile, old, rural and male. Nowadays this group is colloquially referred to by the acronym NORMS. Each term had its own justification. Informants should be non-mobile, so that they had not been sub-ject to interference from another dialect, i.e. they spoke the 'pure' dialect of their native locality. They had to be old, because the aim was to record the speech of about fifty years previous, i.e. the speech of approximately the beginning of the twentieth century. I have already explained the motivation for choosing rural speakers. Males were preferred over females because it was thought that females were more subject to pressure from standardised forms of the language. In hindsight we might well regret some of the decisions that were made about informants, but whatever the case might be (at least the decision to interview only older speakers seems absolutely right under the circumstances), we have to accept those decisions as a fact of life.

One feature which at first sight most surprises present-day readers of the *SED* is the small number of informants. The number appears equally small when compared with the number of speakers used in the German and French dialect atlases compiled at the end of the nineteenth century and the beginning of the next; see here Chambers & Trudgill (1980: 18ff.) for a comparative view. But there is a good explanation for the small number. The *SED* was organised on the basis of a set questionnaire with a variety of questions, often to be presented in an indirect manner, so that we find questions such as:

What's in my pocket? [show an empty pocket] (*nothing, nought*)

Given that in total there were approximately 1,200 questions, all formed in the same manner, and that those questions were required to be asked in a set order, this took about 20 to 24 hours to administer, and often one informant would be replaced by another in order to complete the task – it should be recalled that informants were generally quite old and relatively uneducated.

What the *SED* provides us with, therefore, is a snapshot of a relatively sta-ble, agriculturally based male community whose members were born around the beginning of the twentieth century. The mass of material which was collected has made it possible to produce a range of maps, in particular maps demonstrating the variety in both the phonological systems and the vocabulary. The two essential texts published by the *SED* are *The Linguistic Atlas of England* (*LAE*) (Orton et al., 1978) and *A Word Geography of England* (Orton & Wright, 1974); see also the Further Reading to this chapter. It must be pointed out that it requires some sophistication in order to read such works as the *LAE* successfully; and the map-ping of isoglosses to distinguish the spread of individual items is a major inter-pretive task. For some of the pitfalls see the very useful remarks in Francis (1983).

If we look at the dialect situation in the mid-to-late nineteenth century, when dialect studies first began to flourish and only a few decades before *SED* infor-mants were born, we find that in many aspects of the language there remained features which we might regard today as not merely dialectal, but frankly archaic. Below I list a few examples from the *SED* material which may help to make read-ers aware of what has now gone, or almost gone, from the language. This list is, of course, at one and the same time, selective and random.

In vocabulary, it is doubtful, for example, that *tab* 'ear' is any longer found in Nottinghamshire or Derbyshire, and *lug*, instead of being found widely throughout the north and east, as far south as Suffolk, is certainly becoming more recessive as *ear* becomes the 'normal' word in so much more of the country (although it remains a possibility for a Scot like me). Other words which have been lost or are almost lost include: *urchin* 'hedgehog' (northern, also Shropshire, Herefordshire); *mind* 'remember' is still common in Scotland, but pockets of *mind* formerly throughout England have lost out except perhaps on the Scottish border; *quist* 'pigeons' was formerly found in the west midlands from Cheshire to Gloucestershire, but is certainly not found in Cheshire today. It would be wrong, however, to suggest that all dialect vocabulary has been lost. For example, my own experience would suggest that *lake* 'play' is still possible in many parts of Yorkshire.

If the above paragraph gives only a tantalising flavour, it is perhaps easier to list significant morphological features. Here I concentrate on aspects of the pronoun system. One important feature which still obtained quite frequently in mid-nineteenth-century local dialects was the preservation of the second-person singular pronoun *thou*, which persisted widely throughout the north and the west, but was always threatened by *you*, a process which today is almost complete although it remains in the speech of at least some speakers from Yorkshire. That is by no means the only change in the pronoun system. Throughout the south midlands, from Leicestershire to Hampshire *his* and *hers* at the time of the *SED* retained the old Middle English midlands forms *hisn*, *hern*, whilst *hissen* for *himself* is still found in Yorkshire, Lincolnshire, Derbyshire and Nottinghamshire, but *hissel*, the form still found quite widely at that time, is probably receding except in Scotland and the northernmost parts of England.

Let us now turn our attention to syntax, which is often regarded as the cinderella of dialect studies. One reason for this is that both vocabulary and phonology provide an easier and almost immediate reaction. If I were to use the word *gallus*, for example (which happens to be part of my native vocabulary), I doubt if more than 10 per cent of the British population would know what I meant. Native speakers of British English can normally detect phonological features in dialects other than their own without much difficulty. But often syntactic features are either unnoticed or dismissed as errors, rather than genuine dialectal variations.

Here I want to consider a small group of historical syntactic features, which are sometimes near to extinction, although they seem to have been quite vigorous 150 years ago, others of which remain viable and sometimes strong. The first of these is found in northern dialects, and is called 'The Northern subject rule'; see Ihalainen (1994: 221–2), also Chapman (1998). The following are typical examples:

They peel them and boil*s* them
Him and me drink*s* nought but water
I often tell*s* him
I tell him not to

The general rule in this construction is that inflectional -*s* is found throughout the present tense, unless the verb is immediately preceded or followed by a single personal pronoun subject. Thus there is both an extension of the inflection, and it is nevertheless absent in the immediate vicinity of a personal pronoun. This feature is one which already existed in sixteenth-century northern English and Scots. William Dunbar writes:

> On to the ded goi*s* all Estatis

Although the dialectal spread of the Northern subject rule may have shrunk a little over the intervening time, it is still alive and well in its core areas. A superficially similar morphology occurs in East Anglian dialects, where there is no inflection throughout the present, so that we find:

> She like him

but this is simply total loss of the inflection. This too appears to remain fully viable, although it has retreated from Essex, where it was formerly strong; see Trudgill (1999b: 101–2).

Southwestern and west midlands dialects have a peculiar feature no longer found elsewhere. This is a process called Pronoun Exchange, and produces sentences such as:

> Her told I

which actually means 'She told him.' But as Trudgill (1999b: 95–8) observes, this feature was also found in Essex in the nineteenth century, which leads him to suppose, plausibly, that it was formerly a quite widespread feature of southern and western dialects before receding under the influence of the standard language. Another southern feature which was already almost lost by the twentieth century is the pronoun *Ich* 'I', as in the phrase *Chill let you go* in *King Lear*. Alexander Ellis (1889) talks of part of Somerset as *The Land of Utch*. It seems to have survived, just, into the 1970s.

So far I have not touched on pronunciation, yet this is perhaps the area where change is most obvious and salient. This omission has been deliberate. For this area has some interesting features, which means that it requires rather different treatment. Of course, most of the emphasis of dialect study has been placed on the phonological material, for reasons that we have already mentioned. As a result, there is a huge amount of material which we could consider, greatly exceeding the bounds of this chapter. But there is a rather more interesting issue. It seems quite clear that the last two hundred years has seen a considerable amount of change in pronunciation; see MacMahon (1998: esp. 373–4). MacMahon is talking about standard English; but the changes in non-standard dialects are even greater. The changes which have occurred in dialects over the last two hundred years, and which are most apparent in the area of phonology, can be classified into three types: (1) standardisation; (2) levelling; (3) innovation. Let us examine each these in turn, starting with standardisation.

Figure 7.5   *Limits of postvocalic /r/ in present-day dialects (from Trudgill,*
1999b)

Most ordinary people have the perception that local dialects are disappearing
under the pressure of standardisation, the result of a variety of factors, amongst
which the rise of literacy due to increased education is perhaps the most obvious.
To this must be added other elements such as the rise of mass media (as much the
result of mass literacy as anything else) and the continuous urbanisation of the
country. And that is indeed true, although, as we shall see, there are counter-effects
which mean that the situation is not quite so simple.

Nevertheless, the effects of standardisation can be very well exemplified by
considering one of the most notable features of standard English English, namely
the loss of postvocalic /r/ in words such as *arm* (/ɑːm/). This is in striking contrast
to the preservation of /r/ in both Scottish English and American English. It is also
in contrast to the dialect situation about 100 years ago. For then, all dialects
south of a line from Shrewsbury to Dover (but, importantly, excluding London)
where equally rhotic, as was the northwest (from Chester northwards) and also
the Tyneside area.

But ever since then the rhotic area has shrunk, so that now only the area southwest of a line from Northampton to Portsmouth and a small enclave centred on Blackburn in Lancashire remain. And everywhere on the margins of these areas, especially those closest to London, the rhotic forms are predominantly found with older speakers only. Other features show a similarly recessive character. Even the northern and midlands use of /ʊ/ in words such as *but* is slowly receding, for standard /ʌ/ seems to have moved 25–50 miles north. Another recessive feature is perhaps the /ng/ in words such as *finger*, which occurs in the northwest midlands from Preston in the north to just south of Birmingham, but appears to be strong only in parts of Lancashire, Staffordshire and the west midlands.

In contrast to such recessive features, it is important to note that there are some innovative features which appear to have gained remarkable strength in a relatively short period of time. One such case involves the vocalisation of postvocalic /l/ in words such as *milk*. In standard English the pronunciation of this work is [mɪʊɫk] with a velarised [ɫ]. But in the southeastern corner of England, from Essex across to Hampshire, the *l* has been lost and we find [mɪʊk]. The same area also shows the replacement of intervocalic /t/ with a glottal stop, as in /bʌʔə/ 'butter'. This is often recognised as a stereotypical Cockney feature, but it is spreading, as is the process of glottalling, as in /ʌʔp/ 'up', although other dialects, such as in Scotland, appear to have independently innovated this change. The set of features we have just mentioned are commonly described as signs of 'Estuary English'. From our point of view they demonstrate the large influence exercised on standard English by the dialects to the northeast of London. It is also important to distinguish this type of increasing use from merely stable or recessive dialect features. Thus the pronunciation of *brother* with a labiodental fricative, i.e. /brʌvə/, remains a particularly Cockney feature (although Wright, 1892, found it near his native Windhill).

There is a widely held view that dialects are disappearing. This view is in many respects entirely correct. It does seem to be quite true that the variety of rural dialects with which we are presented in a work such as the *SED* is diminishing rapidly. This is due to obvious factors which we have already mentioned, such as the urbanisation of former countryside, the growth of mass media with its influence on the young, and the role of education and literacy in stigmatising local dialect. Yet this view does not reveal the full picture. Although rural dialects are indeed under threat, as they have been for a century or more, the history of urban dialects is rather different. To some extent, this is a historiographical issue. As we have seen, the rise of the study of dialects was essentially a nineteenth-century phenomenon which was gradually refined until the time of the *SED*. Both for good reasons, such as the desire to record forms which were thought to be dying out, and for ideological reasons, connected with the desire to record 'pure' dialect, information about urban dialects was often ignored.

But there is also a methodological issue here, for the traditional approach was difficult to apply in urban areas, where the situation was very different. A solution to the difficulties only became possible with the emergence of what is now known as sociolinguistics. The first systematic sociolinguistic studies were undertaken by William Labov in New York in the mid-1960s; see Labov (1972) or, for a more detailed and extended account, Labov (1994). Britain had to wait for the studies of Norwich produced in the early 1970s by Peter Trudgill; see especially Trudgill (1974). Since then there have been an increasing number of important studies, several of which are mentioned in the Further Reading to this chapter.

It is important to recognise that sociolinguistics is not a rival to traditional dialectology. Yet it brought new methods of working and permitted an investigation of a much wider segment of the population, so that now younger, as well as older, informants could be sampled, and women, as well as men, were seen as proper subjects of study; also, in contrast to the *SED*, these sociolinguistic approaches were concerned with the interaction of different social classes. The consequences of such a revolution (that seems a more appropriate word than 'evolution') may not redraw the dialect geography of Britain, in the sense that the historical maps still hold. On the other hand, we now can draw new maps which can alter our perceptions of what is happening to dialects today.

This brings us back to the view that dialects are disappearing. Most of the socio-linguistic studies are based on precisely delimited areas: for example, Trudgill (1974) was a study of the sociolinguistics of Norwich; see also, for example, Milroy (1980), Cheshire (1982). This is inherent in the methodology. Nevertheless, there has been some geographically quite large-scale work done which is of the highest importance in assessing the state of present-day dialects. Perhaps the most interesting of these is Cheshire et al. (1993). This work was a first attempt to assess the language of schoolchildren throughout the British Isles. Although, for reasons outside the authors' control, the study was not as fruitful as had been hoped, it still remains a foundation for further work in the area.

Perhaps the most important general result from this survey, and one which has been confirmed by more local studies, is that there has indeed been a process of dialect levelling, that is to say, there has been a decline in dialectal variety throughout Britain (although Scots and Ulster English tend to go their own way, presumably for reasons of national identity). But this decline in variety is not in the direction of standard English. Instead, what seems to be happening is that the different urban dialects are becoming more and more alike whilst remaining distinct from the standard.

In this survey the six most frequent usages (all with a percentage score of 85 per cent or higher) were:

them (Look at them big spiders)
should of (You should of left half an hour ago!)
'no plural marking' (. . . you need two pound of flour)
what as subject relative (The film what was on last night was good)
never as past-tense negator (No, I never broke that)
there was with notional plural (There was some singers here a minute ago)

Even if there are some problems with this survey, the general outline is indisputable. Over a very wide range of urban dialects there has been a noticeable trend to level dialect forms so that it becomes sensible to consider the whole urban spread in England as tending to become a single unit. By and large these urban forms remain unacceptable in standard English, although there are signs that usages such as *never* and *there was*, as exemplified above, are acceptable in colloquial standard. Against this, the use of, for example, *should of* and relative *what* are both heavily stigmatised.

Perhaps an even more important aspect of this study is that the authors are able to demonstrate that in some features we can find evidence that there is a quite clearcut division between urban dialects and the dialects of surrounding regions. One interesting division occurs in a split between core Manchester dialects and other northwestern dialects. Core Manchester dialects use *youse* 'you plural', whilst the form is rare elsewhere; on the other hand, the same northwestern dialects regularly use demonstrative *this here*, *that there*, which is infrequent in Manchester, where *them* is preferred.

There is some temptation to assume that the phenomenon of dialect levelling will follow the pattern established in the standard language, where the predominant influence is from the southeastern part of the country. However, this seems to be less the case in the context of dialect levelling. One important example of levelling which seems to be spreading from other parts of the country is the replacement of present participle forms by past participle in the verbs *sit* and *stand*. Thus, where standard English has *She was sitting there*, *He was standing there*, in the urban dialects we are talking about, we find *She was sat there*, *He was stood there*. The latter forms are widely felt to be common only in the northwest of England, but in Cheshire et al. (1993) the evidence quite clearly shows the forms have become diffused over a large part of the country, including through much of the south.

A further result from this survey, which is of considerable interest, is that some usages in Scotland are quite divergent from those in England and Wales. For example, where the English schools reported demonstrative *them* (see above), the Scottish schools (all Glaswegian) reported *thon*, *thae*, *yon*. Similarly *ain't*/*in't* was absent from Scottish schools. Although this divergence could be trivial, it seems most likely that it is an indication of the continuing separation of Scots as a semi-autonomous variety of English.

There are, indeed, a great many dialect differences between Scots and any form of English. Not all these differences are merely the result of continuity from earlier periods, from the situation in the sixteenth and seventeenth centuries, as we discussed in Section 7.4. This does not mean that there are no remnants of the earlier language, for there are: thus we can mention the mid-high front vowel /ʉ/ in *buik* 'book' together with the merger of /u/ and /ʊ/ in that new phoneme, and the retention of postvocalic /r/; see the earlier discussion of loss of rhoticity in almost all English dialects. Remaining with phonology, the most obvious other aspect of Scots is the phenomenon known as Aitken's Law; see Aitken (1981), Aitken & Macafee (2002), Lass (1974), Wells (1982), McClure

(1994). Throughout Scots all vowels are short, except before a stem boundary, a voiced fricative or /r/. Typical examples, where English dialects have a long vowel, are Scots *bead* /bid/, *lace* /les/, cf. English /biːd/, /leɪs/. Perhaps the most obvious examples occur before inflectional forms so that there is a clear contrast between *need* /nid/ and *knee+d* /niːd/.

In syntax also, there are significant differences from English. Perhaps the best known of these concern modal verbs and negative marking. As in many other dialects, the variety of modal verbs is more restricted than in standard varieties, but Scots dialects have a distinctive usage not found elsewhere in Britain (except the contiguous area of Northumberland), although there are some parts of the US where the usage is found, notably in the Ohio–Pennsylvania area. The construction is called the Double Modal construction, and can be exemplified by sentences such as:

> He might could do it if he tried ('He would be able to do it ...')
> She should can go tomorrow ('She ought to be able to go tomorrow')

The term Double Modal may not be fully accurate, since the following triple modal is equally possible:

> He'll might could do it for you ('He might be able in the future to do it for you')

Double modals are, of course, inherently interesting, since they break the usual assumption about English that there can only be one modal per verb phrase. But Scots also has a negation system which is different from that found in English dialects and which interacts with modals, so that we find sentences such as:

> She couldnae hae telt him ('It is not possible for her to have told him')
> She could no hae telt him ('It was possible for her not to have told him')

and even:

> He couldnae hae no been no working ('It is impossible that he has not been out of work')

See further Brown (1991), Brown & Millar (1980). I have such forms in my own native dialect.

The evidence that we have just reviewed, from both English and Scottish dialects, supports quite strongly the belief that dialect levelling is taking place. This, however, should not lead us to assume that traditional rural dialects have completely disappeared, although they are undoubtedly on the decline, despite, I think, the comments of Trudgill (1999b: 108). But they are being replaced not so much by standard English as by a generalised non-standard variety. And this variety is different in the two countries, and could even be increasing because of external influences, such as the distinctive political atmosphere in Scotland.

The type of dialect levelling we have just discussed is sometimes reminiscent of the 'colourless' language which we noted in later Middle English. There are differences, to be sure, but there are also resemblances. However, there is another type of change, studied in Britain by Paul Kerswill and others. Kerswill has studied dialect variation in the 'new town' of Milton Keynes, where the developments take a different shape. In such cases a new levelled form appears to replace any earlier form very abruptly and with complete loss of earlier forms in the whole area. Kerswill calls this type of levelling 'koine formation'. Examples of this in Britain seem most obvious in the southern part of the country, where there is considerable levelling in any case, yet the process seems to be markedly different from the usual types of levelling; see further Kerswill & Williams (2000).

7.7   Other dialects

So far in this survey there has been virtually no mention of Welsh or Irish dialects of English. The reasons for this are rather different. In the case of Welsh English the local dialects are all quite subordinate to the English dialects to their east, either, in the case of south Wales, to the southwestern dialects of England, or in north Wales to the dialects centred, in particular, on Liverpool and the Wirral. As such, dialectal features particular to areas of Wales are thin on the ground. Parry's *Survey of Anglo-Welsh Dialects* (1977, 1979) begins to fill the gaps, as does Coupland's (1988) sociolinguistic study of Cardiff English; for these and others, see Thomas (1994).

At first sight the situation in Ireland seems similar, but the similarities are actually insignificant. In Wales, English was introduced into indigenous areas from the fourteenth century. Irish English (I use the term preferred in Kallen, 1994) was first introduced in 1169, and texts are first found from about around 1250. But in Ireland there was competition between three languages – English, French and Irish – possibly, if we include Latin, four. Furthermore, the loss of French appears to have enhanced the status of Irish, rather than of English, at least until the seventeenth century. At this time there was a deliberate attempt to resettle Ireland and establish British rule. The most important attempts involved the Plantation Settlements, firstly in Leix and Offaly and later, and more crucially, in the northeast of Ulster, by Scots. As a result, English now had two bases in Ireland, one around Dublin and Wexford, the other around Antrim. Since then English has become the dominant language over the whole country. Although its spread has been irregular and patchy, native-speaker ability in Irish may now be as low as 3 per cent; see Kallen (1994: 164).

In terms of medieval inheritance of English, much attention is paid to the speech of the baronies of Forth and Bargy in Wexford, first commented upon by the chronicler Stanyhurst in 1577:

> Howbeit to this day, the dregs of the olde auncient Chaucer English, are kept as well as in Fingall. As they term a spider, attercop, a wispe, a wad . . .
> (Görlach, 1991)

Many of the present-day features of Irish English appear in these Wexford dialects, which appear to have survived until the nineteenth century. Thus the dentalisation of the fricatives /θ, ð/ to [t̪, d̪] in words such as *thin*, *thirty* appears to have been established very early on. Equally early is the shift of /f/ to bilabial /ɸ/, hence *faat* 'what'; compare the form *fit* in Buchan in northeast Scotland. The influence of Irish Gaelic is at least as obvious in syntax as in phonology. Even in early Modern Irish, therefore, the use of *after* as a perfective mark, as in:

> I'm after missing the bus ('I have missed the bus')

is extensive.

It is often remarked that Irish dialects are typically more conservative than those on the mainland. One obvious sign of this is that Irish dialects are almost uniformly rhotic. Another feature is the failure of the so-called FLEECE-merger (Wells, 1982: 194–6), so that *meet* and *meat* are not homophones, although today this failure is lost from all but the most conservative dialects; see further Harris (1985). In syntax it is noticeable that Irish dialects make rather more use of *do*-periphrasis than elsewhere:

> They *does be* lonesome by night, the priest does, surely (Filppula, 1999)

although similar constructions also occur in the southwest of England, and this is one of the principal sources for the earlier settlement of Ireland by English speakers. However, it is also possible that the periphrasis is the result of Gaelic influence, and the question remains unresolved; see Filppula (1999: 130–50).

We have already mentioned the existence of the later Plantation Settlements of Antrim and this led to marked features of Ulster English which are due to Scots, including, for example, the presence of Aitken's Law. It would be wrong, however, to see linguistic variation in Irish English, essentially a mélange created from southwestern English, Scots and substratal Gaelic, which operate on a continuum, as in any way reflecting the sharply divided political (and quasi-religious) cultures in parts of the island.

As we reach the conclusion of this chapter, there remains one further distinctive dialect which we must mention, namely British Black English (BBE; see Sutcliffe, 1982). This refers to the creole-type of English used by English descendants from Caribbean migrants who came to Britain in the decades after the Second World War. Amongst these speakers the mainly Jamaican-based creole has been maintained to a considerable degree, particularly in peer-to-peer interaction; see Sebba (1993). There are signs, however, that British speakers are losing some of the Caribbean structures even in their creole. And, of course, most speakers of BBE are fluent in either some local British dialect or standard English. Most studies have worked with southeastern subjects, in particular from London, and as Sebba (1993) shows, his subjects, when speaking English (as opposed to creole), share many of the features of the local dialect. Whether BBE will survive, or for how long, is an open question. And it should be noted that some BBE forms have entered other non-standard dialects, for example the widespread use of *bad* 'good'.

8 English in North America
Edward Finegan

8.1 The colonial period: 1607–1776

In 1607, following several failed attempts, the English succeeded at Jamestown, Virginia, with their first permanent settlement in the New World. In the decades to follow, other English settlements were made at Massachusetts Bay, Plymouth, Providence and elsewhere.

8.1.1 Explorers and settlers meet Native Americans

Along the Atlantic seaboard, explorers and settlers met, mixed with and sometimes married Native Americans and used Native American names for many artifacts in American life and culture, as well as for places and for unfamiliar plants and animals in the new environment. For other places and things English speakers invented new names or invoked familiar ones. Even before 1607, scores of Algonquian words already peppered English. In *A Briefe and True Report of the New Found Land of Virginia*, first published in 1588, Thomas Harriot, an astronomer working for Sir Walter Raleigh, described *openauk* as 'a kind of roots of round forme, some of the bignes of walnuts, some far greater', and *sacquenummener* as 'a kinde of berries almost like vnto capres but somewhat greater which grow together in clusters vpon a plant or herb that is found in shallow waters'; the berries would later be called cranberries. For various acorns, Harriot used their Algonquian names (*sagatemener, osamener, pummuckoner, sapummener, mangummenauk*), as he did for many New World plants, but these names did not survive in English. Among familiar 'beastes', he reported abundant *deare, conies, squirels* and *beares*, but for unfamiliar animals he again borrowed from Algonquian, calling two 'small beastes greater then conies which are very good meat' *maquowoc* and *saquenuckot. Maquowoc*, probably referring to mink or muskrat, did not stick, but *saquenuckot*, reinforced by related Algonquian words in other colonies, has become today's *skunk*.

Other New World terms found their way into English before Jamestown, sometimes via Spanish, as with *chocolate* (through Spanish from Nahuatl), *canoe* (through French and Spanish from Cariban), *cocoa* (through Spanish from Nahuatl), *maize* (through Spanish from Arawakan) and *savannah* (through Spanish from Taino). Appearing early in the 1600s and still in use are *moose, raccoon, opossum, moccasin, persimmon, tomahawk, terrapin, powwow, wigwam, hominy, squash, papoose, pone* and *squaw*. More than a hundred others appeared later in the century and hundreds more later again, but many colonial borrowings and innovations flourished only temporarily. No one can determine how many New World words spoken by the colonists are now as alien as Harriot's *sagatemener* and *maquowoc*. Nor could any colonist have predicted which borrowings and innovations would last. As Bailey (2004) notes, the history of North American English cannot be assessed adequately by what survives. To estimate the vocabulary and sounds of a language in earlier times would require familiarity with abundant contemporary documents, the less tutored the better.

8.1.2   Maintenance and change

A modern glossary of colonial English (Lederer, 1985) identifies 3,000 expressions no longer widely familiar at least in their colonial use, including names for fabrics, clothing, food, drink, household items, games, dances, musical instruments, law and punishment, and medicine. It contains expressions for places and people first encountered in the New World and for flora and fauna previously unknown to the colonists. Entries from a single page include *bark* 'a bed of Cyprus bark', *barkentine* 'a particular three-masted vessel', *barleycorn* 'one third of an inch or one gram', *barley water* 'a liquid used for inflammatory disorders', *barm* 'the scum that forms on top of fermenting beer', *burnish* 'to grow fat', *barony* 'a political division of a county in Pennsylvania and South Carolina', *barracan* 'a thick material like camlet', *barrow* 'a castrated hog', *basilicon* 'an ointment of beeswax, rosin and lard', *bason* 'a work bench with a heated metal plate', *basset* 'a certain card game', *bastard* 'a sweetened wine'.

Some expressions known regionally today can be traced to the colonial period (Carver, 1992). New England terms used in the 1960s and also in colonial Massachusetts, Connecticut or New Hampshire include *alewife* 'herring-like fish', *banker* 'fisherman, fishing vessel', *basket-fish* 'brittle star', *beaver meadow* 'an open grassy area', *black ash* 'American ash', *bonnyclabber* 'solidified sour milk', *buttery* 'pantry', *caboose* 'cook's galley on a ship', *case* 'general health', *chamber* 'upper room or floor', *clapboard* 'wooden siding', *deacon seat* 'front-row seat in church', *dresser* 'sideboard, cupboard', *fare* 'a catch of fish', *flitch* 'salt pork', *green corn* 'sweet corn'. Among 1960s Southern terms traceable to colonial Virginia and the Carolinas are *amber* 'tobacco spit', *baldface* 'a white face', *bat* 'nighthawk', *black gum* 'tupelo', *brake* 'thicket', *branch* 'stream', *case* 'a condition of tobacco leaves', *cat* 'catfish', *chinquapin* 'chestnut', *fever and ague* 'malaria', *Frenchman* 'a spindly tobacco plant', *fresh* 'stream', *ground worm* 'cutwork', *(hog) crawl* 'enclosure for hogs', *honey tree* 'honey locust'.

We can infer a good deal about colonial English from what is known of English in Britain in the 1600s and 1700s, but by the ordinary forces of language evolution the English spoken by the disembarking colonists began immediately to differentiate itself from the English they had spoken in Britain. Besides vocabulary borrowed from colonists speaking other European languages and from Native Americans, some English words developed new senses, while other linguistic features continued in the colonies but changed or fell into disuse in England. With divided usages one variant may have flourished in the colonies, the other in England. *Gotten*, the more common seventeenth-century past participle of *get*, remained favoured in America, while *got* grew stronger in England. After *fall* and *autumn* travelled to the colonies, *fall* mostly triumphed, as *autumn* did in England. *Mad* meant 'crazy' or 'angry', but in England (except regionally) it has mostly lost what is now its chief American sense of 'angry'.

8.1.3   Waves of immigrant colonists

Evidence for the origins of immigrants in four major colonial settlement areas has been gathered by Fischer (1989), drawing on British and transplanted folkways, including ways of speech, building, religion, learning, family and marriage, and food and dress. Viewing seventeenth-century Britain as comprising regions 'defined primarily by broad ethnic, cultural and historical processes', he draws parallels between specific English and colonial regions and identifies four major waves of British migration before the War of Independence.

1.   *New England settlement.* In the first migration, 21,000 Puritans chiefly from East Anglia sailed to Massachusetts between 1629 and 1640. Among them were well-educated magistrates and Puritan ministers, as well as yeoman and artisans. About 90 per cent arrived with other family members, and they settled around Massachusetts Bay, whence their children later moved south and west into Rhode Island, Connecticut, New York and New Jersey, or north into Vermont and Maine. Men outnumbered women by only three to two.

2.   *Virginia settlement.* The second large-scale migration comprised 45,000 Anglican cavaliers, labourers and servants. Between 1642 and 1675 they left the south and west of England and settled in Virginia. Sixty per cent were farmers, 30 per cent artisans; men outnumbered women five to one.

3.   *Delaware valley settlement.* In this migration, 23,000 emigrants, mostly Friends (Quakers) from the English north midlands (including Yorkshire, Derbyshire, Lancashire, Nottinghamshire, Cheshire and Staffordshire) and parts of Wales, settled in the Delaware valley between 1675 and 1715. About 40 per cent were farmers, 40 per cent artisans; men outnumbered women five to two.

4.   *Backcountry settlement.* The largest migration from 1717 to 1775 saw some 250,000 'borderlands' emigrants from the Scottish lowlands, the north of Ireland, and the six northernmost counties of England reach Pennsylvania and the colonial backcountry. Mostly Presbyterians and Anglicans, mostly tenants and cottagers, mostly families, they shared

a common border culture. As many as two-thirds of these Scotch-Irish arrived in the decade immediately preceding 1775. The 1790 census places them largely in the backcountry areas of southwestern Pennsylvania, western Maryland, Virginia, North and South Carolina and Georgia, and in Kentucky and Tennessee.

8.1.4   Character of colonial English

To gauge the character of colonial speech, recall that in 1607 when Jamestown was settled Shakespeare was active in Stratford. Roger Williams, who founded the Providence plantation in Rhode Island, was born in London in 1603, the year Queen Elizabeth died, and wrote his *Key into the Language of America* in 1643, before becoming friends with John Milton, who was born the year after the Jamestown settlement. Naturally, the English spoken in Massachusetts, Providence, Virginia and Pennsylvania reflected the late sixteenth- and seventeenth-century varieties of English the colonists had spoken before embarking for the New World. In the colonies, the regional and social backgrounds of the settlers became thoroughly mixed and yielded different linguistic complexions in different colonies.

During the colonial period, English in Britain was varied and variable. The language of the court, London and the nearby southeast carried prestige, but variation distinguished region from region (see Chapters 5 and 7). Pronunciation in England during the colonial period is treated in Chapter 2; here we underscore the prevalence of variation and emphasise that colonial speech reflected different mixes of English and Irish dialects and the emerging London standard. Colonists disembarking in the New World spoke the dialect of their native region and town, embodying its grammar, vocabulary and accent. Most ships embarking from Bristol, Plymouth, Liverpool and the other ports carried emigrants from different regions, thus mixing dialects before the ships reached the colonies. Then, disembarking in Boston, Philadelphia or Jamestown, new arrivals met a mixture of dialects. The colonial dialect pattern was paisley, not plaid, to borrow Laird's (1970: 162) metaphor.

8.1.5   Regional origins of colonial English

The English spoken in the New England colonies originated chiefly in East Anglia, London and parts of the southeast; that of Virginia echoed heavier immigration from the southwest; that of Pennsylvania reflected the north of England and the Scotch-Irish. In Ulster, the Scotch-Irish already represented a colony of dialects – with immigrants from the Scottish lowlands, Ireland and parts of northern England, and by the time they arrived in the New World, principally through Philadelphia and Delaware, and moved west through Pennsylvania and south into the backcountry of Virginia, their dialect reflected a mixed linguistic heritage (Montgomery, 2001).

Still, a stark reminder that the English spoken by the colonists reflected their geographical and social origins can be spied in the role accents played in identifying runaways. Many English and Irish immigrants arrived in the colonies as indentured servants and fled their servitude prematurely. In Pennsylvania, Maryland, Virginia, Massachusetts, New York, South Carolina and Georgia, newspaper notices often identified a runaway's accent: 'a West-country man and talks like one'; 'born in the West of England, and speaks that Country Dialect'; 'a Yorkshireman who talks very broad'; 'speaks the North Country Dialect'; 'born in Cheshire, and speaks in that dialect'; 'born near Manchester in England, and speaks much with that dialect'; 'her Speech is the North of England Dialect, and says she was born in Lincolnshire'. Notices also identified Irish and Scottish runaways by their speech: 'a Scotchman and talks as such'; 'talks pretty broad Scotch'; 'has the Irish Brogue on her tongue'; 'speaks pretty good English, but has a little brogue on it'; 'talks with the Irish accent very much'; 'by his dialect may be known to be a native of the north of Ireland' (Read, 2002: 89–92). From the observation that among hundreds of such notices none identified a runaway as speaking the dialect of East Anglia or the southeastern counties (the dialect nearest to London was that of a runaway from Wiltshire), we infer that that dialect was the norm throughout the colonies (Read, 2002: 86–8).

For over 150 years the colonists remained British, and especially those along the eastern seaboard remained closely tied to England, Ireland or Scotland. From the outset, English-speaking colonists also had contact with speakers of other languages. Besides continuing intercourse with Britain, colonial English swam in the polyglot tides around it, not only local Indians, but Dutch in New Amsterdam, French in Louisiana and Canada, and Spanish in New Spain, among others.

8.1.6   Tracing linguistic features to Britain

Dialect geographers have with little success tried tracing New World linguistic features to their origins in standard London English or particular regions of the British Isles. The classic position was stated by Hans Kurath, first director of the Linguistic Atlas of the United States and Canada:

> Most American practices can with some probability be related to specific features once current in Standard British English or still in use in one or another of the regional folk dialects of England. It is also fairly clear that most, if not all, regional variants in American cultivated speech of today can be traced to British cultivated usage of the seventeenth and the eighteenth centuries, and that features of pronunciation confined to certain subareas of the Atlantic seaboard [e.g., the vowel in *half, glass*, etc. and loss of postvocalic /r/] were not fashionable in the London area until shortly before the American Revolution.   (Kurath & McDavid, 1961: vi–vii)

The task is complicated in several ways, including inadequate data (Montgomery, 2001) and the fact that the most significant large-scale investigations of dialects in the eastern US were completed before the major studies of regional British English (see Chapter 7), which will now help researchers track linguistic relations between North America and the British Isles.

Kurath's is not the only interpretation of the origins of North American English, and other views will likely influence the eventual understanding of the origins of NAE. Dillard (1992: 22) has emphasised the early sixteenth-century arrivals from Europe in Newfoundland and along the Atlantic coast and the great mixing of tongues in the colonies. He notes, for example, that Manhattan was reported to be home to speakers of sixteen languages in 1644 and that once it became English in 1664 its multilingual character increased further. Similarly, the Delaware valley settlers met Swedes and Finns who had settled earlier, and the Puritans in Massachusetts met Dutch and other Europeans, along with Indian groups. Colonists met Indians speaking 221 languages in four distinct families (Axtell, 2000:16). Such an extraordinary mixing of languages and dialects may point to a radical colonial levelling that gave rise after the Revolution to the major American dialects (Dillard, 1992). However accurate the levelling hypothesis, several British visitors to the colonies in the late 1700s remarked on the homogeneity of English in America (all quoted by Read, 2002: 44–6):

William Eddis in 1770:

> In England, almost every county is distinguished by a peculiar dialect; . . . but in Maryland and throughout adjacent provinces . . . a striking similarity of speech universally prevails; and it is strictly true, that the pronunciation of the generality of the people has an accuracy and elegance, that cannot fail of gratifying the most judicious ear.
>
> The colonists are composed of adventurers, not only from every district of Great Britain and Ireland, but from almost every other European government. . . . Is it not, therefore, reasonable to suppose, that the English language must be greatly corrupted by such a strange intermixture of various nations? The reverse is, however, true. The language of the immediate descendants of such a promiscuous ancestry is perfectly uniform, and unadulterated; nor has it borrowed any provincial, or national accent, from its British or foreign percentage.
>
> . . . This uniformity of language prevails not only on the coast, . . . but likewise in the interior parts . . .

Seven years later, Nicholas Cresswell of Derbyshire, having spent three years in Virginia, Kentucky, Pennsylvania and New York:

> Though the inhabitants of this Country are composed of different Nations and different languages, yet it is very remarkable that they in general speak better English than the English do. No Country or Colonial dialect is to be distinguished here, except it be the New Englanders, who have a sort of whining cadence that I cannot describe.

The London editor of Ramsay's *History of the American Revolution* in 1791:

> It is a curious fact, that there is perhaps no one portion of the British empire, in which two or three millions of persons are to be found, who speak their mother-tongue with greater purity, or a truer pronunciation, than the white inhabitants of the United States. This was attributed, by a penetrating observer, to the number of British subjects assembled in America from various quarters, who, in consequence of their intercourse and intermarriages soon dropped the peculiarities of their several provincial idioms, retaining only what was fundamental and common to them all; a process, which the frequency or rather the universality of school-learning in North America, must naturally have assisted.

A well-known preacher who lived in Maryland or Virginia between 1759 and 1775 noted that 'in North America, there prevails not only . . . the purest Pronunciation of the English Tongue that is anywhere to be met with, but a perfect Uniformity'.

We conclude that, in contrast with the dialect diversity of England, colonial English was strikingly homogeneous although not necessarily of a single kind. Eddis speaks of uniformity in Maryland and the 'adjacent provinces'; Cresswell distinguishes between a more general colonial variety and that spoken in New England. From such comments and from information in other sources, we infer that colonial English had become somewhat levelled as a consequence of people from diverse parts of England, Ireland and Scotland mixing together and mixing with speakers of Dutch, German, Swedish and Finnish.

8.1.7   Place-names: Native American, French, Dutch, Spanish, English

As noted, English colonists exploring the New World met Native Americans and colonists from other nations. Along with thousands of other names, *Manhattan*, *Massachusetts*, *Mississippi*, *Missouri* and *Alabama* echo Native American ones. Reminders of contact with Europeans appear in the Dutch *Harlem* and *Brooklyn*; the French *Montreal*, *Quebec*, *Vermont* and *Maine*; and, farther west, the Spanish *Rio Grande*, *Sierra Nevada* and *Santa Fe*. English, French and Dutch nobles, explorers and government officials are honored in *Carolina* (Charles I) and *Charleston* (Charles II), *Maryland* (Queen Mary) and *Virginia* (Elizabeth I, the Virgin Queen); *Louisiana* (Louis XIV) and *Lake Champlain* (the French explorer Samuel de Champlain); *Block Island* (the Dutch explorer Adriaen Block) and *Cape May* and *Stuyvesant Falls* (named for governors of New Netherlands).

English names include *New Hampshire*, *New Jersey*, *New London*, *New York*, *New England*; *Boston, Brighton, Essex, Norfolk, Sussex*; and hundreds of others. Suggesting strong Dutch influence in the New York City and Hudson valley regions are *Flushing* (*Vlissingen*), *Staten Island* and the *Bowery* ('farm'). *Wall Street* takes its name from the fact that Walloons inhabited lower Manhattan in the seventeenth century. The *Spuyten Duyvil Creek* separates the upper end of Manhattan Island from the mainland. Dutch *kill* 'creek, small stream' appears in New York's *Catskill Mountains* and town names like *Sparkill* and *Peekskill*, as well as in Pennsylvania's *Schuylkill River*. In the nineteenth century, *kill* was extended to a minnow-like fish inhabiting creeks around New York City, where the *killie* or *killifish* still swims. The origin of some Dutch names lies hidden in their anglicised forms, as with *Grammercy* (*krom-marisje* 'crooked marsh'), *Saybrook* (*Zeebroeck* 'sea river'), *Rhode Island* (*'t Roode Eylandt* 'red island') and *Tarrytown* (*tarwe* 'wheat'). *Hook* 'angle' appears in names like *Sandy Hook* and *Red Hook*, and, famously, as part of *OK*, shortened from *Old Kinderhook*, an 1840 nickname for US president Martin van Buren, a native of the Hudson River town of Kinderhook. A year earlier, *OK* represented the jocular spelling 'oll korrect', so van Buren was *OK* in both senses. Abundant North American place-names with origins in languages other than English testify to the complex settlement of North America and the profound influence of early contacts.

An English fashion for names in *-ville*, perhaps encouraged by that favourite resort of rich English tourists, Deauville in Normandy, was adopted in America for primary settlements. The first element ('E1' in the terms used in Section 6.5.4) was typically a personal name or surname – only local knowledge can decide which in some instances – either uninflected or in the genitive (*Morrisville*, *Swoyerville*). A further favourite in America as anglophone settlement proceeded gave *Levittown*, *Jewett City* and many similar forms. Soon ordinary lexical elements could appear as first element, as in *Pleasantville*, *Truthville* and *Lineville* on a state boundary. America also went for *-borough*, usually in the form *-burgh* or *-boro*, and later as *-burg* (*Pittsburgh*, which survived the official attempt to replace all names in *-burgh* with *-burg*), *Greensboro*, *Harrisburg*. Place-names were formed by analogy with established English ones, with many new creations in *-ton* (*Princeton*, *Lumberton*, *Thomaston*). Other concessions were made to naming practices current in Europe; the use of *port* with either a preposed or a postposed specifier was common, resting on established models such as *Newport* and the French model also widely adopted by the English abroad, so that we find such names as *Hyannisport* and *Port Jefferson*. Far greater onomastic freedom with English resources was made than in the old country, but other resources were also drafted in, for instance the Classical Latin suffix *-ia* seen in *Robesonia* and *Fredonia* (from *freedom*), and the Greek element *-polis* (*Annapolis*, *Indianapolis*).

8.2   The national period: 1776–1900

In 1776, the colonists declared independence from England, and in 1783 New Hampshire, Massachusetts, Rhode Island, Connecticut, New York, New Jersey, Pennsylvania, Delaware, Maryland, Virginia, North Carolina, South Carolina and Georgia united under the Articles of Confederation. Especially in the northeast, however, many colonists remained loyal to the crown, and these United Empire Loyalists headed north to Canada, often carrying their New England speech patterns. Thus, the colonial dialect of the northeast formed the bedrock of Canadian English in the east. Newfoundland had been settled much earlier, and its linguistic history (like that of Quebec with its French traditions and language) is independent of most of Canada's.

When the first US census was taken in 1790, the 13 states and three districts included 3.9 million people. Virginia, the most populous, had nearly 750,000 residents, including 293,000 slaves, while Rhode Island and Delaware had fewer than 70,000 residents each, including slaves. In 1800, the western border of the nation extended only to the Mississippi River, and the population stood at 5.1 million, including nearly 900,000 slaves. The purchase of Louisiana from France in 1803 doubled the nation's territory, and the frontier proved to be a magnet (see Bailey, 2003; Eble, 2003 commemorates the bicentennial of the Lewis and Clark expedition exploring the new territory). By 1850 the population swelled to 23 million and ten years later to 31 million, including nearly 4 million slaves and 4 million foreign-born free persons. Such heavy immigration followed that, of the 49 million residents in 1880, 163,000 had been born in Scotland, 700,000 in England or Wales, and 1.8 million in Ireland. There were also 1.9 million German-born residents, mostly in Illinois, Missouri, Ohio, Pennsylvania, Wisconsin and New York, while from Sweden and Norway had come 350,000 immigrants. Spurred by the need for workers on the transcontinental railroad, nearly 75,000 Chinese-born immigrants lived in California. That state also had 9,000 Mexican-born residents, while Texas had 43,000. (Arizona and New Mexico were not yet populous enough to enter the Union.)

8.2.1   American language or American English? Noah Webster schools the nation

Much has been written about the effect of national independence on Americans' views of their language. Two perspectives are conveniently, if anachronistically, suggested by the titles of Mencken's *The American Language* and Krapp's *The English Language in America*. Sometimes one person wavered between the two perspectives. In 1800, when Noah Webster projected a *Dictionary of the American Language*, he called it 'a work ... absolutely necessary, on account of considerable differences between the American and English language' (Read, 2002: 17). But when it appeared in 1828, it bore the strikingly different title, *An American Dictionary of the English Language*, and its author said in the preface that 'It is not only important, but, in a degree necessary, that the people of this country, should have an *American Dictionary* of the English Language; for, although the body of the language is the same as in England, and it is desirable to perpetuate that sameness, yet some differences must exist.' He noted that some US words were unknown in England or unknown in their American senses, citing as examples *land-office*, *land-warrant*, *consociation* of churches, *regent* of a university, *intendant* of a city, *plantation*, *selectman*, *marshal*, *senate*, *congress*, *court* and *assembly*. His dictionary represented an assertion that American English (a term Webster had used in 1806) needed codification, and he aimed 'to furnish a standard of our vernacular tongue, which we shall not be ashamed to bequeath to three hundred millions of people, who are destined to occupy, and . . . adorn the vast territory within our jurisdiction' (1828, Preface).

With great vigour Webster tackled the codification of American English, claiming as early as 1789 that, 'As an independent nation, our honor requires us to have a system of our own, in language as well as government. Great Britain . . . should no longer be *our* standard . . .' Despite such nationalistic fervor, Webster wavered about linguistic independence and occasionally looked to Britain as the source of good English, as when he claimed never to have heard 'an improper use of the verbs *shall* and *will*, among the unmixed English descendants in the eastern states' (1789: 240). Webster's politics were nationalist, but his heart was a New Englander's, and New England English struck him as most euphonious. Concerning the pronunciation in the middle Atlantic states of *once* and *twice* with a final *t* (*oncet* and *twicet*), he would have overlooked it, he said, 'but for its prevalence among a class of very well educated people; particularly in Philadelphia and Baltimore' (1789: 111). Generally recognising speech as the basis for writing, he asked why we should 'retain words in writing which are not generally recognized in oral practice!' and in that vein endorsed the use of past-tense forms for past participles (e.g. *have broke, have shook, have chose, have drank*) and such simple past-tense forms as *rung, sprung, sunk, sung, forbid, begun* and *writ* (1807: 186–9).

Webster's linguistic influence is most palpable in American spelling practices. In 1789, he had proposed phonetic spellings like *bred, tru, tuf, dawter, bilt* and *arkitect* but laid aside those reforms in his first dictionary (1806) and ultimately left little in the spellings of his mammoth *American Dictionary* of 1828 to be judged radical. In his dictionaries and spelling books he propelled American preferences for *-or* in *color, labor, parlor, behavior, -er* in *center, meter, meager* (but listed both *theater* and *theatre*), *-ize* in *generalize, liberalize, subsidize* (but not *advertise*), *-se* in *license, offense*. Among words from which he pruned letters are the *judgment* class (without *e*), the *public* class (without *k*), and the *catalog* class (not *catalogue*). He eliminated double consonants in such words as *leveled*, and endorsed *check, curb, tire, maneuver* and *encyclopedia*. He entered *czar* and gave its pronunciation as *tzar*, entered *jail* and condemned *gaol*. Needless to say, not all his endorsements succeeded, as with *tun* for *ton*.

8.2.2   Prescriptivism

The nineteenth century saw the rise of a strong prescriptive streak in the United States, no better exemplified than by Richard Grant White (1821–85). He would have experienced variable usage in nearly all he heard and read, and support for the principle that usage was the basis of correctness was in the air. In Oxford, citations were being gathered as the basis for describing usage in the *Oxford English Dictionary*, and White contributed some of those citations, but in

New York he and others were having none of the *OED*'s descriptivism: 'There is a misuse of words which can be justified by no authority however great, by no usage, however general' (White, 1870). As an example, he said that even if fifty instances of *both* applying to three things could be uncovered in Chaucer, Spenser, Shakespeare and Milton, the word's etymology and its usage elsewhere mandated that it not be used for more than two: 'it is impossible that the same word can mean two and three'.

English in America was ablaze with innovation, but White urged his readers to reject neologisms and putative neologisms, including the verbs *donate*, *jeopardize*, *resurrect* and *initiate*; the nouns *campaign*, *practitioner*, *photographer*, *pants*, *conversationalist* and *standpoint*; the adjectives *accountable*, *answerable*, *tangential*, *exponential*, *gubernatorial*, *shamefaced* and *reliable*; he was particularly exercised at the progressive passive forms like *is being built* and penned an entire chapter condemning them. He could be amusing, and some of what he wrote rings true today: in objecting to the 'blatant Americanism' *presidential campaign* he asked, 'Is it not time that we had done with this nauseous talk about campaigns, and standard-bearers, and glorious victories, and all the bloated army-bumming bombast which is so rife for the six months preceding an election? To read almost any one of our political papers during a canvass is enough to make one sick and sorry . . . We could do our political talking much better in simple English' (1870: 218–19).

Like Webster and others, White recognised regional patterns of expression. He noted that what people properly called *overshoes* went by the name *gums* in Philadelphia and *rubbers* elsewhere (1870: 5). About one of the hot usage topics of his day, he claimed the proper distinction between *shall* and *will* likely to be disregarded by anyone lacking 'the advantage of early intercourse with educated English people'. In New England, he claimed, 'even the boys and girls playing on the commons use *shall* and *will* correctly' (1870: 264), and in New York, New Jersey, Ohio, Virginia, Maryland and South Carolina, 'fairly educated people of English stock' do the same – but not Scotchmen or Irishmen or the 'great mass of the people of the Western and South-western States'. Though not shy about his prejudices, this critic acknowledged differences among ethnic groups and geographical regions.

8.2.3   Lexical borrowings

A land of immigrants, the US and North America more generally have experienced waves of immigration from the start, and immigrant groups have left an imprint on NAE. Both for convenience and because the nineteenth and early twentieth centuries witnessed significant immigration, we treat borrowed words in this section, including those borrowed both before and after the national period.

Especially in the early periods, borrowings from French abound, including *gopher*, *pumpkin*, *chowder*, *jambalaya*, *praline*, *butte*, *chute*, *crevasse*, *levee*, *prairie*, *rapids*, *bureau*, *depot*, *shanty*, *cache*, *carry-all*, *toboggan*, *voyageur*, *cent*, *dime, picayune, rotisserie* and *sashay*, all cited by Marckwardt (1958). Even the French suffix *-ee*, used in English for a long time, was revitalised in the US in words such as *employee, parolee* and recently *exoneree* 'a prisoner exonerated by DNA evidence'. Among borrowings from Dutch are *cole slaw, cookie, cruller, pit* 'stone, seed', *waffle, bush* 'back country', *caboose, scow, sleigh, stoop* 'porch', *boss, patroon, Yankee, dope, dumb* 'stupid', *poppycock, Santa Claus, snoop* and *spook* (Marckwardt, 1958).

Borrowings from German, as Marckwardt notes, come from an immigrant group that settled among colonists or Americans, unlike those from French, Dutch and Native American languages, who were competitors for the land occupied now by English speakers in the New World. Among terms associated with food and drink, he lists *delicatessen, dunk, frankfurter, hamburger, lager beer, liverwurst, noodle, pretzel, pumpernickel, sauerkraut, schnitzel, stollen* and *zwieback,* and in other domains *festschrift, semester, seminar, beer garden, Christmas tree, Kris Kringle, pinochle, stein, bum, fresh* 'impudent', *hex, katzenjammer, loafer, nix, ouch, phooey, spiel* and *wunderkind.* When residents of Milwaukee talk about being *by Aunt Mary's* rather than *at Aunt Mary's,* they are reflecting the semantics of German *bei,* a consequence of earlier concentrations of German settlers there (Preston, 2003: 235), and a similar German influence likely explains the same phenomenon among working-class residents of the New York metropolitan area.

Spanish is the most prolific contributor to New World English words, including these (Marckwardt, 1958): among plants and animals, *alfalfa, marijuana, mesquite, yucca, armadillo, bronco, burro, barracuda, bonito, pompano, chigger, cockroach, coyote, mustang, palomino* and *pinto*; associated with ranch life, *buckaroo, chaparral, cinch, corral, hacienda, lariat, lasso, peon, ranch, rodeo, stampede* and *wrangler*; associated with food and drink, *chile con carne, enchilada, frijole, mescal, pinion nuts, taco, tamale, tequila, tortilla*; in building, *adobe, cafeteria, patio, plaza* and *puebla*; in legal and penal contexts, *calaboose, desperado, hoosegow, incommunicado* and *vigilantes*; among toponyms, *arroyo, canyon, key, mesa, sierra*; in races and nationalities, *coon, creole, dago, mulatto, octoroon*; in clothing, *chaps, poncho, serape, sombrero* and *ten-gallon hat*; in a miscellaneous group, *fiesta, filibuster, hombre, loco, marina, mosey, pronto, rumba, savvy, stevedore, temblor, tornado* and *vamoose.* The *ten-gallon hat* worn by cowboys takes its name not from its capacious size, as folk etymology would have it, but from *galon* for 'ribbon or lace', referring to the custom of placing decorative bands around men's headgear (Laird, 1970: 318).

Among borrowings from West African languages spoken by slaves brought to North America, Marckwardt identifies *gumbo, goober, buckra, juba, juke* (as in *juke box*), *voodoo* and *hoodoo,* and Carver (1987: 149) adds *cooter, juju, okra, pinder* and *poor joe.* The verb *tote* is often cited as an African borrowing, but according to the *OED* that association lacks foundation.

From Yiddish, too, mostly in the twentieth century, have come loanwords, many of which are better known in metropolitan areas where Jewish immigrants settled in large numbers. Terms borrowed from Yiddish and cited first in the *OED* from

US authors are *klutz, kvetch, mensch, nudnik, pisher, schlepper, schlock, schmaltz, schmooze, schnook, shtik, tchotchke, tochus* and *yenta. Already,* as in *So tell it already!* or *Enough, already!,* is another Yiddishism, as is the formulation *You want I should . . . ,* which is used in self-conscious imitation of Yiddish. According to the *OED, schlemiel, chutzpah, dreck, schlep* and the interjection *oy!* entered English in Britain, not North America.

Other languages have also contributed to the American lexicon, and many such borrowed words have then found their way into other varieties: from Italian, *spaghetti, ravioli, minestrone, antipasto*; from Swedish, *smorgasbord* and *lutefisk*; from Chinese, *chow, chow mein* and *chop suey* (Marckwardt, 1958); *feng-shui,* popular in the US today, is not an Americanism but debuted in the *Encyclopaedia Britannica* more than 200 years ago.

8.3   Modern period: 1900-present

By 1900, the population of the US stood at 75 million, one million of whom had been born in England or Scotland and 1.6 million in Ireland. By 1950, it would double to 150 million and by 2000 to 281 million. In this section we focus on linguistic variation in North American English across regions and social groups. We begin with a brief description of selected syntactic features distinguishing NAE from British English, but for lack of space do not treat pronunciation differences.

8.3.1   Syntactic patterns in American English and British English

NAE and BrE share most, but not all, syntactic patterns. In NAE, collective nouns such as *family, staff* and *committee*, and names referring to sports teams, companies, organisations and institutions generally require singular verbs, as in these headlines: *Shadow Government Is at Work in Secret; Ballard Team Has High Hopes for Deep-Water Robot*; and *Ford Is Adopting EPA's Stringent Standards.* Ordinarily, sentences in which a plural verb agrees with a collective noun would be ungrammatical, as in these from the British National Corpus (BNC): *Once ITV realize the BBC are going ahead . . .* ; *the Government were driven to the desperation of calling upon alchemy.* A few collective nouns such as *police* require a plural verb in NAE and BrE.

NAE commonly uses singular forms in compounds like *drug enforcement unit* and *new fair market rent policy* (cf. *drugs enforcement unit* and *market rents policy*). When the first element of a compound is itself a compound containing a plural form (*hate crimes*), the larger compound incorporates that plural (*hate crimes policy*). American and British journalistic styles use appositives of the form *David Owen, a staff writer for the New Yorker*, but American style is more tolerant of lengthy noun string modifiers: *department spokeswoman Darla Jordan*; *death penalty opponent Helen Prejean*; *celebrity capital punishment opponent Susan Sarandon*.

In restrictive relative clauses, both *that* and *which* occur, but in news writing NAE shows a somewhat stronger preference for *that* than BrE, and in conversation a preference twice as strong (Biber et al., 1999: 616).

In reply to a question such as *Have you finished the assignment?*, NAE and BrE permit *Yes, I have*, but only BrE permits *Yes, I have done*. Asked whether flying time from London to Chicago varies, British flight attendants may respond *It can do*, while their American counterparts are more likely to say, *It can* – and NAE speakers are more likely to judge sentences like these (taken from the BNC) ungrammatical: *Yeah, they can do* and *I could do, I suppose*, preferring instead *Yeah, they can* and *I could do it, I suppose*.

Sometimes the same alternatives occur in both NAE and BrE, but with notably different frequencies. Twice as frequent in NAE conversation is mid-sentence ellipsis of the auxiliary: *When you coming back?* (cf. *When are you coming back?*) and *How you doing?* (cf. *How are you doing?*) (Biber et al., 1999: 1108). Generally, though, NAE shows less ellipsis, as with combined subject and auxiliary in *Like it?* and *Wanna clear a crowded room?* (cf. *Do you like it?* and *Do you want to . . . ?*), and with combined subject and main verb, as in *Serious?* and *Too early for you?* (cf. *Are you serious?* and *Is it too early . . . ?*). NAE also shows half as much initial and final ellipsis (Biber et al., 1999: 1108), as in *I tried to* and *Yes, no question about it* (cf. *I tried to press charges* and *Yes, there's no question about it*). In questions and replies, NAE shows an overwhelming preference in conversation and fiction for auxiliary *do*, as in *Do you have any . . . ?* (cf. BrE conversational *Have you got any . . . ?* and fictional *Have you any . . . ?*) (Biber et al., 1999: 216).

In NAE, *got* serves as a simple past tense meaning 'became' (*She got tired*) or 'arrived' (*when she got home*), and both *got* and *gotten* serve as past participles, though not equivalently. *Gotten* is strongly preferred, as in *Most Americans have gotten over the shock and gotten on with their lives* (cf. BrE *No amount of NATO pressure would have got it even on to paper*). *Have you got one?* is a frequent NAE equivalent to BrE *Do you have one?* (also used in NAE) and underpins an advertising campaign that asks, *Got milk? Gotten* often means 'received, acquired', as in *Have you gotten any?*, and *have got* means 'have' (*We've got ID cards now*; *We've got locked gates*).

In some contexts, NAE tends to omit the infinitive marker *to* after the verbs *come*, *go*, *help* and some others (Todd & Hancock, 1986: 477), as in *You wanna go get some water?* and *Proceeds will help establish a wetlands protection fund*. Alternatively, NAE compounds the two verbs, as in *I feel it's only right that I come and help out*. With patterns of negation, NAE conversation prefers *do not have the* (*don't have the time*) and *have no* (*have no doubt, has none of your character, has nothing to fear*) over the BrE forms *have got no* (as in *have got no one to love* or *have got nothing to hide*), *have not got a/any* (as in *has not got an easy task*) and *have/has not the* (as in *has not the strength*) (Biber et al.,

1999: 161). Use of modals also differs somewhat. In conversation, *must, will, better* and *got to* are less frequent than in BrE, whereas *going to* (or *gonna*) and *have to* (*hafta*) are more common than in BrE (Biber et al., 1999: 488). Except in some legal registers, the use of *shall* is diminishing drastically in NAE and BrE, probably more so in NAE.

NAE displays characteristic adverb use, as with the amplifier *real*, as in *real good* and *real fast*. At least in conversation, US residents prefer the amplifier *pretty* (*pretty easy, pretty good*) over *quite* (Biber et al., 1999: 567); *quite* as an amplifier (*quite big, quite easy*) occurs in NAE only one-seventh as often as in BrE. Both varieties use *quite* and *pretty* with the adjectives *sure* and *good*, but AmE tends to limit *quite sure* to negative contexts: *not/never quite sure. Now* and *immediately* function as adverbs but not conjunctions in NAE, and to make these examples from the BNC grammatical in NAE, the underscored subordinators have been added: *Now that they're older they can do it* and *They took off immediately after the passengers were on board.*

With noun phrases that denote a point in space or time, NAE sometimes requires an article where BrE does not: *in the hospital* and *the next day*. In some expressions, both varieties omit the article for relatively general senses of the noun: *in school, to class, in college, to church.*

In NAE the preposition may be omitted from certain time references and after certain verbs, as in *a doctor's appointment Monday*; *see you this weekend*; and *departed New York on time* (cf. *on Monday, at the weekend, from New York*). Preposition choice or form may differ: *a store on Main Street* (cf. *a shop in the High Street*), *different than* or *different from* (*different to*), *around the city* (*round*) and *toward the light* (*towards*).

8.3.2   Regional patterns in American English

A picture of North American dialects, particularly in the eastern US, has been available since the mid-twentieth century, but our understanding is complicated by the vast geographical expanse of the country and the fact that several areas west of the Mississippi River remain to be adequately investigated, and existing surveys employed different techniques and were carried out at different times; in addition, some studies focussed on pronunciation, others on vocabulary. While the general processes that establish dialects are similar for diverse kinds of features, distributions of phonological and lexical variants seldom coincide. Indeed, distributions for any two lexical items seldom coincide. In addition, much of what was investigated earlier characterised rural speakers, while later sociolinguistic interest preferred urban speakers. Finally, especially the western states and provinces continue to develop with in-migration and immigration, so dialect patterns remain unsettled.

Regional atlases have been completed for New England (Kurath et al., 1939–43), the Upper Midwest (Allen, 1973–6), and the Gulf States (Pederson et al., 1986–93). For some other regions (North Central States, Middle and South

Atlantic States, Pacific West), fieldwork has been completed and some findings published. (For current information about regional atlases, see the Linguistic Atlas Projects website < http://us.english.uga.edu/ >.) A widely, but not universally, accepted view is that American English has four main regional dialects (North, Midland, South, and West), each with subdivisions, twenty-one in all, as listed in Pederson's (2001) thorough overview. With its settlement history across a great expanse, the US has a complex pattern of regional dialects, with some broad strokes differentiating regions essentially from east to west, but with subdivisions within those dialects. Features of several regions have been mentioned above, although regions are best described in terms of sets of features rather than uniquely characteristic ones.

North American English, as we have seen, has several sources: the English brought from England to the New World by the original colonists; the English brought by later immigrants from England and other parts of Britain and Ireland; innovation in North America; and borrowings from Native Americans and from immigrant groups speaking other languages. But agreement diminishes in tracing particular expressions, grammatical forms and pronunciations, particularly to their British sources. Krapp (1925) and Kurath (1949; Kurath & McDavid, 1961) underscored the links between AmE and the standard English of southeast England, and many dialect maps in *The Pronunciation of English in the Atlantic States* (Kurath & McDavid, 1961) contain insets of the southeastern counties of England with pronunciations matching those along the American seaboard. More generally, these interpretive studies tend to discount the likelihood of regional features of British or Irish English surviving in American regional dialects. Commenting, for example, on South and South Midland pronunciations of *because* with [e] in the second syllable, Kurath & McDavid (1961: 162) report 'no evidence' for the phenomenon in English dialects, but Montgomery (2001: 139) identifies the pronunciation in Ulster dialects and on that basis and others objects to their claim that 'distinctive features of the dialects of the northern counties of England, of Scotland, and of Northern Ireland rarely survive in American English'.

8.3.3   *Dictionary of American Regional English (DARE)*

Besides the regional atlases, a promising tool for addressing regional associations between NAE and Britain is the *Dictionary of American Regional English. DARE* treats regional words and expressions and displays many findings on maps that represent population distribution rather than strict geographical boundaries and thus shape state borders and state sizes only roughly as compared to a traditional map. A *DARE* map encloses a grid of the 1,002 communities canvassed in its 1960s survey. If a particular variant occurred in a community, a filled circle appears on the map for that feature in that community; if not, the space designating that community remains empty. For a feature used in every community, the map would contain no empty spaces. Figure 8.1 shows a *DARE* map and a traditional map of the United States. (Full names for abbreviations

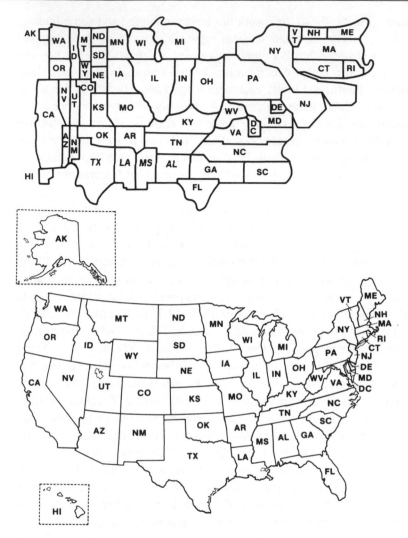

Figure 8.1   DARE *map and conventional map, with state names*
Source: Dictionary of American Regional English, *I, 1985*

such as ME 'Maine' and MN 'Minnesota' can be found in the Appendix to this chapter.)

We illustrate *DARE*'s treatment with regional terms for a long sandwich made on an Italian roll or French bread. *Hero* (shortened from *hero sandwich*) is common in Metropolitan New York City, with some use in nearby New Jersey and upstate New York, but only sporadic use elsewhere (Figure 8.2). *Hoagie* is the term used almost exclusively in Pennsylvania and New Jersey (Figure 8.3). *Poor boy*, commonly pronounced 'po'boy' or 'pore boy', originated in Louisiana and spread west into Texas and California, east into Mississippi and Alabama, and northeast into Tennessee; a few communities in northern Illinois also used *poor*

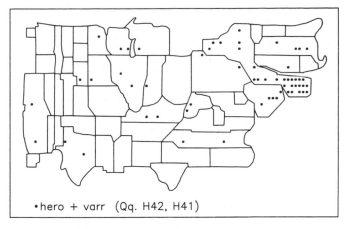

•hero + varr (Qq. H42, H41)

Figure 8.2 *Distribution of* hero *on a* DARE *map*
Source: Dictionary of American Regional English, *II, 1991*

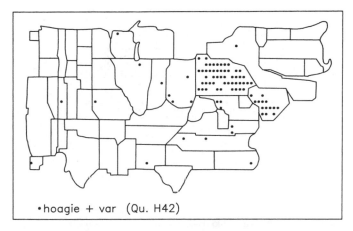

•hoagie + var (Qu. H42)

Figure 8.3 *Distribution of* hoagie *on a* DARE *map*
Source: Dictionary of American Regional English, *II, 1991*

boy, but most states show no occurrences (Figure 8.4). *Submarine sandwich* (Figure 8.5) appears mostly in the north central and northeast states, although the distribution of *submarine* and *sub* is likely to be far more widespread than that represented in Figure 8.5 because in 1965 the popular 'Subway' chain of fast-food restaurants was launched. Besides these terms, *grinder* is the preferred name in New England (except for Maine), while *Cuban sandwich* is used in Miami, Florida.

From *DARE*'s findings, a map of American dialects has been proposed, as we will see. First, we describe the traditional method for determining dialect boundaries by plotting occurrences of a single feature on a map and drawing isoglosses at the boundary delimiting occurrences of the feature. Reflecting this method, maps in *Word Geography of the Eastern United States* (Kurath, 1949)

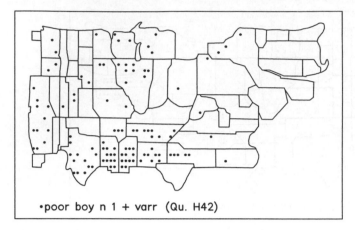

•poor boy n 1 + varr (Qu. H42)

Figure 8.4   *Distribution of* poor boy *on a* DARE *map*
Source: Dictionary of American Regional English, *IV, 2002*

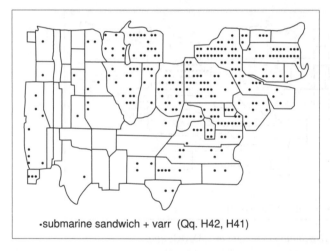

•submarine sandwich + varr (Qq. H42, H41)

Figure 8.5   *Distribution of* submarine sandwich *on a* DARE *map*
Source: Dictionary of American Regional English, *V, forthcoming*

show the distribution of variants of a linguistic feature on a traditional map. Dialect maps are then drawn, in effect, by overlaying several maps to reveal bundles of isoglosses. Where isoglosses bundle together, dialect boundaries are proposed, such as those in Figure 8.6. Kurath's map of the eastern US depicts three main dialects – North, Midland and South – a word-based division used later again when Kurath laid out regional patterns of pronunciation, despite his recognising and acknowledging noticeable differences between word boundaries and pronunciation boundaries.

Taking a different approach and using *DARE* materials, Carver (1987) relied on the number of isoglosses shared by a community to create 'layers' that enabled him to identify stronger and weaker dialect boundaries. He proposed a new dialect map

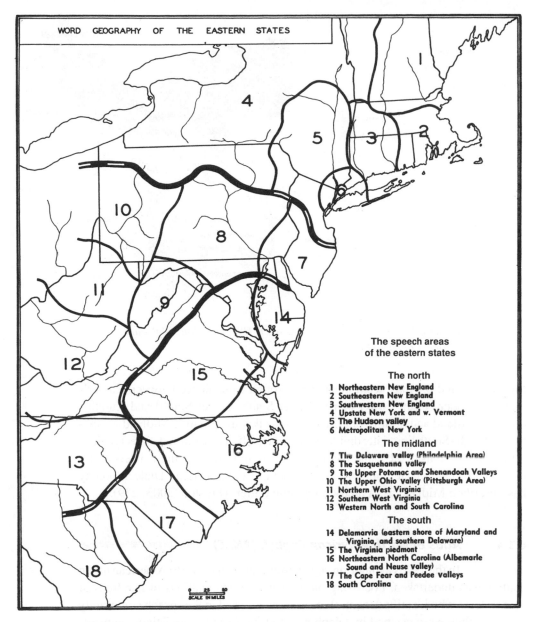

Figure 8.6   *Kurath's dialect regions of the eastern states, based on vocabulary*
Source: Kurath, 1949

that generally resembles earlier maps, but postulates only two major US dialects –
North and South – each with upper and lower sections and each with subsections
(see Figure 8.7). He also identified a weaker West dialect, an extension largely
of the North, and argued that the traditional division into Northern, Midland and
Southern dialects overlooked a fundamental divide between North and South.

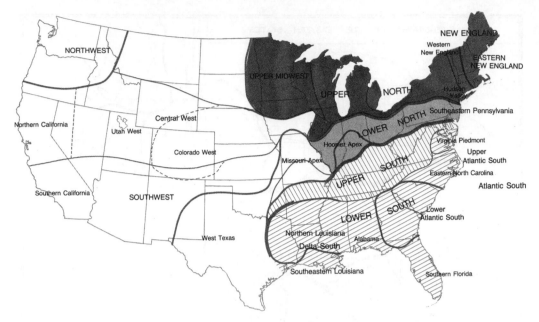

Figure 8.7   *Carver's dialect regions of the USA, based on vocabulary*
Source: Carver, 1987

Figures 8.6 and 8.7 may seem to suggest a rough equivalence between Carver's regions (Upper North, Lower North, Upper South, Lower South) and Kurath's (North, Midland and South), but Carver insists that the putative Midland is 'split by the North–South linguistic divide' and is not itself 'a true unified dialect region' (1987: 161). Considerable ink has been spilled arguing over the existence of a distinct Midland dialect, and even a president of the American Dialect Society has described Midland as 'a pretty puny little critter' (Preston, 2003: 239).

8.3.4   *Atlas of North American English (ANAE)*

In the 1990s a major survey of pronunciation in North American urban centres was undertaken. Focussing on the vowel pronunciations of hundreds of respondents who identified themselves as born or raised in the speech community in which they were reached by telephone, it utilised impressionistic judgements of pronunciation, as had other dialect studies, but combined them with rigorous acoustic analysis. The investigators (Labov et al., 2005) acknowledge the skepticism of dialectologists concerning the boundaries between dialects and offer as one reason for such skepticism the fact that classifications of dialects and dialect boundaries relied on sets of isoglosses for individual vocabulary items, which are idiosyncratic and not systemically related to one another. By contrast, the telephone survey project ('Telsur') relied on vowel patterns, an integral part of every linguistic system, and explored a huge geographical area within a period of only a few years. Despite its focus on vowel systems and its non-traditional telephone

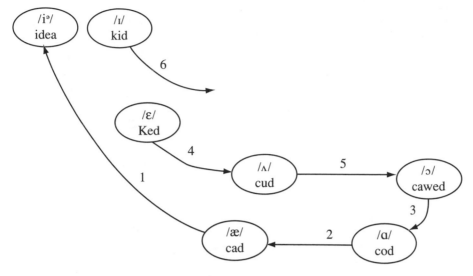

Figure 8.8   *Northern Cities Shift*
Source: Adapted from Labov et al., 2005

methodology, *ANAE* uncovered dialects strikingly similar to those proposed in earlier studies of regional vocabulary.

Critical to the Telsur investigation is its focus on patterns of vowel mergers and vowel shifts that are currently restructuring North American pronunciation. Traditional pronunciations of *cot* and *caught* distinguish them as [kʰɑt] versus [kʰɔt], a distinction that supports a perceptual contrast in pairs such as *don/dawn* and *hock/hawk*. In many US regions and most of English-speaking Canada, however, speakers have merged these vowels; besides losing the distinction between these word pairs, many other words, such as *daughter*, *water* and *lock*, are also affected by this low-back merger. Another vowel merger, with a narrower geographical reach, involves /ɪ/ and /ɛ/ before nasals in such words as *pin/pen*, *lint/lent* and *cinder/sender*, which are distinct in most regions of the US and nearly all of Canada, but which, across a swath of southern states, are homophonous. Related to these mergers are two vowel shifts currently underway, potentially as dramatic in their consequences as the Great Vowel Shift (see Chapter 2).

Northern Cities Shift
Across a set of northern US cities (Syracuse, Rochester and Buffalo, NY; Cleveland and Akron, Ohio; Detroit, Michigan; Chicago and Rockford, Illinois; Milwaukee and Madison, Wisconsin) and in cities in southern Canada, a set of vowel shifts is radically altering the way words are pronounced and perceived. The effect is so drastic that speakers from dialect regions not participating in the shift report mishearing, for example, 'stacks and bands' for *stocks and bonds* and 'battle' for *bottle*. Figure 8.8 lays out the shift in six steps. The first step got underway no later than the 1940s, though it went unnoticed for some time.

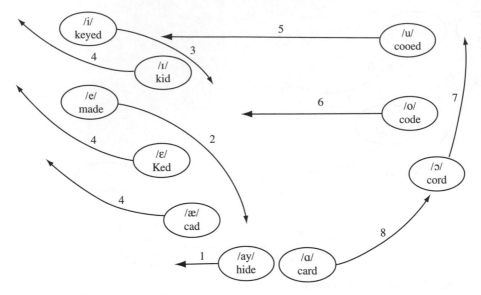

Figure 8.9   *Southern Shift*
Source: Adapted from Labov et al., 2005

1.   /æ/ is raised and fronted to [iᵊ] so that *man* and *bad* are heard with the underscored vowel of *idea*: [miᵊn] and [biᵊd]
2.   /ɑ/ is fronted to [æ] so that *block* and *stocks* are heard as *black* and *stacks*
3.   /ɔ/ is lowered and fronted to [ɑ] so that *cawed* is heard as *cod*
4.   /ɛ/ is lowered and centred to [ʌ] so that *Ked* and *steady* are heard as *cud* and *study*
5.   /ʌ/ is backed to [ɔ] so that *cud* is heard as *cawed*
6.   /ɪ/ is lowered and backed

Southern Shift

Remarkably, in a large part of the American South, vowels are shifting in opposing directions to those of the Northern Cities Shift. This Southern Shift begins with a simple process in which the diphthong /ay/ loses its offglide, often with compensatory lengthening of the nucleus. Figure 8.9 provides a schematic of the shift in eight steps.

1.   /ay/ is monophthongised to [a] or [aː] so that *hide* is heard as [had] or [haːd]
2.   /e/ is lowered and centralised to [aj] so that *slade* is heard as *slide*
3.   /i/ is lowered and backed
4.   /ɪ/, /ɛ/, /æ/ are raised and fronted so that *kid* is heard as *keyed*, *red* as *rid*, *pat* as *pet*
5.   /u/ is fronted so that *cool* is heard as 'kewl'
6.   /o/ is fronted so that *code* and *boat* are heard as [kɛᵒd] and [bɛᵒt]

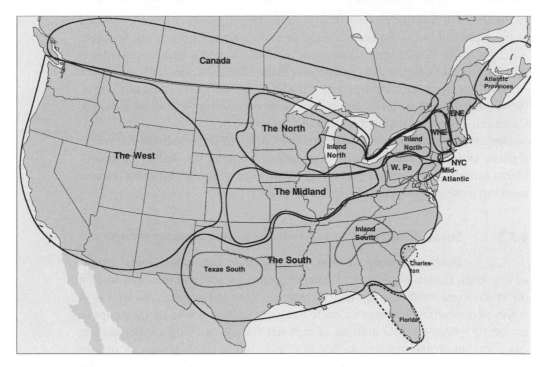

Figure 8.10   *Dialect areas of North America, based on vowel pronunciation*
Source: Adapted from Labov et al., 2005

7.   /ɔ/ is raised
8.   /ɑ/ is raised

Using vowel pronunciations from Telsur (see <http://ling.upenn.edu/phono_atlas/home.html>) *ANAE* proposes four main US dialect regions, with subdivisions: North, South, Midland and West. (Mid-Atlantic, New York City, Eastern New England, Boston, Providence, Western Pennsylvania and a few others carry separate designations.) Canada, of course, is a separate dialect region, with its own subdivisions. Below are summarised some characteristics of regional pronunciations identified in the urban areas surveyed, and Figure 8.10 is the resulting map of NAE dialects.

NORTH	less fronting of /o/ than elsewhere
Inland North	Northern Cities Shift
Western New England	less advanced Northern Cities Shift
SOUTH	monophthongisation of /ay/ (word-finally and preceding voiced consonants)
Inland South	Southern Shift
Texas South	Southern Shift
MIDLAND	transitional low-back merger fronting of /o/
WEST	low-back merger fronting of /u/ but not /o/
CANADA	low-back merger

In Figure 8.10, note that Florida, though geographically southern, is not included in the dialect of the South because Floridians do not participate in the Southern Shift generally, despite some fronting of /u/. Note, too, that speakers in what is labelled the 'St Louis Corridor' participate in the Northern Cities Shift, unlike the Midland speakers surrounding them. Finally, note that, unlike most of Canada, Newfoundland and the Maritime provinces do not exhibit the low-back merger (or certain other characteristic Canadian features).

Despite the rapid rate of change uncovered by Telsur's findings, the investigators emphasise that the basic boundaries separating the dialect regions of North America have remained relatively stable, even while the particular features marking those dialects have changed over time.

8.3.5   Social dialects

Besides regional varieties, language may vary across social groups of any kind. Ethnic groups, socioeconomic status groups, and men and women differ from one another in vocabulary, pronunciation and grammar, as well as in styles of interaction. It is convenient to think of variation across social groups as occurring within regional dialects, of regional dialects as being a superordinate category, but characteristics ascribed to ethnic groups, status groups, or men or women may transcend regions, and social group variation of one kind typically interacts with that of other kinds. For example, pronunciation of the final consonant in the *talking/running* class of words varies between [n] and [ŋ]. Both variants appear in most dialects, but [ŋ] appears more frequently in Northern US dialects than in those of the South, more frequently among women than men, and more frequently among higher-socioeconomic status groups than lower-ranking ones.

8.3.5.1   Socioeconomic status

Principally for methodological reasons, recent investigations of language use across socioeconomic status groups have focused on pronunciation. In a trailblazing study of New York City, Labov (1966, 1972b) examined the vowels (æ) and (ɔ) and the consonants (ð), (θ), (r) and (ŋ). The respondents participated in sociolinguistic interviews designed to elicit styles in a range from casual to formal. Across four ranked groups, New York City residents showed remarkable similarity in overall patterns of variation, though they differed systematically in actual realisations of the variables. For example, pronunciations of /æ/ in words like *ham* and *crash* varied from [æ] to raised and fronted [ɛː] and [iə]. Pronunciations of the stressed vowel in the *coffee* and *fought* class varied from low back [ɑ] to mid back [ɔ] and high back [uə]. The lowest-ranking SES group showed higher percentages of raised vowels than higher-ranked groups.

Among consonants, (θ) and (ð) represent variable pronunciations of the sounds represented by initial *th* in words like *thin* and *then*, respectively. In a wide range of dialects, these consonants are variably pronounced as fricatives ([θ] or [ð]) or stops

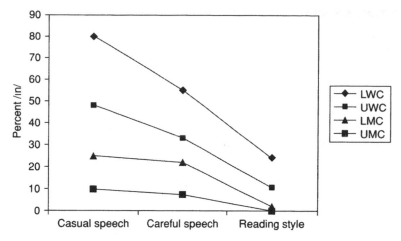

Figure 8.11   *Pronunciation of -ing as /ɪn/ by four SES groups in three*
situations in New York City
Source: Labov, 1996

([t] or [d]). Frequent stop pronunciations underlie the reputation of New Yorkers
for saying 'dis', 'dat', 'dem', and 'dose'. These and a few other phonological
variables (ŋ~n, θ~t, ð~d) have remained stable over long periods of time and
showed similar patterns of use among all SES groups in New York City. Upper-
middle-class speakers scored higher than lower-middle-class speakers, who in
turn scored higher than working-class speakers, who scored higher than lower-
class speakers. A typical display for stable variables appears in Figure 8.11; it
shows index values for the four SES groups in 'styles' ranging from casual to
reading style. Note the roughly parallel pattern: the indexes for the variables
across SES groups mirror the indexes for styles; pronunciations that all SES
groups favour in more formal styles are the ones favoured by higher-ranked SES
groups more generally.

The /r/ variable showed a somewhat different pattern. In the most formal
styles, index values were higher for the second highest-ranking group than for the
highest-ranking group, creating a pattern of 'hypercorrection' that is thought to
reflect a sound change in progress. This interpretation is supported by analysis of
patterns across 'apparent time', where younger New York City residents showed
higher realisations of /r/ than older residents in the same SES group. In other
words, lower SES groups more frequently dropped /r/ in the *car ~ card* word
class than did higher SES groups, and all groups pronounced /r/ more frequently
in careful styles than in casual ones. For these same phonological variables, similar patterns have been found elsewhere in the US (as in Britain; see Trudgill,
1974). Other phonological variables that correlate with SES include consonant
cluster reduction, where lower-ranking social groups show a stronger tendency
to reduce word-final clusters such as /ʃt/ in words like *wished* and /rnd/ in words
like *turned*.

8.3.6   Ethnic dialects

Over time, ethnic dialects might be expected to converge with local non-ethnic vernaculars, if not with regional or national standards, and this seems to be what has happened in the US with German-American English and Irish-American English, for example. Today, however, several ethnic varieties of AmE remain distinct, including those spoken in the Amish community (McArthur, 2002: 179), certain urban Jewish-American communities (McArthur, 2002: 198–200) and American Indian communities (Leap, 1993); limitations of space prevent our describing those varieties here. Two other ethnic varieties are particularly salient. African American English has been the focus of considerable scholarly, political and even legal attention. Latino English, less well studied and described, is sometimes wrongly viewed as learner English.

8.3.6.1   African American English (AAE)

Researchers disagree about the origins and evolution of African American English, particularly the extent to which it is based on a creole in the process of decreolisation or is a development of dialects first learned by African slaves chiefly on southern plantations (Mufwene, 2001). From the score of enslaved Africans first brought to Virginia on a Dutch boat in 1619, the tobacco and cotton plantations at the base of the South's economy grew in reliance on slave labour, so that in 1790 the first US census showed nearly 48,000 families holding slaves in eight states. Coming mostly from West Africa and speaking many languages, slaves speaking the same language were systematically separated from one another. Today, across the thousands of miles separating New York and Los Angeles, and in urban centres throughout the US, AAE shows remarkably uniform grammatical, phonological, lexical and interactional patterns.

Besides a few unique features and some uncommon ones, AAE shares features with other varieties especially in the rural South, although speakers may display those features to a greater extent or in different linguistic environments. For example, in several varieties, *desk*, *wild* and *passed* may be pronounced [dɛs], [waɪl] and [pʰæs], but such consonant cluster reduction occurs to a greater extent in AAE than in other varieties, so much so that some speakers who pronounce the plural of *desk* as *desses* presumably have underlying /dɛs/ rather than /dɛsk/. Word-final stop consonants are variably deleted in words like *side* and *borrowed*, producing *sigh* and *borrow*. When the stop represents a separate morpheme (as in *followed* and *tried*), /d/ is preserved much more frequently than when it is part of a larger morpheme (e.g. *side* and *rapid*). Final stops in strongly stressed syllables (e.g. *tried*) tend to be preserved more than in weakly stressed syllables (e.g. *borrowed*, *rapid*). A following vowel most strongly preserves a final stop, as in *side angle* and *tried it* (cf. *tried hard* and *side street*).

The consonant represented by *th* in words like *with*, *both* and *Bethlehem* may be pronounced as a labiodental fricative ([wɪf], [bof], [bɛfləhɛm]), while the underlying interdental fricative in words like *smooth*, *bathe* and *brother* may be pronounced as a labiodental ([smuv], [bev], [bɹʌvə]). AAE's non-rhotic character is suggested by [bɹʌvə] for *brother*, and AAE also permits variable absence of intervocalic /r/, as in [pʰæs] for *Paris*. Two lexical pronunciations characteristic of AAE are *aunt* as [ant] or [ɑnt] (not [ænt]) and *ask* as [æks] (with metathesis), although the first also occurs in some standard varieties of New England and the South, the second in non-standard varieties throughout the US. Speakers of AAE show little or no participation in the Northern Cities Shift, even in urban centres where the shift is otherwise well advanced.

Among notable grammatical features are copula deletion, habitual *be*, negative concord, preterit *had*, existential *it*, and the verbal markers *come* and *steady*. Copula deletion occurs variably in present-tense expressions where standard English allows contraction: *He my friend* and *The coffee cold* (cf. *He's my friend*). Habitual *be*, also called invariant *be*, signals recurring or repeated action, as in *Yeah, the boys do be messin' around a lot* and *I see her when I bees on my way to school*. Negative concord, a feature widespread in non-standard dialects, appears in utterances like *Don't nobody never help me do my work* and *He don't never go nowhere*, in which more than one word is marked for negation, and the sense remains unmistakably negative.

Arising since the middle of the twentieth century and characteristic mostly of urban speakers is preterit *had*: the use of *had* with a past-tense verb to represent a simple past tense – a preterit – rather than the past perfect tense, as in standard varieties. Thus, urban AAE permits *I had wrote* and *We had went* (cf. standard *I wrote* and *We went*). 'Existential *it*' refers to the use of *it is* instead of *there is* in sentences such as *Is it a Miss Williams in this office?* and *She's been a wonderful wife and it's nothin' too good for her* (cf. *Is there a Miss Williams in this office?* and . . . *there's nothing too good for her*). Two verbal markers appear to be unique to AAE: *come* used as a modal to express speaker indignation (*Don't come telling me all those lies*) and *steady* used as a modal to express an intense and continuous action of the verb (*When I would talk to her, she wouldn't pay me any attention. She would just steady drive*) (Green, 2002: 22–4; see also Rickford, 1999).

AAE speakers also use characteristic vocabulary items and word senses not generally known by outsiders. Some words refer to phenomena associated with African American dress and personal care, such as *ashy* 'the whitish coloration of black skin' and *kitchen* 'the hair at the nape of the neck'; others relate to patterns of behavior or interaction, as with *saddity* meaning 'uppity' or *get over* meaning 'to take advantage of', as in *The students tried to get over on the teacher* (Green, 2002).

Two interactional practices have been much discussed. *Call and response* occurs during church services and certain kinds of secular events at which a leader – a preacher, minister or speaker – says something and the congregation or audience responds spontaneously, though not necessarily in unison or harmony. The other, *the dozens*, can be illustrated from the work of African American novelists. Here, from a short story by Nora Zeale Hurston, is an example of playing the dozens, 'the age-old black ritual of graceful insult' (Gates, 1996: 291):

> Yo' mama don't wear no Draws
> Ah seen her when she took 'em Off
> She soaked 'em in alcoHol
> She sold 'em tuh de Santy Claus
> He told her 'twas aginst de Laws
> To wear dem dirty Draws
> ('Hurricane', 1946: 152)

Despite the popular sense that dialects are disappearing in the US largely as a consequence of nationwide television programmes, considerable evidence points to AAE's becoming increasingly differentiated from mainstream varieties (see Butters, 1987).

8.3.6.2   Latino English

Varieties of Latino English are spoken by residents of Puerto Rican, Cuban, Mexican and Latin American descent in many parts of the US. The best studied variety is that spoken by residents of Mexican descent in urban areas throughout the US and in rural areas of the southwest. Known as Chicano English (ChE), it is spoken natively by many Americans of Mexican ancestry, and as with other varieties of Latino English it would be inaccurate to characterise it as English spoken with a foreign accent. Still, some features characteristic of Latino English likely arose in situations where English was spoken as a second language, and some features may be supported by the continuing vitality of Spanish in Latino communities throughout the US. ChE exhibits consonant cluster reduction, as in [ɪs] for *it's*, [kaɪn] for *kind*, [ol] for *old* and [bɛs] for *best*. *Hardware* may be pronounced [hɑwɚ] (Fought, 2003: 69) and *It's kind of hard* [ɪskɑnəhɑɹ]. Consonant cluster reduction may appear within words, as in [ʌnəɹstæn] for *understand*. For the standard fricatives represented by *th*, speakers variably pronounce stops (typically apico-dental stops); thus, [t] or [t̪] for [θ] in *thick* and *with* and [d] or [d̪] for [ð] in *then*. Earlier reports suggesting that ChE devoices /z/, especially in word-final position, have not been confirmed, perhaps because those studies did not distinguish adequately between native speakers of ChE and speakers of learner English or because ChE has changed in the intervening decades. Support for the evolutionary view appears in a finding of occasional use in older but not younger speakers of ChE (Fought, 2003). Words like *sing* and *long* that end in *-ng* (not verbal *-ing*) are pronounced with both a velar nasal and a velar stop: [sɪŋg] and [lɔŋg] instead of standard [sɪŋ] and [lɔŋ].

The ChE vowel system is close to that of standard varieties, but shows less gliding and less reduction of unstressed vowels. In standard AmE, long vowels tend to be glided and are often represented, even phonemically, as diphthongs: /iy/ and /ey/, /uw/ and /ow/. Possibly as an abiding influence from Spanish, whose vowels are not glided, speakers of ChE pronounce long vowels more nearly as monophthongs, especially [i] and [u]. Because unstressed vowels are reduced less than in standard varieties, words like *together*, *delivery* and *university* are likely to be pronounced [tʰugɛðɚ], [dilɪvəɹi] and [junɪvəɹsɪɾi] rather than [tʰəgɛðɚ], [dəlɪvəɹi] and [junəvəɹsəɾi]. In many AmE varieties, as we have seen, /æ/ is raised and pronounced [ɛ] or even [iᵊ] in words like *ham* and *hand*, but in ChE this class of words is pronounced with [æ].

The stereotype suggesting a merger or confusion of [i] and [ɪ] is inaccurate for native speakers of ChE, though it may characterise learner English among Spanish speakers. The stereotype may receive support from the frequent pronunciation of verbal *-ing* as 'een' [in] rather than [ən] or [ɪŋ]. There is evidence that /ɪ/ is sometimes realised as a sound somewhere between [ɪ] and [i], but ChE does not interchange [ɪ] and [i]. As with speakers of AAE, speakers of Latino English do not participate in the Northern Cities Shift, at least to the same extent as their non-Latino peers.

Other pronunciations earlier associated with ChE appear to have died out (or are characteristic of learner English), among them substitution of *ch* [tʃ] for *sh* [ʃ] (as in *she*, *shoes*) and the reverse substitution of *sh* [ʃ] for *ch* [tʃ] (as in *preach*, *check*).

In its grammatical features, ChE exhibits negative concord, as in *You don't owe me nothing* and *Us little people don't get nothin'*. It also regularises some verb forms, using past-tense forms as past participles, and shows frequent use of *ain't*. Some speakers also use features of AAE, such as habitual *be* (*The news be showing it too much*), existential *it* (*It's four of us, there's two of them*), and preterit *had* (*The cops had went to my house*).

Among characteristic lexical items are the verbs *clown* 'tease', *talk to* 'date', *kick it* 'hang around', and *tell* 'ask', as in *If I tell her to jump up, she'll tell me 'how high'*; the phrase *from somewhere* 'in a gang', as in *I told him I wasn't from anywhere* and *I'm not from nowhere*; the adjective *American* 'European-American or white', as in *It wasn't the American lady, it was the other one*; and the adverb *barely* 'just recently', as in *He just barely got a job you know back with his father* and *These were expensive when they barely came out*. One feature that shows Spanish influence is the use of *brothers* for 'brothers and sisters' or 'siblings' (cf. Spanish *hermanos*), as when a sixteen-year-old girl in a family with one boy and five girls said, *To my brothers I usually talk English*. Another borrowing from Spanish occurs with the discourse marker *ey*, glossed as 'yeah' and exemplified in *If a girl's pretty you know and she feels the same for me, ey, I got it right there* (examples from Fought, 2003: 103–6).

8.3.7   English in Canada

A further form of English in North America which we must consider separately is Canadian English, and Newfoundland and Quebec must be distinguished from other provinces. Claimed by England as early as 1497, Newfoundland remained independent of Canada until joining the Confederation in

1949. For centuries, then, it had a history independent of most of Canada's. Likewise, Quebec province is largely francophone, with strong French cultural ties that separate it from the provinces to its east and west. Canada is strikingly uniform in its class structure, being highly urban and 'overwhelmingly middle-class' (Chambers 1991: 90). Newfoundland and Quebec aside, Canada is also relatively uniform in its use of the English language.

Canadian English has roots in several sources (Brinton & Fee, 2001), whose work we follow, together with Chambers (1993, 1998): American English spoken by some Loyalists who immigrated to Canada during and after the War of Independence; subsequent immigration from the British Isles and Ireland; interaction with French in Quebec; and government policies, including bilingualism and multiculturalism. Four major immigrant groups can be identified (Chambers, 1991). The Loyalists arrived chiefly between 1776 and 1793 and included as many as 40,000 to Nova Scotia (and then, for some, on to England or Sierra Leone) and perhaps 12,000 to Upper Canada (Ontario). The second wave of British settlers, particularly Irish and Scots, peaked in 1851–61 and went mostly to Upper Canada. A third wave comprising British (mostly Scots) settlers and Germans, Dutch and Belgians immigrated between 1901 and 1911. Then, between 1951 and 1961, arrived a group of Germans, Italians, Ukrainians, Greeks, Chinese and Portuguese.

Partly because both BrE and AmE exert strong influence on it, CanE is defined by a set of features peculiar to it and by the particular mix drawn from its wellsprings. One notable feature is its exceptional homogeneity. Newfoundland aside, 'the accents of second-generation middle-class Anglophones from Halifax or Ottawa or Winnipeg or Edmonton are indistinguishable', even though those cities are farther apart than New York City and Richmond, Virginia, which are noticeably different in their dialects; put strongly, standard CanE is 'almost indistinguishable from one end of the country to the other' (Chambers, 1998: 253–4).

Other characteristic features combine to make CanE a distinct national variety. The most prominent pronunciation feature involves the vowels in the *bite~bike~life* and *bout~shout~house* word classes. In the nucleus of the diphthongs /ay/ and /aw/, a phenomenon usually called Canadian raising produces [ʌɪ] before voiceless consonants, as in *wipe, white, strike, lice* and *life* (but not *bribe, wide, lies, Clive*) and [ʌʊ] in *about* and *house* (but not *proud* and *houses*). Currently, there appears to be a change underway in the pronunciation of this vowel, a change that would threaten this distinctive feature. Especially in inland urban areas, younger Canadians increasingly pronounce the diphthong in the *how, houses, house* class with a low front onset vowel, just like their American counterparts (Chambers, 1991: 93). As noted earlier, the vowels in *caught* and *cot, pawned* and *pond* are pronounced alike in a merger traced in Canada to the mid-1800s (Chambers, 1993: 11). CanE likewise flaps intervocalic /t/ in words with certain stress patterns, producing [ɾ] (or [d]) for /t/ and creating homophones of pairs like *latter/ladder* and *metal/medal*. CanE flaps intervocalic /t/ in more contexts than US varieties do, including between /f/ and a vowel (as in *after*), between

/s/ and a vowel (*sister*), between /ʃ/ and a vowel (*washed out*), and between /k/ and a vowel (*picture*) (Brinton & Fee, 2001).

CanE is rhotic. Loyalists arriving from New England may have brought an *r*-less variety and afterwards restored *r*-pronunciations, perhaps in part to create distance from the Americans and thereby underscore Canadian loyalty to the crown (Bailey, 1982). Alternatively, New England dialects of the 1770s and 1780s may have been non-rhotic to some degree. Pronunciation of postvocalic /r/ (*fear, storm*) was in flux in England, with /r/ having been 'sporadically' lost as early as the fifteenth century; it was 'on its way out in the 1770s', such that 'by the 1790s /r/-less pronunciations must have been very common and increasing' (Lass, 1999: 115). Consequently, rather than carrying an *r*-less variety to Canada and later restoring /r/, Loyalists may have spoken a dialect with variable /r/ pronunciation and subsequently increased its frequency, exactly the opposite of what their neighbours to the south did. In distancing their speech from that of New Englanders, if that is what happened, the Loyalists likewise distanced it from the speech of southern England, which went on to become non-rhotic.

A few word classes and a few isolated words differ in their Canadian and American pronunciations, although Canadian usage typically varies. The first syllable of the *process* ∼ *progress* class is pronounced with /o/ (but in the US with /ɑ/); *schedule* has initial /ʃ/ or /sk/ (in the US only /sk/); the second syllable of *again* may rhyme with *pain* or *ten* (in the US typically with *ten*); the first vowel of *drama* is pronounced /æ/. A sensitive matter is the name of the last letter of the alphabet – Canadian *zed*. Apparently influenced by kindergarten alphabet songs seeking a rhyme for the letter *tee*, children living in parts of southern Ontario call the letter *zee*, but *zee* is such a shibboleth that, as children mature, the percentage using *zed* increases dramatically (Chambers, 2003: 207–8).

While most vocabulary items are shared across NAE, some expressions for Canadian customs are unfamiliar in the US. In other matters, too, government structure or political history differs, and terms routinely used in one nation may be unfamiliar in the other. In Canadian courts, the *Crown* prosecutes; in US jurisdictions, the *State* or *Commonwealth*. The head of a province is the *premier*, of the federal government the *prime minister*. The *hydro* is an 'electric bill'; *washroom* is usual for 'toilet'; *Grade 13*, equivalent to the British sixth form, is unknown in the US. Some vocabulary items that have been distinctively Canadian – e.g. *chesterfield* 'sofa' – are being lost, while for others Canadians use several terms, including the generally used American one. Recent local surveys (see Chambers, 1998) have found that Canadians use *washcloth* and *facecloth*, Americans only *washcloth*; Canadians call post-secondary institutions *college* or *university*, Americans almost invariably *college*. For the prank in which schoolboys pull up another boy by the back of his underpants, Americans use only *wedgie*, while Canadians also say *gotchie, rooney* and *snuggy*.

In grammar, a few characteristic features have been identified, including (1) *after* plus a past participle (*He's after telling me all about it* 'He has just told me all about it'), found in parts of Newfoundland, Nova Scotia and 'other places founded by Celtic settlers'; (2) *ever*-exclamations (*Is he ever stupid!*), also known in the US; (3) sentence-initial *as well* (*He told Mary to be careful. As well, he asked all of us to help her*) (Chambers, 1986: 9–10).

In spelling, Canadians draw sometimes on British precedents (*cheque* not *check*), sometimes on American (*tire* not *tyre*); Canadian style manuals urge drawing selectively on one tradition or the other and, within a given pattern, not to mix British and American spellings – for example, not to use both *neighbour* and *color* or both *criticise* and *initialize* (Brinton & Fee, 2001). Spelling differs somewhat from province to province (Brinton & Fee, 2001; Ireland, 1979 as reported in Chambers, 1986). By contrast, publications throughout the US draw on the standardised spellings propagated in a few nationally distributed dictionaries, as Noah Webster had hoped when he published his *American Dictionary* as a national standard of usage.

8.3.8   Social meaning and attitudes

Attitudes play an important role in forming and judging people's language. We describe four instances of social meaning attaching to pronunciation – one each related to local and class values, a third to urban and traditional values, and one to ethnic identity. On Martha's Vineyard, an island off the coast of Massachusetts that is home to a small group of year-round residents with an influx of summer tourists and vacationers, characteristic pronunciation shows centralisation of the nucleus in the diphthongs of the *nice* and *shout* word classes. Year-round residents vary between centralised [nʌɪs] and [ʃʌʊt] and the mainland pronunciations [naɪs] and [ʃaʊt]. In the 1960s, resident young men planning to raise families on the island showed the highest incidence of centralised variants, while those intending to take up careers on the mainland showed the least (Labov, 1972a). Vowel centralisation thus represented island values. Elsewhere, in a suburban Detroit secondary school, students showed varied realisations of the diphthong /ay/. Representing middle-class suburban values, 'jocks' showed least raising and backing, while 'burnouts', representing working-class urban values, had much higher indexes for this feature (Eckert, 2001: 125). Another kind of social meaning attaches to pronunciations of the final vowel in *Missouri*, where 'Missouree' with final [-i] is associated with urban and refined values, while 'Missouruh' with [ə] signals traditional rural values. Reflecting larger cultural trends, the more urban pronunciation closer to the spelling is on the increase (Lance, 2003).

The final example involves pronunciations with a distinctly non-English flavour. In the US one readily hears Latino television and radio correspondents reporting from the field in standard varieties of English, unmarked by features of Latino English. In signing off, however, these same correspondents may use markedly ethnic pronunciations of their own names. Maria Hinojosa identifies herself as [mɑriɑ inohosɑ] with a trill [r] and full vowels rather than the reduced vowels characteristic of unstressed syllables in NAE. Geraldo Rivera calls himself [hɛraldo], and others identify themselves as [dɛlakrus] 'de la Cruz', [fwɛntɛs] 'Fuentes', [garsa] 'Garza', or [ɛrnandɛs] 'Hernandez', using pronunciations that affirm their Latino identity.

8.3.9   Official languages in a multilingual North America

Benjamin Franklin argued for limiting languages other than English in America, and John Adams suggested that the Continental Congress create an academy to 'purify, develop, and dictate usage', both to no avail. More than a century later, President Theodore Roosevelt claimed 'We have but one flag. We must also learn one language, and that language is English.' From the outset, some North Americans have been troubled by linguistic diversity, and especially in periods of political or international conflict or heavy immigration, citizens of both Canada and the US have tried legislating restrictions on language use. After the start of World War I, the states of Iowa, Ohio, Nebraska and several others forbade teaching youths any subject in the German language, but in 1923 the US Supreme Court declared such laws unconstitutional. In 1981, a proposed amendment to the Constitution would have made English the official language of the US, but at the federal level nothing came of it. More than twenty states have designated English their official language, although state supreme courts have ruled certain of these statutes unconstitutional. Hawaii is the only state with two official languages – English and Hawaiian – although Louisiana law recognises both English and French.

As in colonial North America English was not the only language, so it remains today. It is not the only language of government, not the only official language, and certainly not the only language of importance in many people's everyday lives. In Canada, English and French are the official languages; likewise for the province of New Brunswick; in Quebec province, French is the sole official language. In 1996, of 28.5 million Canadian residents, 6.6 million claimed French as a mother tongue (more than 85 per cent of whom lived in Quebec), and an additional 4.6 million claimed a mother tongue other than English or French.

The US has no official language, and the 2000 census found that 47 million residents over the age of five speak a language other than English at home. (That's 18 per cent of that age group, up from 11 per cent in 1980.) Twenty-eight million of those claim Spanish, but many other languages are represented, including Chinese with 2 million claimants, and French, German, Tagalog, Vietnamese and Italian with a million or more each. Korean is spoken by 900,000, Russian and Polish by 700,000 each, Arabic by 600,000. Each of the fifty states is home to speakers of Arabic, Hindi, Hungarian, Korean, Tagalog, Thai, Urdu and Vietnamese. In seven heavily populated states, at least one in four residents claims a home language other than English. In Los Angeles, election ballots are available to citizens in English, Spanish, Vietnamese, Chinese, Japanese, Korean and Tagalog. Native American languages are spoken in every state, but the misleading character of that fact is underscored by acknowledging that the 175,000 speakers of

Navajo – the most vital among these languages – are spread across 47 of the 50 states. Despite great diversity and despite pockets particularly of French in Canada and of Spanish in the USA, English continues to predominate throughout most of North America.

8.3.10   The future of North American dialects

One often reads that regional and ethnic dialects of NAE are disappearing. While it is too early to judge how much linguistic levelling national television broadcasts may promote, evidence suggests that American regional dialects remain vital. 'In spite of the intense exposure of the American population to a national media with a convergent network standard of pronunciation . . . the local accents of Boston, New York, Philadelphia, Atlanta, Buffalo, Detroit, Chicago, and San Francisco are more different from each other than at any time in the past' (Labov & Ash, 1997: 508). Some regional dialect features are new, but they do not spread independently of traditional dialect boundaries. Likewise for features such as preterit *had* in African American English. Social dialects gain and lose particular features, but the dialects remain. Canadian English is more homogeneous than American English, and younger speakers in Newfoundland are absorbing features of the national standard, but their dialect is not disappearing. Characteristic features of regional and social dialects may evolve, but for a long time to come the dialects of North American English are expected to survive.

Appendix: abbreviations of US state-names

AL	Alabama	ME	Maine
AK	Alaska	MD	Maryland
AZ	Arizona	MA	Massachusetts
AR	Arkansas	MI	Michigan
CA	California	MN	Minnesota
CO	Colorado	MS	Mississippi
CT	Connecticut	MO	Missouri
DE	Delaware	MT	Montana
FL	Florida	NB	Nebraska
GA	Georgia	NV	Nevada
HI	Hawaii	NH	New Hampshire
ID	Idaho	NJ	New Jersey
IL	Illinois	NM	New Mexico
IN	Indiana	NY	New York
IA	Iowa	NC	North Carolina
KS	Kansas	ND	North Dakota
KY	Kentucky	OH	Ohio
LA	Louisiana	OK	Oklahoma

OR	Oregon	UT	Utah
PA	Pennsylvania	VT	Vermont
RI	Rhode Island	VA	Virginia
SC	South Carolina	WA	Washington
SD	South Dakota	WV	West Virginia
TN	Tennessee	WI	Wisconsin
TX	Texas	WY	Wyoming

9 English worldwide

David Crystal

9.1 Introduction

The final quinquennium of the twentieth century saw an unprecedented interest in the topic of global English, articulated at both popular and academic levels, and a discernible step forward in the generality with which the phenomenon was discussed. To the media of the time, the global spread of English was an established and straightforward fact. 'English Rules' (*The Globe and Mail*, Toronto, 12 July 1997) was just one of many newspaper headlines presenting to the world an uncomplicated scenario that took for granted the universality of the language's spread, the speed with which it had happened, and the likelihood of its continuation. A statement prominently displayed in the body of the associated article, memorable for its alliterative ingenuity but for little else, reinforced the initial impression: 'The British Empire may be in full retreat with the handover of Hong Kong. But from Bengal to Belize and Las Vegas to Lahore, the language of the sceptred isle is rapidly becoming the first global lingua franca.' Millennial retrospectives and prognostications continued in the same vein, with several major newspapers and magazines finding in the subject of the English language an apt symbol for the themes of globalisation, diversification, progress and identity addressed in their special editions (e.g. Ryan, 1999). Certainly, by the turn of the century, the topic must have made contact with millions of popular intuitions at a level which had simply not existed a decade before.

There was considerable movement, also, at an academic level, but here a more complex picture was beginning to emerge. The largely article-driven literature of previous decades had typically been exploratory and programmatic, restricted to individual situations, anecdotal in illustration, lacking a sociolinguistic frame of reference, and focussing on the written (and usually literary) language. By contrast, the 1990s saw the emergence of a more comprehensive perspective in which spoken varieties became prominent, there was a real increase in the amount of descriptive data, and attempts were made to arrive at explanations and to make predictions of an appropriately general and sociolinguistically informed character. In particular, several book-length treatments by individual authors appeared, each providing a personal synthesis of previous observations and speculations, and focussing on the phenomenon of global English as an end in itself. Three of these treatments illustrate the kinds of theoretical issue being addressed: Crystal

(1997/2003), Graddol (1998) and McArthur (1998). Significantly – and contrary to the general impression provided by the popular media – the perspectives adopted by these authors, and the conclusions they reached, were by no means identical.

My own book is predominantly a retrospective account, examining the range of historical factors which have led to the current position of English in the world. Although avoiding firm predictions about the future, I think it likely that English 'has already grown to be independent of any form of social control' (1997: 139/2003: 290). In my view the momentum of growth has become so great that there is nothing likely to stop its continued spread as a global lingua franca. Graddol looks towards the future, beginning with the present-day situation, and examining the contemporary trends likely to affect the language's eventual role. For him, English is certainly stoppable. Emphasising the unpredictability inherent in language use, he suggests that 'the current global wave of English may lose momentum' (1998: 60) and sees the real possibility of new language hierarchies emerging in the next century, with English holding a less global position. McArthur, adopting a more synchronic perspective, moves away from a monolithic concept of English. He investigates the kinds of variation encountered in the language as a consequence of its global spread, and suggests that English is undergoing a process of radical change which will eventually lead to fragmentation into a 'family of languages'.

The arrival of these books, published within twelve months of each other yet seeing the issue in very different ways, well illustrates the naivety of the populist account, with its simplistic and often suggestively triumphalist tone. Their role has been to underline some of the parameters of inquiry which must influence the next wave of empirical studies. From a stage when there were few general hypotheses to motivate research, we now have a multiplicity of them. Some are issues relating to language use: several political, economic, demographic and social factors have been identified as potential influences on world language presence, all of which have been recognised as operating at local regional levels, such as in relation to minority languages (Edwards, 1992) or endangered languages (Grenoble & Whaley, 1998); however, the role of such factors at a global level remains virtually unexplored. Others are issues affecting language structure: the way in which regional and social factors influence the growth of language varieties and foster linguistic change has formed much of the subject-matter of sociolinguistics and dialectology; but here too, there is as yet little understanding of what happens when these processes begin to operate at a macro level. To take just one example: the radical diversification envisioned by McArthur could have several outcomes, certainly including the development of an English family of languages, but also resulting in various forms of multiglossia (going well beyond current conceptions of diglossia), the emergence of more complex notions of 'standard', and different kinds of multidialectism. We have as yet no adequate typology of the remarkable range of language contact situations which have emerged as a consequence of globalisation, either physically (e.g. through population movement and economic development) or virtually (e.g. through internet communication and satellite broadcasting).

The emergence of English with a genuine global presence therefore has a significance which goes well beyond this particular language. Because there are no precedents for languages achieving this level of use (if we exclude Latin, which was in a sense 'global' when the world was much smaller), we do not know what happens to them in such circumstances. The investigation of world English therefore provides a fresh testing-ground for sociolinguistic hypotheses which previously had only regional validity, and a domain where we may encounter new kinds of phenomena which might one day motivate a global reconceptualisation of that subject. What happens to a language when it is spoken by many times more people as a second or foreign language than as a mother tongue? What happens in the long-term when children, born to parents who communicate with each other through a lingua franca learned as a foreign language, go on to acquire that form of language as their first language? If English does one day go the same way as Latin and French, and have less of a global role, the next languages to rise (the potential of Spanish, Chinese, Arabic and Hindi/Urdu is highlighted by Graddol, 1998: 59) will doubtless be subject to the same governing factors. So far, although we have a general sense of what these factors are, we have very little understanding of how they interact, and of what happens to the structural character of a language when it achieves a global presence.

This chapter therefore has three main sections, which in turn look at the past, the present and the future of English as a world language. I begin with a brief look backwards, to identify the factors which have enabled the language to achieve its global spread. I then examine the chief linguistic features which characterise the 'New Englishes' which have arisen as a result of this spread. And I conclude with some speculation about future trends. A pervasive theme is the lack of empirical data about the nature and rate of current change, which makes the chapter somewhat anecdotal in its references to individual locations, and promotes a certain statistical indeterminacy when making statements about world English as a whole. The chief reason for the lack of knowledge is the recency of the phenomenon.

9.2   The recency of world English

People have been predicting the emergence of English as a global language for at least two centuries (see Bailey, 1991: ch. 4), but in a genuine sense of 'global' the phenomenon is relatively recent. A language achieves a truly global status when it develops a special role that is recognised in every country. The notion of 'special role' is critical. It is obviously present when large numbers of the people in a country speak English as a first language, as happens in the USA, Canada, Britain, Ireland, Australia, New Zealand, South Africa and a scattering of other territories. It is also present when it is made the official language of a country, or is given joint-official or special-regional status (the terms vary in different dispensations), and comes to be used as the primary medium of communication in such domains as government, the law courts, broadcasting, the press and the educational system. English now has some kind of special administrative status in over seventy countries, such as Ghana, Nigeria, Zimbabwe, India, Singapore and Vanuatu. Then, in a different way, English achieves a special role when it is made a priority in a country's foreign-language teaching policy; it has no official status, but it is nonetheless the foreign language which children are most likely to encounter when they arrive in school, and the one most available to adults in further education. Over 100 countries treat English as just a foreign language (chiefly in Europe, Asia, North Africa and Latin America), and in most of these it is now recognised as the chief foreign language being taught in schools, or the one which a country would most like to introduce (if only more trained staff and teaching resources were available).

The term 'global English' thus had a genuine application in the year 2000. However, it could not have had such an application a half-century before. Although the notion of a lingua franca is probably as old as language diversity itself, and although a pre-Babelian romanticism is regularly encountered in the history of ideas (Eco, 1995), the prospect that a lingua franca might be needed as a practical tool for the whole world is something which has emerged strongly only since the 1950s (notwithstanding the efforts of the various artificial language movements during the first half of the century). Not only was there then a postwar demand for a mechanism enabling nations to talk and listen to each other on a regular basis, the actual number of nations in the world participating in that mechanism was soon to increase significantly. The United Nations had only 51 member states when it began in 1945, but this had risen to 191 members by 2002. The consequence was an increasing reliance on the concept of a 'working language', as an alternative to expensive and often impracticable multiway translation facilities, with English more likely to be the mutually accessible language than any other. Although the point has not received the historical study it should, relevant anecdotes abound. Alex Allen, High Commissioner for Australia in the late 1990s, recalls being present at the meetings which led to the formation of the European Bank for Reconstruction and Development: simultaneous translation took place routinely into various languages, but only until 10 o'clock, when the interpreters had to go off-duty – at which point discussion would often continue into the early hours, with everyone using English (Allen, 1999). Reports of this kind of thing happening at political gatherings are commonplace now, notwithstanding the pressure to safeguard and maintain other languages at an official level, and are reflected in the daily realities of interaction in the worlds of business and education.

Translating daily experience into reliable linguistic statistics is virtually impossible, given the absence of routine data-gathering procedures about language use in the population censuses of the world. And when it comes to global statistics, we are in the business of informed guesswork. Still, international organisations,

Table 9.1 *Some recent estimates of World English speakers as a first, second and foreign language (in millions)*

Source	First	Second		Foreign	Total
Quirk, 1962: 6	250	100			350
1970s [cf. McArthur, 1992: 355]	300	300		100	700
Kachru, 1985: 212	300	300–400			600–700
Ethnologue, 1988 [*Time*, 1986 estimate]	403	397	800		
Quirk & Stein, 1990: 60	350				
Bright, 1992: II.74	403	397			800
Columbia Encyclopedia, 1993	450	400			850
Crystal, 1997/2003 [based on 1995 populations]	337–77	235–350		100–1000	1200
Graddol, 1998: 8	372				
Ethnologue, 1992 [*World Almanac*, 1991 estimate]	450	350			
Crystal [current]	400	400		600–700	1400–1500

linguistic surveys and individual authors, using various criteria, have come up with some figures, and as they are the only ones available, we must use them, cautiously, as guidelines for thinking (see Table 9.1). Each category has an in-built uncertainty, the nature of which needs to be appreciated before the totals can be used with any cogency.

The first-language totals cited in the 1990s were swinging between 350 and 450 million, a considerable range – probably because of differences of opinion as to what should be included under this heading. The chief factor must be the status of pidgins and creoles historically derived from English. If these are considered now to be 'varieties of English', then their speakers will be included, and we will move towards accepting the higher total; on the other hand, if they are thought to be separate languages, whether on grounds of mutual unintelligibility or sociopolitical identity or both, then their numbers will be excluded, and the lower total will be more acceptable. As they are not a coherent group, linguistically, many possible decisions could be made; but significant numbers of people are involved. There are over thirty such entities (Crystal, 1995/2003: 346), which in the 2004 *Encyclopaedia Britannica* language survey are said to be represented by some 73 million speakers.

The second- and foreign-language totals, often considered together (as in parts of Table 9.1), are even more difficult to be sure about, for the obvious reason that fluency is a continuum, and commentators differ in their view about how much competence in English a person needs before being allowed to join the community of world English users. A criterion of native-speaker-like fluency would clearly produce a relatively small figure; including every beginner would produce a relatively large one. A widely circulated British Council estimate – more informed than most, as it was based on reports of numbers attending courses and taking examinations, as well as on market intelligence provided by its English 2000 project – has referred to a billion (i.e. thousand million) people engaged in learning English (British Council, 1997). That figure needs to be interpreted cautiously, because it includes all learners, from beginners to advanced. If we take, as a criterion, a medium level of conversational competence in handling domestic subject-matter, then one might expect between half and two-thirds of this total to be counted as 'speakers of English as a foreign language'. However, there need to be only small variations in percentage estimations in the more populous countries (chiefly, India and China) to produce a large effect on the figures. In India, for example, estimates of the numbers of English speakers have varied between 3% (Kachru, 1986: 54), 19% (Encyclopaedia Britannica, 1999: 772) and 33% (Kachru, 2001: 411, reporting a 1997 *India Today* survey) – which in real terms represent a range between 30 million and over 330 million (for comprehension, with a somewhat lower [sic] figure, 200 million, for speech production).

Faced with such notable variations, in which people with particular political agendas can argue for English being stronger or weaker, a cautious temperament will use averages of the most recent estimates – as shown in the final line of Table 9.1, which gives a grand total of around 1,500 million speakers from all sources. This figure permits a convenient summary, given that world population passed the 6 billion mark during late 1999. It suggests that approximately one in four of the world's population are now capable of communicating to a useful level in English.

Two comments must immediately be made about this or any similar conclusion. First, if one quarter of the world's population are able to use English, then three-quarters are not. Nor do we have to travel far into the hinterland of a country – away from the tourist spots, airports, hotels and restaurants – to encounter this reality. Populist claims about the universal spread of English thus need to be kept firmly in perspective. Second, there is evidently a major shift taking place in the centre of gravity of the language. From a time (in the 1960s) when the majority of speakers were thought to be first-language speakers, we now have a situation where there are as many people speaking it as a second language, and many more speaking it as a foreign language. If we combine these two latter groups, the ratio of native to non-native is around 1:3. Moreover, the population growth in areas where English is a second language is about 2.5 times that in areas where it is a first language (see Table 9.2), so that this differential is steadily increasing. Graddol (1999: 61) suggests that the proportion of the world's population who have English as a first language will decline from over 8 per cent in 1950 to less than 5 per cent in 2050. The situation is without precedent for an international language.

Table 9.2 *Annual growth rate in population, 1998–2003: selected countries*

	%	Total pop. 2003
Australia	1.2	19,880,000
Canada	0.9	31,590,000
New Zealand	1.0	4,001,000
UK	0.3	59,164,000
USA	1.1	291,587,000
Average population increase	0.9	
Cameroon	2.1	15,746,000
India	1.6	1,065,462,000
Malaysia	2.9	25,225,000
Nigeria	2.9	125,275,000
Philippines	2.1	81,161,000
Average population increase	2.32	

Data from Encyclopaedia Britannica (2004).

9.3   The reasons for the emergence of world English

Uninformed popular opinion often sees the global spread of English in terms of intrinsic linguistic factors, believing that there are properties in the language which make it especially attractive or easy to learn. The imagined simplicity of English is frequently cited, with the relative lack of inflectional endings, the absence of grammatical gender and lexical tone, or the non-use of honorifics sometimes cited as evidence. Ignored by this account are such matters as the language's syntactic, lexical and stylistic complexity, or the proportion of irregularity in its spelling system. Linguists, respecting the axiom that languages are equivalent in their structural complexity, have no difficulty rejecting intrinsic arguments of this kind. It need only be pointed out that languages which are strongly marked by inflection and grammatical gender, such as Latin and French, have been international languages in their day, to demonstrate that global stature has nothing to do with linguistic character.

A language becomes a world language for extrinsic reasons only, and these all relate to the power of the people who speak it. 'Power', in this connection, has a variety of applications in political (military), technological, economic and cultural contexts. Political power is seen in the form of the colonialism that brought English around the world from the sixteenth century, so that by the nineteenth century, the language was one 'on which the sun does not set' (Quirk et al., 1985: 1). Technological power is present in the sense that the Industrial Revolution of the seventeenth and eighteenth centuries was very significantly an English-language event. The nineteenth century saw the growth in the economic power of the United

States, rapidly overtaking Britain as its population grew, and adding greatly to the number of world English speakers. And in the twentieth century, cultural power manifested itself in virtually every walk of life through spheres of American influence. The core of Crystal (1997/2003: chs. 3–4) is the identification of several domains within which English has become pre-eminent in this way: politics, economics, the press, advertising, broadcasting, motion pictures, popular music, international travel and safety, education, and communications. Given this spread of functionality, it is not surprising that so many countries have found it useful to adopt English as a medium of communication, either for internal or external purposes.

9.3.1 Politics

As just suggested, pre-twentieth-century commentators would have had no difficulty giving a single, political answer to the question, 'Why world English?' They would simply have pointed to the growth of the British Empire, a legacy which carried over into the twentieth century. The League of Nations was the first of many modern international alliances to allocate a special place to English in its proceedings: English was one of the two official languages (along with French), and all documents were printed in both. English now plays an official or working role in the proceedings of most major international political gatherings.

9.3.2 Economics

By the beginning of the nineteenth century, Britain had become the world's leading industrial and trading nation (Parker, 1986: 391). Its population of 5 million in 1700 more than doubled by 1800, and during that century no country could equal its economic growth, with a gross national product rising, on average, at 2 per cent per year. By 1800, the chief growth areas, in textiles and mining, were producing a range of manufactured goods for export which led to Britain being called the 'workshop of the world'. Over half of the leading scientists and technologists during the Industrial Revolution worked in English, and people who travelled to Britain (and later America) to learn about the new technologies had to do so through the medium of English. The early nineteenth century saw the rapid growth of the international banking system, especially in Germany, Britain and the USA, with London and New York becoming the investment capitals of the world. The resulting 'economic imperialism' brought a fresh dimension to the balance of linguistic power.

9.3.3 The press

The English language has been an important medium of the press for nearly 400 years. The nineteenth century was the period of greatest progress, thanks to the introduction of new printing technology and new methods of mass production and transportation. It also saw the development of a truly independent press, chiefly fostered in the USA, where there were some 400 daily newspapers by 1850, and nearly 2,000 by the turn of the century. Censorship and other restrictions continued in continental Europe during the early decades, however, which meant that the provision of popular news in languages other than English developed much more slowly. Today, about a third of the world's newspapers are published in countries where English has special status (Encyclopaedia Britannica, 2004: 818ff.), and the majority of these will be in English. This high profile was reinforced by the way techniques of news gathering developed. The mid-nineteenth century saw the growth of the major news agencies, especially following the invention of the telegraph. Paul Julius Reuter started an office in Aachen, but soon moved to London, where in 1851 he launched the agency which now bears his name. By 1870 Reuters had acquired more territorial news monopolies than any of its continental competitors. With the emergence in 1856 of the New York Associated Press, the majority of the information being transmitted along the telegraph wires of the world was in English. Some degree of linguistic balance would later emerge, but not for a considerable time.

9.3.4   Advertising

Towards the end of the nineteenth century, a combination of social and economic factors led to a dramatic increase in the use of advertisements in publications, especially in the more industrialised countries. Mass production had increased the flow of goods and was fostering competition; consumer purchasing power was growing; and new printing techniques were providing fresh display possibilities. In the USA, publishers realised that income from advertising would allow them to lower the selling price of their magazines, and thus hugely increase circulation. Two-thirds of a modern newspaper, especially in the USA, may be devoted to advertising. During the nineteenth century the advertising slogan became a feature of the medium, as did the famous 'trade name'. The media capitalised on the brevity with which a product could be conveyed to an audience: posters, billboards, electric displays, shop signs and other techniques became part of the everyday scene. As international markets grew, the 'outdoor media' began to travel the world, and their prominence in virtually every town and city became one of the most noticeable global manifestations of English language use. American English ruled: by 1972, only three of the world's top 30 advertising agencies were not US-owned. Today (as of 2004), the American bias has decreased, because of the increased role of British and Japanese agencies, but the English-language dominance is still there, in 17 out of 30 agencies (and, of course, several Japanese agencies now handle a great deal of English-language work).

9.3.5   Broadcasting

It took many decades of experimental research in physics before it was possible to send the first radio telecommunication signals through the air, without wires. Marconi's system, built in 1895, carried telegraph code signals over a distance of one mile. Six years later, his signals had crossed the Atlantic Ocean; by 1918, they had reached Australia. English was the first language to be transmitted by radio. Within twenty-five years of Marconi's first transmission, public broadcasting became a reality. The first commercial radio station, in Pittsburgh, Pennsylvania, broadcast its first programme in November 1920, and there were over 500 broadcasting stations licensed in the USA within two years. A similar dramatic expansion affected public television twenty years later. We can only speculate about how these media developments must have influenced the growth of world English. There are no statistics on the proportion of time devoted to English-language programmes the world over, or on how much time is spent listening to such programmes. But if we look at broadcasting aimed specifically at audiences in other countries (such as the BBC World Service, or the Voice of America), we note significant levels of provision – over a thousand hours a week by the former, twice as much by the latter, at the turn of the millennium. Most other countries showed sharp increases in external broadcasting during the postwar years, and several launched English-language radio programmes, such as the Soviet Union, Italy, Japan, Luxembourg, the Netherlands, Sweden and Germany.

9.3.6   Motion pictures

The new technologies which followed the discovery of electrical power fundamentally altered the nature of home and public entertainment, and provided fresh directions for the development of the English language. The technology of this industry has many roots in Europe and America during the nineteenth century, with England and France providing an initial impetus to the artistic and commercial development of the cinema from 1895. However, the years preceding and during the First World War stunted the growth of a European film industry, and dominance soon passed to America, which oversaw from 1915 the emergence of the feature film, the star system, the movie mogul and the grand studio, all based in Hollywood, California. As a result, when sound was added to the technology in the late 1920s, it was spoken English which suddenly came to dominate the movie world. And despite the growth of the film industry in other countries in later decades, English-language movies still dominate the medium, with Hollywood coming to rely increasingly on a small number of annual productions aimed at huge audiences. It is unusual to find a blockbuster movie produced in a language other than English, and about 80 per cent of all feature films given a theatrical release are in English (British Film Institute, 1996), though this figure needs to be set against the amount of dubbing into other languages, which is steadily increasing.

9.3.7   Popular music

The cinema was one of two new entertainment technologies which emerged at the end of the nineteenth century: the other was the recording industry.

Here too the English language was early in evidence. When in 1877 Thomas A. Edison devised the phonograph, the first machine that could both record and reproduce sound, the first words to be recorded were 'What God hath wrought', followed by the words of the nursery-rhyme 'Mary had a little lamb'. Most of the subsequent technical developments took place in the USA. All the major recording companies in popular music had English-language origins, beginning with the US firm Columbia (from 1898). Radio sets around the world hourly testify to the dominance of English in the popular music scene today. By the turn of the century, Tin Pan Alley (the popular name for the Broadway-centred song-publishing industry) was a reality, and was soon known worldwide as the chief source of US popular music. Jazz, too, had its linguistic dimension, with the development of the blues and many other genres. And by the time modern popular music arrived, it was almost entirely an English scene. The pop groups of two chief English-speaking nations were soon to dominate the recording world: Bill Haley and the Comets and Elvis Presley in the USA; the Beatles and the Rolling Stones in the UK. Mass audiences for pop singers became a routine feature of the world scene from the 1960s. No other single source has spread the English language around the youth of the world so rapidly and so pervasively.

9.3.8   International travel and safety

For those whose international travel brings them into a world of package holidays, business meetings, academic conferences, international conventions, community rallies, sporting occasions, military occupations, and other 'official' gatherings, the domains of transportation and accommodation are chiefly mediated through the use of English as an auxiliary language. Safety instructions on international flights and sailings, information about emergency procedures in hotels, and directions to major locations are now increasingly in English alongside local languages. A special aspect of safety is the way that the language has come to be used as a means of controlling international transport operations, especially on water and in the air. English has emerged as the international language of the sea, in the form of Essential English for International Maritime Use – often referred to as 'Seaspeak' (Weeks, Glover, Strevens & Johnson, 1984). 'Airspeak', the language of international aircraft control, emerged after the Second World War, when the International Civil Aviation Organisation was created, and it was agreed that English should be the international language of aviation when pilots and controllers speak different languages (a principle which is not always respected in practice, as air disasters sometimes bring to light).

9.3.9   Education

English is the medium of a great deal of the world's knowledge, especially in such areas as science and technology; and access to knowledge is the business of education. When we investigate why so many nations have in recent years made English an official language or chosen it as their chief foreign language in schools, one of the most important reasons is always educational. Since the 1960s, English has become the normal medium of instruction in higher education for many countries – including several where the language has no official status. Advanced courses in the Netherlands, for example, are widely taught in English. No African country uses its indigenous language in higher education, English being used in the majority of cases. The English language teaching (ELT) business has become one of the major growth industries around the world in the past half century. However, its relevance to the growth of English as a world language goes back much further. In the final quarter of the eighteenth century, we find several examples of English grammars, such as Lindley Murray's, being translated into other languages (Tieken-Boon van Ostade, 1996b).

9.3.10   Communications

If a language is a truly international medium, it is going to be most apparent in those services which deal directly with the task of communication – the postal and telephone systems and the electronic networks. Information about the use of English in these domains is not easy to come by, however. It is thought that three-quarters of the world's mail is in English; but as no one monitors the language in which we write our letters, such statistics are highly speculative. Only on the internet, where messages and data can be left for indefinite periods of time, is it possible to develop an idea of how much of the world's everyday communications (at least, between computer-owners) is actually in English. The internet began as ARPANET, the Advanced Research Projects Agency network, in the late 1960s, in the USA. Its language was, accordingly, English; and when people in other countries began to form links with this network, it proved essential for them to use English. The dominance of this language was then reinforced when the service was opened up in the 1980s to private and commercial organisations, most of which were (for the reasons already given) already communicating chiefly in English. However, as the internet has spread, the dominance of English has significantly reduced. By 2000, the proportion of internet hosts in English had fallen to around 80 per cent (Crystal, 2001), and by 2003 this figure was less than 70 per cent. The proportion of internet users in English-speaking countries showed an even more dramatic fall in the new millennium, according to Global Reach Surveys (http://www.glreach.com/globstats/) – to 43 per cent by December 2001 and to 35.8 per cent by March 2004. Internet usage will in due course probably reflect the balance of linguistic power in the outside world. On the other hand, the headstart English has had means that there is more high-quality content on the web in English than in other languages, so that even if the number of English websites falls further, the number of hits on those sites (i.e. individuals calling up specific web addresses) may remain disproportionately high for some time.

9.4   The future of English as a world language

Language is an immensely democratising institution. To have learned a language is immediately to have rights in it. You may add to it, modify it, play with it, create in it, ignore bits of it, as you will. And it is just as likely that the course of the English language is going to be influenced by those who speak it as a second or foreign language as by those who speak it as a mother tongue. Fashions count, in language, as anywhere else. And fashions are a function of numbers. As we have seen, the total number of mother-tongue speakers in the world is steadily falling, as a proportion of world English users. It is perfectly possible for a linguistic fashion to be started by a group of second- or foreign-language learners, or (as the example of rapping suggests) by those who speak a creole or pidgin variety, which then catches on among other speakers. And as numbers grow, and second/foreign-language speakers gain in national and international prestige, usages which were previously criticised as 'foreign' – such as a new concord rule (*three person*), variations in countability (*furnitures, kitchenwares*) or verb use (*he be running*) – can become part of the standard educated speech of a locality, and may eventually appear in writing.

What power and prestige is associated with these new varieties of English? It is all happening so quickly that it is difficult to be sure; there have been so few studies. But impressionistically, we can see several of these new linguistic features achieving an increasingly public profile, in their respective countries. Words become used less self-consciously in the national press – no longer being put in inverted commas, for example, or given a gloss. They come to be adopted, often at first with some effort, then more naturally, by first-language speakers of English in the locality. Indeed, the canons of local political correctness, in the best sense of that phrase, may foster a local usage, giving it more prestige than it could ever have dreamed of – a good example is the contemporary popularity in New Zealand English of Maori words (and the occasional Maori grammatical feature, such as the dropping of the definite article before the people name *Maori* itself). And, above all, the local words begin to be used at the prestigious levels of society – by politicians, religious leaders, socialites, pop musicians and others. Using local words is then no longer to be seen as slovenly or ignorant, within a country; it is respectable; it may even be 'cool'.

The next step is the move from national to international levels. These people who are important in their own communities – whether politicians or pop stars – start travelling abroad. The rest of the world looks up to them, either because it wants what they have, or because it wants to sell them something. And the result is the typical present-day scenario – an international gathering (political, educational, economic, artistic . . .) during which senior visitors use, deliberately or unselfconsciously, a word or phrase from their own country which would not be found in the traditional standards of British or American English. Once upon a time, the reaction would have been to condemn the usage as ignorance.

Today, it is becoming increasingly difficult to say this, or even to think it, if the visitors have more degrees than the visited, or own a bigger company, or are social equals in every way. In such circumstances, one has to learn to live with the new usage, as a feature of increasing diversity in English. It can take a generation or two, but it does happen. It happened within fifty years between Britain and America: by 1842, Charles Dickens (in his *American Notes*, revised in 1868) made some observations about American linguistic usage – such as (in chapter 9) his amazement at the many ways that Americans use the verb *fix* – all expressed in tones of delight, not dismay. But, whatever your attitude towards new usages – and there will always be people who sneer at diversity – there is no getting away from the fact that, these days, regional national varieties of English are increasingly being used with prestige on the international scene.

If these New Englishes are becoming standardised, as markers of educated regional identity, what is taking their place elsewhere within the social spectrum of these communities? Here, very little descriptive research has been done, but there are enough anecdotal reports to suggest the way things are going. When actual examples of language in use are analysed, in such multilingual settings as Malaysia and Singapore, we immediately encounter varieties which make use of the different levels of code-mixing illustrated above. Conversations of that kind, between well-educated people, are now heard at grass-roots level in communities all over the English-speaking world (Mesthrie, 1992; Siegel, 1995). However, establishment attitudes towards these varieties are still generally negative. In 1999, for example, Prime Minister Goh Chok Tong of Singapore devoted several minutes of his National Day Rally speech to a plea for Singaporeans to cut down on their use of Singlish (a hybrid of English, Chinese and Malay) and to maintain the use of standard English, if the country's aims for a greater international role were to be realised. He illustrated this part of the speech with some Singlish expressions, then focussed his anxiety on the influence of the media, and in particular the leading character from the country's highly popular television sitcom, Phua Chu Kang ('PCK'), known for his rapid, fluent Singlish. The prime minister then approached the Television Corporation of Singapore, and asked them to do something about it; they then agreed to enrol PCK in some basic English classes so that he could improve his standard English. The action was widely reported both within the country (e.g. *The Straits Times*, 23 August 1999) and abroad, and not without scepticism. As the *Independent* put it (17 October 1999), the chastising of Phua Chu Kang 'was something like the Queen rebuking Del Boy during the opening of parliament'.

That language should receive such a high profile in a 'state of the union' address is itself surprising, and that a head of government should go out of his way to influence a television sitcom is probably unprecedented in the history of language planning! But it well illustrates the direction in which matters are moving. Singlish must now be a significant presence in Singapore for it to attract this level of attention and condemnation. And the nature of the reaction also well illustrates the nature of the problem which all New Englishes encounter, in their early stages. It is the same problem that older varieties of English also encountered: the view that there can only be one kind of English, the standard kind, and that all others should be eliminated. From the days when this mindset first became dominant, in the eighteenth century, Britain and a few other countries have taken some 250 years to confront it and replace it with a more egalitarian perspective, in educational curricula (Crystal, 2004). The contemporary view, as represented in the UK National Curriculum, is to maintain the importance of standard English while at the same time maintaining the value of local accents and dialects. The intellectual basis for this policy is the recognition of the fact that language has many functions, and that the reason for the existence of standard English (to promote mutual intelligibility) is different from the reason for the existence of local dialects (to promote local identity). The same arguments apply, with even greater force, on a global scale. There is no intrinsic conflict between standard English and Singlish in Singapore, as the reasons for the existence of the former, to permit Singaporeans of different linguistic backgrounds to communicate with each other and with people abroad, are different from the reasons for the emergence of the latter, to provide a sense of local identity. Ironically, the prime minister himself recognised the importance of both these goals, in emphasising that the future of Singapore needed both an outward-looking set of economic and cultural goals as well as an inward-looking sense of the 'something special and precious' in the Singaporean way of life. A bidialectal (or bilingual) policy allows a people to look both ways at once, and would be the most efficient way of the country achieving its aims. Fostering standard English is one plank of such a policy. Condemning Singlish is not.

Similar attitudes will be encountered in all parts of the world where English is developing a strong non-native presence, and at all levels. Teachers of English as a second or foreign language have to deal with the situation routinely, with students increasingly arriving in the classroom speaking a dialect which is markedly different from standard English. The question of just how much local phonology, grammar, vocabulary and pragmatics should be allowed in is difficult and contentious. But there seems no doubt that, gradually, there is a definite ameliorative trend around the English-speaking world, with expressions which were once heavily penalised as local and low-class now achieving a degree of status. How fast this trend develops depends on economic and social factors more than on anything else. If the people who use mixed varieties as markers of their identity become more influential, attitudes will change, and usages will become more acceptable. In fifty years time, we could find ourselves with an English language which contains within itself large areas of contact-influenced vocabulary, borrowed from such languages as Malay or Chinese, being actively used in Singapore, Malaysia and emigrant communities elsewhere. First-language speakers from those areas would instinctively select this vocabulary as their first choice in conversation. Everyone else would recognise their words as legitimate options – passively, at least, with occasional forays into active use. It is a familiar story, in the history of the English language, though operating now on a global scale.

Indeed, such a scenario would not be so different from that already found in English. There are over 350 living languages given as vocabulary sources in the files of the *Oxford English Dictionary*. And, for example, there are already over 250 words with Malay as part of their etymology in the *OED*. So the foundation is already laid. The contact-language words of the future will of course include more alternative rather than supplementary expressions – localised words for everyday notions, such as tables and chairs, rather than for regionally restricted notions, such as fauna and flora – but the notion of a lexical mosaic as such is not new. It has always been part of the language.

9.5   An English family of languages?

The future of world English is likely to be one of increasing multidialectism; but could this become multilingualism? Is English going to fragment into mutually unintelligible varieties, just as Vulgar Latin did a millennium ago? The forces of the past fifty years, which have led to so many New Englishes, suggest this outcome. If such significant change can be noticed within a relatively short period of time, must not these varieties become even more differentiated over the next century, so that we end up, as McArthur (1998) argues, with an English 'family of languages'?

The question does not have a single answer. The history of language suggests that fragmentation has been a frequent phenomenon (as in the well-known case of Latin); but the history of language is no longer a guide. Today, we live in the proverbial global village, where we have immediate access to other languages and varieties of English in ways that have come to be available but recently; and this is having a strong centripetal effect. With a whole range of fresh auditory models becoming routinely available, chiefly through satellite television, it is easy to see how any New English could move in different directions at the same time. The pull imposed by the need for identity, which has been making New Englishes increasingly dissimilar from British English, could be balanced by a pull imposed by the need for intelligibility, on a world scale, which will make them increasingly similar. At the former level, there may well be increasing mutual unintelligibility; but at the latter level, there might not.

None of this disallows the possible emergence of a family of English languages in a sociolinguistic sense; but mutual unintelligibility will not be the basis of such a notion in the case of New Englishes, any more than it has been in relation to intra-national accents and dialects. Although there are several well-known instances of dialect unintelligibility among people from different regional backgrounds, especially when encountered at rapid conversational speed – in Britain, Cockney (London), Geordie (Newcastle), Scouse (Liverpool) and Glaswegian (Glasgow) are among the most commonly cited cases – the problems largely resolve when a speaker slows down, or they reduce to difficulties over isolated lexical items.

This makes regional varieties of English no more problematic for linguistic theory than, say, occupational varieties such as legal or scientific. It is no more illuminating to call Cockney or Scouse 'different English languages' than it would be to call Legal or Scientific by such a name, and anyone who chooses to extend the application of the term 'language' in this way finds a slippery slope which eventually leads to the blurring of the potentially useful distinctions between 'language', 'variety' and 'dialect'.

The intelligibility criterion has traditionally provided little support for an English 'language family'. But we have learned from sociolinguistics in recent decades that this criterion is by no means an adequate explanation for the language nomenclature of the world, as it leaves out of consideration linguistic attitudes, and in particular the criterion of identity. It is this which allows us to say that people from Norway, Sweden and Denmark speak different languages, notwithstanding the considerable amount of intelligibility which exists between them. It seems that if a community wishes its way of speaking to be considered a 'language', and if they have the political power to support their decision, there is nothing which can stop them doing so. The present-day ethos is to allow communities to deal with their own internal policies themselves, as long as these are not perceived as being a threat to others. However, to promote an autonomous language policy, two criteria need to be satisfied. The first is to have a community with a single mind about the matter, and the second is to have a community which has enough political-economic 'clout' to make its decision respected by outsiders with whom it is in regular contact. When these criteria are lacking, any such movement is doomed.

There are very few examples of English generating varieties which are given totally different names, and even fewer where these names are rated as 'languages' (as opposed to 'dialects'). There are some cases among the English-derived pidgins and creoles around the world (e.g. *Tok Pisin, Gullah*), but any proposal for language status is invariably surrounded with controversy. An instance from the mid-1990s is the case of *Ebonics* – a blend of Ebony + phonics – proposed for the variety of English spoken by African Americans, and which had previously been called by such names as *Black Vernacular English* or *African-American Vernacular English* (McArthur, 1998: 197ff.). Although the intentions behind the proposal were noble, and attracted some support, it was denounced by people from across the political and ethnic spectrum, including such prominent individuals as the education secretary Richard W. Riley, black civil rights leader Rev. Jesse Jackson and writer Maya Angelou. Quite evidently the two criteria above did not obtain: the US black community did not have a single mind about the matter, and the people who had the political-economic clout to make the decision respected also had mixed views about it.

By giving a distinct name, Ebonics, to what had previously been recognised as a variety of English, a hidden boundary in the collective unconscious seems to have been crossed. It is in fact very unusual to assign a novel name to a variety of English in this way, other than in the humorous literature, where such names as *Strine* (a spelling of an imagined casual Australian pronunciation of the word 'Australian') can be found. There are indeed many world English locations which have generated their regional humour book, in which the local accent or dialect is illustrated by comic 'translations' into standard English (see Crystal, 1998). Exchanges of this kind, however, are part of the genre of language play, and recognised as such by author and reader. They are not serious attempts to upgrade the status of the dialect into a separate language. The notion of translation which they employ is purely figurative. Indeed, the humour depends on a tacit recognition of the fact that we are dealing with a variety which is 'non-standard', and that people can recognise what it is saying. There is no true intelligibility problem and no problem of identity status.

There is one clear case where a specific regional variety of English has acquired a new name as part of its claim to be recognised as a standard in its locality: Scots. Here is McArthur's summary of the situation (1998: 138):

> The people of Scotland occupy a unique historical and cultural position in the English-speaking world. They use the standard language (with distinctive phonological, grammatical, lexical, and idiomatic features) in administration, law, education, the media, all national institutions, and by and large in their dealings with Anglophones elsewhere, but in their everyday lives a majority of them mix 'the King's English' with what in an earlier age was called 'the King's Scots'.

How does Scots stand in relation to the two criteria referred to above? The situation is complex, because the Scots community does not have a single mind about the matter, nor has it had enough political-economic power to make any decision respected by outsiders. In relation to the former point, the case in favour has been strongly argued by the leading scholar on Scots, Jack Aitken. After reviewing the arguments, he concludes (1985: 44):

> All the phenomena just recounted – the distinctiveness of Scots, its still substantial presence in daily speech, the fact that it was once the national language, its identifiably distinct history, its adoption (some Gaels would call it usurpation) of the nation's name, and the massive and remarkable and still vital literature in it, mutually support one another and one further and remarkable phenomenon – the ancient and still persistent notion that Scots is indeed 'the Scottish language'.

But the missionary tone of this quotation, along with the indication that at least one section of the Scottish community thinks differently, suggests a complex sociolinguistic situation; and at the end of his article even Aitken pulls back from the brink:

> I believe what I have written suggests that if Scots is not now a full 'language' it is something more than a mere 'dialect'. A distinguished German scholar once called it a *Halbsprache* – a semi-language.

In relation to the second criterion, it remains to be seen whether the changing political situation in Scotland (the 1997 referendum on devolution agreeing the formation of a new Scots Assembly) will produce a stronger voice in favour of Scots. McArthur is doubtful (1998: 138):

> Any political change in the condition of Scotland is unlikely to have a direct influence on the shaky condition of Scots or Gaelic, because the movement for Scottish autonomy (within the EU) does not have a linguistic dimension to it.

If he is right, then that eliminates the strongest traditional contender for a separate identity within an English family of languages.

In all these cases of emerging linguistic status, however, the number of speakers involved has been a minority, within a much larger sociopolitical entity. We have yet to see whether the same situation will obtain in countries where the New English speakers are in a majority and hold political power, or in locations where new, supranational political relationships are being formed. For example, although several languages are co-official in the European Union, pragmatic linguistic realities result in English being the most widely used language in these corridors (see above). But what kind of common English emerges, when Germans, French, Greeks and others come into contact, each using English with its own pattern of interference from the mother tongue? There will be the usual sociolinguistic accommodation (Giles & Smith, 1979), and the result will be a novel variety, of 'Euro-English' – a term which has been used for over a decade with reference to the distinctive vocabulary of the Union (with its *Eurofighters, Eurodollars, Eurosceptics* and so on), but which must now be extended to include the various hybrid accents, grammatical constructions and discourse patterns encountered there. On several occasions, I have encountered English-as-a-first-language politicians, diplomats and civil servants working in Brussels commenting on how they have felt their own English being pulled in the direction of these foreign-language patterns. A common feature, evidently, is to accommodate to an increasingly syllable-timed rhythm. Others include the use of simplified sentence constructions, the avoidance of idioms and colloquial vocabulary, a slower rate of speech, and the use of clearer patterns of articulation (avoiding some of the assimilations and elisions which would be natural in a first-language setting). It is important to stress that this is not the 'foreigner talk' reported in an earlier ELT era. These people are not 'talking down' to their colleagues, or consciously adopting simpler expressions, for the English of their interlocutors may be as fluent as their own. It is a natural process of accommodation, which in due course could lead to new standardised forms.

It is plain that the emergence of hybrid trends and varieties raises all kinds of theoretical and pedagogical questions, several of which began to be addressed during the 1990s (see the range of issues addressed in Schneider, 1997 and Foley, 1999). They blur the long-standing distinctions between 'first', 'second' and 'foreign' language. They make us reconsider the notion of 'standard', especially when we find such hybrids being used confidently and fluently by groups of people who have education and influence in their own regional setting. They present the traditionally clear-cut notion of 'translation' with all kinds of fresh problems, for (to go back to the Malaysian example) at what point in a conversation should we say that a notion of translation is relevant, as we move from 'understanding' to 'understanding most of the utterance precisely' to 'understanding little of the utterance precisely ("getting the drift" or "gist")' to 'understanding none of the utterance, despite its containing several features of English'? And, to move into the sociolinguistic dimension, hybrids give us new challenges in relation to language attitudes: for example, at what point would our insistence on the need for translation cause an adverse reaction from the participants, who might maintain they are 'speaking English', even though we cannot understand them? There have been analogous situations earlier in the history of English. William Caxton was the first to comment on it, in his Prologue to Virgil's *Booke of Eneydos* (see Section 5.2.4). We are being faced again with *egges* and *eyren*, but on a global scale.

Further reading

We give here some initial suggestions for further reading on selected topics in each chapter, sometimes with information on referencing. The website associated with this book has some more detailed recommendations.

1   Overview

Among the many excellent histories of the English language which you might wish to consult alongside this one, we are tempted to recommend those by Strang (1970) and Lass (1987) for their individual and insightful views of the whole picture, and *The Cambridge History of the English Language* (1992–2001) for the fullness of coverage permitted by six volumes. It is impossible to make short recommendations for books on the external history of English – of 'English-land' and the English-speaking peoples: they are too many and too various. Among books on the topic of recent change, some of which are now themselves period pieces, are Barber (1964) (updated by the author in Barber, 1985), Potter (1975), Bauer (1994).

2   Phonology and morphology

For more detailed treatments of the material in this chapter see Hogg (1992b), Lass (1992, 1999), MacMahon (1998) and the references there.

All quotations from named ME manuscripts are from the data-base of the *Linguistic Atlas of Early Middle English* (*LAEME*), transcribed from the original sources by Margaret Laing. To save space, Roger Lass has not given precise sources for many of the shorter illustrative quotations; unless otherwise specified, data outside of early ME is from Lass (1992, 1999), and referenced there.

Lass writes that an apparently self-satisfied preponderance of his own name may be observed in the list of references; this is because he has assumed the ready availability of standard sources and treatments of these matters, and referenced mainly his own more controversial claims and the literature supporting or arguing against them. Other references are to particularly interesting or useful recent contributions to the topics discussed here.

3   Syntax

Throughout this chapter, heavy use has gratefully been made of *CHEL* 1 to 4, in particular the chapters on syntax by Traugott (1992) for OE, Fischer (1992) for ME, Rissanen (1999a) for eModE and Denison (1998) for late ModE. More detailed explanations and references for further reading can be found there. Here we will mainly refer to work that has appeared after the dates of the various *CHEL* volumes. Other standard works (and important sources for this chapter) are Mitchell (1985) for OE syntax; Mustanoja (1960) for ME syntax (really on morphology, but containing a lot of syntax); Görlach (1991) and Barber (1997) for eModE; Görlach (2001) for eighteenth-century English; Bailey (1996) and Görlach (1999) for nineteenth-century English; Brunner (1962) for the whole period, especially the relation between morphology and syntax; Visser (1963–73) for a complete historical overview of verbal syntax (including verbal arguments); Denison (1993) for a more recent overview and critical interpretation of this same area; Strang (1970) and Jespersen's (1909–49) *magnum opus* for all periods.

For works focussing on the language of individual authors, see several volumes in the Language Library of Blackwell/André Deutsch. These often contain insightful observations about the relation between an author's usage and the contemporary language.

Some recent examples of theoretical work grounded in detailed empirical investigation are Warner (1993) on auxiliaries; Pintzuk (1993, 1995) on word order in OE; Kroch & Taylor (1997, 2000) on dialectal differences in early ME syntax; and Los (2005) on infinitives in OE and ME.

4   Vocabulary

Undoubtedly the most authoritative study of English lexical morphology is Marchand (1969). For recent usage and description this is well-supplemented by the relevant sections in Quirk et al. (1985). There are quite a few books which offer a range of approaches to the topic, and amongst those which may be cited are Bauer (1983, 1988), Dressler (1985) and Lipka (2002). The *OED*, of course, is a constant source of material, and Finkenstaedt et al. (1970), despite its shortcomings, is also extremely useful. Schäfer (1980) provides a useful corrective to the *OED*'s analysis of the Renaissance period. In the area of lexical semantics Cruse (1986) provides an invaluable overview.

For the origins and development of the language, one general work which has yet to be superseded is Serjeantson (1935), and this work provides an excellent account of the processes of borrowing into English. For the Old English period two works lead the way to others, namely Gneuss (1955) and Schabram (1965). For the Middle English period the material has rarely been offered in other than highly specialised sources not always accessible to the interested reader.

5   Standardisation

For examples of individual attempts at normalisation and standardisation, see Anderson & Britton (1999), Osselton (1984a) and Monaghan (1983). Gotti (1996) analyses the attempts of one writer, Robert Boyle (1627–91), at adapting English vocabulary as a medium suitable for the language of science. An overview of normative studies produced in England since the beginnings of the early modern period may be found in Tieken-Boon van Ostade (2000). Taavitsainen et al. (1999) is a collection of articles on various aspects of the history of *non*-standard English.

For more information on the grammatical features discussed in Section 5.3.3, see Nevalainen & Raumolin-Brunberg (2003). On Section 5.3.4, see also Gramley (2001), who pays particular attention to words and word meanings used in the national varieties of English around the world. A popular introduction to Estuary English (Section 5.3.7) can be found in Coggle (1993).

6   Names

The indispensable tools for English name study are as follows. On given names, Hanks & Hodges (1990a) is the most reliable recent general guide; especially good on the international dimension, while Dunkling & Gosling (1991) is especially good on modern developments in personal naming. The standard reference work on surnames is Reaney & Wilson (1991), while the only complete modern descriptive history is McKinley (1990). Hey (2000) provides a useful tool for those with a genealogical interest as well as a historical or philological one. Note also the county volumes of the English Surnames Survey, published by Leopard's Head Press.

The standard reference manual on place-names for over forty years has been Ekwall (1960). Watts (2004), intended to replace it, has many virtues but needs some expertise in its users because of errors and inconsistencies. A compact, reliable guide to scholarly work on names, now in paperback, is Mills (1998). Foundational guides to topographical terms in place-names and to the relation between place-names, history and archaeology are Gelling & Cole (2000) and Gelling (1997), respectively. Field (1993) provides a highly readable general history. For reference there are the county volumes of the Survey of English Place-Names, published at the University of Nottingham.

Improved interpretations of individual place-names, and occasional debunkings, are frequently carried by the journals *Nomina* and *Journal of the English Place-Name Society*, as are refinements in the understanding of the regional and demographic sources of particular surnames. These two journals both carry substantial annual bibliographies, and there is an annual report on English onomastics in *The Year's Work in English Studies*. For those who do not share Richard

Coates' scepticism about the value of the study of character-names from an aesthetic or psychoanalytical viewpoint, there is the journal *Literary Onomastics*. A major general resource for all onomastics, begun in 2005, is the new bibliographical database of the International Council of Onomastic Sciences. The Council also publishes an annual journal *Onoma*, each issue of which is devoted to a general, as opposed to a regional, theme, such as names in literature, the teaching of onomastics, or name theory (the topics for publication years 2004–6). *Onoma* and *Names*, the journal of the American Name Society, are the only truly general journals of onomastics published (at least in part) in English.

7   English in Britain

The fundamental work dealing with dialects in England is Orton (1962–71), namely *A Survey of English Dialects*, from which many important works have been subsequently derived, in particular dialect atlases based on the material in the *SED*, such as Orton & Wright (1974) and Orton, Sanderson & Widdowson (1978). The *SED* continues to flourish and one interesting, more, theoretical work from the *SED* group is Kirk, Sanderson & Widdowson (1985), which, amongst other things, has chapters on the theory of dialectology as it applies to the *SED*. The *SED*, because of its aims and methods, has much of value to offer historical dialectology, and this is explicit in the further related dialect atlas of Kolb et al. (1979). Current work on regional variations partly related to the *SED* can be found online at the BBC website: http://www.bbc.co.uk/voices/

Naturally for historical dialects themselves the indispensable source must be *LALME* (McIntosh, Samuels & Benskin, 1986) and currently research proceeds on producing parallel material for early Middle English, as noted in Laing (1993). On the same topic the various studies by Kristensson contain much material of interest; see, for example, Kristensson (2001) and his earlier studies in the same project. There is no substantial work available for the Old English period as we await the publication of Kitson's massive work on Old English charters; see, for example, Kitson (1993). Current views on dialectology in the medieval period can be found in Hogg (forthcoming) and Laing & Lass (forthcoming). For the postmedieval period one necessary work is Ihalainen (1994), and Nevalainen & Raumolin-Brunberg (2003) offer an important sociolinguistic approach which opens promising avenues for success.

Returning to the present day, we can note a variety of essential texts on dialects outside England, such as, for Scotland, Mather & Speitel (1975–86); for Ireland, Filppula (1999); and for Wales, Parry (1977, 1979). There are an enormous number of books on modern varieties of English and it is difficult to pick and choose. However, four works which offer different, yet equally valuable perspectives are Chambers & Trudgill (1998), Francis (1983), Trudgill (1974) and Wakelin (1977).

8   English in North America

For American English in general, consult Finegan & Rickford (2004); there are also the books by Krapp (1925), Kurath (1949), Marckwardt (1958), Mencken (1963), Dillard (1992), Labov, Ash & Boberg (forthcoming). For regional words, phrases, and pronunciations, Cassidy & Hall's *Dictionary of American Regional English* (1985–forthcoming) is invaluable; Montgomery & Hall (2004) focuses on Smoky Mountain English. For African American English see Rickford (1999) and Green (2002), for American Indian English, Leap (1993).

Considerable published information describing Canadian English exists, including broad surveys (e.g. Bailey, 1982; Chambers, 1993, 1998; Clarke, 1993; Brinton & Fee, 2001), a historical dictionary (Avis, 1991), a description and dictionary of Newfoundland English (Kirwin, 2001; Story et al., 1990), a dictionary of Prince Edward Island English (Pratt, 1988) and bibliographies of writings up to 1987 (Avis & Kinloch, n.d.; Lougheed, 1988).

9   English worldwide

Three books from the 1990s provide a perspective for the issues discussed in this chapter. Crystal (1997, 2nd edn 2003) is predominantly a retrospective account, examining the range of historical factors which have led to the current position of English in the world. Graddol (1998) looks towards the future, examining the contemporary trends likely to affect the language's eventual role. McArthur (1998) investigates the kinds of variation encountered in the language as a consequence of its global spread. 'Classic' collections of areal reviews include Bailey & Görlach (1982), Cheshire (1991), Burchfield (1994) and Schneider (1997). The global story of English is placed in a more general historical linguistic setting by Ostler (2005).

References

Adamson, S. 1989. With double tongue. In M. Short (ed.), *Reading, Analysing and Teaching Literature*. London: Longman, 204–40.

Adamson, S. 2000. A lovely little example: word order options and category shift in the premodifying string. In Fischer et al. (eds.), 39–66.

Aitchison, J. 1987. *Words in the Mind: an Introduction to the Mental Lexicon*. Oxford: Blackwell.

Aitchison, J. 1994a. 'Say, say it again Sam': the treatment of repetition in linguistics. In A. Fischer (ed.), *Repetition* (SPELL 7). Tübingen: Gunter Narr, 15–34.

Aitchison, J. 1994b. *Words in the Mind: an Introduction to the Mental Lexicon*, 2nd edn. Oxford: Blackwell.

Aitchison, J. 2001. *Language Change: Progress or Decay*, 3rd edn. Cambridge: Cambridge University Press.

Aitken, A. J. 1981. The Scottish vowel-length rule. In M. Benskin & M. L. Samuels (eds.), *So Meny People Longages and Tongues*. Edinburgh: Benskin & Samuels, 131–57.

Aitken, A. J. 1985. Is Scots a language? *English Today* 3: 41–5.

Aitken, A. J. & C. Macafee. 2002. *The Older Scots Vowels*. Glasgow: The Scottish Text Society.

Algeo, J. 1998. Vocabulary. In Romaine (ed.), 57–91.

Algeo, J. (ed.). 2001. *The Cambridge History of the English Language*, vol. 6, *English in North America*. Cambridge: Cambridge University Press.

Algeo, J. & A. S. Algeo (eds.). 1991. *Fifty Years 'Among the New Words': A Dictionary of Neologisms, 1941–1991*. New York: Cambridge University Press.

Allen, Alex. 1999. Communication at the English Speaking Union world members conference, Sydney, August.

Allen, C. L. 1995. *Case Marking and Reanalysis: Grammatical Relations from Old to Early Modern English*. Oxford: Oxford University Press.

Allen, C. L. 1997. The origins of the 'group genitive' in English. *Transactions of the Philological Society* 95: 111–31.

Allen, Harold B. 1973–6. *The Linguistic Atlas of the Upper Midwest*, 3 vols. Minneapolis: University of Minnesota Press.

Alston, R. C. 1965. *A Bibliography of the English Language from the Invention of Printing to the Year 1800*, vol. 1, *English Grammars Written in English*. Leeds: E. J. Arnold & Son.

American Fact Finder. 2002. http://factfinder.census.gov/servlet/BasicFactsServlet

Anderson (Arngart), O. 1941. *Old English Material in the Leningrad Manuscript of Bede's Ecclesiastical History* (Acta Regiae Societatis Humaniorum Litterarum Lundensis 31). Lund: University of Lund.

Anderson, J. & D. Britton. 1999. The orthography and phonology of the *Ormulum*. *English Language and Linguistics* 3: 299–334.

Anon. 1695. *The Writing Scholar's Companion*, ed. E. Ekwall 1911. Halle: Niemeyer.

Anshen, F. & M. Aronoff. 1988. Producing morphologically complex words. *Linguistics* 26: 641–55.

Aronoff, M. 1980. The relevance of productivity in a synchronic description of word formation. In J. Fisiak (ed.), *Historical Morphology* (Trends in Linguistics. Studies and Monographs 17). The Hague: Mouton, 71–82.

Aronoff, M. 1987. The orthographic system of an early English printer: Wynkyn de Worde. *Folia Linguistica Historica* 8: 65–97.

Ashley, Leonard R. N. 2003. *Names of Places*. Bloomington, IN: 1st Books Library.

Atkinson, D. 1996. The *Philosophical Transactions of the Royal Society of London*, 1675–1975: a sociohistorical discourse analysis. *Language in Society* 25: 333–71.

Atwood, E. Bagby. 1953. *A Survey of Verb Forms in the Eastern United States*. Ann Arbor: University of Michigan Press.

Austin, F. 1994. The effect of exposure to Standard English: the language of William Clift. In D. Stein & I. Tieken-Boon van Ostade (eds.), *Towards a Standard English 1600–1800*. Berlin and New York: Mouton de Gruyter, 285–313.

Australian National Dictionary: Australian Words and their Origins, ed. W. S. Ramson. 1988. Melbourne: Oxford University Press.

Avis, Walter S. 1967. *A Dictionary of Canadianisms on Historical Principles*. Toronto: Gage. Repr. 1991.

Avis, Walter S. & A. M. Kinloch. n.d. *Writings on Canadian English, 1792–1975: an Annotated Bibliography*. Toronto: Fitzhenry and Whiteside.

Axtell, James. 2000. Babel of tongues: communicating with the Indians in eastern North America. In Edward G. Gray & Norman Fiering (eds.), *The Language Encounter in the Americas, 1492–1800*. New York: Berghahn Books, 15–60.

Ayto, J. 1999. *Twentieth Century Words*. Oxford: Oxford University Press.

Baayen, R. H. 1989. *A Corpus-Based Approach to Morphological Productivity: Statistical Analysis and Psycholinguistic Interpretation*. Amsterdam: Centrum voor Wiskunde en Informatica.

Bækken, Bjørg. 1998. *Word Order Patterns in Early Modern English, with Special Reference to the Position of the Subject and the Finite Verb* (Studia Anglistica Norvegica 9). Oslo: Novus Press.

Bailey, Richard W. 1982. The English language in Canada. In Bailey & Görlach (eds.), 134–76.

Bailey, Richard W. 1991. *Images of English: a Cultural History of the Language*. Cambridge: Cambridge University Press.

Bailey, Richard W. 1996. *Nineteenth-Century English*. Ann Arbor: University of Michigan Press.

Bailey, Richard W. 2003. The foundation of English in the Louisiana Purchase: New Orleans, 1800–1850. *American Speech* 78: 353–84.

Bailey, Richard W. 2004. American English: its origin and history. In Finegan & Rickford (eds.), 3–17.

Bailey, Richard W. & Manfred Görlach (eds.). 1982. *English as a World Language*. Cambridge: Cambridge University Press; Ann Arbor: University of Michigan Press.

Baker, R. 1770. *Reflections on the English Language*. London. Repr. in facs. by R. C. Alston, 1974, *English Linguistics 1500–1800* (English Linguistics 87). London: Scolar Press.

Barber, C. 1964. *Linguistic Change in Present-Day English*. Edinburgh and London: Oliver and Boyd.

Barber, C. 1985. Linguistic change in Present-Day English. In S. Backman & G. Kjellmer (eds.), *Papers on Language and Literature: Presented to Alvar Ellegård and Erik Frykman* (Gothenburg Studies in English 60). Gothenburg: Acta Universitatis Gothoburgensis, 36–45.

Barber, C. 1997. *Early Modern English*, 2nd edn (1st edn 1976). Edinburgh: Edinburgh University Press.

Bardsley, Charles W. 1880. *Curiosities of Puritan Nomenclature*. New York: R. Worthington.

The Barnhart Dictionary Companion. 1997. http://www.m-w.com/mw/textonly/info/barn/barn3.htm.

Barry, Herbert III & Aylene S. Harper. 1982. Evolution of unisex names. *Names* 30: 15–22.

Barry, Herbert III & Aylene S. Harper. 1995. Increased choice of female phonetic attributes between first names of boys and girls. *Sex Roles* 32: 809–19.

Barry, Herbert III and Aylene S. Harper. 2003. Final letter compared with final phoneme in male and female names. *Names* 51: 13–34.

Bauer, L. 1983. *English Word-Formation*. Cambridge: Cambridge University Press.

Bauer, L. 1988. *Introducing Linguistic Morphology*. Edinburgh: Edinburgh University Press.

Bauer, L. 1994. *Watching English Change: an Introduction to the Study of Linguistic Change in Standard Englishes in the Twentieth Century* (Learning about Language). London and New York: Longman.

Baugh, A. C. & T. Cable. 1978. *A History of the English Language*, 3rd edn. 5th edn, 2002. London: Routledge.

Beier, A. L. & R. Finlay (eds.). 1986. *London 1500–1700: the Making of the Metropolis*. London and New York: Longman.

Benskin, Michael. 1994. Descriptions of dialect and areal distributions. In M. Laing & K. Williamson (eds.), *Speaking in Our Tongues*. Woodbridge, Suffolk: D. S. Brewer, 169–87.

Bermúdez-Otero, Ricardo, David Denison, Richard M. Hogg & C. B. McCully (eds.). 2000. *Generative Theory and Corpus Studies: a Dialogue from 10 ICEHL* (Topics in English Linguistics 31). Berlin and New York: Mouton de Gruyter.

Bernstein, Cynthia, Thomas Nunnally & Robin Sabino (eds.). 1997. *Language Variety in the South Revisited*. Tuscaloosa: University of Alabama Press.

den Besten, Hans. 1977. The interaction of root transformations and lexical deletive rules. MS, University of Amsterdam. Published in *Groninger Arbeiten zur Germanistischen Linguistik* 20 (1981): 1–78.

Biber, D. 1988. *Variation Across Speech and Writing*. Cambridge: Cambridge University Press.

Biber, D. 1995. *Dimensions of Register Variation*. Cambridge: Cambridge University Press.

Biber, D. & E. Finegan. 1997. Diachronic relations among speech-based and written registers of English. In T. Nevalainen & L. Kahlas-Tarkka (eds.), *To Explain the Present:
Studies in the Changing English Language in Honour of Matti Rissanen* (Mémoires
de la Société Néophilologique de Helsinki 52). Helsinki: Société Néophilologique,
253–75. Repr. in Conrad & Biber (eds.), 2001.

Biber, D., E. Finegan & D. Atkinson. 1994. ARCHER and its challenges: compiling and
exploring a representative corpus of historical English registers. In U. Fries, G. Tottie
& P. Schneider (eds.), *Creating and Using English Language Corpora*. Amsterdam
and Atlanta: Rodopi, 1–13.

Biber, D., S. Johansson, G. Leech, S. Conrad & E. Finegan. 1999. *Longman Grammar of
Spoken and Written English*. London: Longman.

Blake, N. F. 1973. *Caxton's Own Prose*. London: Deutsch.

Blake, N. F. 1987. The spread of printing in English during the fifteenth century. *Gutenberg
Jahrbuch*, 26–36.

Blake, N. (ed.). 1992. *The Cambridge History of the English Language*, vol. 2, *1066–1476*.
Cambridge: Cambridge University Press.

Bloomfield, L. 1935. *Language*. London: Allen & Unwin.

Blount, T. 1656. *Glossographia*. London: T. Newcomb for H. Moseley.

Bodine, A. 1975. Androcentrism in prescriptive grammar: singular 'they', sex-indefinite
'he', and 'he or she'. *Language in Society* 4: 129–46.

Bolinger, D. 1952. Linear modification, *PMLA* 67: 1117–144.

Bolinger, D. 1972. *Degree Words*. The Hague: Monton.

Bosworth, Joseph & T. Northcote Toller. 1898. *An Anglo-Saxon Dictionary*. Oxford:
Oxford University Press, with supplements by Toller (1921) and by A. Campbell
(1972).

Branford, J. 1987. *A Dictionary of South African English*, 3rd edn. Cape Town: Oxford
University Press.

Bright, William (ed.). 1992. *International Encyclopedia of Linguistics*. Oxford: Oxford
University Press.

Bright, William. 2004. *Native American Placenames of the United States*. Norman, OK:
Oklahoma University Press.

Brightman, Joan. 1994. Why Hillary chooses Rodham Clinton. *American Demographics*
16 (March): 9–10.

Brinton, L. 1988. *The Development of English Aspectual Systems*. Cambridge: Cambridge
University Press.

Brinton, L. J. 1996. *Pragmatic Markers in English: Grammaticalization and Discourse
Functions*. Berlin: Mouton de Gruyter.

Brinton, Laurel J. & Margery Fee. 2001. Canadian English. In Algeo (ed.), 422–40.

British Council. 1997. *English Language Teaching*. London: The British Council.

British Film Institute. 1996. *Film and Television Handbook*. London: British Film Institute.

British National Corpus. www.natcorp.ox.ac.uk/.

Britton, D. 1991. On Middle English *she, sho*: a Scots solution to an English problem.
NOWELE 17:52.

Britton, D. (ed.). 1996. *English Historical Linguistics 1994: Papers from the 8th International Conference on English Historical Linguistics (8. ICEHL, Edinburgh, 19–23
Sept. 1994)*. Amsterdam: Benjamins.

Britton, D. 2000. Henry Machyn, Axel Wijk and the case of the wrong Riding: the south-west Yorkshire character of the language of Machyn's diary. *Neuphilologische Mitteilungen* 101: 571–96.

Brook, G. L. 1955. *Introduction to Old English*. Manchester: Manchester University Press.

Bronstein, A. 1990. The development of pronunciation in English language dictionaries. In S. Ramsaran (ed.), *Studies in the Pronunciation of English*. London and New York: Routledge, 137–52.

Brown, K. 1991. Double modals in Hawick Scots. In P. Trudgill & J. K. Chambers (eds.), *Dialects of English: Studies in Grammatical Variation*. London: Longman, 74–103.

Brown, K. & M. Millar. 1980. Auxiliary verbs in Edinburgh speech. *Transactions of the Philosophical Society* 78: 81–133.

Brunner, K. 1962. *Die englische Sprache, Band II*. Tübingen: Niemeyer.

Bullokar, W. 1586. *Pamphlet for Grammar*. London.

Burchfield, R. (ed.). 1994. *The Cambridge History of the English Language*, vol. 5, *English in Britain and Overseas*. Cambridge: Cambridge University Press.

Burchfield, R. W. (ed.). 1996. *The New Fowler's Modern English Usage*, 3rd edn. Oxford: Clarendon Press.

Burnley, D. 1992. *The History of the English Language: a Source Book*. London and New York: Longman.

Burrow, John A. & Thorlac Turville-Petre. 1992. *A Book of Middle English*. Oxford: Blackwell.

Butters, Ronald R. (ed.). 1987. Are Black and White vernaculars diverging? Papers from the NWAVE XIV Panel Discussion. *American Speech* 62.1.

CHEL = Cambridge History of the English Language, 6 vols. *CHEL* 1 = Hogg, 1992a; *CHEL* 2 = Blake, 1992; *CHEL* 3 = Lass, 1999a; *CHEL* 4 = Romaine, 1998; *CHEL* 5 = Burchfield, 1994; *CHEL* 6 = Algeo, 2001.

Cameron, D. 2000. Styling the worker: gender and the commodification of language in the globalized service economy. *Journal of Sociolinguistics* 4: 323–47.

Cameron, Kenneth. 1961. *English Place-Names*. 5th edn, 1996. London: Batsford.

Cameron, Kenneth. 1965–71. Scandinavian settlement in the territory of the Five Boroughs (parts I–III). Published in separate periodicals; collected and reprinted in Cameron (ed.), 1977: 115–71.

Cameron, Kenneth (ed.). 1977. *Place-Name Evidence for the Anglo-Saxon Invasion and Scandinavian Settlements*. Nottingham: English Place-Name Society.

Cameron, Kenneth (with a contribution by John Insley). 1998. *A Dictionary of Lincolnshire Place-Names*. Nottingham: English Place-Name Society.

Campbell, Alistair. 1959. *Old English Grammar*. Oxford: Clarendon Press.

Caon, L. 2002. Final -*e* and spelling habits in the fifteenth-century versions of the *Wife of Bath's Prologue*. *English Studies* 83: 296–310.

Carlsson, Stig. 1989. *Studies on Middle English Local Bynames in East Anglia* (Lund Studies in English 79). Lund: Lund University Press.

Carney, E. 1994. *A Survey of English Spelling*. London and New York: Routledge.

Carr, C. T. 1939. *Nominal Compounds in Germanic* (St Andrews University Publications 41). London: Oxford University Press.

Carver, Craig M. 1987. *American Regional Dialects: a Word Geography.* Ann Arbor: University of Michigan Press.

Carver, Craig M. 1992. The Mayflower to the Model-T: the development of American English. In Tim William Machan & Charles T. Scott (eds.), *English in Its Social Contexts: Essays in Historical Sociolinguistics.* New York: Oxford University Press, 131–54.

Cassidy, F. G. & J. H. Hall. 2001. Americanisms. In Algeo (ed.), 184–218.

Cassidy, F. G. & R. B. Le Page (eds.). 1980. *Dictionary of Jamaican English.* Cambridge: Cambridge University Press.

Cassidy, Frederick G. & Joan Houston Hall (eds.). 1985–. *Dictionary of American Regional English,* 5 vols. Cambridge, MA: Belknap. [= *DARE*]

Catto, J. I. 1984. Citizens, scholars and masters. In J. I. Catto (ed.), *The History of the University of Oxford,* vol. 1, *The Early Oxford Schools.* Oxford: Clarendon Press, 151–92.

Cawdrey, R. 1604. *A Table Alphabeticall.* London. I. R. for E. Weaver.

Chambers, J. K. 1986. Three kinds of standard in Canadian English. In W. C. Lougheed (ed.), *In Search of the Standard in Canadian English.* Kingston, Ontario: Strathy Language Unit, Queen's University, Occasional Papers Number 1, 1–15.

Chambers, J. K. 1991. Canada. In Cheshire (ed.), 89–107.

Chambers, J. K. 1993. 'Lawless and vulgar innovations': Victorian views of Canadian English. In Sandra Clarke (ed.), *Focus on Canada* (Varieties of English Around the World). Amsterdam & Philadelphia: John Benjamins, 11–26.

Chambers, J. K. 1995. *Sociolinguistic Theory.* Oxford: Blackwell.

Chambers, J. K. 1998. English: Canadian varieties. In John Edwards (ed.), *Language in Canada.* Cambridge: Cambridge University Press, 252–72.

Chambers, J. K. 2002. *Sociolinguistic Theory: Linguistic Variation and its Social Significance,* 2nd edn (Language in Society). Oxford: Blackwell.

Chambers, J. K. & Peter Trudgill. 1980. *Dialectology.* 2nd edn, 1998. Cambridge: Cambridge University Press.

Chapman, Carol. 1998. A subject–verb agreement hierarchy: evidence from analogical change in modern English dialects. In R. M. Hogg & L. van Bergen (eds.), *Historical Linguistics 1995.* Amsterdam: John Benjamins, 35–44.

Charles, B. G. 1938. *Non-Celtic Place-Names in Wales* (London Mediaeval Studies 1). London: University College.

Cheshire, J., V. Edwards & P. Whittle. 1993. Non-standard English and dialect levelling. In J. Milroy & L. Milroy (eds.), *Real English: the Grammar of English Dialects in the British Isles.* London and New York: Longman, 53–96.

Cheshire, Jenny. 1982. *Variation in an English Dialect.* Cambridge: Cambridge University Press.

Cheshire, Jenny (ed.). 1991. *English around the World: Sociolinguistic Perspectives.* Cambridge: Cambridge University Press.

Ching, M. K. L. 1982. The question intonation in assertions. *American Speech* 57: 95–107.

Chomsky, N. 1965. *Aspects of the Theory of Syntax.* Cambridge, MA: MIT Press.

Chomsky, N. & M. Halle. 1968. *The Sound Pattern of English.* New York: Harper & Row.

Claridge, C. 2000. *Multi-Word Verbs in Early Modern English: a Corpus-Based Study* (Language and Computers: Studies in Practical Linguistics 32). Amsterdam: Rodopi.

Clark, Cecily. 1979. Clark's first three laws of applied anthroponymics. *Nomina* 3: 13–18.

Clark, Cecily. 1982. The early personal names of King's Lynn: an essay in socio-cultural history, part I: baptismal names. *Nomina* 6: 51–71. Repr. in Jackson (ed.), 1995: 241–57.

Clark, Cecily. 1983. The early personal names of King's Lynn: an essay in socio-cultural history, part II: by-names. *Nomina* 7: 65–89. Repr. in Jackson (ed.), 1995: 258–79.

Clark, Cecily. 1987a. English personal names ca. 650–1300: some prosopographical bearings. *Medieval Prosopography* 8: 31–60.

Clark, Cecily. 1987b. *Willelmus rex? vel alius Willelmus? Nomina* 11: 7–33. Repr. in Jackson (ed.), 1995: 280–98.

Clark, Cecily. 1992a. Onomastics. In Hogg (ed.), 452–89.

Clark, Cecily. 1992b. Onomastics. In Blake (ed.), 542–606.

Clark, Cecily. 1992c. The myth of the Anglo-Norman scribe. In Rissanen et al. (eds.), 117–29. Repr. in Jackson (ed.), 1995: 168–76.

Clarke, Sandra (ed.). 1993. *Focus on Canada* (Varieties of English around the World 11). Amsterdam: John Benjamins.

Coates, Richard. 1988. *Toponymic Topics*. Brighton: Younsmere Press.

Coates, Richard. 1989. *The Place-Names of Hampshire*. London: Batsford.

Coates, Richard. 1997a. The scriptorium of the Mercian Rushworth Gloss: a bilingual perspective. *Notes and Queries* 242: 453–8.

Coates, Richard. 1997b. The plural of singular -*ing*: an alternative application of Old English -*ingas*. In Rumble & Mills (eds.), 26–49.

Coates, Richard. 1998. Onomastics. In Romaine (ed.), 330–72.

Coates, Richard. 1999. New light from old wicks: the progeny of Latin *vicus*. *Nomina* 22: 75–116.

Coates, Richard. 2000. Singular definite expressions with a unique denotatum and the limits of properhood. *Linguistics* 38.6 [370]: 1161–74.

Coates, Richard. 2005a. A new theory of properhood. In Eva Brylla and Mats Wahlberg (eds.), *Proceedings of the 21st International Congress of Onomastic Sciences, Uppsala, August 2002*. Uppsala: SOFI.

Coates, Richard. 2005b. A speculative psycholinguistic model of onymization. *Rivista Italiana Onomastica* (International series 1), 3–13.

Coates Richard. forthcoming a. Properhood. *Language*.

Coates, Richard. forthcoming b. The grammar of Scandinavian place-names in England: a preliminary commentary. To appear in Doreen Waugh et al. (eds.), *Cultural Contacts in the North Atlantic Region*. Proceedings of the SNSBI conference at Lerwick, Shetland, April 2003.

Coates, Richard & Andrew Breeze, with David Horovitz. 2000. *Celtic Voices, English Places*. Donington, Lincs.: Shaun Tyas.

Cobban, A. C. 1988. *The Medieval English Universities: Oxford and Cambridge to c.1500*. Aldershot: Scolar Press.

Coggle, P. 1993. *Do You Speak Estuary? The New Standard English*. London: Bloomsbury Publishing.

Cohen, G. & D. M. Burke. 1993. Memory for proper names: a review. *Memory* 1: 249–63.

Cole, Ann. 1990. The origin, distribution and use of the place-name element *ōra* and its relationship to the element *ofer*. *Journal of the English Place-Name Society* 22: 26–41.

Cole, Ann. 1992. Distribution and use of the Old English place-name *mere-tūn*. *Journal of the English Place-Name Society* 24: 30–41.

Cole, Ann. 1993. The distribution and use of *mere* as a generic in place-names. *Journal of the English Place-Name Society* 25: 38–50.

Cole, Ann. 1994. The Anglo-Saxon traveller. *Nomina* 17: 7–18.

Coles, E. 1676. *An English Dictionary*. London: S. Crouch.

Colman, Fran. 1984. Anglo-Saxon pennies and Old English phonology. *Folia Linguistica Historica* 5: 91–143.

Colman, Fran. 1988a. Heavy arguments in Old English. In John Anderson & N. MacLeod (eds.), *Edinburgh Studies in the English Language 1*. Edinburgh: John Donald, 33–89.

Colman, Fran. 1988b. What *is* in a name? In Jacek Fisiak (ed.), *Historical Dialectology*. Berlin: Mouton de Gruyter, 111–37.

Colman, Fran. 1990. Numismatics, names and neutralisations. *Transactions of the Philological Society* 88: 59–86.

Colman, Fran. 1992. *Money Talks* (Trends in Linguistics Studies and Monographs 56). Berlin and New York: Mouton de Gruyter.

Conrad, S. & D. Biber (eds.). 2001. *Variation in English: Multi-dimensional Studies*. Harlow: Pearson Education.

Cooper, C. 1685. *Grammatica linguae Anglicanae*. London: Tooke.

Cooper, C. 1687. *The English Teacher*. London: The Author.

Coplestone-Crow, B. 1989. *Herefordshire Place-Names*. London: British Archaeological Reports (British series 214).

Corpus of Middle English Prose and Verse. University of Michigan. 2000. http://www.hti.umich.edu/c/cme/

Coseriu, E. 1973. *Probleme der strukturellen Semantik*, ed. D. Kastovsky (Tübinger Beiträge zur Linguistik 40). 2nd edn, 1976. Tübingen: Narr.

Coseriu, E. & H. Geckeler. 1981. *Trends in Structural Semantics*. Tübingen: Narr.

Cottle, Basil. 1978. *The Penguin Dictionary of Surnames*, 2nd edn. Harmondsworth: Penguin.

Coupland, Nikolaus. 1988. *Dialect in Use: Sociolinguistic Variation in Cardiff English*. Cardiff: University of Wales Press.

Cowie, C. & C. Dalton-Puffer. 2002. Diachronic word-formation and studying changes in productivity over time: theoretical and methodological considerations. In J. E. Díaz Vera (ed.), *A Changing World of Words: Studies in English Historical Lexicography, Lexicology and Semantics*. Amsterdam and New York: Rodopi, 410–37.

Cox, Barrie M. 1976. The place-names of the earliest English records. *Journal of the English Place-Name Society* 8: 12–66.

Cox, Barrie. 1988. Furze, gorse and whin: an aside on Rutland in the Danelaw. *Journal of the English Place-Name Society* 20: 3–10.

Cox, Barrie. 1990. Rutland in the Danelaw: a field-names perspective. *Journal of the English Place-Name Society* 22: 7–22.

Cresswell, Julia. 1990. *Dictionary of First Names*. London: Bloomsbury.

Cressy, D. 1980. *Literacy and Social Order: Reading and Writing in Tudor and Stuart England*. Cambridge: Cambridge University Press.

Croft, W. 2000. *Explaining Language Change: an Evolutionary Approach* (Longman Linguistics Library). Harlow: Longman.

Crowley, E. T. & R. C. Thomas. 1973. *Acronyms and Initialisms Dictionary*, 4th edn. Detroit: Gale Research Co.

Cruse, D. A. 1986. *Lexical Semantics* (Cambridge Textbooks in Linguistics). Cambridge: Cambridge University Press.

Cruse, D. A. 2000. *Meaning in Language: an Introduction to Semantics and Pragmatics.* Oxford: Oxford University Press.

Cruttenden, A. 1994. *Gimson's Pronunciation of English*. London: Edward Arnold.

Crystal, D. 1980. Neglected grammatical factors in conversational English. In S. Greenbaum, G. Leech & J. Svartvik (eds.), *Studies in English Linguistics for Randolph Quirk*. London: Longman, 153–66.

Crystal, David. 1997. *English as a Global Language*. 2nd edn, 2003. Cambridge: Cambridge University Press.

Crystal, David. 1995. *The Cambridge Encyclopedia of the English Language*. 2nd edn, 2003. Cambridge: Cambridge University Press.

Crystal, David. 1998. *Language Play*. London: Penguin.

Crystal, David. 2001. *Language and the Internet*. Cambridge: Cambridge University Press.

Crystal, David. 2004. *The Stories of English*. London: Penguin.

Cullen, Paul. 1997. The place-names of the lathes of St Augustine and Shipway, Kent. PhD dissertation, University of Sussex (unpublished).

Culpeper, J. & P. Clapham. 1996. The borrowing of Classical and Romance words into English: a study based on the electronic *Oxford English Dictionary*. *International Journal of Corpus Linguistics* 1 (2): 199–218.

Cutler, Anne, James McQueen & Ken Robinson. 1990. Sound patterns of men's and women's names. *Journal of Linguistics* 26: 471–82.

Dalton-Puffer, C. 1996. *The French Influence on Middle English Morphology: a Corpus-Based Study of Derivation* (Topics in English Linguistics 20). Berlin and New York: Mouton de Gruyter.

Dalton-Puffer, C. 2002. Is there a social element in English word-stress? Explorations into a non-categorial treatment of English stress: a long-term view. In D. Kastovsky & A. Mettinger (eds.), *The History of English in a Social Context: a Contribution to Historical Sociolinguistics* (Trends in Linguistics 129). Berlin and New York: Mouton de Gruyter, 91–113.

Dalton-Puffer, C. & I. Plag. 2000. Categorywise, some compound type morphemes seem to be rather suffix-like: on the status of *-ful, -type* and *-wise* in Present Day English. *Folia Linguistica* 34: 225–45.

Dalton-Puffer, C. & N. Ritt (eds.). 2000. *Words: Structure, Meaning, Function. A Festschrift for Dieter Kastovsky*. Berlin: Mouton de Gruyter.

Danchev, A. 1997. The Middle English creolization hypothesis revisited. In J. Fisiak (ed.), *Studies in Middle English Linguistics* (Trends in Linguistics / Studies and Monographs 103). Berlin and New York: Mouton de Gruyter, 79–108.

Danielsson, B. (ed.). 1963. *John Hart's Works on English Orthography and Pronunciation (1551, 1569, 1570)*, part 2, *Phonology*. Stockholm: Almqvist & Wiksell.

Daunton, M. J. 1985. *Royal Mail: the Post Office since 1840*. London and Dover, NH: Athlone.

Davidse, K. 1996. Functional dimensions of the dative in English. In William van Belle & Willy Langendonck (eds.), *The Dative*, vol. I, *Descriptive Studies*. Amsterdam: Benjamins, 289–338.

DeCamp, David. 1958. The genesis of the Old English dialects: a new hypothesis. *Language* 34: 232–44.

Dekeyser, X. 1975. *Number and Case Relations in 19th Century British English: a Comparative Study of Grammar and Usage*. Antwerp and Amsterdam: De Nederlandsche Boekhandel.

Denison, David. 1985. The origins of periphrastic DO: Ellegård and Visser reconsidered. In Roger Eaton, Olga Fischer, Willem Koopman & Frederike van der Leek (eds.), *Papers from the 4th International Conference on English Historical Linguistics: Amsterdam, 10–13 April 1985* (Current Issues in Linguistic Theory 41). Amsterdam and Philadelphia: John Benjamins, 45–60.

Denison, D. 1993. *English Historical Syntax* (Longman Linguistics Library). Harlow: Longman.

Denison, D. 1998. Syntax. In Romaine (ed.), 92–329.

Denison, D. 2000a. Combining English auxiliaries. In Fischer et al. (eds.), 111–47.

Denison, D. 2000b. So what's new? How do we recognise linguistic change. Paper given at ESSE 5, Helsinki.

Digital Library Production Services/Program Development, June 2000. University of Michigan. http://www.umdl.umich.edu/monthly/200006

Dillard, J. L. 1992. *A History of American English*. Harlow, Essex: Longman.

Dobson, Eric J. 1957. *English Pronunciation 1500–1700*, 2 vols. Oxford: Clarendon Press.

Dodgson, John McNeal. 1966. The significance of the distribution of the English place-name in *-ingas, -inga-* in south-east England. *Medieval Archaeology* 10: 1–29. Repr. in Cameron (ed.), 1977: 27–54.

Dodgson, John McNeal. 1967. Various forms of Old English *-ing* in English place-names. *Beiträge zur Namenforschung* (new series) 2: 325–96.

Dodgson, John McNeal. 1968. Various English place-name formations containing Old English *-ing*. *Beiträge zur Namenforschung* (new series) 3: 141–89.

Dressler, Wolfgang U. 1985. *Morphonology: the Dynamics of Derivation*. Ann Arbor: Karoma.

Duggan, Deborah A., Albert A. Cota & Kenneth L. Dion. 1993. Taking thy husband's name: what might it mean? *Names* 41: 87–102.

Dunkling, Leslie & William Gosling. 1991. *Everyman's Dictionary of First Names*, 3rd edn. London: Dent.

Eble, Connie C. 2003. The Louisiana Purchase and American English. *American Speech* 78: 347–52.

Eckert, Penelope. 2001. Style and social meaning. In Penelope Eckert & John R. Rickford (eds.), *Style and Sociolinguistic Variation*. Cambridge: Cambridge University Press, 119–26.

Eco, Umberto. 1995. *The Search for the Perfect Language*. Oxford: Blackwell.

Education: Elementary and Secondary Schools. Public Record Office. 2001. http://catalogue.pro.gov.uk/Leaflets/ri2172.htm

Edwards, John. 1992. Sociopolitical aspects of language maintenance and loss: towards a typology of minority language situations. In Willem Fase, Koen Jaspaert & Sjaak Kroon (eds.), *Maintenance and Loss of Minority Languages*. Amsterdam: Benjamins, 37–54.

Ekwall, Eilert. 1928. *English River-Names*. Oxford: Clarendon Press.

Ekwall, Eilert. 1947. *Early London Personal Names*. Lund: Gleerup.

Ekwall, Eilert. 1956. *Studies on the Population of Medieval London* (Filologisk-filosofiska series 2). Stockholm: Almqvist and Wiksell.

Ekwall, Eilert. 1960. *The Concise Oxford Dictionary of English Place-Names*, 4th edn. Oxford: Clarendon Press.

Elenbaas, M. 2003. Particle verbs in early Middle English: the case of *up*. In L. Cornips & P. Fikkert (eds.), *Linguistics in the Netherlands 2003*. Amsterdam: Benjamins, 45–57.

Ellegård, Alvar. 1953. *The Auxiliary 'do': the Establishment and Regulation of its Growth in English* (Gothenburg Studies in English 2). Stockholm: Almqvist & Wiksell.

Elliott, R. W. V. 1974. *Chaucer's English*. London: Deutsch.

Ellis, A. J. 1869. *On Early English Pronunciation* (Early English Text Society, Extra Series 2). Repr. 1968. London: Greenwood Press.

Ellis, A. J. 1874. *Early English Pronunciation, with Especial Reference to Shakspere and Chaucer*, part 4. London: Asher.

Ellis, Alexander J. 1875. On the classification of Modern English dialects [summary only]. *Transactions of the Philological Society* 16 (Minutes of meetings): 15–16.

Ellis, Alexander J. 1889. *On Early English Pronunciation*, vol. 5, *The existing phonology of English dialects compared with that of West Saxon* (Early English Text Society, Extra Series 56). London: Oxford University Press.

Elsness, J. 1997. *The Perfect and the Preterite in Contemporary and Earlier English*. Amsterdam: Benjamins.

Elworthy, T. 1875. The dialect of West Somerset. *Transactions of the Philological Society* 15: 197–272.

Encyclopaedia Britannica. 1999. *Britannica Book of the Year*. Chicago: Encyclopaedia Britannica.

Encyclopaedia Britannica. 2001. DVD-ROM, Encyclopaedia Britannica Inc.

Encyclopaedia Britannica. 2004. *Britannica Book of the Year*. Chicago: Encyclopaedia Britannica.

Engel, D. M. & M.-E. A. Ritz. 2000. The use of the present perfect in Australian English. *Australian Journal of Linguistics* 20: 119–40.

Ethnologue. 1988, 1992. Texas: Summer Institute of Linguistics.

Evans, Cleveland Kent. 1992. *Unusual and Most Popular Baby Names*. Lincolnwood, IL: Publications International.

Faarlund, J. T. (ed.). 2001. *Grammatical Relations in Change* (Studies in Language Companion Series 56). Amsterdam: Benjamins.

Fanego, T. 1996a. The gerund in Early Modern English: evidence from the Helsinki Corpus. *Folia Linguistica Historica* 17: 97–152.

Fanego, T. 1996b. The development of gerunds as objects of subject-control verbs in English (1400–1760). *Diachronica* 13: 29–62.

Fanego, T. 1998. Developments in argument linking in early Modern English gerund phrases. *English Language and Linguistics* 2: 87–119.

Fellows-Jensen, Gillian. 2000. Vikings in the British Isles: the place-name evidence. *Acta Archaeologica* 71: 135–46.

Fellows-Jensen, Gillian. 1972. *Scandinavian Settlement Names in Yorkshire* (Navnestudier 11). Copenhagen: Institut for Navneforskning.

Fellows-Jensen, Gillian. 1978. *Scandinavian Settlement Names in the East Midlands* (Navnestudier 16). Copenhagen: Institut for Navneforskning.

Fellows-Jensen, Gillian. 1985. *Scandinavian Settlement Names in the North-West* (Navnestudier 25). Copenhagen: Institut for Navneforskning.

Fellows-Jensen, Gillian. 1992. Place-names in *-thorp*: in retrospect and in turmoil. *Nomina* 15: 35–51.

Field, John. 1972. *English Field-Names: a Dictionary*. Newton Abbot: David & Charles.

Field, John. 1993. *A History of English Field-Names*. Harlow: Longman.

Fillmore, C. J. 1968. The case for case. In E. Bach & R. T. Harms (eds.), *Universals in Linguistic Theory*. New York: Holt, Rinehart and Winston, 1–88.

Filppula, Markku. 1999. *The Grammar of Irish English*. London: Routledge.

Filppula, M., J. Klemola & H. Pitkänen (eds.). 2002a. *The Celtic Roots of English* (Studies in Language 37). University of Joensuu: Faculty of Humanities.

Filppula, M., J. Klemola & H. Pitkänen. 2002b. Early contacts between English and the Celtic languages. In Filppula, Klemola & Pitkänen (eds.), 1–26.

Finegan, E. 1998. English grammar and usage. In Romaine (ed.), 536–88.

Finegan, Edward & John R. Rickford (eds.). 2004. *Language in the USA: Themes for the Twenty-first Century*. Cambridge: Cambridge University Press.

Finkenstaedt, T., E. Leisi & D. Wolff. 1970. *A Chronological English Dictionary Listing 80,000 Words in Order of their Earliest Known Occurrence*. Heidelberg: Winter. [= CED]

Finkenstaedt, T., E. Leisi & D. Wolff. 1973. *Ordered Profusion. Studies in Dictionaries and the English Lexicon*. Heidelberg: Winter.

Finlay, R. & B. Shearer. 1986. Population growth and suburban expansion. In A. L. Beier & R. Finlay (eds.), *London 1500–1700: the Making of the Metropolis*. London and New York: Longman, 37–59.

Fischer, David Hackett. 1989. *Albion's Seed: Four British Folkways in America*. New York: Oxford University Press.

Fischer, John L. 1958. Social influences on the choice of a linguistic variable. *Word* 14: 47–56. Repr. in Hymes (ed.), 1964: 483–88.

Fischer, O. 1992. Syntax. In Blake (ed.), 207–408.

Fischer, O. 1997. Infinitive marking in late Middle English: transitivity and changes in the English system of case. In J. Fisiak & W. Winter (eds.), *Studies in Middle English Linguistics*. Berlin: Mouton de Gruyter, 109–34.

Fischer, O. 2000. The position of the adjective in Old English. In Bermúdez-Otero et al. (eds.), 153–81.

Fischer, O. 2004. Developments in the category adjective from Old to Middle English. *Studies in Medieval English Language and Literature* 19: 1–36.

Fischer, Olga, Ans van Kemenade, Willem Koopman & Wim van der Wurff. 2000. *The Syntax of Early English* (Cambridge Syntax Guides 1). Cambridge: Cambridge University Press.

Fischer, O. & F. van der Leek. 1987. A 'case' for the Old English impersonal. In W. F. Koopman, F. van der Leek, O. Fischer & R. Eaton (eds.), *Explanation and Linguistic Change* (Current Issues in Linguistic Theory 45). Amsterdam: Benjamins, 79–120.

Fischer, O. & M. Nänny (eds.). 2001. *The Motivated Sign. Iconicity in Language and Literature 2*. Amsterdam: Benjamins.

Fischer, O., A. Rosenbach & D. Stein (eds.). 2000. *Pathways of Change: Grammaticalization in English*. Amsterdam: Benjamins.

Fisher, J. H. 1996. *The Emergence of Standard English*. Lexington, KY: University of Kentucky Press.

Fisher, J. H. 2001. British and American, continuity and divergence. In Algeo (ed.), 59–85.

Fisiak, J. 1977. Sociolinguistics and Middle English: some socially motivated changes in the history of English. *Kwartalnik Neofilologiczny* 24: 247–59.

Flint, M. 1740. *Prononciation de la langue angloise*. In H. Kökeritz, 1944, *Mather Flint on early English pronunciation. Skrifta Utgivna af Kungl. Humanistiska Vetenskapsamfundet i Uppsala*, 37.

Foley, James A. (ed.). 1999. *English in New Cultural Contexts*. New York: Oxford University Press.

Fought, Carmen. 2003. *Chicano English in Context*. Houndmills: Palgrave Macmillan.

Fowler, H. W. 1926. *A Dictionary of Modern English Usage*. Oxford: Clarendon Press.

Fowler, H. W. 1965. *A Dictionary of Modern English Usage*, 2nd edn. Oxford: Oxford University Press.

Francis, W. Nelson. 1983. *Dialectology: an Introduction*. Harlow: Longman.

Fransson, Gustav. 1935. *Middle English Surnames of Occupation, 1100–1350* (Lund Studies in English 3). Lund: C. W. K. Gleerup.

Funke, O. 1914. *Die gelehrten lateinischen Lehn- und Fremdwörter in der altenglischen Literatur von der Mitte des X. Jahrhunderts bis um das Jahr 1066*. Halle: Niemeyer.

Gammeltoft, Peder. 2003. 'I sauh a tour on a toft, tryelyche i-maket' part II: on place-names in toft in England. *Nomina* 26: 43–63.

Garmonsway, G. N. 1954. *The Anglo-Saxon Chronicle* (Everyman's Library 624). London: Dent.

Gates, Henry Louis, Jr. 1996. Afterword. In *The Complete Stories by Zora Neale Hurston*. New York: Harper Perennial.

Geipel, J. 1971. *The Viking Legacy: the Scandinavian Influence on the English and Gaelic Languages*. Newton Abbot: David & Charles.

Gelling, Margaret. 1984. *Place-Names in the Landscape*. London: Dent.

Gelling, Margaret. 1997. *Signposts to the Past*, 3rd edn. Chichester: Phillimore.

Gelling, Margaret & Ann Cole. 2000. *The Landscape of Place-Names*. Stamford: Shaun Tyas.

Gelling, Margaret, W. F. H. Nicolaisen & Melville Richards. 1970. *The Names of Towns and Cities in Britain*. London: Batsford. [Sometimes catalogued under Nicolaisen.]

Gil, A. 1619. *Logonomia Anglica*. In B. Danielsson & A. Gabrielsson (eds.), 1972, *Alexander Gil's Logonomia Anglica, 1619*, 2 vols. Stockholm: Almqvist & Wiksell.

Giles, H. & P. Smith. 1979. Accommodation theory: optimal levels of convergence. In H. Giles & R. St Clair (eds.), *Language and Social Psychology*. Oxford: Blackwell.

Gimbutas, M. A. 1982. *The Goddesses and Gods of Old Europe, 6500–3500 BC: Myths and Cult Images*, 2nd edn. London: Thames & Hudson.

Gimson, A. C. 1962. *An Introduction to the Pronunciation of English*. 2nd edn, 1970; 3rd edn, 1980. London: Arnold.

Gneuss, H. 1955. *Lehnbildungen und Lehnbedeutungen im Altenglischen*. Berlin: Schmidt.

Gneuss, H. 1972. The origin of Standard Old English and Æthelwold's school at Winchester. *Anglo-Saxon England* 1: 63–83.

Gneuss, H. 1985. Linguistic borrowing and Old English lexicography: Old English terms for the books of liturgy. In A. Bammesberger (ed.), *Problems of Old English Lexicography. Studies in Memory of Angus Cameron*. Heidelberg: Winter, 109–29.

Godden, M. R. 1992. Literary language. In Hogg (ed.), 490–535.

Gordon, I. A. 1966. *The Movement of English Prose.* London: Longman. Repr. 1972, 1980.

Görlach, M. (ed.). 2001. *A Dictionary of European Anglicisms: a Usage Dictionary of Anglicisms in Sixteen European Languages.* Oxford: Oxford University Press.

Görlach, M. 1986. Middle English – a creole? In D. Kastovsky & A. Szwedek (eds.), *Linguistics across Historical and Geographical Boundaries: in Honour of Jacek Fisiak on the Occasion of his Fiftieth Birthday,* vol. 1 (Trends in Linguistics. Studies and Monographs 32). Berlin: Mouton de Gruyter, 329–44.

Görlach, M. 1991, *Introduction to Early Modern English.* Cambridge: Cambridge University Press.

Görlach, M. 1991. *Englishes: Studies in Varieties of English, 1984–1988.* Amsterdam: Benjamins.

Görlach, M. 1994. *Einführung ins Frühneuenglische* (Sprachwissenschaftliche Studienbücher. 1. Abteilung), 2nd edn. Heidelberg: Quelle & Meyer.

Görlach, M. 1995. *More Englishes: New Studies in Varieties of English, 1988–1994.* Amsterdam: Benjamins.

Görlach, M. 1998. *Even More Englishes.* Amsterdam: Benjamins.

Görlach, M. 1999. *English in Nineteenth-Century England: an Introduction.* Cambridge: Cambridge University Press.

Görlach, M. 2001. *Eighteenth-Century English* (Sprachwissenschaftliche Studienbücher). Heidelberg: Winter.

Görlach, M. 2002. *Still More Englishes.* Amsterdam: Benjamins.

Gotti, M. 1996. *Robert Boyle and the Language of Science.* Milan: Guerini Scientifica.

Graddol, David. 1999. The decline of the native speaker. In David Graddol & Ulrike H. Meinhof (eds.), *English in a Changing World. AILA Review* 13: 57–68.

Graddol, David. 1998. *The Future of English.* London: The British Council.

Gramley, S. 2001. *The Vocabulary of World English.* London: Arnold.

Green, Lisa J. 2002. *African American English: a Linguistic Introduction.* Cambridge: Cambridge University Press.

Greenwood, J. 1711. *An Essay towards a Practical English Grammar.* London. Repr. in facsimile by R. C. Alston, 1974, *English Linguistics 1500–1800* (English Linguistics 128). London: Scolar Press.

Grenoble, Lenore A. & Lindsay J. Whaley. 1998. Toward a typology of language endangerment. In Lenore A. Grenoble & Lindsay J. Whaley (eds.), *Endangered languages.* Cambridge: Cambridge University Press, 22–54.

Guppy, H. P. 1890. *Homes of Family Names in Great Britain.* London: Genealogical Publishing Co.

Guy, G. & J. Vonwiller. 1989. The high rising tone in Australian English. In P. Collins & D. Blair (eds.), *Australian English: the Language of a New Society.* St Lucia: University of Queensland Press.

Guy, G., B. Horvath, J. Vonwiller, E. Daisley & I. Rogers. 1986. An intonational change in progress in Australian English. *Language in Society* 15: 23–51.

Haeberli, E. 2002. Inflectional morphology and the loss of verb-second in English. In Lightfoot (ed.), 88–106.

Haegeman, L. 1997. Register variation, truncation, and subject omission in English and in French. *English Language and Linguistics* 1: 233–70.

Haiman, John. 1983. Iconic and economic motivation. *Language* 59: 781–819.

Halliday, M. A. K. 1993. Some grammatical problems of scientific English. In M. A. K. Halliday & J. R. Martin, *Writing Science: Literacy and Discursive Power*. London: Falmer Press, 69–85.

Hamerow, Helena F. 1991. Settlement mobility and the 'Middle Saxon Shift': rural settlements and settlement patterns in Anglo-Saxon England. *Anglo-Saxon England* 21: 1–17.

Hanks, Patrick. 1993. The present-day distribution of surnames in the British Isles. *Nomina* 16: 79–98.

Hanks, Patrick & Flavia Hodges. 1990a. *A Dictionary of First Names*. Oxford: Oxford University Press.

Hanks, Patrick & Flavia Hodges. 1990b. *A Dictionary of Surnames*. Oxford: Oxford University Press.

Hanley, J. Richard & Janice Kay. 1998. Proper name anomia and anomia for the names of people: functionally dissociable impairments? *Cortex* 34: 155–8.

Hansen, B. H. 1984. The historical implications of the Scandinavian linguistic element in English: a theoretical evaluation. *NOWELE* 4: 53–95.

Harriot, Thomas. 1590 [1972]. *A Briefe and True Report of the New Found Land of Virginia* [facsimile edition of the complete 1590 Theodor de Bry edn, with intro. by Paul Hulton]. New York: Dover.

Harris, A. C. & L. Campbell. 1995. *Historical Syntax in Cross-Linguistic Perspective*. Cambridge: Cambridge University Press.

Harris, John. 1985. *Phonological Variation and Change*. Cambridge: Cambridge University Press.

Hart, J. 1569. *An orthographie, conteyning the due Order and Reason, howe to Write or Paint Thimage of Mannes Voice, most like to the Life or Nature*. London.

Hartman, James W. 1985. Guide to pronunciation. *Dictionary of American Regional English*, vol. 1. Cambridge, MA: Belknap, xii–lxi.

Healey, Antonette diPaolo & Richard L. Venezky. 1980. *Microfiche Concordance of Old English*. Toronto: University of Toronto (Centre for Medieval Studies). [= *MCOE*]

Heikkonen, Kirsi. 1996. Regional variation in standardization: a case study of Henry V's Signet Office. In Nevalainen & Raumolin-Brunberg (eds.), 111–27.

Hellinga, W. & L. Hellinga. 1984. Between two languages: Caxton's translation of Reynaert de Vos. In G. A. M. Janssens & F. G. A. M. Aarts (eds.), *Studies in Seventeenth-Century English Literature, History and Bibliography*. Amsterdam: Rodopi, 119–131.

Hey, David. 1998. *The Distinctive Surnames of Staffordshire*. Earl Lecture (Staffordshire Studies 10). Newcastle under Lyme: Keele University.

Hey, David. 2000. *Family Names and Family History*. London and New York: Hambledon and London.

Hill, David. 1981. *An Atlas of Anglo-Saxon England*. Oxford: Blackwell.

Hiltunen, R. 1983. *The Decline of the Prefixes and the Beginnings of the English Phrasal Verb* (Annales Universitatis Turkuensis, Ser. B., Tom. 160). Turku: Turun Yliopisto.

Hirschberg, J. & G. Ward. 1995. The interpretation of the high-rise question contour in English. *Journal of Pragmatics* 24: 407–12.

Hjertstedt, Ingrid. 1987. *Middle English nicknames in the Lay Subsidy Rolls for Warwickshire* (Studia Anglica Upsaliensia 63). Uppsala: Almqvist and Wiksell.

Hodges, R. 1643. *A Special Help to Orthography; or, the true-writing of English*. London: Cotes.

Hodges, R. 1644. *The English Primrose*. London: Cotes.

Hofland, K. & S. Johansson. 1982. *Word Frequencies in British and American English*. Bergen: The Norwegian Computing Centre for the Humanities.

Hofstetter, W. 1987. *Winchester und der spätaltenglische Sprachgebrauch. Untersuchungen zur geographischen und zeitlichen Verbreitung altenglischer Synonyme* (Texte und Untersuchungen zur englischen Philologie 14). Munich: Fink.

Hofstetter, W. 1979. Der Erstbeleg von AE. *pryte/pryde*. *Anglia* 97: 172–75.

Hogg, R. M. 1988. On the impossibility of Old English dialectology. In Kastovsky & Bauer (eds.), 183–204.

Hogg, R. M. (ed.). 1992a. *The Cambridge History of the English Language*, vol. 1, *The Beginnings to 1066*. Cambridge: Cambridge University Press.

Hogg, R. M. 1992b. Phonology and morphology. In Hogg (ed.), 67–167.

Hogg, R. M. 1992c. *A Grammar of Old English*. Oxford: Blackwell.

Hogg, R. M. 1997. Using the future to predict the past: Old English dialectology in the light of Middle English place-names. In J. Fisiak (ed.), *Studies in Middle English Linguistics*. Berlin: Mouton de Gruyter, 207–20.

Hogg, R. M. 2004. North Northumbrian and South Northumbrian: a geographical question? In M. Dossena & R. Lass (eds.), *English Historical Dialectology*. Munich: Peter Lang, 241–55.

Hogg, R. M. forthcoming. Old English dialectology. In van Kemenade & Los (eds.).

Hopper, P. J. 1991. On some principles of grammaticization. In E. C. Traugott & B. Heine (eds.), *Approaches to Grammaticalization*, vol. 1, *Focus on Theoretical and Methodological Issues*. Amsterdam: Benjamins, 17–35.

Hopper, P. J. & S. A. Thompson. 1984. The discourse basis for lexical categories in Universal Grammar. *Language* 60: 703–52.

Horgan, D. M. 1980. Patterns of variation and interchangeability in some Old English prefixes. *Neuphilologische Mitteilungen* 81: 127–30.

Horovitz, David. 2005. *The Place-Names of Staffordshire*. Brewood: David Horovitz.

Hughes, G. 2000. *A History of English Words*. Oxford: Blackwell.

Hurston, Zora Neale. 1946. Hurricane, Repr. in *The Complete Stories/Zora Neale Hurston*. 1996. New York: Harper Perennial, 149–61.

Hymes, Dell (ed.). 1964. *Language in Culture and Society*. New York: Harper & Row.

Iglesias-Rábade, L. 2001. Composite predicates in Middle English with the verbs *nimen* and *taken*. *Studia Neophilologica* 73: 143–63.

Ihalainen, Ossi. 1994. The dialects of England since 1776. In Burchfield (ed.), 197–274.

Ilson, R. F. 1985. Usage problems in British and American English. In S. Greenbaum (ed.), *The English Language Today*. Oxford: Pergamon Press, 166–182.

Insley, John. 1987. Regional variation in Scandinavian personal nomenclature in England. *Nomina* 3: 52–60.

Insley, John. 1994. *Scandinavian Personal Names in Norfolk: a Survey Based on Medieval Records and Place-Names* (Acta Academiae Regiae Gustavi Adolphi 62). Uppsala: Almqvist & Wiksell.

Insley, John. 2002. The study of Old English personal names and anthroponymic lexika. In Dieter Geuenich, Wolfgang Haubrichs & Jörg Janut (eds.), *Person und Name: methodische Probleme bei der Erstellung eines Personennamenbuches des Frühmittelalters*. Berlin and New York: Walter de Gruyter, 148–76.

Ireland, R. J. 1979. Canadian spelling: an empirical and historical survey of selected words. Ph.D. thesis. York University.

Jack, G. B. 1978. Negation in later Middle English prose. *Archivum Linguisticum* 9 (n.s.): 58–72.

Jack, G. B. 1988. The origins of the English gerund. *NOWELE* 12: 15–75.

Jackson, K. H. 1953. *Language and History in Early Britain*. Edinburgh: Edinburgh University Press.

Jackson, Peter (ed.). 1995. *Words, Names and History: Selected Writings of Cecily Clark*. Cambridge: D. S. Brewer.

Janda, R. D. 1980. On the decline of declensional systems: the overall loss of Old English nominal case inflections and the Middle English reanalysis of -ES as HIS. In E. C. Traugott, R. Labrum, S. Shepherd & P. Kiparsky (eds.), *Papers from the 4th International Conference on Historical Linguistics*. Amsterdam: Benjamins, 243–52.

Jespersen, Otto. 1914. *A Modern English Grammar on Historical Principles*, part 2: *Syntax*, vol. 1. Heidelberg: C. Winter. Repr. London: Allen & Unwin, 1961.

Johnson, F. R. 1944. Latin versus English: the sixteenth-century debate over scientific terminology. *Studies in Philology* 41: 109–35.

Johnson, S. 1755. *A Dictionary of the English Language: in which the Words are deduced from their Originals, and illustrated in their Different Significations by Examples from the Best Writers*, 2 vols. London: J. F. & C. Rivington.

Jones, C. 1994. Alexander Geddes: an eighteenth century Scottish orthoepist and dialectologist. *Folia Linguistica Historica* 15: 71–103.

Jones, D. 1917. *An English Pronouncing Dictionary*. London: Dent. 14th edn, 1991. Cambridge: Cambridge University Press.

Jones, D. 1918. *An Outline of English Phonetics*. Leipzig: Teubner. 9th edn, 1963. Cambridge: Heffer.

Jones, J. 1701. *Dr John Jones' Practical Phonography*. London: Richard Smith.

Jönsjö, J. 1979. *Studies on Middle English Nicknames, I: Compounds* (Lund Studies in English 55). Lund: C. W. K. Gleerup.

Jonson, B. 1640. *The English Grammar. Made by Ben. Johnson. For the benefit of all Strangers, out of his Observations of the English language now spoken, and in use*. In *The Works of Benjamin Ionson*, II.31–84. London: Richard Bishop.

Kachru, Braj. 1985. Institutionalized second-language varieties. In Sidney Greenbaum (ed.), *The English Language Today*. Oxford: Pergamon, 211–26.

Kachru, Braj. 1986. *The Alchemy of English*. Oxford: Pergamon.

Kachru, Braj. 2001. World Englishes and culture wars. In T. C. Kiong, A. Pakir, B. K. Choon & R. B. H. Goh (eds.), *Ariels: Departures and Returns: Essays for Edwin Thumboo*. Singapore: Oxford University Press, 392–414.

Kallen, Jeffrey L. 1994. English in Ireland. In Burchfield (ed.), 148–96.

Kärre, K. 1915. *Nomina agentis in Old English*. I. Uppsala: Akademiska Bokhandeln.

Kastovsky, D. 1968. *Old English Deverbal Substantives Derived by Means of a Zero Morpheme*. [PhD dissertation, Tübingen University 1967]. Esslingen/N.: Langer.

Kastovsky, D. 1980. Zero in morphology: a means of making up for phonological losses? In J. Fisiak (ed.), *Historical Morphology* (Trends in Linguistics. Studies and Monographs 17). The Hague: Mouton, 213–50.

Kastovsky, D. 1982. *Wortbildung und Semantik* (Studienreihe Englisch 14). Tübingen/Düsseldorf: Francke/Bagel.

Kastovsky, D. 1985. Deverbal nouns in Old English and Modern English: from stem-formation to word-formation. In J. Fisiak (ed.), *Historical Semantics. Historical*

Word-formation (Trends in Linguistics. Studies and Monographs 29). Berlin: Mouton de Gruyter: 221–62.

Kastovsky, D. 1986. Diachronic word-formation in a functional perspective. In D. Kastovsky & A. Szwedek (eds.), *Linguistics across Historical and Geographical Boundaries: in Honour of Jacek Fisiak on the Occasion of his Fiftieth Birthday* (Trends in Linguistics. Studies and Monographs 32). Berlin: Mouton de Gruyter, 409–21.

Kastovsky, D. 1989. Morphophonemic alternations and the history of English: examples from Old English. In M. Markus (ed.), *Historical English. On the Occasion of Karl Brunner's 100th Birthday* (Innsbrucker Beiträge zur Kulturwissenschaft. Anglistische Reihe 1). Innsbruck: University of Innsbruck, 112–23.

Kastovsky, D. 1990. Whatever happened to the ablaut nouns in English – and why did it not happen in German? In H. Andersen & K. Koerner (eds.), *Historical Linguistics 1987* (Current Issues in Linguistic Theory 66). Amsterdam: Benjamins, 253–64.

Kastovsky, D. 1992. Semantics and vocabulary. In Hogg (ed.), 290–407.

Kastovsky, D. (ed.). 1994a. *Studies in Early Modern English* (Topics in English Linguistics 13). Berlin: Mouton.

Kastovsky, D. 1994b. Historical English word-formation. From a monostratal to a polystratal system. In R. Bacchielli (ed.), *Historical English Word-Formation. Papers Read at the Sixth National Conference of the History of English*. Urbino: Quattro-Venti, 17–31.

Kastovsky, D. 1996. Verbal derivation in English: a historical survey. Or: Much ado about nothing. In Britton (ed.), 93–117.

Kastovsky, D. 1999. Hans Marchand's theory of word-formation: Genesis and development. In U. Carls & P. Lucko (eds.), *Form, Function and Variation in English: Studies in Honour of Klaus Hansen*. Frankfurt am Main: Peter Lang, 19–39.

Kastovsky, D. 2000. Words and word-formation: morphology in the *OED*. In L. Mugglestone (ed.), *Lexicography and the OED: Pioneers in the Untrodden Forest*. Oxford: Oxford University Press, 110–25.

Kastovsky, D. 2002a. The derivation of ornative, locative, ablative, privative and reversative verbs in English: a historical sketch. In T. Fanego, M. José López-Couso & J. Pérez-Guerra (eds.), *English Historical Syntax and Morphology: Selected Papers from 11 ICEHL, Santiago de Compostela, 7–11 September 2000* (Current Issues in Linguistic Theory 223). Amsterdam and Philadelphia: John Benjamins, 99–109.

Kastovsky, D. 2002b. The 'haves' and the 'have-nots' in Germanic and English: from *bahuvrihi* compounds to affixal derivation. In K. Lenz & Ruth Möhlig (eds.), *Of Dyuersitie and Chaunge of language: Essays Presented to Manfred Görlach on the Occasion of his 65th Birthday*. Heidelberg: C. Winter, 33–46.

Kastovsky, D. & G. Bauer (eds.). 1988. *Luick Revisited. Papers Read at the Luick-Symposium at Schloß Liechtenstein, 15–18.9.1985*. Tübingen: Gunter Narr Verlag.

Kastovsky, D. & C. Dalton-Puffer. 2002. Sexist German – non-sexist English or non-sexist German – sexist English? Historical observations on a pragmatic question. *Language Sciences* 24: 285–96.

Keast, William R. 1957. The two Clarissas in Johnson's *Dictionary*. *Studies in Philology* 54: 429–39.

Keene, D. 2000. Metropolitan values: migration, mobility and cultural norms, London 1100–1700. In L. Wright (ed.), *The Development of Standard English, 1300–1800: Theories, Descriptions, Conflicts*. Cambridge: Cambridge University Press, 93–116.

van Kemenade, A. 1987. *Syntactic Case and Morphological Case in the History of English*. Dordrecht: Foris.

van Kemenade, A. 1997. V2 and embedded topicalization in Old and Middle English. In van Kemenade & Vincent (eds.), 326–52.

van Kemenade, A. & N. Vincent (eds.). 1997. *Parameters of Morphosyntactic Change*. Cambridge: Cambridge University Press.

van Kemenade, A. & B. Los (eds.). forthcoming. *The Handbook of the History of English*. Oxford: Blackwell.

Kenyon, J. & T. A. Knott. 1944/1953. *A Pronouncing Dictionary of American English*. Springfield, MA: Merriam.

Kerswill, P. & A. Williams. 2000. Creating a New Town koine. *Language in Society* 29: 65–115.

Kirk, J. M., S. Sanderson & J. Widdowson. 1985. *Studies in Linguistic Geography*. London: Croom Helm.

Kirkby, J. 1746. *A New English Grammar: a Guide to the English Tongue, with Notes*. London: Manby & C.

Kirwin, William J. 2001. Newfoundland English. In Algeo (ed.), 441–55.

Kitson, Peter. 1992. Old English dialects and the stages of transition to Middle English. *Folia Linguistica Historica* 14: 27–87.

Kitson, Peter. 1993. Geographical variation in Old English prepositions and the location of Ælfric's and other literary dialects. *English Studies* 74: 1–50.

Kitson, Peter R. 1995. The nature of Old English dialect distributions, mainly as exhibited in charter boundaries, part I: Vocabulary. In Jacek Fisiak (ed.), *Medieval Dialectology*. Berlin: de Gruyter, 43–115.

Kitson, Peter R. 1997. Worth(y). *Studia Anglica Posnaniensia* 31: 105–15.

Kitson, Peter. 2002. How Anglo-Saxon personal names work. *Nomina* 25: 91–131.

Klemola, J. 2002. Periphrastic DO: dialectal distribution and origins. In Filppula, Klemola & Pitkänen (eds.), 199–210.

Kohnen, T. 2001. The influence of 'Latinate' constructions in Early Modern English: orality and literacy as complementary forces. In D. Kastovsky & A. Mettinger (eds.), *Language Contact in the History of English* (Studies in English Medieval Language and Literature 1). Bern: Lang, 171–94.

Kolb, E., B. Glauser, W. Elmer & R. Stamm. 1979. *Atlas of English Sounds*. Bern: Francke Verlag.

Kornexl, L. 2001. 'Unnatural words'? Loan formations in Old English glosses. In D. Kastovsky & A. Mettinger (eds.), *Language Contact in the History of English* (Studies in English Medieval Language and Literature 1). Frankfurt a. M.: Lang, 195–216.

Krapp, George Philip. 1925. *The English Language in America*, 2 vols. New York: Modern Language Association. Repr. New York: Frederick Ungar, 1960.

Kripke, Saul A. 1980. *Naming and Necessity*, 2nd edn. Oxford: Blackwell.

Kripke, S. A. 1982. *Wittgenstein on Rules and Private Language*. Cambridge, MA: Harvard University Press.

Kristensson, Gillis. 1967. *A Survey of Middle English Dialects 1290–1350: the Six Northern Counties and Lincolnshire* (Lund Studies in English 35). Lund: Gleerup.

Kristensson, Gillis. 1987. *A Survey of Middle English Dialects 1290–1350: the West Midland Counties*. Lund: Lund University Press.

Kristensson, G. 2001. *A Survey of Middle English Dialects 1290–1350: the Southern Counties*. Lund: Lund University Press.

Kroch, A. & A. Taylor. 1997. Verb movement in Old and Middle English: dialect variation & language contact. In van Kemenade and Vincent (eds.), 297–325.

Kroch, A. & A. Taylor. 2000. Verb–object order in Early Middle English. In Pintzuk et al. (eds.), 132–63.

Kroch, A., A. Taylor & D. Ringe. 2000. The Middle English verb-second constraint: a case study in language contact and language change. In S. Herring, P. van Reenen & L. Schøsler (eds.), *Textual Parameters in Older Languages* (Current Issues in Linguistic Theory 195). Amsterdam and Philadelphia, PA: Benjamins, 353–91.

Kroesch, S. 1929. Semantic borrowing in Old English. In K. Malone & M. B. Rund (eds.), *A Miscellany in Honor of Frederick Klaeber*. Minneapolis: University of Minnesota Press, 50–72.

Kurath, Hans. 1949. *A Word Geography of the United States*. Ann Arbor: University of Michigan Press.

Kurath, Hans, M. Hanley, B. Bloch & G. S. Lowman Jr. 1939–43. *Linguistic Atlas of New England*, 6 vols. Providence, RI: Brown University Press.

Kurath, Hans & Raven I. McDavid Jr. 1961. *Pronunciation of English in the Atlantic States*. Ann Arbor: University of Michigan Press.

Kytö, Merja & Andrei Danchev. 2001. The Middle English *'for to* + infinitive' construction. In Dieter Kastovsky & Arthur Mettinger (eds.), *Language Contact in the History of English* (Studies in English Medieval Language and Literature 1). Bern: Lang, 35–55.

Labov, William. 1966. *The Social Stratification of English in New York City*. Washington, DC: Center for Applied Linguistics.

Labov, William. 1972a. *Sociolinguistic Patterns*. Philadelphia: University of Pennsylvania Press.

Labov, William. 1972b. The social motivation of a sound change. In Labov, 1–42.

Labov, W. 1994–2001. *Principles of Linguistic Change*, vol. 1, *Internal Factors*, vol. 2, *Social factors*. (Language in Society). Oxford and Cambridge, MA: Blackwell.

Labov, William & Sharon Ash. 1997. Understanding Birmingham. In Bernstein et al. (eds.), 508–73.

Labov, William, Sharon Ash & Charles Boberg. 2005. *Atlas of North American English*. Berlin: Mouton de Gruyter.

LAEME = Laing, M. & R. Lass in prep. *Linguistic Atlas of Early Middle English*. Edinburgh: University of Edinburgh, Institute for Historical Dialectology.

Laing, M. 1993. *Catalogue of Sources for a Linguistic Atlas of Early Medieval English*. Cambridge and Rochester, NY: Brewer.

Laing, M. 1999. Confusion *wrs* confounded: litteral substitution sets in early Middle English writing systems. *Neuphilologische Mitteilungen* 100: 251–70.

Laing, M. & R. Lass. 2003. Tales of the 1001 nists: the phonological implications of litteral substitution sets in some thirteenth-century South-West Midland texts. *English Language and Linguistics* 7: 279–308.

Laing, M. R. Lass. forthcoming. Early Middle English dialectology. In van Kemenade & Los (eds.).

Laird, Charlton Grant. 1970. *Language in America*. Cleveland: World Publishing.

LALME = McIntosh, A., M. L. Samuels & M. Benskin. 1986. *A Linguistic Atlas of Late Mediaeval English*, 4 vols. Aberdeen: Aberdeen University Press.

Lance, Donald M. 2003. The pronunciation of *Missouri*: variation and change in American English. *American Speech* 78: 255–84.

Language Resource Program: Heritage Languages. 2001. University of California at Los Angeles. http://www.isop.ucla.edu/lrp/survey-hl.htm

Lasker, Gabriel Ward. 1985. *Surnames and Genetic Structure*. Cambridge: Cambridge University Press.

Lasker, Gabriel Ward & C. G. N. Mascie-Taylor (eds.). 1990. *Atlas of British Surnames*. Cambridge: Cambridge University Press.

Lass, Roger. 1974. Linguistic orthogenesis? Scots vowel quantity and the English length conspiracy. In J. M. Anderson & C. Jones (eds.), *Historical Linguistics*. Amsterdam: North Holland, 311–52.

Lass, R. 1987. *The Shape of English: Structure and History*. London and Melbourne: Dent.

Lass, R. 1988. Vowel shifts, great and otherwise: remarks on Stockwell and Minkova. In Kastovsky & Bauer (eds.), 395–410.

Lass, R. 1989. How early does English get modern? Or, what happens if you listen to orthoepists and not to historians. *Diachronica* 6.1: 75–110.

Lass, R. 1990a. A standard South African vowel system. In S. Ramsaran (ed.), *Studies in the Pronunciation of English*. London and New York: Routledge, 272–85.

Lass, R. 1990b. Where do Extraterritorial Englishes come from? Dialect input and recodification in transported Englishes. In S. Adamson, V. Law, N. Vincent & S. Wright (eds.), *Papers from the 5th International Conference on English Historical Linguistics*. Amsterdam: John Benjamins, 245–80.

Lass, R. 1992. Phonology and morphology. In Blake (ed.), 23–155.

Lass, R. 1994. Proliferation and option-cutting: the strong verb in the fifteenth to eighteenth centuries. In D. Stein & I. Tieken-Boon van Ostade (eds.), *Towards a Standard English 1600–1800*. Berlin: Mouton de Gruyter, 81–114.

Lass, R. 1997. *Historical Linguistics and Language Change*. Cambridge: Cambridge University Press.

Lass, R. (ed.). 1999a. *The Cambridge History of the English Language*, vol. 3, *1476–1776*. Cambridge: Cambridge University Press.

Lass, R. 1999b. Introduction. In Lass (ed.), 1–12.

Lass, R. 1999c. Phonology and morphology. In Lass (ed.), 56–186.

Lass, R. 2001. Language periodization and the concept "middle". In I. Taavitsainen, T. Nevalainen, P. Pahta & M. Rissanen (eds.), *Placing Middle English in Context* (Topics in English Linguistics 35). Berlin and New York: Mouton de Gruyter, 7–41.

Lass, R. & M. Laing. forthcoming. Are front rounded vowels retained in West Midland Middle English? Paper delivered at the 4th International Conference on Middle English, Vienna 2002. To appear in the proceedings.

Leader, D. R. 1988. *A History of the University of Cambridge*, vol. 1, *The University to 1546*. Cambridge: Cambridge University Press.

Leap, William L. 1993. *American Indian English*. Salt Lake City: University of Utah Press.

Lederer, Richard M., Jr. 1985. *Colonial American English, a Glossary*. Essex, CT: Verbatim.

Lehmann, W. P. 1993. *Theoretical Bases of Indo-European Linguistics*. London: Routledge.

Levins, P. 1570. *Manipulus vocabulorum*. In H. B. Wheatley (ed.) 1867, *Manipulus vocabulorum: a Rhyming Dictionary of the English Language, by Peter Levins (1570)*. EETS OS 27.

Lieberson, Stanley & Eleanor O. Bell. 1992. Children's first names: an empirical study of social taste. *American Journal of Sociology* 98: 511–54.

Lieberson, Stanley & Kelly S. Mikelson. 1995. Distinctive African American names: an experimental, historical, and linguistic analysis of innovation. *American Sociological Review* 60: 928–46.

Lightfoot, D. W. 1974. The diachronic analysis of English modals. In J. Anderson & C. Jones (eds.), *Historical Linguistics* (Proceedings of the 1st ICHL). Amsterdam: North Holland, vol. 1, 219–41.

Lightfoot, D. W. 1979. *Principles of Diachronic Syntax*. Cambridge: Cambridge University Press.

Lightfoot, D. W. 1997. Shifting triggers and diachronic reanalyses. In van Kemenade & Vincent (eds.), 253–72.

Lightfoot, D. W. 1999. *The Development of Language: Acquisition, Change, and Evolution*. Oxford: Blackwell.

Lightfoot, D. W. (ed.). 2002. *Syntactic Effects of Morphological Change*. Oxford: Oxford University Press.

Lipka, L. 2002. *English Lexicology. Lexical Structure, Word Semantics and Ford-formation*, 3rd edn. Tübingen: Narr.

Longobardi, Giuseppe. 1994. Reference and proper names. *Linguistic Inquiry* 25: 609–65.

Los, B. 2005. *The Rise of the to-Infinitive*. Oxford: Oxford University Press.

Lougheed, W. C. 1988. *Writings on Canadian English, 1976–1987: a Selective, Annotated Bibliography*. Kingston, Ont.: Queens University, Strathy Language Unit, Occasional Papers Number 2.

Lowth, R. 1762. *A Short Introduction to English Grammar*. London. Repr. in facsimile by R. C. Alston, 1974, *English Linguistics 1500–1800* (English Linguistics 18). London: Scolar Press.

Lyall, R. J. 1989. Materials: the paper revolution. In Jeremy Griffiths & Derek Pearsall (eds.), *Book Production and Publishing in Britain, 1375–1475*. Cambridge: Cambridge University Press, 11–29.

Lyons, J. 1977. *Semantics*, 2 vols. Cambridge: Cambridge University Press.

MacMahon, M. K. C. 1998. Phonology. In Romaine (ed.), 373–535.

Maddison, A. 1991. *Dynamic Forces in Capitalist Development: a Long-run Comparative View*. Oxford and New York: Oxford University Press.

Maddison, A. 1995. *Monitoring the World Economy 1820–1992*. Paris: OECD.

Mallory, J. P. 1989. *In Search of the Indo-Europeans: Language, Archaeology and Myth*. London: Thames & Hudson.

Marchand, H. 1969. *The Categories and Types of Present-day English Word-formation*, 2nd rev. edn. Munich: Beck.

Marckwardt, Albert H. 1958. *American English*. New York: Oxford University Press.

Mather, J. Y. & H. H. Speitel. 1975, 1977, 1986. *The Linguistic Atlas of Scotland*, vols. I–III. London: Croom Helm.

Mathews, Mitford M. (ed.). 1951. *A Dictionary of Americanisms on Historical Principles*. Chicago: University of Chicago Press.

McArthur, Tom. 1992. *The Oxford Companion to the English Language*. Oxford: Oxford University Press.

McArthur, Tom. 1998. *The English Languages*. Cambridge: Cambridge University Press.

McArthur, Tom. 2002. *The Oxford Guide to World English*. Oxford: Oxford University Press.

McClure, J. Derrick. 1994. English in Scotland. In Burchfield (ed.), 23–93.

McClure, Peter. 1979. Patterns of migration in the late Middle Ages: the evidence of English place-name surnames. *Economic History Review* (2nd series) 32: 167–82.

McClure, Peter. 1982. The origin of the surname *Waterer. Nomina* 6: 92.

McClure, Peter. 1998. The interpretation of hypocoristic forms of Middle English baptismal names. *Nomina* 21: 101–31.

McIntosh, Angus. 1956. The analysis of written Middle English. *Transactions of the Philological Society* 55: 26–55.

McIntosh, Angus. 1963. A new approach to Middle English dialectology. *English Studies* 44: 1–11.

McIntosh, Angus. 1983. Present indicative plural forms in the later Middle English of the North Midlands. In D. Gray & E. G. Stanley (eds.), *Middle English Studies Presented to Norman Davis*. Oxford University Press, 235–44. Repr. in M. Laing (ed.), 1989, *Middle English Dialectology. Essays on Some Principles and Problems*. Aberdeen University Press.

McIntosh, Angus, M. L. Samuels & Michael Benskin. 1986. *A Linguistic Atlas of Late Mediaeval English*, 4 vols. Aberdeen: Aberdeen University Press.

McKinley, Richard. 1975. *Norfolk and Suffolk Surnames in the Middle Ages* (English Surnames series 2). London and Chichester: Phillimore.

McKinley, Richard. 1977. *The Surnames of Oxfordshire* (English Surnames series 3). Oxford: Leopard's Head Press.

McKinley, Richard. 1981. *The Surnames of Lancashire* (English Surnames series 4). Oxford: Leopard's Head Press.

McKinley, Richard. 1988. *The Surnames of Sussex* (English Surnames series 5). Oxford: Leopard's Head Press.

McKinley, Richard. 1990. *A History of British Surnames*. London: Longmans.

McLemore, C. 1991. The interpretation of L*H in English. *Texas Linguistic Forum* 32: 175–96.

McMahon, April. 2003. On not explaining language change: Optimality Theory and the Great Vowel Shift. In R. Hickey (ed.), *Motives for Language Change*. Cambridge: Cambridge University Press, 82–96.

McWhorter, John H. 2002. What happened to English? *Diachronica* 19: 217–72.

MCOE = Healey & Venezky, 1980.

Meillet, A. 1937. *Introduction à l'étude comparative des langues indo-européennes*. Paris: Hachette.

Mencken, H. L. 1963. *The American Language: an Inquiry into the Development of English in the United States*, 4th edn and two supplements, abridged. With annotations and new material by R. I. McDavid Jr. New York: Knopf.

Merry, Emma. 1994. *First Names: the Definitive Guide to Popular Names in England and Wales*. London: Her Majesty's Stationery Office.

Mesthrie, Rajend. 1992. *English in Language Shift*. Cambridge: Cambridge University Press.

Microsoft Encarta 97 Encyclopedia. 1996. CD-ROM. Microsoft, Redmond, WA.

Miles, Joyce. 2000. *Owls Hoot: How People Name Their Houses*. London: John Murray. [See also her MPhil dissertation, 'The naming of private houses in Britain since 1700' (Bristol 1978).]

Miller, J. 2004. Perfect and resultative constructions in spoken and non-standard English. In O. Fischer, M. Norde & H. Perridon (eds.), *Up and Down the Cline – the Nature of Grammaticalization*. Amsterdam: Benjamins, 229–46.

Mills, A. D. 1991. *Oxford Dictionary of English Place-Names*. 2nd edn, 1998. Oxford: Oxford University Press.

Mills, A. D. 1976. *The Place-Names of Lancashire*. London: Batsford.

Milroy, J. 1992. *Linguistic Variation and Change: on the Historical Sociolinguistics of English*. Oxford and Cambridge, MA: Blackwell.

Milroy, J. 1993. On the social origins of language change. In C. Jones (ed.), *Historical Linguistics: Problems and Perspectives* (Longman Linguistics Library). London and New York: Longman, 215–36.

Milroy, J. 1994. The notion of standard language and its applicability to the study of Early Modern English pronunciation. In D. Stein & I. Tieken-Boon van Ostade (eds.), *Towards a Standard English 1600–1800*. Berlin and New York: Mouton de Gruyter, 19–29.

Milroy, James. 1998. Children can't speak or write properly any more. In L. Bauer & P. Trudgill (eds.), *Language Myths*. London: Penguin Books, 58–65.

Milroy, J. & L. Milroy. 1991. *Authority in Language. Investigating Language Prescription and Standardisation*, 2nd edn. London and New York: Routledge.

Milroy, L. 1980. *Language and social networks*. 2nd edn, 1987 (Language in Society 2). Oxford: Blackwell.

Minkova, D. & R. P. Stockwell. 1990. The early Modern English vowels: more O'Lass. *Diachronica* 7: 199–214.

Minkova, D. & R. P. Stockwell. 1998. The origins of long–short allomorphy in English. In J. Fisiak & M. Krygier (eds.), *Advances in English Historical Linguistics* (Trends in Linguistics 112). Berlin and New York: Mouton de Gruyter, 211–39.

Mitchell, B. 1985 *Old English Syntax*, 2 vols. Oxford: Oxford University Press.

Mittins, M. H., M. Salu, M. Edminson & S. Coyne. 1970. *Attitudes to English Usage*. London: Oxford University Press. Repr. 1975.

Mizobata, K. (ed.). 1990. *A Concordance to Caxton's Own Prose*. Tokyo: Shohakusha.

Moerenhout, M. & W. van der Wurff. 2000. Remnants of the old order: OV in the *Paston Letters*. *English Studies* 81: 513–30.

Monaghan, E. J. 1983. *A Common Heritage. Noah Webster's Blue-Back Speller*. Hamden, CT: Archon Books.

Montgomery, Michael B. & Joseph S. Hall. 2004. *A Dictionary of Smoky Mountain English*. Knoxville: University of Tennessee Press.

Montgomery, Michael. 2001. British and Irish antecedents. In Algeo (ed.), 86–153.

Moore, S., S. B. Meech & Harold Whitehall. 1935. Middle English dialect characteristics and dialect boundaries. *Essays and Studies in English and Comparative Literature*. 1–60.

Moralejo-Gárate, T. 2001. Composite predicates and idiomatisation in Middle English: a corpus-based approach. *Studia Anglica Posnaniensia* 36: 171–87.

Morgan, Jane, Christopher O'Neill & Rom Harré. 1976. *Nicknames, Their Origins and Social Consequences*. London: Routledge.

Morrill, John Stephen (ed.). 1991. *The Impact of the English Civil War*. London: Collins & Brown.

Mortelmans, T. 1994. Understanding German dative verbs and their English and Dutch equivalents: a contrastive study in cognitive grammar. *Antwerp Papers in Linguistics* 78: 1–124.

Morton, H. C. 1998. Burchfield on usage: remaking Fowler's classic. *American Speech* 73: 313–25.

Mufwene, Salikoko S. 2001. African-American English. In Algeo (ed.), 291–324.

Mugglestone, L. (ed.). 2000. *Lexicography and the OED. Pioneers in the Untrodden Forest*. Oxford: Oxford University Press.

Mugglestone, L. 2003. *"Talking Proper": the Rise of Accent as Social Symbol*, 2nd edn. Oxford: Oxford University Press.

Mulcaster, R. 1582. *The First Part of the Elementarie*. London: Vautrollier.

Murray, L. 1795. *English Grammar, Adapted to the Different Classes of Learners*. York. Repr. in facsimile by R. C. Alston, 1974, *English Linguistics 1500–1800* (English Linguistics 106). London: Scolar Press.

Murray, Thomas E. 1997. Attitudes toward married women's surnames: evidence from the American Midwest. *Names* 45: 163–83.

Mustanoja, T. 1960. *Middle English Syntax*. Part I. Helsinki: Société Néophilologique.

Nares, R. 1784. *Elements of orthoepy: containing a Distinct View of the Whole Analogy of the English Language: so far as it relates to Pronunciation, Accent, and Quantity*. London: T. Payne & Son.

National Statistics – the official UK statistics site. 2001. http://www.statistics.gov.uk/

Nevalainen, T. 1987. Change from above: a morphosyntactic comparison of two Early Modern English editions of *The Book of Common Prayer*. In L. Kahlas-Tarkka (ed.), *Neophilologica Fennica* (Mémoires de la Société Néophilologique de Helsinki 45). Helsinki: Société Néophilologique, 295–315.

Nevalainen, T. 1997. Recyling inversion: the case of initial adverbs and negators in early Modern English. *Studia Anglica Posnaniensia* 31: 203–14.

Nevalainen, T. 1999. Early Modern English lexis and semantics. In Lass (ed.), 332–458.

Nevalainen, T. 2000a. Processes of supralocalisation and the rise of Standard English in the early Modern period. In Bermúdez-Otero et al. (eds.), 329–71.

Nevalainen, T. 2000b. Mobility, social networks and language change in Early Modern England. *European Journal of English Studies* 4: 253–64.

Nevalainen, T. & H. Raumolin-Brunberg. 1993. Early Modern English. In Rissanen et al. (eds.), 53–73.

Nevalainen, T. & H. Raumolin-Brunberg (eds.). 1996. *Sociolinguistics and Language History: Studies Based on the Corpus of Early English Correspondence*. Amsterdam and Atlanta, GA: Rodopi.

Nevalainen, T. & H. Raumolin-Brunberg. 2000. The third-person singular -(E)s and -(E)TH revisited: the morphophonemic hypothesis. In Dalton-Puffer & Ritt (eds.), 235–48.

Nevalainen, T. & H. Raumolin-Brunberg. 2003. *Historical Sociolinguistics: Language Change in Tudor and Stuart England* (Longman Linguistics Library). London: Longman.

Nicolaisen, W. F. H. 2001. *Scottish Place-Names: Their Study and Significance*, 2nd edn. London: Batsford.

Nicolaisen, W. F. H. 1970. See Gelling et al., 1970.

Oakden, J. P. 1930–1935. *Alliterative Poetry in Middle English*. Manchester: Manchester University Press.

Ogura, Mieko. 2001. Perceptual factors and word order change in English. *Folia Linguistica Historica* 22: 233–53.

Ohlander, U. 1943. Omission of the object in English. *Studia Neophilologica* 16: 105–27.

Orton, Harold. 1962–71. *A Survey of English Dialects*. Leeds: E. J. Arnold.

Orton, Harold, Stewart Sanderson & John Widdowson (eds.). 1978. *The Linguistic Atlas of England*. London: Croom Helm. Repr. London: Routledge, 1998.

Orton, Harold & Natalia Wright. 1974. *A Word Geography of England*. London: Seminar Press.

Osselton, N. E. 1963. Formal and informal spelling in the 18th century. *English Studies* 44: 267–75.

Osselton, N. E. 1984a. Informal spelling systems in Early Modern English: 1500–1800. In N. F. Blake & C. Jones (eds.), *English Historical Linguistics: Studies in Development*. Sheffield: CECTAL, 123–37.

Osselton, N. E. 1984b. Orm and the improvement of English spelling. In J. Kerling & J. Perryman (eds.), *Studies in Early Middle English Literature*. Leiden: University of Leiden, English Department, 39–50.

Ostler, Nicholas. 2005. *Empires of the World*. London: HarperCollins.

Oxford English Dictionary. 1989, ed. J. A. Simpson & E. S. C. Weiner, 2nd edn. Oxford: Clarendon Press. *OED online*: www.oed.com.

Padel, Oliver. 1985. *Cornish Place-Name Elements*. Nottingham: English Place-Name Society.

Padel, O. J. 1988. *A Popular Dictionary of Cornish Place-Names*. Penzance: Alison Hodge.

Page, R. I. 1973. *An Introduction to English Runes*. London: Methuen.

Palsgrave, J. 1530. *Lesclarcissement de la langue francoyse*.

Parker, Geoffrey (ed.). 1986. *The World: an Illustrated History*. London: Time Books.

Parry, David. 1977. *The Survey of Anglo-Welsh Dialects*, vol. 1, *The South-East*. Swansea: University College.

Parry, David. 1979. *The Survey of Anglo-Welsh Dialects*, vol. 2, *The South West*. Swansea: University College.

Parsons, David. 1997. How long did the Scandinavian language survive in England? Again. In J. Graham-Campbell et al. (eds.), *Vikings and the Danelaw. Select papers from the Proceedings of the 13th Viking Congress*. Oxford: Oxbow, 299–312.

Parsons, David N. & Tania Styles, with the collaboration of Carole Hough. 1997– . *The Vocabulary of English Place-Names* (in progress; 3 vols. by 2005). Nottingham: Centre for English Name Studies.

Pederson, Lee et al. (eds.). 1986–93. *Linguistic Atlas of the Gulf States*, 7 vols. Athens: University of Georgia Press.

Pederson, Lee. 2001. Dialects. In Algeo (ed.), 253–90.

Pesetsky, D. 1995. *Zero Syntax: Experiencers and Cascades*. Cambridge, MA: MIT Press.

Peters, H. 1981a. Zum skandinavischen Lehngut im Altenglischen. *Sprachwissenschaft* 6: 85–124.

Peters, H. 1981b. Onomasiologische Untersuchungen. Zum skandinavischen Lehngut im Altenglischen. *Sprachwissenschaft* 6: 169–85.

Pine, L. G. 1965. *The Story of Surnames*. Newton Abbot: David & Charles.

Pintzuk, Susan. 1993. Verb seconding in Old English: Verb movement to Infl. *The Linguistic Review* 10: 5–35.

Pintzuk, Susan. 1995. Variation and change in Old English clause structure. *Language Variation and Change* 7: 229–260.

Pintzuk, Susan. 1998. *Phrase Structures in Competition: Variation and Change in Old English Word Order* (Outstanding Dissertations in Linguistics). New York: Garland.

Pintzuk, S., G. Tsoulas & A. Warner (eds.). 2000. *Diachronic Syntax: Models and Mechanisms*. Oxford: Oxford University Press.

Piroth, Walther. 1979. *Ortsnamenstudien zur angelsächsischen Wanderung* (Frankfurter historische Abhandlungen 18). Wiesbaden: Harrassowitz.

Plag, Ingo. 1999. *Morphological Productivity: Structural Constraints in English Derivation*. Berlin and New York: Mouton de Gruyter.

Plank, F. 1983. Coming into being among the Anglo-Saxons. In M. Davenport, E. Hansen & H. F. Nielsen (eds.), *Current Topics in English Historical Linguistics*. Odense: Odense University Press, 239–78.

Plank, F. 1984. The modals story retold. *Studies in Language* 8: 305–64.

Poole, J. 1646. *The English Accidence*. London.

Poppe, E. 2002. The 'expanded form' in Insular Celtic and English: some historical and comparative considerations, with special emphasis on Middle Irish. In Filppula, Klemola & Pitkänen (eds.), 237–70.

Postles, David. 1995. *The Surnames of Devon* (English Surnames series 6). Oxford: Leopard's Head Press.

Postles, David. 1998. *The Surnames of Leicestershire and Rutland* (English Surnames series 7). Oxford: Leopard's Head Press.

Potsdam, E. 1997. NegP and subjunctive complements in English. *Linguistic Inquiry* 28: 533–41.

Potter, S. 1975. *Changing English*, 2nd edn (The Language Library). London: André Deutsch.

Pound, L. 1914. *Blends: Their Relation to English Word Formation*. Heidelberg: Winter.

Poussa, P. 1982. The evolution of early Standard English: the creolization hypothesis. *Studia Anglica Posnaniensia* 14: 69–85.

Poussa, P. 1990. A contact-universals origin for periphrastic *do*, with special consideration of OE-Celtic contact. In S. Adamson, V. A. Law, N. Vincent & S. Wright (eds.), *Papers from the 5th International Conference on English Historical Linguistics: Cambridge, 6–9 April 1987* (Current Issues in Linguistic Theory 65). Amsterdam and Philadelphia: Benjamins, 407–34.

Pratt, T. K. (ed.). 1988. *Dictionary of Prince Edward Island English*. Toronto: University of Toronto Press.

Preston, Dennis A. 1996. Where the worst English is spoken. In E. Schneider (ed.), *Focus on the USA*. Amsterdam: Benjamins, 297–361.

Preston, Dennis R. 2003. Presidential address: where are the dialects of American English at anyhow? *American Speech* 78: 235–54.

Preusler, W. 1956. Keltischer Einfluss im Englischen. *Revue des Langues Vivantes* 22: 322–50.

Prokosch, Eduard. 1939. *A Comparative Germanic Grammar*. Baltimore, MD: Linguistic Society of America.

Puttenham, G. 1589. *The Arte of English Poesie*. London. Repr. 1968 (English Linguistics 110). Menston: Scolar Press.

Quirk, Randolph. 1962. *The Use of English*. London: Longman.

Quirk, Randolph. 1985. The English language in a global context. In Randolph Quirk & H. G. Widdowson (eds.), *English in the World*. Cambridge: Cambridge University Press, 1–6.

Quirk, R., S. Greenbaum, G. Leech & J. Svartvik. 1985. *A Comprehensive Grammar of the English Language*. London: Longman.

Quirk, Randolph & Gabriele Stein. 1990. *English in Use*. London: Longman.

Raftery, D. 1997. *Women and Learning in English Writing, 1600–1900*. Dublin: Four Courts Press.

Raper, P. E. 1989. *Dictionary of Southern African Place-Names*, 2nd edn. Johannesburg: Jonathan Ball.

Raumolin-Brunberg, H. 1998. Social factors and pronominal change in the seventeenth century: the Civil War effect? In J. Fisiak & M. Krygier (eds.), *Advances in English Historical Linguistics*. Berlin and New York: Mouton de Gruyter, 361–88.

Rayburn, Alan. 1997. *Dictionary of Canadian Place-Names*. Toronto and Oxford: Oxford University Press.

Read, Allen Walker. 2002. Milestones in the history of English in America, ed. Richard W. Bailey. *Publication of the American Dialect Society* 86.

Reaney, P. H. 1967. *The Origin of English Surnames*. London: Routledge & Kegan Paul.

Reaney, P. H. & R. M. Wilson. 1991. *A Dictionary of English Surnames*, 3rd edn. London: Routledge.

Redin, Mats. 1919. Studies on uncompounded personal names in Old English. Uppsala: University of Uppsala (inaugural dissertation).

Redmonds, George. 1973. *Yorkshire: West Riding* (English Surnames series). Chichester: Phillimore.

Redmonds, George. 1997. *Surnames and Genealogy: a New Approach*. Boston, MA: Genealogical Society.

Renfrew, C. 1987. *Archaeology and Language: the Puzzle of Indo-European Origins*. London: Jonathan Cape.

Riddle, E. M. 1985. A historical perspective on the productivity of the Suffixes -*ness* and -*ity*. In Jacek Fisiak (ed.), *Historical Semantics, Historical Word-Formation*. Berlin: Monton, 435–61.

Rickford, John R. 1999. *African American Vernacular English*. Malden, MA: Blackwell.

Rissanen, M. 1967. *The Uses of One in Old and Early Middle English*. Helsinki: Société Néophilologique.

Rissanen, M. 1998. *Isn't it?* or *Is it not?* On the order of postverbal subject and negative particle in the history of English. In Tieken-Boon van Ostade et al. (eds.), 189–205.

Rissanen, M. 1999a. Syntax. In Lass (ed.), 187–331.

Rissanen, M. 1999b. Language of law and the development of Standard English. In Taavitsainen, Melchers & Pahta (eds.), 189–204.

Rissanen, M. 2000. Standardisation and the language of early statutes. In L. Wright (ed.), *The Development of Standard English 1300–1800: Theories, Descriptions, Conflicts*. Cambridge: Cambridge University Press, 117–30.

Rissanen, M., O. Ihalainen, T. Nevalainen & I. Taavitsainen (eds.). 1992. *History of Englishes: New Methods and Interpretations in Historical Linguistics*. Berlin: Mouton de Gruyter.

Rissanen, M., M. Kytö & M. Palander-Collin (eds.). 1993. *Early English in the Computer Age: Explorations through the Helsinki Corpus*. Berlin and New York: Mouton de Gruyter.

Ritt, N. 1994. *Quantity Adjustment: Vowel Lengthening and Shortening in Early Middle English*. Cambridge: Cambridge University Press.

Roberts, I. 1993. *Verbs and Diachronic Syntax: a Comparative History of English and French*. Dordrecht: Kluwer.

Roberts, I. 1997. Directionality and word order change in the history of English. In van Kemenade & Vincent (eds.), 397–426.

Romaine, S. (ed.). 1998a. *The Cambridge History of the English Language*, vol. 4, *1776–1997*. Cambridge: Cambridge University Press.

Romaine, S. 1998b. Introduction. In Romaine (ed.), 1–56.

Room, Adrian. 1992. *The Street-Names of England*. Stamford: Paul Watkins.

Room, Adrian. 2003. *Penguin Dictionary of British Place-Names*. London: Penguin.

Rosenbach, A., D. Stein & L. Vezzosi. 2000. On the history of the *s*-genitive. In Bermúdez-Otero et al. (eds.), 183–210.

Rothwell, W. 2001. English and French in England after 1362. *English Studies* 82: 539–59.

Rumble, Alexander R. & A. D. Mills (eds.). 1997. *Names, Places and People: an Onomastic Miscellany for John McNeal Dodgson*. Stamford: Paul Watkins.

Ryan, Keith (ed.). 1999. *The Official Commemorative Album for the Millennium*. London: Citroen Wolf Communications.

Salmon, V. 1989. John Rastell and the normalisation of early sixteenth-century orthography. In L. Egil Breivik, A. Hille & S. Johansson (eds.), *Essays on English Language in Honour of Bertil Sundby*. Oslo: Novus Forlag, 289–301.

Samuels, M. L. 1963. Some applications of Middle English dialectology. *English Studies* 44: 81–94.

Samuels, M. L. 1971. Kent and the low countries. In A. J. Aitken, A. McIntosh & H. Palsson (eds.), *Edinburgh Studies in English and Scots*. London: Longman, 1–19.

Sapir, E. 1921. *Language*. New York: Henry Holt.

Savory, T. H. 1967. *The Language of Science*. London: Deutsch.

Schabram, H. 1965. *Superbia. Studien zum altenglischen Wortschatz*, vol. 1, *Die dialektale und zeitliche Verbreitung des Wortgutes*. Munich: Fink.

Schäfer, J. 1980. *Documentation in the 'O.E.D.': Shakespeare and Nash as Test Cases*. Oxford: Clarendon Press.

Schäfer, J. 1989. *Early Modern English Lexicography*, 2 vols. Oxford: Clarendon Press.

Schama, Simon. 1995. *Landscape and Memory*. London: HarperCollins.

Scheler, M. 1977. *Der englische Wortschatz* (Grundlagen der Anglistik und Amerikanistik 9). Berlin: Schmidt.

Schendl, H. 2000. Third person present plural in Shakespeare's First Folio. In Dalton-Puffer & Ritt (eds.), 263–76.

Schneider, E. 1992. *Who(m)*? Constraints on the loss of case marking of *wh*-pronouns in the English of Shakespeare and other poets of the Early Modern English period. In Rissanen et al. (eds.), 437–52.

Schneider, E. W. (ed.). 1997. *Englishes around the World*. Amsterdam: Benjamins.

Schneider, E. W. 2000. Feature diffusion vs. contact effects in the evolution of New Englishes: a typological case study of negation patterns. *English World-Wide* 21: 201–30.

Schwartz, R. M. 1999. Railways and population change in industrializing England: an introduction to historical GIS. http://www.mtholyoke.edu/courses/rschwart/rail/intro_hist_gis.htm

Scragg, D. G. 1974. *A History of English Spelling*. Manchester: Manchester University Press.

Searle, W. E. 1897. *Onomasticon anglo-saxonicum*. London: Whiting.

Seaton, M. 2001. Word up. *The Guardian*: 21 Sept.

Sebba, Mark. 1993. *London Jamaican*. London: Longman.

Seltén, Bo. 1972, 1979. *The Anglo-Saxon Heritage in Middle English Personal Names: East Anglia 1100–1399*, vols. I, II (Lund Studies in English 43; Acta Reg. Soc. Hum. Litt. Lundensis 73). Lund: Gleerup.

Semenza, Carlo. 1995. How names are special: neuropsychological evidence for dissociable impairment and sparing of proper names. Knowledge in production. In R. Campbell & M. Conway (eds.), *Broken Memories: Neuropsychological Case Studies*. Oxford: Blackwell.

Semenza, Carlo. 1997. Proper names specific aphasias. In H. Goodglass & A. Wingfield (eds.), *Anomia: Neuroanatomical and Cognitive Correlates*. New York: Academic Press, 115–34.

Semenza, Carlo & Marina Zettin. 1989a. Generating proper names: a case of selective inability. *Cognitive Neuropsychology* 5: 711–21.

Semenza, Carlo & Marina Zettin. 1989b. Evidence from aphasia for the role of proper names as pure referring expressions. *Nature* 342: 678–9.

Serjeantson, M. S. 1935. *A History of Foreign Words in English*. London: Routledge & Kegan Paul.

Sheridan, T. 1780. *A General Dictionary of the English Language*. London: J. Dodsley, C. Dilly & J. Wilkie.

Shuman, R. B. 1985. English language in the secondary school. In S. Greenbaum (ed.), *The English Language Today*. Oxford: Pergamon Press, 314–26.

Siegel, J. 1995. How to get a laugh in Fijian: code-switching and humour. *Language in Society* 24: 95–110.

Simon, J. 1980. *Paradigms Lost. Reflections on Literacy and its Decline*. London: Penguin.

Sisam, Kenneth. 1921. *Fourteenth Century Verse and Prose*. Oxford: Clarendon Press.

Smart, Veronica. 1979. Moneyers' names on the Anglo-Saxon coinage. *Nomina* 3: 20–8.

Smith, A. H. 1956. *English Place-Name Elements*, 2 vols. (EPNS vols. 25, 26). Cambridge: Cambridge University Press.

Smith, Jeremy J. 1996. *An Historical Study of English*. London: Routledge.

Sørensen, K. 1957. Latin influence on English syntax; a survey with a bibliography. *Travaux du Cercle Linguistique de Copenhague* 16: 131–55.

Stanley, E. G. 1971, Studies in the prosaic vocabulary of Old English verse. *Neuphilologische Mitteilungen* 72: 385–418.

Statistical abstract of the United States. 2001. http://www.census.gov/prod/www/statistical-abstract-us.html

Stein, G. 1978. English combining forms. *Linguistica* 9: 140–7.

Stewart, George R. 1967. *Names on the Land: a Historical Account of Place-Naming in the United States*, 3rd edn. Boston: Houghton Mifflin.

Stewart, George R. 1970. *A Concise Dictionary of American Place-Names*. Oxford: Oxford University Press.

Stewart, George R. 1979. *American Given Names, their Origin and History in the Context of the English Language*. New York: Oxford University Press.

Stockwell, R. P. & D. Minkova. 1988. The English vowel shift: problems of coherence and explanation. In Kastovsky & Bauer (eds.), 395–410.

Stone, L. 1964. The educational revolution in England 1560–1640. *Past and Present* 28: 41–80.

Stone, L. 1969. Literacy and education in England 1640–1900. *Past and Present* 42: 69–139.

Story, George Morley, William J. Kirwin & John David Allison Widdowson (eds.). 1990. *Dictionary of Newfoundland English*, 2nd edn. Toronto: University of Toronto Press. Digital version at <www.heritage.nf.ca/dictionary>.

Strang, B. M. H. 1970. *A History of English*. London: Methuen.

Ström, Hilmer. 1939. *Old English Personal Names in Bede's History* (Lund Studies in English 8). Lund: Gleerup.

Sutcliffe, David. 1982. *British Black English*. Oxford: Blackwell.

Svensson, Ann-Marie. 1997. *Middle English Words for 'Town': a Study of Changes in a Semantic Field* (Gothenburg Studies in English 70). Gothenburg: University of Gothenburg.

Sweet, Henry. 1876. Dialects and prehistoric forms of Old English. *Transactions of the Philological Society* 16: 543–69.

Sweet, H. 1877. *A Primer of Phonetics*. Oxford: Clarendon Press.

Sweet, Henry. 1890. *A Primer of Spoken English*. Oxford: Clarendon Press.

Sykes, Bryan, & Catherine Irven. 2000. Surnames and the Y chromosome. *American Journal of Human Genetics* 66: 1417–19.

Taavitsainen, I. & P. Pahta. 1997. Corpus of Early English medical writing 1375–1750. *ICAME Journal* 21: 71–8.

Taavitsainen, I., G. Melchers & P. Pahta (eds.). 1999. *Writing in Nonstandard English*. Amsterdam and Philadelphia: Benjamins.

Tanaka, T. 2000. On the development of transitive expletive constructions in the history of English. *Lingua* 110: 473–95.

Taylor, A. & W. van der Wurff (eds.). 2005. *Aspects of OV and VO Word Order in the History of English*. Special issue of *English Language and Linguistics*.

Tengstrand, Erik. 1940. *A Contribution to the Study of Genitival Composition in Old English Place-Names* (Nomina Germanica 7). Uppsala: Almqvist & Wiksell.

Thomas, Alan R. 1994. English in Wales. In Burchfield (ed.), 94–147.

Thomason, S. G. & T. Kaufman. 1988. *Language Contact, Creolization, and Genetic Linguistics*. Berkeley, Los Angeles and London: University of California Press.

Thompson, S. A. 1995. The iconicity of 'dative shift' in English: considerations from information flow in discourse. In M. E. Landsberg (ed.), *Syntactic Iconicity and Linguistic Freezes: the Human Dimension* (Studies in Anthropological Linguistics 9). Berlin: Mouton de Gruyter, 155–75.

Thompson, S. A. 1988. A discourse approach to the cross-linguistic category 'adjective'. In J. Hawkins (ed.), *Explaining Language Universals*. Oxford: Blackwell, 168–85.

Tieken-Boon van Ostade, I. 1982. Double negation and eighteenth-century English grammars. *Neophilologus* 66: 278–86.

Tieken-Boon van Ostade, I. 1985. 'I will be drowned and no man shall save me': the conventional rules for *shall* and *will* in eighteenth-century English grammars. *English Studies* 66: 123–42.

Tieken-Boon van Ostade, I. 1996a. Social network theory and eighteenth-century English: the case of Boswell. In Britton (ed.), 327–37.

Tieken-Boon van Ostade, Ingrid (ed.). 1996b. *Two Hundred Years of Lindley Murray*. Muenster: Nodus Publikationen.

Tieken-Boon van Ostade, I. 1998. Standardization of English spelling: the eighteenth-century printers' contribution. In J. Fisiak & M. Krygier (eds.), *English Historical Linguistics 1996*. Berlin: Mouton de Gruyter, 457–470.

Tieken-Boon van Ostade, I. 2000. Normative studies in England. In S. Auroux, E. F. K. Koerner, H.-J. Niederehe & K. Versteegh (eds.), *History of the Language Sciences*. Berlin and New York: Walter de Gruyter, 876–87.

Tieken-Boon van Ostade, I., G. Tottie & W. van der Wurff (eds.). 1998. *Negation in the History of English*. Berlin: Mouton de Gruyter.

Tierney, J. E. 1988. *The Correspondence of Robert Dodsley 1733–1764*. Cambridge: Cambridge University Press.

Todd, Loreto & Ian Hancock. 1986. *International English Usage*. London: Croom Helm.

Townend, M. 2002. *Language and History in Viking Age England: Linguistic Relations between Speakers of Old Norse and Old English* (Studies in the Early Middle Ages 6). Turnhout: Brepols.

Trask, R. L. 1996. *Historical Linguistics*. London: Arnold.

Traugott, E. C. 1992. Syntax. In Hogg (ed.), 168–289.

Tristram, H. L. C. (ed.). 1997. *The Celtic Englishes* (Anglistische Forschungen 247). Heidelberg: Winter.

Tristram, H. L. C. (ed.). 2000. *The Celtic Englishes II* (Anglistische Forschungen 286). Heidelberg: Winter.

Tristram, H. L. C. (ed.). 2003. *The Celtic Englishes III* (Anglistische Forschungen 324). Heidelberg: Winter.

Trudgill, Peter. 1974. *The Social Differentiation of English in Norwich*. Cambridge: Cambridge University Press.

Trudgill, P. 1986. *Dialects in Contact*. Oxford: Blackwell.

Trudgill, P. 1999a. Standard English: what it isn't. In T. Bex & R. Watts (eds.), *Standard English: the Widening Debate*. London and New York: Routledge, 117–128.

Trudgill, Peter. 1999b. *The Dialects of England*, 2nd edn. Oxford: Blackwell.

Trudgill, P. & J. Hannah. 1994. *International English: a Guide to Varieties of Standard English*. London: Edward Arnold.

Tucker, A. [pseud. Edward Search, Esq.] 1773. *Vocal Sound*. London: T. Jones.

Uchida, M. 2002. From participles to conjunctions: a parallel corpus study of grammaticalization in English and French. In T. Saito, J. Nakamura & S. Yamazaki (eds.), *English Corpus Linguistics in Japan*. Amsterdam: Rodopi, 131–46.

Ukaji, M. 1992. 'I not say': bridge phenomenon in syntactic change. In Rissanen et al. (eds.), 453–62.

University of Michigan. 2001. http://www.lib.umich.edu/govdocs/frames/sttranfr.html

van Lancker, D. & K. Klein. 1990. Preserved comprehension of proper names in global aphasia. *Brain and Language* 39: 511–29.

Vennemann, T. 2001. Atlantis Semitica: structural contact features in Celtic and English. In L. J. Brinton (ed.), *Historical Linguistics 1999: Selected Papers from the 14th International Conference on Historical Linguistics, Vancouver, 9–13 August 1999* (Current Issues in Linguistic Theory 215). Amsterdam and Philadelphia, PA: John Benjamins, 350–69.

Victorians. 2001. http://www.thesite.org/victorians/communications/the_postal_service. html

Visser F. Th. 1963–73. *An Historical Syntax of the English Language*, vols. I–IIIb. Leiden: Brill.

Wakelin, Martin. 1977. *English Dialects: an Introduction*. London: Athlone Press.

Walker, J. 1790–1. *A Critical Pronouncing Dictionary and Expositor of the English Language*. London: G. G. J. & J. Robinson.

Wallenberg, J. K. 1931. *Kentish Place-Names*. Uppsala: Lundequist.

Wallenberg, J. K. 1934. *The Place-Names of Kent*. Uppsala: Appelberg.

Wallis, J. 1653. *Grammatica Linguae Anglicanae*. Oxford. Repr. in facsimile by R. C. Alston, 1974, *English Linguistics 1500–1800* (English Linguistics 142). London: Scolar Press.

Wallmannsberger, J. 1988. The 'creole hypothesis' in the history of English. In M. Markus (ed.), *Historical English: on the Occasion of Karl Brunner's 100th Birthday* (Innsbrucker Beiträge zur Kulturwissenschaft, Anglistische Reihe 1). Innsbruck: Institut für Anglistik, Universität Innsbruck, 19–36.

Ward, I. C. 1929. *The Phonetics of English*. Cambridge: Heffer.

Wareing, J. 1980. Changes in the geographical distribution of the recruitment of apprentices to the London companies 1486–1750. *Journal of Historical Geography* 6: 241–9.

Warner, A. 1983. Review article on Lightfoot (1979). *Journal of Linguistics* 19: 187–209.

Warner, A. 1993. *English Auxiliaries. Structure and History*. Cambridge: Cambridge University Press.

Warner, A. 1997. The structure of parametric change and V-movement in the history of English. In van Kemenade & Vincent (eds.), 380–93.

Watts, V. E. 2002. *A Dictionary of County Durham Place-Names*. Nottingham: English Place-Name Society.

Watts, V. E. 2004. *Cambridge Dictionary of English Place-Names*. Cambridge: Cambridge University Press.

Weale, Michael E., et al. 2002. Y chromosome evidence for Anglo-Saxon mass migration. *Molecular Biology and Evolution* 19: 1008–21.

Webster, Noah. 1789. *Dissertations on the English Language*. Boston. Facsimile edn. Menston: Scolar Press, 1967.

Webster, Noah. 1807. *A Philosophical and Practical Grammar of the English Language.*

Webster, Noah. 1828. *An American Dictionary of the English Language.* New York: S. Converse. Facsimile edn. New York: Johnson Reprint, 1970.

Weeks, Fred, Alan Glover, Peter Strevens & Edward Johnson. 1984. *Seaspeak Reference Manual.* Oxford: Pergamon.

Weerman, F. 1993. The diachronic consequences of first and second language axcquisition: The change from OV to VO. *Linguistics* 31: 903–931.

Wells, J. C. 1982. *Accents of English*, 3 vols. Cambridge: Cambridge University Press.

Wells, J. C. 1990. *Longman Pronunciation Dictionary.* London: Longman.

Wenisch, F. 1979. *Spezifisch anglisches Wortgut in den nordhumbrischen Interlinear-glossierungen des Lukasevangeliums* (Anglistische Forschungen 132). Heidelberg: Carl Winter.

White, D. L. 2002. Explaining the innovations of Middle English: what, where, and why. In Filppula et al. (eds.), 153–74.

White, Richard Grant. 1870. *Words and their Uses, Past and Present: a Study of the English Language.* New York: Sheldon & Co.

Williams, J. M. 1975. *Origins of the English Language: a Social and Linguistic History.* New York: The Free Press.

Williams, Roger. 1643. *A Key into the Language of America*, eds. J. J. Teunissen & E. J. Hinz. Detroit: Wayne State University Press, 1973.

Wilson, Stephen. 1998. *The Means of Naming: a Social and Cultural History of Personal Naming in Western Europe.* London: UCL Press.

Withycombe, E. G. 1977. *Oxford Dictionary of English Christian Names*, 3rd edn. Oxford: Oxford University Press.

Wolfson, Nessa. 1979. The conversational historical present alternation. *Language 55*: 168–82.

World Bank country data. 2003. http://www.worldbank.org/data/databytopic/databytopic.html

Wright, Joseph. 1892. *A Grammar of the Dialect of Windhill.* London: Kegan Paul, Trench, Trübner.

Wright, Joseph. 1898–1905. *The English Dialect Dictionary.* Oxford: Oxford University Press.

Wrigley, E. A. & R. S. Schofield. 1981. *The Population History of England, 1541–1871: a Reconstruction* (Studies in Social and Demographic History). London: Edward Arnold for the Cambridge Group for the History of Population and Social Structure.

van der Wurff, W. 1989. A remarkable gap in the history of English syntax. *Folia Linguistica Historica* 9, 117–59.

Zachrisson, R. E. 1924. The French element. In A. Mawer & F. M. Stenton (eds.), *Introduction to the Survey of English Place-Names* (part I). Cambridge: Cambridge University Press (EPNS vol. 1), 93–114.

Index

acronyms 214, 270
Adams, John 417
Adamson, S. 126, 303
adjectives 56, 111, 115–16, 122; *see also under*
    Middle English, Old English
  attributive 122
  predicative 122, 124
  weak and strong forms 117, 124, 125,
    126
adjuncts 125
adverbial phrases 190
adverbs 113, 125, 126, 190, 245, 398
  position of 156, 190, 192
advertising 428
Ælfric 35, 218, 355, 358, 359
  Grammar and Vocabulary 215
  vocabulary 358
African American English 410–12
  features of 411
  grammar 411
  pronunciation 410, 411
  vocabulary 411
air travel 24, 430
Airspeak 430
Aitchison, J. 205
Aitken, A. J. 380, 437
  Aitken's Law 380, 383
Alfred 11, 35
  standardisation 271, 273
  writings 30, 218, 355
Algeo, J. 266
Algonquian words 384, 399
Allen, Alex 423
Allen, C. L. 119, 168
Allen, H. B. 398
Alston, R. C. 285
American Dialect Society 404
American English 22, 247, 300, 309, 399
  adverbs 398
  African American English 410–12
  Atlas of North American English 404–8
  borrowing 385, 394–6, 399
    from French 394
    from German 395
    from Spanish 395

    from West African languages 395
    from Yiddish 395–6
Chicano English 412
codification of 393
collective nouns 396
colonial 384–91
  character of 388
  origins of 387–90
consonants 408
dialects 401, 404, 412, 418
Dictionary of American Regional English
  399–404
Ebonics 436
ellipsis 397
ethnic dialects 410
French loan words 394–5
got 397
homogeneity of 389
infinitive markers 397
innovation 394, 399
interrogatives 397
Latino English 412–13, 416
negation 397
Northern Cities Shift 405–6, 408, 411, 413
nouns 396–7, 398
official languages 417–18
personal names 324
place-names 390–1
pluricentric 309
prepositions 398
/r/ 409
regional patterns 398–9
relative clauses 397
social dialects 408–9
social meanings and attitudes 416–17
Southern Shift 406–7, 408
Spanish influence 413
St Louis Corridor 408
standardisation 273
syntax 396–8
ValSpeak 42
verbs 397, 398
vowels 405–8, 416
American Name Society 351
Anderson, O. 319

Anglo-Saxon Chronicle 14, 35, 224, 318, 355
Anglo-Saxons 1, 9–10, 217
Anshen, F. 260
Aronoff, M. 260, 289
articles 55, 117, 121
Ash, S. 418
Ashley, L. R. N. 336
Atkinson, D. 306
Atlas of North American English 404–8
Auchinleck MS 275
Austen, Jane 36
Austin, F. 291
Australia 22, 41, 437
    Australian Question Intonation 41
    dictionaries 266, 309
    place-names 336
Axtell, J. 389

Baayen, R. H. 260
Bailey, N. 283
Bailey, R. W. 385, 392, 415, 422
Baker, R. 285
Barber, C. 279
Barbour, John 366
Bardsley, C. W. 322
Barnes, William 273
Barry, H. III 324
Bauer, L. 210
Baugh, A. C. 220, 221, 274, 283, 284
Bede 3, 9, 10, 318
Bell, E. O. 323
Beier, A. L. 18
Benedictine Reform 217, 218, 220, 221
Benskin, M. 359, 362
Beowulf 186, 219, 220, 355
den Besten, H. 182
Biber, D. 304, 305
    LGSWE 297, 298, 299, 301
    objects 190, 297
    subordinate clauses 171, 297
Bible, translations and versions 28
    Authorised Version 28, 46, 96, 295
bilingualism 14, 224, 246, 272
Blake, N. 277
Bloomfield, L. 205
Blount, Thomas 301
Bodine, A. 274
Bokenham 97, 368
Bolinger, D. 123
Book of Common Prayer 28, 294
borrowing 17, 202, 203, 205, 206, 215, 270, 279,
        385; *see also* under American English,
        Early Modern English, Middle English,
        Old English
Boyle, Robert 305
Breeze, A. 336, 337

Bright, William 317, 336
Brightman, J. 335
Brinton, L. 135, 137, 414, 415, 416
Britain 15, 18, 21, 24, 247
    French language use 246
    immigration and emigration 17–29
    imperial power 21–2, 259–427
    linguistic variation in 15
British Black English 383
British National Corpus 34
Britton, D. 74, 369
broadcasting 34, 377, 428–9
Bronstein, A. 309
Brown, K. 381
Bullokar, W. 284
Burchfield, R. 297, 310
Burke, D. M. 312
Burnley, D. 230, 249, 251, 290
Burrow, J. A. 365
Butters, R. 412
Bybee, J. 48

Cable, T. 220, 221, 274, 283, 284
Cambridge History of the English Language xiii
Cameron, D. 34
Cameron, K. 335, 349
Campbell, Alistair 354, 356
Canada 22, 23, 391, 392, 413–16
    grammar 415–16
    homogeneity of 414
    rhotic character 415
    spelling 416
    vocabulary 415
    Newfoundland 413
    official languages 417
    pronunciation 414–15
    Quebec 414, 417
canals 24
Caon, L. 290
Cape Town Standard English 107
Carlyle, Thomas 32
Carney, E. 290
Carr, C. T. 233, 234
Carroll, Lewis 269
Carver, C. 385, 395, 403, 404
case 111, 211
    agreement 163
    loss of 115, 187, 189
Cassidy, F. G. 25, 266
Cawdrey, Robert 257, 302
Caxton, William 256, 277–9, 301, 439
    pronouns 75
    spelling 289, 294
    vocabulary 279
Celtic languages 8, 9
    substratum for English 136, 154, 225–6

Chambers, J. K. 39, 299, 374
  Canadian English 414, 415, 416
Chancery English 275, 277, 287, 294, 303, 368,
    369
  institutional role 287, 293
  selection as standard 274, 275
  Statutes of the Realm 304
change, language 36, 37–42, 43–6, 109, 110, 293
  from above or below 272, 274, 282, 294
  description and explanation 110
  factors in 38–9
  laws of 74
  and names 313
  radical 147–9
  sound change 356, 359
  synchronic and diachronic 114, 115
  vertical and horizontal 46
Chapman, C. 375
Charles, B. G. 336
Chaucer 32, 62, 71, 72, 117, 126, 273, 275
  Canterbury Tales 15, 68, 77, 79, 287, 360, 364
  consensus MSS 71, 75, 81
  dialect 275
  The Grocers' Ordinances 78
  stress 67, 69
  tense 133, 135
  Treatise on the Astrolabe 78
  Troilus & Criseyde 44–5, 67
Cheshire, J. 298, 299, 379, 380
Chicano English 412
  grammar 413
  pronunciation 412–13
  vocabulary 413
Chomsky, N. 205, 252
Christianity, influence on English 28, 271, 358
Chronicle of Robert of Gloucester 14
Church of England 28
civil war 25, 32
Clapham, P. 274
Claridge, C. 192
Clark, C. 314, 320, 349
clauses, constituents of 160–81
  impersonal constructions 166–8
  infinitival clauses 172–7, 193–5
  objects 164–6
  passive voice 168–71
  relative clauses 127–8, 397
  subjects 160–4
  subordinate clauses 171–2, 177–9, 180–1, 182
Clift family letters 291
Cnut 12
Coates, Richard 312–51, 359
Cohen, G. 312
Cole, A. 335, 340
Cole, Elisha 301, 340
Colman, F. 187, 314, 318, 319

Combe, William 316
communication 18, 22, 24–5, 33, 423, 431
comparative reconstruction 6–7
Cooper, Christopher 83, 97, 99–100
  postvocalic /r/ 92
  stress 94
  verbs 99–100
  vowels 85, 86, 88, 90, 91
  vowels 85, 86, 88, 90, 91; lengthening of
    vowels 86, 89, 90
Coote, Edmund 370
Coplestone-Crow, B. 335
Corpus of Early English Correspondence 41, 293
Coseriu, E. 205
Cota, A. A. 335
Coupland, N. 382
Cox, B. 347
creole languages 16, 17, 424, 436
Cresswell, Nicholas 389, 390
Cressy, D. 290, 295
Croft, W. 39
Cromwell, Thomas 296
Crowley, E. T. 270
Cruse, A. D. 205
Cruttenden, Alan 308
Crystal, David 1, 190, 300, 302, 308, 420–6
Cullen, P. 335
Culpeper, J. 274
culture 18, 39, 201, 224
Cursor Mundi 201, 361
Cuthwulf, King 325
Cutler, A. 323

Dalton-Puffer, C. 251, 252
Danchev, A. 16, 180
Danelaw 11, 16, 224, 338
Danielsson, B. 306
Davidse, K. 166
DeCamp, D. 354
Dekeyser, X. 299
Denison, David 1–38, 115
  auxiliary 157, 158
  determiners 120, 121
  do 155, 157
determiners 56, 70, 71, 111, 116–21
dialects 353, 376, 388
  levelling 352, 379, 380, 381, 382, 389
  study of 352–3, 379
  survival of 378, 379, 412
  unintelligibility 435
  urban and rural 378, 379, 380
Dickens, Charles 433
dictionaries 256, 257, 266
  specialist 302
  standardisation and 279–82, 283, 296, 299,
    307, 308

Dictionary of American Regional English (*DARE*) 399–404
Dieth, Eugen 372
diffusion 37–8, 39, 64, 177, 288, 295
Dillard, J. L. 389
Dion, K. L. 335
diphthongs 49, 53, 60–1
Dissolution of the Monasteries 35
do 154–5, 157
  causative 154–5
  as an empty operator 112, 154, 155
Dobson, E. J. 370
Dodgson, J. M. 343
Dodsley, Robert 283
Domesday Book 12, 317, 339, 348
Donne, John 103
Dressler, W. 227
Duggan, D. A. 335
Dunbar, William 376
Dutch 129, 137, 152, 194

eager-to-please constructions 175, 176, 177
Early Modern English 81–104, 367–70
  borrowing 257–9
    from Celtic languages 259
    from Dutch 259
    from French 258
    from Greek 259
    from Italian 259
    from Latin 257–8
    from Portuguese 259
    from Spanish 259
  clipping 213
  dialects 369
  evidence, historical 367, 376
  orthography 256
  phonology 81–3
  standardisation 256
  vocabulary 256
  voiceless fricatives 370
  word formation 256, 260
    acronyms 265
    blending 265
    clipping 265
    compounding 260–1
    prefixation 260, 261–3
    suffixation 260
    verbs 265
    zero derivation 265
East India Company 23
easy-to-please constructions 175, 176
Eble, C. C. 392
Ebonics 436
Eckert, P. 416
Eco, U. 423
Eddis, William 389, 390

education 290, 311, 367, 377, 430–1, 434
  and religion 28–9, 273
  universities 20, 247
Edward the Confessor 12, 226
Edwards, J. 421
Ekwall, E. 335, 361
electronic mail 33
Elizabeth I 322
  writings 90, 95, 102, 104, 290, 294
Ellegård, Alvar 157, 158
Elliot, R. W. 279
ellipsis 40, 397
Ellis, A. J. 92, 106, 307
  dialects 371, 376
  vowels 104, 105
Elsness, J. 140–1
Elworthy, T. 371
Encyclopaedia Britannica 424
England 8–17, 258, 272, 274, 354
  bilingualism 272, 273
English 2, 3–8, 48, 276–7, 282–4, 300
  acceptance as standard 275–6
  in Britain 352–83, 385–6, 387
  British Black English 383
  colonial 384–8, 390, 391
  East Midland dialect 275
  Estuary English 311, 378
  Euro-English 438
  as a family of languages 435–9
  as a first language 1, 424, 438
  French loanwords 14, 16
  global: *see* global English
  Greater London variety 275
  hybrids 438, 439
  inflection 45, 72, 109
  London English 295, 387
  New Englishes 422, 433, 435
  number of speakers 424, 425
  onomastics 317–18
  prestige of 432–3
  as a second language 424, 434, 438
  for special purposes 301, 305
  special role 423, 427
  syntax 282, 284, 396–8
  varieties of 2, 48, 107, 266, 432–3, 437–8
  Welsh English 382
  Wycliffite 275
English Academy 283
English Dialect Dictionary 300
English Dialect Society 371
Essential English for International Maritime Use 430
Estuary English 311, 378
Ethelred 12
etymologising movement 280–1
Euro-English 438

European Union 423, 438
evidence, historical 29–35, 104, 217
    Anglo-Saxon period 318
    lack of 7, 201, 355–6, 358, 388, 422
    Middle English 63
    Old English 35–6, 52–3, 217
Exceptional Case Marking construction 193–5
Exeter Book 355

Farman 359
Fee, M. 414, 415, 416
Fellows-Jensen, G. 347, 348
Field, J. 337
Fielding, Henry 291
Fielding, Sarah 291
Fillmore, C. J. 207
films 34–5, 429
Filppula, M. 136
Finegan, Edward 300, 384–418
Finkenstaedt, T. 256, 266, 267
Finlay, R. 18, 24
First World War 26
Fischer, D. H. 386
Fischer, Olga 109, 131–59, 164, 299,
    366
Fisher, J. H. 25, 275, 276, 287, 288
Flint, Mather 89, 90, 92
Florio, John 96
focussing 287–311
    grammar 291, 299
    institutions 294
    pronunciation 306
    vocabulary 306
Foley, J. A. 438
Fought, C. 412, 413
Fowler, H. W. 285, 303
France 247, 249, 258, 267, 372
Francis, W. N.
Franklin, Benjamin 417
Fransson, G. 330
French 248
    word order 209
French influence 12, 14–16, 17, 246, 247,
    248
    in learned and public spheres 59, 247, 274
    syntax 185, 187
French loanwords 16, 165, 274
    in America 394–5
    ecclesiastical words 249–50
    government and administrative terms 249, 271,
        338, 382
    legal terms 250
    in Middle English 247
    and personal names 322
    words for fashion, food, social life 250
Frisian 6, 226

Gammeltoft, P. 347
Garmonsway, G. N. 11
Gates, H. L. 412
Gawain and the Grene Knight 364, 366
Geckler, H. 205
Geipel, J. 223
Gelling, M. 335, 336, 340
gender 52, 55, 70, 115
genealogy 317
General English 298
German 47, 129, 137, 152, 194, 372
Germanic language 3, 5, 8, 109
    case 55
    names 319
    pronunciation 68, 93
    verbs 57, 80, 146
    vocabulary 204
    vowel attrition 61
    word formation 208
Germanic Stress Rule 54, 67, 69, 94
gerunds 178–9, 181
Gil, Alexander 87, 93, 288, 369
Gimbutas, M. P. 5
Gimson, A. C. 308
global English 266, 310, 420–5, 426–31, 432–5
    economic factors 427
    factors in its spread 422, 427
    future of 432–5
Gloucester Chronicle 179
Glover, A. 430
Gneuss, H. 216, 218, 222
Godden, M. R. 218
Goh Chok Tong 433
Gordon, I. A. 281, 300
Görlach, M. 16, 34–5, 256, 266, 267, 303
Gower 81, 275
Graddol, D. 421, 422, 425
Graeco-Latin loanwords 68, 303
Gramley, J. 298
grammar 38, 204, 211, 291–9, 371
    focussed 289
    standard and non-standard 299
    variability in 45
grammar books 283, 296, 297
grammaticalisation 116, 130, 142, 155, 160,
        213
    of the auxiliaries 133, 160
    of the future tense marker 133
    of the modal verb 145
    of the perfect tense 139, 140
    of periphrastic constructions 137, 144, 153,
        154
    of the progressive 137
Great Vowel Shift 81–3, 252, 370, 405
Greek 6, 28
Green, L. 411

Greenwood, James 100–1, 284
Grenoble, L. A. 421
Grimm's Law 7
Grote, David 300
Guildhall Letter Books 275

Haegeman, L. 161, 162
Haiman, J. 39
Hall, J. H. 25
Halle, M. 252
Halliday, M. A. K. 306
Halliwell, 371
Hamerow, H. F. 337
Hancock, I. 397
Hanley, J. R. 312
Hannah, J. 309
Hansen, B. H. 16, 223
Harley, Lady Brilliana 290
Harley, Sir Robert 290
Harold 12
Harper, A. S. 324
Harriot, Thomas 384
Harris, A. C. 130, 149
Harris, J. 383
Hart, John 83–4, 306
   adjectives 95
   consonants 84, 93
   palatals and palatalisation 86, 93
   vowels 84, 88, 90
      mergers of 86, 87, 88, 90
Hartman, James 308
Hebrew 28
Heikkonen, K. 275
Hellinga, L. 279
Hellinga, W. 279
Helsinki corpora of texts and correspondence 41,
      293, 301
Henry II 15, 247
Henry III 35
Henry V 274, 339
Heptarchy of kingdoms 10
high rising terminal contour 41
Hiltunen, R. 137, 223, 235, 236
historiography 81
history 8, 43–6, 83, 104
Hodges, Richard 85, 88, 93, 103
Hofland, K. 301
Hofstetter, W. 218
Hogg, Richard 1–38, 79, 238, 352–83
Hopper, P. J. 122
Horgan, D. M. 236
Horovitz, D. 335
Hughes, G. 217
Hundred Years' War 25
Hurston, Nora Zeale 411
hyponymy 205

Iglesias-Rábade, L. 165
Ihalainen, T. 371, 375–6
Ilson, R. F. 285
India 23
Indo-European language 3, 5, 69, 204, 245
industrialisation 21, 24, 427
Ine, King of Wessex 272, 274
infinitival clauses 172–7, 193–5
infinitive 57, 172, 175, 397
   changes in 174, 175
inflection 45, 51–2, 109, 212
   loss of 118, 139
   and word-formation 211, 238, 245
Inkhorn Controversy 27, 257, 280
innovation 37, 39, 378
Inns of Court 20
Insley, J. 319
International Civil Aviation Organization 430
International Council of Onomastic Sciences 351
International Phonetic Alphabet 307
international travel 430
internet 431
interrogatives 112, 156, 184, 197, 397
Ireland 24, 382–3
   Ulster English 383
   Wexford dialects 382
isoglosses 6, 24–5, 402

Jack, G. B. 179
Jackson, K. H. 221
Janda, R. D. 119
Jespersen, O. 214, 299
Johansson, S. 301
John, King of England 247, 274
John of Trevisa 360–1, 368
Johnson, E. 290
Johnson, F. R. 282
Johnson, Dr Samuel 96, 256, 283, 286, 299, 302
Johnson, J. 293, 295
Johnson, S. 296
Jones, C. 309
Jones, Daniel 307, 308, 309
Jonson, Ben 92, 284
journalism 32
Junius manuscript 355
Jutes 9

Kachru, B. 425
Kallen, J. L. 382
Kärre, K. 234
Kastovsky, Dieter 199–270
Kaufman, T. 16
Kay, J. 312
Keast, W. R. 299
van Kemenade, A. 182, 183, 186, 196
kennings 219, 234

Kenyon, John 309
Kerswill, Paul 381–2
King James Bible 294
Kirkby, John 94, 100
Kitson, P. 341, 358, 359
Klein, K. 312
Klemola, J. 154
Knott, Thomas 309
Krapp, G. P. 392, 399
Kripke, S. 314
Kristensson, G. 357, 361
Kroch, A. 16, 184, 187
Kroesch, S. 222
Kurath, Hans 388–9, 398, 399, 401
Kynvett, Thomas 97
Kytö, M. 180

Labov, William 41, 379, 404, 408, 416, 418
Laing, M. 61, 63, 66, 360
Laird, C. G. 387, 395
Lance, D. M. 416
language 90, 92, 94, 199, 201
    approaches to analysis of 43, 110
    codification of 99
    endangered 421
    fragmentation 435
    functions of 434
    High 272, 275, 413
    minority 421
    official languages 423
    special role 422, 423
    structural approach 43, 110
    supralocalisation 288, 291, 292, 293, 294
    vernacular 272
    working language 423
    world language 426
    written and spoken 29, 201, 220, 275, 369
language community 287
language contact 109, 187, 421, 435
language death 224, 246, 247
Lass, Roger 43–108, 309, 380, 415
    standardisation 275, 306, 360
Latin 6, 8, 248, 282
    and Celtic 225
    contribution to English lexicon 15–16
    government and administrative terms 338
    and personal names 322
    role of in England 59, 247, 271–2
    speakers of 8
    Vulgar and Classical 220, 221
    written language 271
League of Nations 427
Lederer, R. M. 385
van der Leek, F. 164
Le Page, R. B. 266
Lehmann, W. P. 5

Leisi, E. 256, 266
letter writing 33
Levins, Peter 94
lexical items 199–200
    complex 206, 208, 209, 219
    dt/dm sequence 209, 210
    function of 206
    simple 206
lexical relations 205
lexical structures 205–6
Lieberson, S. 321, 323, 324
Lightfoot, D. W. 130, 147–9, 151, 185
Lindisfarne Gospels 70, 359
Linguistic Atlas of Early Middle English (LAEME)
    61, 102
Linguistic Atlas of England (LAE) 374
Linguistic Atlas of Late Mediaeval English
    (LALME) 102, 293, 362–3, 368
Linguistic Atlas of the United States and Canada
    388
linguistic atlas projects 399
Lipka, L. 205
literacy 32, 256, 290, 306, 377
Litteral Substitution Sets 63
Lively, P. 310
London 18, 292
    importance of 18, 25, 86
London English 295, 387
Longman Grammar of Spoken and Written
    English 297, 298, 301
Longobardi, G. 314
Los, B. 175
Louis XIV 258
Lowth, Robert 101, 283, 284, 285
Luther, Martin 47
Lyons, J. 205

Machyn, Henry 369
MacMahon, M. K. C. 106, 307, 376
Macquarie University 336
Maddison, A. 21
Mallory, J. P. 5
Marchand, H. 214, 244, 261
    compound verbs 242
    compounds 210, 215, 253, 255
    prefixes and suffixes 251
    word formation 208, 213
    zero derivation 211
Marckwardt, A. H. 395
Maxwell, James Clerk 305
McArthur, T. 421, 435, 436, 438
McClure, J. D. 360, 380
McClure, P. 325, 326, 332
McDavid, R. I. 399
McIntosh, A. 103, 293, 362
McKinley, R. 328, 330, 331, 334

McQueen, J. 323
McWhorter, J. H. 16, 141
meanings, new 40–1
Meech, S. B. 361
Meillet, A. 5
Mencken, H. L. 392
Mercia 10
Mesthrie, R. 433
methodology 7, 362, 378, 379
Middle English 2, 35, 48, 59–81, 94, 359–65
    adjectives 95, 122, 126
    adverbial clauses 180
    articles 117
    borrowing 222, 246, 251
        from French 15, 249–50, 254
        from Latin 250, 254
        from Scandinavian 249
    case 164
    consonants 91–4
        palatals and palatisation 93
        postvocalic /r/ 91-2
        /x/ 65–6, 93-4
    dialects 361–2
    diphthongs 61, 88
    do 155
    evidence, historical 360, 362, 365
    exploratory expressions 150
    French loanwords 168, 224, 247, 248, 360,
        364
    gender 71
    genitive 119, 120
    impersonal constructions 167
    infinitive 80–1, 149, 175
    inflection 116, 118, 129, 255
    innovation 364
    lexical fields 248
    loan words 222
    Middle English Open Syllable Lengthening 64
    modal markers
    mood 145, 150
    morphology 69–70, 81, 212
    nouns 70–2, 252–3
    null dummy subjects 161
    number 69
    objects 165
    participles 80–1, 138, 177
    particles and adverbs 192
    passive voice 153, 169, 173, 174
    phonology 63–70
        'dropping aitches' 65–6, 94
        fricative voice contrast 62
        loss of final -e 66–7
    place-names 339
    plurals 71
    prepositional stranding 196, 198
    progressive 136
pronouns 72–5, 96, 97, 364
    pro-drop 162
    'she' 363
Scandinavian influence 224, 360, 364
spelling 62–3
standardisation 248, 273
stress 67–9, 251–2
tense 69, 76–8
    future tense 133, 150
    past tense 131, 134, 141
    perfect tense 132, 139, 150
texts 35
that-clauses 171
verbs 75–6, 78–9
    'to be' 79–80
    periphrastic constructions 133, 158
    person and number 78–9
    pre-modals 148, 150, 151
    verb-second sentences 184–5
vocabulary 204, 246–55, 364
vowels 61–2, 63–5, 69, 78, 84–91, 105
    /a/ 85–6
    before liquids 90–1
    /ɔ/ 86
    /i/, /u/ and /o:/ 84–5
    /iu/, /eu/ 88
    Lengthening I and II 89–90, 104–8
    monophthongisation and merger 86–7
    long mid-vowels and /a:/ 87–8
    /oi, ui/ and /i:/ 88-9
wh-relative 128–9
word formation 227, 250–5
    adjective compounds 253–4
    compound verbs 254
    compounding 253
    loss of patterns 252
    native-based 250
    noun compounds 253
    prefixation 251, 254
    stem-based 250, 251
    suffixation 254–5
    zero derivation 255
word order 124, 186, 189, 190, 192
Middle English Open Syllable Lengthening 63–5,
    67
Mikelson, K. S. 321, 324
Miles, J. 347
Miller, J. 139
Mills, A. D. 335
Mills, D. 335
Milroy, J. 39, 286, 288, 292, 379
    standardisation 273–4, 285, 288, 292
Milroy, L. 39, 273–4, 285, 286
Minkova, D. 85, 252
Mitchell, B. 134, 165
Mitchell, Margaret 323

Mittins, M. H. 286
Mizobata, K. 279, 289, 301
Modern English 3, 35–6, 81–104, 310, 370–82
  adjectives 95–6
  adverbial clauses 180
  borrowing 267
    from Arabic 267
    from French 267
    from India 267
    from Italian 267
    from Scots 267
    from Spanish 267
  case 51–2
  consonants 50, 91–4
  dialects 370–4, 376
  fricatives 62
  gender 52
  gerund and present participle 80
  history of 104–8
  inflection 51–2
  innovation 378
  loss of postvocalic /r/ 91–2
  monophthongisation and merger 86–7
  morphology 51–2, 95–104, 375
  nouns 95–6
  number 52
  objects 165
  palatals and palatalisation 93
  periphrasis 95
  phonology 52
  pronouns 96–8, 375, 376
  pronunciation 376–8
  stress 51, 94–5
  suffixation 95, 96, 213
  syntax 375–6
  tense and aspect 52
  texts 35–6
  verbs 98–104
  vocabulary 266–70, 375
  vowels 48–50, 59, 90–1
    contrastive vowel length 49
    Lengthening I 89–90, 92, 104–6
    Lengthening II 106–8
  word-formation 208, 211, 268–70
    acronyms 270
    blending 269
    clipping 269
    compounding 268
    prefixation 268–9
    suffixation 269
Moerenhout, M. 187
Montgomery, M. 388, 399
Moore, S. 361
Moralejo-Gárate, T. 165
morphology 43–108, 212
  derivational 17

Middle English 69–81
  stem-based 212
  word-based 212
Morrill, J. S. 25
Morton, H. C. 299
motion pictures 34–5, 429
Mufwene, S. S. 410
Mugglestone, L. 307, 371
Mulcaster, R. 93
multilingualism 435
Murray, Lindley 285, 431
Murray, T. E. 335
Mustanoja, T. 118

names 315, 351
  bestowal of 313, 315–16
  compound 314
  function of 313
  inflection 315
  onomastics 312, 314, 317–18, 350
    confraternity books 318
    discipline of 317
    source materials of 317–18
  Onymic Default Principle 313
  personal names 315, 318–27
    earliest 319–20
    elements of 319, 320
    fashion in choice of 323
    foreign influences 320, 321, 322, 323
    impact of the Norman Conquest 320–1
    influence of popular music and films 324
    male and female 321, 324
    modern 322–4, 325
    monothematic and dithematic 319
    Old Testament 322
    pet-names (hypocoristics) 325–6, 327, 333
    and Puritanism 322
    recent trends 324–5
    Renaissance and Reformation 321–2
    Scottish or Irish 323
    social psychology of 317
    surnames 325, 326, 327–35
  place-names 314, 335–50, 361
    context of 336–8
    descriptive 340
    elements of 341–3, 344, 391
    English-language 340–5
    explanation of 338–40
    French names 349–50
    house names 346–7
    inversion compounds 338, 348–9
    languages other than English 347–50
    modifiers in 344–5
    postmodification by a
    recording of 349

names (*cont.*)
    rivers 336
    Scandinavian 338, 348, 349
    in Scotland 345
    settlements 337, 344
    street-names 345–6
    surnames and 344
    and urban history 345–7
  proper names 312–15, 316–17
  spelling 317
  surnames 325, 326, 327–9, 330, 335
    after 1500 334–5
    by-names 330
    derived from family relationships 330, 332–3
    derived from locations 329, 332
    derived from occupational terms 330, 333–4
    descriptive 329, 331–2
    double-barrelled 334
    from languages other than English 334
    linguistic nature of 331–4
    origin of 327–8
    types of 329–31
    women's 328, 334, 335
  tropes 316–17
Nares, Robert 93, 94
  vowels 89, 90, 91
Native Americans 384–5, 399
negation 112, 124, 157–8, 193, 397
  multiple 292, 295
  negative contraction 357
  Scots 381
Neo-Latin/Greek Internationalisms 303
Neogrammarian movement 353, 356, 371
Nevalainen, T. 261, 271–98
  social factors 25, 39
  verbs 102, 185, 252
New Fowler's Modern English Usage 297, 299, 310
New Shorter Oxford English Dictionary 300
New York City Standard English 107
New York English 41
New Zealand 23, 41, 309, 432
newspapers 32
Nicolaisen, W. F. H. 336, 345, 349
nominalisation 207
non-rhotic dialects 41, 91, 327
Norman Conquest 12, 14, 16, 59, 225, 271, 272
  impact on personal names 320–1, 327
  writing systems following 31
North America, English in 384–418
  Canada: *see* Canada
  colonial period 384–91
  identifying accents in 388
  immigration 386–7
  maintenance and change 385–6
  mixing of languages in 389

  in the modern period 396–418
  National Period 391–6
  New England terms 385
  origins of 387–90
  place-names 390–1
  prescriptivism 393–4
  settlements 386–7
  Southern terms 385
Northern Cities Shift 41, 49, 405–6, 408, 411, 413
Northern present-tense rule 103
Northern subject rule 375–6
Northumbria 10, 355
noun compounds 396–7
  with adjectives 232
  with adverbs 233
  with a linking element and a noun 231–2
  with a noun 229–33
    types of 229–30
    verbal and non-verbal 231
    with participles 233
    with three lexemes 231
  with a verb 232–3
noun phrase 110-29, 398
  dative 195
  determiners 116–21
  genitive 118
  head noun 114–16
  modifiers 122–9
  word order in 114
nouns
  collective 396
  as modifiers 125
  and place-names 339
  proper nouns 314

Oakden, J. P. 361
objects 113, 164–6, 188–90
  direct 166
  indirect 166
  that-clauses 171
  who as 297
Ogura, M. 187
Old English 2, 48, 353–9
  adjectival derivatives 244
  adjectives 95, 122, 123–4, 125
    compound 233–4
    inflection 56, 72, 115–16
  adverbial clauses 180
  adverbs 145, 180
  articles 55, 117
  borrowing 217, 220, 222, 224–5
  case 55, 163
  Celtic influence 225–6
  consonants 54
  cultural contact 224

determiners 56
dialects 217, 218, 356, 358, 361
    Anglian 358
    diachronic evolution of 356, 357
    diocesan boundaries 358
    Kentish 355
    Mercian 355
    Northumbrian 355, 357
diaphasic variation 218
diminutives 240
diphthongs 53
evidence, historical 358
exploratory expressions 130
French influence 62
gender 55, 70
genitive 119
and German 47
gerunds 80, 178
history of 44
indicative mood 142
inflection 56
influence of Christianity 220, 222, 226
interrogatives 128
Latin influence 217, 220, 221, 222, 246
lexical families 217, 218
loan creation 202, 216, 222, 223
loan-renditions 223
loan-translation 215, 222, 223
modifiers, finite and non-finite 126
mood 143, 145
morphology 55–8, 212, 227, 245
nominal derivatives 243–4
nouns
    compounds 229–33
    noun paradigms 55
    noun phrase 55–6, 70
objects 164, 186
particles and adverbs 191–2
passive voice 152, 153, 169, 170, 173
periphrastic constructions 133
phonology 224, 357
place-names 338, 339, 340, 341
pre-modals 148, 149
predicative phrases 145
prefixes 54, 236–7
prepositional stranding 195, 198
prepositions 223
present participle 137–8
progressive 135–6
pronouns 56, 72, 96, 186, 223
    pro-drop 162
    wh-pronouns 128
relative clauses 127
Scandinavian influence 223–5
semantic fields 217
sound change 359

stress 54–5, 67
subjects 161, 162
subjunctive 130, 131, 142, 145
suffixes 238–42, 252
syntactic variation 357
tense 75, 132, 140
texts 35, 52–3
transition to Middle English 59–62
verbs 57–8, 151, 166, 167, 191
    be 79–80
    compound 235–46
    inflection 78–9
    have 158
    morphology 75–6
    prefixes 236-7
    suffixes 238–42
    verb-second sentences 182–4
vocabulary 204, 216–26, 246, 358
voiced fricatives 54
vowels 53, 61, 63, 69, 357
West Saxon dialect 355, 357, 358
    negative contraction 357
    vocabulary 358
word formation 208, 217, 220, 226–46,
        358
    adjectival suffixes 241–2
    adverbs 245
    compounds 228, 229–33, 235–46
    prefixation 228
    stem-allomorphy 227
    stem-formatives 238
    stress 227
    suffixation 228, 238
    suprasegmental alternation 227
    typological status of 245–6
    zero derivation 242–3
word order 189, 194
writing system 30–1
Oldmixon, John 283
onomastics 312
Onymic Default Principle 313
open syllable lengthening 64
Orm 273, 360
Ormulum 66, 71, 72
orthoepists 36
Orton, H. S. 295, 372, 374
Osselson, N. E. 290
Owun 359
Oxford English Dictionary 1, 202, 256, 266, 299,
        300, 393, 435
    historical bias of 300
Oxford Movement 323
Oxinden, Henry

Padel, O. J. 335
Page, R. I. 30

Pahta, P. 281
Palsgrave, J. 256
paper 32
parchment and vellum 30, 35
Parker, G. 427
Parry, D. 382
Parsons, D. 335, 348
passive voice 152, 166, 168–71
    indirect 169
past participle 57
Paston family letters 290, 295, 352, 368–9
Pederson, L. 398, 399
periphrastic constructions 130, 137, 139, 141,
        144, 150
Pesetsky, D. 166
Peterborough Chronicle 14, 63, 72, 78, 271
Peters, H. 224–5
Philological Society 371
phonology 47–8
    basis for 48
    changes in 46, 50, 59–60, 62
    consonants 91–4
    Great Vowel Shift 81–3
    Modern English 52
    and morphology 43–108
    and place-names 339
    vowels 60–2
Phua Chu Kang 433
pidgin languages 16, 424, 436
Pintzuk, S. 183, 186
Piroth, W. 336
place-names: *see under* names
Plag, I. 260
Plank, F. 147, 149, 164
Poema morale 76
poetry 35, 217, 218, 219, 272, 355
    kennings 219
    word order 187
Pogatscher's Line 356–7
politics 427
Poole, Joshua 284
Pope, Alexander 88, 323
Poppe, E. 136
popular music 324, 429–30
population 27
postal system 32, 33
Postles, D. 330
Pound, L. 269
Poussa, P. 8, 16, 223
power 18, 21, 426, 427
prefixation 210, 235
prepositional stranding 113, 193–8
prepositions 398
present-day English 3
    adverbial clauses 180
    articles 116

determiners 120, 121
genetive phrases 118
mood 145
noun phrase 114
null dummy subjects
    object 188
    participles 178
    passive voice 168, 170
    relative clauses 127
    subject 161
    tense 131, 133, 136, 139, 140–1
    that-clauses 171–2
    vowels 65
    word order 114
Preston, Dennis 309, 395, 404
Preusler, W. 8
printing 32, 256, 277–9
    and personal names 321
    and spelling 282, 289, 290
    standardisation and 248, 293, 311, 367
Prokosch, E. 353
pronouns 296, 297
    de-cliticisation of 113, 185
    demonstrative 127–8
    dropping of 162
    indefinite 121, 296
    Middle English 72–5
    modifiers of 115
    in noun phrases 115
    plurals 74–5
    possessive 119
    Pronoun Exchange 376
    relative 128
    Scandinavian paradigm 75
    she 73, 74
    Shetland theory 74
    thou 375
pronunciation 306–10, 311, 376, 387
    fricatives 50, 54, 62, 370
Proto-Indo-European 55
Puttenham, George 306, 367
Pynson, Richard 289

quantifiers 111
Quirk, R. 179, 201, 217, 297, 426

Raftery, D. 290
railways 24–5
Ramsaran, Susan 308
Ramsay, David 389–90
Raper, P. E. 336
Raumolin-Brunberg, H. 25, 39, 102, 290, 296
Ray, John 371
Rayburn, A. 336
Read, A. W. 388, 389, 392
Reaney, P. H. 330

Received Pronunciation 29, 107, 289, 300, 307
  varieties of 308
recording media 34
Reformation 20, 28, 321–2
register 2, 217, 281, 289
  diachronic evolution of 304
  specialist 304, 310
  spoken and written 296, 297
  and standardisation 303–6
  variation in 15, 311
relative clauses 127–8, 397
relative markers 296
Renaissance 27–8, 281, 321–2
Renfrew, C. 5
Reuter, Paul Julius 428
rhotic dialects 25, 41, 91, 377
rhymes and puns 36
Richardson, Samuel 299, 323
Rickford, J. R. 411
Riddle, E. M. 260
Ringe, O. 16
Rissanen, M. 120, 121, 266, 287, 296, 304
Ritt, N. 60
Roach, Peter 308
Roberts, I. 130, 188, 193
Robinson, K. 323
Romaine, S. 288, 309
Romance languages 68, 208, 323
Romance Stress Rule 68, 69, 94
Romans, occupation of Britian 10, 220
Room, A. 336, 345–6
Rosenbach, A. 119
Royal Court 295
Royal Society 281, 305
Rule of St Benet 184
Rushworth texts 358, 359
Ruthwell Cross 365
Ryan, K. 420

safety regimens, English in 430
Salmon, V. 290
Samuels, M. L. 275, 354, 362
Sanskrit 6
Savory, T. 303
Saxons 9, 226
Scandinavian influence 11, 12, 14–16, 74, 248
  names 348, 349
  word order 184, 185, 187
  verbs 16, 141
Schabram, H. 218
Schäfer, J. 266
Schama, S. 347
Scheler, M. 203, 217, 301
Schendl, H. 103, 104
Schneider, E. 297, 438
Schwartz, R. M. 24

science 27, 301–3
Scotland 20, 25, 151, 366
  dialects 365–7, 380
  English place-names in 345
  French loanwords 20, 366
  Gaelic language 20, 366
  language 360, 437
  negation 381
  syntax 381
Scott, Sir Walter 267, 323
Scragg, D. G. 280–1, 282, 289, 290
Seaspeak 430
Sebba , M. 383
Second World War 26
Semenza, C. 312
Serjeantson, M. S. 220
Shakespeare, W. 32, 104, 162, 282
  compounds 261
  grammar 162, 164, 297
  Inkhorn Controversy 280, 281
  names 321, 323
  neologisms 256
  rhymes 87, 102
Shearer, B. 24
Sheridan, Thomas 91, 257, 307, 367
Shorter Oxford English Dictionary 266
Shuman, R. B. 286
Sidney, Sir Philip 323
Siegel, J. 433
Simon, J. 285
Singapore 433
Singlish 433, 434
Sisam, K. 366
Smart, V. 318
Smith, A. H. 335
Smith, J. J. 287, 289, 368
Smith, P. 387
social prestige and language 15, 16, 38
social structures 13, 15, 105
sociolinguistic methods 41, 362, 379, 420, 422,
    436
Sørensen, K. 282
South Africa 23, 25, 309
Southern Shift 406–7, 408
Spanish influence 267, 384
speech communities 199, 200, 201
spelling 276, 291, 426
  changes in 282
  occasional 36
  private writing and 290
  reform of 85, 289, 290
  regularisation 289.
  spelling pronunciation 94, 281
  standardisation of 32, 273, 289–91,
    310
  of surnames 331

Spenser, Edmund 93, 279, 323
spoken word, transmission of 33
Sprat, Thomas 281–2
Standard British 307, 309
standard English 273, 300, 434
  development of 274–87
  codification 307
  elaboration of functions 301, 304, 306
  focussed 288
  genre-specific styles 304
  grammar 303, 310
  influence of dialects 378
  loss of postvocalic /r/ 377
  pronouns 292
  verb phrase 291–2
  vocabulary 303
  written 301
standard Scottish 308
standardisation 99, 107, 271–98, 367, 369, 433,
    438
  acceptance stage 275–6
  belief in 285
  codification stage 282–4
  definition of 273
  and dialects 377
  diffusion stage 276–7
  effects of 377
  elaboration of function stage 279–82, 304,
    306
  and focussing 288
  goal of 288
  grammar 291–9
  institutional support for 274, 275, 276, 282,
    283, 287, 292, 310
  maintenance stage 277–9, 385–6
  prescription stage 284–6
  processes of 289
  pronunciation 306–10, 311
  registers 303–6
  requirements for 310
  selection stage 274–5
  spelling 289–91, 310
  stages of 273
  vocabulary 299–303
  of written language 39, 297, 360
Stanley, E. G. 219
Stanyhurst, Richard 382
Steele, Sir Richard 323
Stein, G. 268
Stevens, P. 430
Stewart, G. R. 336
Stockwell, R. P. 82, 85, 252
Strang, Barbara xiii, 136, 221, 359
stress 17, 51, 238
  Middle English 67–9
  morphology and 51

Old English 54–5, 227
  secondary 51
Ström, H. 319
subjects 112, 160–4, 170
  empty 161, 163, 167, 168
  as experiencer 166, 168
  subject predicatives 163
  that-clauses 171
subjunctive 130, 141, 142, 144, 145
  Middle English 145, 150
  Old English 145
subordinate clauses 171–81, 182
  adverbial 180–1
  infinitival clauses 172–7
  with an *ing*-participle 177–9
  that-clauses 171–2
suffixation 119, 210, 238–42
supralocalisation 288, 291, 292, 293, 294
Survey of English Dialects 373–4, 375
Survey of English Place-Names 335
Sutcliffe, D. 383
Svensson, A.-M. 341
Sweet, Henry 105, 106, 307, 353, 355, 371
Swift, Jonathan 214, 283, 323
syntax 109–13, 159
  clauses 160–81
  noun phrase 110–29
  verbs 129–60
  word order 181–98

Taavitsainen, I. 281
Taylor, A. 16, 184, 187
technical terms 301, 306
television 34
Tengstrand, E. 344
Tennyson, Alfred, Lord 323
texts, historical 35–6
Thomas, A. R. 365, 382
Thomas, R. C. 270
Thomason, S. G. 16
Thompson, S. A. 166
Three Hunderd Years' War 20
Tieken-Boon van Ostade, I. 271–98, 431
to-infinitival clauses 180
Todd, L. 397
Toronto *Dictionary of Old English* 35
transportation 18, 24–5, 32
Traugott, Elizabeth 41, 132
Treaty of Wedmore 11, 224
Tristram, H. L. C. 8
Trisyllabic Laxing 252
Trudgill, P.
  dialects 371, 374, 376, 381
  focussing 287
  grammar of Standard English 291, 292
  phonology 409

Pronoun Exchange 376
Received Pronunciation 308, 309
regional varieties 298
sociolinguistics 379
Tucker, Abraham 85, 92
Turville-Petre, T. 365

Uniformitarian Hypothesis 8
Union of the Crowns 20
United Empire Loyalists 391, 414
United Nations 423
United States 25, 29
  economic status 21, 24, 26
  immigration 394, 399
  languages spoken 22
  population 22, 392, 396
  pronunciation 309
  see also American English and North America,
    English in
univerbation 197
universities 20, 247
urbanisation 24, 377, 378

ValSpeak 42
van Buren, Martin 391
van Lancker, D. 312
variation, linguistic 37, 43–6
Velar Softening 252
verbal phrase 110, 129–60
verbs 129–60
  ablaut series 57, 204
  anomalous 58, 98–101
  aspect 111, 135–42
  auxiliary 148, 151, 158–60
  classes 57–8
  compound 235–45, 246
    derivation of 243–4
    prefixes 236–7
    suffixes 235, 238–42
  do 154–8
  gan/gangan 'to go' 203
  have 140
  light verb combinations 165
  modal 143, 158, 398
    double 151–2, 158, 159, 381, 382–3
  mood 112, 142–4, 146
  Northern present-tense rule 103
  past participle 153
  periphrastic constructions 130, 137, 139, 141,
    144, 150, 156, 158
  person and number 78–9
  phrasal 113
  plurals 78
  pre-modals 147
  present tense 134
  preterite tense 139, 140, 149

progressive 138
strong 57, 58, 77–8, 99
  grade reduction 77, 98
tense 52, 75, 76–8, 112, 131–5
  future markers 132, 133, 138, 296
  past 134
  perfect 139, 140, 141
third-person -s ending 101–4
'to be' 58, 79–80, 141, 142
verbal complementation 149
verbal prhase 129–60
voice 112, 152–4, 168–71
weak 57–8, 76–7, 238
Vercelli Book 355
Vespasian Psalter 359
Vikings, invasions of Britian 11
Visser, F. Th. 138, 148, 149
Vennemann, T. 8
vocabulary 257, 270
  associated and dissociated 203, 257
  changes in 200, 201–4, 213, 215–16
  compounds 209
  core 301, 303, 310
  Early Modern English 256
  expansion of 270, 279
  formal-morphological structures 205–6
  French influence 248, 271
  growth pattern 266
  history of 202
  languages that have contributed 203
  Latin influence 248
  learned and technical 256
  lexical change 201–4
  lexical structures 204–6
  lexicalisation 210
  loan creation 216
  loan translation 215
  Middle English 246–55
  Modern English 266–70
  Old English 216–46
  scientific 266, 268
  semantic structures 205
  size of 208
  standardisation 299–303
  stratification of 201, 217–20
  taboo and 216
  technical terms 256, 261, 266
vowels 49, 61, 84–8, 91
  bird vowel 49
  homorganic lengthening 60, 77
  lengthening and shortening of 246
  Lengthening I 104–6
  Lengthening II 106–8
  lot vowel 49
  low 60–1
  Middle English breaking 61

vowels (*cont.*)
  pre-cluster shortening 60
  trisyllabic shortening 60

Walker, John
  pronunciation dictionary 90, 92, 307
  vowels 90, 104
Wallenberg, J. K. 335
Wallis, John 83
  Grammatica Linguae Anglicanae 284
  postvocalic /r/ 92
  pronouns 96
  verbs 99
  vowels 85, 86, 88
Wallmannsberger, J. 16
Walter of Bibbesworth 248
war, effect on English 25–7
Ward, Ida 105
Wareing, J. 293
Warner, A. 130, 146, 147, 149, 150, 159–60
  grammaticalisation 160
Wars of the Roses 25
Watts, V. E. 335
Weale, M. E. 10
Webster, Noah 392–3
  codification of American English 273, 309,
      393
  spelling 32, 393
Weeks, F. 430
Weerman, F. 187
Wells, John 91, 106, 380, 383
  Longman Pronunciation Dictionary 308,
      309
Welsh English 382
Wenisch, F. 218
Wenkler, Georg 371
Wessex 11
West Saxon dialect 35, 246, 271, 355
Westminster 18
Whaley, L. J. 421
White, D. L. 136
White, Richard Grant 393–4
Whitehall, H. 361
Williams, J. M. 220
Williams, Roger 387
Wilson, S. 321
Wolff, D. 256, 266
Wolfson, N. 134
Woolf, Virginia 46
Worcester, Joseph 309
Worcester Tremulous Script 71, 73
word formation 17, 203, 205
  adverbs 245
  affixation 210, 212
  bahuvrihi compounds 215, 229
  blending 214

categories of 210
clipping 213–14
  back-clipping 269
  change, language 269
  clipping compounds 269–70
  fore-clipping 269
comparison 208
compound adjectives 233–4
compound verbs 235–46
  adjectival derivatives 244
  adverbs 245
  dt/dm sequence 209
  inseparable and separable 235
  nominal derivatives 243–4
  prefixation 235
  verbal derivation 244
  verbal prhase 242
compounds 210, 212
conversion 210, 211
derivations 214, 242
expansions 214, 242
functional classification of 214
nominalisation 207
noun compounds 228, 253, 268
  copulative 261
  sex-denoting types 253
phonetic symbolism 213
prefixation 210
  attitudinal 262–3
  intensifying 263
  locative 262
  negative prefixes 261
  pejorative 263
  privative 261–2
  quantitative 263
  reversative 261–2
  temporal 262
principles of 206–15
processes of 213
stem-based 245
suffixation 210
  adjective-forming 264–5
  noun-forming 263–4
  verb-forming 265
and syntactic constructions 209, 210
syntactic recategorisation 206
word-based 245
word manufacturing 214
zero derivation 211, 220, 242–3
word order 109, 124, 139, 156, 173,
      181–98
changes in 181, 193–8
decline in the use of verb-second sentences
      184-5
direct and indirect objects 188–90
fixation of 156–7

  information structure requirements 120
  object and verb 185–8, 195
  particles and adverbs 190–3
  of subject and verb 182–5
words, new 40
Wright, Joseph 300, 371, 372, 374, 378
writing systems 29–31, 338
van der Wurff, Wim 109, 131–59, 187,
    282

Wycliffites 28
Wynkyn de Worde 289, 290

you
  and thou 97
  diffusion 295, 296

Zachrisson, R. E. 349
Zettin, M. 312